# ST PETERSBURG

## SHADOWS OF THE PAST

Catriona Kelly

YALE UNIVERSITY PRESS
NEW HAVEN AND LONDON

First published in paperback in 2016



For information about this and other Yale University Press publications, please contact:
U.S. Office: sale.press@yale.edu www.yalebooks.com
Europe Office: sales@yaleup.co.uk www.yalebooks.co.uk

Set in Minion Pro by IDSUK (DataConnection) Ltd
Printed in Great Britain by Hobbs the Printers Ltd, Totton, Hampshire

Library of Congress Cataloging-in-Publication Data

Kelly, Catriona, author.
St Petersburg: shadows of the past / Catriona Kelly.
pages: illustrations, maps ; cm
Includes bibliographical references and index.
ISBN 978-0-300-16918-8 (alk. paper)
1. Saint Petersburg (Russia)—Description and travel. 2. Saint Petersburg (Russia)—History. I. Title.
DK552.K45 2013
947′.21—dc23

2013018605

A catalogue record for this book is available from the British Library.

ISBN 978-0-300-21940-1 (pbk)

10 9 8 7 6 5 4 3 2 1

FOR MY FRIENDS FROM ST PETERSBURG

# Contents

# List of Illustrations

Unless otherwise stated, all images are the author's own.

## Plates



## Figures

## Maps

# Preface and Acknowledgements

Late Soviet Leningrad was a complicated city. It was repulsive to outsiders but comparatively open to international links, puritanical but with an extraordinarily vital artistic and intellectual life, and with a political leadership that was at once paternalistic and callous. Twenty years after its renaming, St Petersburg is a different city, and a much more diverse one, but with contradictions of its own. At times, the cavalier attitude to people's needs and safety could make you weep. The idea that Russia is the home of spiritual values, however badly things go materially, could hardly survive contact with the self-interested and go-getting behaviour of some members of the local elite. If Moscow, proverbially, does not believe in tears, Leningrad-Petersburg has never been inclined to notice them.

Extreme beauty is unsettling and difficult to live with. Petersburg has the faintly disapproving, troubled narcissism of a place whose inhabitants measure others' ideas of what matters against their own historical tragedies. Yet locals also have a huge appetite for new experience, a capacity to take nothing for granted, and a winning sense of intelligent irony. Raw as life in the city may be, and inspirationally boring at times, it is almost never dull. This book is an attempt to capture all that; the essence of somewhere that has a victim complex the size of a city, but also makes light of its unbearable past.

Soviet culture was highly integrated, and had a strong drive to homogeneity. But during the 1960s, Leningraders became increasingly convinced their city was unique. It is this central tension that I grapple with here. I look at how people consciously interacted with the local and national past, and at how they simply lived alongside it; at the things and spaces which shaped conscious perceptions, and those people barely noticed. At one level, I am preoccupied with how Leningrad-Petersburg and its culture have been imagined; at others, with concrete layers of experience as they are now remembered.

Present and past interact, in that there can be no conscious reaction to anything that is not to some extent the product of memory. A diary is no closer to the events recalled than a memoir or oral testimony: the act of writing requires even so-called 'naïve writers' to formulate a position towards what they have witnessed. Myth and reality fuse, since practical activities (for example, deciding where to work and live) are driven by shared ideas about what a given place 'is like'. In showing how shared memories of the past impacted on the present between the late 1950s and the 2010s, I interweave different sources – from official documents to works of literature and art, to memoirs and oral history, to the material traces of change that are on show in city streets and buildings. And I draw on my own experience and impressions as well as citing and describing those of others.

No one could aim, even in a book that addresses a relatively short stretch of time, to sum up everything that is important about a big city to all its inhabitants, permanent or temporary. As Olga Lukas's parody of 'St Petersburg and Moscow studies' puts it, 'Petersburgers will take offence at anything, even a misplaced comma'. Those who also know and love the city will certainly argue, loudly, with some or all of the things I have said. But existing treatments of St Petersburg often seem constricted by artificial boundaries: on one corner of the map are discussions of historic buildings without reference to those who live in them; on another, discussions of a supposed 'Soviet and post-Soviet identity' that is more or less undifferentiated by place and person; in a third place, treatments that elevate personal experience or that of some particular circle into insights that stand for an entire culture. What I have tried to do is to move in the direction of an integrated treatment of local life – one that acknowledges, for instance, that not everyone in St Petersburg is an artist or aesthete; that the 'Leningrad' past has not simply disappeared; and that city experiences may vary depending on what generation one comes from.

Guidebooks aim to offer a view of the city that is at once homogeneous and definitive (selecting only monuments that are 'worth a detour' or the latest hard-to-get-into bar). This book is precisely concerned with the many different ways of looking at one city. For the tourist, London is Tower Bridge, the British Museum, black cabs, red buses, and Buckingham Palace. For me, brought up in London, all of these have resonance, but no more so than Richmond Park, where we walked as children and which I cycled through as a student; the bravely cultivated garden of West Kensington Station back in the 1970s; the Wallace Collection, one of the first museums I visited on my own; the city churches my father took us to see one memorable Sunday; the square gardens of Bloomsbury, where I ate lunch as a young lecturer in the 1990s; and, of course, the areas where I have actually lived – Barnes and Bermondsey, both of them close to the ultimate focus of my London patriotism, the Thames embankments. And if one can't write about London now without recognising the work of Peter Ackroyd and Iain Sinclair (just to begin with), then discussions of Petersburg need not end with Pushkin and Dostoevsky and time-honoured clichés about the sting of the cold and the vodka, or more recent ones about unwavering dirigisme and top-to-bottom corruption. In the days before the fledgling Soviet state was recognised, Westerners used to offer 'the view from Riga'; so far as Leningrad-St Petersburg is concerned, they have tended to offer 'the view from the Astoria', not venturing beyond the Moika-Fontanka-Neva triangle into the areas where most people actually live.

* * *

The intellectual debts that I have accumulated over the decade or so that I have been working on the book are as varied as the material itself. Financial support for the costs of research visits to St Petersburg and Moscow (where, to the irritation of patriotic locals, some sources about the 'city on the Neva' not available locally are held) was provided by the Arts and Humanities Research Council, the Leverhulme Trust, the University of Oxford, and the Ludwig Fund, New College. I am extremely grateful to these funding bodies, and to the often extraordinarily helpful staff in libraries and archives in St Petersburg, and in Moscow, Helsinki, and London, as well as my home institutions in Oxford. I also thank everyone I work with at New College and in the University of Oxford for their intellectual company and good fellowship, particularly Josie von Zitzewitz, who took over my teaching while I was on Leverhulme-sponsored and university research leave; and my graduate and undergraduate students, whose enthusiasm for Russian culture helps keep mine going. Many thanks also to the research facilitators in the Humanities Division, particularly Vicky Drew, Sam Sneddon, and Andrew Fairweather-Tall.

The group project sponsored by the AHRC, 'Russian National Identity from 1961', was an amazing source of intellectual stimulation and support. My heartfelt thanks to those involved, particularly Andy Byford, Josie von Zitzewitz, Victoria Donovan, and Edmund Griffiths in Oxford, Hilary Pilkington and Rowenna Baldwin at the University of Warwick, Birgit Beumers at Bristol, Stephen Lovell at King's College London, and in St Petersburg, Albert Baiburin, Dmitry Baranov, Anna Kushkova, and Elena Omelchenko. Participants in the conferences on Eurasian culture and on Soviet history held at New College and Wolfson College, Oxford, and the European University, St Petersburg, and a comparative workshop on Irish and Russian history at Dugort, Achill Island, also contributed in many and diverse ways. Gratitude goes to those who have helped with interviewing, in particular Natalia Galetkina, Evgenia Gulyaeva, Ekaterina Izmestieva, Alexandra Kasatkina, Veronika Makarova, Irina Nazarova, Alexandra Piir, and Marina Samsonova.

Colleagues at the European University, the Likhachev Foundation, and the St Petersburg branch of Memorial, including Boris Firsov, Irina Flige, Oleg Kharkhordin, Alexander Kobak, Boris Kolonitsky, Tatiana Kosinova, Alexander Margolis, and Tatiana Voronina, have all offered invaluable advice and support. I would also like to acknowledge the helpful suggestions and comments from seminar organisers and participants and readers for journals in a variety of locations across St Petersburg, and also in Finland, France, Germany, the USA, and the UK, including Evgeny Dobrenko and Andrey Shcherbenok, Catherine

Merridale and Andreas Schönle, Alain Blum, Claudio Ingerflom, and Isabelle Ohayon, Dina Khapaeva and Nikolai Koposov, Aleksandr Bikbov and colleagues at *Laboratorium* journal, Jurij Murashov, Igor Smirnov, Marina Mogil'ner and colleagues at *Ab Imperio*, Sang Hyun Kim and colleagues at *Journal of Eurasian Studies*, Sara Jones and Debbie Pinfold, Valery Vyugin, Alexander Etkind, Muireann Maguire, Seth Graham, Konstantin Barsht, Nariman Skakov, Grigory Freidin, Monica Greenleaf, Yoram Gorlizki and Vera Tolz. Especial thanks to Gerry Smith, Barbara Heldt, Stephen Lovell, Ekaterina Golynkina, and Alina Kravchenko, who were kind enough to read the entire draft text. Steve Smith's comments were extremely useful at an early stage of writing. Valuable suggestions about things to read, look at, and do were also made by Yury Basilov, Catriona Bass, Vadim Bass, Arkady Bliumbaum, Konstantin Bogdanov, Svetlana Boym, Catherine Clark, Shura Collinson, Alexander Genis, Anton Glikin, Larissa Haskell, Ol'ga Kuznetsova, Mark Lipovetsky, Lev Lurie, Lyubov' Osinkina, Serguei Oushakine, Judy Pallot, Maria Pasholok, Alexandra Smith, Elizabeth Stern, Dar'ya Sukhovei, Gleb Tsipursky, Polina Vakhtina, and many others. Richard Davies generously presented me with a copy of his wonderful book on wooden churches in north-western Russia.

Among members of my family, I would particularly mention my niece Millie Davan-Wetton, who came with me on a visit to the city in October 2011. I owe to her fresh eyes some interesting observations about the city, including the comments about dogwear in Chapter 7, and am grateful for her good humour and sangfroid, even when a brick only just missed her head on Bol'shoi Sampsonievsky prospekt. My husband, Ian Thompson, has also provided welcome company on numerous visits, beginning with the freezing December of 1988, when snell winds raced round the bleak sea front. He has maintained a lively vicarious interest throughout.

Above all, I am grateful to the many people in St Petersburg – some, but by no means all, already mentioned by name – who have, by invitation or spontaneously, shared their love, at times frustrated or sorely tried, for this haunting place. A number have been my friends for more than thirty years; with others, I have developed warm relations in the more recent past; some I barely know at all. St Petersburg is, as even the casual visitor knows, not a cosy city, but if I feel that I have the right to describe myself as at least an honorary St Petersburger – that is the gift of the real locals, and I dedicate the book to them.

St Petersburg,
April 2013

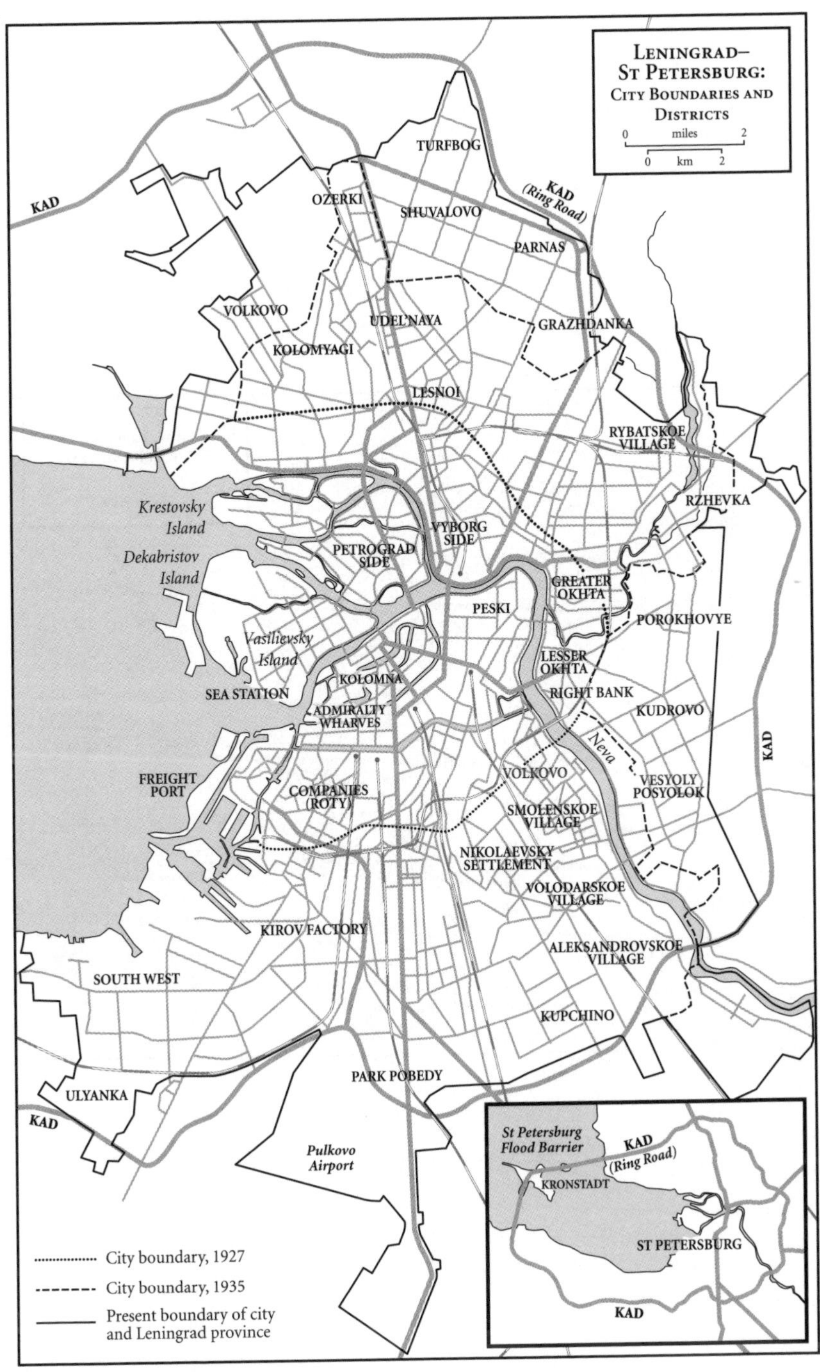
LENINGRAD–
ST PETERSBURG:
CITY BOUNDARIES AND
DISTRICTS
0 miles 2
0 km 2
KAD
KAD
(Ring Road)
TURFBOG
OZERKI
SHUVALOVO
PARNAS
VOLKOVO
UDEL'NAYA
GRAZHDANKA
KOLOMYAGI
LESNOI
RYBATSKOE
VILLAGE
RZHEVKA
Krestovsky
Island
VYBORG
SIDE
PETROGRAD
SIDE
Dekabristov
Island
GREATER
OKHTA
PESKI
POROKHOVYE
Vasilievsky
Island
LESSER
OKHTA
KOLOMNA
SEA STATION
RIGHT BANK
ADMIRALTY
WHARVES
KUDROVO
Neva
KAD
FREIGHT
PORT
VOLKOVO
VESYOLY
POSYOLOK
COMPANIES
(ROTY)
SMOLENSKOE
VILLAGE
NIKOLAEVSKY
SETTLEMENT
VOLODARSKOE
VILLAGE
KIROV FACTORY
ALEKSANDROVSKOE
VILLAGE
SOUTH WEST
KUPCHINO
PARK POBEDY
ULYANKA
KAD
Pulkovo
Airport
St Petersburg
Flood Barrier
KAD
(Ring Road)
KRONSTADT
ST PETERSBURG
KAD
City boundary, 1927
City boundary, 1935
Present boundary of city
and Leningrad province

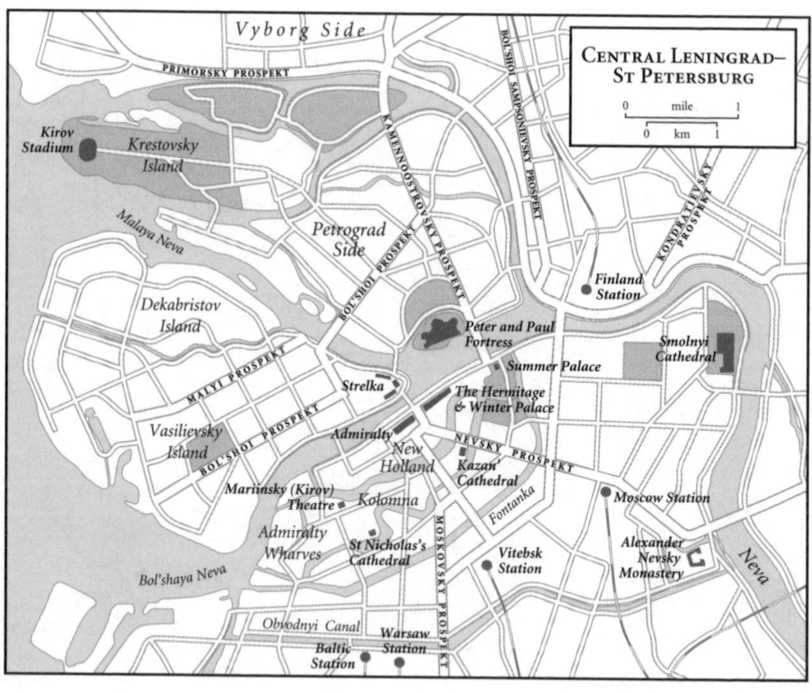

Central Leningrad–St Petersburg
0 mile 1
0 km 1
Vyborg Side
Primorsky Prospekt
Kirov Stadium
Krestovsky Island
Kamennoostrovsky Prospekt
Bol'shoi Sampsonievsky Prospekt
Kondratievsky Prospekt
Malaya Neva
Petrograd Side
Bol'shoi Prospekt
Finland Station
Dekabristov Island
Peter and Paul Fortress
Smolnyi Cathedral
Summer Palace
Malyi Prospekt
Strelka
The Hermitage & Winter Palace
Bol'shoi Prospekt
Vasilievsky Island
Admiralty
New Holland
Nevsky Prospekt
Kazan' Cathedral
Mariinsky (Kirov) Theatre
Kolomna
Moscow Station
Fontanka
Admiralty Wharves
St Nicholas's Cathedral
Moskovsky Prospekt
Vitebsk Station
Alexander Nevsky Monastery
Neva
Bol'shaya Neva
Obvodnyi Canal
Baltic Station
Warsaw Station

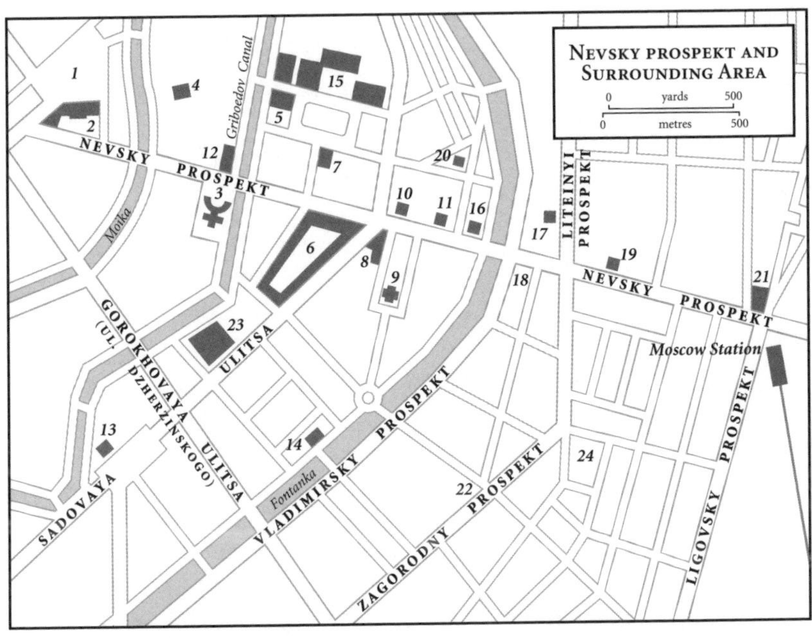


1 *Palace Square (Dvortsovaya ploshchad')*
2 *General Staff building*
3 *Kazan' Cathedral*
4 *DLT (Dom Leningradskoi Torgovli)*
5 *Malyi (Mikhailovsky) Theatre*
6 *Gostinyi dvor*
7 *Philharmonia*
8 *Public Library (Russian National Library)*
9 *Alexandrinsky (Pushkin) Theatre*
10 *Sever (Café Nord)*
11 *Eliseev Stores*
12 *Dom Knigi (House of Books)*
13 *Haymarket (Sennaya ploshchad')*
14 *Bolshoi Dramatic Theatre*
15 *Russian Museum*
16 *Writers' Bookshop*
17 *'Subscription Editions' Bookshop*
18 *Site of Saigon Café (now the Radisson Royal Hotel)*
19 *Dom Aktyora (House of Actors)*
20 *Dom Kino (Cinema House)*
21 *Nevsky Passage Shopping Centre*
22 *'Five Corners'*
23 *Apraksin dvor*
24 *Kuznechnyi Market*

# Introduction: City Panorama

*My homeland is not Russia.*
*My homeland is Petersburg.*[1]

If one mentions the words 'memory' and 'modern Russia' in the same breath, certain expectations surface. Often, these will relate to the suppression of the past. There are the doctored photographs where a crowd is airbrushed to leave only Stalin.[2] There is print censorship of the kind that required librarians to efface an article in the *Great Soviet Encyclopedia* honouring the former police chief Lavrenty Beria, denounced in 1953 as an 'enemy of the people', by pasting over it a conscientiously long article on the 'Bering Sea'.[3] More recently, there are the efforts to encourage patriotic history in the schoolroom, and triumphalist commemorations of the Great Patriotic War in city squares, while large numbers of documents recording the detailed history of that conflict remain inaccessible to most historians.[4] An impressive literature speaks of 'traumatic memory', or the scarring effects of political repression and the horrors of war on the individual and collective consciousness.[5] Here, Russians appear not only as victims, but also as perpetrators: 'scavengers' of local cultures, and oppressors of their neighbours.[6]

In the context of city landscapes, 'memory' is likely to be just as indelibly associated with editing, adjustment, and rupture: the statues that have disappeared, the place-names that have changed, and the buildings that have been demolished, or altered beyond recognition.[7] Even Westerners who have never visited a 'socialist city' will have a clear picture of such a place: grey tower blocks, red flags, and somewhere in the centre an enormous monument to a political leader sneering down on the local population. 'Post-socialist', on the other hand, suggests a comparably drear architectural landscape, but now accessorised with lingerie advertisements and the Marlboro cowboy, where sinister men with stubbly heads and chins cruise the streets in black-windowed SUVs.

As the Russian writer Peter Vail' humorously claimed in his travelogue, *Genius Loci*, stereotypes are never wrong.[8] Certainly, it would not be hard to find places across Eastern Europe and the former Soviet Union resembling the imaginary city that I have just sketched.[9] No wonder that 'nostalgia', in the context of such places, comes across as a pathological condition – an affliction of sadly deluded individuals who have no idea just how awful the place they live in is. At most, it will seem an attempt to salvage a shred of dignity in the face of enduring deprivation, as in the old Soviet joke about the baby maggot who asks his dad why, if some maggots get to live in apples, and others in meat, 'we have to live here in this pile of shit'. The father maggot draws himself up and replies, 'Son, remember this: the motherland is always the motherland!'[10]

What happens, though, when the 'post-Soviet' or 'post-socialist' city concerned is somewhere with a substantial and dignified past predating its role as a Warsaw Pact metropolis – a place such as St Petersburg? Then the temptation is to see the socialist period as an aberration, an era that has nothing to do with the 'real' identity of the city. Foreigners have always been inclined to draw a firm boundary between the city's pre-revolutionary past and its Soviet reality (or recent past). A British teacher, visiting in the 1980s, asked whether she liked Leningrad, replied that she had no idea. When her hosts expressed astonishment, she replied, 'You showed me St Petersburg, and it was magnificent. As for Leningrad – I've never seen the place.'[11]

For locals, making this kind of distinction (as the story also shows) is far harder. The vote to change the city's name from 'Leningrad' to 'St Petersburg' in 1991 produced only a slim overall majority in favour (54.9 per cent, versus 35.5 per cent against). Certainly, there were variations by district: in Kronstadt, only 39.1 per cent approved, and in Dzerzhinsky district (a particularly attractive part of the centre), 60.8 per cent. But in no case was support for the change clear-cut.[12] The restoration of the earlier name meant, after all, the effacement of its Soviet past – and most particularly, of the city's wartime record of dreadful suffering and staunch resistance during the Leningrad Blockade.[13]

Yet what a city is called is only part of a local's relationship with it, and perhaps not the most important part. Westerners' fixation on obvious, external changes of this kind tends to provoke, among Russians, a mixture of irritation and bemusement, as the anthropologist Natal'ya Kosmarskaya has pointed out. Researchers who arrive in post-Soviet cities and assume that monuments must be 'beacons of change' are misguided; for locals, the symbolism of the city lies elsewhere.[14] This is all the more true of St Petersburg, where very few major Soviet-era monuments have in fact disappeared. Perhaps because of the legacy of enthusiastic demolition after the 1917 Revolution and into the 1930s, there was never an episode of demonstrative statue-toppling of the kind that swept across other parts of Eastern Europe, including Moscow (where the pioneering police chief Felix Dzerzhinsky was removed from his pedestal in August 1991). The most important displaced statue in the city is a pre-revolutionary one: behind railings in a quiet courtyard outside the Marble Palace rises the Russo-Italian sculptor Paolo Trubetskoi's surly, hulking memorial to Tsar Alexander

0.1 Paolo Trubetskoi's monument to Alexander III, which originally stood on ploshchad' Vosstaniya, in its current location outside the Marble Palace (once the central Lenin Museum, now an annex of the Russian Museum), photographed in October 2011.

III that used to stand on ploshchad' Vosstaniya (Uprising Square), until it was displaced by a square garden, and then the pedestal for a Lenin statue, and then finally, in 1985, the obelisk commemorating the Great Patriotic War that still stands there now with, behind it, the last surviving red banner, proclaiming Leningrad's status as hero city.[15]

If you live continuously in one place, statues are mainly places for meeting by, but otherwise not noticing.[16] A favourite building may be a place 'to wait out/the cold rain', as the colonnade of the Stock Exchange was in Joseph Brodsky's magnificent poem, 'Almost an Elegy'.[17] Your own memories will be enacted in your everyday behaviour, in the paths around the city, the way you furnish your home, in the things you do at work and when you have free time. This 'mundane memory', as one might call it, primarily focuses on spaces and objects, rather than the official institutions of memory, such as monuments and museums.[18] 'Mundane' memory (which includes what the sociologist Paul

Connerton has termed 'bodily memory', or the physical recollection of space, gesture, etc.)[19] did not have to efface a sense of history. Events impacted on the everyday as well.[20] For those who had lived through it, the Blockade was an indelible experience, as the historian Vladimir Lapin has recalled of his aunt:

> Kirov Bridge was always the place, in her stories, where she first experienced an air-raid, right when she was walking across it. And whenever Kirov Bridge was mentioned, whatever the context, Auntie would start talking about it. At the very least she'd say, 'Yes, that bridge was where I got caught in an air-raid for the very first time.' But that was only the start. If she had the chance, she'd tell you how a policeman dragged her by the arm and didn't let her cross, and how she'd said, 'What difference does it make, I'm half-way across already.' All the details, what the policeman said and what she said to him.[21]

People from Piter (the affectionate local name that effaces the difference between Leningrad and Petersburg)[22] cannot visualise their own identity without the Blockade. As late as the 2010s, the deadliest insults used by fans of Moscow football clubs against Zenit supporters were 'Blockade rats' and '*Vashi dedy lyudoedy*' (Your granddads were cannibals).[23] This does not, however, mean that wartime experience was the *only* way of defining Piter in the half-century and more after the war ended.

In Daniil Granin's 1967 story, 'The House on the Fontanka', the protagonist mused: 'Something had happened. The past appealed to me more than the future.'[24] This transformation of vision – from the bright promise of socialism to the seductive past of old Petersburg, symbolised in Granin's story by the family of Vadim, a young Leningrader who died in the War – ran through the culture of the city at the period Granin was writing. This was not remotely accidental. One of the political hobbyhorses of Nikita Khrushchev was the promotion of regionalism, to a large extent effaced during the Stalin era. The effects could be quite comic – the makers of local TV programmes being told by the centre they were not 'regional' enough, for instance – but in Leningrad, the change of policy was extremely significant.

Between 1949 and 1954, the city was under a dense political cloud, as a result of a large-scale purge of the local political elite, the so-called 'Leningrad Affair'. At the core of the 'Affair' was the supposed assertion of autonomy by local Party officials, who had paid with long prison sentences, or with their lives, for what was seen as a subversion of strict centrism. In 1954, Khrushchev, as part of his struggle for power, accused Beria and Malenkov of having fabricated the Affair: the surviving prisoners were freed (though many were not formally rehabilitated till the glasnost era), and Khrushchev made a landmark speech in which he stirringly claimed that the disgrace of Leningrad had acted as the disgrace of the entire country.[25] Slowly, Leningraders became more assertive. In 1957, the 250th anniversary of the city's founding was celebrated (four years late), along with the twentieth anniversary of the October Revolution: this was marked by the striking of medals and by the publication of albums and histories.[26] An entire cult of 'Leningrad Communism' developed, and guidebooks and tours ceaselessly harped on the city's connections with Lenin and its role in the revolutionary past. Schoolchildren learning languages were taught to say, in resounding if not perfectly correct English, 'Leningrad is Cradle of the October Revolution'.

But attention to the pre-revolutionary past was also rising. Once again, there was a nationwide background to this. The founding of the All-Russian Society for the Protection of Monuments of History and Culture (VOOPIiK) in 1965 – right at the start of the Brezhnev era – both testified to, and fostered, the transformation of attitudes to heritage. The society had its own, extremely active, branch in Leningrad, and activities were mainly concerned with the pre-1917 architecture of what was now coming to be called 'the historic centre'. In reflection of the new preoccupations, the contents of guidebooks gradually shifted from a concentration on monuments associated with the October Revolution to a chronological order that put in first place the buildings and structures raised in the eighteenth and nineteenth centuries.[27] Lists of protected architectural monuments began to include the banks and shops, and even churches, dating from the so-called 'capitalist era', once considered hideous and ripe for demolition.[28] Textbooks and stories for children, and even board games, paid tribute to local places and local history.[29] *The Agitator's Notebook*, whose title bespoke its politically engaged role, started to celebrate the local past. As one woman remembered, 'It was this horrid trade union magazine. Dreadful. Horrid. But you'd always find a little note on the history of some street. A street, or a house, or a square, the stations – that kind of thing. And everyone collected them.'[30]

The Museum of the City of Leningrad, one of the more heavyweight institutions that championed this turn to the past, became an important refuge for young intellectuals who channelled their dislike for the present into state-sponsored work on local history. It was a way of escaping a world where every 7 November you might ask yourself why on earth the country was celebrating 'the suppression of Russia's first democratic government by the Red storm troopers', and where 'the shadow of absurdity' fell over everything.[31] The alternative intelligentsia especially favoured eras, such as the so-called 'decadence' of the early twentieth century, which attracted official disapproval. A canonical interpretation – not by a Leningrader, but widely admired in the city – was Vladimir N. Toporov's *The Petersburg Text in Russian Literature*, which traced how generations of writers had created a literary myth of Petersburg's doomed, depressive, phantasmical character. Modern writers such as Andrei Bitov and

Joseph Brodsky represented Leningrad in comparable ways: crumbling imperial buildings enveloped in the antagonistic weather of fogs and rainstorms.[32]

All of this was very far from the official Soviet spirit of future-oriented optimism. Yet interest in local history was by no means always a cloak for political subversion: at once permitted and mildly scandalous, the enthusiasm for Petersburg culture was consensual. Lyudmila Belova, Director of the Museum of the City of Leningrad, was a highly-placed Communist who retained many of the enthusiasms of her Komsomol youth: on one occasion, she announced to her horrified staff that she proposed to adorn the concert hall of the museum with a piano painted in Soviet scarlet. An enlightened despot with a virtuoso command of the Russian language's enviably rich store of unprintable expressions, she left museum curators in no doubt who was in charge. At the same time, she allowed them free imaginative space, and defended them if there was trouble with the Party and city administration.[33] The constantly expanding collection of pre-revolutionary objects housed in the Peter and Paul Fortress was used for innovative displays and temporary exhibitions that resembled less those in the 'local studies' museums elsewhere in the Soviet Union than those in the city museums of London and Paris.[34]

Long before the renaming of the city in 1992, St Petersburg was undergoing a process of local renaissance. The 1988 hit film *Gentleman Artist* was adapted from a story by Aleksandr Grin (a Soviet writer shelved in the Stalin era), but was explicitly 'decadent' in feel, and had a soundtrack by the rock-jazz musician Sergei Kuryokhin, whose popularity was mainly a phenomenon of unofficial Soviet culture. It typified the paradoxes of the time.[35] Yet the retrieval of pre-Soviet history never went uncontested. The Communist leadership of Leningrad was primarily preoccupied with the city's role as a military-industrial stronghold. The most powerful Party bureaucrat of the 1970s and 1980s was Grigory Romanov, the longest-serving and most effective local leader since Andrei Zhdanov in the 1940s. Romanov was an ambitious technocrat who had no time for sentiment about heritage. Malicious Leningrad tongues said that he had commandeered the *Aurora*, the warship whose guns are alleged to have heralded the outbreak of the October Revolution, and had it sailed down the Neva with his daughter's wedding reception on board. Not content with this sacrilegious assault on a sacred Communist relic, his guests had (so gossip recorded) smashed plates from Catherine II's Wedgwood Frog Service to bring the young couple luck.[36] Improbable as they may have been (the sea- or even river-worthiness of the *Aurora* is an open question, just to begin with), urban legends of this kind emphasised Romanov's indifference to the material past of Leningrad, and still more St Petersburg. Romanov was detested by the local intelligentsia: under his dictate, the city – despite a persistent myth of 'Leningrad Communism' as being somehow more liberal than the Moscow variant – was one of the most repressive places in the Soviet Union. If the Romanov years saw some attempts at cultural management, such as the founding of the KGB-sponsored 'Klub-81' centre for 'vocal and instrumental ensembles', or officially sanctioned rock groups, they also witnessed a crackdown on dissidence, accompanied by searches, arrests, and in some cases physical attacks, mysterious car accidents, and other manifestations of thuggish official disapproval. (Indeed, before Romanov came to power, the Leningrad authorities had stood out for their vicious handling of the cultural opposition: the trial of Joseph Brodsky for 'parasitism' in 1965 not only created a scandal among many members of the intelligentsia, but attracted the covert disapproval of high-level administrators in Moscow.)[37]

However, the different interpretations of Leningrad culture were not just down to 'official' versus 'unofficial', or 'Communist' versus 'non-Party'. A sense of local belonging united all groups. As Academician Dmitry Likhachev, one of the champions of the local heritage movement, put it in 1965, few people who had actually seen pre-revolutionary Petrograd would have called it a beautiful city. That Leningrad was beautiful now was 'the achievement of Soviet town planners'.[38] The preservation of the city's historic fabric was integrated into official documents such as the General Plan of 1966, and decrees of the city authority, Lensovet, emphasised the importance of protecting architecture and monuments. It was the failure of the authorities to live up to their own legislative ideals that generated the fury of oppositionists, rather than the nature of those ideals. And those defending heritage often did so on principles that underlined characteristically Soviet views about propriety – as in cases where members of VOOPIiK fretted about the authorities' intention to locate a public lavatory in an eighteenth-century building as inappropriate, or fumed about the fact that sunbathing was permitted next to the Peter and Paul Fortress.[39] For Likhachev himself, modernism was entirely acceptable – but not in the centre of Leningrad.[40] The appalling quality of most modern buildings in both the post-Stalin and post-Soviet eras came as a kind of self-fulfilling prophecy.[41]

What happened from the late 1950s onwards was that people began arguing about the past – sometimes in extraordinary ways. One instance of this was a poster published in 1980 to celebrate the opening of the Alexander Blok Museum, which was immediately banned as 'too pessimistic' because it represented the world-worn and prematurely aged Blok at the end of his life, rather than the handsome young idealist familiar from collections of his poetry. (See figure 0.2.)

Even within the cultural establishment, a surprising sense of uncertainty could prevail. In 1965, a Leningrader wrote to the Board of Culture of Lensovet to complain that the monument erected in 1937 to commemorate the famous feat of the *Aurora* was historically inaccurate. The ship had in fact heralded the outbreak of revolution not with 'salvos' from its cannons but with 'a salvo' (in the singular). Not surprisingly, this objection did not lead to the text being

0.2 Poster to advertise the Museum-Apartment of Alexander Blok, 1980.

corrected. What borders on the astonishing is that the official in Lensovet who received the letter spent a great deal of time and effort to assure her correspondent that his objection was entirely reasonable, and that she would certainly pass it up the line.[42] Communist myth was starting to lose the struggle with materialism of a kind inimical to Marxism-Leninism: the passionate attachment to unconsidered historical trifles.

The retrieval of the past had practical, as well as intellectual and emotional, resonance. The year 1957 marked not merely Leningrad's postponed 250th anniversary, but the start of a crash building programme that surrounded the city with new concrete suburbs. Between 1959 and 1979, more than 1.5 million people settled in Leningrad.[43] A sense of alienation gripped incomers, removed from villages and small towns to the Soviet Union's second-largest city (and one of the four largest cities in Europe). Old-timers complained that the city was no longer their own, that it was flooded with migrants (*ponaekhali* – 'too many of them have arrived', in the standard phrase).[44] Yet the inhabitants of new districts included large numbers of 'native' (*korennye*, literally 'rooted')

Leningraders, who came high up the housing list for the much coveted separate apartments. Hundreds of thousands of people left the early-Soviet-style 'communal apartments', horizontal tenements where cooking and washing facilities were sometimes shared by dozens of people, many in decayed historic buildings.[45] This was not the first time that the city had attracted waves of incomers – the same had happened during the First Five-Year Plan and the post-war years[46] – but it was the first time that 'native' Leningraders had lost their automatic connection with the city's material past.

In this context, 'memory spaces' of an informal kind – the city's different districts, its cafés, its shops and offices, bars, cultural venues, the surrounding villages and dacha settlements, and individual homes – acquired an extraordinary resonance.[47] The point was not so much that these places were self-consciously 'retro' (they usually were not) but that the aggressive modernity of some of them helped foster an *imaginative* search for an alternative. Vasily Solov'yov-Sedoi and Aleksandr Churkin's *Evening Song*, written for the 1957 jubilee, and later one of Leningrad's unofficial anthems, evoked Komsomol youth on the 'free Neva', but also the 'rustling leaves' of the city's 'parks and gardens'.[48]

Homely things also acquired a commemorative function, as shown in Daniil Granin and Vladimir Vasil'kovsky's album, *The Leningrad Catalogue*, first published in 1986. Granin introduced the book as an effort to commemorate the objects of his youth just as they began to disappear from his memory: 'We decided to collect everything we remembered; the artist would draw them, and I'd tell stories, so as somehow to record the image of that reality, since, sad to say, there are no museums of the history of our Soviet daily life. Of course, in time there will be, but there are things that won't end up there, which can't be displayed there – for instance, the crackle of birch logs burning in a stove.'[49] The book was a lyrical inventory of individual objects – oil lamps, portières, paper knives, fire-tongs, flat-irons – that had no place in the present, being neither 'useful' nor 'antique'. From these, Granin's book expanded into an entire history of daily life, including the laundry suspended in yards and the trams that plied the streets. He moved from objects to be found in individual homes to those which summarised the lost communal life of an entire city. While the late Soviet period was a time of deficit, when what people did not own was of crucial importance, it was also a time when what you did own, or had once owned, carried great weight.[50] In retrospect, ordinary things and practices were to acquire a near-metaphysical status, as the signifiers of a time now lost. As Nonna Slepakova put it in a poem about a demolished house, to remember was to exist – with inanimate things as well, and her own poetry helped them along, making tributes to used bus tickets and to bottles of glue at the post office.[51] In the émigré stories of Sergei Dovlatov, the prized possessions of the Soviet past were at once signifiers of futility, useless in one's exiled present, and more permanent than anything else. 'That entire world has disappeared. Only my belt remains.'[52]

* * *

The practices of memory dissolved the usual division between 'intellectual history' and 'the history of the everyday', since the everyday became highly self-conscious.[53] In turn, writing a history of local memory means working 'between the historical sensitivities of townspeople and the standard conventions of professional ethnography and historiography'.[54] It means placing archival documentation, with its focus on *commemoration*, the official construction of the relationship with the past, alongside memoirs and oral history, where the imaginative processes of *remembrance* and *tradition* can be explored. Rather than attempt to debunk 'myth', and expose the mechanisms of 'invented tradition', we need to understand their functions as ways of explaining the world, as forces that shape, as well as reflecting, reality.[55] As Yosef Yerushalmi argued decades ago, it is history that is, historically speaking, the peculiar and

0.3 'Close the Door After You Leave!' – a sign on the door of the Tram Museum, 2010.

artificial exercise, rather than the creation of legends.[56] If we study areas that are easy to document historically, such as town planning, we can understand the exterior facts of life, for instance how the spaces in which people lived got created, but in order to understand the process of living, we need to make a leap of faith, to rely on people's own narratives, to work from the inside out, as it were.[57]

A theme that will come up again and again in this book is the notion of Leningrad-St Petersburg as an *interior* city. The city's waterfront sweep, where pillared frontages stand under a vast sky, is completely open – too much so, visitors have sometimes worried.[58] But the tourist trails, such as the route from Palace Square to the Peter and Paul Fortress, are not followed by locals. Given what Anthony Cross calls 'the Russian aversion to *walking*', the inhabitants teeter, prance, strut, trudge or saunter from car to café, mini-bus to metro, and only naïve first-time visitors are left to freeze as they range the expanses.[59] If locals do walk round their city in a purposive way, the views they see are not mobile picture-postcards.[60] Much of the city's life is lived away from what is often described as the 'theatre set' of the Neva embankments: as the cultural critic Igor' Smirnov puts it, 'backstage lies everyday life, which is not open to just anyone's gaze'.[61] During the Soviet period, courtyards, with their blank yellow walls and offset windows, had a secret existence. In the post-Soviet years, people often turned completely indoors.[62] The Romantic traditions of secret love and secret knowledge remained strong throughout the twentieth and the early twenty-first centuries.[63] The fact that this was a city where, since the early twentieth century, gay and lesbian culture had been a vital part of local life, but often clandestine, was another element in its hidden existence.[64]

Many Leningrad institutions were secret in the most literal sense. The 'secret section' of Lensovet dealt with vast numbers of everyday processes, down to underpants for army officers and where to put park benches.[65] Large numbers of people worked for so-called 'numbered factories' or 'post-box institutes', too secret to have ordinary names. Researchers at 'post boxes' took notes in special books with numbered and stamped pages, published in closed-circulation journals. They had to evade questions about work even from close relations.[66] Vladimir Maramzin's 1966 story 'The Secrets' showed two classified institutes sharing the same block, yet cut off from each other entirely, the yard divided by barbed wire, and the two canteens at opposite ends so that no careless talk should seep through the walls. At the tram stop, wives and husbands ceased having anything to do with each other, 'preparing to spend their entire day apart, so that the secret might be kept as it should be'.[67]

The waywardness of the city's inner life has often puzzled visitors. In the memorable lament of a German woman doctor from Heidelberg, missing the Gemütlichkeit of the Rhineland: 'It's tough when you can't find anywhere to rest your feet, eat an omelette, have a cup of coffee and do a bit of people-watching.'[68] The poet Viktor Krivulin, in his memoir *Hunting the Woolly Mammoth* (1998), prided himself on offering an 'anti-tour' of Piter. He emphasised that the real life of the city was to be found in the rabbit-warren of garrets and cellars; the more authentic a party, the more likely it was that refreshments would be limited to Snickers and Pepsi. 'This life is closed to tourists,' he insisted.[69]

As this comment suggests, those living in 'the Northern Capital' could be formidably reserved. Those from other Russian cities often associated this with snobbery. This was, after all, the fictional home of Tolstoy's Alexei Karenin, and the place where Ivan Ilich received his legal education. Real-life Petersburgers had a mania for hierarchical classification, ranging down to individual streets. As the novelist E. M. Almedingen remembered, Bol'shoi prospekt on Vasilievsky Island 'was eminently respectable at its eastern end; *Sredny* was just "possible", except for the dinginess of its shops, and *Maly* was quite obviously a slum.'[70] Vladimir Nabokov's constant harping on first-, second-, and third-rateness in aesthetic and philosophical achievement, as though perpetually immured in the staff-room of some Parnassian boarding school, was very much a 'Petersburg' trait.[71] Yury Lotman's touching tribute to the city as an 'eccentric' and hence open capital represented an ideal that was not shared by everyone.[72]

The sheer size of the city was one factor, of course. People who moved from smaller places might either regret, or relish, the fact that communities were less close-knit, yet always sensed this.[73] But that is not all. As types, intellectuals from the city recall their Viennese or Parisian (rather than Berlin or London) counterparts. They traditionally prefer to keep their distance, and may employ the polite snub to virtuoso effect. Igor Kon, later a leading sociologist, recalled in 2004 that when he, as a young man, visited the rare books room of the Leningrad Public Library in order to try and trace Milton's library, he was met by the lawyer and bibliophile Petr Lublinsky, then on the staff, who acidly observed, 'Well, you've a rather provincial way of going about things, I must say, but since you're here, let's see what we can do.'[74] Being cut down to size was the least of the worries faced by complete incomers, as the poet Nikolai Rubtsov recalled in 1960. 'They've registered me, but that's an exception, because here they hold with a steely and sacred resolve to the City Executive Committee's directive not to register people from outside the city, and above all people from different provinces. If Diogenes were to turn up, he'd need to bring his own barrel.'[75] The fact that it could be harder to settle in the city than to settle in Russia generally was reflected by the prices that fixers charged at the start of the twenty-first century to get you a registration, which stood at more than double those asked for arranging Russian citizenship.[76]

0.4 'The Territory of Your Rights', an advertisement for a St Petersburg company providing registrations and other official paperwork.

The persistence of suspicion towards outsiders into the post-Soviet period has been sketched by the writer Il'ya Stogov in a blog entry called 'A Couple of Slaps on the Face to Put You in Your Place':

> A few weeks ago I decided to take a trip into the Russian boondocks, but not just any old where: I wanted to see what the archaeologists were up to. [. . .] The weather was great and the archaeologists were all waving their spades around cheerfully. I turned up and introduced myself, and usually the first question I got was, 'Are you hungry? Want some lunch?'[. . .]
>
> The last stop on my itinerary was Ryurikovo Settlement near Novgorod. Previously, all the people I'd met had been from Moscow or the provinces. I felt the difference straight away. I introduced myself to my fellow Petersburgers, and they nodded politely, but in a preoccupied way. Lunch was somehow never mentioned. A young blond man heard me out and then advised me to leave. Why? I blurted. I tried to insist, saying I'd come 400

> kilometres to have a word with them. The answer was curt: we've no time for chatter here. Lev Lurie, a clever man and a sharp-eyed observer, told me that the Petersburg style means first of all giving someone a slap in the face, and only then condescending to talk to them. But in ten days going round the welcoming, smiling Russian boondocks I'd managed to forget what a complex and unfriendly place Petersburg is.[77]

St Petersburg was, Stogov argued, a supercilious city, one where *no* outsiders (even if *from* the city) were really welcome. When Anatoly Sobchak described the city's character as 'a characteristic mixture of superiority and vulnerability', he was referring to a potentially uncomfortable combination.[78] Attachment to the idea of 'the cultured capital', and the conviction that it is a local virtue to be polite, may be expressed in behaviour recalling the old joke about English gentlemen never being rude by mistake.[79]

An anecdote survives about how, at the 1946 meeting of the Central Committee to discuss what disciplinary measures should be imposed on the editors of the journals *Leningrad* and *Zvezda* for their supposedly anti-Soviet recent publications, Stalin was annoyed to see a group of Leningrad apparatchiks chatting over a cigarette. 'What's all this?' he snarled. 'I'm from Piter too, you know [*ya tozhe piterets*].'[80] Yet, if the exclusive hobnobbing was a quintessentially Piter phenomenon, then Stalin's own persona – arrogantly modest, militaristic, given to a schedule that ran from late morning till very late at night – had a flavour of 'Petersburg style' too (not that the leader himself articulated the connection, or that it would have been warmly regarded in his short-lived home).[81] The exclusivity of the place, over the years, played a part in driving some Petersburgers away from their home town, and may also explain the phenomenon whereby some of the best writing about the city has come either from migrants into Piter, or from migrants out of it.[82]

The self-perception of the detached citizen of the 'cultural capital' may get sucked into ruminations on the distinction between 'Piter' and 'Moscow', a subject on which locals love to expand.[83] In this perspective, detachment can be seen positively – as financial disinterest, ascetism, a refined sense of humour.[84] But of course not all Leningraders or Petersburgers were or are fastidious and refined (or, from another point of view, bloodless snobs). This was and is a city where proletarian identity matters, where working for, say, the Kirov Factory is one of the most prestigious jobs around. Yet, right through the Soviet period, the official ideology of egalitarianism was undercut by a great deal of status-consciousness. Different groups, such as the Party apparat, the 'creative intelligentsia', engineers, skilled workers, unskilled recent incomers – to name only a few – had their own attitudes and behaviour patterns. To some extent, central planning generated uniformity of taste, but precisely for this reason any differences in consumption patterns and perception were highlighted.[85]

The intelligentsia itself was diverse. Different generations, to begin with, had their own attitudes and preferences, all sharpened by the ingrained habit of regarding generations as separate entities. If the '1960-ers' were often socially-conscious utopians, their '1970s' successors were more given to mysticism, and entered adult life determined to forge 'alternative' and 'non-Soviet' paths (itself, of course, a thoroughly 'Soviet' life-choice). The '1980s' generation, on the other hand, took a livelier interest in Western mass culture and consumer goods.[86] In whichever age group, the style of the nineteenth-century Russian radicals – direct to the point of bluntness – had its adherents, and intellectual debate was often robust. The first words of Dovlatov's *The Suitcase* – 'And in the visa department that bitch went and said to me . . .' – cut against any idea that restraint of expression was an essential local characteristic.[87] At the same time, the idea that Leningraders were 'different' because they were more courteous (or, to use the Soviet term, 'cultured') was found even in surprising places. 'Our city is not only the most beautiful in the world, but also the most courageous,' read a characteristic piece of juvenile boosterism in the Leningrad Young Pioneer newspaper, *Leninist Sparks*. 'Our city is very hospitable [. . .] and its inhabitants are very polite.'[88]

Leningraders expressed a relationship with the past not just by thinking about, writing about, and portraying their city, but also by living in it, working in it, and spending their leisure hours in it. The concept of 'memory spaces' (*lieux de mémoire*) in play was broader than the one invoked in Pierre Nora's famous collection of essays under that name. Where Nora and his team distinguished between 'memory' and 'traditions' (as in the contention that the French have 'memory', the English 'traditions'), in actual fact institutions, material culture, and practices of memory, intersected.[89] As anyone living in a city will tell you, the 'memory spaces' important for them are not only, and probably not mainly, the ones listed in the guidebooks. They will include favourite cafés and shops, parks, places where they have worked and lived, and all the other points on familiar trajectories that may be evoked in conversational shorthand.[90]

Michel de Certeau's book *Arts de faire* (1974: translated as *The Practice of Everyday Life*, 1984) gives a wonderful depiction of how city-dwellers find their own paths through the built fabric, imaginatively adjusting the world around them. At the same time, Certeau's distinction between 'official' norms and 'unofficial' practices (in his words, 'strategies' and 'tactics') is a little too neat. Those living in cities may behave normatively – forming their own concepts and standards – while reacting to the practices that are organised 'from above'. Complaining about proliferating refuse (which 'they ought to take away') and holes in the road (which 'they ought to mend') is one obvious case where the relationship between norms and practices that Certeau posits is reversed.[91]

The issue of how much to remember is always an open one. Few people want to live in 'a museum', even where history is as closely associated with local identity as in Piter. As Orhan Pamuk has described in his beautiful book about a former capital with a comparably melancholic air, Istanbul, people are terrified of being not so much antique as merely 'old-fashioned'. While it is debatable whether Petersburg, given the restrictive migration policies obtaining throughout its history, could be described as a 'world city', turning it into a semblance of one became, after 1991, the ambition of a large section of its political and business elite.[92] Already in 1996, Anatoly Sobchak dreamt of converting industrial areas to shiny new apartments, and the Obvodnyi Canal into an 'Autobahn' (sic). Petersburg, Sobchak concluded, was 'still waiting for its Haussmann or a new Leblanc, who would be able not just to "touch up" old districts of the city centre, but essentially to give them a completely new identity.'[93]

At the same time, even radical modernisers often paid lip-service to the 'Petersburg ideal'. After 1992, the past began to be a foundation stone of the legitimacy of the new political leadership, with the old Communist festivals on 7 November and 1 May replaced by 'City Day', a commemoration of the putative founding of St Petersburg on 27 May 1703. No local celebration was complete without a gaggle of figures in eighteenth-century dress; tall moustachioed versions of Peter himself stood on every street corner.[94] The United Russia party ran its December 2011 election campaign under the banner 'Vote Petersburg', and posters offering 'European' levels of service in the new integrated certification centres sat alongside an advertising campaign to get locals to speak 'like Petersburgers' – avoiding bad grammar, slang, and swearing.[95]

* * *

A look inside a city is impossible without drawing on significant amounts of 'local knowledge'. Far fewer people have written about post-revolutionary Piter than about the city before 1917 (it's a question of dozens rather than thousands of studies). In general books, the city's recent past is presented as an afterword.[96] But this book could not have been written without the work of historians, sociologists, and anthropologists such as Aleksandr Kobak, Sergei Yarov, Ekaterina Gerasimova, Il'ya Utekhin, Oleg Pachenkov, Julia Obertreis, Blair Ruble, Finn Sivert Nielsen, and Aleksandr Vakser.[97] Helpful also are some of the less cerebral exercises in local history – particularly, the absorbing books about the city's daily life by Natal'ya Lebina.[98]

At the same time, the *recent* past has remained largely the preserve of autobiography and displaced autobiography – the composition of which is an important Leningrad and Petersburg tradition.[99] Writing of this kind often deploys the key trope of nostalgia, whose central paradox is embodied absence: as the opening paragraph of Gogol's *Old World Landowners*, written in St Petersburg, puts it, 'I see all this clearly [. . .] because I no longer see it.' Often, seeing-yet-not-seeing nostalgia is identified with 'Petersburg memory' overall.[100]

But memory strays widely, and its practices are entangled. The nostalgic or elegiac vein, with its sentimental evocation of the vanished material world (as in Andrei Khrzhanovsky's *One-and-a-Half Rooms*, in which Joseph Brodsky's early life becomes a parade of period knick-knacks and girls in fetching shift dresses) is only one possible way of looking at the past.[101] Indignation or self-disgust are equally likely emotions. A case in point is Mikhail German's remarkable autobiography, *Past Imperfect*, notable for its recall of detail as well as its self-critical stance. German makes no attempt to conceal that the Leningrad intelligentsia was often rather average in its spiritual range, and that there was a great deal of conformity, timidity, and just plain habit in the way life was lived.[102]

If locals are prepared to see themselves as ordinary, however, they believe their city is remarkable. This is expressed not just in the many tributes to the 'most beautiful city in the world', but in the tendency to see the everyday life of the city as exceptional. In truth, there are few things, from building styles to the weather, that cannot be matched in other northern European cities. But the cultural isolation of the Soviet period made other Soviet cities the first point of comparison, and in this context it was not hard to see Leningrad as unique. This attitude endured in the post-Soviet period: the newly renamed 'St Petersburg' was naturally a leader in the reassertion of regional identity that took place after 1991.[103]

All the same, when 'the entire country ripped down the seams', Piter also shared in the marginalisation endured by every urban centre except booming Moscow. From a major manufacturing centre with full employment, it turned in a matter of months into rust-belt territory, undergoing a post-industrial revolution that left many bewildered about how to survive.[104] The bland term 'transition' does no justice to an exceptionally complicated process of adjustment, requiring people to learn new ways of dealing with money and new work practices, and to grapple with value systems that often seemed alien.[105] Though there was a semblance of myth in the image of St Petersburg as 'crime city', during the 1990s levels of violent assault and murder rose steeply, and people also talked far more about danger than in the past. If the ten dollars in your pocket is at once the value of a month's wages, and the cost of three days' food, it is natural to wonder whether it is also the price of your own life.[106] But local memory could offer comfort – suggesting either that things had once been better, or that they had once been worse.[107] Perceived crisis became an arena in which not just personal autonomy, but the dignity of place and its heritage, could be repeatedly rehearsed.[108]

* * *

My own recollections are part of this tissue of memories. I first visited the city then called Leningrad in 1979, as a first-year university student attending a vacation language course. This was also my first ever visit to the Soviet Union, a place that inspired both regret for the lost past and a sense of revulsion among the 'first wave' émigrés in London from whom I had learned Russian. I was put up in a hostel (three or four to a room) out at ploshchad' Muzhestva station on Vyborg side. The place – which I now know to be a well-regarded area, the site of elite Soviet housing as well as the famous Polytechnic, a masterpiece of 1900s neo-classicism – seemed to me then like a desolate wasteland of grimy beige concrete blocks, interrupted by rough grass and scrub.

The city centre – six widely-spaced metro stops away – was a different world, and one with which we had little contact, since most of our excursions were to canonical Soviet sites such as the Piskaryovka Cemetery (the main memorial to Blockade victims) or the various Lenin museums. Apart from a single bus tour on the day we arrived, and a trip to Petrodvorets (Peterhof), where we saw the then bedraggled gardens only since no admissions tickets had been bought for us and the fountains were not playing, there was no effort to show us the historic city. Even the Hermitage was left to personal initiative. (I have discovered since, from Soviet official reports, that this experience was typical – throughout the 1960s and 1970s, foreign visitors were complaining that the balance between factory tours and culture was far too strongly in favour of the former.)[109]

There was a frankly shattering contrast between this experience and later visits, when I was lucky enough to be befriended by Leningraders who themselves were professionally interested in what was coming to be called 'the historic centre'. Then, I spent hours learning about the local past on walks that criss-crossed the old city from end to end, and imbibing my friends' contempt for the mediocrity of contemporary Soviet culture (and a good deal of vodka, gin, and whisk(e)y from the Beriozka hard currency stores too). By the mid-1980s, 'Leningrad' meant for me the pre-1917 fabric of the city as well as the official sites that we had been shown on that first visit, not to speak of the modern buildings where some of my friends lived, and the surviving natural landscape. Like most people, I was particularly struck by the Blockade memorabilia – the desiccated bread rations, and the pages of Tanya Savicheva's diary, with its famous last line: 'Everyone has died. Only Tanya is left'. But just as unforgettable was climbing the narrow, dank stairs of buildings in the streets where *Crime and Punishment* is set, or visiting Stone and Elagin Islands, where avenues lined by plaster Young Pioneers and a boating lake did little to alter the atmosphere of a pre-revolutionary pleasure-ground. In some of the streets, the ornamental wooden dachas were starting to stoop slightly and had gone grey, but the silence would be broken by the plick of a tennis ball hitting an unseen racket, and the hiss of a garden sprinkler, or of a passing limousine.[110]

This book is partly a reflection of that multiple exposure. But it also draws on many later visits to Piter both before and after the renaming, including a

0.5 'The Putsch Will Not Succeed! We are True to Freedom!', from *Smena* newspaper, 20 August 1991.

great deal of time spent there in the last decade. In August 1991, I stood on Palace Square, on the fringes of the crowds gathered to listen to anti-coup speeches, feeling the strange vacuity common to witnesses of major historical events. The stirring calls-to-arms were audible only on someone's transistor, but the whole square erupted when a banner flung out of the windows of the General Staff building unfolded to read, 'The Air Force is With You'.[111]

This was the most dramatic, but not necessarily the most memorable, of many stays. For work reasons – research on a massive history of Russian childhood – I began visiting several times a year from the start of the 2000s, and in 2005 became the owner of an apartment on the northern edge of the city centre. I have lived in all sorts of places: a Khrushchev-era flat where the book overflow was moved to clear the spare divan, but eventually the books won, so I slept on a stiff-spined folding bed, the traditional perch for out-of-town relations; a hotel next to the Moscow Station where my neighbours were men in singlets and tattoos and frowsy blondes paid by the hour; rented or borrowed flats where the water was likely to vanish over the summer, entering and leaving required a sweaty struggle to engage unfamiliar keys in almost immovable locks, where cats had to be fed (condensed milk and chopped steak only), and windows conscientiously opened, or conversely closed, at particular times. I have negotiated on the telephone with the police watch when the instructions I was given about how to lift the anti-burglar surveillance didn't work, suffered the embarrassment of turning off an apparently empty fridge only to have the owner's face creams inside dissolve into rancid pools, dealt with dangerously petulant water-heaters and unfathomable ovens. After all that, buying a flat and getting it redecorated felt like a rest cure, and having a 'city project' to work on was a good way to keep sane on endless trips to builder's merchants out in obscure 'industrial zones', or when winding through the labyrinth of the Maxi-Dom DIY store.

If you work on a city history, the boundaries between 'research' and 'life' become fluid. To attend meetings of the co-operative association is both a matter of intense personal interest to the owner-occupier, and an introduction to the (now remarkably informal) way in which local democracy works. Sitting in one of the city's archives, you have a vivid sense of the material past, as well as what is reflected in the documents. The Russian National Library's headquarters is still in the structure built for it between 1796 and 1896,[112] which recent renovations have left divided between pomp (entrance halls splendidly done up in marble-effect pastel and replacement parquet flooring) and dilapidation. In the reading room for periodicals, volumes are delivered by a mechanism like a perilously wobbly chair-lift in miniature, suspended over acrid druggets, and the dust of ages lies on shelves. The RNL's newspaper hall inhabits part of the former Catherine Institute (1803–7), built by Quarenghi in a particularly imposing style of severe classicism, the impact enhanced by the fact that the echoing corridors are almost always completely empty. Sofas in maroon plush provide dozing points for the weary, while downstairs a Soviet iconostasis enshrines the accusing stares of generations of librarians.

Archives reflect history differently. The Central State Archive, which contains most of the documents of Lensovet and its predecessors, occupies a five-storey exercise in post-Stalinist minimalism surrounded by factories and freight railways, with the melancholy hoots of engines coming through the windows as one works. The Party archives, on the other hand, live on resplendently, at the edge of the city's administrative nerve-centre, Smol'nyi. Readers sit in a tiered, marble-clad auditorium designed to hold Party conferences; next door is the reading room of the city's photography archive, moved from its former premises in a back street behind the Apraksin Market. The Central State Archive of Science and Technology, in the old plebeian area of the Sands (Peski, behind Moscow Station), inhabits what was once a monastic hall of residence (*poddvor'e*), with its church converted to storage.

0.6 The author in the Kazan' Cemetery, Tsarskoe Selo, 1985.

Beyond the state archive network, the sense of how research stretches to the documents' setting is even stronger. Sitting in the Monuments Inspectorate, UGIOP, in ulitsa Rossi (once Theatre Street), you hear the strains of a ballet piano floating over from the Vaganova School across the road, as boys and girls in regulation black-and-white stretch at the barre, or flit past the windows at a running leap. The Archive of the St Petersburg Eparchy occupies part of a wing in the Alexander Nevsky Monastery, looking out on an overgrown walled garden.

In many of these places, the readers include people with a compelling practical need of material from the past – birth and registration certificates so that they can claim benefits, historical plans to support the restoration of old buildings, church records in order to write a brochure for the faithful of a particular parish or simply to work out what a long-demolished chapel once looked like. Thus, archives and libraries are not just, and maybe not even primarily, places where material is retrieved for (or denied to) professional historians, but institutions with their own history and culture.

Combining cultural analysis with personal reminiscence can generate an unpleasant effect of stylistic jarring. So, on the whole, I have decided to stand 'outside the frame'. But first-hand observation, and the questions that it raises, have been an essential part of trying to grasp how the native, adopted, and temporary inhabitants of Piter understand their city's past, and through that, their own and the city's lives, even if the voices of the city's permanent inhabitants are those to which I lend most authority.

## 1

# Moscow Station and Palace Bridge

*The cosy jangle of the crawling tram,*
*Its apple smell of the holiday's first vodka . . .*
(Nonna Slepakova)[1]

In terms of metaphor, Petersburg is a ship-haunted city. The municipal crest, introduced in 1730 and used again from 1991, is decorated with sea and river anchors. A miniature ship – marine life seen through the other end of the telescope – tops the Admiralty building, and anchors decorate its entrances. The building inhabited by many Leningrad writers in the 1920s was known as 'the crazy ship'.[2]

By legend, a salvo from another famous nautical symbol, the cruiser *Aurora*, began the Revolution. The ship became a museum in 1948. Lovingly preserved (indeed, according to a widespread rumour, completely rebuilt to mark the seventieth anniversary of the Revolution), the *Aurora* formed part of a major monumental complex on Petrograd Side, moored alongside the cabin built by Peter the Great, founder of the first Russian fleet. The *Aurora* was only one of the hero ships preserved at different points down the embankments. On Vasilievsky Island stood the icebreaker *Krasin*, dispatched to the rescue of Umberto Nobile's expedition to the Arctic, and returned on 5 October 1928 to a city-wide celebration.[3]

Majestic and ominous, the sea dominated literary representations of the city. For Alexander Blok, the forlorn, drunken sailor on the docks stood for human tragedy in the broadest sense.[4] Mandelstam's apocalyptic post-revolutionary poems about listing, doomed 'Petropolis' identified sea location and watery catastrophe. The air of the Baltic blew through Joseph Brodsky's poems, and the sea figured regularly in the poet's drawings as well.[5] In 1981, the cultural historian Yuri Lotman, a native of the city, saw the association more concretely: 'Petersburg met me with squally winds, the smell of the sea and the thaw. I even had the feeling that Nevsky Prospekt was rocking like a deck. [. . .] As I went down Nevsky at night, I had a poetic moment or two, sensing the city like a vast boat.'[6]

The insistent recrudescence of the maritime in metaphors was partly a displacement. In Petrine days entire sections of the centre were given over to rigging and bales of tow, but in the twentieth century the sea made a muted impact on Petersburg's historic centre – bursts of brackish air and the odd perpetually indignant seagull aside.[7] In the Soviet period, private seafaring craft were as far beyond the reach of Soviet citizens as personal planes.[8] Leningrad was not even visited by long-distance ocean-going ferries.[9] There were no hovercrafts from Tallinn or ro-ros from Helsinki. Sea links with the outer world took the form of luxury cruises, with the huge white ships acting as temporary hotels for Western tourists come to sight-see (and in the case of Finns, drink the town dry). Occasionally they would take some privileged Soviet traveller in the other direction – to Denmark, Germany, and, until the end of the 1970s, England.[10]

There was also a considerable distance between the heart of the city and its marine extremities. Sometimes a cruise liner might be moored in the centre, looking as though someone had dropped it, but the main passenger port was the 'Sea Station' out on the western end of Vasilievsky Island, a vast concrete stack topped with a notional mast, completed in 1982. Before reaching the station, the hopeful traveller had been exposed to mile upon mile of crumbling concrete docks, as the ship slowly made its way up the 'sea canal' from the coast.

The indignity of this approach – as a local historian I know put it in 1990, 'From the sea, Leningrad is an appalling city' – was a recognised embarrassment for the city's administration. In the late Soviet period, the construction of a 'marine façade' became one of the preoccupations of city planners. The tower

1.1 The approach to Leningrad by sea, May 1990. On the right, the 'marine façade' is visible.

blocks created on reclaimed land at the western end of Vasilievsky Island in order to effect this frontage became one of the most prestigious housing zones in the city.[11] But by the early twenty-first century, they too were regarded as graceless, and plans for a new 'marine façade' on reclaimed land in front of the 1970s one were set in train. Constructed as a joint state-private finance initiative, the complex was – according to the company building it – 'an impressive European façade for the Northern capital on its seaward side, with high-rise business centres, shopping malls, leisure facilities, parks, new housing.' It would 'present a modern and convenient marine gateway for guests arriving in St Petersburg', as well as much-needed office space within easy reach of the historic centre.[12]

This ambitious scheme was intended to transform the functionally landlubber existence of the Neva's major city.[13] In the early Soviet period, the banks of the river were still used for freighting, but embankment-building in the post-war years turned the shores of Vyborg Side and Okhta, and the Neva banks south of the Alexander Nevsky Monastery, into ordinary urban thoroughfares.

Throughout the Soviet period, sailing had been the preserve of professional mariners – the sailors based out at Kronstadt, the sea cadets in the Makarov College, and the merchant seamen manning the Soviet Union's largest cargo port. Sailors were a specific sub-cultural group, given their relative freedom to travel. In the late Soviet period, merchant seamen were among the key suppliers of the city's lively black market.[14] Naval officers and ratings inspired much more affection than ordinary army officers and 'Navy Day' was a genuine local holiday, with its brass bands, dress uniforms, and sometimes naval visitors from afar.[15] There was also a 'mariner literature', such as Nikolai Rubtsov's poem 'On the Ocean', which recalled the spattered appearance and cod stink of a sea-going trawler, with its tireless procession of seabirds behind:

> And the waves bulged crimson
> like muscles,
> foam-flecked,
> drunken,
> on the ocean's nervy chest,
> and the seals dived into the waves.[16]

For most locals on ordinary days, though, Leningrad's relationship with the sea recalled Edinburgh rather than Venice or Stockholm. Leningrad was a major training centre for marine architects, and thousands of people were employed in ship-building and marine ballistics. But as activities of strategic significance, these lay below the surface: an open secret, but still a secret.[17] The city's naval base was at Kronstadt, accessible only by special permit. The freight docks lay on remote Kanonersky Island, beyond the end of the city's most proletarian waterway, the Obvodnyi Canal. Only in the summer did the city's connections with the sea revive, with improvised kebab bars down at the docks, and the Neva embankments at the western end of Vasilievsky Island thronged by nautical traffic waiting for the opening of the city's drawbridges.[18]

On summer nights down by the embankments, the lit ships preparing for the off gave a sense of freedom unusual in a country with closed borders. (Along the Estonian coast, villagers who had once worked as fishermen were allowed to keep their boats only if they had these sawn in half; the remnants were used to ornament people's gardens.)[19] But Leningrad's status as harbour was not celebrated in Soviet mythology. It was Moscow, the capital, which had to have primacy here, its landlocked position dissolved in the title 'Port of Five Seas'.[20]

Once 'Leningrad' became 'Petersburg', its relationship with the sea remained ambiguous. With the Baltic Fleet run down, Kronstadt became functionally a normal city suburb, accessible by bus over the flood dam, though still with a military air to its spruce, cobbled streets.[21] However, the 300th anniversary of the foundation of the Russian navy was commemorated by a spate of new monuments.[22] The city filled up with tall ships, suddenly resembling once more the magnet for 'all flags' planned by Peter I in Pushkin's *The Bronze Horseman*. But the flotilla soon dispersed.

Petersburg continued to be one of the Russian Federation's leading cargo ports, with a turnover exceeding that of every other city bar Novorossiisk.[23] Yet this did not put it even in the top fifty internationally (indeed, world leaders

1.2 Tall ships on the Neva for the 300th anniversary of the Russian navy, July 1996.

such as Shanghai and Singapore handled more cargo than all the ports in the Russian Federation put together);[24] rather, the figure was comparable with the slimmed-down Port of London.[25] At the same time, Petersburg's role as a centre for the marine defence industry survived, at least outwardly. In the new world, factories openly advertised themselves as 'Submarine Factory' (on the Neva, beyond Admiralty Wharves), or 'Underwater Ballistics Concern' (on Bol'shoi Sampsonievsky).[26]

Privatisation, while creating problems for the city's professional sailors,[27] did not lead to a surge in boat-purchasing. Sea travel largely remained the preserve of professional sailors and the prosperous – the very rich moored their yachts in Monaco, not on Krestovsky Island.[28] To visit the sea, most locals were likely to take a train out to the Gulf of Finland (the local 'riviera', with its resorts of Zelenogorsk, Sestroretsk, Repino, and Komarovo), rather than head to the city shores.

The sea was thus not so much an essential component of city life as a reminder, at times an awkward reminder, of the potential for elemental nightmares. In 2004, drunks lifted a commemorative anchor on Vasilievsky Island off its pedestal in order to use the marble base as a table, as though such lèse-majesté could reduce the ocean itself to size.[29] In Il'ya Averbakh's film *Monologue* (1972), the teenage heroine's attractive but heartless seducer was a keen amateur sailor, with sexual transgression and wandering the deep at will symbolically associated. The marine haunted the imagination of the city's artists, but in its physical actuality St Petersburg was a river city of a quintessentially Russian kind. The double identity of St Petersburg as marine yet non-marine was poetically captured by Alexander Sokurov's film *Father and Son* (2003), set in a city which, like St Petersburg, was bounded by the grey ocean – but in fact mostly filmed in Lisbon.[30]

The city and sea remained uncomfortable neighbours. Before work started on the protective dam alongside Kronstadt (begun in 1979), major floods were a constant threat. As building slowly advanced (it was interrupted in 1990 for more than a decade, and continued into the 2010s), the possible ecological damage (stagnation, rise in pollution and in topsoil salinity levels) made the thinking public anxious.[31] Artists took refuge in an imaginative retreat to the period of great deluges (as in Andrei Chezhin's 2003 series, *The Neva* [Baptismal] *Font*, which showed the city's landmarks surrounded by churning floods). Hemmed in by increasingly fetid water, the actual St Petersburg – despite the promise of the new 'Marine Façade' – seemed cut off from the ocean to a greater extent than at any time in its history.

## Airborne and Overland

By the late twentieth century, the vast majority of international travellers, and many from within the country, were arriving by air rather than water. Passenger traffic had begun in the 1930s at the airfield to the south of the city later known as Shosseinaya. But flights were few in number, and travellers were mainly those on official business – what Soviet usage referred to as the 'commanded'. A second airfield, Smol'noe (later known as Rzhevka), was opened in 1941, in order to service warplanes (the airfield to the south had been swallowed by the front line). After the war, Smol'noe continued in use, servicing short-range flights in small aircraft.[32] However, it was Shosseinaya airfield that was developed for large-scale traffic. Reopened in 1948, it acquired its first arrival hall (a building of modest size in the conservative neo-classical style contemporary Western architects would have used for a bank) in 1951.

In the late 1950s, the place was still a modest operation, with fewer than 100 flights a day (at the same period, New York-La Guardia was handling over 1000).[33] From the early 1960s, the number of flights started increasing rapidly. By the late 1960s, this was the second busiest airport in the Soviet Union, serving 1.2 million passengers in 1967.[34]

Reconstructed by the leading Leningrad architect Aleksandr Zhuk, it reopened in 1973 as 'Pulkovo'; the design, awarded a State Prize in 1974, attracted a great deal of flattering press coverage.[35] It was later to be on most lists of the leading modern buildings in the city. If the first hall at Pulkovo had resembled a Soviet station (for example, that at Vyborg), the new one looked

1.3 Leningrad airport in the late 1960s.

like an enormous liner with five central funnels (once again, marine metaphors surfaced as the importance of the sea receded). Inside, however, functionalism dominated – by the late twentieth century, rather dilapidated functionalism.

From the late 1980s – as international travel suddenly became possible for Russians – the focus in reporting switched from the airport's splendours to its deficiencies. Among the 'all too earthly concerns' of the aviation authorities, as one journalist put it, was the absence of a city terminus, not to speak of hotels for transit passengers.[36]

The terminal for foreign traffic, the original Shosseinaya arrivals hall, was particularly cramped. Those meeting and seeing off passengers milled aimlessly in an ill-defined arena, with just one café squeezed into a side aisle. In early January 2003, with outside temperatures down to minus 30, it was so cold in the area where passengers were herded to wait for passport control that you had to unpeel the skin of your hand from the surface of a fake marble pillar after using this as a prop for signing off the arrival paperwork. Large-scale reconstruction had to wait till a new pavilion, in the steel and glass style of neo-globalism, was built for the 2003 Jubilee. Even this was hardly adequate to numbers when not being used just by VIPs, particularly as almost all the flights – presumably, for the convenience of customs and passport control staff – arrived and departed in the late afternoon.

All the same, air travel remained a prestige form of long-distance travel into the twenty-first century. In the Soviet period, this was also the only kind of domestic transport for which one could buy a return ticket. Any other type of travel often required the passenger either to trust fate, or to badger friends or connections at the far end to obtain the return *before* the outward journey was booked. Since the main direction of traffic was into Leningrad (as with Moscow), voyaging on spec meant being stranded at the provincial end of the trip, where tickets would be harder to get than reservations in one of London or New York's most fashionable restaurants.[37]

At the other end of the scale from planes lay long-distance buses. In the 1960s, these seemed (at least to provincial travellers) quite luxurious: 'brand new Ikarus vehicles, pretty chic for the times,' remembered a Russian living in Estonia.[38] With the same Ikarus in service for decades, the main virtue came to be cheapness. Concessions to comfort were almost non-existent. At best, there might be a 'relaxer seat' on long-distance routes – though this would not necessarily work – and curtains that, in summer, flapped in the hot, dusty air from the windows. Tickets were till receipts faintly printed out on fibrous, buff-coloured paper. Relegated to a site on Obvodnyi Canal, and built in late-Soviet *style économique*, the Leningrad bus station was the most shame-faced of major entry points.[39]

The bus station was reconstructed for the Jubilee of 2003, and ticketing systems modernised. Bus travellers could now, if they liked, travel considerably more comfortably than in the past, but in that case, tickets cost much the same as by rail.[40] However, bargain-basement bus travel still existed, as was clear from the vehicles lined up outside the Moscow Station in the late evening. Destinations – Elista, the capital of the Kalmyk Republic, Vladikavkaz – made clear that a sizable cohort of passengers were the so-called *gastarbaitery*.[41] Buses to Berlin, Düsseldorf, Helsinki or Paris offered Petersburgers on tight budgets an economical route to the West. Those who could not afford even the bus fare were likely to hitch lifts – though a small sum often needed to be paid for these too.[42]

But for travellers living above the breadline, as well as for many people who had been 'commanded' (that is, were arriving on official business), the train was the most likely mode of transport.[43] It offered a permissively wide tariff for all from VIPs (who, in the Soviet years, might contact the authorities to have a couple of extra carriages added to the country's number one train, the 'Red Arrow')[44] down to those packing the shelf-bunks of the 'general carriages' or occupying an ordinary seat.[45] A sense of occasion was conferred by the playing of Reinhold Glière's 1949 anthem, 'Hymn to a Great City', over the tannoy as the passengers of the premier trains descended to the platforms and made their way to the covered entrance.[46] But whatever their status, rail gave its users access to the heart of the city.

The slow progress into the terminus gave a sense of the extent to which Leningrad, criss-crossed by lines and dotted by stations, was a railway city.[47] Moscow Station, however, was a wan remnant of the city's imperial past, as indeed were the other main stations. In some cases, the rundown air extended to the traffic as well. By the late Soviet period, the Baltic Station was exclusively used by local trains.[48] The Finland Station also mainly had this role, though trains still departed and arrived from Helsinki – always, as was proper to their status, to and from Platform One.

The rebuilding of this station, begun in 1950, was attributable less to infrastructural needs than to its symbolic status as the place of Lenin's triumphant re-entry to revolutionary Petrograd in 1917. The memorial complex included not only the monument in Lenin Square outside the station itself, but Engine no. 293 which had drawn the train used by the Bolshevik leader to reach Petrograd on 7 August 1917. It had lived out its pensioner years in Tampere; in 1964, it was ceremonially presented to the Soviet government, and placed on a special pedestal that was unveiled on 4 November, just before the revolutionary holidays.[49] Huge amounts of effort, not to speak of money, were expended. The budget for constructing the pavilion to house the train was agreed by the Leningrad Regional Committee of the Communist Party on 23 September 1958 at a cost of 1,982,000 roubles, which at that stage would have paid the wages of 200–300 factory workers for a year.[50] As well as revolutionary memories, the station had wartime associations: it had been the start of the 'Road of Life', used to bring supplies and evacuate Leningraders, and a monument was placed to mark this history in 1973. Alongside the monuments themselves, a section of the pre-1950 building, with its incised and cream-painted brickwork, was left standing to symbolise the structure that had actually witnessed the past.

In the case of the Tsarskoe Selo Station, the historical echoes were less convenient, since the terminus of the oldest railway in the country was named for the royal residence. A rare case of a Russian station with an engine shed (so that imperial personages should not, unlike most passengers, be exposed to the weather), the building was a resplendent example of *style moderne*. It was renamed Detskosel'sky Station in 1918 (when Tsarskoe itself became 'Detskoe'). In 1935, on the other hand, it became 'Vitebsk Station', though the vast majority of passengers continued to use it for travel to the Leningrad suburbs. It therefore represented an exceptional instance where Leningrad's nationwide role was actually emphasised during the Soviet period.

This was, though, the exception that proved the rule. Even before the revolution, the decision had been made to develop Moscow, rather than St Petersburg, as the Russian Empire's functional rail hub. The Nikolaevsky Station, serving Moscow, was also by far the most prominent in the city, situated halfway down Nevsky prospekt. Naturally, this situation was further consolidated after 1917. From 1923, the terminus bore the title October Station in commemoration of the Bolshevik Revolution, but from 1930 it became 'the Moscow Station', underlining the new priorities. The decline of Leningrad's national and international connections continued in the post-Soviet era as well. The Warsaw Station, which had carried traffic to Western Europe, was permanently closed in 2001, leaving passengers wanting to travel to those destinations by train to route themselves through Moscow. It reopened as a shopping centre and railway museum.[51]

Only one major rail station was raised in the twentieth century: the Ladoga Station, whose primary purpose was the decongestion of the Moscow Station. Built by N. I. Yavein, it was one of the few reasonably distinguished modern buildings in post-Soviet St Petersburg, partly because of its intelligent reflection of architectural tradition. The roof span, with its heavy half-timbered look, echoed notable arts-and-crafts buildings such as the dacha of Grand Duke Boris Nikolaevich at Tsarskoe Selo. Yet the materials and techniques used were post-industrial, given a retrospective intonation. By contrast, Finland Station's pared-down functionalism (also impressive in its way) had derived from an earlier interpretation, according to which transport junctions were supposed to be thoroughly 'modern'.

In the 1960s, 1970s, and 1980s, old stations had, from the Soviet point of view, no romanticism. The main impulse was to try and update them. So the Moscow Station was thoroughly reconstructed, with glass side booths. Press coverage emphasised the upgrading of the line. The tide turned only in the mid-1980s, when the proposed demolition of the Warsaw Station started to attract opposition.[52] Another sign of altered priorities was that Vitebsk Station became a site of official memory, with the placing of a monument to the first train ever to use the terminus – 'a kind of counter-balance', as one local historian observed in the 1990s, 'to the "Lenin relic"' at the Finland Station.[53] A few years later, in 1993, the Lenin bust at the Moscow Station was one of the most prominent casualties of post-Soviet iconoclasm, replaced by a bust of Peter I, though the city's founding tsar probably had even less claim to commemoration in that particular spot than the Party leader.[54] A decade later the Vitebsk Station, restored for the 2003 Jubilee, became once more a showpiece of Petersburg art nouveau.

Stations, though, were not generally of interest to the authorities as *lieux de mémoire*. Old trains might be cherished, but the modernisation of transport connections was an abiding obsession. However, though press coverage revolved round the high-speed trains shortly to appear on the tracks,[55] the most splendid trains remained way beyond the pocket of most travellers. Even

1.4 The main staircase of the Vitebsk Station, 2011.

in the 2010s, the old style of travel – slow, not very slick, but convenient and cosy – looked set to continue into the foreseeable future.[56]

## 'Cashiers Do Not Give Information'

Arrival in the city brought not just contact with a specific entry point, but transition at many other levels. Piter was rare among major European Russian cities in its closeness to a border zone. For foreign travellers, it might well be their point of entry to Russia itself. The publisher Ray Pierre Corsini, who visited in the early 1960s, noted that foreigners arriving at the airport spent their first minutes in waiting rooms 'with leather armchairs and a round table strewn with travel brochures in several languages', overlooking 'a flower-bordered patch of lawn'. However, then followed a grilling by customs officers about money and valuables ('"you must declare your gold!"').[57] The grilling, rather than the luxury lounge, became many foreign travellers' most lasting memory of arrival – particularly as scrutiny became more and more cursory in other places. (The Russian Federation went over to the international norm of a spot-check system only in the early twenty-first century.)[58]

For Russian travellers, the border was less significant. The city had lost its highroad checkpoints for incomers, *zastavy*, in the late 1850s.[59] The international border had a strong symbolic presence in mass culture – but as a barrier for miscreants from abroad, who were regularly, if the press was to be believed, foiled by the ever-vigilant members of the border police.[60] Border-crossing as an actuality was of greater cultural importance when it took place in the other direction. The rare Soviet travellers to the West were likely to undergo close scrutiny – above all those intending to emigrate for good. Customs officials would assert their rights to any possession that they chose to define as valuable: books, manuscripts, personal jewellery (right up to wedding rings). The check-in staff, seldom pleasant at the best of times, would manifest Soviet patriotism by rudeness and a hawk-like vigilance towards overweight bags.[61] Given the scale of emigration from Leningrad in the 1970s and 1980s, such scenes were widely endured, and still more widely witnessed. They cast a pall even over departures that were not intended to be permanent. The *otval'naya*, or leaving party, and *provody*, seeing people off, were abiding rituals.[62] As one émigré later remembered, 'The banal metaphor of the funeral always came to mind'. The airport was also the first place in Leningrad to acquire self-closing doors.[63]

But arrivals presented challenges of their own. Pulkovo – a sterile, forbidding place about 15 kilometres from the city centre – was uncongenial but closely regulated, apart from a lawless few years in the 1990s when the baggage carousels, groaning with imported Western technology, were regularly robbed.[64] Arrivals anywhere else brought the traveller closer to the edge. Even in the Soviet period, Moscow Station in particular was said to be the haunt of petty thieves and prostitutes.[65] In the early 1990s, the station was, as *Leningradskaya panorama* reported, 'a reeking den of cheap prostitutes, dossers, drug addicts, and hustlers of all descriptions'. In parts of the station, gypsies (widely regarded as a 'criminogenic' population) were camping out; in others, street drinkers glugged freely; yet other spots were the territory of homeless children. Visiting the lavatory was likely to lead to the loss of one's bag or hat at the very least; up to twenty crimes were recorded in the average day.[66] Moral panic aside, railway stations at this period were by any standards a hostile environment.[67]

The impact of the criminal underworld on the station environment was particularly blatant in the post-Soviet era; but neither were stations comfortable places earlier than that. Seating was in chronically short supply, and the food provided at kiosks sparse and often stale. Apart from VIPs, the only members of the public given special treatment were mothers with small children, who had their own waiting, reception, and ticketing facilities. Other travellers could use left-luggage offices, and have some kind of a snack or a meal, but orientation was limited to departure boards and to signs saying, 'Cashiers do not give information'. Beyond this, travellers had to rely on general city-wide 'information offices', which were mainly used to trace the addresses and telephone numbers of friends and relations, making up for the non-availability of telephone directories.[68]

In the post-Soviet period, official coverage dwelt as frequently on the improvement of stations as on the improvement of trains. The latest systems had been introduced to regulate queuing at the ticket offices; facilities in station malls had been transformed. A new culture of *servis* was everywhere.[69] In reality, the termini stubbornly resisted improvement. Standards of decoration and service remained ramshackle, sanitary and refreshment facilities basic at best. In short, they were like real European stations rather than the 'Europeanisation' ideal propounded by the city government.[70]

## 'I Just Started Moving Backwards, Backwards, Backwards!'

Even for those certain of their rights to be there, Piter, on arrival, had a forbidding nature. In his memoirs, written at the end of the 1920s, the painter Kuz'ma Petrov-Vodkin recalled how dispiriting it was, after time spent in Paris, 'to come back to oneself in the bureaucratic bareness of Petersburg avenues'.[71] Decades later, the art historian Mikhail German, also returning from Paris, was to have the same impression.[72] Newcomers might well be positively daunted. In an unpublished short story, Dmitry Mukhin (originally from Vologda) has sketched the confusion of an early twenty-first century arrival:

> *It took me all day to study the city.* And now I more or less know where the main points of convergence of the endless streams of tourists are. But the

> evening made me feel very unhappy. It had got much colder outside, you couldn't say the real chill had set in, but the thought of somewhere cosy and warm was very appealing. It turned out, though, that I wasn't welcome anywhere but in museums and shops. I hadn't even got anywhere to stay. I'd somehow never been bothered by the question before, but now it turned out that, given my budget, finding a place for the night was a lot more difficult than adding two and two.
>
> I strode into the nearest hotel, which happened to carry a grimy plate by its door with the words, 'Hostel – at a price for anyone's pocket'. Both the state the plate was in and what it said gave me hope that I wouldn't be spending the next night on the street. But it turned out that I wasn't the 'anyone' mentioned, nor did my 'pocket' fit the bill. I moved on. Night was really setting in now, but I just couldn't find anywhere cheap. And so, once I'd thought things over and wandered round aimlessly for a bit, I went back where I'd come from – straight to the railway station.[73]

It did not help that the areas surrounding the main termini were notably squalid. A proportion of locals actually preferred things that way: 'Stagnation', an unreconstructedly 'Soviet' shop next to the Vitebsk Station, even attracted poetic tributes as a grease-smeared shrine of local memory.[74] But this was no consolation to those struggling to adjust to the city's hard welcome.

Different groups of new arrivals were likely to feel disoriented for different reasons. For Westerners who could not read or speak Russian, orientation in the most basic sense presented considerable challenges, since the conventions of explaining space were different. Even in the twenty-first century, inhabitants of Piter (like most Russians) did not think in terms of 'north' and 'south', and did not talk about locations in that way. Instead, they might say, 'over towards Griboedov Canal'. Instructions for finding places would be given according to transport routing and local landmarks – 'opposite the Russian Museum', or 'turn left by the beer bar'.[75] For a native of Paris or London, the non-sequential numbering of buildings might cause problems, particularly in the new suburbs.[76] And in the Soviet period, the only maps available where schemas showing the vague location of famous monuments – totally useless for finding a hotel, let alone an apartment block.[77]

Russian arrivals were in a different position. Like the incomers in Protazanov's 1927 film *The End of St Petersburg*, they would primarily rely on word-of-mouth as the standard aid to orientation. In this respect, street-finding remained pre-literate. A witty DHL advertisement from 2008 played on this 'interior knowledge' ethos by showing city views embellished with exhortations: 'Careful! This door opens inwards' and 'You can only get to the yard along Svechnoi pereulok, the other end's blocked off'. 'No one knows St Petersburg like we know it,' boasted the slogan at the bottom. (Similar

1.5 Detail of a 1979 map of Leningrad's architectural monuments.

advertisements were posted for other Russian cities too, along with a generic one for the countryside; this supposedly 'Western' city was placed in the same series as other Russian places.)

More likely to be bewildering to a visitor used to the Russo-Soviet urban environment were the first contacts with the local transport system. Even in the 2010s, there was no direct transport to the city. As in Naples (and perhaps also for reasons to do with local graft), a planned high-speed rail link persisted in not getting off the ground. Those who were not met by car could either pay for a taxi (at rates which were likely to be many times higher than it would have cost to take a taxi *to* the airport), or get ground transport to a stop at the far south of the metro and ride the rest of the way in.[78] At one stage in the late 1980s and early 1990s, even this none-too-convenient service was not working and rapacious cab drivers cleaned up. There were dark rumours about actual robberies, as well as daylight robbery in terms of fares.

While less remote than this, the Sea Station also had poor transport connections – with no metro station within walking distance, and ground transportation a 200-metre hike through the car-park and beyond. While other places of entry lay closer to the centre, onward travel could still be unnerving for new arrivals, particularly on the metro. As a Petersburg student remembered in 2007, when he first arrived from Pskov,

> I was terrified to get off the escalator. I mean, I just couldn't step off that running band back on to fixed ground, so to speak. I remember seeing us getting closer to the end, closer, and I just started moving backwards, backwards, backwards, till eventually this local lady took me by the hand and stepped across with me, right? So at first I was just terrified of all that. Those are my first memories of Petersburg.[79]

## River Crossings

Getting round was not simple even for the initiated. A waterlogged city in some respects (certainly climatically), Leningrad also lived a semi-detached life from its rivers and canals. The waterways – originally used for deliveries – were, by the 1960s, essentially for pleasure craft.[80] A few hydrofoils plied the routes to outlying tourist attractions: Petrodvorets (Petergof), Lomonosov (Oranienbaum); river boats, known affectionately as 'river trams', offered 'Excursions Round the Rivers and Canals'.[81] But otherwise, the river acted as a barrier to transport, rather than a means of getting about. The first electric trams had been laid across the ice, and older Leningraders could remember taking short cuts across the frozen Neva in the 1940s.[82] Whether because of warmer winters, or different ideas about safety, or both, such crossings had become very unusual by the end of the twentieth century. Indeed, the authorities had an ice-breaker cut channels so no one should feel tempted. At whatever season, the Neva could now only be crossed on bridges – of which (contrary to the testimony of a million postcards), it was short, compared with other major rivers. Twenty-two crossings spanned it at different points, as compared with the thirty-two across the Thames at London and thirty-seven across the Seine at Paris.[83]

The river, an important route back in the nineteenth century, was more or less empty of business traffic in the second half of the twentieth. The poet Viktor Krivulin, visiting Hamburg, was struck by the busyness of the Elbe, 'this vast loaded river, so unlike my own Neva, forced into extinction by command of the powers that be, with their abiding fear of open stretches of water.'[84]

Even compared to the Thames at London, with its dinghies, rowing boats, and police launches, and with occasional barges and water-buses, the Neva was scantily plied. Its waters came to life only on select occasions. Apart from Navy Day, the most important of these was the festival for school-leavers, 'Scarlet Sails'.

Introduced in 1968 as the first city-wide Graduation Day event (previously each district had organised celebrations), 'Scarlet Sails' was associated with the water from the very beginning.[85] Concerts were set up along the embankment, and school-leavers could take part in competitions. As an organiser later remembered, 'The prizes were just amazing: a trip on a boat down the Neva, say, or on a taxi round Leningrad by night'. As a result, crowds soon lined up.[86]

The pièce de résistance, though, was a river-boat rigged out in scarlet, carrying a tableau based on Aleksandr Grin's touching and sentimental novel, *Scarlet Sails* (1924). Two school-leavers, a boy and a girl, sailed on a cutter to the Rostral Columns with a torch and lit beacons there; a sailing-ship, rigged with red sails, brought a girl dressed as the heroine of Grin's novel to greet them. Marina Basina, then a school-leaver, remembered the enchantment of that first occasion: 'The sailing-boat was so beautiful. It just went floating by with a searchlight playing on it, to the sounds of some music, carrying these real scarlet sails, not just coloured lights. It was enchanting.'[87]

Aleksandr Grin's novel had been written in Leningrad, though set in an invented wonderland; its lure had been enhanced by a long stretch of political purdah.[88] The point, though, was less the novel's history, or the details of the scenario, than the fact that this was enacted on the river. Decked out with the banal trappings of Soviet ritual though it might be, 'Scarlet Sails' was a latter-day adaptation of 'the Marriage of the Sea' as celebrated in Venice. Though in due course the festival acquired all sorts of additions (fireworks, and, by the early twenty-first century, a 'laser show' with an enormous outdoor screen), the river remained the focus, with thousands who had no connection to the graduation ceremony lining the embankments to watch. As well as a lavishly funded official occasion, 'Scarlet Sails' was a celebration for small boats, dozens of which

1.6 Small boats on the Neva for 'Scarlet Sails', 2010.

charged up the river towards the launch of the main occasion, scudding like beetles beside the sailing ships and the pleasure-boats of school-leavers. On this particular day, *pitertsy* took back the river.

Yet 'Scarlet Sails' remained an exception, in the post-Soviet period too. The relaxation of Soviet economic dirigisme was not accompanied by a sudden surge of private boat ownership along the Neva, any more than it was by a surge in the keeping of marine vessels. Unlike London, let alone Stockholm, the city had no moorings for small craft or house-boats in the centre. Rather, the effect of privatisation was to make the river-boat business a key target of interest among the more piratical local businessmen. In 2005, two new pleasure boats, built to imitate the elegant sailing ships portrayed in engravings of the Petrine era, were blown sky-high. The owner blamed a rival for the atrocity. He claimed that since the Committee for the Management of State Property (KUGI) had taken over the administration of moorings from Mostotrest (the bridge management agency in the Soviet period) 'people get all anxious and that's how they sort out their differences'.[89]

For most locals and visitors, though, taking to the water was a special occasion. The little 'party cutters', with restaurants and bars on board, offered 'excursions round the rivers and canals', and hiring these boats was a popular and pleasant way of marking a special event. From Liteinyi Bridge up to Smol'nyi, past the submarine factory, out to the very edge of the city where a few wooden houses and gardens still cling on, and then back again by the same route, filled a couple of hours on a summer evening at relatively low expense.[90] A slightly more expensive and pretentious type of evening could be spent in a restaurant-ship, a type of entertainment that had been available since the late 1960s when *The Dolphin* and *The Sail* pioneered the trend.[91] The entire concept of a *fixed* ship (and these were often historical fakes, with 'traditional' rigging and portholes) embodied the mannered relationship of late twentieth-century Piter with the water.

That said, the 2000s saw the introduction of 'water taxis', suggesting that there might be a future for regular river transport (badly needed to relieve the horrendously crowded roads).[92] And there were still working ferries to Kronstadt – mainly in use for people coming into the city, but sometimes taking the odd official (in suit, with briefcase) out on the early boats, and occasional visitors on the later ones.[93] Generally, there was enough navigation to justify keeping the city's drawbridges open nightly during the summer season. In the small hours, shipping reconquered the city.[94]

For landlubbers, the situation was less convenient. An elaborate bridge-opening timetable operated, but though in theory different parts of the city should always have been accessible, crossing might require a long detour. You could end up spending over an hour at Lieutenant Schmidt Bridge, only to find that it was closed at the advertised hour, and Palace Bridge (half an hour's walk away) open instead.[95] Bridges could thus be impediments to travel. They were closed for major festivals, as well as summer sailings. In Georgy Daneliya's classic film comedy *Autumn Marathon* (1979), the hero, a university teacher shuttling helplessly between his wife and mistress, used the fact that he had been 'caught by the bridges' as a way to excuse a late arrival home.[96] Aleksandr Medvedev's striking poster, 'Lucky Me –I'm a Leningrader', taking its title from a song of 1944, punned on an open bridge and camp bed. It evoked the city's ambiguous welcome to outsiders, while also domesticating the bridge as an essential part of lives led in the city.[97] The image also parodied the standard ways of celebrating the city in mass-market images; a collection of postcards published in 1979 had represented the same crossing, Palace Bridge, as an example of Leningrad's ineffable beauty.

Piter has always had a hardy group of anglers, hugging the banks in most weathers, bait and warming (or cooling) drinks at the ready.[98] There was at least one employee of the Academy of Sciences institutes on the University Embankment who, preferring the company of fish to that of his colleagues, would nip out to the river in the lunch hour.[99] And the river kept people alive during the Blockade, when the water system failed, and buckets and cans had to be taken there for vital supplies. But in normal times water was mostly for looking *at*, rather than engaging *with*. A view of a river, or, at a pinch, a canal,[100] was a token of prestige and the object of envy. Anna Akhmatova, satirising the pretensions of Larisa Reisner, a leading member of the Leningrad Bolshevik

1.7 Aleksandr Medvedev, 'Lucky Me – I'm a Leningrader' poster, *c.* 1980.

1.8 'White Night on the Neva', postcard, 1979.

establishment in the 1920s, referred ironically to her 'three windows on the Bronze Horseman, and three on the Neva'. 'She said as she left, "I would give up everything to be Anna Akhmatova." What a silly thing to say, eh? Everything? Three windows on the Neva?'[101]

## Temples, UFOs and the Struggle with Quicksands

In the overwhelming majority of cases, moving about the city, like arriving in it, was a matter for dry land. Among such land-based means of transport, the showcase in Soviet times was the metro which, in the 1950s, became the main symbol of the romantic future. As the art historian Mikhail German remembered, the opening of the first line turned into a celebration:

> There were queues waiting at the stations – or to be more accurate, eager, expectant, joyful throngs. Once they got inside the metro, people would spend ages there – having ride after ride. They would get out at every single stop and walk up and down, admiring it all. Children didn't want to leave, ever. It smelled like the Moscow metro – warm and damp, with a metal tang. [. . .] Trains came and went with always the same staccato roar, the emptying platforms shone, and the conductors in their red hats, just like the Moscow ones, shouted 'Ready', the pneumatic doors hissed to, while coloured lights at the entrances to the tunnels flashed on and off [. . .][102]

It was not just the smell and look of the metro that resembled Moscow's, on this first line. The basics of engineering – lines, escalators, the trains

1.9 V. M. Bobkov's photo of Vyborgskaya metro station, 1975.

themselves – followed the capital's lead too. The Baltic Station–Lenin Square stretch had the Soviet Baroque encrustations and embellishments of Moscow's Sokol'niki-Lenin Hills and Circle Lines. Vladimirskaya, by Leningrad's Central Collective Farm Market, had vast mosaics of Soviet Circes with grains and fruit, promising the 'abundance' that was trumpeted in the canonical cookbook of the time, *The Book of Tasty and Nutritious Food*. Gilded mouldings and marble were the basic decorative mode. Above the pavement, the ticketing vestibule in the metro's cynosure, ploshchad' Vosstaniya, rose like a neo-classical mausoleum (it had replaced the Church of the Sign as the key architectural feature of the square).[103] Later stations, on the other hand, were showpieces of the steel-and-glass functionalism of the post-Stalin era.

But Leningraders – from builders to passengers – did their best to ensure that the metro had a proper, local identity. It acquired its own mythology. Texts about the metro dwelled on the heroism of building it: the tense burrowing through the unreliable geology of the Neva delta, with always the possibility of hitting quick-sand, *plyvun*, which would make the drilling dangerously unstable.[104] The plat-form areas of stations adopted a 'house style': severely sumptuous, with grey marble and elegantly soaring vaults.[105] And, of course, there were the usual city legends of secret tunnels, despite official assurances that the only creatures who could pass freely through the metro routes were rats.[106]

The metro was not 100 per cent reliable, even in the Soviet period. In 1969, a cable failure paralysed the entire blue line outside Park Pobedy station for an hour during the morning rush. Unusually, the glitch was reported in the press, with an assurance that it was the only such occurrence in the fourteen years of the Leningrad metro's history.[107] In the mid-1990s, there were two far more serious incidents. In 1994, the red line (leading north from ploshchad' Vosstaniya to the Vyborg Side) suddenly flooded to the suburban side of ploshchad' Muzhestva, leaving a 'replacement bus service' to operate for nearly a decade before the affected stretch of the line reopened.[108] While this seems to have been an 'act of providence', there were also starting to be signs of defective building at some of the stations. In 1999, a concrete awning collapsed at one of the entrances to Sennaya (then only twenty-five years old), causing seven deaths.[109] In 2008, Gor'kovskaya Station was closed so that the entrance pavilion could be demolished and completely rebuilt, after seeping damp had caused extensive damage to the construction. Even after work had been done, facilities were still not really modern: as late as 2011, only one station on the entire network offered passengers a ramp for pushchairs or wheelchairs.[110]

A loss of design confidence was also starting to become obvious. In the 1990s, the original severe style was retained for the stations constructed north of the Neva on the line out to ulitsa Dybenko. Particularly striking were the two-storey platforms at Sportivnaya (so two trains could run at once and allow fast clearance of the neighbouring stadium). But a decade later, a much more opulent style (with a flavour of the 'Luzhkov baroque' preferred by the contemporary mayor of Moscow) became the norm. The rebuilt booth of Gor'kovskaya Station resembled a beached UFO clad in patinaed copper. The new Spasskaya Station's name commemorated the church that had once stood on the square outside; it was decorated by a florid marble and gilt monument, 'To the Architects of Petersburg', that most of those honoured would have found appalling.

However, the system's functionality did not match its grandeur. Even in the Soviet period, building lagged behind demand.[111] After the retraction of public financing after 1991, the pace of construction slowed down significantly. The next stretch of line was opened in 1997, two years behind schedule with only two of the four planned stations completed. By the late 2000s building was around two decades behind what had been anticipated in 1985.[112] It was reported in 2003 that 21 new stations would be completed by 2015, along with 41.5 kilometres of track. But since the report also claimed that Admiralteiskaya Station would be ready in 2005 (it was finally opened in December 2011), these projections seemed over-optimistic.[113] The Petersburg metro went into the new century with its traditional hydra sprawl intact, without a circle line, and with only dozens of stops rather than the hundreds in Moscow, London, Paris or New York.

Yet despite the weak development of the network, the metro remained the prestige form of transport into the twenty-first century. There were no rivals to it in terms of rapid transit. An elevated railway was planned in the 1910s, but never built.[114] Indeed (in contrast to London, Paris, Tokyo, or New York and

Chicago), Leningrad had no inner-city railway network of any kind. In principle, one could take the local trains going out to places in Leningrad province, but the halts (literally, 'platforms') were inconveniently sited, the pace glacially slow, and using this system was the recourse of the insolvent and desperate.[115] The metro was an indispensable way of getting round the city at speed.

As well as taking people from A to B, the metro imposed its own spatial organisation on the city. The first stations to be built, as in Moscow, were in ceremonial places: the Finland Station and ploshchad' Vosstaniya, the Kirov Factory, the 'worker aristocracy' suburb of Avtovo.[116] North-south connections were developed earlier and more thoroughly than east-west ones.[117] Alongside this, the system made it quicker and more convenient to get from new suburbs to the centre than to cross the centre, which enhanced the appeal of settling some way out.[118] Above all, the metro was a means of socialisation, an instrument for schooling passengers in the rules of Soviet 'culturedness'. According to the first set of rules for passengers, produced in 1955, users were forbidden not only from sitting on the escalator steps and running down the platform but also from travelling on the metro when in a drunken condition, singing and playing instruments, and wearing 'stained or splashed clothing'.[119] Throughout the Soviet period, passengers indeed used the metro in a spirit of due solemnity. Even loud talk and laughter, let alone shouts, song, or kissing, attracted looks of disapproval.[120]

In the post-Soviet era, the rigidity of etiquette loosened: to run up, and more particularly down, the escalator at high speed became a display of daring by young men (and the occasional young woman). It was common to see couples cuddling up and talking animatedly. Low-level damage to rolling stock (especially graffiti etched on windows) was far from unknown. But the metro still remained a special world. Sometimes a Chechen veteran with no legs, begging for cash, or a person who wanted to sell an 'indispensable' gizmo (plasters that didn't stick, torches guaranteed to last till you got out of the train) would come through. But usually there was a kind of hypnotic calm. When a balloon squealed all down a carriage on its way to deflation, only one head turned.[121] While ads became a fixture in carriages and on the escalators from the late 1980s, the platforms themselves held only route signage. It was – at least until the introduction of new, brightly-coloured direction indicators in the early 2010s – easy to believe oneself back in the Soviet Union.

## 'The Leningrad Tram'

Other means of transport did not drill their passengers to the same extent. A 1965 article that praised a trolleybus driver for making informative announcements about buying multiple tickets showed how unusual taking initiative of this kind was.[122] Riding ground transport was primarily a question of what you

1.10 A parade of trolleybuses on Liteinyi prospekt, 1969. Photographed by Galina Lisyutich.

could force yourself on to, since overcrowding was endemic. Once there, the pressing issues were how to get out again, and in the meantime how not to lurch into your neighbour when the vehicle braked, and how to pay for your ticket. Conductors disappeared in the late 1960s; passengers were expected to cast a few coins into an honesty box and receive tear-off tickets in return. Whichever way, making payment usually required a passenger to ask others, 'please pass [the fare] along'; the person at the end of the chain then started the long process of returning the purchased ticket. It was less the size of the fine than the loud social disgrace of being caught without a ticket that one feared.[123] In order to acculturate foreigners, language courses always included lengthy and boring sessions on public transport etiquette.[124]

If the metro stood for modernity and culturedness, ground transport was simply a means of getting from A to B – in unpleasant propinquity with other passengers. Yet one type exceeded this basic brief, coming to embody the spirit of the city. This was the 'Leningrad tram'.

The reason for the tram's iconic status was not necessarily its perceived virtues, though it had become a symbol of the brisk efficiency of the 'model socialist city' in the 1930s. In the 1960s and 1970s, it was still represented as a symbol of modernity – as in a 1975 article from *Leningradskaya pravda* praising a recently released new model.[125] Tram drivers also were often represented as civic heroes – not just in their own professional paper, *Leningradskii tramvai* (The Leningrad Tram), but in the mainstream press as well.[126] Such copy, in its admiring representation of flawless engineering and perfect order, always silently suggested that what was expected was the opposite. And in fact riding the trams was often hell. As a means of transport, the Leningrad tram was thoroughly unappealing, 'a living embodiment of Soviet indigent excess, with sweaty people strap-hanging on the steps; a concentration of embittered overcrowding, a communal apartment on wheels, causing hatreds to boil ("as rude as a tram passenger").'[127]

These memories of Mikhail German go back to the 1940s, when trams still had outside steps, and passengers could still hang in 'tormented bunches' from them. Late twentieth-century versions of the tram were sleeker and less crowded.[128] But interiors were still extremely basic, with a few wooden seats (some paired, some single) by the walls.

Below the surface of cheerful propaganda public transport, and particularly the tram system, was under constant stress. Overcrowding was endemic, above all in new districts where metro stations were distant. In some places, according to official planning figures, up to 45,000 people an hour were expected to use overground transport.[129] In these circumstances, trams were likely to resemble cattle-trucks. The three-tier fare system ranged metro and bus at the top (five kopecks), trolleybus next (four), and trams at the bottom (three). The difference in cost was not enough to deter most Leningraders, since all the fares were extremely cheap – barely half the cost of a briquette of vanilla ice-cream, twenty times less than a basic set lunch in a canteen. The tram's cheapness made it not so much accessible as a 'third class' mode of transport. Already in 1957 special rules visualised considerably more possibilities of deviance than those presumed to be likely among metro passengers. Those riding trams might not 'get the carriage dirty', 'distract the staff with ordinary chat', carry axes, rakes, skates, or spades without wrapping these, transport animals other than muzzled dogs on leads or birds in cages, and allow children to stand or kneel on the seats.[130]

German's comparison of the tram to a 'communal apartment' (one often made by Leningraders) evoked the yelling and squalor likely to be encountered there. It had a topographical logic too. As tramlines were removed in favour of buses, surviving routes tended to serve proletarian districts of the city – Kolomna, lying between the markets of Sadovaya ulitsa and the docks; Ligovsky prospekt, leading from the Moscow Station to the factory zones of the south;

Nevsky and Narva districts. These were also places with above average proportions of communal apartments and barracks housing, often in decayed blocks.

But the tram–communal apartment comparison also suggested the shared tensions of enforced collective existence in a space where no one was in charge. 'A row in a tram' was a disapprobatory expression for vehement, illogical argument. Though the Five-Year Plan of 1966 still envisaged the tram as 'the basic, mass form of transport', in fact, only just over a third of passengers travelled by this method in 1967. Buses were spreading rapidly.[131] By the late 1970s, the tram network was starting to be reduced – a process that continued inexorably over the following decades.[132] By 1989 a journalist could remark, 'The tram used to be everyone's favourite, but now it's the object of universal irritation and complaint.'[133]

As the tram network shrank so it became less appealing, and as it became less appealing the level of service got worse. By the mid 1990s, a twenty-minute wait for a tram was by no means unusual; sometimes communications broke down altogether, forcing passengers to walk or flag down a lift, as resources and opportunity dictated. Once the tram arrived, it might well be a draughty, leaking bone-shaker, its carapace peeling and distorted, its electric horns forever ready to slide from the overhead wires. At the same time, tickets became ever more expensive. Honesty boxes were replaced by *kompostyory* (composteurs), miniature steel vices that clipped a unique pattern of holes into pre-bought tickets. At this point inspectors – an occasional nuisance in the 1960s and 1970s when some passengers, such as students, would 'ride like hares' (with no tickets) on a regular basis – became much more conspicuous and authoritarian, and fines larger.[134] Eventually, dwindling revenues and the emergence of a new class of fake inspectors, prone to extort fines even from those who actually held tickets, led to the reintroduction, for the first time in decades, of bus and tram conductors.[135]

Decay continued to be all too obvious into the 2000s as well.[136] Particularly solicitous conductors provided newspapers or plastic bags for passengers – otherwise in wet weather up to half the seats might be unusable.[137] A tram even nearly full was a rare sight. The tram seemed locked in an unstoppable downwards spiral: the wages of drivers and conductors were based on passenger numbers, so staff refused to work the less profitable routes, making closures inevitable.[138] Car drivers' contempt for the tram was palpable: in contravention of road rules and common sense, they would cut up trams on the inside, charge down the rails, dodging an approaching engine, and accelerate at tram-stops so as not to stop for alighting passengers. Every descent was a heart-stopping moment, and average speeds hardly rose above walking pace.[139]

Even the guide at the Tram Museum, when I visited in September 2010, was gloomy. The network was terminally superannuated ('the kind that America got rid of in the 1940s') and the traffic problems beyond amelioration. He predicted that the tram would survive only in outlying areas, as onward transport from the metro. Most of the visitors, he complained, were school-children dragged there by their teachers: 'When I say, "Are there any questions?" someone always says, "When will the visit be over?"' On my own guided tour, I was the single visitor in the enormous hangar.[140]

Yet city-dwellers' love-hate relationship with the tram as a local phenomenon continued. The tram was an important part of Blockade mythology. The system, as the public was regularly reminded, shut down for only four months, from 8 December 1941 to 15 April 1942. 'A former worker at the Leonov Tram Park recalls, "The population of the city joyfully welcomed the trams. They wept and laughed with happiness, handed the conductors and drivers bunches of the first spring flowers. They said, if the trams are running, we'll certainly survive to Victory Day . . ."'[141] As with communal flats, people were astonished to hear that trams were an important fact of life in Moscow, let alone anywhere else.[142] The city authorities' lack of concern about supporting the network provoked regret and indignation: 'tram nostalgia' ripened.

It helped that the tram was the only local means of transport with a literary pedigree. One of the most famous Russian modernist poems, Nikolai Gumilyov's ballad 'The Lost Tram', based on a contemporary report of an electric tram that had wandered from its shed after a short circuit, took recent history and personal biography on a lurching, demonic ride.[143] In 1955, the underground poet Roal'd Mandel'shtam was to rework the idea:

Who will halt those wagons?
The loop makes our heads spin.
Like a dead iron crow
The weather slaps our faces.

The burning edge of the sky
Splits like a dead barrel.
Into the drizzle of night stars
Rushes the scarlet tram.[144]

Leningrad's premier poet of the 1970s, Viktor Krivulin, saw things differently, writing beautifully of 'the two-stringed tram, wind instrument of the spirit'.[145] Thus, an uncomfortable ride kept one in touch with the city's culture, even if – or perhaps precisely because – it was getting nowhere fast.

As the tram network itself reached the point of no return, so nostalgia for the tram mounted. The first tram museum was set up in 1967 at the Vasilievsky Island Tram Park (no. 62). Other tram parks in due course acquired similar 'museums'. In 1982 – just as the last ever generation of Soviet trams was rolled out on to the rails – a central 'Museum of City Electrical Transport' was established in Park no. 62, and in the following years salvage and restoration of the vehicles themselves began.[146] In 1987, it became possible to tour the city on a retro-tram.[147] This practice continued in the following decades as well, with the Tram Museum earning money by taking people round in the restored vintage trams that were on display.[148] Alongside this kind of 'living tribute', memorialisation of a fixed kind took place as well. In 2004, the pedestrian zone on 6–7 Liniya of Vasilievsky Island acquired a life-size model of the Petersburg horse tram, placed in unconsciously ironic juxtaposition to the metro station.[149]

'Tram nostalgia' reached a high point in 2007, the centenary of Petersburg's electric tram system. In the immediately preceding years, the collection of the Museum of Electrical Transport acquired several more reconditioned vehicles.[150] The jubilee year itself saw the publication of a lavishly illustrated album, dedicated to the 'past and present' of the St Petersburg tram.[151] Yet even this celebratory publication recorded the system's inexorable decline, down to a mere 39 routes and 1114 drivers. The system now had only 11,352 employees overall, of whom 21 per cent were of pensionable age and only 9.2 per cent under 30.[152]

Increasingly, the tram was the vehicle of memory, sometimes going back a generation or more:

> My grandmother told me they first met in this amazing way. She lived on Malaya Okhta, on ulitsa Stakhanovtsev, where Dad was born, and spent quite a lot of time living there, in a communal flat, a big one. And she used to travel by tram – that was before they built Alexander Nevsky Bridge. And she would get the tram from there to the Polytechnic. And my grandfather used to get on somewhere along the route. So they met up every day. And that's how they met, then they got married. [. . .] And now trams don't do that route, it's all the metro now. And it's not so easy to meet people on the metro . . .[153]

The tram of memory was much more than a mode of transport: it was a symbol of lost innocence. Even Mikhail German shared this double vision, remembering, alongside the sweaty claustrophobia of tram interiors, the 'poetry' of their bells, and lamenting the demise of the old multi-coloured lights that had once given each route its own face. A process of aestheticisation through distance was taking place, with the lapsing years working to mute rawness, just as spatial distance turned the screech of moving trams into a curlew cry. Increasingly, the tram was placed at an imaginative remove. So advertisements in trams during the centenary year of 2007 showed, alongside the 'tram of the future' (an extraordinary-looking vehicle straight out of *Blade Runner*, certainly never seen on St Petersburg's tracks), 'the tram of the past'. What figured nowhere was 'the tram of the present'.[154]

## Riding the Tin 'Gazelle'

The tram was by no means the only means of transport that had become dysfunctional by the early 1990s. At this point, overground routes generally reached their nadir. Waits for buses and trolleybuses were potentially endless; only the metro continued to roll up reliably every couple of minutes.[155] The inevitable result was that the metro also became unbearably crowded, and that travel in the many areas not covered (expansion of the system had ground to a halt because of underfunding)[156] was tortuous. Transport deregulation in the early 1990s brought shoals of private buses (prefixed 'K'), but these were significantly more expensive than the ordinary kind.[157]

By the end of the 1990s the differences between commercial and municipal buses had started to level off. The former were slightly more expensive, but the main distinction now was that they did not offer concessionary fares. With newer models of bus arriving, the city routes were in better shape than some commercial ones, though these buses also filled up more quickly. However, with the removal of many tram and trolleybus routes, and long gaps between services on most bus routes as well, the logic of the Soviet transport system had collapsed. Beyond Nevsky prospekt, *marshrutki* or *tezhki*[158] – minibus taxis running fixed routes, like the Turkish dolmas – were the only form of transport that offered anything resembling a unified network of transport coverage.

*Marshrutki* had existed in the Soviet period (they were introduced to Leningrad in 1965).[159] However, they were not that much used because they were significantly more expensive than other forms of transport (15 kopecks rather than 3, 4, or 5). From the late 1980s, the first private ('co-operative') vehicles started appearing, in competition with municipal routes, which themselves became increasingly commercial in nature.[160] By the late 1990s they spread everywhere. Though they were still the most expensive form of public transport in the city (costing around 25 per cent more than the metro fare), these Soviet-made 'Gazelle'[161] buses were not in any other sense 'elite'. Dilapidated to the point of no return, they had seats crammed into any available space. Passengers would sit practically on each other's knees or – if no seats were left – clutch frantically at the seat backs, heads down under the unforgiving arch of the roof. An entrance or exit required one to squeeze past, flailing at the side-door, and brave the ferocious yells of the driver if this stuck. Once, when the door jammed completely, a contingent of passengers had to climb over the driver's seat and out through his door – which all of them, from micro-skirted beauties to babushka with shopping bags, managed remarkably nimbly.[162]

Striking were the efforts made to maintain order in the tiny space. Drivers had change neatly arranged next to the driving seat so it could be doled out quickly. Notices pleaded (not unsuccessfully) for a spirit of courtesy and understanding among passengers. If the load factor allowed, you could look at the

1.11 Marshrutka interior, 2012. Note the carpets on and below the shelf for the money, and the box for stacking change. Despite its dilapidated condition, this is one of the ‘European’-style larger buses, rather than a Gazel’ van.

ads posted up on the walls or – in some marshrutki by the end of the 2000s – at video ads on a screen, proudly presented by ‘First Popular Television.’[163]

While passengers generally had the sepulchral detachment of those trapped in big-city transport anywhere, the forced propinquity sometimes fostered human contact. As Easter 2009 approached, a lady of 90 told anyone who would listen the story of most of her life, beginning with a rant about priests (‘on the TV all the time! To f . . . with them!’), and ending with her plans to get her Easter loaf blessed in the church.[164] I have heard of marshrutka passengers suddenly yelling into a mobile telephone, ‘Sashka! Know what? I’ve *forgotten the bribe!*’[165] or launching into emotional tirades. ‘For me,’ one woman remembered, ‘this is the only space I manage to get involved in arguments with people I don’t know, and last year [I] even said to a slightly drunken man, who was slagging Russian women off and then asked me to corroborate his views, that this was “impotent’s talk” (believe me, it’s very uncharacteristic of me – definitely something about *marshrutki*!). I must say he was not lost for words, and said to the rest of our co-travellers: "I told you, they never have enough!" – but I thought the women there were on my side.'[166]

Marshrutki thus provided not just an essential service, but also a highly specific social environment. Lurching round the city on a stop-at-request basis, they could be hailed down almost anywhere – except on bridges, an obstacle in that respect too.[167] They had taken over from the tram not just as the most characteristic main means of transport, but as the transport that everyone loved to hate. They were erratic – not even pretending to work to a timetable but leaving when the number of passengers was considered viable – and often grimy inside and out. Because of this, and because their drivers were almost always from the Caucasus or Central Asia, they fitted badly into the 'Window on Europe' ideal. Ordinary passengers, antennae primed by the drivers' status as ethnic Untermenschen, would often treat them casually, even rudely. Some passengers thought it was perfectly in order to shave a rouble or two off the fare, knowing the driver had no real redress. As one Uzbek driver described, you got blamed for everything, even when another driver crashed straight into you:

> This Russian bloke, his fault no question, slams straight into my wing. The whole bus looks at him and at me. They're working out who's right and who's not. I got out, put out my warning signs, got back in the bus and said, 'There'll be another bus here in a minute to take you.' And they're like, 'So why do you drive like . . .' And I'm like, 'So what've I got to do with it? The bastard doesn't know how to drive, where's he coming from?!' and the entire bus is looking out through the window and you can see some of them knew what had happened, what was just going to happen. [. . .] But no, it's me to blame. You're an Uzbek, you bought your licence, you're out on the road for the first time today, and you sat in a car for the first time in your life yesterday. [*Laughs*]. That's all. We're no good at anything else. Only riding donkeys.[168]

Marshrutki were disliked by the city administration too, ostensibly on safety grounds. In 2007 there were 498 accidents involving marshrutki on the roads of St Petersburg, leading to 6 deaths and 206 injuries.[169] But given the hair-raising accident statistics overall – 12,667 accidents and 1444 fatalities in Petersburg and Leningradskaya province, taken together, in 2007[170] – marshrutki hardly stood out. Trams had been a traffic hazard right back to the early twentieth century, but had not been regarded as dispensable on those grounds.[171] Mainly, the municipal authorities of St Petersburg saw the ubiquity of these battered minibuses as an affront to their civilising ambitions. From 2005, the companies running the services were required to bring these up to 'European' standards.[172] The Russian-made Gazel' minibuses were indeed replaced on many routes – by Chinese ones.

The introduction of the new buses gave marshrutki passengers more space, but as the transport system further declined, they too became crowded, and signs of wear and tear began appearing.[173] As a dingy, if convenient, form of transport that was clearly making *someone* money, the marshrutka had much the same status as minicabs in Central London – indispensable and detested.

As for real taxis, back in Soviet days, these were considerably more expensive than any other way of getting around, but there was no sense of bourgeois luxury about them. Taxis were simply used by the carless at times when other transport was not available, for shifting something heavy, say, or in cases of urgency (such as getting someone with labour pains to the maternity home). Passengers had many little strategies for reducing the already quite low cost of a ride. 'They didn't like throwing money around,' a driver remembered. 'And whenever the meter got near a round sum – a rouble or two or three – they were quite capable of stopping you before you got to the original destination, so the fare didn't creep up to 2 roubles 14 kopecks or whatever' – thus avoiding the need to 'round up' more than a few kopecks for a tip.[174]

Soviet press reports treated *taksisty* as members of the broad class of 'professional drivers' (*voditeli*), not as entrepreneurs. Abuses – such as drivers who arrogantly refused to take passengers where they wanted to go – were regarded as scandalous, but did not tar the entire profession.[175] Unofficial taxis attracted more animus, but generally the money involved was so trifling that this sector of the black market was hardly worth police time. Among members of the public, drivers had a reputation of acting as the eyes and ears of the KGB, and were much disliked for their arrogance. But they were also known to be a good source of vodka out of shop hours.[176] They were, all in all, thoroughly integrated into the everyday life of the city.

In the 1980s, however, as other transport worsened demand on taxis increased, generating a scarcity that was sharpened also by decaying stock. There was now a chronic deficit of taxis, and their drivers, along with those of cowboy cabs (*chastniki*, or 'privates'), had started to demand vast sums. By 1995, St Petersburg was, according to official estimates, 5000 taxis short of the necessary level.[177] Conditions in the job were also becoming increasingly unappealing, with one or two murders a week reported in the summer of 1998.[178] On the other hand, banditry among cab drivers themselves was starting to be a fact of life.[179] By the start of the 2000s, though, things had settled down, and prices returned to and remained at a reasonable level – maybe five times the bus fare for a short hop in the city centre.[180]

Given the cheapness of getting a lift, whether in an official taxi or a cowboy one, this mode of transport had no 'snob' freighting in the way that it would with the kind of Londoner who uses a black cab to get from employment in Bond Street to home in Kensington, or the Baltic Exchange to Wapping. In many ways – though firms might have more or less fanciful names – the service offered by taxis (and private drivers) still remained 'socialist' in flavour. No driver would ever have opened a door for a passenger, though he[181] might well have helped take luggage to the door; tips were not obligatory any more than courtesy was; and most passengers rode in the front. It was in the use of the private car that the social transformations of the late Soviet and post-Soviet eras made themselves felt.

## 'The City Was Not Built for Cars'

Since the first years of Soviet power, it had been accepted that members of the elite should be allowed access to car transport. This included not just Party officials but also senior employees of the Academy of Sciences. In 1946 a Leningrad historian boasted to a colleague in Moscow, 'I've now got the right to use the Academy car (on a call-out basis). The tram has fallen by the wayside.'[182] But the Khrushchev years saw an attack on 'wasteful' car use to official ends, and it was not until the 1970s that Soviet state planners moved to the view that the car should be a mainstream form of transport.[183] Before that, it was common for Leningrad journalists to draw smug contrasts between the ridiculous all-out dependence on the car in the US and the rational state of things in Soviet society.[184] Economics followed ideology: it was hard to get cars (the single outlet in the city was on Apraksin dvor), and few people had them. In 1963, there were 27,304 private cars in Leningrad, an increase of over 150 per cent on the 1959 figures, but still a small number compared with the city's population.[185]

By the 1970s, things were beginning to change. One sign was the alterations to the licence system in 1976, which did away with the old term 'amateur driver'; allowed drivers themselves to keep their licence, rather than forcing them to lodge this at the traffic police (GAI); and classified vehicles in terms of their size.[186] Right across the Soviet Union, car production was upped, and mass car usage started to be built into national and city planning.[187] Images became increasingly seductive too, as with a 1973 image of cars progressing in stately fashion down the Neva embankment (figure 1.12).

But car owners were still a minority and the roads were, by contemporary Western European (let alone American) standards, practically deserted. As Colin Thubron, a rare car-driving visitor, recorded:

> Trams and concertina-like Hungarian buses wobbled along the streets, but often the ways were half deserted. In every other lane my car would hit a heaving slipstream of cobbles. Open manholes gaped without warning in the middle of thoroughfares, and twice I nearly dropped the car into one. Every street was a long, seductive ambush. Tram-lines erupted like swords from their cobbled beds; and once I almost crashed into one of the black official limousines, bullying its way down a road's centre.

1.12 A leisurely ride along the Neva, 1973.

'The city was not built for cars,' he concluded.[188]

Nevertheless, traffic was starting to build up, and with that, some unpleasant side-effects of motorisation. Already in 1910 the British journalist George Dobson had pointed out that motor vehicles were not only much less practical in a city with six months of winter, requiring constant snow clearance, but also far more aurally intrusive. 'St Petersburg has been the last of great European cities to be invaded on an extensive scale by motor carriages, taxi-cabs, and other motor vehicles, which, together with the electric tramways, have simply transformed it in the cold season from a quiet into a noisy city.'[189] By the end of the 1960s such noise pollution had become a major irritant.[190] There was increasing anxiety also about the number of accidents. According to a report in *Leningradskaya pravda* published in June 1975, this increased from 4704 in 1973 to 5459 in 1974, with a staggering 3796 accidents the fault of the driver.[191]

The social cost of the car, however, was offset by its appeal from an individual perspective. Though more expensive than using public transport, in almost every other way it was preferable – one got around faster, and in pleasanter conditions. Above all, the car had flexibility, allowing owners a partial escape from the paternalistic central planning of Soviet lives. Car drivers could choose their own itineraries within the city, and take holidays when and where they wanted, and with the company they wanted. Increasing car use both reflected and fostered the development of the new middle class. Those who were sending their children to prestigious schools outside the official catchment area, and who had chosen to move outside the centre to an area of new co-operative flats – both of which were important indicators of middle-class status – found it hard to do without.[192]

But to see the transition to car ownership as purely a shift to 'bourgeois individualism' would be crude.[193] Giving lifts, or at the very least dropping a visiting friend or fellow guest at the nearest metro station, was a recognised social duty. Drivers would be expected to take a sick friend to the doctor, to scour the city for someone's essential medicines, to meet arrivals at the station, to help with moves.[194] Ferrying strangers who hitched lifts was also widespread, usually for money, but not always. Sometimes the prompt was a desire to help out, or a desire for company on a trip that had become routine.[195]

In the 1990s and 2000s, as the quality of public transport declined, car ownership rose commensurately.[196] An *inomarka*, foreign car (particularly, in the early days, a Mercedes), became the most widely current symbol of social status. Yet as more and more people turned to private cars, conditions for drivers worsened. Infrastructure decayed under pressure from the floods of vehicles, and the pace of road repairs was desperately inadequate.[197] Parking space – at a premium even during the Soviet period – could not cope with the volume of new traffic. The city government's only contribution was to impose a ban in some places – for example, Nevsky prospekt – while others turned into a free-for-all. With cars shoaling over every pavement, even finding a place to double-park could take a ten-minute search.[198] But as in many other Russian cities, it was above all the formidable traffic jams that provoked drivers' frustration. By the 2000s they were so bad that the touts, rather than offering to clean windows, sold sex magazines to cheer drivers up.[199]

Official solutions to the problem were less colourful, but not necessarily more effective. Attempts to reroute traffic were bedevilled by the slow development of the outer beltway. Within the city, a mind-bending one-way system concentrated the flow in bottlenecks, such as the junction of Nevsky and Ligovsky prospekt.[200] Drivers engaged in anecdotal competition: 'And it took me an hour and forty minutes to go only 600 metres!'[201] Some joined the militant drivers' rights group 'Freedom of Choice', but the 'grumbling majority' was many times larger.[202] The high-ups of the city, like those in Moscow, dealt with the problems by travelling in convoy, illuminated by flashing blue lights (*migalki*); drivers who did not automatically give way would be called to order by police speaking through loud hailers: 'Clear the road!' The thoroughfares that they used, 'government roads' (*pravitel'stvennye trassy*), were tended assiduously. On ul. Shpalernaya, leading to Smol'nyi, pedestrian crossings like red carpets lay on the silkiest tarmac in the city. The road was overlooked by the Tauride Palace, once the home of Grigory Potemkin; there was a long heritage of putting the best face on anything the powerful might pass along the way.

## Racing the Second-Counter

Walking might have seemed like a preferable alternative, since even the infirm could probably have covered 600 metres in a tenth the time. Walkers also had more to look at than the (probably grimy) back end of the car in front. But walking in order to get somewhere (as opposed to promenading)[203] was a great anti-tradition in this city. 'Vitya used to work in a medical publishers on the corner of Sadovaya and Apraksin pereulok. The Saigon was a short trip away, but it was a nuisance to get there; you had to ride a tram first, then a trolleybus,' the poet Viktor Krivulin's first wife, Anna Katsman, remembered.[204] The 'awkward journey' in question covered perhaps one-third of a mile.

Krivulin, who had been lamed by polio, had, of course, special reasons for not wanting to walk. But many other Leningraders who were perfectly able-bodied regularly used public transport for equally insignificant stretches. Maiya Borisova's gently didactic insistence on walking, in a poem for children, acknowledged the temptation was to do otherwise – 'If you're in no hurry/If you know the town/Don't ride public transport/Walk there on your own!'[205] Weather was one factor in this, and (by the 2000s) fear of pollution another, though experience would suggest that hanging round at stops or waiting to enter a packed metro station is colder and worse for the lungs.[206]

It was not just the weather that made foot travel unpleasant. While not the most nerve-stretching way of getting about the city – that honour had to be given to cycling – it was often frankly dangerous. Little was done to aid the passage of pedestrians in Soviet days, and the numbers of accidents were starting to become a concern even in the 1930s.[207] The worst period was the late 1980s and early 1990s, when the general sense of social licence, combined with the appearance of larger and larger numbers of drivers, generated wild road conditions. Pedestrians ignored lights – since, after all, the drivers did too – and hot-footed it across the road when and where they could. Only in the 2000s did the numbers of lights increase. Some even acquired second-counters, useful for those who preferred not to risk being mowed down when they were only part-way across a vast thoroughfare. Even so, the odds were stacked – pedestrians had to shift as though recording times for the Olympic walking race. But this was still better than crossings without lights, next to some of which wreaths hung on lamp-posts as memorials to those who had not got across fast enough.

There were constant blocks to forward progress. Long stretches of Palace Embankment and Suvorovsky Embankment – two of the major tourist strolling routes in the city – completely lacked crossings; the drunkards who decided to make a dash often came to a fatal end.[208] Vehicles too, if travelling below motorway speed, could be at risk. In 2007 Valeria Kolodyazhnaya, the five-year-old daughter of the Mayor of Sochi, was on a trip in a pony carriage

1.13 Floral tribute by a lightless crossing on the Pirogov Embankment, 2009.

outside the Winter Palace when a car behind slammed into the vehicle. She died in hospital from abdominal injuries.[209]

Accidents of this kind might be infrequent but lower-level ones, often involving broken bones, were commonplace. Even if pedestrians escaped actual injury, they were often subject to random abuse: a tram-driver shouting 'Right under the wheels, you goat!', car drivers taking revenge on pedestrians by pulling across to spray them with rain or slush, or by making the car jump a foot forward when stopped at a pedestrian crossing, frantic hooting, peremptory acceleration round slow walkers on crossings . . .[210] The worst offenders were the drivers with blue lights. Detested by the general population, they provoked mutterings of disdain when glimpsed – but also envy.[211]

Bridges – or those on the Neva, at any rate – were particularly formidable obstacles for pedestrians, and not just because there were so few of them. The concept of 'tow path' was alien (freight had traditionally been brought into the city down the canals and minor waterways). The embankment walkway was interrupted by almost every bridge (only Liteinyi was an exception, having ramps to ensure access to the lifting gear for the bridge's exceptionally long drawbridge sections). Most bridges had pedestrian lights – if at all – on only one bank of the river, so that novice walkers disinclined to make a nightmare dash across six lanes of boiling traffic might find themselves forced to cross to the far side of the waterway and back in order to return to a spot thirty metres away from where they had first been standing. For all their wrought-iron elegance, bridges did not appeal as places to stand and stare either: the city's cutting winds were particularly sharp here, and in any case, as 'strategic objects', they were not places to hang around.

As post-Soviet obsession with the car took hold, the embankments themselves became the territory of screaming traffic. Planners' ideal was to turn them into an urban motorway ('a non-stop through-route') with the help of tunnels. This led to the closure, in 2010, of the entire walkway between Liteiny and Samson Bridges, banishing pedestrians to the façade of the Military-Medical Institute in a literalisation of the saying, 'the weakest must go to the wall'.[212] In 2012 there was a plan to turn historical 'routine buildings' into covered parking lots, the tiers of cars masked by reconstructed façades.[213] The surge in cars made Petersburg as busy as anywhere in Western Europe, but the sheer pace of development had cut out forty years of reforms: box junctions, let alone bus lanes, were a promise of the bright future.

If civil engineers still handled road management much as they had in the Soviet period, the pervasive hostility to pedestrians was a distant echo of *ancien régime* social organisation. *The Table of Carriages and Liveries* had limited the use of personal carriages to persons from the gentry and nobility (*dvoryanstvo*), with the obvious effect that people who mattered invariably got around on wheels. This was the case in the Soviet era as well. Not being able to use transport of some kind was associated with catastrophe – the Revolution, the Blockade.[214] Road manners were by all accounts erratic before 1917: 'Our drivers are not given to dreary caution when going about, and care little for the safety and even the lives of their passengers,' F. E. Enakiev's *The Tasks of Transforming St Petersburg* reported in 1912. Dostoevsky's Marmeladov was a fictional example of a road death way back in the 1860s.[215]

But by the early twenty-first century, even staying on the pavement was not necessarily safe. Cars and other traffic contested this territory, as people barrelled their cars into courtyard parking places or made a loop round roadworks.[216] Vast falling icicles, renamed *sosuli* ('icicks') in 2009 (when someone in the city administration decided the diminutive was inappropriate), were another hazard, particularly during extreme winters.[217] You were lucky to end up in situations that were merely undignified – such as failing to notice ice-blocks hidden under the snow at an uncleared, dimly-lit stretch; if you slipped on one block, the struggle to get up would reduce you to a stranded beetle, a sheep turned on its back.

The Petersburg pavement has never been much associated with motion in a pleasurable sense, with walking for the sake of it. Pushkin's Evgeny in *The Bronze Horseman*, hunted by grief and madness, and Dostoevsky's Raskol'nikov, driven by guilt, show the connection of forward movement and pain. In 1964, Georgy Daneliya's *I Stride Round Moscow* portrayed a group of young people delightedly exploring that city on foot; his *Autumn Marathon* had the hero frenetically rushing round Leningrad, hounded by the commitments of university teaching and free-lance translation, not to speak of his wife and mistress. The cult film *The Stroll*, made by Andrei Uchitel' in 2003, continued this maniacal progress: shot with a queasily lurching hand-held camera, it focused on a young woman who alleged that she *must* walk and walk, because a riding accident had damaged her spine.[218]

The very configuration of the city encouraged such moods. Walking was for the obsessive, for those who infrequently needed to stop and rest, let alone take refreshments. In parts of the city – for instance, the Trinity Bridge, or Nevsky – there were, by the late 2000s, as many cyclists and roller-bladers (darting maniacally through the knots of strollers) as purposive walkers.[219] The latter were left to odd stretches of pavement, disconnected places.

In late Soviet times, the most prestigious buildings completely failed to engage with the street (as in the case of the Hotel Leningrad, with its 100 metres of car parking between entrance and passers-by). This spawned a similar

1.14 Europa turns her back on the city, Kutuzov Embankment, August 2008.

soullessness in post-Soviet prestige developments, such as the luxury blocks of Krestovsky Island and Shpalernaya. The idea was to keep out, rather than lure inside. The expensive conversions of nineteenth-century mansions serving the imagined needs of twenty-first century 'VIPs' made the same point in a different way: inside the ground-floor window of a would-be fancy hotel on Kutuzov Embankment, a porcelain reclining Europa turned her ample bottom on passers-by.

Given the ready availability of credit to buy new vehicles, more and more people turned to the road. Some drivers claimed on the basis of personal observation that the 2008 crisis had led to a drop in cars.[220] But the effects, if any, were strictly temporary. In an oil-producing country, running a car was sufficiently cheap to offset the relatively high purchase price, and the high costs of insurance.

Getting round the city was not always hellish. Jeremiads about appalling traffic might be an indispensable genre of city folklore, but congestion had not in fact brought Petersburg to a standstill – or not every hour of every day. It was still possible to get a sense of what the place felt like before anyone drove – if you got up before ten o'clock on a summer Saturday or Sunday, or walked around during the long holidays at the start of January.

Car travel itself had done more than condemn people to a zomboid existence of standing in jams, or alternatively, speeding so fast they could see nothing. Built to be seen from a carriage, the city opened its best vistas to drivers and passengers. Driving around also created new imaginative possibilities. A wonderful poem by Elena Shvarts written in 1995 celebrated the 'canary colours' of night cars as one shot past the city's landmarks in an 'ancient dream of motion'.[221] At an everyday level, the surge in circulation of maps represented an important shift not just in the culture of freedom of information but also in ways of getting around. People had to know the layout of the city better because they could no longer expect to drive to point A and cruise around looking for point B, or not unless they were prepared to risk getting stuck in three or four unnecessary traffic jams. Those using public transport needed to know about marshrutki as well as buses and trams. Now it was foreigners who had to make do with approximate representations of topography, as they went the customary round from the Bronze Horseman to the Winter Palace, from the Peter and Paul Fortress to the Kunstkamera. True, the end of the 2000s saw the introduction of handsome, detailed micro-topographical guides of the YOU ARE HERE kind, posted on boards near major landmarks. But these could play strange tricks: in 2007, the map standing next to the Catherine Institute on the Fontanka provided a beautifully accurate view – but of the area round Vasilievsky Island, some two miles to the west.[222]

Like the increase in building, the build-up of traffic was seen by some as a deprovincialisation of the city. The Russian equivalent of 'busy' (as in 'busy junction') is 'enlivened' (*ozhivlyonnyi*). The major roads did indeed come to life

1.15 The end of the line, Nevsky district, April 2011.

in the post-Soviet period, and they also began to be much more brightly lit. Around New Year, most major squares acquired enormous New Year trees, and often coloured lights as well. Even public transport sprouted decorations – such as a no. 6 tram in 2008, shimmering in blue, white, and red Christmas bulbs. Some might snort about 'Las Vegas' tastes, but some – larger numbers, probably – were glad the place was getting less drab.[223]

Yet a few enclaves even managed to outlast post-Soviet 'enlivening'. In Volkovo, peace was ensured by the enormous cemetery, which not only imposed a territory of silence but defied rational road-planning round it. The low-rise houses – neo-classicism at its plainest, as in some towns in the Irish midlands – were sunk in timeless provincial quietude. Kolomna, much loved by writers (Pushkin, Blok in particular),[224] stretching down the Griboedov Canal between Sennaya ploshchad' and the docks, and cut through only by secondary through-routes, seemed a miraculous reserve, though the *grands projets* planned for the area, particularly the transformation of New Holland wharves, threatened transformation into the kind of cultural centre considered essential for a 'world city'. And from here, another survivor, the no. 3 tram, one of the oldest routes in the city, struggled its way up perpetually choked Sadovaya Street and across Nevsky, arriving, after literally hours of shuddering motion, eventually at the Finland Station.

2

# Making a Home on the Neva

*It is not the palace and hovel that represent the two ends of the scale of prosperity and destitution, but the room in the communal apartment and the three-room separate flat.*
(Lidiya Ginzburg)[1]

Among Westerners, the words 'Petersburg style' conjure up an existence of supreme refinement, perhaps in some neo-classical palace overlooking the Fontanka. A long line of spacious, elegant rooms connected by double doors, hand-painted wallpaper, etchings with panoramas of eighteenth-century firework displays . . . 'Petersburg style' is sometimes evoked like this by post-Soviet Russian glossy magazines as well.[2] Yet even in the eighteenth century, the city was, by contemporary standards, already a high-density environment. A decree of 1763 ordained the construction of 'multi-storeyed stone buildings with no gaps between them',[3] so that no precious land was wasted. Palatial *enfilades* made up only a small proportion of the housing stock. Most families, even from the cultural elite, lived in quite different conditions. From the 1840s, the standard genre of new building was the *dokhodnyi dom* or tenement, a multi-storeyed block usually constructed around an internal courtyard, often ill-lit, and sometimes presenting the viewer with the sight of a blank, windowless *brandmauer*.[4] Particularly in the upper floors of such buildings, ceilings were generally quite low, and room sizes modest.[5] When the composer Sergei Prokofiev joined the junior department of the St Petersburg Conservatoire in 1904, his family rented a flat on Sadovaya, in the centre of the city, with three bedrooms, two of which looked into the building's internal courtyard, a sitting-room, and a dining room, alongside a kitchen and a tiny bathroom and lavatory. Though generous compared with the hostel accommodation or dank cellars occupied by the very poor, these quarters seemed cramped to a family from the provinces, such as the Prokofievs, used to much more spacious conditions.[6]

Petersburgers themselves tended to be less fussy, in part because it was common – as Dmitry Likhachev recalled in his memoirs – to rent accommodation for only part of the year before departing, furniture and all, to a rented dacha, and returning to another rented apartment in the autumn.[7] Birds of passage are by custom not house-proud. Certainly, during the economic boom of the late nineteenth and early twentieth centuries, the top of the housing market began to develop rapidly. Speculative builders started constructing a new type of apartment block, this time aimed at moneyed tenants, where the traditional closed courtyards were replaced by open garden courtyards (*cours d'honneur*). Rooms were spacious, ceilings very high (up to four metres), and decoration lavish. Profitability was ensured by concentrating construction in areas where land values were relatively low, such as Petrograd Side, formerly a sleepy backwater, the lower reaches of the Fontanka, and the edge of Kolomna.[8] But most of the buildings in the city were smaller-scale. As late as 1930, Leningrad still contained large numbers of low buildings. Only sixteen buildings (all in the centre) had eight storeys and 236 had seven storeys, as opposed to over 17,000 buildings with one or two storeys. Wooden structures were also still common, particularly in the city's outskirts.[9]

After the Revolution the palaces and mansions were nationalised and handed over to museums, government departments, and institutions. The state rooms were used as public reception rooms, for instance, lecture halls, and the ancillary and service quarters as living accommodation.[10] Conditions were at best rough and ready. It was only the Soviet elite who lived in anything resembling the conditions enjoyed by high-status Petersburgers before 1917. These included not just Party leaders such as Sergei Kirov, whose magnificent apartment (complete with shiny American refrigerator) stood on ulitsa Krasnykh Zor', but the intellectual dignitaries of the city. On Lieutenant Schmidt Embankment was the neo-classical block owned by the Academy of Sciences, encrusted in memorial plaques, where academic bigwigs enjoyed a direct view of the Neva from their long windows.[11] A fictional representation of domestic life at this level of society is the 'vale of science' (*yudol' nauki*) in Bitov's novel *Pushkin House* (1971), with its academic inhabitants, 'old people in the process of extinction with their decanal children and graduate-student grandchildren', and its soft voices and soft light falling on book-cases and piles of papers.[12]

From 1935 planning for the new centre of the city, on Mezhdunarodnyi prospekt, laid out an avenue of high-rise blocks whose style owed much to the architecture of Petrograd Side. While some flagship projects of the 'cultural revolution' (1928–32), the Lensovet Building and the House of Political Prisoners, were built on the *dom-kommuna* principle – with collective facilities for catering, child-care, laundry, and so on – these developments represented only one trend.[13] Leningrad contained no apartment blocks with the lustre of the top Moscow developments – for example, D. N. Chechulin, A. K. Rostovsky, and L. M. Gokhman's Stalinist wedding-cake on the Kotel'nicheskaya embankment opposite the Kremlin (1948–52), with its marble halls and ball-room, as well as specialist shops.[14] But conditions in elite apartment blocks were significantly better than average, with higher ceilings, bigger rooms, and above all superior levels of maintenance.[15]

Accommodation for Leningraders outside the upper echelons of the Party elite was much more basic. An open tender organised in 1929 for a brick or concrete structure to be constructed on the corner of ulitsa Krasnykh Zor' and Pesochnaya (now ul. Professora Popova), specified ceilings of up to 2.85 metres (3 metres on the first two floors). The three-room or four-room flats with a total area of 50 square metres (or 65 in the case of four-roomed ones) were to have a kitchen of 7 square metres, a hall at least 1.5 metres wide, and separate kitchens and bathrooms.[16] By the standards of the time, this was generous. In other buildings of the day, facilities were constructed on the 'corridor' principle, with 'conveniences' shared between groups.

Facilities of the 'corridor' kind remained the norm throughout the Soviet period in the *obshchezhitie*, the bottom rung of the state housing ladder, and the precarious foothold of incomers to the city. Hostels were to be found almost everywhere, but they clustered in areas such as the streets around the Leningrad Institute of Technology, the location for many factory hostels as well as student ones. In 1970, nearly 200,000 people, or around 5 per cent of the city's population, were living in the city's 969 hostels.[17] The majority of hostel occupants (around 70 per cent) were under thirty, and they were likely to live there for a few years at most – though there were cases where residents spent their whole lives in one, not having anywhere else to go. Hostels were also one of the destinations of those who were living illegally.[18]

The floating population of hostel-dwellers had few resources to lobby the authorities, and space was cramped (six to eight people in one room was not unknown, even in the late Soviet period). Conditions were therefore often uncomfortable or plain squalid. In 1970, a generally optimistic meeting about factory hostels identified serious problems in some places: rooms that were provided with either lockers or cupboards but not both; hostels where the age of inhabitants ran from the teens to the early thirties; and in the worst instances, truly dreadful living conditions: 'There is no hot water, no chairs. The furniture is completely worn out, as are the kitchen tables. 40 people using the kitchen have only one small cupboard between them,' said a representative of one local factory.[19]

As in Soviet 'total institutions' generally (orphanages were another example) regulations often went unheeded. Despite a ministerial decree of 1966, and a Lensovet measure of 1968, in 1970 fewer than a third of hostels offered food to their inhabitants, many had still not phased out damp basements, and over 4000 were in need of redecoration and repairs.[20]

Hostels had a bad reputation for rowdiness as well as for squalor.[21] According to official reports, boozing, card-playing, theft, rows, and indeed fights were all typical.[22] Some were better regulated than this. Nikolai Rubtsov noted in 1960 that his hostel (at the Kirov Factory) was 'in very good order'. 'There's gas, central heating, a "red corner" with a TV, books, magazines, and nice girls using it, there's a hall with a big mirror opposite the entrance from the street, it's got lots of tables there too. They even have flowers on them.' His own room was 'always pretty well quiet, like a cell in a monastery'.[23]

But Rubtsov had been brought up in an orphanage. The conditions seemed less homely to others. Walls were generally painted the 'hospital green' favoured in all Soviet institutions. Furniture included – at best – a few beds, also of the 'hospital' kind, *tumbochki* (bedside lockers), a table for eating, reading, or working at, and a wardrobe. Elaborate rules forbade inhabitants not just from moving rooms but also from altering the position of the furniture.[24] This latter rule was at times breached with impunity, but the absence of privacy and the lack of security for personal possessions (items placed inside someone's locker were generally preserved untouched, but anything on view was subject to 'borrowing') acted as disincentives to individual attempts at decoration. Usually the 'personal touch' was represented by a person's own bedspread and perhaps a few ornaments and a photograph or two.[25]

For a family, too, the essential private space was the bed and its immediate surroundings. In the recollection of Mikhail E., born in 1944: 'And she [my mother] tramped round from hostel to hostel, and I went along with her. And so she lived, well, how did people used to live in those hostels? [. . .] In the middle a table, a screen here, a screen here, a screen here, a screen here, that's how people used to live.'[26] In a space of this kind, 'home' would be limited to the area inside the screens, which might contain, besides the inevitable *tumbochka*, shelves over the bed, hooks for hanging, and a suitcase placed under the bed for storage. Sometimes wardrobes and cupboards might be used instead of screens to divide up the room into different 'cubicles'.[27] But the end result in whatever case was a remarkably small amount of personal space for each family – perhaps 3–4 square metres at most.

However, the population of hostels was often glad enough to be living there. As Vyacheslav Rezvov remembered in 2000, 'Just a little more patience, a decade or so, and the factory will find you a flat, and then you can get yourself a family, have children, bring them up.'[28] He was not intending to be sarcastic. Hostel conditions might be basic to grim, but the costs of living were commensurately low – getting a bed was a bigger problem than paying for it. Foreign students might (and did) complain,[29] but the Soviet inhabitants of hostels were all too aware that they were privileged. The alternative was renting a room, or more likely a bed (or, as Russian parlance has it, a 'berth' or a 'corner') from some private individual at an unregulated price.[30] Or, of course, sleeping rough, as an amorphous population of tramps had done since the city was created.[31] For members of the hippy *sistema*, 'home' was portable objects stuffed into a rucksack (some basic food items, a few clothes, and a sleeping bag), transported round various 'crash pads' (in Russian, *flety*) or squats (*skvoty*).[32]

Such willed indigence was beyond the compass of many and even in the post-Soviet period hostel living had its advocates, as in the case of an elderly woman, Fedos'ya Spiridonovna, interviewed by a local newspaper in 1995. Aged 89, she had then lived for 60 years in the tram park hostel on Degtyarnyi pereulok, in the Peski area of the city. She counted herself lucky. After first moving to the city to escape economic devastation in her collectivised village, she had spent five years 'renting out corners here, there, and everywhere'. The hostel had been a huge improvement, despite the crowding then prevalent (twenty-two people to a room). Once you married, there was one room to each two families, so you could at least get half a room to yourself. Widowed when her husband died of exposure in the Finno-Soviet War of 1940, Fedos'ya Spiridonovna had never been offered a flat of her own (though a Blockade survivor). She associated the hostel with human warmth and fellow-spirit – people boiling potatoes for each other, ready company at all times. Finding a room privately – no doubt somewhere in a cellar, or in a flat with drunks – did not appeal.[33] By now the city authorities were committed to phasing out hostels, and many had also been illegally privatised – but it was not clear what the alternative, for cash-strapped incomers or elderly people who had lived communal lives since childhood, might realistically be.[34]

## The Boundaries of Privacy: the *kommunalka*

If hostels and barracks (comparable accommodation offered by factories) represented the most basic form of communal living in the Soviet period, those living in them were aware of still less attractive alternatives. This was the difference between them and denizens of the infamous Leningrad *kommunalka*, or communal apartment, tirelessly evoked in memoirs, literature, and academic studies.[35] The peculiarity of this type of dwelling was that the surroundings acted as a reminder of something better – albeit in a vanished past. After *uplotnenie*, or 'compression', in the 1920s (the forcible billeting of further inhabitants on one-family households), large apartments were broken up into multiple units with plywood partitions used to divide up larger rooms. Sometimes, the decayed splendour was very splendid indeed. One of my own informants happened to live in a 'communal' apartment shared by only two families; her own family's territory included the former ballroom. But she was the daughter of a top-ranking 'Red Commander', and even in these circumstances life had its stresses. She and her parents did not get on with the distant relations who lived in the other half of the flat, a situation that provoked all kinds of petty persecution (for example, on one occasion these relatives organised a relay so that the lavatory was occupied for the entire evening when guests were visiting).[36]

Another woman with particularly unhappy memories of communal life was brought up in a flat inhabited by several generations of the same family. A bad-tempered grandmother used constantly to nag the children about leaving the light on in the lavatory after they left it, 'even though electricity cost only kopecks back then'.[37]

While moaning about supposedly differential use of utilities was a common experience with communal flat neighbours who were not relations, the more usual kind of *kommunalka* also presented another kind of stress – the need to share accommodation with people of radically different social background. In these conditions the room itself became 'home', with a sharp distinction between the family or individual's own territory and the 'common parts' (*mesta obshchego pol'zovaniya*, literally 'spaces in common use'). The only place in the 'common parts' that might to a limited extent be 'personalised' by tenants was the kitchen, which was used not just for cooking, and often also for hanging laundry, but as the 'social centre of the [communal apartment], the basic place for meeting neighbours and interacting with them, the main stage for public events in the life of the flat'.[38] Bathrooms and lavatories were strictly functional places, subject to an elaborate system of hygiene rules; for example, tenants usually had their own lavatory seats and were careful to avoid contaminating, or being contaminated by, the common tub.[39]

'Communal living', in the peculiar circumstances of the communal flat, was something quite different from the shared existence of the traditional co-operative, or *artel'*, or indeed the hostel. A strict sense of personal ownership was in operation. In kitchens each family would have its own primus, or, after gas was introduced, its own gas ring or rings. While food was not, as a rule, left in kitchens for fear of theft, pans and other bits of kitchen equipment were usually stored there, and such items were not held in common. The kitchen was a kind of extension of 'home' into shared space.[40]

Otherwise, the main opportunity to place territorial markers was the small amount of floor immediately outside the door of the individual room. Here, the light bulb was likely to be supplied by the individual family, and only switched on by them as well, and there might well be a doormat, racks for shoes, and so on.[41] Among children the corridor usually served as a common playroom, so that toys might make their way out here.[42]

Within people's individual rooms, space was organised round a small number of larger possessions. Some of these were functional – the dining-table, the divan for sitting and sleeping on, wardrobes for storing clothes or cupboards for household items (both these pieces of furniture are known in Russian as *shkafy*). The *shkafy* might also be given a screening function, to allow minimal privacy to someone's sleeping arrangements: 'So, the wardrobes divided off Mum and Dad's bed. But our [beds] simply stood there in the room, as divans. The big [bed], they partitioned that off in the corner. [. . .] And there

2.1 *Kommunalka* kitchen, 2011. Note the multiple stores of china and utensils.

was a TV there, and there was this kind of . . . not a secretaire exactly, but a desk for the eldest, since he was the first to go [to school]. So. And a big dining table, where I used to do my homework.'[43]

The TV that the informant mentions was not just a functional item. To own a set at all was prestigious in the early years of the medium, and in later years the type of set one owned could have cachet.[44] Another item with status links was the *servant*. This was the mid- to late twentieth-century word for what in traditional usage was called a *bufet*. Both words referred to a piece of furniture with shelves and glass-fronted doors (as variously known in English by the words *dresser, sideboard, display cabinet, shelving unit*, etc.) This was the place for keeping particularly valued or delicate possessions – porcelain teacups, crystal vases, photographs, etc. – and also treats such as chocolate or alcoholic drinks.[45] Bookcases also took up much wall space in many families.[46] Apart from chairs, this more or less exhausts the list of standard items (it is common for informants to describe their homes as 'nothing special').[47] The main variation took place at the level of individual possessions – which particular bits of glass and china, ornaments and trinkets, house-plants, books, pictures, etc. were on display.

The communal apartments of Leningrad, often seen retrospectively as unique to the city, had analogues in other cultures – in the tenements and rooming houses of Berlin, Paris, London, and Glasgow, to name only a few examples.[48] But there were important differences. One of these lay in the cultural capital of some of the *kommunalka*'s inhabitants, who were able to commemorate their existence in authoritative ways, writing about the stresses of enforced collectivism from the inside.[49] Another lay in the fact that many of Leningrad's communal apartments had originally been built as high-status accommodation. Poorly maintained after 1917, they rapidly declined into a state of Gothic decay. As the journalist Alexander Werth recalled in 1944, the building where he had once lived on Malaya Morskaya (known in the Soviet period as ulitsa Gogolya) was in an almost unrecognisable condition: 'The white imitation marble walls were covered with dark, dirty-brown paint, and there was no sign of the well-scrubbed wooden steps with the red carpet and the carefully-preserved brass carpet rails [. . .] The hall was dark and empty. No mirror, no coat-hangers – nothing.'[50] While the emptiness of this apartment may have been attributable to the effects of the Blockade, the general squalor was the result of longer-term processes.

However, Werth, an outsider in Soviet Leningrad, was seeing communal life with an alienated eye. Diaries of the 1920s, 1930s, and 1940s record many causes for irritation, but details such as damage to 'white imitation marble walls' were not among these.[51] In the 1920s, 1930s, and 1940s, most Leningraders seem simply to have accepted the *kommunalka* as home – there was, after all, no choice – and not seen their existence as particularly bleak or degraded.[52] But as the quantities of one-family accommodation expanded, the sense that the communal apartment represented a social anomaly, yet also somehow encapsulated 'Petersburg life', started to strengthen.[53]

### Mass Building, Standard Homes

In Leningrad, as in other cities, the crash building programme begun in 1957 fundamentally altered the profile of accommodation available to citizens. The percentage of those living in communal dwellings remained high. In 1970, an article in *Leningradskaya pravda* newspaper gave it as 40 per cent; in 1990, it was between 19 and 65 per cent, depending on district, with an average of 23 per cent across the city.[54] Because of pressure on housing, flats built as 'separate family accommodation' were sometimes settled communally.[55] However, the view that this was undesirable eventually prompted a decision to reduce the number of larger apartments in new projects, and concentrate on one-, two-, and three-roomed units,[56] and the main weight of the population gradually transferred into 'separate flats'.

What was just as important, Leningraders with 'cultural capital' were particularly likely to be rehoused in such separate flats. A significant role in this process of selection was played by the rise of the housing co-operative, reintroduced in the late 1950s as a way of tempting the cash-rich Soviet population to help fund new building, with the opportunity to shorten the wait in the housing queue as an incentive. Co-operative members made an advance payment of 40 per cent of the cost price of a new apartment, set according to a state tariff that priced 12 metres of living space at 2800 roubles and allowed members to acquire the right to inhabit up to 60 metres of living space. The remaining 60 per cent of the fee was payable over fifteen years at a rate of 1 per cent interest.[57] An unspoken factor in the process was that co-operative members were much more likely to end up living next to people like themselves, since co-operatives were – from 1 January 1964 – generally formed by enterprises or organisations (including 'creative unions' for actors, writers, etc.).[58] And as old buildings in the centre were cleared, they underwent *kompleksnyi kapital'nyi remont* (a process by which wooden partitions were replaced by concrete blocks, wooden staircases by metal ones, and pre-revolutionary apartment layouts were altered to accommodate single-family apartments that approximated to the ground-plan of new apartments).[59] The result was a shift in the symbolic, if not the real-life, role of the communal apartment. Such apartments increasingly became linked, in the local imaginary, with social marginals – from alcoholics to lumpenproletarians to bohemian artists.[60]

*Kommunalki* were in fact often preferred by non-official artists, because there was more space for organising exhibitions, concerts, and seminars, and the neighbours were less likely to make a fuss about noise than those in thin-walled modern apartments. As the poet Viktor Krivulin put it, the kitchen was: 'the *kommunalka's* holy of holies, the sanctuary of any Leningrad apartment, an agora and forum, a place for meeting people and for talking about politics and the economy. People here wept aloud, shouted and gesticulated, like the characters in a Dostoevsky novel. In their own rooms, they whispered.'[61]

With the revival of interest in pre-revolutionary St Petersburg, the very squalor of the *kommunalka* came to seem authentic, given the history of regarding the city, with a kind of melancholy pride, as the capital of crime and degradation.[62] And living with others cut down the amount of energy expended on domestic life.[63] While the communal apartment began to be associated primarily with an anti-homemaking drive, the 'nesting instinct' shifted to new family apartments. Now, a crucial concept started to be *uyut* – usually translated as 'cosiness' but probably the closest equivalent to the English word 'home'.[64]

As in every other Soviet city, low-rise blocks (five to eight storeys) were built at a relentless pace (between 1966 and 1969 alone, over 4.5 million square metres of accommodation was brought into use).[65] The grey concrete boxes surrounded by scrubland had little individuality. In the words of a British architect and planner who visited Leningrad in 1957, just as the first developments were beginning: 'The first impression on this estate [Ivanovskaya ulitsa] is of rather poor workmanship, the blocks of flats being hastily thrown together. The flats, too, are on the whole dull and stereotyped.'[66] The pervasiveness of poor workmanship was frequently noted in Soviet official sources, not just in the 1960s but at later stages too.[67] In 1982 the Executive Committee of Lensovet observed, 'Justified complaints from those moving into new homes are inspired by work that has not been properly completed, where there are problems with electricity and fire safety, and where lifts and plumbing do not work.' Provision of gas and water lagged behind construction, and even sometimes behind the arrival of the tenants.[68] In systems-built blocks where no outer brick 'skin' was provided (the so-called *blochnye doma* or *panel'nye doma*), water, condensation and draughts often seeped through the gaps, damaging the interior decoration and furnishings and making the dwellings unpleasantly cold.[69]

At the same time, the British architect who recorded his negative first impressions added that 'on examining finished work, however, the impression is rather better, a certain amount of modest craftsmanship being carefully concealed. The one, two, and three bedroomed flats (priced at 33, 70, and 105 roubles a month) are really very pleasant.'[70] If Leningrad new building is compared with Western social housing of the same period, it is not clear that aesthetics and standards were so very far adrift.[71] From the start of the crash building drive, the architects and engineers responsible for mass housing exercised their minds about how to construct buildings in which it would be possible to live reasonably pleasant lives. Their concerns are revealed by the behind-closed-doors discussions in Lenproekt, the architectural institute responsible for the planning of individual buildings, blocks (*kvartaly*), and entire districts in the city.

In 1957, for example, A. S. Ginzberg, a participant in a session of the Technical Council of Lenproekt, complained that plans for pattern-book architecture often saw industrial production as the purpose of the process, not as the means. 'Creating cheap, well-built, comfortable blocks' was in fact the end that everyone should keep in mind. V. F. Railyan was even more frank:

> I've got a 2.6 metre wide room in my flat, and it's not very comfortable. 2.27 metre wide would be really uncomfortable. You can't even put the bed-head up against that wall, or you only have 15 cm. left, so you have to jump across the bed, but if you put it along the long wall, then it looks like you were in a barracks, and if you have two beds, you can't cross the room. There's

an access route on the sketch, but you can put anything on a sketch. You have to leave 5 cm between a bed and the wall, and here the width is shown as 75 centimetres, but if you add in the coverlets, it's 90 cm, and then you won't be able to get between the two beds at all. It's just a cheat to put in that four-panel glass door, what use is there in that, you'll still have to jump across the beds, and if some guest arrives and they're sitting in the living room, then you'll be stuck there. [. . .] Comrades, we've lost our way trying to carry out all these orders and directives from Gosstroi [the state building authority], they've just muzzled us, they've put blinkers on us and we can't see anything and we're completely off the right track. You have to work in a principled way, the whole design of these blocks should be completely different.[72]

A few months later, the Novye Cheryomushki development, a prestige housing complex in south-west Moscow which the Leningrad architects were being instructed to see as exemplary,[73] also attracted adverse comment. There was simply not enough room for what one would expect in one's home, a member of Lenproekt complained.

We've reached the full pitch of absurdity – if we put a toilet bowl in, we take the wash-hand basin out. OK, so why don't we take the main basin out, people can just use the toilet bowl?

This project is so cramped you pretty well can't chuck anything out. When the discussion of small-scale apartments started, no one said they had to be less comfortable. But now we're removing the wash-hand basin, we're starting to get rid of the built-in cupboards. So if we do remove them, and people end up having to use ordinary furniture in small-scale apartments, what then? [. . .]

VOICE FROM THE FLOOR: But we're supposed to be going for a cost reduction.

MACHERET: You can't talk about cost reduction for its own sake. There are people involved here. After all, Viktor Viktorovich, imagine putting you and your furniture in one of these flats. Think of what that would look like. There'd be no room to hang a coat, even. You just can't do things like that.[74]

In 1961, the latest plans for high-rise blocks were criticised with equal vigour. Participants in the discussion described the plans as creating 'nothing more than a roof over people's heads' and 'living space, not real flats'. One speaker was especially doubtful about one aspect of the design: 'The main room [*obshchaya komnata*, lit. 'common room'] should be a good size, it should have plenty of space, it should have room for a bed. And here [pointing at the artist's impression] it's a through room and there's nowhere here for a bed.'[75] The comment made clear the expectation that living space would remain multi-functional; every room would serve as someone's bedroom, as well as being used for other purposes. A 'through room' (*prokhodnaya komnata*) therefore meant somewhere that another person would need to walk through to get to *their* bedroom.

Aside from the cramped conditions in the main room, and the inconvenience of 'through rooms', a particular focus of disquiet was the size of the kitchens in these new apartments. In 1961, members of the Technical Council at Lenproekt pointed out that a kitchen sized only 2.15 by 2.17 metres would leave less than half a square metre of workspace once the units and table were fitted in – and this only if the fridge were banished to the corridor.[76]

Later generations of high-rise blocks were more generously sized (a 9-square-metre kitchen was standard by the late 1960s, and by the 1970s ceiling heights had also risen).[77] But as basic designs improved, criticism shifted to the *otdelka*, the fittings and interior decorations put into the apartment shells. It was general practice for Soviet builders to kit new flats out, from taps to wallpaper, but, as time wore on, this practice came in for increasing criticism from professionals. A Leningrad newspaper for the construction industry complained in 1973 that Kolpino linoleum, the sole type locally available, was really horrible, that rubbish chutes were manufactured to a standard which would have made a village blacksmith blush, and that it was possible to buy just one type of parquet block. State building companies (*stroitresty*) were not allowed to raise spending on items such as this, yet tenants, once they moved in, immediately ripped out unsatisfactory lino, changed doors on fitted cupboards, tore out useless locks, etc., so that installing poor-quality fittings was an obvious waste of money. The article pointed to cases where tenants had cheerfully paid 193 roubles (significantly more than the average monthly wage) for specially designed kitchens, and suggested that everyone should be given the opportunity of choosing whether to stick with the default or pay for an alternative.[78] The newspaper regularly carried articles about new types of bathroom fitting, wallpaper, tiles and other household objects.[79]

## Living in a 'Cubby-Hole'

The discussions in Lenproekt, and Leningrad journalism of the 1960s and 1970s, leave one in no doubt about the importance of *uyut* as an objective of the planning and propaganda of the day. In the post-Stalin era, there was extensive coverage of the 'house-warming' (*novosel'e*), the arrival in the new family apartment as a key point in the Soviet city-dweller's existence.[80] At the same time, the mechanics of home-making were not dwelt on in detail by official sources; one needs oral history and other forms of personal remembrance to get at these.

The lyrical reminiscences that one often comes across in interviews or on the internet about, say, food[81] contrast with the considerably less nostalgic recollections of what home-making was like. One woman recalled the shock effect of arriving at her new block in Kupchino, right next to a 'bog', after the solidly built and rather gracious building next to Obvodnyi Canal where her communal apartment had been located: 'So they gave us a separate apartment. Of course, it actually was bigger, metre for metre, than the one we'd had. Naturally. But as a separate apartment, it was really small. Or at least, the kitchen was small, and the passageway was small, and the ceilings were really low. It was a complete shock.'[82]

Another woman's recollections were similar:

> My parents had got the flat through an official order [*po raspredeleniyu*]. Before they got it, my parents lived with my father's parents and his younger sister. And where they lived, it was this micro-district on Leninsky . . . round Leninsky prospekt. In this really typical Khrushchev-era apartment, on the first floor. Officially it was called a 'four-room' flat, but the space was more like a modern . . . well, a big one-roomed flat or a small two-roomed one [i.e. about 25–30 square metres]. There was one slightly bigger room, this hall thing in the middle, and three of these little cubby-holes [*zakutochki*], practically, see . . . And my parents were in this room . . . I think it was about five metres, five square metres. And so when they unfolded their double divan, they had about 20 cm of free space left to get in the room and lie down.[83]

However, here she is describing a type of layout, nicknamed *raspashonka* or 'baby's jacket', which became obsolete in the early 1960s.[84] Later, doors opened off a hall, and the minimum size of rooms was larger. At the same time, space was always limited: in 1970, the average allocation per person was given by the head of the Leningrad City Soviet board responsible for distributing accommodation as 8.6 square metres per person.[85] With ceilings of 2.4 metres, those used to the high ceilings of some pre-revolutionary Leningrad *kommunalki* could feel particularly cramped.[86]

Home-makers could do nothing about this: to alter the layout of one's apartment by 'replanning' (e.g. demolishing walls or even moving a doorway) was forbidden. The amount of choice that the average householder could exercise about decoration was also limited. One type of parquet flooring, one type of linoleum, one type of ceiling finish, identical bathroom fitments, kitchen cabinets, and even wallpaper and paint, remained the norm. Not everything about this was bad – the quantity of built-in storage in a post-Stalin-era flat would have put the average British dwelling of the period to shame.[87] Great efforts were made to design 'small-scale' furniture that would actually fit the new apartments.[88] But provision was inflexible; new inhabitants could not decide where and what storage and fittings they needed.

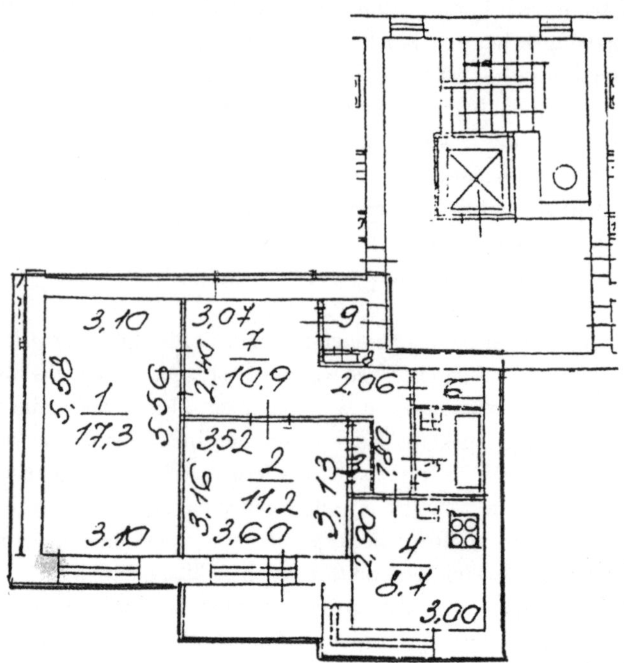


2.2 Plan of a two-room flat, standard layout, 1987 – but similar designs were used routinely from the late 1960s onwards.

Even if the will was there, making alterations was not easy. The operative word even professionals used for obtaining building materials was *dostat'*, 'to get hold of', meaning to wangle supplies through one's connections.[89] Without such connections, obtaining bathroom fittings, say, was difficult. There was accordingly a restricted range for the imagination of the person or people who moved in. 'Soviet redecoration consisted of two things,' a friend of mine remembered: 'new wallpaper and new paint.'[90]

One other place where people were able to, or had to, make choices of their own was in selecting curtains.[91] In a major textile-producing city such as Leningrad, upholstery and curtain material was readily available in shops with the generic name *Tkani* (Fabrics), as well as in the different department stores. What was on sale was serviceable, but usually rather drab, with a limited colour palette and patterns that tended to follow the principles of Soviet 'good taste': small scale, geometrically stylised rather than representational prints. Browns and beiges predominated. Wallpaper, too, tended to look like the foxed pages of a well-loved nineteenth-century novel. While the interior lines of post-Stalin flats had the geometrical lines of Baudrillard's 'urban chic', the shades used for decoration were quite different.[92]

Given that curtain-rails and hooks were extremely basic, it did not occur to anyone to attempt elaborate 'window treatments'. At most, people might hang inner net curtains or ruched blinds alongside the plain oblong strips suspended at the edges of the windows. Furniture was also, for most people, predictable in character: small, boxy units, usually constructed in plain deal with mahogany veneering.[93]

In circumstances of such unpretentious, indeed stark, decoration, the room for creating a 'home' in an individual sense was rather limited. Indeed, today many informants, asked what they remember about their family's home at this period, will produce the phrase '*vsyo kak u vsekh*' (everything like in everyone's home), just like those recalling life in communal apartments. At the same time, standardisation was not necessarily a barrier to *uyut*. One of the most important factors in making somewhere 'cosy' was that it should be warm. By the 1960s, district-wide heating supply systems had become ubiquitous in Leningrad, replacing the picturesque, but unpredictable and labour-intensive, solid fuel stoves of the past. Few regretted the disappearance of individual heating, and into the post-Soviet period the provision of abundant warmth that could be individually moderated only by opening a window remained one of the core assumptions of urban existence, both in Petersburg and all over Russia.[94]

## 'Family Relics'

Modern Leningrad apartments were very different from the collectors' treasure-houses that signal 'Petersburg style'. Inherited possessions were rare. Few people remember even one thing in this category. Here is an exception: 'And on the other side they had a double wardrobe and this really old desk, it had been my great-grandmother's . . . [. . .] You couldn't get a pram in the room. They used to fold it up and put it in the big room – there just wasn't room in the corridor.'[95] The desk must have dated from the 1900s at the earliest, but this counted in most people's minds as 'really old'. It was rare to have any heirlooms (*semeinye relikvii*, literally 'family relics') at all.[96] This was a standard situation in Soviet cities, given the amount that people tended to move about, the difficulties of transporting furniture, especially large pieces, and the vulnerability of burnable objects in times of crisis. In Leningrad oral history the Blockade, with this as everything else, marks a symbolic border: it is common to be told that few things survived this catastrophe.[97] Informants from later generations sometimes remember how things that were the wrong size or simply looked 'odd' in new flats went to the state 'commission stores', where private citizens could sell items on payment of a small premium. By the late Soviet period, it was generally furniture of an obviously functional kind (as in the case of this 'old desk') that survived. A certain ascetism – 'Why do people need to clutter their lives?' – was characteristic.[98] Occasional tables, what-nots (*etazherki*), and silk-upholstered sofas were found only in the houses of devotees.

Getting antiques during the Soviet period was, in principle, perfectly possible. They could be 'acquired' if you took over a room in a communal flat and previous inhabitants' belongings happened to turn up there. Sometimes, they could simply be picked up on household dumps.[99] Among the diverse 'used' clutter in the commission shops were some real treasures: 'On the one hand, collecting things was easy, but on the other, it was kind of hard. Why easy? Because everything was very cheap. And kind of hard, because the collectors used to turn up at the commission shops out of opening hours, and look at what they had. And they did their best to buy whatever took their fancy – if there were some good paintings there and so on, they'd have them.' The most avid collectors usually developed personal relationships with the sales staff ('they had their own assistants'). As well as this advantage, you needed an eye, since nothing was filtered or classified: paintings, of whatever quality, were priced according to size (so that an art student's copy of a work by a nineteenth-century Russian academician measuring three foot by six foot would have been four times the price of a miniature sketch by Rubens or Rembrandt).[100]

In fact, though, many people either did not like old furniture or did not have the space to house it.[101] It was quite typical of the older intelligentsia to consider collecting rather vulgar.[102] Inherited possessions were likely to be small-scale: watches, maybe, small bits of jewellery, perhaps a few silver spoons.[103] Families from a rural background might treasure – carefully concealed – an icon.[104] And people did not necessarily treat old things with much piety: 'I remember now, we do have one family heirloom – it's a bronze clock. I think that's all that's left from before the war. [. . .] It was real once, it had a special movement, an old one. But I couldn't get it to work again, so I just stuck a new movement in there. But all the rest is left, that clock . . . it even looks like one I saw in the Hermitage.'[105]

This sense of 'heritage' in a collective sense – the link to Leningrad as locality ('a clock like one in the Hermitage') – was relatively rare. Separate apartments presented their inhabitants with an environment that was not specific to the city. A dilapidated *kommunalka* might include pre-revolutionary architectural features such as tiled stoves, stained glass, or a plasterwork ceiling. As L. V. Vlasov (born in 1926 and brought up on Kuznechnyi pereulok, in the heart of the city) remembered:

> Until it was reconstructed in 1956, Flat no. 4 was out of the ordinary. There was a big hall with two niches for wardrobes next to the doors into the rooms. The kitchen had a roomy stove with an oven, 'embellished' with

> many flaps and a highly efficient ventilation system. There were cool boxes in the windows. The bathroom, a full 12 metres square, had a 'family tub' and a water-heater with a metal airing cupboard. The flower-painted lavatory pan stood on a little platform behind a door with decorated glass. [. . .]
>
> The room we lived in had a beautiful moulded ceiling. The imitation fabric wallpaper had a kind of airy look to it. The parquet floor, set to an unusual pattern, was where I loved playing war games with my little tin soldiers. In the room was a beautiful tiled stove decorated with silhouettes of lads and lasses, and with a whole picture on its front. I often remember the warmth and *uyut* with which it filled our room in the evenings.[106]

Separate apartments lacked such features, even if they had been carved out of old buildings.[107] This was one of the reasons why some members of the artistic bohemia preferred to remain in *kommunalki*. In such circles, the cultivation of *uyut* was also considered a rather dubious objective, an expression of *meshchanstvo* (petit-bourgeois values).[108]

However, this was a minority view. Most flat-dwellers do not seem much to have missed relics of the Petersburg past, or attempted to replace them by other 'historical' items. The one item of a 'local heritage' kind that might be on display was porcelain, from the Lomonosov Factory (the former Imperial Porcelain Factory).[109] Tea, coffee, and dinner services were all regularly offered as wedding presents, or gifts on holidays and birthdays. Novelty items in Lomonosov porcelain – presentation plates, statuettes, decorative ink-wells, candlesticks – might also be on show. This china, along with other precious things, tended to be arranged in the *servant*, which formed the cynosure of living-rooms in family flats as it had in families' rooms in the collective apartment. At the same time, it was normally not antique 'Imperial' porcelain but modern Soviet designs that were placed in this family sanctum.

Despite the growing prominence of pre-revolutionary St Petersburg in representational terms, Leningrad homeowners often evoked associations with the past in their homes in ways that were typical for other Soviet cities too. For instance, craft-style souvenirs picked up on trips round the Soviet Union brought a pleasurable sense of temporal and spatial exoticism.[110] In terms of *objects*, Soviet-era Leningrad homes tended not to be specific to the locale. The situation is caught by Georgy Daneliya's film comedy *Autumn Marathon*, where only the most negative character – the fat translator who passes off the hero's work as her own – inhabits a palatial apartment steeped in Petersburg history. The protagonist himself is housed in a pattern-built block somewhere on the city's outskirts, where only the piano and a couple of pictures speak of the pre-Soviet world.

The arrangement of space in separate apartments was also 'Soviet' in character – a situation displaced into fantasy by Vadim Shefner's story 'A Palace

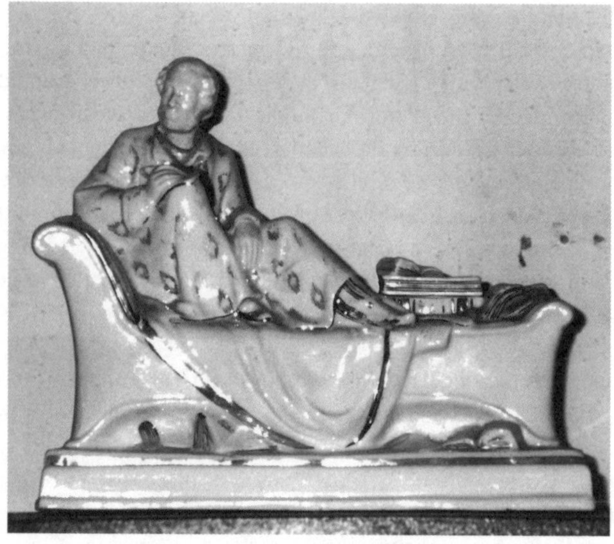

2.3 A 1940s inkwell with a figurine of Pushkin, Lomonosov Factory.

2.4 A glass-fronted cabinet (*servant*) in a communal flat, showing examples of Lomonosov porcelain on the left and on top, 2011.

for Three, or The Confessions of a Bachelor'. Presented with the flat of his dreams by a magician, the narrator has difficulty in 'thinking big':

> Stunned by the exact way in which my creative commission had been fulfilled, I went to look at the finished apartment. Apart from the hall, it consisted of a single enormous room, a kitchen, a bathroom and toilet, and one more small room. The little room was really to make up numbers. [. . .] I couldn't really think of anything to do with the second room, and I decided that it could probably serve as something like the sick-bay in an orphanage – you'd go there when you were ill.[111]

In the real world, multi-functionality continued to be taken for granted.[112] A couple with a two-room flat was unlikely to create a 'children's corner' in the room they used as their own bedroom and use the other as a full-time living room. Instead, the standard pattern was for the largest room to be used both as a living room and as the parental bedroom, while the child's room also served as a spare room for guests, and also somewhere for temporary storage. If space allocation officially included a study (the perk for those with higher degrees),[113] then this room might serve as a spare room, and possibly also a secondary sitting room if more than one person in the family had guests. Arrangement of furniture tended also to be replicated – as with the continuing use of the *servant* as a marker of 'display' space.

The 1980s saw increasing public expression of interest in preserving the past, encouraged by publications such as Daniil Granin's *Leningrad Catalogue*, which underlined the importance of family memory: 'Family archives aren't the past; they are the future. Every family should have its archive – the roll of honour [*pochyotnaya gramota*][114] of grandfathers and fathers, the history of their achievements, their labours, the history of a lineage, a family name'.[115] Yet it is unclear how many people actually compiled such 'archives'. As in earlier generations, it was the photograph album that often acted as the repository of family history, along with the stories told about it on the occasions when it was produced.[116] Albums were not only showcases for the talents of amateur photographers and records of memorable events, earlier phases of life, and precious family *lieux de mémoire* such as the dacha, but, in a sense, official chronicles. As is well known, in the 1930s pictures of 'enemies of the people' would often be carefully removed; in what Anna Akhmatova termed 'vegetarian times', this was uncommon, but the images of divorced spouses and other *personae non gratae* might be excised with a vengeful pair of scissors.[117]

All in all, the items by which people fashioned a past in the home tended to be related to Soviet preferences generally, rather than being specifically local. Paintings of the city were a habitual wall-hanging among the old intelligentsia (as a visit to the flat once shared by Anna Akhmatova and the Punin family indicates).[118] But if you lived half an hour from the real thing, you were unlikely to pin up a city view, or a calendar showing the Bronze Horseman, and high-quality reproductions of eighteenth- and nineteenth-century panoramas of the kind that might have found favour were not generally available.[119] The explicit repository of local memory, among educated Leningraders, was the home library. Most educated readers had at least a small collection of books about St Petersburg and Leningrad and, of course, also copies of books by the classic authors of the city, the collection of which became a major manifestation of permissible consumerism in the late Soviet era.[120] The *kommunalka*'s *material* connection with the past was offset, in newbuild, by an *imaginative* connection with the past.[121]

### The 'Piter Kitchen'

In some respects, home life in separate apartments represented a continuation of life in the *kommunalka*, with the separate rooms, particularly the 'common room', organised much as the single family room in the *kommunalka* had been. What had undergone significant change were the functional areas of the apartment. Secluded social contact between members of the same family was possible in the hall, the bathroom, and the kitchen. This last had now slid from its previous role as somewhere where families precariously established a small private foothold in a generally public realm, to a largely private place that occasionally acquired a public function. Meals, apart from those on major festivals (state holidays, such as New Year, Victory Day, or 7 November, and family birthdays and other special occasions), would be eaten here, including when guests were present. Entertaining was centred round the provision of food, as Yakov Fridman's 'Conversations about Nothing in a Kitchen in Piter' lyrically recalled:

> Have you never sat in a tiny kitchen in Piter, when black December foul weather is raging outside the window, but in the kitchen, it's warm and cosy? When there's a dish of hot fried potatoes on the table, and salt herring with chopped onion, and a bottle of decent vodka, with half of it already downed. When your friends are there at the table, and there's chat about nothing and about everything. About the theatre, about politics, about women, about history, about literature, about the state of the nation and the people. The Russian people and the peoples of Europe. Have you never sat there? Too bad for you, then.[122]

From a place squabbled over by different communal tenants, the kitchen had become somewhere crucial to expressing the personality of a specific group of people.

To what extent this personality had local colour is debatable. Before 1917, what Petersburgers put on the table had been dependent on means and opportunity. In the richest households, certain traditions – the *zakuska* table, tea with jam round the samovar, the serving of Easter foods – were token signifiers of 'Russianness', but much was international. At the other end of the scale was the food served in working-class households and *arteli* (worker co-operatives), where peasant custom – *kasha*, soups, and stews eaten out of a shared dish – prevailed. One local peculiarity was that coffee was at least as widely drunk as tea, even among the poor, but foodstuffs were generally not place-specific. Important here was not just the anonymity of any big city, but also the traditional domination of the population by single males, who made do with meals in a chop-house (*kharchevnya*) or with what a servant provided.[123]

Gastronomic adventurousness was further inhibited in the Soviet period, partly because of famine. Kuz'ma Petrov-Vodkin's still lifes of the early 1920s, with smoked fish on newspaper next to a faceted glass, suggested greater abundance than many could hope for. Near-famine conditions took hold again in 1931–32, and during the Blockade 'recipes' were more likely to include melted-down buttons, boiled leather belts or goosefoot salads than recognisable foodstuffs.[124] Thereafter, people returned with relief to familiar foods: bread, meat, sausage, potatoes above all, with vegetables or pickles according to season.

There was also a Soviet culinary 'high style', but this took the form of 'socialism in one country', without reference to regional culinary traditions. The canonical *Book of Tasty and Nutritious Food* (1939) included mainly dishes with purely descriptive names – 'Fried Fish with Mushrooms'. Identification by place-name was generally limited to 'ethnic' foods that were considered suitable for mass dissemination in simplified form ('Uzbek Plov', 'Ukrainian Borsht'). In a class by itself was 'Moskovsky' or 'stolichnyi' ('from the capital'), meant to signal sophistication. This principle was retained in later editions as well: in fact, emphasis on mass-produced ingredients, particularly bottled mayonnaise, further enhanced standardisation. The ultimate fusion of 'taste' and 'nutrition' was what might be called the 'stalad' (Stalinist salad): a mixture of chopped vegetables dressed in *maionez*, a dish that owed little to Russian (as opposed to American) culinary traditions.[125]

Leningraders did recognise some dishes as 'local'. 'Leningrad shchi' was a variant of the generically Russian cabbage soup that happened also to contain mushrooms. Pickled lampreys (*minogi*) were a delicacy served at parties.[126] Another tradition that survived 'socialism on one table' was the habit of eating *koryushka* (smelt),[127] which shoaled abundantly in the Gulf of Finland and Neva delta during spring, and might be eaten fried or marinated, or salted or smoked for later use. Unlike lamprey, this was not a party food: 'He used to catch that fish in the lake, and our family didn't have much money, so we more or less lived on fish. And my mother made these really tasty fishballs. It was mostly what they call "Sestroretsk *koryushka*"."[128] Even if people needed to buy it, the cost was low – you could even afford to buy it as a treat for the cat.[129] For the poet Nonna Slepakova, the smell of tired *koryushka* was associated with the disillusioned final moments of a love affair.[130]

At the same time, it had its own historicising mythology. There were family traditions about how, in the Blockade years, 'surviving till *koryushka* time' brought the promise one would live till the end of the year. The food had powerful sentimental associations:

> I was overjoyed when I was once living way away from Leningrad and I got a food parcel with a round rye loaf and marinated *koryushka*. It wasn't just food, it was the smell of home. I remember that when there were the food crises of the early 1990s and everything was rationed, the *koryushka* helped us through, and the whole population of both banks of the Neva by the Volodarsky Bridge, everyone of all ages was fishing for *koryushka* –no rods, just a *zakidushka* [a line with a metal ring and a net at the bottom]. Sometimes you could catch a whole kilo or even two in an evening. We felt this deep joy . . .
>
> And when I brought my son back from the maternity hospital, it was spring, and on the festive table was *koryushka* . . .[131]

The fish only became a 'speciality' of the drumroll kind in the post-Soviet era, with the initiation of a '*koryushka* festival', accompanied by much ersatz traditionalism, in 2002[132] – a time that also coincided with growing scarcity of the fish, so that it now qualified in terms of price as a 'delicacy' too.[133] But people continued to prepare it at home (fried, in a dusting of flour) and to associate it with the season: stalls at food markets carried the traditional waft of cucumber into the air of the modern city.

*Koryushka* was typical of Leningrad food in its simplicity and dependence on what happened to be available.[134] Culinary initiative was saved for special occasions. The tenants of communal flats might fire up their solid-fuel stoves, normally replaced by primuses, to bake pies and Easter loaves, and families living in separate flats did their best to put on a real party spread.

The 'family recipe', handed down through the generations, was as rare as other forms of 'family relic'. Even assuming such lore had survived the attrition of the human population, many traditional ingredients were unavailable. Techniques such as baking in a Russian stove could not be reproduced in the cramped kitchens of separate flats, with their gas or electric burners and their often crotchety single ovens. But many keen cooks had their *firmennye blyuda* (literally, 'house specials'), lovingly revived as family recipes. The *firmennoe blyudo* quintessentially put a slightly offbeat spin on something standard (the phrase itself is derived from Soviet commercial cooking).[135] However, such

2.5 *Koryushka* seller, Kuznechnyi Market, April 2012.

dishes would become encrusted with experience at the different occasions when they had been served – and their arrival was fraught with anticipation if also, sometimes, with anxiety (would they turn out as well as usual?).[136]

In standard Soviet and post-Soviet usage, 'kitchen talk' was associated with political criticism (the kind of 'private conversation' one could not have elsewhere). But the topics of discussion were quite varied. Apart from the ones Fridman mentions, others included family and friends, the socialisation of children (*vospitanie*) – prompted by the presence of the subject under discussion – and likewise the ever-present issue of how to 'get hold of' scarce goods.[137] Decorous flirtation (*ukhazhivanie*), particularly on the part of the host with woman guests, was also the order of the day.[138] But the more festive the occasion, the more likely it was that food and drink would be at the centre of attention – with the hostess congratulated on a particular dish and asked how to make it, and perhaps also on her particular *nastoika* (flavoured vodka).

Not everyone was a keen 'putter by', but typically there would be at least some preserved vegetables and fruits around – presents or purchases, if not products of the family's own cottage industry. Dominating the landscape would also be a large refrigerator, essential for storing food supplies that were more perishable than the preserved items.[139] Fridges were a reflection of deficit, housing more food than the 'cold cabinet' in the wall or gap between the double windows, and keeping it more reliably cold. But because they allowed stockpiling of items to be eaten or bartered later, they were also a mechanism of deficit – allowing individual families to purchase substantial quantities of desirable items so that these sold out faster.

The term 'hostess' is precise: in nine homes out of ten, kitchen work was strongly gendered. Men might help with some outside tasks, such as bringing *in* food and/or bottles of liquor, and carrying *out* rubbish, but the business of preparing and serving food was generally left to female members of the household.[140] However, cooking was not necessarily seen as a chore. Being able to dispose entirely over *one's own* kitchen – however small – was a significant difference from communal life, with its constant background of wrangling. At the same time, cooking for special occasions was still often undertaken collectively, with friends and relations pitching in to help with preparation (a practice that may be one factor behind the prevalence of dishes relying on simple techniques, such as chopping, on the party table).[141]

Memory played a central role in the kitchen. The process of cooking – certainly when it became a performance for guests, or at strongly ritualised family occasions – was also a process of re-creation. The convention of refusing to pass on recipes (as though these were a form of magic knowledge) was less

2.6 Party table, Leningrad, 1988. In this particular flat, the kitchen was too small for eating, so this meal was laid out in the living room. Note the chopped salads, pickles and supplies of Western gin and tonic.

common than a burning desire to impart exactly how to make a particular dish, and thus perpetuate tradition. But the kitchen was a 'memory space' not just in the sense that it was a place for recollection and recreation. As somewhere for displaying objects – ceramics, a samovar, old pans, vases, treasured pieces of cooking equipment – the kitchen was second only to the *servant* (and in families where the *servant* was considered a bit petit-bourgeois, not necessarily even second).[142]

In many ways, the kitchen was the most 'Soviet' room in the Leningrad apartment. Even in homes where antiques were on show in the main rooms, mementos here were unlikely to have city links. Yet at the same time, the kitchen was very much the centre of the home, and hence highly individual: the primary space for *uyut* and for social contact, and the primary space of family memories.

## Post-Soviet Homes

In 1991, after arguments that had rambled on for the best part of two years, the flat-dwellers of Leningrad were given the opportunity to 'privatise' their living space.[143] As in other parts of the Soviet Union, the new circumstances caused bewilderment. People were inclined to grumble that 'privatisation' had essentially represented an offloading of the financial burden of maintenance on to the individual, without the compensation of security of tenure that would have balanced the new monetary responsibilities. The authorities retained formidable powers of compulsory purchase, and if the building was cleared for reconstruction the new owner was entitled only to replacement accommodation of similar size in a given city district, not in the same building or street.[144] Bureaucratic regulation of interior space continued to be tight: not only were the new owner-occupiers forbidden from assailing load-bearing walls, but smaller changes, such as moving doors or demolishing partitions, also required agreement from the authorities.[145] Rather than signalling new freedom of action, privatisation generated anxiety – both because people living in unprivatised accommodation were vulnerable to buyouts by developers, and because those who had arranged a purchase felt bereft of practical support.[146]

All the same, the new owner-occupiers (who by 2006 made up around 70 per cent of immovable property owners across the city)[147] quickly acquired a much greater sense of involvement with their surroundings, and a desire to improve these. The earliest signs of this were purchases of consumer goods. In the late Soviet period, people had already made efforts to acquire items such as cassette recorders, which they might purchase on the black market, or get as gifts from Western friends.[148] More substantial purchases included imported furniture. At the top end of possible aspirations was Finnish furniture, particularly the *stenka* – the modernist equivalent of a *servant*, a system of wall units with glass doors. A rung or two below came furniture from Yugoslavia and also from the Baltic states, considered the most civilised of the Soviet republics.[149] In the post-Soviet era, there was an explosion of outlets selling furniture from different European countries – Spain, France, Italy, as well as all over Scandinavia – and Russian manufacturers started to imitate imported styles as well.[150] Not everyone could afford to buy new furniture but, for most, Soviet-era items had no cachet: they were for disposal as soon as one could manage to purchase something else.[151]

If they had the money, people also hurried to arrange redecoration (*remont*) of their quarters. The ideal was a so-called *evroremont*, 'redecoration in the European style', which included not just new paint and wallpaper but wide-ranging structural alterations.[152] Windows were likely to be replaced with UPV-framed sealed-unit double glazing (*steklopakety*) imported from Germany; the rough boards exposed when lino was removed would be covered by wooden laminate. Soviet doors would be stripped out, and new veneered ones with bright brass handles installed. (All this, it should be said, applied to home owners at the modest end of the scale. The plutocracy, if prepared to live in old buildings at all – many preferred newbuild, with or without a pastiche-old façade – expected complete reconstruction. *Their* homes were supposed to have heated garages, separate water supplies – to stop designer clothes and bathrooms going rust-coloured from the particles in the main city system – special electricity generators, heated garages, and, of course, round-the-clock security.)[153]

As interior design norms diversified, it became a point of honour among some of the better off *not* to use the kitchen as a place for general socialising. One strategy adopted in smaller flats was to convert what had formerly been a kitchen into a dining room, and use corridor space to carve out a small galley kitchen.[154] A 'kitchen for eating in' was not envisaged by glossy magazines, or even humbler advice literature publications. One publication in the latter category, published in Moscow in 1998, included, alongside cosy living-rooms with overstuffed sofas and armchairs, rocking-chairs, dining tables, and slightly sterile kitchens with pull-down flaps for food preparation rather than eating space. One picture showed an attempt to divide off a 'dining end' by using a unit with studiedly unfunctional curtains and decorations.[155] This latter strategy was adopted by some Petersburgers too – say, replacing plain emulsion with William Morris-style wallpaper, to emphasis the separate character of the niche with the table.[156]

Yet some sense of the kitchen as a family 'shrine' (*ochag*) remained. Even idealised images sometimes had 'nostalgia value'. For instance, a picture in the 1998 household manual showed old-fashioned enamel cans for collecting milk (*bidony*), long made functionally invalid by the arrival of the TetraPak; on the shelves sat woven baskets, even if an alien bottle of olive oil had usurped the table.[157]

2.7 Petersburg kitchen as nineteenth-century mock-up: note Raskol'nikov's axe hanging on the wall.

Similar kitchens were displayed on the home forum run by the local newspaper (with strong online presence) *Moi raion*. This included a page where people swapped information about the decoration of their kitchens. As in the past, *uyut* often required the accumulation of significant amounts of clutter, including patterned ceramic plates, earthenware mugs and bottles, Soviet-era aluminium or enamel bowls and tubs, folksy calendars and pictures, and so on. A host of shops had sprung up in St Petersburg offering 'bygones' of this kind for sale.[158]

By no means all the kitchens on this site were 'folksy'; some were done out in the kind of sleek chrome and tiling envisaged by magazines. But efforts at making the place 'cosy' usually bore relation to a Soviet vision of 'traditional culture' (lace curtains and embroidered hangings).

Occasionally, there would be signs of attachment to a kind of 'retro-Petersburg style'. For instance, one of the kitchens on the *Moi raion* site (reposted from another internet site) had heavy, mahogany-style furniture and rather formal lace curtains and lamps, though also (a completely inauthentic touch in this context) exposed brickwork. But more widespread were types of individualisation rather than 'localisation' – as in the fashion (widespread in the West as well) for multi-coloured letters and other kinds of fridge magnet. For the solvent, the fridge had been transformed from its Soviet-era role as a vital repository of food stores to a visual amenity, stuffed with brightly-coloured Westernised yoghurt pots on the inside, and decorated on the outside. One of the most popular pieces of furniture for a kitchen was an arrangement of benches known as a 'kitchen corner' that allowed plenty of 'sitting' round the table, perhaps while drinking tea or watching the TV (or both at once).[159]

There was no one canonical understanding of 'the Petersburg kitchen'. Indeed, a blogger on Live Journal explicitly addressing the topic carried three totally disparate images: a *kirovka* (constructivist building dating from the early 1930s, named for the then Party leader Sergei Kirov) in the Finland Station area, a quite palatial nineteenth-century block, and a building from the 1930s.[160] Only one of these kitchens self-consciously evoked the classic Petersburg past, and then in an obviously ironic way (Raskol'nikov's axe, suspended on the wall). If there was a unity between these images, it lay mainly in eclecticism itself: paper napkins, plastic toys, fridge ornaments *and* folk ceramics; brocade curtains, novelty wine-bottles, *and* fridge ornaments; Soviet-era cooking utensils *and* a mobile telephone next to Westernised wrapping-paper and gift presentation. All precision of a historical kind vanished. Chandeliers may be 'authentic' in St Petersburg apartments, but hardly in the kitchen; folk ceramics and plastic worktops have a tense and paradoxical relationship to each other. Buying antiques and 'old' items had become commoner, but that did not mean that people lived in historically exact St Petersburg interiors.[161]

Amid the confusion, though, the Soviet-era concept of *uyut* persisted.[162] In the words of a participant in another *Moi raion* forum, 'Uyutnyi dom' (Cosy Home):

> For me *uyut* means a sense of relaxation, calm, being secure. Warmth. Spiritual and physical. The things that surround you give you associations and invisible links with events and people who are dear to me.
>
> And the people round you, of course.

Another participant said much the same, while being more specific about the types of objects:

> For me, it's the little details that create *uyut* – something on the walls. And mats (on the floor). Lots of mats.
>
> My home isn't *uyutnyi*, I don't want to spoil the walls.[163]

The post-Soviet era gave people vastly increased opportunities to buy new things, and imposed new kinds of taste. But the basic sense of how to handle space – and particularly that space should be *filled* – persisted. The key compliment to any home-maker was to say that their space was 'cosy'.[164] On the whole, too, the relationship with the past continued to be expressed in generically 'retro' objects (folksy prints and knick-knacks), rather than in items with a specifically 'local' connection.

The leading idea was caught by the forum participant who wrote: 'The things that surround you give you associations and invisible links with events and people who are dear to me'. A central place in home decoration was played by the *suvenir*, a word that in some European languages is applied mainly to a memento brought back from a holiday, but which in Russian primarily signified a gift object, such as might be purchased for New Year or a birthday. Objects of this kind, often representing something animate (dinky animals or people in cartoon style) were favoured precisely because they did not conform to strict canons of taste; since the Soviet era, advice literature had been exhorting readers *not* to buy items like this. In the words of two priggish young contributors to a newspaper discussion called 'The Museum of Bad Taste' in 1965, 'Everyone wants to decorate their room. But it is best to do so with an etching, not a china pussy-cat or a rug'.[165]

Mostly, *suveniry* lacked city resonance. An enterprising initiative by the Lomonosov Porcelain Factory Mit'ki was to manufacture artist Vladimir Golubev's series of angels in traditional Russian male winter-wear: padded jerkins and hats with ear-flaps.[166]

2.8 One of the Lomonosov Factory angels designed by Vladimir Golubev.

However, on the whole, 'souvenirs' were not 'designed', and even if they showed Petersburg scenes, they might well be made in Hong Kong.[167] In their whimsical and even ugly nature, they spoke of informality, and hence of intimacy, 'peopling' (in a nearly literal sense) otherwise bleak expanses, turning a standard space into something inhabited by one individual or individuals.[168] They were the expression of an emotional and communicative network stretching out beyond the apartment's walls. In this sense, commemorative objects in the apartment expressed not a vertical relationship with the city (stretching down into the past), but a horizontal relationship – they honoured a set of ties to other people living at different points of the city topographically, but within a unified temporal world. This also worked in reverse. As a woman in her twenties put it in 2011, 'My family is my city for me.'[169]

3

# 'The Hermitage and My Own Front Door': City Spaces

*Where in Leningrad do you live?*
*On the front line [= in the suburbs]*
(post-war Leningrad joke)[1]

In 1958 a book for Leningraders, *The City We Live In*, began its armchair excursion round the city with a chapter on 'Where We Live'. Looking back to the late Tsarist era, it recalled the 'dreadful conditions' in which workers had been housed, perching on narrow beds in damp cellar accommodation. The Soviet era, however, had changed everything. In place of wooden houses, shining new quarters were rising. As for the Nevsky Gate, formerly a notoriously deprived spot, this was now 'one of the most beautiful areas of Leningrad'. At what had once been the city limits, on Shchemilovka, 'Quarter no. 122' was going up. 'Many high-rise blocks have been built here, joyful to the eye with their superb appearance.'[2]

In 1862 Petersburg had become the Russian homeland of the socialist utopia, when Nikolai Chernyshevsky's novel, *What is to be Done?*, made the 'crystal palace' the central symbol of the new world of rational egotism.[3] The imagery of the book possessed the minds of Leningraders too. In 1961, the leading architect Sergei Speransky, directing the project to build a new hotel opposite the mooring of the *Aurora*, recalled his vision of the site:

> Long ago, before we even began planning the hotel, I was once making a speech at the [Technical] Council [of Lenproekt Planning Institute] and, odd as it may seem, I once had this dream of a tall crystal palace standing next to the [Pirogov] Museum and it all looked very beautiful, just as things always do in dreams. And, well, you know, things like that do happen – I got this idea that there should be a tall glass building on that spot. Many years later, it has become possible to realise that structure, and we think it will be the kind of accent that will unite all that fairly classic horizontal building [. . .] and it should be a sculptural form in terms of its composition and placing, up to 70 metres tall at its highest point.[4]

3.1 Kantemirskaya ploshchad', Vyborg Side, 1931. Note the surviving wooden buildings as well as the new blocks.

As the outskirts of the city were transformed into new districts, attitudes to the centre also changed and its 'horizontal building' came to seem, in the eyes of some, 'provincial'. From the early 1930s, indeed, spaces in the outlying districts had been the focus of the drive to turn Leningrad into an 'exemplary socialist city'. The construction of 'International prospekt' (later 'Stalin prospekt'), an enormous avenue resembling a Moscow thoroughfare in scale and style, was supposed to give the city a new administrative centre, leaving the banks of the Neva as a 'museum city'. (In a poem completed in 1963, Ol'ga Berggol'ts recalled how back then, 'Before my eyes arose the mountain ranges/of Greater Leningrad').[5] The Narva Gate was 'reforged' into a comparable arena, providing a geometrical focus for prospekt Stachek (Strike Avenue), lined on both sides with modern blocks.[6] These districts continued to be showcased after the war as well. For example, a lavish album of city panoramas published in 1954 contained photographs of various new developments, including Narva, Neva, and Vyborg districts, as well as the Strelka, Palace Square, and the other historical sites.[7]

From the late 1950s onwards, the same principle of making the outskirts a model for the centre applied. The Sovetskaya Hotel, constructed on the Fontanka, the Press House, further along that river, and the new apartment block for leading officials on Petrovsky Embankment were built in the same pared-down style as the avenues rising in outlying districts.[8] It was fashionable to heighten the dissonance between a new building and its neighbours. The

3.2 New apartment block on Vyborg Side, 1957.

Vasilievsky Island metro station of 1967 was a steel-and-glass box set back from the street line, in radical contrast to the late nineteenth-century apartment blocks to either side. Ya. D. Bolotin, the architect, commented approvingly on the effects of his design when it was at the planning stage:

> I have known this area since 1936. The whole of Vasilievsky Island, Sredny, Maly, Bol'shoi prospekt has the streets clearly delineated. And it is good that here, suddenly, in one particular place, there will be a structure like this, one with a quite different character, one that emerges from the run-of-the-mill building. Which is why we have to treat this section in a more characteristic way, a more modern way [. . .] and exactly this treatment, based on a contrast between a modern glass building that is not on the ordinary street frontage, but set back, but which does not disrupt the system set up by Sredny prospekt and 7-ya liniya is, in our opinion, the right resolution for the situation in question.[9]

Bolotin's argument (unlike his building) was circular. The structure needed to be of a 'characteristic' kind because the site required a 'characteristic' structure (by implication, Vasilievsky Island was 'modern' before its time). For planners, there *was* no historical distinction between 'Petersburg' and 'Leningrad'. The entire city was one whole – as suggested in the paradoxical trope used about new buildings, which, despite their entirely man-made character (glass, concrete, and steel), were supposed to 'blend organically' into the surrounding area.[10] It was customary to emphasise uniformity with paint: while the city's premier architectural landmarks were individual in turquoise, blue, or pink, carefully restored from paint scrapings, secondary buildings were mainly veiled in two colours: dun and the smudgy grey of clouds coming on to rain.[11]

But by the late 1960s, some were coming to criticise this uniformity. As one contributor to an architecture journal bluntly remarked in 1970, naming two of the showpieces of recent building, 'It's boring in Kupchino. And on the Right Bank of the Neva as well'. The forum in which he was participating had set out to examine whether such areas deserved to be considered part of 'Leningrad' (the term then used for the historic city). On the whole, the conclusions drawn were sceptical.[12]

Indeed, if one walks along Maly prospekt on Vasilievsky Island, the undemonstrative modernism of the early twentieth-century 'lines' and the gargantuan masses of Communist International prospekt impact on each other like tectonic plates. Metro lines splay out from Nevsky into Giant's Causeways of greying concrete. But locals have ways of making a 'no-place urban realm' their own, and do not necessarily see where they live in terms of a simple contrast between new and old. 'Small cities that all have their centres on Nevsky prospekt', was how one woman summed up her sense of the metropolis.[13]

I can speak from personal experience here. The neighbourhood where I began living in 2005 is typical in its ambiguity – somewhere that is both the 'centre' and not. At its southward end is the Neva embankment; to the north lie the major arterial roads of Bol'shoi Sampsonievsky and Lesnoi prospekt, each with its own specific built environment (a mixture of pre-revolutionary housing and Soviet model developments – mostly from the late 1940s and early 1950s on Bol'shoi Sampsonievsky, and from the 1930s on Lesnoi). Also dominant are the enormous and ugly bulk of the Hotel St Petersburg with attached business centre and – stretching from the river to the Finland Station – the severe neoclassical façades of the Military-Medical Academy, painted in regulation yellow.

Though the place (with the exception of the Military-Medical Academy, the oldest institute of higher education in the city) does not form part of the so-called 'historic centre' in planning terms, it has plenty of history. It has always been a kind of borderland, originally between official St Petersburg and the old 'Vyborg side' of market gardens and wooden houses evoked in Goncharov's *Oblomov*. By the late nineteenth century, it marked a standoff between the military and the industrial life of the city. After the emergence of 'savage capitalism', a third factor was added, as the embankments got turned into an embryonic St Petersburg CBD.

By the 2000s, the triangle of residential development between the river and Bol'shoi Sampsonievsky, denominated on the third side by Finlyandsky prospekt (a street about 100 metres long whose name most residents of the city don't know, and which is often left unmarked on maps), made up a small, precarious, socially diverse area, with communal flats, revamped

3.3 Prospekt Karla Marksa (now Bol'shoi Sampsonievsky), *c.* 1958. (The archive this photograph is taken from dates the photo to 1938, but this is clearly wrong: the car on the left is a 'Victory' (Pobeda), first built in the late 1940s, and the blocks in the background are also post-war.)

nineteenth-century tenements, late Stalin houses for the 'worker aristocracy', and a slightly decaying but still respectable co-operative block from the Brezhnev era.

When I first arrived, I found the place chilling compared with the covered market, cafés, and specialist shops of 'Five Corners', where I had lived immediately before. But it rapidly acquired its own appeal: the red-brick factories reflected in the sometimes silver, sometimes charcoal-grey water of the Neva, or offset by fretted ice; the musical-comedy sight of cadets, spruce in their dark greatcoats, coming in well-drilled groups to shovel snow off the pavement; the calls of a bugle challenging the snarls of traffic. After protests, efforts to relocate the Military-Medical Academy have ceased (brought to a halt by President Putin, no less).[14] Life in this spot has showed me how a 'district' may to all intents and purposes be invisible to those who don't live there, yet represent a definite 'somewhere' to those who do.

In fact, from the beginning, the division between 'centre' and 'outskirts' in Petersburg was less than clear-cut. The geography of the Neva delta divided the city into many different territories. The capital's oldest permanent structure, the Peter and Paul Fortress, was on an island, Petersburg (later Petrograd) Side; the embankments of Vasilievsky Island housed many of the premier buildings of the 'Golden Age'; settlement on Vyborg Side went back to the Petrine era. While the nineteenth century saw the south side of the Neva (Nevsky prospekt and the streets and embankments around) emerge as the fashionable centre, the reconstruction of Petersburg (later Petrograd) Side in the 1910s as a luxurious new residential district started to challenge this hierarchy. In the Soviet era, this was where the Party elite preferred to live.[15]

Even within the area that came to be known in the 1980s as the 'historic centre', there were in fact many different 'centres': Palace Square, where tourists thronged; ploshchad' Vosstaniya, the hub for incomers and also for many locals arriving on public transport; Nevsky prospekt; the Party administrative headquarters out at Smol'nyi; the city administration in the Mariinsky Palace on St Isaac's Square. There were also areas that were central, but which lay beyond the boundaries of the official city myth, such as Ligovsky prospekt, leading off ploschad' Vosstaniya, or Kolomna at the seaward end of the Fontanka. The early twentieth-century architecture of Petrograd Side, 'The Sands' (Peski), or 'Five Corners' might be painted the same dun as the nineteenth-century ranges along the Moika, but window and door sizes, as well as roof angles and the shapes of balconies and decorative features, were very different; turrets and bay windows sprouted from the long flat ranges. And for residents in their day-to-day lives, perception of the city was tied to the city's sprawling topography, its land-masses divided by water, with the most intense impressions, of course, connected with the immediate area where they lived. The initial sense of surrounding space, indeed, was bound up with areas too microscopic to be mapped – within a person's own building, and in the territory immediately surrounding it.

## The Approaches to Home

For Leningraders who lived in separate apartments, the dividing line between 'home' and the wider world was much clearer than it was for inhabitants of communal flats. There, contact with the 'common parts' was frequent and unavoidable – washing, and for many people cooking, could only take place in shared space. In blocks of separate apartments, on the other hand, such shared space was peripheral and almost completely anonymous. Indeed, the *pod"ezd*, or entryway, was one of the key sites of Soviet collectivism, with doors and mailboxes numbered, rather than named, and painted in regulation green.[16] The halls, stairways, and lifts often had to be cleaned by tenants themselves on a rota basis (as with the 'common parts' of *kommunalki*), and people were expected to keep these places free of personal clutter. One of the tasks of the 'elder' of each *pod"ezd* was to chivvy anyone who deposited trash – whether of a culinary kind or furnishing and building detritus. Neighbours also might take upon themselves this admonitory role. All the more remarkable as a sign of transition was the symbolic privatisation of hallway space in the late 1980s, as people began purchasing new doors, and sometimes even caging off sections of the corridor, to deny entry to uninvited strangers.

3.4 and 3.5 *Pod"ezd* in a municipal building (top) and in a building from the late Soviet period (bottom), 2012. In the former, while the space is maintained to a reasonable level, the conditions are comparable to those in Soviet days, including the characteristic use of green paint. In the latter, the block is cared for, as shown by the replacement plastic windows and radiators, and repainted walls (in a prim pinkish brown), with even an attempt at decoration (the cloud design in the corner) – but it is still anonymous.

Sometimes the word *paradnaya* ('parade staircase', used in the Tsarist era for the main entranceway to an apartment block, as opposed to the *chernaya lestnitsa*, 'black staircase') was still used for the entryways to apartment blocks. However, applied to modern blocks – as opposed to the decaying stairs of communal apartments, degraded as the latter might be by neglect, with grubby stairs and walls, and cracked or vanished mirrors – the term *paradnaya* was pretentious.[17] The *pod"ezd*, as opposed to the *paradnaya* in its original manifestation, was bleakly functional.

In time, 'privatisation' of security features moved outwards to the barrier between the *pod"ezd* itself and the street. During the Soviet period, outer doors to blocks were generally not locked; human watchers fended off intrusion. In the first decades of the new era, a survival of the pre-revolutionary past, the *dvornik* or 'yardman', the equivalent of a janitor or concierge, kept an eye on all comings and goings. Alongside keeping the street frontage of the block clean, and also its internal courtyard, he or she was supposed to monitor the *pod"ezd*.[18] However, in the post-war years, yardmen disappeared from many places.[19] Instead, the principles of 'socialist competition' and collective voluntary work were invoked: 'social housing committees' were supposed to organise tenants into cleaning up after themselves.[20] Though having a yardman to do the work was a matter of pride among those with social capital, the horizontal surveillance carried out (or not) by the denizens of a given block was often the only mechanism regulating whether a given block and the courtyard next to it were clean and respectable, or quite the opposite.[21] Often, elderly women (the generic *babushki*) were the main enforcers, intervening directly but also acting as conduits of information to the official body of house management, the *zhek* ('office for the exploitation of dwellings').

This association between the maintenance of order and interference, added to the stresses of urban life, meant that the collectivism imposed on residents of Leningrad blocks did not always translate into communal spirit of a tangible kind. People tended to rely on relatives and friends, rather than neighbours, to keep a set of keys and water plants and feed pets while they were away. Neighbours who were *already* your friends were treated with great warmth, but to introduce yourself to neighbours when you arrived, or greet them with slices of pie and tips about attractions in the locality, would have been, to put it mildly, eccentric. 'Good neighbourly relations' often meant to say hallo on the stairs, and perhaps know a person's first name.[22] An important gripe about new apartments was that the sounds of your neighbours were ever-present – another indication of the fact that people preferred to live 'without neighbours' where they could.[23]

Privatisation in the post-Soviet period made no difference to this situation. Indeed, since one main effect of the reform was to give former tenants a greater financial and emotional investment in their own space, neighbours who allowed plumbing or noise to leak through walls and ceilings might generate even more aggression than in the past.[24] An interesting side effect of 'anti-neighbourliness' was that it could be difficult to broker collective agreement to the installation of an entryphone. To begin with, some people did not wish to pay (indeed, even enforcing payment of utilities was not always possible).[25] People might also resent the control on movement in and out – if you had a lot of guests, it was more convenient to leave the door open than to keep rushing to the buzzer.[26] In any case, the hypothetical bandit out on the street could seem a lesser threat than the alcoholic or drug addict across the hallway.[27]

The collapse of Soviet power also brought the demise of institutions such as 'staircase elder' – the person responsible for order within a particular *pod"ezd* (organising clean-up sessions and sometimes even a 'wall newspaper' with optimistic news, cheery slogans and snide little pieces badmouthing slackers). Self-management by tenants reached a low ebb, particularly in former state (as opposed to co-operative) blocks. The 2005 reforms to housing management attempted to reverse this trend and to set up 'owner-occupier corporations' (TSZh) – democratically-accountable residents' associations of the kind that had existed before then in housing co-operatives.[28] By popular vote at a 'general meeting' that reached its official quorum, improvements could be agreed that were paid for by general levy. In some blocks, the TSZh even funded restoration of the historic fabric – the replacement of missing tiles and mirrors, the repair of plasterwork.[29] However, in many dwelling-houses, the reform remained, in its early years at least, a theoretical measure. Even in effective TSZh, the active work of management was done by scantily paid representatives of the inhabitants rewarded, often enough, by the loud complaints of the otherwise supine majority.[30] Meetings were held in a spirit of more or less cheerful confrontation, as people milled in and out, loudly applauded, or shouted comments from the floor ('if you don't get this sorted out, they'll evict the hell out of us!'). Pungent comments about current and former members of the management committee were exchanged. But meetings happened only annually, and were poorly attended; meanwhile, issues of the day rolled on. Minor repairs might get organised; fundamental problems, such as the purchase of the land on which the building stood, were deferred year after year.[31]

The *pod"ezd* thus remained the main place where neighbours saw each other, though contact might well be superficial. This was a liminal zone: an intrinsic part of a given block, but also accessible to passing strangers. Given that Soviet cities were extremely short of facilities for those 'just passing through', the *pod"ezd* commonly acted as a site for improper assignations, whether mercantile or sexual. But it was also somewhere you might go to find out whether and where your tights were laddered, and perhaps even to change your clothes. It was a place to drink (as in Venedikt Erofeev's famous novel

*Moskva-Petushki*), to wait out an eddy of bad weather, and, by the late 1990s increasingly, to shoot up. The rank stenches in many a *pod"ezd* testified to usage that was promiscuous in every sense of the word.[32] Even in the post-Soviet period, passers-by sometimes got past the entryphone system and reasserted these ancient rights, as a despairing notice posted in a city-centre *pod"ezd* in 2005 recorded:

> Dear residents!
>
> Let's take care that strangers don't get into our *pod"ezd*.
>
> Right now the under-stair space on the ground floor is being used as a public toilet, and someone is regularly sick on the landing between the second and third floors, and there are syringes scattered all over the staircase.
>
> When we specially put in an entryphone and metal door so that shouldn't happen.
>
> Let's be vigilant!
>
> And if we manage not to forget bags of litter in the *pod"ezd* and throw cigarette ends and cans on the floor, that would be really wonderful! Is cleanliness really so bad?[33]

The main means of communicating in the *pod"ezd* was indeed usually by notice. Unlike the inhabitants of literary dystopias, the residents of Soviet blocks did not all leave for work or come back at the same time; you could enter and depart on repeated occasions without seeing anyone at all.[34] This state of things persisted into the post-Soviet period too, though some blocks – once the crime panics of the early 1990s had died down – started to acquire a more relaxed feel. Mats appeared outside doors; sometimes plants were put out to decorate passageways and staircases. Smokers forced to indulge their passion outside home proper might colonise the landings of staircases as nooks of self-indulgence, with a used can to act as a receptacle for stubs, placed next to a chair that had got too shabby for domestic use. As one would expect, the area immediately outside front doors was prime territory for minor self-assertion of this kind.[35]

But the *pod"ezd* – particularly in the post-Soviet era – was also a favoured place for another type of text: the graffito. Petersburg had its population of dedicated graffiti artists, carefully selecting their sites to emphasise their own daring, or seeking inspiration in the facture of a peeling wall.[36] Their work was mostly out in yards or in eye-catching positions out on the street, emphasising its status as silent public performance or two-dimensional installation. Another type of graffito testified to the presence of adolescents and pre-teens, marking territory or exchanging statements with each other.[37] Graffiti of this kind tended to be in liminal places – on the walls of lifts, by doors, round the outside of the *pod"ezd*.

3.6 '108 School' graffito near the Nobel Buildings, 2008.

In the Soviet era, graffiti were reticent – occupying inconspicuous places, literally scratched into the walls.[38] Even in the 1990s, simple paint predominated. The arrival of marker pens and aerosol paint transformed the inscriptions, particularly as graffitists became aware of 'international best practice' on the internet. The younger graffitists followed these models, using acronyms to label group identity. But older types of identifier, such as the school number, diminutives and nicknames, were favoured as well. Sometimes graffiti would be placed right by some official text – for example, an advertisement for some company in the building – as though acting as an alternative claim to territory. Those who created graffiti also expressed a creative relationship with a concrete place, adjusting their designs to the facture and layout of the walls. To older adults, though, their presence was an irritant, regarded as 'hooliganism' – a disorderly and inappropriate incursion into neutral shared space.[39]

## Back Yards and Through Routes

For graffitists, the *pod"ezd* and the courtyard were part of one territory. In a sense, they were for ordinary tenants as well. Both areas were traditionally

3.7 'Rap is Shit' – a (mis-spelled) graffito in a *pod"ezd*, Udel'naya, 1997.

under the jurisdiction of the yardman, who was responsible for keeping them clean and respectable – though not always to noticeable effect. At the start of the 1860s, a British visitor was startled by the contrast between the 'well-lighted, airy, and tall' rooms that he rented and the approach to these over a 'paved and puddly' courtyard and 'long passages, angular, dark, and smelling atrociously of tom-cats.' Similar descriptions abounded in fiction of the period.[40] One difficulty was that the courtyards had inalienable practical functions, as George Dobson remarked in 1910. 'There is no house without one or more of these court-yards, where the contents of cesspools (as long as there is no drainage) are periodically removed in carts, and logs of firewood are daily chopped up to be delivered to the occupants of different flats.'[41]

In the Soviet period, this situation altered only gradually, with the development of mains drainage, piped water, and electricity and gas supplies – a process not completed until the 1960s. At this point, privies and log piles, along with communal laundries, disappeared from inner-city courtyards leaving behind bleak paved or asphalted yards.[42] In the new districts rising round the city limits, on the other hand, a 'courtyard' was not the traditional enclosed 'well' of late nineteenth-century tenement blocks (as in the Glaswegian 'close'), but a large open space, a stretch of the natural environment that had existed before the building of the new blocks at its fringes. But systematic landscaping of courtyards, whether in the centre or outside, was more or less unknown.

3.8 'In the Courtyard', photograph by Galina Lisyutich, 1969. A photograph of the popular singer Edita P'ekha has ended up at the bottom of a rusty bucket.

Some straggling grass and a few trees, small groups of benches, and erratic clusters of sheds and garages, were the main features.[43]

Rather than provide tenants with amenities, or, from the early 1960s, yardmen, the authorities tried to make tenants themselves do the work. As well as co-ordinating cleaning, 'social housing committees' were expected to organise sport and other healthy, consciousness-raising activities, with help from Komsomol and Pioneer workers.[44] Communal clearing sessions, *subbotniki*, were supposed to inculcate a sense of shared responsibility for cleanliness and order. But in practice, yards were places that were used for a variety of different functions and activities, sometimes conflicting. It was common for tension to arise between those who valued the yard as safe space for children and people who wanted to park or garage their cars; between people who used the yard for playing dominos and the grannies sitting by the door of the *pod"ezd*; between advocates of sand-pits and supporters of football pitches.[45]

In addition, most courtyards were *prokhodnye*, open to use as a through-route by people cutting between streets. Children and teenagers often became possessive about space, and courtyard to courtyard fights, as well as fights

3.9 Back courtyard with a blank firewall (brandmauer), 2007. Note the straggling bushes.

within one's own courtyard, were an abiding experience. 'We'd get into punch-ups [. . .] So people didn't raid our territory, our trash heaps. We used to collect bottles and paper. Hand them in and get money. We needed it for ice-cream,' remembered a man born in 1960.[46] At the same time, adults accepted that the courtyard was not somewhere 'private', and access was possible round-the-clock and without restriction.

During the post-Soviet years, the potential for conflict increased. The proliferation of private cars made ever-increasing demands on space, with efforts on the part of some to designate some particular spot as 'mine' for parking (in former municipal blocks, there were no official named spaces, or even anything resembling residents' parking).[47] But chaotic 'territorialisation' of this kind was not the only dynamic. Groups of residents might join up in an effort to denominate space for collective use, mounting barriers to impede access by cars to a courtyard or part of this. In some cases, gates taken down in the era of the First Five-Year Plan began reappearing, and yards became 'residents only' for the first time since 1917.

However, the late 1990s and 2000s also saw a drive to 'ennoble' courtyard space on the part of the city government.[48] Benches, flowerbeds, swings and slides started to appear, meant for use by a wider community, not just by the courtyard-dwellers themselves. In many places, yardmen again held sway, clearing snow and keeping an eye on courtyard traffic. This reinforced the sense among local residents that keeping communal space orderly was someone else's job. In the words of a local newspaper in 1998, 'Better a good yardman right through the year than a communal clearing-up session in the spring.'[49] While *subbotniki* (communal clearing-up sessions) were still organised, they were not universal and participation in them could no longer be enforced, since the house management did not have the capacity to evict non-complying owner-occupiers.[50]

Despite the efforts of residents and officials, the negative connotations of the courtyard survived. It remained essentially an abject space, where activities impossible in well-run homes and parks (for instance, gambling) were furtively indulged. Noise pollution – whether because people were playing music, or because of conversations or arguments carried on through the window at full pitch – was another hazard.[51] New playground facilities notwithstanding, parents were now less likely to let their children out than in the past.[52] And one of the courtyard's traditional functions proved impossible to eradicate. In the twenty-first century as in earlier centuries, this remained the place where domestic refuse was stored, usually in a large rusting tank (*bak*) that concealed fetid layers of detritus. Efforts to 'ennoble' this particular part of the courtyard were in vain: new pink walls concealed the trash only from certain angles, and stray bits of paper and plastic, not to speak of reeks, regularly eluded containment.

In Leningrad literary tradition, the communal dump had a humble but secure niche. For some creative artists, it was an exciting and even fertile place, the metaphor for acquisitive creativity:

> The ruined wreck of an ottoman
> Lies cramped in a pool of lilac shade,
> Whispering tales of hookahs by the Golden Horn
> To lionising clumps of willowherb.[53]

More ambiguously, it could stand for the type of memory resistant to logical ordering, but stimulating to the imagination. In a poem by Boris Khersonsky, the speaker regretted his inability to jettison hurtful recollections:

> high time they went on the dump but
> there's still hurt there
> in the chest the drawer of Petersburg
> in the raincoat lining

through the hole in the pocket the valves
        of the heart
        three tough lads
had the boy pinned down right mate let him have it[54]

In day-to-day life, refuse was not seen as creative; it simply provoked disgust.[55] Children might hunt through it for 'treasure', but skips piled with stinking, deliquescent food remains repelled most adults.[56] A form of tactful filtering was practised, so that anything which might possibly have value to someone else – old doors and window-frames, last year's sweaters, anthologies of folk epics – was placed alongside the container, rather than inside this.[57] On the whole, those who helped themselves to discarded waste were socially marginal: pensioners looking for glass that could be taken to a recycling point in exchange for small payments to keep body and soul together, and above all dossers (*bomzhi*).[58] The most easily portable items tended to disappear most quickly. Veneer divans of the Soviet period, their primly flowered cushions still fairly clean, hung around for entire days; two hats of imitation fur, a man's in beaver brown and a woman's in an extraordinary luminous emerald, vanished in a matter of hours.[59]

3.10 Items placed for informal recycling by rubbish skips, 2007. Note the two hats, which disappeared almost immediately.

In contrast to the *pod"ezd*, the dump was notice-bare. No one needed to place neatly written cards saying 'help yourself' or 'free', of the kind found in Britain or America in the 2000s. People just took things. Or, alternatively, did not, since the post-Soviet era saw a marked increase in the amount of rubbish that had no value even in terms of informal recycling.[60] As late as the end of the 1980s, Leningrad cars left on the street were likely to be stripped of any removable parts; less than ten years later, abandoned cars, disintegrating with painful slowness, had become a regular eyesore.[61]

## From Okhta to Kupchino

The *pod"ezd* and the courtyard formed the borderline of contact between 'home' and the wider world. But people's sense of their 'home patch's' relationship with the surrounding city did not stop at this boundary.

In a famous study of the urban environment, the geographer Yi-Fu Tuan argued that 'the street where one lives is part of one's intimate experience. The larger unit, neighbourhood, is a concept'.[62] If anything, the situation in Leningrad and St Petersburg was the other way round. Streets, particularly in new districts, were often far from 'intimate'. People often knew their backyard better than the street frontage – particularly if they lived in a block some way back in a new area. The capricious numbering systems meant that a building might officially 'belong' to a street that it had spatially little to do with. Few streets, even old ones, had the picturesque self-sufficiency of the Amsterdam street described by Edward Soja, with its line of narrow seventeenth-century houses, neat apartments on each floor, and the specialist food shops, craft shops, designer dress-makers, secondhand bookshops and antique shops at street level.[63] The most 'picturesque' St Petersburg streets (such as ul. Rubinshteina, with its line of cafés, or Stremyannyi pereulok, a cluster of imaginative antique shops) were very short of facilities such as food stores, and few, if any, proprietors 'lived over the shop'. Viktor Kosakovsky's offbeat documentary film, *Hush!* (2003), an obsessive, almost narrative-less close-up of one small stretch of street, filmed from inside the windows of an apartment in a standard nineteenth-century block, worked as 'art' because its pedantic illusionism was undercut by the fact that no one would normally have been so engrossingly preoccupied with the life of the street outside.[64]

But the precise neighbourhood where Petersburgers lived had a considerable impact on their lives in practical and emotional terms. Certainly, 'districts' in the administrative sense were to some extent abstractions, partly because they were vast (up to 400,000 in population). Even people's day-to-day contact with bureaucrats was likely to be with a district subdivision, or 'micro-district'.[65] The boundaries had also changed quite frequently over the decades – most recently, a spate of reshaping and renaming took place on 21 March 1994.[66]

This left some with post-Soviet, politically neutral, names (Central rather than Kuibyshev, Dzerzhinsky, and Smol'nyi; Admiralty and not October and Lenin), while others retained their Soviet appellations (Kalinin, Red Guard). Still others had non-Soviet names to begin with (for example, Nevsky, known before 1917 as 'Neva Gate', or Vyborgsky, from Vyborg Side).

Whichever way, most of the official district names lacked any folkloric resonance – they conferred no real sense of 'location' of a semiotic kind.[67] More often, people would use denominators related to the city's physical geography – say 'Okhta', 'Vasilievsky Island' or 'Petrograd Side' to describe where they lived. (Sometimes, an affectionate diminutive – 'Vas'ka' or 'Petrogradka' – might be used, though there were older locals who frowned on this habit as vulgar, even, oh horror, 'Muscovite'.)[68] But above all, it was the neighbourhood or *kvartal* (or unofficially, *pyatachok*, 'patch') that was resonant. Some names evoked pre-revolutionary areas that had once had a distinctive character, for instance, *Roty* ('Companies' [in the military sense], behind the Trinity-Izmailovsky Regiment Cathedral).[69] But there were also large numbers of modern names, often related to major thoroughfares or metro stations. The area around prospekt Prosveshcheniya, for instance, was known as 'Prosvet'. The metro station 'Ulitsa Dybenko' gave its name to the entire quarter.[70]

What residents saw as their home territory involved a large number of different and perhaps even contradictory concepts: 'location' in the house-agent's sense (the convenience and prestige of a given neighbourhood), topography, landscape, building styles, and the essential 'character' – both human and non-human – of a given place. It was really everything about living somewhere that the inhabitants felt to be special.

In the Soviet period, the neighbourhood led a more or less unremarked existence. Only the official districts were commemorated in official mythology. For instance, each 1 May and 7 November columns of marchers would form up in each district and then converge from their different directions on Palace Square, an action that at once honoured the contribution made by outlying areas to the revolutionary past and acted as an expression of their subordination to the centre. The so-called 'people's museums' that enshrined the history of particular districts were embodiments of a similar expression of autonomy combined with subordination.[71]

Housing policy was also 'location blind'. Though every district had its own presiding architect, concepts of rational planning were set at city level, and there was no 'local' style of buildings specific to a particular neighbourhood. Leningraders were, in any case, not encouraged to discriminate between different types of housing. Resettlement schemes worked on the principle 'out of substandard dwellings into beautiful new apartments', irrespective of location. Whether people were moved from communal flats into reconstructed apartments in old buildings, or into new blocks, was purely incidental. As in the 1920s, formerly elegant buildings on the Moika were likely to have their contingent of factory workers.[72]

For those lucky enough to have individual flats and for the increasingly miserable inhabitants of communal ones, location was also not a primary consideration. Legally, the housing norm was in square metres, and the dwellers of communal flats would denominate their dwelling-place primarily in these terms ('I grew up in a twenty-seven square metre room . . .'). However, with the proliferation of separate family apartments, the number of rooms also began to have social weight. In practice, people would say that they lived in a three-roomed apartment, rather than an apartment of 60 square metres (the standardisation of space in new buildings and in conversions of old ones meant that the room number gave a clear picture of exactly how much space one had).[73]

Yet the emphasis on space in terms of the private environment, *locale*, rather than in terms of *location*, did not preclude the sense that some places were more pleasant to live in than others. Families could exercise leverage at the point of rehousing, perhaps turning down a larger apartment on the outskirts in favour of a smaller one in an old part of the city – 'If one's living in Leningrad, then the historic centre is the only place to live'.[74] The same could happen in reverse. Those with most clout would attempt to get permission to move to better accommodation in the same district, or even in the same house, if they were aware of something suitable. The files of one of the leading Leningrad theatres contain numerous examples of special pleading on behalf of employees. A star actor needed a separate apartment that could offer the tranquillity and comfort required by a talented person, and was close to the theatre (i.e. central); a particularly deserving make-up artist who had regularly done the faces of actors playing Lenin should be allowed a larger room.[75]

People also had the legal right to exchange apartments privately – for instance, two one-roomers for a two-roomer when getting married, or vice versa when divorcing.[76] While the main factor here was juggling square metres, the belief that district X was rough and dirty, or alternatively, sterile and dreary, also had influence.

There was also a lively sense of place that came from reading literary texts and from city folklore. This had little or nothing to do with official monuments, which tended to be treated ironically. There was, for instance, a joke about a drunk who woke up with a befuddled head and no idea at all where he was. 'You're by the Narva Gates,' a passer-by explained, referring to the triumphal arch built by Vasily Stasov in 1824–37 to commemorate the victory of 1812. To which the drunk replied, in a quavering voice, 'Close the gates, will you, there's a draught blowing down me neck!'[77]

In literature, too, attachment to neighbourhood was usually expressed by a proud emphasis on the place's marginal character – a tradition that went back to nineteenth-century writers such as Blok and Pushkin, who celebrated the

3.11 Kolomna, 2012, with the Admiralty Wharves in the background. This was one of the few areas of the city where traffic was still at Soviet levels into the twenty-first century, though the arrival of the New Holland arts centre in 2011, a haven of boho-chic Western culture, was set fair to change this.

quasi-provincial backwater of Kolomna, and Dostoevsky, whose Petersburg prose was rooted in the areas round the Catherine (later Griboedov) Canal. While official Leningrad writing was usually vague as to spatial setting, unofficial writing made up the deficiency, with Roal'd Mandel'shtam's tribute to New Holland, Lev Losev's celebration of the districts beyond Obvodnyi Canal, and Sergei Dovlatov's focus on 'Five Corners' all cases of texts that looked beyond the 'posh [*paradnye*] quarters' of the city.

At the same time, celebration of neighbourhoods was mainly limited to peripheral areas of the *old* centre.[78] In Andrei Bitov's novel *Pushkin House* (1978), the protagonist's visit to his grandfather in a new district put him among 'the very last houses' (in the area, and by implication perhaps the city and the world as well):

> Lyova had never been there before. He was startled to find himself thinking that he'd probably never left the old city either, he'd actually *lived* in that museum, none of his daily routes had taken him beyond those museum prospekt-corridors and square-halls . . . odd. He'd heard about the newbuild

> on the outskirts, but the names got confused in his mind. Right now, he'd forgotten what this place he was in was called: Obukhovka, maybe, or was it Proletarka? Yet again he checked his note-book.
>
> He had the sense of being in a different city.[79]

Partly such attitudes derived from a sense of social status as a result of zoning policy in the Soviet era. The development of some of the outlying areas of Leningrad-St Petersburg, for example Narva district, turned these into heavily industrialised landscapes, *promzony*, where the ecological conditions were as unappealing as the architecture: as the poet Nonna Slepakova put it: 'snow is the only natural thing'.[80] One might live in squalor in the old centre, but there could be compensations: 'One loo between twelve people, no hot water in the bathroom, and a single stove with four burners. But in return, the Summer Garden was five minutes' walk away.'[81] Yet, if the outlying suburbs lacked obvious aesthetic appeal, this did not mean that living there was left to philistines. Some areas on Vyborg Side, north of the Neva (for example 'Grazhdanka', Grazhdansky prospekt), were intelligentsia enclaves.[82]

Suffice it to say that two of the leading cultural gurus of the era, Alexander Panchenko and Dmitry Likhachev, lived in these new districts in their later years. But for the younger generations, the monotony of the new buildings made these constrictive. In the words of a song by Viktor Tsoi that spoke for those 'born in the cramped flats of the new districts':

3.12 New block on prospekt Morisa Toreza, Vyborg Side, early 1970s.

We want to see further
Than the windows of the block in front,
We are long-lived as cats,
And we've come to assert our rights.
Do you hear the rustle of raincoats? It's us,
And from now on we'll be calling the shots.[83]

For the poet Elena Shvarts, newbuild was a place where one could imagine the birth of Christ, after the rape of his mother by a drunken carpenter, but definitely not the Archangel Gabriel.[84]

The precise part of the city one came from was a badge of local identity. To say 'I'm from Okhta' had resonance to a Leningrader in a way that it did not for an outsider.[85] In working-class areas, people would even enforce boundaries by fighting:

> People always fought. So, eh. I remember, Vit'ka was standing in the wrong place, so he got it as well. [. . .] And we had this [prospekt] Kul'tury down our way, with Vyborgsky district on one side and Kalininsky on the other. He lived in Kalininsky district, but the stop was on Vyborg [Side] . . ., in Vyborgsky district. So he got it on the gob. And it was always like that![86]

The sense of district as offering a personal sense of belonging began to develop especially strongly in the post-Soviet era. Once newspaper advertisements seeking an exchange began appearing in the early 1990s, these often specified what location the would-be exchanger considered acceptable:

> *Wish to exchange*: one-room flat, 16 sq. m., privatised, and a 28 sq. m. room, P[etrograd] S[ide], for a high-ceilinged three-room apartment, P[etrograd] S[ide]. Will throw in dacha plot with wooden hut, pick-up.
>
> Two-room flat, 30 sq. m., kitchen 5.5 sq. m., on third floor (of 4), large enclosed balcony, all mod cons, in a communal apartment with only a few other tenants, swap with three-room flat, at least 45 sq. m. total, nothing in 'ship' blocks, no ground- or top-floor flats, no old districts.[87]

The earlier criterion of square meterage remained in force, and people were now very fussy about what type of building was acceptable (the 'ship' mentioned in the second advertisement was a particularly unloved type of systems-built concrete block, with very small windows like portholes). But where the flat was also had weight – and not just in terms of universals, like closeness to a metro station. For instance, the widespread liking for 'high-ceilinged' (*krupnogabaritnye*) apartments actually entrenched the appeal of Petrograd Side and Moskovsky prospekt, two areas built to a generous scale.[88] Thus, growing sensitivity to variables in the domestic environment was matched by a growing sense of the specificity of particular districts.

What was 'prestigious' in the Soviet period retained its lustre, partly because back then it had been more inaccessible to ordinary mortals than the most expensive new block with heated underground garage was in the 2000s. While the 1999 list of top addresses compiled by Dmitry Gubin, Lev Lurie, and Igor' Poroshin looked slightly out of date a decade later, some of the locations listed on it, such as the Tauride Garden, were still reckoned as desirable.[89] The glamour of the areas specified was precisely a *Soviet* phenomenon: few of the 1999 addresses would have figured on a list compiled in 1910.[90] The status of the Tauride Garden was attributable to the concentration of housing for Party and local government officials because the Party headquarters at Smol'nyi was next door.[91]

To the outsider's eye, the explosion in the 2000s of expensive 'town houses' and quality apartments out at Udel'naya, an area to the north of the city, looked odd. But insiders knew this was a 'good' place to live, the site of co-operative blocks built for members of the cultural intelligentsia back in the 1970s and 1980s. Certainly, Krestovsky Island – once an enclave of factory housing – became one of the most expensive districts in the city. But this was because it neighboured Stone (Kamennyi) Island, a park reserve that had housed the summer residences of Party, and later city, bigwigs.[92] Conversely, the handsome pre-First-World-War worker apartments of Gavan' and the Nobel Settlement off Lesnoi prospekt remained proletarian enclaves, and therefore much less sought-after than the concrete blocks around Primorskaya, Udel'naya, and Politekhnicheskaya metro stations.[93]

Such attitudes affected property development, since high-specification apartments in previously unprestigious areas often did not sell well.[94] Conversely, there was an explosion of brash new minigarch havens round Tauride Garden and down the Kamennoostrovsky prospekt 'corridor' on Petrograd Side. As in Moscow, residents of sought-after areas who lacked economic capital were likely to find themselves evicted – whether or not they owned their dwellings. A standard procedure was to declare an entire building 'unfit for human habitation' and clear it, making space for luxurious housing or a boutique hotel. As a local joke put it, 'Red Riding Hood comes to visit her granny and finds the place empty and the wolf sitting there with a broad grin. "What's happening here?" she asks. "Dunno," says the wolf. "S'pose it'll be an office or something." '[95]

But commercial gentrification made only modest inroads on St Petersburg (compared with its impact on London, or even Moscow). Gentrification by personal initiative was even more limited. In practice, people's first association with a location was often accidental. You were either born in a district, or you ended up there when you arrived as an outsider with little else to choose from.

The disproportionate cost of housing, compared with salary levels, meant that the average denizen of St Petersburg had, for much of the time, to put up with what he or she could get. When people moved into the city, they often lived with friends, and then transferred to a flat share or to renting a room in a *kommunalka* – often a whole series of rooms all over the place – or indeed a squat.[96] As in other cities, people were unfamiliar with the concept of the mortgage and dubious about what they saw as a threateningly large and cumbersome loan.[97] Only if they were much better off than average would they immediately acquire an apartment. And once housing of a half-way satisfactory kind had been tracked down, moving meant taking a large number of risks. What state would the new apartment and the block housing it be in? Would it be too noisy, dusty, hot, cold, or perhaps (depending on one's tastes) so quiet it was claustrophobic? Would the neighbours be acceptable? With all this to worry about, moving was not undertaken lightly.

Yet when people *did* move, districts played some role in their manoeuvring. The usual way of operating (for the solvent) was to employ a realtor, and to name the district and the price you wanted to pay. And people were starting to see where they lived as an expression of personal choice. The new market in privatised property did not, as outsiders might expect, lead to an obvious binary divide between 'the centre' and 'the outskirts'. In fact, there was a surge of 'newbuild patriotism', partly as a result of the growing awareness of ecological issues. In the words of a man born in 1938 who had lived all his life in Leningrad, he liked Vasilievsky Island, but much of the centre was dirty (Nevsky prospekt, for instance, was 'spit-soaked' and 'hideous'). He was delighted to live in Krasnogvardeisky district (a flagship project of the 1960s and 1970s), which was convenient, as well as quiet and green. The modernist values of light, fresh air, and landscaping were widely shared.[98] The association between modernist housing projects and uncongenial and unsafe city space made canonical by Jane Jacobs's 1961 classic *The Death and Life of Great American Cities* did not work in this city.[99]

Outlying districts were beginning to acquire their own written traditions as well. In 2005, the writer Il'ya Stogov took issue with received opinion that the city should be defined entirely in terms of its 'historic centre'. He himself had then been living for several years in Kupchino, and that was just how he liked it:

> I chose it myself. Everyone thinks Petersburg is the square kilometre round the Hermitage. No, we have our own South Bronxes and West Harlems. It's time we began to love them – Kupchino, Prosvet. Right opposite where I live is 'Twin Peaks', two thirty-storey skyscrapers, the only ones in town, and I'm proud of that. If someone gave me a T-shirt saying 'Kupchino', I'd wear it.[100]

3.13 Brezhnev-era *kirpichnyi dom* (brick-clad apartment block) on prospekt Nepokoryonnykh, in the northern suburbs near Piskaryovka Cemetery. This is regarded as a 'good' area – note the branch of the bookshop chain Bukvoed ('Bookworm') in the building.

For Andrei Astvatsaturov in *Skunkamera* (2011), the area round ploshchad' Muzhestva on Vyborg Side provoked intensive, self-ironising scrutiny of the local micro-environment. Cut off by his new German plastic sealed-unit double glazing, in a modern block now covered in parti-coloured ceramic tiles (many of the originally pristine white tiles had come unstuck and been unexpectedly replaced, after years of decay, by new ones of a brownish hue), Astvatsaturov looked back with tongue-in-cheek regret to the Soviet past, when a throng of beer-stalls stood around the square:

> What sense in fattening your arse in a proper bar? There's no romanticism in that, no movement, no dynamism. Even if your bar does happen to be called 'Grenada'. A beer-stall is quite different. You can take a proper tour round them. You can ask for a little one in the first, a big one in the second, chill off in the third, have a smoke in the fourth, make a new friend in the

> fifth, then grab him by the chest, and get a smack in the face for your pains. It's a trip round a whole empire – a local one. The pissheads hereabouts, the ones who called the hostel 'the monkey-house', used to call it 'a tour round the Golden Ring'.[101]

Once again, the local's insight was ironically juxtaposed to the tourist's: 'the Golden Ring' was the official 'brand' under which selected Old Russian cities were packaged for Soviet and international consumption.[102]

Local photographers also relished the new districts, with the vast concrete shells of incomplete new buildings (*nedostroiki*) and the Cyclopean towers of the housing estates.[103] Some of the most important local poems of the post-Soviet era, including Nailya Yamakova's 'Cities Keep Growing: A Visit to Poklonnaya Gora', and Dar'ya Sukhovei's 'remembrance of prospekt veteranov', dealt with comparable outlying areas – interesting precisely in their dearth of obvious landmarks.[104] In the words of Nailya Yamakova:

> From the frozen earth up to the sky new cities arise,
> salt-pillars of wayside and telegraph poles, along run the wires,
> the glitter of memory – of forehead and ice-rink – off toothed edges of skates,
> all covered in scratches – of our days,
> our dear doubles
> our records of dates.

There were none of the buildings that acted as cultural 'markers' in the old centre, but a peculiar, innovative sacral topography was visible:

> there are no stadiums, head-colds, no foreheads with scabs,
> no dome to be seen from that rift – and no songs of praise.
> but lo! look now! all is concrete and glass,
> from the bell-towers of those little churches pour raspberry notes.[105]

These representations stood in contrast to, say, Sergei Stratanovsky's vision in a 1972 poem of the new houses as 'places where there will never be *domovye*', referring to the traditional house spirit, and to the newbuild as haunted by a 'mad Orpheus' and 'the wandering eyes/Of tipsy wastelands'.[106]

In fact, the choice not to live in the centre did not mean retreating to alcoholic emptiness. The suburban areas included not just some of the earliest traces of human habitation, settlements that preceded 'Petersburg' (such as the Swedish settlement Nyen on Okhta), but important historic buildings. In the vicinity of the largely Stalinist Moskovsky prospekt stood the Chesme Church, an exquisite sugar-pink masterpiece of Russian neo-Gothic. Until the 1970s, the lodge designed by Rastrelli for Empress Elizabeth also survived, in badly

3.14 The Chesme Church and Palace, in the southern suburbs of Leningrad, surrounded by modern newbuild, 1981. This aerial photograph bears a stamp indicating it was cleared for publication by the Leningrad military censors.

mutilated form, at Srednyaya Rogatka, a junction at the south end of the prospekt.[107] Vyborg Side sheltered the Samsonievsky Cathedral, one of the earliest surviving churches in Piter.

Locals knew of these landmarks and took pride in them, but there were also more esoteric places of historical interest, such as the splendid neo-classical abattoir designed by Joseph Charlemagne in 1823–26, and used as the Petromol milk factory until the late 2000s (in Moskovsky District), the beautiful church 'in the English style' out at Shuvalovo Park, or the *style russe* lunatic asylum in the remote northern area of Fermskoe shosse.[108] About a mile from the grimy railway and metro interchange of Devyatkino, on the city's northern border, stood Murino, with one of the finest small eighteenth-century churches in the area, built in the late 1780s by Nikolai L'vov (much decayed in the Soviet period, but lovingly restored in the 1990s and 2000s).

By the end of the twentieth century, specialist guidebooks and newspaper articles were starting to catalogue such places.[109] The very standardisation of newbuild lent a new value to old architecture.[110] Also an influence on the rise of 'district' loyalty were the popular books by Naum Sindalovsky, which recorded jokes and legends about individual places and buildings beyond the centre as well as in it.[111] From the 1990s, local history at district level also played a role in school education, with pupils asked to write essays about their 'home patch'.[112] In the 2000s, commercial culture also began to celebrate the city outskirts. Stogov's praise of Kupchino was inspired by the appearance of a line of T-shirts with local district names, including 'Prosvet' and 'Grazhdanka'. The T-shirts reportedly found a ready market.[113] While the number of occasions where district administrations could contribute to the ceremonial side of the city was limited (new festivals such as City Day, Russia Day, Youth Day, or the St Petersburg Beer Festival did not have a 'local' presence in the way Communist demonstrations once had), district-level ceremonies were proliferating. Some event organisers had considerably more ambitious ideas, too, than the people annually recycling Petrine motifs for City Day. For instance, the planners for Frunzensky district at the start of the 2010s pointed to the avant-garde exhibition space 'Loft-proekt "Etazhi"' as the inspiration for their work, and their local magazine, *No Dormitory Suburb*, had design values that put to shame some commercial publications.[114] While the idea of putting customs posts on the bridges to Vasilievsky Island and issuing a new currency called *vasyuki* was simply a joke (as in the classic London film *Passport to Pimlico*), district pride was perfectly serious.[115]

The newspaper that ran the story about Kupchino T-shirts, *Moi raion*, pointed in its title to the importance of local patriotism.[116] Beginning with editions aimed at the public in the centre of the city, it rapidly expanded to cover city districts well beyond 'the square mile in front of the Hermitage'. It claimed a print-run of 933,000 and circulation of 1.3 million in 2008, and launched an internet edition in 2006.[117] Online, the paper carried local stories in a format allowing readers to click on their own district and access information. These publications might include anything from traffic problems to local history, from human interest items about sick children or struggling alcoholics or bizarre acts of violence ('Wife Crushes Husband with Folding Bed', 8 July 2008) to stories about notable local events ('Petropavlovka Beach to Get Sand Sculptures', 9 July 2008). Often, the material tried precisely to promote the individuality of outlying areas. For example, an article published on 3 July 2008 reported on efforts to provide dormitory suburbs with their own monuments, and gave information about what to do in order to get a sculpture set up in your own city courtyard.[118]

## Lived Districts

The sense of neighbourhood was not just absorbed by locals from written sources such as literature and newspapers. It came from direct observation. The area round Lomonosov metro station, with its streets named after polar explorers (and skinning winds blowing off the lake during the winter months), the decayed magnificence of its Stalin-era porticos, and its special flyover for trams, was tangibly different from the Brezhnev-era avenues of Kupchino just a couple of miles away.

Whatever the district, locals had landmarks of their own, such as the untidily silvered sputnik moored outside the doors of an otherwise unremarkable block on the sprawling campus of the Military-Medical Academy.[119] In the most unpropitious circumstances, people would search out places of interest. 'It's almost two decades since we moved to the north-west, to Primorsky district, and now Petersburg newbuild has become "familiar territory". And we're still making an effort to discover something there that isn't actually hideous,' wrote a blogger in 2007. But she also wrote that she and her family were doing all they could to find out about local history, regularly organising expeditions round the area to look at places of possible interest.[120] And some found the decayed utopias of the suburbs appealing in themselves. 'There's a kind of romanticism in it,' one Rzhevka local observed.[121] 'I got interested in [the rock group] "Kino", read books about them. They were always walking round somewhere,' a young woman recalled of her adolescence at the end of the 90s. 'So where did they live? Round [prospekt] Veteranov, Kosmonavtov, they were always wandering round there, walking. And I thought, Well, I'm no worse than them, am I? And started walking round myself.'[122]

Exploring your area was a way of making it imaginable and habitable. But people also made their environment familiar through words. As a woman born in the Ukraine who now felt completely at home in the city where she had lived since her student days in the 1970s put it, 'In my own district, I'm like in my village.'[123] Still more poetically, a St Petersburg schoolboy writing in 1998 observed: 'Everyone has his Motherland. It's the place where someone was born and where he still feels drawn to, where everything is familiar, near, dear. In my case, this dear corner is Petrograd Side.'[124]

In the Soviet period, assigning names to particular areas was a commoner strategy of indicating familiarity with the city than nicknames for individual buildings – though there were some famous exceptions, such as 'The Nest of Gentry' for the opulent 1964 Party block next to Peter the Great's cottage on Petrograd side.[125] Not much was done to 'domesticate' the various new buildings of the post-Soviet era either, partly because many were assigned fanciful names by developers in any case (a case in point being the 'Twin Peaks' mentioned by Stogov).[126] St Petersburgers had a well-developed sense of the ridiculous with regard to their built environment – unpopular new white-on-black house numbers introduced in the early 2000s were rapidly nicknamed 'coffins with light-bulbs on', and a temporary pontoon bridge adopted during repairs to Lieutenant Schmidt Bridge in 2007 was immediately dubbed 'Son of Lieutenant Schmidt'. But it was rarely directed at landmarks.[127]

However, nicknames for places – 'Three Idiots' Avenue' for the Communist-era streets officially commemorating Enthusiasts, Guides, and Bolsheviks, 'The Winter Garden' for the arcaded exit to Nevsky prospekt metro station, 'Gribanal' for the Griboedov Canal, and 'Obvodka' for Obvodnyi Canal – were ten a kopeck.[128] They worked not just to claim 'our' territory but also to poke fun at places where 'others' lived, as in the spiteful name for an area of well-appointed co-operative housing on the Vyborg Side: 'Jewish Pauper Zone'. Such names could also 'domesticate' little-known parts of the city for those who did not travel outside their district very often, but wanted to distinguish themselves from the 'official' naming patterns used by complete outsiders.

Whatever St Petersburgers felt about 'the centre', they always claimed some acquaintance with it. Like most inhabitants of big cities, however, they tended not to feel they knew districts beyond the centre – other than the place where they lived, assuming that was on the periphery. It was typical for someone in their late 30s to confess to having visited Kupchino for the first time just a few days ago, or not having even a mental picture of Grazhdanka. Just so, a local *vade mecum* presented outlying districts as the unexplored territory of dangerous tribes: 'We needed an aboriginal guide.'[129] While this was a symptom of snobbery, people often admitted to not knowing other districts with a rather more lustrous reputation, as in the case of a woman who described Petrogradka as 'a dark forest' to her.[130]

The reluctance to do much non-armchair-exploring meant that people's perception of places they did not like was often based on hearsay. For instance, ulitsa Dybenko was said to be a 'druggy' area, while the areas along Obvodnyi Canal were stigmatised because they were allegedly full of factories and the canal was thick with sewage.[131]

While the familiar nicknames for different districts had high recognition value, informants often reacted to them with a parade of hostile stereotypes:

> 'Grazhdanka' has two halves, there's Akademichesky, well, everything there is more slobbish, has its own kind of separate character, down by Akademicheskaya metro station. But there are dreadful bits down Grazhdanka way too, kind of ghettos [. . .] I know this for sure too, they never leave their neighbourhood, not once in their lives.[132]

The informant's uncertainty about where the places at the end of prospekt Prosveshcheniya that he is talking about actually are offsets his certainty that he knows exactly what they are like. Vast areas may be condemned like this – as Londoners living on the north bank of the river lump together very diverse districts in the shuddering term 'South London', so Petersburgers living elsewhere use 'The Right Bank' (of the Neva) as a signifier of the drear. In both cases, the river acts as a boundary of bearable society.

3.15 The embankment of Obvodnyi Canal, 2009.

Notions of 'unacceptable' districts were usually formed at long distance and were subject to general, folkloric notions of what a place was like. 'Ligovka' (Ligovsky prospekt) had an evil reputation that went back to the 1920s. This reputation was attractive to writers and artists (the most famous artists' squat, Pushkinskaya 10, was minutes away), but less so to other members of the public. Decades after the place had become a humdrum shopping street, the words *ligovskaya shpana* (Ligovka mob) typed into an internet search produced many dozens of hits.

Attitudes to places people did know were much more concrete in social terms. Krestovsky Island was remembered as a traditional, close-knit working-class community, and prospekt Kosmonavtov, off Moskovsky prospekt, as a place with a concentration of mainly Jewish intellectuals; even in the 1990s you could still hear Yiddish in the streets.[133] People who lived in a district that was traditionally thought to be 'crime ridden' would assign the danger zone to one or two streets, while regarding, say, the foul-mouthed alcoholics on their own corner as part of the local 'micro-climate'.[134]

Of course Petersburgers did not just imagine their city in terms of their 'home patch'. But the visitor's automatic classification into 'Petersburg' (the centre) versus 'Leningrad' (the outskirts) was replaced by a polarisation between the *imaginary* city (of literature and art, viewed panoramically) and the *lived* city (of 'my' humdrum everyday experience, viewed microscopically):

> When people talk to me about Petersburg, I've two pictures in my head – one of them is an illustration from that famous edition of Dostoevsky's White Nights [by Mstislav Dobuzhinsky], those famous black-and-white illustrations, where there are those kind of bridges and canals and embankments and wrought-iron fences, where everything is so beautiful. There were pictures like that in the Soviet period too, sometimes they published them – instead of the ads you get now on Channel Five, you'd get views of the city, black-and-white, with some kind of music playing lyrically, boom-boom-boom, I mean it really was quite beautiful. Something like that. And the other picture is the complete opposite, it's my own *pod"ezd*, with its lovely smell [laughs], its wonderful heaps of rubbish, and people staggering around – definitely.[135]

Neighbourhood solidarity could also be generated by external threats, such as aggressive eviction, and the infill building that swallowed green space. In the summer of 2008, there was large-scale action by the inhabitants of the Sergievsky gorodok quarter in the city centre, a large enclave of modest nineteenth-century housing (in the former royal laundries) on whose territory developers hoped to build expensive apartment hotels. Another focus for energetic activity was the area round Lomonosovskaya metro station, where there were plans to develop the site of the Imperial Porcelain Factory's Church of the Transfiguration, converted into a park after its demolition in 1932, into a shopping and amusement arcade.[136] In a city largely gripped by political apathy, alterations to localities provoked people into action.

The search for community could take other forms as well. The rise of the internet was not necessarily the cause of withdrawal into virtual relationships, as opposed to real ones. Some sites were meant to help people meet others near where they lived. In the words of the website www.sosedi.ru: 'Living in this vast megalopolis, do you know your neighbours? On our site you can meet interesting people living in your block, on your street, in your district [*raion*]! You may find new friends, fellow spirits, and maybe even the love of your life'. A partial resurgence of local identity was also in progress through a revival of church parishes, though places of worship were still few and scattered compared with the size of the city population.[137]

At the same time, local issues occupied a less important space in the life of post-Soviet St Petersburg than they did in, say, London or New York. There were no permanent forums for local concerns such as residents' associations, and the only district newspapers had municipal funding.[138] Local issues were not terribly important even to the forum participants of *Moi raion*: while a posted discussion of the flight paths from Pulkovo airport and the districts these overflew had attracted 32 comments by 8 July 2008, there was considerably more interest in city-wide topics such as 'Automobile Arson' (111 comments), or 'Whither Russia?' (123).[139]

Sense of belonging was not limited to one's home patch. According to figures from 2005, St Petersburg was overwhelmingly a commuting city: 87 per cent of the economically active population lived outside the centre, yet 40 per cent of this population worked in the centre. As the cultural critic Boris Groys put it in a 1995 discussion, people lived according to 'planes'. For some, this 'plane' might comprise factory, beer-bar, flat, for others library, university department, lecture hall, and for still others, cathedral and bar. 'The real city consists of "my route", "my trajectories".'[140]

Long-term residents also saw their 'trajectories' as part of their lives in a diachronic sense. They were part of sentimentally recalled childhood experience:

> Where did I hang out? [. . .] Ovsyannikovsky Park. Yes. That was what it was. Later, and that was kind of round the Sovetskie [ulitsy],[141] you'd be coming back from school, and you'd make sure you set every garbage tip on fire. Along the way. And there was another fetish, in winter: you had to break the ice [i.e. on puddles etc.]. When you were going along in the winter, snap-snap, you've gone through the ice. I loved that.[142]

This referred to an area right in the centre. But children growing up in new areas could feel equally attached to them. In an online memoir, a woman who grew up in the north of the city remembered that in her area, with its raw blocks in an unlandscaped waste, children were drawn to the aerodrome and to older, low-rise yellow houses standing a short distance away.[143] For some children, the wasteland itself would have been the area of rich fantasy.[144]

Another phase of life where temporal and spatial nostalgia was fused was the recollected love affair: 'My favourite place, my kind of memory spot, is the corner of ul. Pestelya, Liteinyi prospekt and Mokhovaya. My wife and I used to walk round there, she'd drop by for me. When I finished my sessions of clinic work. That was where we, so to speak, wandered round the area.'[145] Thus, people might define themselves not just by where they live at the time of telling their stories, but by where they had lived. And there might be different locations for different identities (a standard trajectory from the late 1960s to the early twentieth century would be early childhood in the centre followed by later childhood years out in a *novostroika*, followed by a move back into the centre during one's student years in the early 1990s, followed by a move out again to improve the quality of life for the children a few years later . . .).[146]

But everyday practices did enforce a sense of neighbourhood too. People tended to shop locally because this was convenient, even if they did not develop a particular sense of loyalty to one local store.[147] The process of finding out what was sold where, or where to go when the local 'twenty-four hour store' happened to have closed for its 'technical break' in the small hours, required local knowledge. And choices of where to shop brought an investment of emotional energy. In the words of a woman standing next to me in the queue at the fruit and vegetable kiosk in my block in June 2008: 'I still do shop here, even though I know I'll get swindled every time.' In the undifferentiated quotidian of big-city life, the familiarity even of being cheated could seem attractive.

Whatever people's particular strategies for day-to-day living, 'local knowledge' was never a matter simply of responding to locality. Rather, locality itself was created through people's preferred trajectories – their conviction (however misguided) that shop *x* had politer staff and shorter queues than shop *y*, their routes for going to the playground or walking the dog, their feeling that they were among 'their own':

> I've got really used to Petrogradka, it's kind of like my own village, you've only to step outside and everyone knows you. [. . .] Even a bit further afield, you know all the faces, people say hallo – who they are, God knows. OK, so if they've said hallo, so will I. 'Give us a cigarette, eh?' 'Oh, yes, of course, right . . . hang on a second . . .'[148]

Precisely the same behaviour would be found offensive outside one's own area. The boundaries of the familiar were defined by a strong sense of what constituted over-familiarity:

> Say you come out of Akademicheskaya [metro station]. You're going along and someone comes up to you [*imitates gruff voice*]. 'Eh, mate, got a smoke, eh? Can I use your mobile a minute?' But if I'm going down Chernyshevskaya, no one would dream of talking to me.[149]

Yet local belonging, dependent as it was on the incidental, was always fragile. An issue that particularly exposed this was the 'privatisation' of former 'through courtyards'. While for the people actually living in the surrounding buildings this was welcome (keeping 'them' out), at the level of the neighbourhood it was experienced painfully. Walking across 'through courtyards' shortened routes to bus and tram stops and metro stations, but their significance was more than practical. Ability to thread one's way through the unmapped maze of arches and paths depended on local knowledge, and was thus a crucial part of 'feeling at home'. When what were once 'trajectories of freedom' disappeared, laments about loss of community spirit and commercialisation were certain to follow.[150]

* * *

However they chose to live their lives, the residents of post-Soviet St Petersburg created a very different kind of 'Petersburg text' from the one elaborated in the famous essay by Vladimir Toporov – a hard-and-fast set of communicative conventions made canonical by the participation in this of great writers. Certainly, people's views of their own lives were influenced both by literature and by culturological analysis, so that even 'anti-literary' statements often had a 'literary' resonance. But the cultural work in which people were engaged was improvisatory. They were engaged in a constant process of familiarising their landscape, of placing themselves and others upon it, of creating relationships between their own small territory and the larger city world. District or 'neighbourhood' quickly became part of a person's identity: stating directly you loathed your area and would gladly move out of it immediately was scarcely a tenable position.

The sense of affinity was just as strong in the areas of newbuild as in the city centre. Petersburg 'aborigines' carefully distinguished between districts and fragments of districts that were habitable and others that were not, and if the

3.16 View down Bol'shoi Sampsonievsky prospekt towards the Sampson Cathedral, 2010.

place where they lived was not quite their dream residence, it was also understood to be infinitely better than many other places where one *might* live. The district represented both a facet in city life that was hard to alter (because the cost of property made it difficult to move) and something that could at some level constantly be altered in the telling – perhaps more so in the case of apparently nondescript districts than with those made famous by canonical literary descriptions. The city centre had plenty of advocates who justified their choice in terms of the anonymity and ugliness of newbuild ('every district is faceless in its own kind of way').[151] But there were also many denizens of outlying areas who represented their choice not just in terms of practicality but in terms of pleasure. There was more light, green space, one was closer to nature. This was the legacy of Soviet utopian plans for new housing, but also expressed a sense of discomfort at the constraints associated with living in the 'museum quarter' of the centre. 'Real' St Petersburgers were determined to create a relationship with the city that was radically different from the foolish staring of the tourist; a sense of landscape unlike that in postcards, panoramas, or snapshots from visitors' albums.

# 4

# Initiation into the Working Class

*Beyond the Baltic Station lies a ragged waste,*
*As though the city were running away from itself; [. . .]*
*The factory makes dust and grease out of bones,*
*And scatters it over tumbleweed and steppe grass,*
*The Petrograd flora.*
*And the tannery is right there, and a pond,*
*Where the spines of whole herds lie sprawling and rot.*
(Elena Shvarts)[1]

In his memoirs, completed and revised in the 1960s though started two decades earlier, Aleksei Gonchukov (born in 1904) recalled his years of service to the pre-eminent industrial enterprise in Leningrad, the Kirov Factory (founded in 1801 as the Putilov Works and renamed Red Putilov Worker after its nationalisation in 1922).[2] His intricate and sometimes annoying chronicle, supported with household bills reproduced verbatim and photographs of personal documents, records the clash between Gonchukov's lasting loyalty to the ideals of Soviet Communism and the petty disappointments and frustrations with which his working life presented him.

Gonchukov, originally from Yaroslavl', had moved to Petrograd in 1923 after service with the Cheka as a teenager.[3] He hoped – but failed – to gain a place at the Polytechnic Institute. After working for a short time at the Nevsky Machine-Building Factory, he became chairman of a housing administration office before joining Red Putilov Worker in 1929 as a political activist (*agitator*). He was to remain with the factory for the rest of his working life, apart from military service as a volunteer during and after the War, and a brief period in the 1950s.

Like another Leningrader of his generation, the poet Ol'ga Berggol'ts (born in 1910), Gonchukov conducted his relationship with Soviet reality like a stormy love affair. His marriage in 1931, and the death of close family members in the Blockade, were passed over in a few sentences; the birth of his children was not even mentioned.[4] But he expanded on Leningrad's sense of grief when Kirov was murdered ('The city had been orphaned'), and on his besetting difficulties in dealing with his superiors. During the War, he could barely stop himself from hitting a drunken commander. He was shocked – against his will – by the destruction of German cities ('there's Russian humanitarianism for you!').[5]

Promoted to the office of acting assistant to the director in 1951, Gonchukov had his boss 'positively foaming at the mouth' with his criticisms. The inequalities of Soviet post-war society infuriated him. Why should he have to struggle to buy shoes and clothes for his family on the 40 roubles left after taxes and compulsory contributions to state loan repayments, while shop assistants could spend 100 times that much on new shoes, and shop directors send their offspring to school with a feast of salami and biscuits in their lunchboxes? He raged at the condition of the factory hostels, sometimes with ten and more families to a room, where damp and dilapidation added to the misery of overcrowding ('and this in Leningrad – the cultural centre of our country!'). Yet he shared the general surge of enthusiasm when Stalin celebrated his seventieth birthday, boasting that the Kirov works had 'completed the entire programme for the quarter under every heading, and won the Banner of the Council of Ministers of the USSR'. Gonchukov recorded the extreme distress when the leader died (in Moscow, 'the people walking round in the streets were literally in tears'), and shared in this himself.[6]

Gonchukov's emotional conflicts continued in the following months. The eve of New Year's Day 1954 had him fretting over his continuing financial worries, and over the discrepancy between the boasts in *Leningradskaya pravda* and the miserable lack of actual achievements on the part of the Kirov Factory.[7] Yet he also launched into a lyrical peroration of pure hope:

> It's about 9 in the evening now, the radio is broadcasting the wonderful successes of our multi-million strong nation and how one would like to join in by showing a genuinely Soviet socialist capacity for organising one's labour and production. And for us, us Kirov workers, that's right up our street.
>
> That's what we'll do!!
>
> It's just time I'm worried about. How long to get there?
>
> I'll stop writing now. It's already 10.
>
> Happy New Year!!!
>
> I want to say, using Chernyshevsky's words,
>
> '. . . the future is radiant and sublime. Love it, strive towards it, work for it, make it come closer . . .'[8]

In 1955, Gonchukov's work as a thorn in the side of the Kirov management came briefly to a stop, when he was transferred from his post there to a lumber works in Leningrad region. Returning penniless in 1957, after working for fourteen months in dreadful conditions, he began getting himself reinstated at the factory, a laborious process that filled him with contempt for the official he had to deal with – 'a drunkard, the son-in-law of some minister, gentry dregs'.[9]

Money worries continued even after Gonchukov started earning again, and his son had found employment too. In 1960, expenditure on essentials left them around 250 roubles for 'repairs to household goods, theatre and cinema tickets, the hairdresser, the banya [public baths], lottery tickets, the odd glass of vodka, celebrating various holidays etc.'[10] Yet even what he saw as the catastrophic disaster of de-Stalinisation (the chapter describing this is headed 'A Tragedy in the Consciousness') did not shake Gonchukov's pride in the Soviet Union's achievements. In an open letter to Churchill, written in 1959, he recalled how Soviet power had transformed his home city:

> Just look at Leningrad now!!!
>
> It's the most beautiful of all beautiful cities in the world.
>
> And what did you leave us in Leningrad-Petrograd in 1917? Some old horse cabs, a few clapped-out trams.
>
> And now Leningrad is a city of world civilisation with a widely developed network of trolleybuses and motor buses. Thousands of comfortable cars, an underground railway like nothing else in the world – excluding the Moscow one, of course.
>
> The city of the glory of the Russian people stands puffed up with pride on the banks of the Neva . . .[11]

Gonchukov's perception of the city that he loved was entirely in tune with the anniversary celebrations of 1957, with their focus on Soviet achievements.[12] The present had improved on the past, and the future would be still better. His memoirs and diary entries give no sign that he was interested in the pre-revolutionary heritage. He might, for all he indicates, never have visited any of the city's museums, or noticed its famous buildings. Pushkin appears only as the author of a poem that could be rephrased in order to express pious hope for the future of the Kirov Factory:

> Comrade, have faith: she will arise
> The dawn of captivating happiness
> Our factory will arise from sleep
> And once again on its scrolls
> They will write wonderful deeds.[13]

If Gonchukov had tried to sum up his life, he could have adapted another line from Pushkin – 'Our fatherland is the Kirov Factory'. The place embodied his pride in, and exasperation with, Soviet existence generally. At the start of his text, he expressed a determination to finish writing up his life history in time for the fiftieth anniversary of the Revolution in 1967.[14] In this, as in everything else, he identified with the nation whose conscious life had run in parallel to his own. But in fact, the conclusion of his narrative coincided with the end of his working life, as though there was now nothing more to say.

### To Direct, to Support, to Celebrate

A text such as Gonchukov's, with its painful mixture of defiant loyalty to the workplace and righteous anger, was a product of a specific generation and time. Only in the immediate aftermath of de-Stalinisation, when sincerity had become a crucial virtue,[15] could such a 'warts and all' portrait of a major factory have been produced – or only then, at any rate, would its author have entertained serious hopes it might be published.

The Thaw years witnessed an agonised scrutiny of conditions in Leningrad industry, as management and workers were encouraged to dwell on the problems of their environment. At a meeting in 1960, directors of textile factories gave a bleak picture of conditions. There were problems with equipment, materials, spare parts, the bureaucratic regulation of incomers, and living space. In the Tel'man factory, modernisation was desperately overdue, but workers had only the factory itself to use as living space, so that improvements were constantly delayed. Lack of accommodation inhibited recruitment, which constantly fell short of the norm. Lighting was so dim that it made using machinery difficult. At the Red Flag Factory the promised foreign machines ('the quality of the ones Soviet factories produce is disgusting') had mostly failed to materialise, and here too there was a shortage of manpower. Other directors told similar tales; all reported serious problems with labour turnover, and some with general commitment too. In the Worker factory, sometimes as few as 800 of the 4000 workers would turn up on a given day, because of sick leave and holidays.[16] A secret report on 'worker moods' of 1962 pointed to grumbling about pay differentials ('even a low-level boss earns more than a skilled worker') and the sense that speaking one's mind was pointless ('go on, criticise – and they'll kick you out straight away').[17]

In the attempt to deal with these problems, the authorities operated three intersecting strategies. The first was to monitor and direct public opinion. Like all Soviet institutions, factories had employee meetings at which issues of the day would be discussed. 'General meetings' were – at least after the end of the 1960s – to a large extent talking shops. By a show of hands, participants would vote unanimously to condemn American imperial aggression in Vietnam or support the Soviet fraternal intervention into Afghanistan. Raising even a slightly unorthodox topic generated a frisson. German Gurevich, who worked as an engineer at Leningrad Energy Repairs (Lenenergoremont), responsible for carrying out major repairs at power stations all over the Soviet Union, was, by his own account, drafted into political activism by default: he was one of only two people in his workshop who spoke and wrote grammatical Russian. At a meeting in 1976 when the draft of the new Soviet constitution was discussed, he suggested that at least two candidates (both from the Party list) might stand in elections, rather than just one. As a result of putting forward an idea that had been discussed openly during the early 1960s, 'I wasn't asked to take part in any political or social work until the perestroika era.'[18]

In this manifestation, meetings blended into the programmes of edifying lectures and pep-talks on the international situation, or the decisions of the latest Party congress or plenum, or the evils of religious belief, that were regularly organised for employees.[19] But at the same time, meetings might also discuss practical questions. For instance, in 1972 at the Worker factory a foreman in a section that had underfulfilled its work quota was deputed to give a talk, 'On the Quality of Goods Produced in the Section.'[20] 'Moral education' and professional education were closely associated: many factories, including the Kirov, had a mentoring system, where older workers would show younger ones the ropes, and also, by design, convey to them the values and traditions of the 'work collective'.[21]

'Socio-political events' were also a way of 'taking the temperature' of the workplace, of finding out about grievances and anxieties. In the Khrushchev era, question-and-answer sessions were sometimes substituted for lectures, and the result of this could be tough interrogation from the floor. Was Khrushchev now becoming the subject of a personality cult? Should NEP be reintroduced so that there might be something to buy in the shops? Why was Soviet radio so biased?[22] In different political circumstances, talk of that kind was immediately nipped in the bud. But as late as 1975, the files of 'typical questions' passed by lecturers to the Obkom included not just comments related to ideological campaigns ('What countries are included in "the third world"?' 'How long is Sakharov going to get away with saying what he does?'), but also many practical ones ('How many families are there in the Leningrad housing queue?' 'Why are there so few shops in the new districts?' 'Are there going to be any bathhouses built there?' 'When will people in Leningrad stop having to work on Saturdays, like in Moscow?').[23]

Canvassing opinion in this way was directly related also to the second strategy of work with employees. Factories and plants were not simply manufacturing centres. They were entire microdistricts, with their own moral economy and provisioning systems.[24] In 1972, the factories of Vyborgsky district contributed 5.5 million roubles to the apartment-building programme and 290,000 roubles to medical services, and spent 3.8 million roubles on expanding their network of public catering, 190,000 on kindergartens, and 1.9 million roubles on summer camps for Young Pioneers.[25] (By comparison, the entire directly funded apartment-building programme across the USSR in that year was budgeted at 1.9 billion roubles.)[26] It was customary in the Soviet period to poke fun at the ameliorative efforts of pre-revolutionary capitalist entrepreneurs, providing their workers with clinics, barrack accommodation, and magic-lantern shows.[27] Yet the administrators of Soviet factories themselves carried out comparable work. The main difference was ideological, with 'culture clubs' replacing factory churches (sometimes in the most literal sense, as in the famous conversion of the church at the former Putilov Factory into a club in 1925). The status of a plant in the Soviet industrial hierarchy was measured by the capacity to provide the facilities of 'cultured life' to its employees, as well as by the importance of its product in terms of the official hierarchy of values (with contributors to the 'military-industrial bloc' at the top).[28]

If major factories were 'cities within the city',[29] this did not necessarily mean that facilities were conveniently organised all in one place. The factory territory was always at least partly virtual, particularly after different enterprises began being welded together into vast conglomerates (*kombinaty*) under Grigory Romanov, a policy that made sense from the planner's desk rather than in terms of the lives of those who might suddenly find themselves re-assigned to a different part of the 'same' enterprise right across the city.[30] Even before this, accommodation might be provided in areas some distance away from the factory. The enormous Svetlana plant had hostels in several totally different districts.[31] However, whatever the practicalities, as an *ideal* the factory was a unit aiming to cater for every aspect of its workforce's needs: housing them, caring for their children, providing medical care and trips to 'houses of rest', as well as an on-site programme of entertainment and education. At the Kirov Factory, even military service was partly subordinated to work life: new conscripts would take their oath of allegiance at the plant itself.[32]

The difficulty with this strategy of universal provision, as with any system of enlightened paternalism, was that employees looked to the factory to solve whatever problems they might have. Enterprises became heirs to the history of expectation that those in authority should 'feed' their subject population (in the sense not just of providing them with sustenance, but of offering general material support).[33] If this trust was betrayed, disillusion and anger might follow – the emotions that come through so strongly in Gonchukov's memoirs.[34]

Not everyone set these feelings down in writing, or had such a sharp sense of exploitation. But mild discontent, particularly about how much one was paid, was common. As a former factory worker born in the 1940s remembered:

> Nikita Sergeevich, he said, 'This generation will see life under Communism!' But then he went, and they forgot all that. Well, Brezhnev let people live a little, he lived a little himself [*laughs*], let others do the same. We relaxed a bit, of course. There was only one minus to the soc . . . socialist state, if you wanted good earnings, they'd not let you have those. [. . .] The foreman used

> to keep my earnings down, he was always on at me. For wanting more money, like, but I needed the cash . . . You'd be on a job. He'd say, 'No, leave it there, finish it next month.' I'd say, 'No, I've earned the money, hand it over now.' The lads would tell me, 'Come on now, you may get an extra 10–15 roubles, but what about the cost to your nerves?' But I'd always get in a row about that. Now, you can work as much as you like – you do it, you get paid. Back then, the upper limit was . . . they'd give you 160 roubles, no more. [. . .] The foreman had to work within the funds they'd given him for that month's wages. He could spend those and no more.[35]

By Soviet standards, 160 roubles was quite good pay. But outgoings in a city the size of Leningrad were high. Former workers, even at leading factories, uniformly remember feeling the pinch.[36] People did all they could to hold out for bonuses (*premii*), which were in the gift of one's immediate boss.[37]

Conditions in Leningrad factories improved during the 1960s and 1970s. As new housing projects were completed, people no longer had to sleep on the factory floor, and imported machinery made conditions better on the production line.[38] Yet labour turnover remained a problem. In 1970, an activist responsible for organising 'moral education' in hostels reported: 'The lads straight out of the army are the worst. They get themselves demobbed three months early, then brought to Leningrad for nothing. They buy some smart clothes, have a look round Leningrad, spend one winter here, and then leave.'[39] A colleague was more sympathetic about the likely stresses of a young worker's day: up at six, with nothing to eat before rushing into work, back twelve hours or more later, in an exhausted condition. A tot of vodka on an empty stomach, and collapse, were the likeliest outcome.[40] The difficulties of adjusting to city life for those straight from the village were widely recognised.[41] The issue was how to retain the workforce in a city that was more attractive to visit than it was to settle in.[42]

These considerations prompted a third strategy on the part of the political leadership and factory administrators: the effort to generate loyalty to the workplace in its own right, a sense of belonging not just to the 'collective' in the abstract but to a specific factory, with its own history and traditions. From the start of the 1960s, there was an explosion of work-related and enterprise-based holidays and festivals. Some of these were national and did not always have much local significance, though this did not mean that people did not enjoy celebrating them:

> On Railwaymen's Day everyone was a railwayman. On Miners' Day everyone was a miner. All those celebrations of different professions, they were pretty popular, you know. Well, you got the chance to down a few. And all perfectly legal as well. I can remember how, sometime back in the 1970s, they put on a celebration in the Moscow Victory Park, a celebration for

> Miners' Day. OK, fine, so Miners' Day down in the Donbass, Kuzbass, Vorkuta, that makes perfect sense. But in Leningrad? All that pomp and circumstance for Miners' Day? It all looked, shall we say, a bit odd . . . But people were enjoying themselves. All those different Days celebrating the professions were like that . . . Celebrations on a mass scale, concerts . . .[43]

Great encouragement was also given to festivals associated with a particular workplace. Enterprises might celebrate 'Factory Day', as at the Kirov: 'Even back in the days when the enterprise was run on special regime lines, its gates would be open wide. You and the family could walk right through its vast grounds, see some of the goods they were making, learn lots of interesting things about the factory's history and traditions.'[44]

Alongside festivals, factory and enterprise museums also developed energetically in the post-Stalin years. Some were actually set up in the 1960s, as in the case of the museum at the No. 62 Tram Park on Vasilievsky Island.[45] The Kirov Museum, set up in 1962, began with two halls; in 1964 another was added, and in 1982 a fourth. The resulting display was exhaustive, running from the early history of the plant to its development in the socialist era, with photographs of production lines, models of machinery, a selection of the 'rotating red banners' that different workshops would compete for, and examples of the decorations awarded to leading workers.[46] It became customary to take new employees round the factory museums, in order to emphasise the traditions of the place that they had joined.[47]

Also encouraged were new rites of passage marking specific phases of an employee's relationship with a given factory or workplace. These were intended as substitutes for the initiation rituals that workers had traditionally organised among themselves. For instance, the *magarych*, a custom dictating that the incomer should stand drinks for all his workmates, was supposed to be replaced by a ceremony called 'Initiation into the Working Class', or the presentation of an employee's first official 'labour book'.[48] Efforts were also made to honour 'worker dynasties'. An article about the Nevsky Factory published in 1984 emphasised not only the long history of the place (opened as the Semyanikovsky Factory in 1857, and the place where the 'first Russian battleships' were produced), but also the personal histories of different workers there, including a father and son, Andrei and Leonid Kuznetsov, who had joined the factory in 1975 and 1950 respectively. But you did not have to be one of a dynasty to be feted: the article also mentioned various individuals who had made their mark on factory life (such as another Kuznetsov, no relation, who had joined in 1957 and received the Order of the Red Banner in 1974).[49] As well as recommending such employees for nationwide decorations, factories could organise their own system of honours: the Kirov, for instance, awarded favoured employees the title of 'Honoured Kirov Worker' (*zasluzhennyi kirovets*).[50]

4.1 Agitation in the factory workshop, Kirov Factory, early 1970s. Note the 'board of honour' to the right.

The period also saw corporate celebrations proliferate. For example, there were regular celebrations of jubilees, both in the sense of round-number birthdays and of milestones reached in terms of work years.[51] Even ordinary birthdays began to be celebrated more widely.[52]

In the 1920s, factories had been testing grounds for new Soviet rites of passage, such as 'Red Christenings'. The babe-in-arms was sometimes officially inducted into a trade union or made a candidate member of the Komsomol.[53] Leningrad factories had always been celebrated in the literature and art of the city.[54] Memorialised with ideologically significant names from the early days of Soviet power ('Red Dawn', 'Bolshevik', 'Red Triangle', and so on), they groaned with honours ('Two Times the Order of Lenin', 'Two Times the Order of Labour') accrued over the ensuing decades.[55] But in the post-Stalin era, the numbers of festivals increased and they now received whole-hearted official support (in the 1920s, some members of the political administration had seen them as providing too much leeway for initiative on the part of the masses).[56] The celebrations also had a different character. Rather than pointing the way to 'new life', they were, at least by ambition, integrated into the ordinary tenor of social existence. Stalin had announced in 1935, 'Life has become cheerier'; in the Brezhnev days, life became cosier. In the words of a conversation between a younger worker and an older worker reported by a brochure progandising the new festivals:

> 'So how are you supposed to love your factory? Like a girl or what?'
> 'Yes, like a girl, and I'd add, like your own mother as well.'[57]

The suggestion that family connections had any relevance as a model for public life marked a radical departure from early Soviet values. In the 1920s, the whole point of social and political activism was to break with traditional family ties; in the Stalin era, it was the Party, and particularly the leader himself, who became the object of grateful filial sentiments.[58]

## 'The Unauthorised Exportation of Production'

The fact that people were prepared to celebrate workplace high days and holidays did not consistently generate behaviour of the sort that political activists considered appropriate. If the factory was a 'family', then – as with families – people had often not chosen to be part of the relationship to begin with. Many had ended up where they were as the result of *raspredelenie*, the system of national service that assigned school-leavers and graduates to a workplace where their skills were required. If the new recruit exercised any leverage at all, the prompting was often a wish to move to, or to stay in, Leningrad rather than an attraction to that specific position.[59] Major enterprises had special arrangements for registering incomers (the so-called *limit*, according to which those coming to fill a vacancy that could not be filled from the labour pool in Leningrad itself were registered on a provisional basis).[60]

One's relationship with the workplace could therefore be less like a love affair than a marriage of convenience.[61] Sometimes attitudes were frankly cynical. In Leningrad's defence factories, work discipline was supported by intensive surveillance from the security services as well as by the unusually good conditions of employment.[62] In less privileged enterprises, such as the textile factories whose directors were lamenting their lot in 1960, or in other types of non-strategic manufacturing, things were rather different. In 1965, official records indicated that many factories across the city had lower than average figures for days worked per year and poor productivity records; the rates for wilfully missed work time (*progul*) were almost twice as high in Leningrad's machine-building factories as in this branch of industry across the USSR generally.[63]

In Leningrad, as in other Soviet cities, the deficit economy made its mark on supplies. In 1971 the 'Fortieth Anniversary of the Komsomol Factory', which produced reinforced concrete, was suffering a shortage of cement – a fact that must have generated rather fundamental difficulties on the production line.[64] As elsewhere in the socialist system, factory managers needed to lobby and hustle in order to secure essentials.[65] Shortages also impacted on the other end of the process – the 'disappearance' of raw materials and useful items as workers and supervisors helped themselves. Vadim Shefner's story 'A Palace for Three' gave a humorous portrait of the situation:

> Gosha was working as a plumber at the Lenzhet cosmetics factory, and he used sometimes to bring perfume back home. Of course, not by the bottle: he used a little hot-water bottle, of the kind you'd put in a cot. He'd tie it to his tummy, under his trousers. It was mainly women working there, including the guards on the door, and they felt embarrassed about groping round inside a man's trousers with reference to the unauthorised exportation of factory production.[66]

'The unauthorised exportation of factory production', or to put it more bluntly, filching, was not just the work of the rank-and-file. A foreman or engineer on a production line where spirit was used for cleaning and polishing machine tools was almost certain to help himself.[67] In 1976 an engineer at the Leningrad television factory was arraigned on charges of theft when it was discovered that he had been systematically removing parts from the factory and using them to assemble TV sets at home, which he then resold.[68] A widespread joke of the day went like this: 'I took a few parts home from the sewing machine workshop to make one for the wife, but all I ended up with was a Kalashnikov.'[69] Sometimes there were crackdowns on particularly blatant cases (as the newspaper stories show), but more often the 'disappearance' of materials was simply ignored.[70] Even more common was 'time theft', where workers got on with their own affairs during work hours. One woman recalled being shocked, after she joined a factory making printing equipment in the early 1980s, by the brazenness with which people conducted romances: 'All these forty-five and fifty-year-olds cuddling up in corners during the lunch hour!' She was considered a 'careerist' for her conscientious attitude, and an older woman advised her, in a parody of Soviet moral discourse, 'A respectable woman gets everything done during the working day.'[71]

Still more common was social contact between members of the same sex – which, in the case of men, was often accompanied by drinking. When the Komsomol newspaper *Smena* organised an anti-alcohol 'raid' in 1980, one man in overalls was deeply indignant. 'It's me own money I've bought this with!' He insisted he would 'sort it' with the people frisking workers at the gate. Vodka shop No. 62 on Pionerskaya ulitsa had become 'a place of pilgrimage for the drunkards from all the factories around'.[72]

Tolerance of such behaviour went up the system. As Sergei Dovlatov's brilliant story 'The Nomenklatura Shoes' (1986) showed, an official celebration of any kind was unimaginable without alcohol; workers would, as a rare concession, begin the day sober, to mark the solemnity of the occasion, before lashing into champagne and cognac as they usually would into vodka. A junior would regularly be dispatched to come back clanking with bottles. In the demented world of the story, the narrator himself repeatedly struggled 600 steps from the depths of an under-construction metro station to fetch the latest order of vodka for his two drunken stone-carver workmates. In the everyday, conditions might be less remarkable, but bibbing was just as heroic. Foremen would cover by saying of so-and-so, 'he's right here, he'll be back any moment'.[73]

There were agitational strategies for dealing with miscreants – 'Boards of Shame' and outraged articles in the wall newspaper or factory newspaper – but in the late Soviet period, at least, these seem to have been employed sparingly.[74] On the whole, managers worked by incentives. The completion of plan targets meant bonuses; individuals who took on voluntary overtime could expect to get extra leave (*otgul*).[75]

Face-to-face confrontation was also common. Bosses as well as foremen had often started life on the factory floor, and shared the same attitudes. Their relationship with those they oversaw could be collusive, but it was also rough. Shouting and thumping the table were more typical than sage moral saws; the use of obscenity was common. 'Where's that shithead Zaitsev?' someone from central factory management might demand, reducing a section head to jelly. But given the prevalence of coarse speech among workers themselves – anyone who talked guff would be known as a *khueplyot*, literally a 'prick-waver' – this kind of address was not necessarily perceived as offensive. If educated staff did find it distasteful, they could get their own back by rephrasing a lewd comment, or repeating it in quotation marks. When one construction bureau chief tried to persuade a top engineer to do overtime by saying, 'The cash might come in handy to buy chocolates for your whores, eh?', the reply, 'Thank you, but I can afford to treat my *lady friends* as it is', produced an apology.[76]

Once people got dug in to work at a factory, life had its compensations. Relations with your immediate workmates were usually friendly. Bosses might be dictatorial, but there was also a sturdy tradition of 'up management' – those officially lower down robustly expressing their views about what was and was not possible.[77] The practice of assigning a responsible role (holding the keys to the stores, say) to one particular individual (not necessarily the director) gave anyone holding such a role power and leverage.[78] People might envy the pay of top management, but the gulf was not enormous (factory directors earned around twice as much as senior engineers), and privileges were sometimes flexibly allocated. At LMZ the food at the ordinary canteens was revolting, but employees with the necessary chutzpah would also use the ones for the bosses, outside the official dinner hour.[79] For workers, there were trips to the factory's house of rest or even abroad, since official delegations were always supposed to have a representation from the city's factories. Engineers and management could hope to be sent 'on command' to other parts of the Soviet Union, expenses paid.[80] Employees exercised some leverage about where they worked, and not just by pulling out when a job did not suit. Personal contacts (family, friends, connections, and connections of connections) could be used to secure a place at a workplace that suited – a practice that was condemned from time to time in Soviet official sources, but never actually prohibited.[81] Or you could make a 'marriage of convenience' not just with the factory but with another person.[82]

## Bureaucrats and Scholars

The celebration of 'worker dynasties' pointed to a feature of life in late Soviet Leningrad that propaganda never mentioned directly: limited social mobility. It was overwhelmingly young people from a white-collar background who made their way into the most prestigious institutions of higher education. At the First Medical Institute, 77.2 per cent of the student body in 1964–5 had this social profile; in the same category were the Institute of Paediatrics (78 per cent), the Electro-Technical Institute (74.6 per cent), and Leningrad State University (75.1 per cent). At the other end of the scale lay the Institute of Trade (37.8 per cent) and the Veterinary Institute (17.9 per cent – this was one of the few Leningrad institutions attended by a significant proportion of students from the countryside).[83] In the Khrushchev years positive discrimination was operated, when selecting candidates for higher education, in favour of those who had done a stint in employment – a system that brought some young people from a non-manual background, at least briefly, into manual work.[84] However, these efforts faded out in the late 1960s. The system of vocational education siphoned off many young people from working-class backgrounds at the age of fifteen.[85] On the other hand, some of the Leningrad schools offering a so-called 'general education' had particularly high standards, and in the early 1960s several superb 'profile schools' for maths and science began educating children.[86] But the children of well-informed intelligentsia parents who knew how to judge quality had a well above average chance of ending up in these places, as with the special language-teaching schools.[87] References to 'worker dynasties' gilded the fact that it was difficult to escape your parents' fate.

The prevailing mythology notwithstanding, Piter was a bureaucratic city as much as it was an industrial city or a 'cultural capital'. In Tsarist times, white-collar workers were predominantly employed in the Russian Empire's vast government service network. In 1918, the ministries disappeared to Moscow, leaving the city with a purely provincial administrative role. The administrative pyramid descended from the First and Second Secretaries of the Regional Committee of the Communist Party (with their entourage of plain 'secretaries'), through the First and Second Secretaries of the City Committee and entourage, to the Chairman of the Executive Committee of Lensovet, and in parallel from the different sections of the Regional and City Committee, and the various standing committees and boards of the city soviet, down to the district committees of the Communist Party and district soviets. The Komsomol and Pioneer organisations, and the trade union movement, all had their officials as well, as did city and district education and health authorities.[88] By the late Soviet period Party and non-Party bureaucracy were, in practice if not formally, more or less identical.[89] The Party's Regional Committee was the highest local authority for all purposes. The route to a high administrative position anywhere (educational and academic institutions, factories, shops, restaurants, aviation, the local railway network . . .) lay through Party membership.

Though only a minority of white-collar workers were Party members, Party policy set the tone everywhere. Non-productive work was far more susceptible to ideological pressure than factory labour. If you had to fulfil an order of tractors to go to the collective farms of Tambov province, or supply turbines for a power station in Kazakhstan, you needed to make large numbers of purely pragmatic decisions. Sections of factory shops might be hung with exhortations to implement the directives of the Twenty-Fifth Congress of the CPSU, or fulfil the targets of the Ninth Five-Year Plan, but the mechanisms of supply and demand were uppermost.[90] However, circulating state directives and filing reports – the kinds of activities demanded by the state bureaucracy in the broadest sense – required close attention to the nature of the commands sent down from above: to the legitimating strategies they used, the authorities they cited, the examples they gave, and the language in which they were written. As Alexander Zinoviev ironically but accurately remarked: 'It is not the content of a report, but the fact of its existence that matters.'[91]

All this left little room for a specific 'Leningrad style' (as evoked in the myth of 'Leningrad Communism'). Though they were sometimes housed in splendid buildings which had been ministries since they were first constructed, and though staff might occasionally use desks and cupboards that went back to the nineteenth century, Leningrad offices were little different from ones anywhere. A Lensovet decree of 10 August 1959 had stipulated that furnishings should be maximally plain and spare: 'superfluous items of equipment and decoration' were to be removed, and 'heavy furniture, expensive lighting, objects in cast bronze, rugs, plush and velvet curtains, expensive writing sets, and the use of marble, leather and fine wood panelling' were all forbidden.[92] Rather than filing cabinets and Venetian blinds (the symbols of bureaucratic authority in their Western counterparts), post-Stalinist offices were accoutred with plywood wall cabinets, faced in toffee-coloured veneer, frilly jalousies, and various types of obstinately unappealing pot plant. Space was invariably communal: even high officials were likely to have a meeting-table in their office. Desks were empty of ornament, though some personal items, particularly cups and plates, might be produced from storage in a cupboard during one of the tea-breaks that punctuated the day.[93] Style varied little whatever part of the bureaucracy

4.2 Top official at the Kirov Factory, 1965. Note the telephone and the near-absence of personal items.

an office happened to serve – from factory managements through academic institutions to directorates in schools and shops. Though not 'cosy' in the sense that home space was, such places were accommodating – at least to those who worked there.

Outsiders were treated very differently. Those calling on an important official would be kept waiting in an anteroom, perched on exhausted sofas or spindly chairs. Once they reached the sanctum, they engaged in unequal competition for attention with an array of telephones – for internal, external, and perhaps also top security network (*vertushka*) calls.[94] Even 'a friend in high places' did not ensure polite treatment. As the writer Mikhail Kuraev remembered:

> A friend of mine, an extremely well-known script-writer for Lenfilm, was making hopeless efforts to get a telephone installed in his new flat. Having experienced all the degradations that one does in such circumstances, he eventually got (through 'protection') right up to Comrade Malinin, the boss of the whole Leningrad telephone network. After running through all the arguments he could muster and realising that the telecommunications grandee wasn't even pretending to listen, my friend decided to try one last desperate measure. [. . .] He blurted, 'But Comrade Malinin, had you not

> heard that the Party takes special care of people working in the cinema industry?' 'The Party takes special care of everybody,' Malinin drilled out, and flatly refused to help.[95]

Lower-level officials aped the dictatorial style of those higher up, constantly citing 'the regulations', as creatively interpreted by them. Contacts with such figures were the subject of a vigorous local tradition of literary satire going back to the stories of Mikhail Zoshchenko in the 1920s. Narratives like *The Squiggle* (1928), in which an unfortunate visitor to an office is repeatedly turned back by the staff at the exit barrier because he needs to get his piece of paper endorsed with the vital mark, raised a laugh into the 1980s.[96] While persecuting the public, officials were not averse to doing themselves well. A detailed investigation in 1961 established that a group of high-ranking employees at the regional consumer union (Oblpotrebsoyuz) had abused their position in order to sell off Pobeda family saloons at inflated prices, and to buy for their own use a number of Volga limousines that had been earmarked for remote rural areas, where public transport was not at all adequate to local needs.[97]

At the same time, Leningrad officials, unlike their Muscovite colleagues, were not a breed apart. There was no local equivalent of 'an apartment facing the Kremlin' for Party dignitaries. Leningrad had its Party housing enclaves, but these were not much more opulent than the top-end housing co-operatives. For example, the 1964 block on the Petrovsky Embankment that became known sarcastically as 'The Nest of Gentry' was a one-off architect-designed project. It had higher ceilings than normal (3 metres), the planning costs were a generous 140 roubles per square metre, and most windows in the larger flats faced south. But the maximum size of the accommodation offered was three rooms, alongside kitchen and bathroom.[98] The development had a magnificent view of the city centre, but was comparable in its appointments to the late 1960s dwellings in the area round Primorskaya metro station, where a wide range of bureaucrats, city as well as Party, had their 'nests'.[99] Top military officials lived on a comparable footing. In the 1970s, the Admiral of the Baltic Fleet had, by Soviet standards, a generous allocation of space for himself, his wife, and two children – 123 square metres – and lived in a block also inhabited by foreigners (a sign of its prestige status).[100] But as this suggests, the top of the scale equated only with modest, middle-class prosperity in the West. And the top of the academic establishment was similarly accommodated, with special institutional blocks (*vedomstvennye doma*), as well as official dachas and generous food supply lines.[101]

This situation reflected Leningrad's provincial status in terms of Party governance. But it also reflected the extraordinary importance of the city's academic elite. Leningrad had dozens of scientific research institutes (NII), many of them dedicated to applied work on topics such as refrigeration and ice-cream production. The status and work conditions of the staff at these resembled those of engineers and researchers directly employed by factories, some of whom also held higher degrees, such as 'doctor of technological sciences', and academic or quasi-academic titles.[102] These places offered secure employment with good prospects of promotion and increased pay.[103] However, above this lay a more rarefied stratum, its members drawn from a small number of leading institutions of higher education (foremost among them the University and the Polytechnic Institute), one or two museums (the Hermitage, the Russian Museum), and the institutions of the Academy of Sciences of the USSR.

All of these institutions had existed before 1917 as well, and efforts to subordinate some of them to their Moscow counterparts in the late 1940s had not removed a certain inherited sense of seniority. (In any case, in the post-Stalin years, the Leningrad institutes started to be allowed a little more autonomy.)[104] Back in the 1920s some academicians, particularly in the field of Russian literary scholarship, had strongly resented the new order, and the original Academy of Sciences had been pitted against the 'Red Academy', specialising in the social sciences.[105] But this heritage did not mean that the Leningrad academy was a haven of intellectual free-thinking. Rather than opposing Soviet rule, some scholars and scientists hastened to accommodate themselves to it as early as they were able.[106] Naturally, this process was entrenched in the 1930s and 1940s, at which point emerged what the acidly intelligent, and socially marginal, literary scholar Lidiya Ginzburg termed 'egoists who have forgotten how to think'. In her essay under that title, a lightly veiled portrait of the one-time Formalist Boris Eikhenbaum, she pointed to the 'constant mild mockery of ministerial schemas, which at the same time prove absorbing and unsettling', the frantic efforts to submit 'applications for personal freedom' – that is, to gain permission for research that was not integrated into top-level plans – and above all, the way in which the new status quo offered senior academics a road to power that they could not have envisaged even a decade earlier.[107]

The Khrushchev years, for all their immense impact on intellectual discussion and (though more mutedly) intellectual production, unsettled the status quo only to a limited degree – partly because academics found Khrushchev's own bluffness and insistence on the links between learning and life crude and constraining.[108] But more importantly, institutes of the Academy of Sciences retained their rigid hierarchy, with 'junior researchers', 'senior researchers', 'section heads', and 'academic council', presided over by the director, deputy director, and 'research director'. So did teaching institutions, where 'professors' and 'docents' were kept in order by 'deans', as well as by the top-level administration, headed by the rector.

Like all Soviet workplaces, academic institutions had their own Party organisations, and their own programmes of 'socially useful work'.[109] Outward ideological rectitude was expected from those who hoped for career advancement. This was something of a dead letter in scientific institutes, where researchers had considerable freedom.[110] Here, the frustrations, for experimental scientists at least, could be more at the level of trying to persuade superiors that one needed essential but expensive equipment.[111] Political control was much more problematic in the humanities and social sciences, where the adventurous, if appointed at all, were likely to remain in the grade of 'junior researcher' until well into their 40s. The fact that academic administrators were often intelligent and cultivated did not necessarily make them liberal or likable.[112] Boris Piotrovsky, Director of the Hermitage from 1964 to 1990, retained unfond memories of a predecessor, I. A. Orbeli, who in the late 1940s 'ran the Hermitage in an exceptionally autocratic way [. . .] he dealt with all the promotions and major conflicts himself, leaving me to handle annoying trivia.'[113] This particular style remained typical of 'academic leadership' in later years too. Sometimes, senior Leningrad academics were even stuffier than their Moscow colleagues – in part because their positions were more precarious.[114] A certain hereditary sense of entitlement could be in play too. If worker dynasties were celebrated in the Soviet media, academic dynasties were a tangible presence in Leningrad. Some of the most prominent scholars during the post-Stalin era were following in the footsteps of a parent, uncle, sister, cousin, or aunt.[115]

In teaching establishments, too, there was a distinctive Leningrad tradition, as expressed in a clipped, precise manner of speech, intellectual self-confidence, and a certain degree of pretension. As a former student at the Leningrad Electro-Technical University recalled:

> Every lecture he [Professor Aleksandr Pikovsky] gave was like a gala performance by some world-famous maestro. It was all worked out to a T: from his impeccably elegant attire to the refined gestures that he used.
>
> He didn't read his lectures, he expounded them – or rather, performed them, soaring rhetorically in a state of semi-ecstasy with his eyes half-closed, like the Delphic Oracle or Cumaean Sibyl in full prophetic flood. [. . .] In the break between lectures, he would read Corneille or Racine (in the original, of course), or flick through *L'Humanité-Dimanche*.

Many of the Leningrad students on the course were doing their best to evolve into similar figures, and outsiders could expect to be subjected to predictable rituals of humiliation when they arrived.[116] Not everyone regarded the local distinctiveness with irony, but most remarked it.[117]

Study at top Leningrad institutes was sometimes socially alienating as well as intellectually challenging. Famous scholars did not necessarily make good teachers; relationships between professors and pupils were generally rather formal; and, above all in ideologically mainstream subjects such as history, social sciences, and Russian literature, the syllabus was strictly regulated.[118] The city had no institution like the University of Tartu, a place much closer to an academic republic, where, particularly in the Russian Department in the days of Yuri Lotman, students were able to have genuine intellectual contact with their teachers.[119]

Whether in universities or Academy of Sciences institutes, academics endured more interference than any other professional group in Soviet Leningrad, with the possible exception of schoolteachers. No one expected factory workers to have much command of Communist rhetoric or economic planning. When dealing with the creative intelligentsia, too, Party officials washed their hands. Expressing amused consternation at plans in Dzerzhinsky district to teach actors the principles of economics, one Party official remarked in 1971, 'You have to know your limits!' Sometimes it was difficult to get actors to say two words during political discussions, 'and ballerinas and opera singers have their little ways as well'. Seminars on Marxist-Leninist aesthetics were replaced, in many theatres, by collective visits to cultural events, followed by discussion.[120] Some did not have Party cells at all.[121]

Theatre directors, when auditioning aspirant actors, did not ask whether their views were ideologically sound, or complain that their performance showed traces of idealism: instead, they concentrated on the niceties of looks, presence, and technique.[122] Leadership in the performing arts was a mixture of brutality and spontaneous kindness (the choreographer Leonid Yakobson would keep his dancers working for hours past the norm, but 'whenever it was someone's birthday or some other big occasion, he would take part energetically; as soon as the rehearsal was over, he'd call over two of the boys, give them some money, and say "Off you go lads, bring us a crate of champagne." ')[123]

In academic institutes, it was different. Marxist-Leninist ideology had been invented by university graduates, and Marxism was supposed to be a science. This generated a strong tendency to identify *nauka* (science and scholarship, Wissenschaft) and ideology. The process of *prorabotka*, or 'working over', when engaged in by educated, articulate people who had a fluent command of the necessary rhetoric, could be harrowing.[124] Intellectually empowered though they might be, rank-and-file academic staff were at the same time socially marginal. The magnificent buildings occupied by institutes and libraries could be a consolation: Nina Koroleva remembered her delight in Pushkin House: 'the marble staircase, Aivazovsky's painting *Pushkin by the Sea* [. . .] the ceremonial style of the meetings [. . .] where graduate students, me included, were allowed the first word'.[125] This was less democratic than it sounds, however, since the tradition was for senior academics to make their authoritative pronouncements once the idle chat was over.[126] And the expansiveness of public space was in striking contrast to the indigent, temporary, cramped air of the everyday working environment. Conference halls occupied the state apartments of former palaces, with frothing plasterwork, bosomy murals, and stamped leather hangings; offices and workrooms their dusty and peeling attics.[127]

The pace of work, though, was permissive. University teachers, while not expected to give much personal attention to students, had a high lecturing load. But academics in research institutes were, if they were not laboratory scientists, able to spend a good deal less time in their official workplace than most other employees. After the holding of simultaneous appointments in universities and Academy of Science institutes was banned in 1949, the only teaching required was supervision of researchers working for their candidate's dissertation (perhaps two or three at a time). For senior academics, attendance was compulsory only twice a week, on the so-called *prisutstvennye dni* (presence days), and by and large the activities consisted of 'sitting', tea-drinking, and academic chat.[128] Those at the top of the hierarchy were also high earners – not just in terms of salary but also in terms of bonuses.[129]

If Leningrad academic life was at one level pompous and hierarchical, attitudes were very different outside official meetings. In this perspective, the mismatch between space and numbers hardly mattered: one could perch anywhere with a cup of tea, perhaps wandering desultorily between there and the 'smoking area' (*kurilka*, some chairs next to an ashtray on the stairs, or a barely-furnished, yellowed small room, always with a partly-open door).

There was a surreal plausibility in Andrei Bitov's novel, *Pushkin House*, where the scholars in the institute where the protagonist worked reached the culmination of intellectual and emotional excitement during a bibulous late-night session when acting as wardens of the almost empty building. That said, most people's 'presence days' were mainly devoted to pleasantly dull academic pursuits. One could drop into the library, or sit out a paper or two at a conference, for decency's sake or even out of real interest. It was common for people to have a whole set of parallel interests and projects that were not declared on the five-year plan, and to collaborate with colleagues beyond the official network, such as the talented scholars who could not gain official employment at the institutes. But discussions in the official workplace could be intense as well – not at formal meetings, certainly, but with colleagues in one's 'section':

> The scene is the Institute of Ethnography at the Academy of Sciences (now MAE RAN) in the 1980s. My desk is on the balcony; beneath us is the exhibition room where a collection of ethnography from Australia and Oceania is displayed. Sitting on that balcony, I argue for hours on end with my supervisor and later with my colleagues, who back then seemed infinitely superior to me. This goes on for months, we argue day in and day out about almost every line of my doctoral dissertation (what attention lavished on

4.3 Smoking corner, 2009. The tiles and paint are new, but the rest is of Soviet vintage.

> the work of a junior researcher!). From time to time we are cut short by the tour guides: 'You're disturbing the tours!' we're told, if, in the heat of an academic argument, we raise our voices too much. At that point we move to the coffee bar of the Akademichka – a canteen for academics located in the building next to the institute.[130]

Leningrad University too was characterised not just by the preferment of mediocre academics who happened to be good at administration (a phenomenon not unknown in other cultures as well), but by genuinely lively seminars at which students also could argue their point, and by classes at which extraordinarily knowledgeable scholars could spend as much time as they liked on imparting their expertise.[131]

The post-Stalin era is sometimes represented in terms of a hard-and-fast distinction between public space and private space, with the latter providing a refuge for people's true thoughts and perceptions.[132] Institutes, with their many different places for social contact, some formal and some less so, presented a more complicated picture; the same person might adopt a whole variety of roles depending on his or her physical surroundings and companions.[133] As in factories, celebrations helped hold the community together – not just official anniversaries, but birthday parties, and also *kapustniki*, a pre-revolutionary tradition of in-house revues, with comic sketches, parody verses, songs and dances. Senior figures were likely to find themselves gently mocked – a process which they regarded as flattering rather than offensive:

> Docent Anikeyev had a smoke by a picket,
> But then the Wood Boss appeared from a thicket,
> Quietly he muttered his terrible spell –
> The lab rat that resulted is still doing well.[134]

While academics were professionally adept in tying themselves up in bureaucratic knots, they were also adept in escaping from these; they enjoyed, if not inner freedom, a sense of purpose and inner conviction.

At the same time, academic institutions acted to exclude as much as to shelter. In the post-Stalin years, outright dismissal was considerably rarer than in the carnivorous 1930s and 1940s, but those who offended against an ideological imperative – for instance, if they propose to emigrate to Israel or had a close relation who did – were likely to find themselves without employment.[135] There was also a constituency of intellectuals who were, whatever their talents, considered unsuitable for employment in academic institutions, because they had the wrong profile (wrong nationality, wrong research topic, wrong family status, such as being divorced – or on the other hand, flamboyantly single . . .) Or such people might not be able to stand life in a place where, as the poet Yury Kolker put it, 'real scholarship was squashed miserably against the wall, like a street beggar'.[136]

One possible survival strategy was to live on freelance earnings (since quite generous royalties were paid for academic articles and books, and there was also a significant 'shadow economy' that embraced activities such as tutoring university entrants and ghost-writing course assignments and dissertations). But this laid a person open to charges of parasitism – a particular anxiety in Leningrad after the Brodsky trial.[137] Hence the recourse of taking up some manual occupation – not in a factory (which would have required skill and the ability to integrate into an alien environment), but on a casual basis.

In time, working as the overseer of a boiler-room supplying heat to an entire micro-district (*kochegar*) became as much a symbol of intellectual-bohemian existence as living in a communal flat. Through word of mouth, people who were not otherwise 'fixed up' (*ustroennye*) would find their way to a network supervisor who was prepared to take on 'someone with a degree and a funny surname' – in practice, large numbers, since willing hands were short, and the members of the genuine working class who signed up tended to be social marginals of a different kind, workshy incompetents with drink problems. Boiler-rooms across the city began to house informal studies, clandestine publishing outfits, even entire seminars – provided the heat kept coming, managers were happy to let their underlings alone.[138]

Unofficial work did not always have this dissident resonance. The word *khaltura*, signifying both 'shoddy work' and 'work on the side', conveyed the ironically dismissive attitude that was typical of many intellectuals.[139] But there was also an important layer of late Soviet Leningrad society that was primarily interested in the informal labour market for financial reasons. Among the Norwegian anthropologist Finn Sivert Nielsen's informants in the late 1970s was a man who ran an underground shoe-making business, with a dozen or so outworkers getting piece-rates for tasks performed in their own homes.[140] If this was plainly illegal, some of the work done by people working in official Soviet occupations fell on an administrative borderline. For instance, though waiting anywhere except at an official rank was forbidden, a taxi driver might choose to hover near Intourist hotels 'at his own risk'.[141] A doctor who performed a termination of pregnancy in the patient's own home (so as to ensure clean conditions and anaesthetic) and a teacher who took private pupils were, like the driver, in the twilight zone of tolerated, rather than permitted, work activities familiar to many Soviet citizens.[142] The system's interstices were as accommodating as its framework was rigid.

## 'Savage Capitalism' and the World of Work

By the mid-1980s, there began to be official recognition of the fact that not everything in Leningrad industry was satisfactory. In 1985, for example, an article in *Leningradskaya pravda* scrutinised one of the city's most famous enterprises, the Lomonosov Porcelain Factory, previously the subject of adulatory coverage, and raised the question of why so little of its output was actually attractive to the customer.[143] Political manoeuvring may have lain behind this. After the designation of Gorbachev as Party leader, Grigory Romanov (who had been promoted to the post of Secretary of the Central Committee in 1983) was removed from high office, to which he was never to return.

Certainly, the policy of technocratic industrial development, strict centrist control, and political repressiveness that Romanov had sponsored was quite out of keeping with the age of glasnost and perestroika. Like other cities, Leningrad acquired its co-operative movement, officially sponsored by the Komsomol, and flourishing particularly in the service sector as video saloons, food bars, and small shops opened in large numbers.[144] But as the consumer sector developed, manufacturing in Leningrad began a downturn that, in the early years of post-socialist transition, turned precipitate. By 1996, the city's share of national industrial output had halved compared with 1970 – a decline that in later years proved irreversible.[145]

In the mid-1960s, the goods produced at Leningrad factories had included, according to an official list, 'steel, sulphuric acid, automobile roofs, turbines, diesels, generators, marine etc. cables, cranes and diggers, cement, fabric, shoes, sweets, pastries, and cakes, bread, macaroni, butter and oil, vodka, champagne, cigarettes, meat, sausage, ice-cream, clocks and watches, radio sets, vacuum cleaners, furniture, crockery, pianos, kettles, and washing machines'. This did not, of course, include the large proportion of the city's output that consisted of military hardware.[146] In turn, the retraction of defence spending left the specialist industries reeling. In a post-Soviet equivalent of the beating of swords into ploughshares, the Kirov Factory began producing, instead of tanks, items such as mincers, at least transiently marketable in circumstances where the availability of quality meat was an open question.[147] But overall, the demand for consumer goods was contracting, as the rising desire for Western products made Soviet ones seem tired and shoddy. As a result, cloth production, for instance, dropped dramatically in the early 1990s.[148]

Over the next decade, the former factory capital of the USSR turned, under the painful effects of economic 'shock therapy', into a post-industrial city. By 2004, only a quarter of the working population was employed in manufacturing.[149] Whole stretches of Vyborg Side, Vasilievsky Island, and the embankments of Obvodnyi Canal, to name only a few of the central areas, became desolate wastelands. In the 2000s the network of streets at the back of what locals call 'Old Nevsky' (the stretch of the famous prospekt beyond Moscow Station) commemorated not just the provincial backwaters of the Russian Empire (Mirgorod, Kremenchug) honoured in their names, but the vanished industrial dreams of the Soviet period. Inside peeling blank walls, the windows of these deserted crystal palaces were veiled with dirt; vast double 'parade doors' stood permanently closed. In some places, clusters of parked cars suggested that some activity was in progress, but mostly the streets were empty except for the occasional driver avoiding the traffic-choked centre. Areas of Vyborg Side were equally decayed. Some of the city's historic factories died twice over: once when they 'came to a standstill', and a second time when they were cleared for new developments.[150]

Even in the twenty-first century, a 'loft apartment' culture showed little sign of emerging. The 'cultural reuse' movement for utilitarian buildings (as represented in Moscow by the Vinzavod gallery, in a former port factory) only slowly gained ground. Founded in 2007, Loft-Proekt Etazhi, the exhibition space housed in what had once been a bakery, was a rare successful initiative to reuse industrial premises.[151] Certainly there was sensitivity in the Monuments Department to the importance of factory architecture, encouraged by the pioneering work of local historian Margarita Shtiglits, who had researched industrial architecture since the late Soviet era, undeterred by criticism that there was no point in working on 'those ugly factory buildings'.[152] But as Shtiglits pointed out, the vast majority of new entrepreneurs were simply not interested in these structures, but rather in the premium development land which they occupied.[153] Developers and journalists dreamed of how 'the tumbledown workshops and tyre replacement joints and wasteland could become respectable hotels, apartment blocks, public buildings and creative districts'[154] – as though one could successfully plan for these last. Generally, the deserted factories become the territory of people looking for picturesque neo-ruins.[155] By 2012, however, conversion was starting to gain more momentum: if some 'creative spaces' devoted large areas to the display of designer clothing and handmade cosmetics and knick-knacks, there was also a growing amount of gallery space. The 'Red Weavers' textile factory on Obvodnyi showed major exhibitions, such as, in spring 2013, Marat Gel'man's 'Icons', with controversial treatments of religious themes; the Rizzordi Art Foundation had a foothold within the Sten'ka Razin Beer Factory in Narva District.[156]

As the brewery showed, not all St Petersburg industry was dead. At the end of the 1990s, defence production started showing signs of a revival. Surviving factories transformed themselves from nameless 'box numbers' into high-profile 'concerns'. A case in point was the Gidropribor torpedo factory, on Bol'shoi Sampsonievsky, which opened its in-house museum in 2004, just as other factory museums were closing. According to the factory's website in 2011, it was manufacturing ten different types of torpedo and mine, as well as equipment for underwater exploration and the ventilation of sea-going vessels.[157] The main entrance to the factory, bearing the concern's new title in gold letters alongside a meticulously restored 'Order of the October Revolution' awarded in 1982, suggested the new pride that was being taken in the manufacture of ballistics – even if the factory's rear end presented a much more battered sight to the world.[158]

Gidropribor was entirely owned by the Russian state, a factor that gave it some degree of financial security.[159] But some industries which were privatised at an early stage were also still in a productive condition. The Skorokhod shoe factory, whose history went back to 1882 (it was one of the few factories not to change its name after 1917), was making a 20 per cent profit on what it produced by 1991.[160] From 1998, it began specialising in children's shoes; in 2005, it was placed in an official list of the top 500 companies in the Russian Federation.[161] By the 2010s, over 10 per cent of Russian-made cars were built in St Petersburg.[162] Whatever the achievements of such companies by international standards of modernity and efficiency (some locals carped that they were no more than 'Potemkin factories' kept alive by public funding), press and promotional materials presented them as success stories.[163]

Another celebratory genre, as trotted out by newspapers and official citations, echoed the tone of press reports in the Soviet period: the tough but fair workshop foreman with the common touch, who would always sit down to a game of dominoes with the lads at the end of the working day; the long-serving accountant in the Institute for Scientific Research in Fats, who enjoyed well-earned authority among her comrades.[164] Factories and enterprises continued to run their in-house newspapers, and occasionally to organise collective holidays (now described as 'corporate' occasions).[165]

Under this veneer lay worry about the future, even among those working for the biggest enterprises. The old communal certainties were gone. Economic liberalisation unleashed a spree of self-advancement, from which those at the bottom were not in a position to benefit. As German Gurevich reported, the new democratic structures set up in the late 1980s, 'soviets of the labouring collective', were freely elected but in practice totally toothless. The director of the factory where he worked was able to fix his own salary at 2000 dollars, while the chief engineer was assigned 100.[166] Not one enterprise in St Petersburg was bought out by its workforce, and the new order did not offer the compensations that had once reconciled people to low wages. As a woman with decades of experience of working at the Kirov Factory put it, 'In the old days, earnings were small, but at least you used to get certificates of congratulation and medals. Now all that's gone.'[167]

Also gone were the so-called 'professional unions', *profsoyuzy*, of Soviet days. Not 'trades unions' in the Western sense (that is, organisations of democratic representation, mutual aid, and collective pay bargaining), these were branches of the state bureaucracy. All the same, they policed employers' adherence to labour protection legislation (for instance, arrangements for holiday leave had to be agreed with the relevant *profsoyuz*),[168] and provided welfare support. The 'free professional unions' that replaced them in 1990 were closer to the Western model, but had far less leverage: membership was low, and strike action infrequent.[169] The social role of their Soviet namesakes, with its formidable combination of 'care' and 'control', was a thing of the past.

The shift in the role of large enterprises also transformed the broader city landscape. No longer were entire districts of the city the fiefdoms of the Leningrad Metal Works or the Karl Marx Plant. Hostels had been closed down, shops turned over to commercial operations, and increasingly, industrial areas were transformed by the arrival of economic activities unrelated to manufacturing – warehouses of electrical and household goods, clothing emporiums, drive-by fast-food outlets, and gaming arcades.[170]

By the end of the 2000s, plans for systematic rezoning – mooted for over a decade – were starting to build up momentum. A survey of 2004 established that so far, despite all the talk, only one factory in the entire city had been transferred at the behest of the city administration. However, of 43 industrial enterprises in four central districts, 20 were in the process of relocating without help from the city authorities, 15 were no longer functioning, and the other 8 would have been happy with a move, had they been able to get premises.[171] Though progress was still slow, by 2011 there was a schedule for the relocation to Kronstadt of the Admiralty Wharves, a process that it was planned to complete by 2020. The Wharves covered an enormous area close to the New

Holland, another industrial site of a different era (the eighteenth century) which was itself scheduled for all-out redevelopment.[172]

Overall, St Petersburg was in the process of turning back into a city where the critical mass of employees sat behind desks, rather than lathes, much as had been the case in the first half of the nineteenth century. Yet the character of non-manual labour had itself altered. The collapse of Soviet economic relations also had an enormous impact on academic institutions – not just those tied to particular industries, but those doing speculative research. Cultural deregulation prompted an explosion of new universities, academies, and institutes of all kinds, offering a plethora of studies, from nanotechnology to astrology. But some of the existing academic institutes had gone into a kind of twilight. From the late 1990s, graduates who might once have worked in academia began moving into the business world; increasingly, young people selected courses with commercial potential (marketing, management, PR, and design in particular), rather than traditional sciences or humanities subjects.[173]

The process was most painful in the case of the formerly most prestigious institutions, the dependencies of the Academy of Sciences. With every other vocational secondary school now renamed an 'academy', and a whole host of organisations calling themselves 'academies' and creating their own 'academicians' of telepathy or water-divining, even the institution's title had become tarnished. But far more important were the problems of recruitment and retention. Institutes became more and more top-heavy in terms of seniority, and pluralism was rife, as people coped with a drop in the real value of salaries by taking other employment. As in the case of factories, rituals and rhetoric survived, but much of the corporate spirit had gone. In the words of a long-term member of academic staff at one institute under the RAN umbrella, 'People come here as though they were collecting their pension.'[174]

An obvious ancillary career for senior academics was teaching, but a gulf had opened up between teaching at schools – which had undergone significant reform in the 1990s – and university teaching, which resembled the Soviet model much more closely. In any case, before the early 1990s those working in research institutes had limited contact with students. Such seminars as there were had been organised by students themselves; otherwise, the graduate student was mainly required to turn up daily at his or her section before disappearing to the library. The only core courses were in 'philosophy' (Marxism-Leninism), which many tried to miss if they could.[175] The result was that not every scholar of distinction had much idea of how to lecture.

This mattered more now that students were used to a livelier and more engaged mode of address in the classroom. If the listeners were sometimes alienated, then their teachers were sometimes frustrated – a situation for which they were occasionally inclined to blame their students.

> They write slowly, in messy handwriting and with solecisms of spelling, grammar, and syntax. They're just not used to writing – they've spent their lives ticking boxes in multiple-choice tests or typing texts straight into the computer (or more often, cut-and-pasting them from the Internet). Making lecture notes is a real ordeal for them. They're inarticulate too: they've got used to the frightful pidgin they hear on trendy youth programmes and to the sound-tracks of trashy US films dubbed into what passes for Russian. At the age when earlier generations of schoolchildren were spending their time reading, they were playing computer games.[176]

A foreign student who returned from temporary study in the St Petersburg Conservatoire in the late 2000s recalled that the behaviour of teachers there was often offensive: comments such as 'You play like a cripple' or 'I regret I accepted you on this course' were common, sometimes accompanied by loud laughter at a student's playing.[177]

High-handedness of this kind was, in fact, nothing new: compare Logan Robinson's recollection of his academic advisor in late 1970s Leningrad: 'She displayed no ability for abstraction or dispassionate analysis, relying instead on rhetoric, party slogans, and derisive laughter'.[178] 'Party slogans' might have vanished, but 'rhetoric' and 'laughter' were still used as weapons. Hardly preferable was the completely uninterested attitude of staff in some other places. 'Your lecturer comes in four hours late stinking of booze and doesn't apologise,' one person complained about a well-known design college.[179] (Part of the background to this was the steep decline in the prestige of teaching generally. By the 2010s, even so august a place as the Herzen Pedagogical University offered courses in languages, law, management, IT, and design alongside pedagogy in order to maximise intake.)[180] The most dedicated university teachers were often those of the older generation, though in subjects where the world had moved on, being taught by those in their sixties, seventies, and even eighties, could have drawbacks too.[181]

Yet some new institutions with an explicitly reforming remit treated their students very differently, modelling their practices on the collegial relations which had characterised informal contact in Soviet research institutes. These institutions deliberately kept student bodies small, allowing a lot of personal contact between teachers and the taught, and effective seminar work. Here, awareness of international research and teaching practices was strong, and discussions were as lively as in leading institutions anywhere in the world.[182] However, places of this kind were scarce, and they had the self-aware character of model establishments – their members pointing with a mixture of regret and relish to the fact that things were done much worse elsewhere.

### Doing *biznes* in the New World

In some parts of post-Soviet Russia, particularly Moscow, the academic elite provided some leading members of the new elite – most famously the ex-physicist and doctor of sciences, Boris Berezovsky. In Petersburg, on the other hand, it tended to be those holding relatively low-level posts in practical subjects who made their way into the business world.[183] Many academics felt that participating in the messy sphere of commerce was beneath their dignity – a hero of 'pure science' being the distinguished mathematician Grigory Perel'man, who refused to accept the Fields Medal and the Clay Prize for his work.[184]

The purist view found amusing expression in 'Petersburg for Tourists', a story that Nataliya Tolstaya published in 1999. Its narrator, trained as a linguist, was faced with the *khaltura* from hell: updating a US sovietologist's tour-guide to Petersburg, apparently written from his armchair somewhere in the Midwest. She was left agonising over whether to correct his peculiar notions about local practices (such as his belief that Leningraders regularly spent their free time going on 'collective walks round lakes'), as well as his extremely vague knowledge of the city's topography and history. The sense that there was something unavoidably lowering in the whole activity of working for money was brought out by the confrontation with this laughable ignoramus.

The experience Tolstaya described made clear the contempt for commercialism felt by many St Petersburgers from the educated elite. Before economic liberalisation, it was rare for Leningrad intellectuals to undertake freelance work of a commercial kind (as opposed to literary or academic writing, or translation). It is hard to imagine a professor of history moonlighting as a film consultant to earn the money for the deposit on a co-operative flat, as some Moscow academics did without hesitation.[185] Relative lack of opportunity was one issue, but another was difference in attitude. It was easier for an architect to switch from state commissions to private commissions than for those who had primarily valued the research they did in their own time to sacrifice that time to paid labour. The sudden pressure to find earnings was painful.[186]

Administrators were another story. In the 1990s, some of the staff working in the 'foreign sections' of universities were able to use their contacts abroad in order to start up highly effective export-import networks.[187] But most often, leading businessmen emerged from the cohort of Komsomol and Party members who had begun to take opportunities when they first offered themselves in the late 1980s and early 1990s. It was sports colleges, rather than the science and humanities faculties and sections of leading universities and Academy of Sciences institutes, where the new business leaders were mainly incubated.[188] Where such people did study at more traditional places, they were often from the provinces. 'You see, they already had their own social networks,' a man born in 1980 explained. 'And they had to fight so hard too; that made them much more successful when it came to business.'[189]

As *biznes* developed, so assumptions about work culture that had evolved in the days of the shadow economy became entrenched. An activist in the co-operative movement explained in 1991 that rules were obstacles to be got round; every official had a price; and if you could not do something openly, you did it 'on the sly'. Before privatisation was allowed, he had made a concealed purchase of a 'clapped out little flour mill in Roshchino', which was soon supplying state shops with 150,000 packets of rolled oats a month, sold at 37 kopecks each.[190] With hard work and commitment, not to speak of lack of inhibitions, there were now fantastic sums to be made.

Not everyone was a rip-off merchant: new businessmen sometimes prided themselves on providing quality goods, and on their own creative gifts.[191] But the new ethos of profit before everything tended to shape people's relations with business, often in a negative sense. 'We bought this boat, we had a plan to make really valuable things, but then it all folded. Well. Obviously. [. . .] You can't do things like that if you're honest,' one man remembered, also commenting that he found organisation 'really soul-destroying'. 'And then you have to find someone else, and the temptation's just too much – hand straight in the till.'[192] The all-out commitment essential to business success was another alienating factor. The widespread sense that life had been more fun back in Soviet days was to a large extent prompted by the fact that there had been more time for your friends back then.[193] On the other hand, the significant rise in the numbers of non-working wives (often successful businessmen considered it prestigious if the family could live on the man's earnings alone) created a body of people who sometimes did not know what to do with their time – as well as a pool of demand for service providers such as beauticians.[194]

Employees were subject to culture-shock too. The evolution of *biznes* brought huge changes in the pace of life. In the past, everyone knew that express post was scarcely worth the extra cost. The equivalent of a courier was sending things 'with the pilots' (you paid an Aeroflot employee to get a package on to a departing plane).[195] Breaks were taken for granted; getting time off was easy. Work was just as much about the production of social relations as about 'productivity' in a time-management sense.[196] From the early 1990s a new equation of time and money took hold, and with it a frenetic, displacement-anxiety emphasis on how busy one was. At first, this could seem exciting, but for those used to a different pace, disillusion, not to speak of exhaustion, was a serious risk.[197]

Another enormous change was in the sheer unpredictability of one's conditions of employment. In the Soviet period, there had been a reassuring sameness about the working cycle, with pressure building up at predictable phases of the latest five-year plan. 'Labour turnover' might be recognised as a problem in factories, but other workers tended to remain in the same position for years. The sense of wholesale disorientation began to subside only in the 2000s, as people began work who had never held jobs under the Soviet system, and did not necessarily expect to stay in one position for life, or to work in a profession directly related to their career. There were now plenty of examples of ex-linguists who worked in travel agencies, mathematicians who had moved into IT management and software production, designers serving as TV journalists, and even artists with successful careers in image counselling or hairdressing.[198]

At the same time, the increasing flexibility of younger staff also made them impatient with peremptory behaviour on the part of their employers: when a salary rise was withheld, or the directors of the firm suddenly reallocated staff to a completely different part of the city.[199] Yet, if arbitrary rule was resented, it was also taken for granted. Even in post-Soviet workplaces the characteristic verb used of a boss's request to do something was 'to order' (*prikazyvat'*), and people were extremely hesitant about doing anything without the sanction of higher authority. (Conversely, since consultation was exclusively associated with asking for permission, communication up and down the management hierarchy was considerably more effective than communication horizontally; people simply did not understand why they should 'clear' anything with their peers.)[200]

An even half-way tolerable boss came into the 'devil you know' category; starting afresh meant dealing with arbitrariness of a more threatening kind. For instance, a new employer might insist on settling up only when a job was complete – a practice that made it easy for the unscrupulous not to pay the employee at all.[201] One side-effect of uncertainty was a proliferation of contracts for the smallest service – booking a sandwich lunch for twenty people at a café would require a written agreement in duplicate.[202] Another was that personal connections became even more important than back in the Soviet period – only that way could one be reasonably sure of decent treatment.[203] Working from home was also on the rise. Until 2013, those who did this were in a kind of official twilight, but in April that year, the thousands of outworkers finally received recognition as employees, from the point of view of the state if not necessarily from the point of view of individual companies.[204]

The wildly differing levels of pay, like the different conditions, also generated anxiety. How much should one's time be worth? People simply had no idea. The 'windfall economics' of the 1990s, when you could earn more in a day at a street market than by working in an office for a month, endured for years in folk memory.[205] Hopes of 'lucking out' were pervasive.[206] Younger people in particular sometimes proved vulnerable to advertisements that promised large salaries for light work – usually, in fact, commission-selling on dreadful terms.[207] In fact, the vast majority of jobs on offer were casual and rather poorly paid – handing out advertising leaflets, doing market research, working in a call centre. On the website www.jobs.ru, offers under the rubric 'Sales' were two or three times as numerous as jobs in manufacturing or construction, but also much worse remunerated.[208] As a result, labour turnover reached levels that would have given Soviet managers heart failure: those running enterprises such as cafés took it for granted that employees would drop in and out as it suited them.[209] Freelancing and informal work – such as selling things at markets – was also widespread; for instance, the Udel'naya flea market, according to a sociological study in the early 2000s, attracted significant numbers of 'downwardly mobile' locals, who were keen to make a bit of money and also welcomed the camaraderie of the place.[210]

But the heritage of disinterested activity under Soviet power (as a friend of mine put it back in the 1980s, 'one works out of cultural instinct' rather than for high pay or career success) also meant that people were capable of remarkable dedication in unpropitious circumstances. This was particularly the case in professions such as medicine and teaching, but not only in those.[211] It sometimes shocked St Petersburgers visiting the West to realise that most office staff expected to go home, come what may, not a minute later than 5 pm (or indeed, 4.30). As one woman put it, 'in Russia, those people are often completely useless, but if they're not, and something's urgent, then they won't get home till the job is done.'[212] Punctual arrival at the start of the day might be rare, but so was clock-watching at the end.[213] There was still a widespread practice of bonus payments (*premii*), which meant that showing *unusual* application was likely to be better rewarded than steady effort day in day out.[214]

Leningrad's enormous bureaucracy went through a rather different process of transformation. One major shift – as everywhere in the Soviet Union – was the demise of the Party administration. After 1991, new administrative structures were built up, with Lensovet (dissolved by Boris Yeltsin in December 1993) replaced in 1994 by the City Legislative Assembly, and its Executive Committee by the Government of St Petersburg. However, even before the elected city leader was replaced by a government-appointed governor in 2006, there were signs of retrenchment on the part of the pre-1991 bureaucracy – not just as a result of Vladimir Putin's commitment to restoring the 'power vertical', but because of dissatisfaction with the personal rule that had characterised the years when Anatoly Sobchak was in charge of the city.[215] By the mid-2000s, the political elite of Petersburg was showing considerable overlap both with the Party and Komsomol elite of the 1980s, and with the sectors of the business elite that had emerged from a comparable background.[216]

Sometimes, the elites were to all intents and purposes identical – as in the case of Yury Molchanov, who continued his activities as a property developer after appointment to the city administration in 2001 (he became one of the vice-governors in 2003), or Vadim Tyul'panov, president of the city's legislative assembly from 2003 to 2011, and leader of the United Russia St Petersburg section party council from 2004, who set up a successful freight company before moving into politics in the late 1990s.[217] At lower levels, on the other hand, there was often direct continuity from Soviet times, with senior officials such as heads of section holding similar positions to the ones they had held back in the days of Lensovet (an example was Vera Dement'eva, the head of the Monuments Office between 2003 and 2011, who had worked in the agency's Soviet predecessor from 1975).

The tenacity of leading officials was only one of the signs of the local bureaucracy's resilience. While employees in the city administration were, by the standards of business, not well paid, they enjoyed far greater job security and a much kinder working schedule. Normally, the time set aside for dealing with members of the public was a few hours on two or three days per week. While these periods could be stressful, there was otherwise quite generous capacity for tea-drinking, social chat with one's workmates, private telephone conversations, and other pleasant diversions. Little serious responsibility was devolved down to lower levels; routine work could be performed on auto-pilot. In other words, work conditions in the bureaucracy were far more 'Soviet' than they were in other places of employment.[218]

The view seen from the other side of the desk had not changed that much either. Those attempting to get government employees to provide them with services were likely to feel extreme frustration. As a journalist put it in 2004:

> Standing in a queue at the passport and visa service is worse than being in the delivery room of a maternity hospital.
>
> You arrive at 7 a.m. and find out that you are No. 37, you stand three hours by the locked door, jumping up and down so as not to die of cold, and then ten minutes before they open you crawl back home, realising that you'll never get to the end of the queue whatever happens.[219]

Long lines were probably resented more than they had been back in the days when queuing was the norm for everything. Certainly, the provision of formal or informal agency services so that those who could afford to pay the fee did not have to queue was a notable money-maker of the post-Soviet period.[220]

But the queue was only the start. It was the attitudes of the staff when one reached them that offended most people:

> Passport offices, housing offices, visa sections [OVIR] and all that – they're the most horrible places in the country. I can't remember ever encountering anything worse. Wherever else you go, you can feel the changes, you don't have to deal with that dreadful *sovdepiya* [a derogatory term for Soviet bureaucracy] and that dreadful attitude to people. It's all changed. Whereas those places – it's a kind of conservation zone of the *sovdepiya* [. . .] Those

> biddies drove me nearly frantic, they were so stupid, and they kept asking for all these ridiculous documents, although the situation was completely clear without any of them. It's obvious, the rules just say you need these papers, so they kept on asking for them in this moronic way [. . .] And then I have to go and see the same people about getting the stairwell redecorated. It's just awful, of course. The rudeness, you should hear them say [*adopting surly voice*]: 'It's lunch time, we need to eat just like anyone else.' Although these days no one takes a lunch hour in companies and offices. But *they* do, and what's more they take forever over it, and at other times – forget it. They're just not there.[221]

There was considerable public amusement when, in February 2011, Valentina Matvienko herself, testing out the assertions by members of the city health committee that there had been remarkable advances in attitudes to patients, rang up one of the city's clinics and tried to make an appointment with an ophthalmologist. After extreme difficulties in getting through, she was told flatly there were no slots available, but just might be if she tried ringing again some days later.[222]

One possible way of dealing with recalcitrance was to offer a 'sweetener'. However, this solution was not as widespread as some Western comment of the day would have suggested.[223] In 2005, an INDEM survey with 3000 participants established that only just over half of the respondents were prepared to give bribes (in 2001 it had been close to 75 per cent). The responses also produced an interesting rundown of the top areas for bribe-giving, as by millions of dollars expended. At the top was higher education (583.4 million in 2005), followed by the health services (401.1). Then came the military call-up board (353.6), registration of living space (298.6), courts of law (209.5), the automobile testing service (183.3), schools (92.4), and the police (29.6). By size of bribe, the call-up board was by far the largest (around 600 dollars on average), with university boards getting around 130 dollars, and medical staff about 50 dollars.[224]

These figures pointed to important differences in practices on the ground. With the traffic police – also notoriously venal back in the Soviet period – most people accepted with annoyed resignation that donations were a fact of life. If one's licence turned out to be out of date, the officer might say, 'I'm supposed to impound your car, but . . .' Offered a choice between struggling home by public transport, then travelling out to the pound and paying a large fine, or handing over a couple of hundred dollars on the spot, many people would understandably choose the latter.[225] Paying a hospital nurse to give a sick relation extra attention was a widespread strategy, and usually not even seen as 'a bribe'.[226] Incomers whose identity papers were not in order regularly expected to pay beat policemen (here again, there was an issue of categories, since in some cases a 'fine' would be demanded even if the documentation was in order).[227] Financial paving of the way when one organised building permissions was so common that it was sometimes cited as a reason for not wanting to start the process again.[228] Buying a son out of military service (with a misleading medical certificate, particularly), was, by the 2000s, all but universal among those who could afford it, and cheaper than the alternative – to send him to study abroad, which in any case solved the problem only for as long as the academic course in question lasted.[229] Bribes to court staff, university admissions and examining boards, and schools, on the other hand, were not widely regarded as normal and acceptable, though attempting to 'pull strings' was a different matter.[230]

'Bribery' was a sub-territory of the much larger concept of *blat*, whose prevalence in Soviet and post-Soviet culture is a truth universally acknowledged.[231] The background of favour-trading meant that hard and fast boundaries were difficult to draw. Paying someone extra to get a job done was not a 'bribe' if you happened to work with them, but if the money was given by a person outside the workplace, things were different.[232] With the retraction of state control, the exchange of favours and exercise of social and cultural capital started to be monetised. In the Soviet period, a teacher might be given a package of some scarce delicacy to persuade her to look favourably on one's precious son or daughter; in the post-Soviet period, arranging private lessons, for a fee, was a likelier strategy.[233] As Valentina Matvienko's brush with the receptionist showed, a municipal bigwig was no longer guaranteed special treatment. This was one reason behind the widespread phrase, 'money decides everything' (an ironic parody of the Soviet slogan, 'cadres decide everything').

The involvement of individuals in irregular payments and 'self-interested gifts' was only the most visible part of the exchange of favours. Far more important, in economic and structural terms, was the vast culture of *otkat* – backhanders paid by companies and general insider dealing. In 2006, the going rate to get a large-scale building project agreed was running at about a million dollars.[234] Companies also paid bribes to obtain work permits for migrant labourers (or alternatively, when illegal migrants were discovered without proper papers). A common dodge was for a public official to create regulations requiring the purchase of some item (for instance, a particular kind of super-efficient smoke detector) – and then to change jobs and begin manufacturing or selling whatever the item was.[235] Such below-the-line calculations, according to one estimate, added 15 per cent to the cost of goods and transactions in 2005.[236] While the rise of the 'strong state' had eroded the power of the mafia, officials now developed their own 'protection rackets'. Actual extortion was not unknown – as in the case of police officials who colluded in a 'fake car crash' scam used to blackmail money out of drivers in 2007.[237]

The city government made a show of grappling with the problem. A 'corruption hotline' was set up in the late 2000s,[238] and in 2009–10 a poster campaign

4.4 'Do You Give Bribes?', 2010. This public information poster warns that this contravenes article 291 of the Criminal Code and carries a sentence of up to 8 years.

was organised, 'DO YOU GIVE BRIBES?', warning miscreants of stiff prison sentences if they attempted to grease palms.

Efforts were also made to come at the problem from the other end. At the central level, a new tariff of fines for corrupt officials was introduced by President Medvedev in 2011, and posters in St Petersburg at the start of 2012 encouraged the public to ring a hotline and denounce bribe-takers.

But once again, the problem of classification raised itself. If an official carrying out an inspection arrived and presented a list of things required for his personal comfort while he was doing the work, you could report this and perhaps a substitute official would be sent, but in the meantime the chit you needed would not be produced.[239] In any case, pronouncing on venality was difficult in a work culture where expensive birthday presents to those in authority were seen as tokens of affection, not just ways of buying goodwill. Enormous amounts of energy were expended on collective gifts to people's 'bosses' in the workplace – but the fuss was relished, just as it was when people selected gifts and organised celebrations for their peers.[240] A poster campaign of 2013, 'A BRIBE IS NOT A GIFT', indicated just how widespread confusion in fact was.[241] Wandering the labyrinth of badly formulated and often contradictory commands from above, people were reliant on occasional acts of spontaneous kindness – including the decision by a given official to ignore what was, strictly speaking, required. In many years of visiting Piter, I have rarely encountered a situation where I was expected to bribe an official.[242] But I have plenty of experience of cases where people have decided to think flexibly about a supposedly inviolable rule – as the Russian phrase would have it, *poshli na vstrechu* ('came over to your point of view').[243] Or alternatively, refused to do something which they certainly ought, in terms of the rules, to have done.

The combination of petty authoritarianism and rule-bending endured, a situation that seemed likely to change only when or if private business interests had become powerful enough to resist obstruction. However, in the boom-and-bust international cycles of the late 1990s and 2000s, and with increasing intervention from the state power-brokers (*siloviki*) at the centre, the independence of the corporate sector was fragile.[244] And among the general public, there was a devastating lack of trust in officials of all hues, as was indicated not just by polls but by private conversation: 'We don't have a thing to our names, do we? Well, loads of fat smug officials, torrents of them – but do we need those?'[245] There was the sense that even the rudimentary competence of the Soviet official had vanished (back then, as one man put it, young incomers were given at least some training in administration, 'they knew what doors to knock on').[246] Now, the old lobbying channels were gone:

> Suppose you've had an accident in the [so-and-so] district, and the boss of the local police happens to be a mate of yours, then you can sort things out. But if he isn't, and the traffic cops, the police there break the rules, then you can spend the rest of your life in the courts and get nowhere. If your boss at work does something to you that's illegal, you're better off resigning and moving to another job than trying to put things right. And so on. While the Soviet system had managed to set up ways of putting pressure on the authorities precisely for so-called ordinary people. If you didn't like what the housing administration was doing, you went to the district soviet. If you didn't like what they were up to, you went to the local party cell. See? And if that didn't work, you could always write to the papers.[247]

Aged eleven when the Soviet Union collapsed, this person was hardly in a position to judge how effective lobbying was back then, but the fact that these views were often second-hand did not diminish their grip.

The new set of relations – based primarily on personal gain and collusion with 'the right people' – excluded those at the bottom end of society; to a greater degree, many felt, than the flawed egalitarianism of Soviet bureaucratic relations. Whether this assessment was objectively true or not, it certainly acted as an engine of political and social dissatisfaction. Not surprisingly, one of the most successful ventures of the Russian opposition was the website rosyama.ru, a kind of moaners' free-for-all where the chance to bombard the authorities with messages about that hole in the road was only the click of a mouse away.[248]

Yet the personalisation of relations was not limited to the state sector: dealings with private companies too were unpredictable. Within the same company, one could find staff who were charming and efficient, and those for whom getting out of bed in the morning seemed to have exhausted all available energy. Complaints websites suggested a preponderance of the latter, as did the rumour network. When I expressed admiration of a telephone engineer who (unlike most in the UK) had turned up on time, as well as sober, and fixed the line in a matter of seconds (and without any charge), I was told by a friend: 'they're all Baptists down there.' Yet the reasons for variation were surely wider than idiosyncrasies of biography. The universal belief that competence was extraordinary might foster cases of extraordinary competence, but it also – and more notably – fostered a great deal of ordinary, 'what else do you expect' *in*competence.[249]

## New Work Places, New Work Ethic?

If the relationship between the past and the present was confused where working practices were concerned, corporate style had undergone appreciable change. Every leading company and institution now had a website, almost always with a historical section that emphasised long ties with the city. The official company history was an expanding genre, and work on such books was a way for professional historians to make money.[250] *A History of St Petersburg Trade*, published to mark the city's jubilee in 2002–3, was an opulent two-volume album that combined chronicles of different famous nineteenth-century factories and shops, an account of Soviet enterprises and their contribution to the defence of Leningrad, and spreads on the 'onward and upward' history of manufacturing and trade in the post-Soviet period: dynamic new directors, latest technology, novel brands and lines, but always with sensitivity to the unique history of the city in which this commercial activity was taking place.[251]

In terms of the face that workplaces presented to actual visitors, things were a little different. During the late 1990s and 2000s, housing one's office in a resplendent historical building became prestigious (a local meaning of

4.5 Restored lift and stairway of the Mertens House, Nevsky prospekt, 2010.

'corporate raiding' (*reiderstvo*) was collusion with the city authorities in order to have lessees of some desirable building evicted).[252] In some cases, such as the Mertens House on Nevsky prospekt, the entrances, staircases, and lifts had been splendidly restored.

But once inside, companies sought to emphasise their 'new age' status with sleek office furniture, electronic equipment in matt monochrome, and vertical, rather than ruched, blinds. In due course (by the mid-2000s), state offices also started to buy in new furniture, usually made of MDF, with veneering in pale wood, such as maple, rather than the toffee hues of the past. In both places, the traditional organisation of space, with the desk as cynosure, continued. The telephone retained its former role as an indicator of status – competing with the mobile and smartphone. But the surrounds looked very different.

In academic offices, things had changed much less. Furniture was still mostly battered and limited to tables and chairs, with perhaps a cupboard or coat-stand for hanging clothes. The main addition to the existing landscape

4.6 Microwave and icon in the eating area of a workplace, 2010.

was the computer (usually surrounded by scary nests of wires), and maybe a microwave or sandwich toaster. But here – as in every other kind of office – there was a notable change, in the sheer number of personal items that were scattered around. Plants had not fallen out of favour, but there was now far more 'extra-curricular action'. Desktops were awash with comfortable clutter: pen-pots, mugs, jolly animal figurines, funny postcards, greetings cards, not to speak of family photographs. Cupboards for storing equipment had patterned paper on the inside; microwaves might be decorated with magnets and slogans.

Even very small spaces might be given the personal touch. In 2008–9, a traffic observation booth by the lights on the intersection of ulitsa Lebedeva and Botkinskaya ulitsa – though only just big enough to hold one chair – had cheerful sprigged curtains, a busy-lizzie plant, plastic flowers, and a landscape photograph. When it was out of use in the late evenings, the curtains would be chastely drawn on this domestic scene.[253]

Yet the prevalence of this pleasant cosiness, a kind of visual and tactile leveller, could not conceal the discrepancies in political and cultural capital between different occupations. By the late 2000s, St Petersburg was a civil-service-dominated city in much the way that it had been in the 1840s. The 1990s dreams of a kind of independent Hansastadt had been replaced by a reality that was more like the German statelet, with its parochially-oriented, obstinate, indolent officials, as represented by Eichendorff's *Life of a Good-for-Nothing*. It remained to be seen whether the relocation of the Constitutional Courts and of Gazprom, as major all-Russian institutions, would transform the status quo. It was, after all, the supposed need to provide the new arrivals with a suitable landscape and facilities that had been the driving force behind the proposal to build Okhta-Centre, the enormous skyscraper that generated huge protests in 2008–10. Could the influx of Moscow bureaucrats, from a more dynamic work culture, change the small details of work life as well? A humorous poll run by Rosbalt news agency during the official 'Year of Spain', 2011, 'Which Spanish traditions would you like to see introduced here?', produced a substantial majority in favour of the siesta.[254] Would a transfusion of Moscow energy and ambition come about, or would these be sapped by the infamous low atmospheric pressure and nagging winds of the Neva delta, the dying fall of the endless nights and belated sunrises of high winter?

# 5

# Eliseev and Aprashka

*An old-old man just like a gnome*
*is dragging from the grocers home*
*a net bag, absolutely crammed.*
*What is in it? Sausage? Ham?*
(Joseph Brodsky)[1]

The austerity of intellectual Leningraders had a particular impact on attitudes to shopping. During the mid-1960s discussions about the future of Nevsky prospekt, there were even suggestions that shops should be completely removed so the street could be turned into a cultural reserve.[2] Nina Katerli's 1977 novella *Sennaya ploshchad'* drew on the classic traditions of Petersburg prose not just because it emphasised the deceptive character of the city, with its 'Barsukov triangle' of inexplicable vanishings centred on Raskol'nikov's home patch, but because it represented shopping as a plunge into degradation:

> Mar'ya Sidorovna Tyutina got up at eight, as was her wont, ate a bowl of porridge, washed up the breakfast dishes she and her husband had used and set off for the local 'dive', where yesterday she had been confidently promised that cod fillet would be on sale this morning.
>
> She decided not to pay for her purchase in advance; instead, she went straight to the counter to get the fish weighed out. After waiting for hours – well, at least half an hour – she reached the end of the queue at last, but then she heard, no receipt – no goods. Mar'ya Sidorovna pleaded with the assistant to let her have half a kilo, even, there was someone laid up at home and she'd joined the queue first thing, and there was a long queue at the cash desk too, but the assistant paid her no mind; she just grabbed a receipt from some man and turned her back on Mar'ya Sidorovna. The other people in the queue yelled at Mar'ya Sidorovna not to hold them up – they had work to go to, so she went to the cash desk after all . . .[3]

In falling victim to a system that required customers to queue up to four times (once to pay, once to request goods, and perhaps also once to correct any error in the payment), Mar'ya Sidorovna was not suffering a peculiarly local torment. Standing in multiple lines was required across the Soviet Union, since there were few self-service stores.[4] In times of scarcity, shop assistants had a crucial role, making sure goods were parcelled out according to a norm per customer (known colloquially as *v ruki*, 'into [a pair of] hands').

Contrary to received stereotypes of Petersburg refinement, sales staff were often brusque at best. In being spared a tide of verbal abuse, Mar'ya Sidorovna had got off lightly. As Sergei Dovlatov remembered, adopting a servile manner was automatic: he would constrict his bulky frame to the smallest possible dimension and adopt a wheedling tone: 'could you *possibly* weigh me out *just a little* butter, say 100 grams, and *just a little*, say 200 grams of some of that *lovely* sausage, not too greasy if you don't mind . . .' – while at the same time aware that the assistant was passing off watered-down sour cream on her customers, and would likely give him a tongue-lashing whatever he said and did.[5]

## 'Acquiring' and 'Chucking Out'

Stores were run in the 'cultural capital' in the same way as they were in other Soviet cities. A salesperson would be assigned to a certain section of the shop where he, or much more likely she, would spend the entire day, irrespective of whether there were actually any customers. Just before the collapse of the Soviet Union, a journalist irritably recorded visiting a shop in Kirov Distict (on the misnamed 'Happy Street') where sixty people were queuing for cakes and sweets, 'while in the next-door section, where margarine and kvas stood in solitary splendour, two assistants were hanging round doing nothing'.[6] Anyone who shopped in the Soviet period could have confirmed this impression from personal experience.

In Leningrad, as anywhere, to be stuck in a long snaking line was a severe test of nerve:

> Of course, you could always walk away, but then you never knew when they'd actually bring something, or indeed if. I was never 100 per cent sure myself. If you did decide to leave, you could always tell someone else or in front or behind that you were nipping away for a while, but people didn't . . . exactly like that much, and likely by the time you got back you'd either find they weren't there, or that they'd forgotten you. [. . .] Though there was no rule they'd not let you back in either.[7]

'You'd be standing in line three hours. And all for some green bananas,' another woman recalled.[8] The compensations could be a certain sense of companionship through sheer misfortune (a queue was one of the few occasions when people in this austere city might start chatting to strangers), not to speak of the triumph conferred by a lucky purchase.[9] But the danger of goods running out before the end of the line was ever-present.

The peculiarly Leningrad feature of Mar'ya Sidorovna's brush with retailing was the venue. The word 'dive' (*nizok*, literally 'bottom bit') referred to a store housed in a cellar or basement. Already in the nineteenth century, cellar stores and bars had been a standard feature of Petersburg life. Such a bar is visited by Raskol'nikov in the hours leading up to his double murder. Low-ceilinged dim places, with blunt (and often misleading) titles such as Food, Milk, Meat, or Bread, 'dive' shops contained, in the Soviet era, a few counters, and perhaps a chiller or two (seldom in full working order) with smeared, cracked glass; the floor was likely to be uneven if not grimy. A persistent smell of slightly stale fat, sometimes with acrid overnotes of smoked fish, hung in the air. Attempts to modernise – by providing new windows and doors, say – only added to the monotony.[10]

The contents of basic food shops were equally dismal: slabs of hacked, oozing meat; waxy, industrial cheese; eggs that were sometimes chalky with age. Expensive things – coffee beans, for example – had often 'lain around' (*zalezhali*). Basic items, on the other hand, ran out fast, if delivered at all. Assistants would shrug: 'They haven't brought it' (*ne privezli*). Even the official press occasionally acknowledged problems, sometimes by the oblique method of insisting that yes there *were* plenty of potatoes, that last year's shortage of

5.1 Food in a Leningrad store, 1960s. To judge by appearances, the items on sale comprise bottled salad, smoked fish and pork fat (*salo*).

onions had been sorted out *almost immediately*, and that supplies were being boosted in time for the next public holiday (a stage when basic foodstuffs often disappeared completely).[11] Discussions behind closed doors were considerably more explicit.[12]

At the same time, the food supply was better in Leningrad than everywhere else, excluding Moscow.[13] Goods such as meat, fresh fish, butter, and eggs were usually available, something that was certainly not true of many provincial cities.[14] There were even some local specialities, such as buttercream, sold in paper cartons; spread on bread, it was known as a 'Leningrad sandwich'.[15] An ordinary district store, such as 'Marxist' (next to the factory of that name on Zheleznovodskaya, Vasilievsky Island), might boast two kinds of sausage and 'cabbage provençale'[16] alongside more predictable staples, such as salt herring; the shop at the nearby Vodniki factory was still better. With a separate bakery, a shop selling milk on draught, and a hut where vegetables were sold, all nearby, inhabitants of this area were by general Soviet standards well off.[17] But all districts would have a *gastronom* within reach – down the length of Bol'shoi prospekt on Petrograd Side, there were three of them.[18]

In fact the pervasiveness of queues, particularly in central Leningrad, was a sign of prosperity: it pointed to the fact that attractive goods were on sale. The relative abundance in the city was the source of wonder to outsiders: 'I remember when we came here for your father's wedding, we went to that shop on Nevsky, that fish one, remember? With your gran, and they had all this stuff there, this smoked salmon, all different kinds, all kinds. [. . .] We didn't have all that in Belorussia. There was much more in the way of food here.[19] The shop referred to here is probably the famous fish shop on the corner of ul.

5.2 A *gastronomiya* on prospekt Marksa (Bol'shoi Sampsonievsky), 1980.

Rubinshteina (the street was jokingly known as 'Rybinshteina', from the Russian word for 'fish').[20]

Another notable food shop was Gastronom, or delicatessen, No. 1, in an opulent early-twentieth-century building by Gavriil Baranovsky, also the author of the city's Buddhist Temple. All curlicues of dark wood, mirrors, and engraved and stained glass, the structure had formerly housed the Eliseev Stores (and no Leningrader would ever have referred to the shop by any other name). In contrast to other shops, this one smelled positively delicious, a waft of smoked ham reaching the nostrils when one opened the door.[21]

But the delicacies had a forbidden air. In the first summer of the war, Izrail' Metter remembered, 'foodstuffs vanished capriciously: the Eliseev Stores was heaped high with tinned crab and champagne.'[22] After the war, people would often visit just to look at what was on sale.[23] In the late 1950s, caviar and olives as well as crab are remembered as abundant – indicating that purchases were rare.[24] Food and drink of this kind was not necessarily extortionately priced but it seemed 'out of reach', something to be enjoyed only on holidays. A rigid division between 'ordinary food' and 'celebration food' was in operation: 'A can of sprats, for instance, you'd keep it till a . . . [special occasion], it was sort of shameful, ridiculous to eat it just like that. Senseless! Daft! You cook your everyday soup – what's the sense of putting bottled peas in it? Are you mad? . . . You need it for a celebration.'[25]

5.3 The Eliseev Stores, photographed in 1959 by V. Kunov.

At the same time, by the 1970s many Leningraders had developed a greater sense of entitlement, bulk-buying celebration foods rather than letting these lie around unsold. As one woman recalled, 'You'd go to Repino in a car, and buy twenty crates of bottled peas at one go'.[26] The result was that items such as these peas (used in the classic party dish, salat Olivier or 'Russian salad'), caviar, and indeed tinned crab, became subject to chronic shortages. Foods like this were known metonymically as *defitsit*, the particular standing for the general.

Also heavily in demand were humbler kinds of delicacies – pastries, biscuits, sweets, and chocolates. It was here that the local imagination flowered. Most Leningrad goods shared the names, packaging, and taste of their counterparts all over the country: 'Ukrainian' and 'Zhiguli' beer, 'Russian' and 'Lithuanian' cheese, 'Milk', 'Kefir'.[27] But alongside the ubiquitous 'cream horns' and 'potatoes' (large, sweet, stodgy truffles, made with potato flour), there were nut biscuits, bouchées soused in sugar syrup with chocolate topping, and Café Sever sponges with buttercream. The entire city had a sweet tooth, nurtured from childhood on 'Queen of Spades', 'Leningrad', and 'Northern Aurora' candies from the Krupskaya Factory.[28]

As with everything else, demand fed demand, and by the 1980s shortages of cakes and chocolates had become endemic. In 1986, the magazine *Leningradskaya panorama* reported that the average customer was now buying six times as much as in the past, putting unbearable pressure on staff and premises. A year later, the same magazine reported that there were huge queues at the 'Oriental Sweets' shop on Nevsky. The journalists complained that people were eating way above recommended norms of sugar, and attributed the run on sticky things to increased prosperity. It suggested price rises as a way out of the situation.[29]

In fact, enhanced purchasing power was only part of the story. The peculiar mechanisms of deficit worked in order to generate demand for what was scarce, and to make what was easily available seem unattractive, creating an ever-tightening spiral. In the post-Soviet period, shortages were recalled, through a fog of nostalgia, as challenges to be overcome by skill, resourcefulness, or cunning.[30] A bus driver boasted of having bought sausage on duty, and one hardheaded shopper claimed that when there was no paper in a shop to wrap salt herring, she demanded the complaints-and-suggestions book, tore out a page, and used it as a wrapping.[31] A technician recalled how, back in the 1980s, some friends who worked at a restaurant had given him a cardboard box of meat to use for kebabs at his birthday party; he found himself the object of horrified stares as he sat in the metro. A trail of bloodstained drips was oozing from the package, 'like something out of Dostoevsky'.[32]

Anecdotes of this kind – *baiki* or 'tall stories' – were a well-loved genre in the Soviet era too, for telling round the kitchen table, perhaps.[33] But in practice shortages were immensely wearing. It was one thing when obvious 'party' foods, such as sprats, went short, another when the entire city ran out of mustard.[34] Inadequate supplies of favourite foods for children caused particular stress.[35] The exigencies of acquisition affected language: mostly, people did not talk about 'buying' or 'purchasing' (*kupit'*) food and other items, but of *getting hold* of them (*dostat'*) or *obtaining goods* (*otovarit'sya*); rather than *prodavat'* (to sell) one said *davat'* (to give out), and instead of 'distribution', the byword was *chuck out* (*vybrasyvat'*, *vykidyvat'*).[36]

Of over 200 letters received in December 1976 by *Leningradskaya pravda* about shopping, around 10 expressed gratitude for positive experiences, but the others consisted of 'complaints, complaints, and more complaints . . .' *Vechernii Leningrad* clocked up another 160, 150 of which were dissatisfied. The goods that readers noted were unobtainable included essential items such as warm shirts and boots for the winter, children's tights, eye-glasses, macaroni, bicarbonate of soda, and various medicines, alongside developing fluid for photography, paper and card for amateur book-binders, vanilla flavouring and spices for home bakers, chicory, batteries, binoculars, guitars and mandolins, and coffee (except in bean form, but then there were no coffee-mills to be had). What *was* on sale was frequently of poor quality – potatoes, for instance, were often rotten.[37] Of course, these complaints indicated that even the more esoteric

5.4 A display of jellies in a local gastronom, 1963.

items were sometimes available (in Soviet parlance, *byvali*, 'to be around occasionally'), but that was not much consolation.

Like other Soviet cities, Leningrad had its closed 'distribution points' (*raspredeliteli*) for members of the Party hierarchy and the *nomenklatura*, who included the holders of high-ranking positions in places such as the Academy of Sciences and in scientific institutes. As a woman with direct experience of these places – her father held a position attached to the Presidium of the Academy of Sciences – recalled, in the 1970s the best shops in the cities even provided a delivery service to the dacha:

> So the Eliseev Stores, it [. . .] fixed the orders for the Regional Committee, and there were these shops, the Eliseev Stores, Dieta on Zagorodnyi, Strela on Novoizmailovsky [. . .] and they'd come out to three dacha settlements, Komarovo, Solnechnoe, and Repino, over the summer [. . .] They served people who'd been Party members from whenever [. . .] and workers from the Regional and City Committees, and high-ups from the Academy of Sciences [. . .] they'd bring the buckwheat and so on they had left over and deliver it right to the station, on Sundays. [. . .] The shops themselves had these lists, and you could ring up, and they brought whatever you needed, only you had to get down on those lists. [. . .] And I could pick whatever I liked, there was nothing they dumped you with. Unlike the way it was at work. Everything was short, and then you'd get stuck with something you didn't need to begin with.[38]

Certainly, all this cost money – both for the goods themselves and for the customary tip to the delivery man. But the opportunity to choose high-quality goods at one's leisure was a significant privilege.

For ordinary mortals, it was commoner to acquire things through the non-choice system known as *prodovol'stvennye zakazy*, or 'food orders'. This referred to packages of items that were sold on a 'take it or leave it' basis in workplaces. Usually, they contained one or two scarce and desirable items such as bottled peas, tinned salmon, tins of Hungarian ham, red caviar, and mayonnaise. Then there would be the *nagruzka*, 'burden', made up of goods that sold poorly on their own: pickled seaweed, 'crabsticks' made of ocean krill, pearl barley, powder for making *kissel'* (fruit compote set with potato starch), and, in one particularly bizarre case, guava purée.[39] Workplaces varied in terms of what was offered and in how often purchases could be made. Usually goods were circulated just before state holidays (to compensate for the fact that the ordinary state shops tended to empty at times like this), but some employees had the chance to buy things rather more often.

The elite of Leningrad society could expect significantly more than a few tins and packets. According to the recollection of a woman whose husband

5.5 Press photograph of food items being packaged in the orders department of the Eliseev Stores, 16 February 1982. The attractive plastic bags decorated with local views were then as big a deficit item as the oranges and condensed milk.

once received the New Year rations of a Party regional committee member as a gift for helping this person write his candidate's dissertation, two kinds of caviar, veal tongues, poussins, cognac, and wine were among the delicacies in the presentation box.[40] It was, however, not just the city high-ups who did better than normal. The principle of assumed need could also mean that people's professional responsibilities got them superior treatment. Those at the most highly-regarded factories and institutes received better rations than those at mediocre enterprises, and top management had first pick when any supplies of anything arrived. At the same time, most of the 'food orders' were allocated on an egalitarian basis. Each package contained the same items and the system usually dictated that, if there were too few packages to go round, a raffle was held, with those who lost out given priority next time.[41]

Alongside the state system, there also existed a whole network of alternative supply lines. Like other Soviet cities, Leningrad had its collective farm markets, some in handsomely appointed, purpose-built halls. The oldest complex,

Andreevsky Market on Vasilievsky Island, went back to the 1780s, though it had been substantially reconstructed in 1959 (the Mal'tsev Market, on ul. Nekrasova, acquired a functionalist new building in 1955; two other old markets, Sytnyi and Kuznechnyi, had been rebuilt in the 1910s and the 1920s respectively). Rows of identical weighing machines and white shelving stood in contrast to the heaps of varied produce – citrus fruit, dried fruit and spices, and year-round tomatoes from Central Asia and the Caucasus; pickled cucumbers, cabbage, and garlic, curd cheese, meat, and honey from northwestern Russia; and, in season, exotic fruit and wood mushrooms. They were the only place to get most of these things – indeed, the only reliable place for any vegetables other than potatoes, cabbage, beetroot, and carrots. From the consumer's point of view, however, markets were expensive, especially for items not available in the state shops.[42] Like the foremost *gastronomy*, they were places where most people shopped for special occasions.

As legal, but non-state, institutions, markets had attracted disapproval since the early Soviet period. In 1924, the Leningrad magazine *Rezets* warned its readers that the Andreevsky Market sold dodgy wares – its snacks were known as 'bow-wow pies' – and that petty crime was rife.[43] Shopping at markets was a case of *caveat emptor* – though also of *caveat vendor*, since officials were always alert to violations of the rules by traders. Markets testified to a transition between fully legal kinds of selling and those in the grey or black economy – what was known in the late Soviet period as 'on the left' (*nalevo*). Among these was 'speculation', or the selling of goods at enhanced prices by enterprising shoppers, and those directly working in the retailing and catering industries.

The proportion of goods sold this way was widely believed to be very large: Soviet comedians, such as Arkady Raikin, regularly joked about 'goods through the back door' and 'things falling off lorries', and members of the general public just as regularly complained about the rapacious behaviour of shop assistants.[44] Deficit goods had a lively circulation beyond the shops. In the late 1970s, tinned stew, *tushonka*, went under the jocular name 'Soviet currency'.[45] If 'markets' blended into 'black markets', the shadow economy shared its other border with the mutual support networks that were vital to surviving deficit.[46] Soviet citizens regularly acted as 'bagmen' to family networks, bringing into one city what was available only in others. Provincial cousins who visited Leningrad to buy supplies, often of consumer goods, would reciprocate the hospitality of the families they visited by bringing whole larderfuls of food.

As Leonid Przhepyurko, who came to Leningrad from Dnepropetrovsk for a visit in 1972 after his wife had a baby, remembered, 'You had to take a present, and it had to have a Ukrainian flavour, of the kind that everyone across the former Soviet Union would recognise: smoked pork fat, sunflower oil and fruit, and all only of private market quality.' He himself set out with twenty-five buckets of sweet cherries, only ten of which actually made it to their final destination (the rest having been sold 'at a substantial profit' en route after the plane was delayed in Minsk).[47] But relations did not necessarily have to visit in order to keep their families supplied: they could use the post, or more likely the kind of informal Soviet courier service that involved paying a guard on an overnight train to take a package, collected at the far end by the lucky recipient.[48]

It was particularly useful, of course, to have a friend or relation who actually worked in a shop. 'Oh yes,' a man born in 1975 remembered of an aunt by marriage, who lived with the family. 'That was our *rich* nan. She was a . . . a book-keeper in a food shop. Oh yes! And so far as my other nan went, and my mum, our rich nan kept the wolf from the door. When things got tough.' At the same time, this woman, with her laughable mispronunciations of common words (*deryovnya*, 'villodge'), her 'ZIL limousine fridge', and love of vodka-drinking parties with mates from the catering sector (as the 'grandson' disdainfully remembered, these included 'a book-keeper in a *chebureki* outlet'), stood out as somehow déclassé within the family: useful, undeniably, but also a source of embarrassment.[49] 'Getting hold' of things was not just a test of nerves; it sometimes made people feel less than good about themselves.

## From *Sintetika* to *Dzhinzy*

No one could avoid food shopping at frequent intervals. Whether to purchase consumer goods was a matter of more choice. Often, membership of the cultural elite meant at least affecting to despise material possessions, as in Viktor Krivulin's scathing anatomisation of the prosperous, aspirant, 'respectable' Soviet person:

> Your wages on the first and twentieth of every month, hockey or figure-skating on the telly when you got back from work, 'The Voice of America' after midnight, three and a half days off in a row if a public holiday happened to fall on a Friday, staying up to the small hours to read a carbon copy of *The Gulag Archipelago* and then doing your quarterly accounts the next morning, a bottle of Camus cognac and a packet of JPS ciggies from the Beriozka, a twin-deck cassette recorder with auto-reverse you bought off a merchant seaman, a trip to Bulgaria, dinner in the restaurant of the Central House of Writers with a general's daughter, a 'no. 7' car without having to wait in the queue, and an order for a three-roomed co-operative flat in your pocket.[50]

Indifference to possessions had deep roots in the Soviet intelligentsia generally, but was particularly entrenched in Leningrad, an ascetic place even before 1917. As George Dobson observed in 1910:

> Russian social life has hitherto been free and unconventional inversely to its want of political liberty. [. . .] One can still go to a theatre in St Petersburg in a morning coat or any other decent attire and present tickets for boxes or stalls without any risk of being turned away at the doors. And if you are invited to an ordinary dinner and omit to put on evening dress, your host and hostess, as well as any other guests, will probably be all the more pleased with you on that very account.[51]

Leningrad intellectuals were well aware of this history, and regarded dressing up with easily as much derision as their predecessors half a century earlier. Never touching a razor, never wearing a suit or tie, missing your own wedding and making your relationship legal only years later – all were calculated gestures of contempt for convention.[52]

An exception to the generally puritanical attitude to accumulating things was made for books, of which intellectuals worth the name were supposed to have large numbers. These were as subject to deficit as the most rarefied foreign *schmutter*. The city's leading outlets, the Writers' Bookshop on Nevsky,

5.6 The back corridor in the Writers' Bookshop, with icons of some famous visitors and patrons, March 2012 (before the redecoration of the shop later that year).

Akademkniga, and the House of Books, had little to offer the casual buyer, though those with accreditation (writers and academics particularly) were able to get priority access to some books and journals. Whichever way, the central bookshops were imposing places to visit, and those who dropped in had the possibility of seeing some local notability come through, or sometimes, of attending a reading.

For serious book-buyers, though, the likeliest spots were the different second-hand or antiquarian shops (*bukinisticheskie magaziny*), which charged high prices, but where treasures could often be found.[53] 'Subscription Editions', on Liteinyi, was where you tried to sign on for collected works (a prestigious acquisition even if you never opened them). As a former director remembered: 'There's a green at the back, and people would queue up for 2–3 days at a time, light bonfires to keep warm. They'd buy anything – the *Great Soviet Encyclopedia*, the *World Literature* series. There were huge queues for Esenin.'[54] Black-market suppliers, of whom there were many, liked to hang round the courtyards behind the Writers' Bookshop, though there was also a much larger market on the fringes of the city.[55]

The possession of sound recordings was also acceptable in circles where other types of acquisition were frowned on. While recordings of classical music were cheap and widely available through the Melodiya shops, forays into adventurous jazz or rock usually meant recourse to unofficial supply lines. State-sponsored recordings of such material were chronically scarce, so most people listened to *magnitizdat* bootleg tapes on home recorders, or to 'rock on the bones', unofficial recordings on X-ray slides. Western records on the black market were beyond the reach of many.[56] Even the austere Viktor Krivulin owned, in the mid-1980s, a modern, high-quality Japanese cassette recorder.[57]

But most Leningraders were less concerned by the disdain of the bohemian underground than they were by explicit perceptions about what was done and not done. While deeming preoccupation with possessions 'petit-bourgeois', late Soviet culture at the same time accorded great weight to personal appearance.[58] Cartoons in the 'wall newspapers' of the Kirov Factory mercilessly mocked those who were eccentric of dress and hairstyle.

'You didn't wear trousers back then, and wearing a dress over your bare body wasn't done either, and no one would have worn anything clinging, so they used to sell these things called *kombinatsii*', a woman born in 1950 remembered of her youth.[59] (A *kombinatsiya* was a slip or a petticoat, which skimmed over more unmentionable undergarments.)[60]

At the same time, by the 1960s, Leningrad culture was beginning to develop the instability of taste characteristic of late modern fashion regimes. The very mockery of clothes such as drainpipe jeans bespoke their popularity. The narrator of the Strugatsky Brothers' fantasy *Monday Begins on Saturday* (1965), visiting a small northern town, was greeted by screeches of *stilyaga*, and after

5.7 'Disgraceful!! Disgraceful!!', from the wall newspaper of the Kirov Factory, 1960s. A young man who regularly skips work is shown wearing drainpipe jeans and other modish clothes.

the inhabitants had stared pointedly at his jeans, 'was glad that I had a work-related smut on my backside – the previous day I'd very luckily sat down on a syringe of lubricant oil'.[61] In the city itself, the word *stilyaga* was rather passé – the trend having lost its currency in the late 1950s.[62] But Western goods, films, and magazines – not to speak of actual Westerners – continued to set the standards of taste. As in contemporary America and Britain, a mania for artificial fibres took hold in the 1960s. 'There was this shop called *Sintetika* on Novoizmailovsky prospekt, people used to start queuing there at 6 in the morning. "*Sintetika*" sounded something like, well, "Mercedes 500", back then. Wow, you're in synthetics today! Underwear made of synthetics! That was really something.'[63]

But a very different ethos of dress – jeans and mini-skirts (alternatively, maxi-skirts) – was becoming the rule among some younger Leningraders. Andrei Lebedev, writing in 2009, was to recall the huge impact of three Georgian students at the Leningrad Railway Institute who arrived 'all done up in American jeans and suede jackets, Apache style, with fringing across the backs'.[64] A 1970s dandy, Mikhail Fainshtein, recalled, 'We took a great deal of care over how we looked, or I did, anyway. We wore grey suede "Playboy" boots, real US button-down shirts with a loop at the back, and Levi-Strauss jeans. I liked that look back then. I sewed my own caps, and for other people as well, not just me.'[65]

As was the case all over Eastern Europe, jeans were the single most important status item in the increasingly Westernised youth culture of the time.[66] They began as a signifier of 'alternative' affinities, much favoured by bohemian artists and Leningrad's dissident or semi-dissident elite. But by the late 1970s, people holding official Komsomol positions had started to don them as well.[67] Even the put-upon hero in Mikhail Veller's *The Purse* (1983) hankered for them. 'It seemed absurd, here he was, 42 years old, and never once worn jeans. And he had the right legs for them too. But they cost a lot – 200 roubles.'[68] This was double the average wage, and five times the official monthly Soviet student grant, making jeans a luxury.

However, the trend spread, as indicated even in the censored medium of film. Il'ya Averbakh's *The Private Life of Valentin Kuzyaev* (1966) showed young women in pencil skirts, hairy pea coats, and headscarves, and young men in woollen trousers under their shapeless jumpers. Fourteen years later, almost all the main characters in Averbakh's *Voice* were got up in jeans and denim jackets. The only item with an unassailable place in the Leningrad wardrobe was the mackintosh.

As the influence of Western casual clothes widened (aided by increasing numbers of foreign students and tourists), coverage of fashion in the Soviet press seemed increasingly out-of-touch. Typical was a double-page spread of short skirts, high heels, and a fluorescent trouser suit in a 1970 issue of *Smena*, the Komsomol newspaper.[69] No wonder that more relaxed clothes were preferred by large numbers of young people.

Although fashion was beginning to be identified with self-assertion, 'looking different', social norms – including those in bohemian circles – were nearly as inflexible as the official perceptions of decency. The disapproving term *samopal* was applied to 'anything home-made or without a prestigious brand-name'.[70] Having the 'right' effect depended on wearing whatever the latest craze happened to be – a light nylon raincoat called a *bolon'ka* in the 1960s; in the late 1970s mini-skirts, platform boots, and tan tights.[71] Often the original inspiration was Western fashion, but foreign students were likely to find that the more unfamiliar trends – the vintage look of the late 1970s and early 1980s in particular – attracted disapproval, as expressed in the ultimate insult, 'Did you buy that here?'[72]

One could not wear any old thing, but the shops were not much help. Just like food, consumer goods had to be ingeniously 'acquired', rather than simply purchased. Certainly, the city had quite a variety of stores, some with a resplendent

5.8 Visitors to the Kirov Museum, dressed in their best, *c.* 1972.

past: Gostinyi dvor on Nevsky, and several less lustrous covered bazaars; Russia's oldest shopping arcade, Passazh; and The House of Leningrad Trade, built as a super-modern steel and concrete department store in the early twentieth century (from 1961 it specialised in items for children).[73] The Soviet period had added some notable retail buildings also, including 'trading co-operatives' (in Narvsky district, for example), and department stores, such as the Frunzensky on International'nyi prospekt (now Moskovsky prospekt), constructed in 1934–38.[74] There was also a variety of outlets in 1960s-internationalist style, known by the generic nickname *steklyashka* (glass box).[75]

Whatever the type of shop, the interiors were functional: plywood and strip lighting were the norm.[76] Even the pre-revolutionary shops had been thoroughly Sovietised inside. Gostinyi dvor was originally an arcade of little individual shops (this layout can still be seen in the covered market on Raz"ezzhaya ulitsa). Remodelling between 1955 and 1967 transformed it into a semblance of a modern department store. As a result, the different sections were strung out along long, cavernous corridors, though at least there was ample room for the queues that built up whenever something inviting was on sale.[77]

There were also far more shoppers than the builders of pre-revolutionary stores, and indeed Soviet stores, had anticipated, making conditions very

5.9 The Gostinyi dvor in the run-up to New Year, 1975.

uncomfortable. A woman who worked in the first-aid section of the House of Leningrad Trade in the 1970s and 1980s remembered: 'The building was in very bad condition. On the top floor there was a café, in summer it would be like a skillet. The floor was just burning, imagine! The roof would get red hot – it was really awful. [. . .] Queues everywhere [. . .] they'd be standing in queues and someone would faint, even start dying . . . anything you like.' As an employee of the store, she had 'inside track' advantages, but ordinary shoppers made their resentment of this felt. 'So the girls let me out of one section into another, I crawled under [the partition], but when I was carrying out the winter coat I wanted, someone grabbed me by the bosoms [. . .] "You weren't standing in that line!" '[78]

'Getting hold of things' could be a test of physical endurance. But creative thinking was also needed:

> Well, as for clothes, it was a question of what you could buy, what you could get hold of. Mainly we bought fabrics and got them made up, there wasn't

> anything else. [. . .] All kinds of crêpe-de-chine, georgette, things like that. I'd buy them and then when I went back home for a holiday, I had this dressmaker there, she'd make them up for me.[79]

Another woman remembered, 'My mother had a dressmaker, all her life, back to whenever, as they say. She always had her coats made, they'd buy coats for me, but Mama had all hers made up: autumn ones, winter ones, sometimes they'd make things over, with fur and stuff. [. . .] She [the dressmaker] charged a packet, but people thought a lot of her, like you would of some designer these days. She made all her patterns herself.'[80]

A less respectable form of self-reliance was represented by purchases 'on the left', that is, buying something outside the state system. Private transactions of this kind were regarded as illegal 'speculation' in Soviet law. At the same time, sales assistants were allowed to buy, quite officially, a limited number of *defitsitnye* goods before these went on sale to the public: for example, blouses in the Gostinyi dvor, or boxed sets of make-up in a central city chemist's shop.[81] It was common for them to pass these on, at a consideration, to favoured customers. But this was only one source of supply. Whether the rumours of underground millionaires that circulated in the 1970s and early 1980s had foundation is hard to say.[82] At all events, Leningrad was certainly notable for large numbers of *fartsovshchiki* (dealers in hard currency and Western goods). The humorous writer Mikhail Veller insisted that the first of these individuals – a certain Fima Bleischitz – had begun his work in 1957.[83] Be that as it may, the US journalist Ray Pierre Corsini certainly remembered being approached by such a person in the early 1960s:

> Footsore, we sat down to rest on a bench near the Kazan Cathedral. Before long, a gangling youth in a leather jacket came striding down the quiet street. He slowed down as he approached us and glanced around as if to make certain no one else was near. Then, in schoolboy English he asked if we could sell him a fountain pen. Andy happened to have an extra one with him and handed it to the young man. When he learned it was a gift, he stammered his thanks. Emboldened, he leaned closer and asked Andy if he had a suit to sell. He would pay well for it, as much as 900 roubles. When asked how he could afford that much, he replied: 'I have friends – they can pay.'

At this point, seeing two men in uniform approach, the youth 'scurried off as fast as his legs could carry him'.[84] In the 1980s, *fartsovshchiki* were recognisable, even before they accosted you, by their affectation of sunglasses, whatever the weather, always with the designer label still neatly stuck to one lens, and by their brash body language.[85]

Statistics assembled by the city-wide Komsomol militias indicated that in 1977, 1503 people across the city were placed under citizen's arrest for 'pestering foreigners', and 4706 for 'selling on the street in unauthorised places'.[86] An indication of priorities in social control, the figures do also point to a lively black market. *Fartsovshchiki* might either sell on directly, or act as middlemen for others – from the small fry who hung round in the shadows of Gostinyi dvor to the underground businessmen and businesswomen who operated from their own well-stocked apartments.[87] Such activities were stigmatised – among ordinary Leningraders, as well as in the Soviet press – but people did not necessarily buy directly: 'commodity laundering' through friendship chains was common.[88]

Alongside tourists, and of course sailors, another source of supply was soldiers on foreign postings. Second World War 'trophy goods' were often stockpiled for many decades, but later generations of soldiers were unofficial bagmen too – such as a man sent to Cuba in 1962, who came back spared a war and with contraband jeans for his girlfriend in his luggage.[89] With larger numbers of Soviet citizens visiting the West as tourists, such channels of supply broadened.[90] There was an expectation that anyone lucky enough to go abroad should share out their good fortune when they got back.

> There was this dreadful system in operation back then: when you arrived back from somewhere abroad, you had to bring presents for your relations [. . .] It was an absolute must. Going abroad was such a rarity, you just had to bring back presents. I remember my brother getting the huff. I'd got back and given him a packet of needles, for a sewing machine, you see, yes. And he gets all upset and says, 'And there's me with nothing to wear . . .'[91]

Those who actually got the chance to earn money abroad sometimes ended up with credits in the so-called 'certificate rouble' shops, which sold scarce consumer items for prices fixed by the state. Merchant seamen, for example, could use the 'Albatross' store down by the docks.[92] Shopping on the sly in one of the *beryozka* stores for visiting foreigners – or getting a foreign friend to take one there – was another way of obtaining access to non-Soviet goods.[93]

The *beryozka* showed how foreign goods were starting to be tacitly endorsed in official culture too – a development which trade exhibitions also fostered. In 1968, an exhibition of foreign-produced fish produce under the unwieldy name *Inrybprom* bowled over locals with its glossy display values: 'People fought over the freebie carrier bags.' At the Admiralty Wharves, a number from a sketch featured a parody of a song from El'dar Ryazanov's hit film *Carnival Night* (1956):

> If you're feeling blue when you go on your daily mission,
> If even the Hermitage offers you no cheer,

Be sure to rush along to *Inrybprom* exhibition,
Where there's a real scrum around the booths with souvenirs . . .[94]

Attempts were made to channel some of the lustre of the exotic into local products. In the early 1960s, a Russian-American boot and galosh factory was set up on Obvodnyi Canal (a kind of local dress-rehearsal for the Pepsi-Cola and Philip Morris 'Soyuz Apollon' cigarette franchises of the 1970s).[95] However, while Pepsi made as much of a hit in Leningrad as anywhere else (though at first tasting to the local palate like 'cough mixture', it became a classic example of a deficit item, to be saved for mixing with vodka on high days and holidays),[96] the footwear was to languish in obscurity. In the world of clothes, there was no substitute for the 'real thing', and Soviet-made jeans had no cachet. 'After we got friendly with India, you couldn't shift them. Suddenly . . . well, to begin with there weren't many around, but later on every shop had them just lying there . . .'[97]

An acceptable compromise was goods from socialist countries: less prestigious than those from the West, but also cheaper and much more freely available. 'You could get really nice viscose things from the GDR, only 12.50 roubles, I can remember the price exactly. Mum gave me a slip made of that for my school graduation [. . .] They always had lace on [. . .] lots of it too, and they were nice colours.'[98] There was a lively second-hand trade in such clothes as well, which might be sold in the huge 'commission store' in Apraksin dvor, the covered market just along from Gostinyi.[99] Also very popular were cosmetics: Polish and Hungarian shampoos, Bulgarian toothpaste, and so forth, which were considered superior to their Soviet equivalents.[100]

Among Soviet goods, however, those made in Leningrad were considered to be above average quality, and developed their own loyal market.[101] Packaging played on this by developing a distinctive 'Leningrad style', which often used the city's famous landmarks (particularly the Admiralty) to aid 'brand recognition'.[102] Local newspapers would excitedly report favourable reactions to Leningrad-made items abroad (or in the socialist countries, at any rate). There was also local gossip about foreigners who marvelled at the quality of the local cosmetics.[103]

These stories have the ring of immortal provincial myth (compare the tales told round this time about how Dubliners, no, *Parisians*, liked to come to Cork to do their shopping). But some items did have genuine prestige among Leningraders themselves. Among the leading shops in the city were the Leningrad House of Models, on Nevsky, and the Leningrad House of Fashion, on Petrograd Side, opened in 1968.[104] The *atel'e* (workshops producing clothes to order) attached to these places were the most prestigious venues for fashion in the city. While there were no official restrictions on who could use them, ordering clothes took money, organisation (there were long waiting lists), and

5.10 The director Aleksei German and stars from *Twenty Days Without War*, 1976. Note the fashionable sheepskin coats. Photographed by Galina Lisyutich.

a certain sense of entitlement. Above all it was people professionally required to dress well – actors and variety stars – who prevailed.[105]

A certain elegance lived on.[106] As Tat'yana Derviz remembered, in the pre-war years, 'everyone wore hats – from the age of eight to eighty. Even women working at pavement stalls, even down-and-outs [. . .] It was just about the only thing that you could get without trouble. There were even special shops.'[107] Viktor Sokolov's film *A Day of Sunshine and Rain* (1967) showed the protagonist's sister, a petite and attractive Bardot blonde, trying on elegant hats in the Frunze Department Store.[108] By the mid-1970s, younger people had stopped wearing hats – at any rate in the summer – but members of the older generation still favoured them. Even in the early twenty-first century, ladies of a certain age could still be seen wearing velvet coal-scuttles and cashmere mixing bowls.[109]

Presenting a decent face to the world mattered. In order to get hold of something better than normal, people thought up all kinds of ruses. One strategy was to sign up for a marriage slot at the registry office, whether or not you were actually engaged, and then use the coupons given out to buy special clothes in the bridal wear department. 'I signed up three times without knowing

5.11 Petersburgers wearing hats, 2012.

who I was marrying,' one woman born in the 1960s recalled. 'People used to help each other out, someone from your year group would say, "There's this boy in our group needs some shoes. Fancy a nice pair of shoes yourself?" And I'd have a look and decide they would suit me. And we'd go along and get signed up, and then take the coupons along . . .'[110]

However Leningrad shoppers grumbled about their lot, those with long memories realised more was available in the 1960s, 1970s, and 1980s than at any previous period in Soviet history. A woman born in 1950 recalled that in the 1960s, people started to wash their hair with shampoo, rather than soft soap, though you often had to queue. 'And then the boom started, all those Polish shops, the famous ones, that "Miraculem" and so on. [. . .] "Polleno" was another one that was usually on sale, quite small bottles, in the special shops, there was one on Liteinyi, for instance.'[111]

By the late 1970s, shopping was becoming an increasing preoccupation, and humorous morality tales portrayed the results. Boris Vakhtin's *The Sheepskin* (1979), updating Gogol's *The Overcoat*, showed a nondescript official in the censorship, obsessed with a beautiful young artist, resorting to the black market for a coat to find favour in her eyes.[112] In Veller's *The Purse* (1983), a similar downtrodden protagonist, suddenly enriched by a magic purse, overcame his scruples and began to lash out:

> In Gostinyi he slipped on the stairs, and the phrase, 'the slippery slope' started to spin round in his head, and he couldn't turn it off when he was paying at the cash-desk for a coffee-coloured Hungarian jacket, an Icelandic sweater, also in coffee-coloured wool, a precocious-looking doll with the muscles of a handball player, when he was taking plastic bags with 'Montana' on from the hands of the impudently deferential gypsies on Kuznechnyi market and filling them with butter-soft pears, transparently ripe grapes, fragrant lime-blossom honey of a colour to put topaz in the shade, when he did a little distracted tap-dance in the wine and spirits shop as he was buying vintage cognac and champagne ('the lad's on a razzle – just back from a stint up north', came the approving murmur behind him), and when he blew the last 47 roubles, including 3.20 of his very own, on an idiotic so-called crystal vase in an antique shop. [. . .] He also bought ten pairs of socks and the same number of hankies, having decided that it was time to cut down on the washing. He wanted a metal watch with a bracelet too, but the money had run out.[113]

Few Leningraders, even those 'back from a stint up north' (that is, having spent some months earning the inflated wage packets that were paid to those working in the Arctic), could actually have afforded such a remarkable binge. But Veller's story captured the furtive appeal of spending in a culture that was now only superficially puritanical, yet where having enough underwear might seem as luxurious a dream as fine clothes or top-of-the-range cognac.

## 'Visiting Cards' and Savage Capitalism

Within a few years, shopping stopped seeming such an innocent pleasure. Sergei Dovlatov's story-cycle *The Suitcase* (1986) was a revision of 1970s culture from the perspective of an émigré who no longer had any practical use for the things that had once seemed so valuable – including even a pair of shoes filched from the Chairman of Lensovet. What was more, the process of devaluation was, Dovlatov showed, intrinsic to the whole system of trading relations in Soviet society. In the opening story, 'Finnish Crepe Socks', a money-making enterprise to sell fashionable nylon hose illegally on the streets was disrupted overnight when Soviet-produced ones became available. The organisers were left with hundreds of unwanted synthetics on their hands.[114] Rather than a means to human dignity, consumption was the opposite – the ideal being a place, such as America, where one would no longer have to worry about everyday things.

Dovlatov's pioneering mixture of nostalgia and disgust did not resonate in his home country immediately. The shopping bonanza went on. A discussion about city preservation in 1988 provoked the editor of *Leningradskaya pravda* to suggest that one of Leningrad's problems was the sheer dearth of shops – people had to visit Nevsky to buy almost everything.[115] The promotion of small businesses in the form of 'co-operatives' (which could be set up with support from the Komsomol) altered this profile, with new retail outlets springing up in kiosks, conventional shops, and corners of state-owned workplaces.[116] They were distinguished by their unpredictable stocks of objects – umbrellas, key-rings, and T-shirts, say – and also by their outlandish names.[117]

But as shopping for desirables had become easier, so essentials were ever harder to get hold of. The combination of increased demand and deficient supply generated ever more critical shortages. At the start of 1990, the city administration introduced ration cards (euphemistically described as 'visiting

5.12 The co-operative store 'Antaeus', 1991.

cards'), for the first time since 1947. As a preliminary measure, shoppers were required to show their passports in order to buy a range of foodstuffs and consumer goods, including meat.[118]

Still, Leningraders were in a relatively advantageous position: many provincial towns had been exposed to rationing a year and more earlier.[119] But rations were seen as a particular affront to their dignity. In January 1990, *Vechernii Leningrad* reported that an employee of the Russian Museum who happened to have forgotten his passport on the day the new rule was introduced had been unable to persuade the assistants to serve him on the basis of his work pass. 'Where does it say that the Russian Museum is in Leningrad?' they demanded.[120] The story was an axiomatic representation of city identity in conflict with locality-blind officialdom.

Restrictions became ever tighter: in June 1990, alcohol and sugar started to be available on coupons only and sausage, butter, eggs, flour and macaroni were added on 1 December that year. Talk of price rises, as well as dwindling supplies and rising demand from people travelling in to the city to buy food, fuelled panic buying. Some people organised raids on local collective farm fields. While in many cities production on allotments offset shortages, the Leningrad tradition of using these mainly as places for relaxation meant that city-dwellers were badly prepared to withstand shortages. On the whole, it was workplaces that filled the gaps. Institutes might dispatch students to fetch in vegetables from a distribution centre (*ovoshchnaya baza*), or arrange mass deliveries of scarce products.[121] The cream of Leningrad's population mucked in along with the rest. When the Composers' Union organised deliveries of *spageti* (sic: this sounded more elegant than 'noodles' or 'macaroni'), the city's leading singers flocked to unload, basses on top and tenors below (inverting the standard choral line-up). When a consignment of ox liver arrived, these delicate individuals hacked it into portions themselves.[122] Among those without access to such arrangements, things were naturally a lot worse. In March 1990, it was estimated that Leningrad contained over 150,000 families living below the breadline.[123]

An inevitable result of the introduction of coupons was to make informal market relations still more important. With some forms of private trading licit, the grey economy was near-impossible to regulate.[124] Non-monetary exchanges became entrenched. Vodka in particular (sometimes jokingly known as 'liquid currency') was a vital bargaining counter. Most workmen expected to be paid or part-paid in this.[125] During democratisation, officials with 'food power' acquired electoral capital. In one academic institution, the winning candidate for the rectorship was someone who had managed to wangle the staff an enhanced meat supply.[126]

Consumer goods were also subject to severe shortages – in particular, cigarettes. For those with the money, Marlboro at 25 roubles a packet (about a quarter the average wage at the time) were freely available, but otherwise getting something to smoke meant standing for many hours in line. Ordinary Russian cigarettes were sold on the black market for up to ten times the state price. The root cause of the problem was a fall in state production, but trading 'on the left' added to the problems. The local police newspaper reported in September 1990 that there had been cases of shop assistants and managers secreting thousands of packets for private sale.[127]

While 'speculation' universally annoyed buyers, the background of political optimism meant that the shortages were at first treated with a degree of understanding. A humorous piece on queuing published in March 1991 included mock-academic comments from a sociologist (on queuing as a leisure activity), a doctor (who referred to 'the queue syndrome'), and so on.[128] People displayed capacity for flexible thinking too. As crisis hit the city's enterprises, factory administrations started to improvise, swapping metal for sugar, TVs for meat.[129]

But the difficult winter of 1991–92, when shortages were everywhere, led to a lowering of spirits. One local paper's New Year vox-pop captured the grim mood. 'There's no feeling of joy at all. You want to weep when you go round the shops. There's been no sausage to buy for 3 months. No meat, no eggs.' One man had been reduced to tins of 'The Tourist's Breakfast' (an even less interesting version of luncheon meat) as a purchase for the party table. By no means everyone could afford the traditional champagne.[130] Even some of the optimistic reactions were hardly encouraging. Ol'ga Sergeevna, a pensioner, reported on 4 January that she had waited 'only ten minutes for bread, I've known it take several hours'. People's misery was redoubled by price liberalisation. In August 1991, a kilo of meat was 35 roubles, and a packet of biscuits 22 roubles. By the start of January 1992, a kilo of curd cheese even in state shops was costing 40 roubles (nearly half the average wage). It had become a treat, rather than a staple.[131]

By an unfortunate historical irony, the food crisis coincided with the fiftieth anniversary of the worst winter of the Blockade. While the shortages certainly did not bear comparison, life was tougher than it had been for decades. Some people spent most of the time living on tea and bread.[132] In the following months, prices rose even more sharply. By the middle of 1992, beef had reached 85–90 roubles a kilo, cheese 100–160 roubles, butter 170–180 roubles, sugar 60–70. A doctor's monthly pay was worth precisely 7 kilos of beef as priced by the collective farm market. Petrol was 6–7 roubles a litre at free prices.[133] In August 1992, grants were introduced for children's clothes, but in order to buy most items, people had to rely on their own resources.[134] This situation persisted in the following years. In January 1995, a report in *Nevskoe vremya* recorded that food had recently increased in price by up to 50 per cent, and that shops still selling at the old prices were besieged by queues. Wages were still not keeping up.[135]

The extremity of the situation led to a re-examination of the traditional Soviet view that voluntary work was 'bourgeois' and politically subversive. From 1989, charitable organisations such as 'Leningrad' began to set up soup kitchens for those struggling to cope, particularly pensioners. 'Humanitarian aid' was also dispatched by foreign agencies.[136] However, the latter became the source of conflict, not just because people complained that distribution was being carried out in a murky, unfair way, but because there were rumours that stale and sub-quality food was being dumped – 'dog sausage', for instance.[137] In any case taking hand-outs, particularly from Germany, was an insult to pride.

With prices in official shops spiralling out of reach, street trading – already mushrooming during the late 1980s as police control subsided – started to function on an epic scale. Traders set up benches on the pavement, held goods in their hands, or balanced a few Western cans on a wall; open spaces, particularly around stations, sprouted with kiosks; entire areas of the city became flea markets (*tolkuchki*):

> On our street, Bukharestskaya, there were all these pavilions, pavilions with food for sale. Everyone's grabbing something, you can't work out what anything costs. And I remember I was going past one day and I thought, 'Hum, need some more cooking oil.' But then I thought, 'Hell, they're not going to run out, are they? I'll buy it tomorrow or the day after.' And exactly a day later, that oil had reached a price when I realised I couldn't buy it anyway.[138]

One of the most notorious areas for informal trade was the Haymarket, already a place of low repute in Dostoevsky's day, and formidably seedy in the Soviet era too. Now, the area pullulated with people, 'some holding up goods for sale, some selling straight from cars or folding stalls, or out of cardboard boxes'.[139] Another phenomenon of the times was Apraksin dvor. 'Aprashka', as it was popularly known, went back to the mid-eighteenth century, but had been totally rebuilt after a fire in 1863. By the late Soviet period, it was a huddle of buildings of diverse dates, mainly dating to the 1870s and 1880s, but including some structures built during the Soviet period. Only partly used for retail in the Soviet period, the site also accommodated warehouses and even living space.[140] In late 1991, perhaps because of Aprashka's established links with the 'commission' trade, it was one of the places used for the resale of goods that had been confiscated from speculators.[141]

By 1992, Aprashka had become a regular market, so much in demand that the organisers were able to charge both traders and customers for entry – there was even a lively secondary market for trader tickets. Already the place was acquiring an evil reputation – allegedly it was not just a favourite haunt for pickpockets, but a positive training ground for them.[142] In 1995, the place received a makeover from the city authorities: paths were tarmacked, and 'frightful-looking kiosks' removed, though the criminal presence proved harder to eradicate.[143] At this period, the place was not only massively popular with customers (as one Petersburger commented, 'we'd buy all kinds of stuff in "Aprashkin [sic] dvor", as we called it, not in shops'),[144] but a source of affection and even pride to the city elite. A journalist expatiated, 'How Lily Row recalls our life in all its current chaos, ugliness, and rich variety!' In 1995, the director of the Piter commercial centre described it as equal to shopping centres in many European cities.[145] Alongside the stalls as such, specialist shops began to appear. For instance, Kantus music shop (founded in 1997) had a line in musical instruments and accessories, synthesisers, light and sound systems, as well as claiming to be the oldest and largest shop selling second-hand musical instruments on commission in the country.

Some of the customers at markets of this kind were starting to generate a new kind of 'alternative' style. Self-styled 'punks', for example, were recognisable not just by their back-combed and lacquered hair, but also by the deliberately provocative clothes they adopted, which ran roughshod over the inflexible Soviet perceptions of decency: 'old clothes of bizarre colours and styles with a powerful dash of provincial chic'.[146] It could hardly have been further from traditional concepts of Leningrad elegance.[147]

Selling at the market was generally held to be dominated by organised crime. Valery Kalugin's *The Markets of Petersburg* (2000) claimed that mafias had taken over all the city markets in the early 1990s, and that some were being used to sell drugs alongside fruit and vegetables. While some had been cleaned up later in the decade (for instance, Mal'tsevsky), others had not: ulitsa Dybenko ('Dyby') had the largest narcotics turnover in Europe. Bribery, armed robbery, and a lively trade in fakes were just some of the other activities that were being perpetrated energetically.[148] Anxiety about counterfeit goods spread round the city. Newspaper reports recorded that, as well as the dodgy jeans, trash handbags, and 'French perfume' from just round the corner that you might find in any street market, there were underground industries for canned beer and vodka, and a roaring trade in illegal caviar. Some of the things sold were not just of poor quality, but actively revolting – bottles of liquor with insect remains in them, for instance.[149]

At the same time, it was not just professional law-breakers who benefited from the new market relations. Importing CDs by the suitcase for resale enabled one young academic to make enough money to buy a flat, and for his father to retire early.[150] Large swathes of the population were trading 'on the side' in this way.[151] Typical was the case of a schoolboy who, with two of his friends, acted as the middleman for sales of Chinese jeans, and quickly discovered that the outlying settlements round Leningrad were an excellent market: 'Out towards the country's better, 'cos there's more choice in town, and they'd come into Gatchina from the villages around. Stick out a mile, don't they? [. . .] And they'd be really grateful, if you were honest. They'd turn up a second time, a third time. "These are great trousers you sold me, look a treat, eh?" [. . .] I'd work weekends regular.'[152] 'I've got this mate from school,' an internet memoirist recalled in 2005, 'and he used to "speculate" in hard currency at the Haymarket. He made a packet by the standards back then, loooads a money. It was a crazy time, a joke really. A schoolboy of 11 or 12 [. . .] used to have sums in his pocket it'd have taken his parents months on end to earn.'[153] If for some the birth of 'savage capitalism' meant suddenly not being able to afford basic goods, for others it meant suddenly being able to afford expensive ones.[154]

The prices of imported goods were, compared with contemporary Western prices, reasonable. In July 1993, a large-screen Sony TV was priced at the equivalent of 3,150 dollars, video players at 210–350 dollars, US men's shoes at 30 dollars, and the wholesale price for butter was 80 cents a kilo, for condensed milk 15 cents a tin, for Dunhill cigarettes 70 cents, and Lucky Strike 55 cents.[155] However, with average monthly pay standing in low double figures by the dollar rate, a gulf opened up between those who had access to hard currency (those working for the new joint venture companies or abroad, those who were able to bring back foreign goods for sale, those could expect handouts from relatives and friends living abroad) and those without such opportunities and support.[156] The 'New Russian' plutocrats at one end of the system, and the desperate pensioners at the other, represented diametrically opposed results of market liberalisation, but the emphasis on them in jokes and gossip masked the complexity of the processes that were in train.[157]

## Select Goods and Prestige Shopping

The late 1990s saw a change of attitudes on the part of local administrators towards the improvised markets. The riot police, OMON, regularly raided, driving away sellers without permits.[158] The city administration began to see trading places of this kind as an embarrassment, expressing the quaint view that street markets were not 'European'.[159] The rows of kiosks round metro stations began to be demolished. In 2007 they disappeared from outside the Finland Station, and at around the same time they also vanished from the area round Udel'naya metro (though the enormous flea market nearby, with its defunct electrical goods and shrivelled acrylic sweaters set out on blankets edged by mud, continued to operate).[160] Now, the only markets left in most of the city were covered ones – the food 'bazaars'. Here, all looked much as it had in Soviet times, but the fruit was now more likely to come from the Canary Islands or Turkey than from the Caucasus or Central Asia.[161]

In 2002 an agency specialising in retail development declared, 'St Petersburg is way behind major European cities in terms of the number and quality of retail premises available.'[162] The following years saw everything possible done to make up this perceived deficiency. There was a boom in shopping centres and malls with a plastic-global look – not so much 'European', in fact, as American. A particularly controversial project was the replacement of an early twentieth-century building on Vladimirskaya ploshchad', in the heart of Dostoevsky's St Petersburg, by a multi-storey shopping centre with a retro-façade that faintly recalled the *style moderne* of the structure demolished to build it. While the shopping centre did have a local heritage – *passages* in the French style had been constructed from the mid-nineteenth century[163] – the new steel-and-glass arcades were nothing like their pre-revolutionary ancestors. The shops inside them also had the anonymity of such places worldwide.

Chain stores proliferated, not just in the centres but outside them too. On Nevsky prospekt clustered Hugo Boss, Benetton, Wolford, Zara, Mango, and Intimissimi. People shopped for food at supermarket chains such as Pyatyorochka, Dixi, Lenta, and Fresh, individual branches of which (with a blow-up Suchard Milka cow in mauve skewbald hanging from the ceiling, perhaps) were more different than the overall shop styles were from each other.[164] (An exception was the 'People's Store' chain, specialising in super-cheap staples such as herring, attracting the hatred of rivals and the disapproval of the city's administration.)[165]

Even the premier stores of the Soviet era had trouble surviving. DLT retained its former name, but ceased to specialise in children's goods and became a normal ('family') department store. Taken over by a Moscow company, in 2012 it reopened after a revamp that refashioned the modernist interior into glib, glittering international luxury, with nearly as many mannequins in designer wear as shoppers.[166] In 1994, a private company, 'Eliseev Stores', took over the site of the former 'Gastronom No. 1', and was assigned a fifty-year lease. While the interior began looking even more splendid after extensive restoration in 2001–3, trade was slack. Except in a cramped hall to the right of the main entrance, where tourists jostled to buy caviar, there were few customers. The contents of the shop – pyramids of fruit with crêpy skin, packets of Hungarian bacon, Estonian parmesan by the wrapped triangle – were far less inviting than those of the city's fancier supermarkets. The eventual outcome was a sad end to over a hundred years of history. In 2007, the company stopped paying the rent on the premises, and in 2009 the city administration had the contract wound up by writ. The company filed for bankruptcy in May 2010. The victors in the tender for the leasehold of the building, Paritet, announced in September that year that they planned to reopen the former Eliseev Stores: here would be a café and what business-speak described as a 'sales and tasting room for the vending of premium foodstuffs.'[167]

What this turned out to mean was an opulent grocery store managed by a former employee of Harrods Food Hall in London. Resplendently restored,

5.13 View through the window of the empty Eliseev Stores, 2010.

and with a gigantic palm as the showpiece, the shop had a 'Eurodeli' spread on show: Parma ham and jamón serrano, Manchego and Grana Padano cheese, *pièces montées* of pastel-coloured macaroons, tiers of sugared fruit pastels in clear plastic heart-shaped boxes. The fish section, once luscious, was reduced to sides of smoked salmon and tins of caviar. Elegantly anonymous, the goods looked straight out of Fortnums or Fauchon. Only the preponderance of pastries (the size, colours, and indeed prices recalling gifts from Fabergé) was a local touch. But the old Eliseev's had vanished as completely as the wafts of smoked ham; in fact, the shop smelled of nothing at all, not even coffee or croissants.[168]

The word 'premium' bandied about when the Eliseev's future was discussed acted as a sign of the times. The use of *otbornoe* ('select') and *elitnoe* ('elite') as adjectives of commendation had become ubiquitous. While the former word had a lengthy pedigree, the latter was new – the term *elita* in Soviet days often had an ironic resonance.[169] The effect could be absurd (compare such marketing terms, in the English-speaking world, as 'luxury bungalow'). To see a skinny and rigid carcase in the Kuznechnyi Market labelled 'Elite Rabbit' could only provoke a smile.[170]

Yet the efforts to ennoble shopping as an activity were not without results. New kiosks in the 'Petersburg style' (some with *style moderne* curves to replace Soviet-era functionalist angularity, others would-be neo-classical, with tiny pediments) appeared in many parts of the centre.[171]

For those who wanted to visit shops in order to gaze, as well as to buy, there were now many more venues to choose from. The shopping centres opening up everywhere in the 1990s and 2000s did not have marble floors and fountains, as the Petersburg malls of pre-revolutionary days had, but customers still flocked there.

Younger people, in particular, favoured places where there was a 'total shopping experience'. 'I like Okei, you can get everything there. From knickers to meat. I remember what it was like coming back from nursery school, you had to visit about five shops to get what you wanted, food, bread . . . And queue up in all of them too, of course,' a woman in her late thirties remembered in 2007.[172] Another woman, in her twenties, admitted that shopping was one of her favourite leisure activities. 'I like walking round the shops. We love going to Mega as well. There's an IKEA there. Me and my friend Lena, we like going to IKEA and just walking round. "Hey look, love, that's just amazing!" We'll put it all in our baskets, then take it out again and put something else in, then take

5.14 New-style kiosk, 2012.

that out, and so on.'[173] For the first time in recent history, browsing the shops was pleasurable. If you did actually want to buy something, the assistants were not necessarily much more helpful than in the past. But in some shops, at least, they were so polite as to be almost obsequious, and the open mockery and rank insults of the Soviet period had generally disappeared.[174]

To a foreigner, the main difference from major Western cities – aside from the perpetual shortage of small change[175] – was the unpredictability of what you could and could not get. A novelty shortbread box in the form of a kilt was no problem; candles, where not white and utilitarian, required a real search.[176] This situation had its own logic. Shop stocks were most abundant in the categories where scarcity had been most pressing in the Soviet past (food, clothes, and furniture). Household goods, on the other hand, had always been available. So, it was down to 'gift sets' of saucepans at hundreds of euro, or basic tinned enamel; and anything less than a presentation canteen of knives and forks meant a choice between IKEA and the *antikvariat*. The ubiquity of credit – shops even offered hire-purchase deals on kettles – made customers more likely to go for upmarket goods, especially since it was taken for granted that more expensive always meant better.[177]

5.15 Credit handbill stuck to a Prada poster, Vyborg Side, March 2012.

## The Perils of Infinite Choice

Petersburg shopping was not just a carnival of gratification and deferred gratification. Under the surface bubbled issues that were not reflected in the shiny chrome and plastic of the new retail outlets.

One issue was prices, which rose more steadily than during the 'shock therapy' of 1990–95, but unremittingly. This process was partly caused by the decline in food produced within the Russian Federation. The default of 1998 put the brakes on imports, and food production rose slightly in the following years.[178] As a result, prices fell back. However, the underlying trend was upward. The next financial crisis, in 2008, also meant that the most expensive goods disappeared – but even the cheap ones now stretched the budgets of many. Some prices were flattened by government subsidy (notably bread and processed grain, such as oats). But many others were not.[179] Medicines – a key sector of retailing, as was made clear by the ubiquity of pharmacies – were extortionately priced relative to local incomes, particularly given that people preferred branded pills to generics, even with aspirins.[180]

The situation was particularly tough on older people, whose pensions barely lifted them above the breadline. In 2008, *Izvestiya* published the diary of Lyudmila Kadilova, a pensioner from Oryol, describing how she kept body and soul together on just over 100 dollars a month. Sticking mainly to staples such as millet, buckwheat, and macaroni, with a dab of cheap margarine, she would occasionally 'lash out' on some fish ('not salmon, whose taste I've long forgotten, or even pollack at 102 roubles [3 dollars] a kilo, but a frozen lump of something shapeless, all heads and tails'). With resignation and humour, Kadilova described the stress of a minor house repair, which could leave you worrying over how to pay for food, and the terror of landing up in debt ('the young get cross with me, they say you should forget the household bills and just buy something for yourself').[181] Conditions were at least equally tough in St Petersburg.

For those who could afford more than the bare minimum, shopping might still not be a pleasure. 'I can see it all changing, all my favourite shops closing down, and God knows what replacing them,' lamented one sixty-something lady in 2009.[182] Even if one had no particular affection for the basic Soviet-era food store in one's own street, its closure would be an inconvenience, and the opening of three more modern ones half a kilometre away no consolation.[183] The sight of an empty bread shop was likely to cause particular distress.

The fact of choice was also bewildering. Leningraders abroad in the late Soviet era had found dealing with Western shops difficult, and even traumatic.[184] Soviet goods might be of variable quality, but people knew their way round the system. People often asked assistants to comment, and valued the disarming frankness that went with lack of responsibility for what you were selling. A salesperson might perfectly well say that sausage was only fit for one's dog, or reply 'Not very' when asked whether something was fresh.[185]

Now, people were left to themselves, only to find that, actually, standards were not always more reliable than before. Short-weight was common in supermarkets, as well as market stalls (in 2005, an investigative journalist discovered that a batch of strawberry punnets all labelled '700 g.' varied in actual weight by a range of half a kilo).[186] Almost every purchase of vegetables, wherever made, would contain a few duds (supermarket pick-and-choose allowed customers to select the best of what was available, but sometimes this had 'lain around'). In any row of grannies selling hand-picked vegetables from 'my allotment', there would likely be one who was actually recycling rejects from a store shelf.[187]

Unsettling also was the disappearance of the old relationships between staples and luxuries. For instance, farmed smoked salmon (traditionally something put on the party table) now cost less than curd cheese, which back in Soviet times had been an everyday foodstuff, considered especially nutritious for children.[188] While shortages were mostly a thing of the past (though the Ukrainian trade embargo in 2005 provoked a temporary salt-buying panic), food shopping still generated high anxiety.

There were also fears that things were less 'healthy' and 'tasty' than they had been in the past. Anxiety about 'fakes' had subsided (though in the world of consumer goods it lived on): instead, people were worried about whether products were 'natural'.[189] In the Soviet past, so people thought, 'chemicals' had not been added to foodstuffs. This was probably an illusion: industrial food production had been the dream of some planners even before 1917, and became the pride and joy of the Stalinist party leadership in the 1930s.[190] The Khrushchev era saw a vast expansion of the chemical industry, and 'natural flavourings' and preservatives were found in Soviet foodstuffs as well, for example bottled drinks, pork products, sweets and biscuits, and sauces.[191] But Soviet labels did not list ingredients, so additives simply did not 'exist' in the purchasers' eyes. For people who had always assumed they were eating traditionally made products, it was a huge shock to read on the back of a packet that the contents contained little other than flavouring, pigment, glucose, and water.[192] It was particularly hurtful when trusted brands, such as Metropole cakes, started using inferior ingredients (margarine instead of butter, for instance) – though the post-Soviet obsession with not eating too much fat gave manufacturers every reason to change the recipes.[193]

In any case, buyers were not always putting 'traditional' purchases into their shopping baskets. Official statistics from the 1990s and early 2000s gave a sense of shifting priorities. Production of most foodstuffs had dropped, but levels of tinned meat had held up better than average, and there were increased levels of production not just of vegetables (a large proportion of which now came from private market-gardens), but of tinned and frozen vegetables, dried whey, and 'liquid and paste milk products', as used for industrially manufactured fruit yoghurts and desserts.[194]

The mystique of Western goods had now worn off, and not just because those who had been sold fake German beer were unlikely to think it was up to much. In some cases things made outside Russia were in fact inferior – for instance, Russian-made 'bitter chocolate' had higher cocoa-butter levels than cheaper brands of imported dark chocolate – or simply not to the local taste. Particularly during and after the default crisis of August 1998, the saturation of the food market with imported goods inspired anxiety and irritation.[195] People were convinced that 'home-produced' meant better. They would select 'Vologda' butter, rather than 'Valio' (though in fact both were made by a Finnish company), and 'Baltika' and 'Nevskoe', rather than Czech or Danish, beer (though both the local breweries were foreign-owned).[196]

The latter two cases marked a trend for emphasising the local connections of food and drink. 'Lady Petersburger' (*Peterburzhenka*) meat products, such as smoked beef and salamis, carried the name in an 'old-fashioned' style surrounded by scrolling, and surmounted by a lady in eighteenth-century costume, with a coronet. The 'Sankt-Peterburg' brand of 'Russian Champagne' had the name in the old orthography on the neck label, and on the main label was an engraved portrait of Peter I in a cartouche, and a reproduction of an early print of the Lomonosov bridge. The Krupskaya confectionery factory, known in Soviet times as the best in the city, did not change its name, but began marketing 'historical' novelty selections, such as Bronze Horseman and Vernissage (with pictures by painters from the World of Art group, such as Alexandre Benois). Other brands harked back to Soviet styling – though usually taking as their models Soviet art in a general sense, rather than packaging as such. 'Retro' packaging sometimes emphasised local credentials too, as in a 2011 packet of 'Leningrad' pickled sprats, with the place name proudly displayed above a pictured trawler (though in fact the sprats were made in Kursk; see plate VIII).[197] Thus the Soviet-era conviction that things made in Piter were of higher than average quality persisted.[198]

Food shoppers' explicit preference for 'our' products impacted directly on producers. The Kirov Meat Conglomerate was able to reinvent itself, first as the then state-owned 'St Petersburg Meat Conglomerate', which launched new lines of 'delicatessen sausage' in 1992, and later as 'Samson'.[199] With consumer goods, on the other hand, the 'local' label had less appeal. The 'Bolshevik Woman' Factory, which began a push to produce attractive clothing for the new consumer in 1995, fell by the wayside.[200] Luxury designer wear sold much less well than in Moscow: a section of Gostinyi dvor selling brands such as Gucci, Dolce and Gabbana, and Christian Lacroix, had the atmosphere of an Egyptian tomb just before sealing of the main door.[201] But foreign goods at the lower end of the market were different. Priced higher than in their places of origin because of customs duty, clothes by companies such as Mango or Zara brought with them a bit of foreign elegance. They had a certain cachet which they might have lacked on the high streets of the cities where they originated.[202]

Yet survival shopping hung on. People still had the mindset of resplendent feasting on holidays, but plain living the rest of the time. A Western-style gourmet supermarket in the Vladimirsky Passage had 80-euro bottles of 'single estate' olive oil, and tanks of live fish, but also packets of porridge oats at a few cents, and 'early bird' discounts for pensioners. One might see a young couple in clothes from Emporio Armani poring over packets of macaroni: no, Russian-made was still best, it didn't fall apart in the boiling.[203] The supermarket in my own block would sell you a kilo pack of chicken hearts or a 'soup selection' of bones for about double the cost of a loaf of bread. But the patisserie next door (which gossip claimed was owned by the mistress of a famous businessman) was often visited (and not just at weekends) by people spending up to 50 dollars on a spread of pastries for their guests. Of course, there were all sorts of options between these two extremes, but the emphasis in most shops was on a modest daily repertoire: pickled fish and pickled vegetables, smoked meat and fish, sour milk products, *kasha*, chopped tomatoes and cucumbers, fried meat and potatoes. In ordinary shops (as opposed to 'elite' ones), produce was highly seasonal. On the tricky cusp of winter and spring, vegetables often looked distinctly wizened below their protective coats of dirt. But by May, 'new-harvest' onions, potatoes, and carrots were plentiful; the autumn was a firework display of apples and berries.

There was also a 'survival market' for consumer goods, as shown by the many *sekond khend* shops (some with the proud boast, 'from Europe', on their doors). Many people, particularly in the outer districts, still visited shops whose presentation of goods had not changed much since Soviet days, with shelves of dry goods, cooking oil, and alcohol stacked high behind tall counters.[204] Markets, with pyramids of fruit, slippers dangling from Formica panels, and scarves displayed on plastic heads, were still widespread in places like the Narva Gates or Lomonosovskaya.

Basic retailing had not completely vanished even from the centre. As late as the 2000s, Apraksin dvor was still a traditional arcade of small shops, selling everything from car parts to fishnet tights and bias binding. At the start of the decade, the city administration resolved to clear the place. The 'Agency for the Reconstruction and Development of Apraksin dvor', intended to turn the place into an expensive shopping centre, was set up in 2002.[205] Eventually, in 2008, the contract for the reconstruction of the territory was awarded to Oleg Deripaska's company, Glavstroi. Grandiose plans for the site were drawn up: huge new galleries and atriums were to be built, and the existing historic buildings mostly demolished. It was announced that the centre would house a

5.16 Booth in a market inside the former 'Sputnik' cinema, near Lomonovskaya metro, January 2012. On the third shelf down, the scarves are displayed on plastic heads.

shopping and culture centre on the model of London's Covent Garden.[206] An alternative site for the market – in the remote suburban location of prospekt Rustaveli – was selected.

But the pace of eviction stalled: the Apraksin traders simply refused to move.[207] As time passed, the financial, legal and preservationist obstacles to the reconstruction project mounted. In July 2010, the city administration's refusal to allow the developers to resubmit their proposal was endorsed by Gosstroinadzor (the State Building Supervision authority).[208] As of the autumn of that year, stalemate had been reached.

Aprashka was loathed by many ordinary Petersburgers, as well as officials. 'You can't possibly have a market like that, stuffed with filth, druggies, and fakes, on one of the main embankments in the city, right next to the Bol'shoi Dramatic Theatre,' protested one contributor to an online forum in November 2009. Another called it 'a shitheap' (*bardak*, literally, 'brothel').[209] The market became a focus for anti-'Asiatic' comment, both from officials and from rank-and-file city-dwellers. In October 2008, the Chairman of the Committee on

Investment and Financial Planning of St Petersburg, Roman Starovoit, asserted: 'Everyone knows that this area can't possibly be left as it is, right in the centre of the city. It's a real Shanghai.'[210] In similar vein, a forum participant saw it as an illustration of how 'Piter is turning into one big *aul*' (mountain village).[211] But in an increasingly expensive city, there was a crying need for cheap places. 'I like Aprashka. You can buy stuff at wholesale prices, and you don't have to go to the back end of beyond to do it,' was a typical view.[212]

Attempting to 'Europeanise' the city by making its shops more glossy, and therefore more expensive, was a viable policy only if earnings started to come closer to European norms. At the start of the 2010s, that objective still seemed a long way off. And in any case, Petersburg had always had its 'belly', its dodgy trading places and rackety markets. Given the new administration's obsession with 'tradition', there was a certain poetic justice in the endurance of Piter institutions that were much more genuine than the new 'Nevsky Passage' shopping centre, a set of rebuilt nineteenth-century houses, sprucely stuccoed and painted, with a multi-storey shopping centre, built to 'European' norms, secreted inside the walls.

5.17 Galleria shopping mall, 2011.

# 6

# Theatre Street

*How I loved the chill expanses*
*In empty foyers at the start of January,*
*When the soprano sobs, 'I am yours!'*
*And the sun strokes the velvet drapes.*
(Lev Losev)[1]

Intellectual Leningraders defined themselves not just by repudiating the interests of commerce and politics (customarily identified with Moscow), but by championing their city as a shrine of alternative values. While the 'Petersburg text' of literature and painting was crucial to this process, the city's status as 'cultural capital' had other foundations too. When the literary and artistic establishment retreated into provincialism in the 1930s, with the departure of most major figures to Moscow, the performing arts became the main area where Leningrad could still pretend to 'all-Soviet' status.[2] Some local stars were lured away – cases in point being Galina Ulanova, probably the finest ballerina of her generation, who worked at the Bol'shoi from 1944, or Dmitry Shostakovich, who after October 1941 was to pay only short visits to his native city. However, these figures – to a greater extent than departing writers such as Osip Mandelstam, Samuil Marshak, or Kornei Chukovsky – remained part of the local landscape. Ulanova was given the signal honour of a bust in the pantheon at the centre of the city's main Victory Park. Shostakovich's Leningrad connections were lovingly celebrated in a volume from a series honouring famous people's links with Leningrad.[3] Even if only occasionally present in the city where they were born, such famous artists still 'belonged' to it.

## The Territories of Technique

In the area of ballet particularly, Leningrad also preserved its own indigenous traditions. The Mariinsky Theatre, known after the Revolution by the unlovely acronym GATOB (the State Academic Theatre of Opera and Ballet), and honoured in 1935 with the name of the dead Party leader Sergei Kirov, housed one of the two premiere companies in the Soviet Union. At the ballet school attached to the company, Agrippina Vaganova (1879–1951) developed a pedagogical system which perpetuated principles of strict classicism into the late twentieth century and beyond.[4] In her honour, the school was renamed the Vaganova School in 1957. Vaganova's system was used in many other places as well, and during the war Leningraders evacuated to other Soviet cities, particularly Perm', took the principles of training with them. Later, the ballet school in Perm' was to supply some notable dancers to the home company, including Lyubov' Kunakova (at the Kirov from 1974) and Olga Chenchikova (who joined in 1977).[5] However, the majority of the Kirov's stars were home-trained, including a group that became world-famous after defection to the West: Rudolf Nureyev, Natalia Makarova, and Mikhail Baryshnikov.

Yet, for all the shock effects of these artists' 'treachery to the motherland' (as it was seen officially), the company proved resilient.[6] Even the tragic death of another Kirov star, Yury Solov'yov, who shot himself in 1977, did not change the character of this magnificent machine. Other stars (such as Gabriela Komleva, Natal'ya Bolshakova, Alla Osipenko, and Sergei Vikulov, and later Altynai Asylmuratova and Farukh Ruzimatov) took the place of those who

6.1 Rudolf Nureyev and Kaleriya Fedicheva in Vakhtang Chabukiani's ballet *Laurencia*, 1959.

6.2 Gabriela Komleva and Vadim Budarin performing *Swan Lake* in the hall of the Leningrad Philharmonic, 1970s.

departed. The glory of the Kirov was its depth of talent, right down to the corps de ballet.[7] Leningraders remained convinced – and not without reason – that they had the best classical ballet troupe in the world.

The colossal amounts expended on subsidies for culture brought certain expectations. In terms of official Party cultural planning, the arts, like museums, were supposed to contribute to the cause of 'Communist education'. It was expected that ideologically and socially relevant shows and films would have due weight. In 1971, for example, a report to the Regional Committee of the Communist Party praised an exhibition currently running in the city: 'A good many interesting sculptures and paintings of leading industrial workers are on show in the Russian Museum and at the "Our Contemporary" exhibition organised on the eve of the Twenty-Fourth Congress of the CPSU.' It went on to list other events planned for the time around the Congress, and stated that the writers and film-makers of Leningrad were in the process of responding positively to requests by leading workers for representations related to topics of interest to them (for example, the struggle with alcoholism).[8] This ritual articulation of the supposed wishes of the proletariat went back to the First Congress of Soviet Writers in 1934, and forty years on, it rang increasingly hollow. Nevertheless, repertoires and exhibition schedules, like the plans of publishing houses, were supposed to make a show of reflecting the supposed preoccupations of workers, and more to the point, the issues which Party congresses themselves proclaimed to be important.

Even such a traditional art form as the ballet was not immune from ideological pressure. In the 1920s, there had been campaigns to create 'drama-ballets' (*drambalety*) that would replace favourite fantasies about swan princesses and corsairs with narratives about the citizens of the new society.[9] From the mid-1930s, however, the stronghold of experimentalism was not GATOB but another theatre with an outlandish acronym, MALEGOT, or the Malyi [Small] State Theatre of Opera and Ballet, scene for the premiere of Shostakovich's *The Bright Stream* in 1935. In the post-war years, new ballets in the city's main house were more inclined to pay tribute to the glorious national past (as with Glière's *The Bronze Horseman* in 1949).[10]

But in the Khrushchev era, the Kirov once again went through a phase of introducing 'agitational' work to its audiences, prompted in part by official pressure.[11] In 1956 were the first performances of Leonid Yakobson and Aram Khachaturian's epic portrayal of slave rebellion, *Spartacus*; Yury Slonimsky and Igor' Bel'sky's *Shore of Hope* was staged in 1957, along with Yury Grigorovich's reworking of *The Stone Flower*. In 1961 came Bel'sky's version of a ballet set to Shostakovich's *Leningrad Symphony*, evoking the heroism of the defence of the city.

Yet such works never dominated the repertoire. Leonid Yakobson, the choreographer of *Spartacus*, who in 1971 revived his Stalin-era *Shurale* (1950), an Oriental spectacular with a didactic plot, became equally well-known for *Choreographic Miniatures* (1958). This anthology of mini-ballets included an appearance by a tragicomic Pierrot, a naturalistic drunk scene in which a young woman propositioned a returning sailor only for both simultaneously to realise that they had been boyfriend and girlfriend before he left, and a hearty rustic dance set to the fairground theme from Stravinsky's *Petrushka*. (This homage to an émigré composer with 'decadent' associations was a daring gesture for the time.) *Choreographic Miniatures* was framed by pas-de-deux, one in a rehearsal studio, and the other in a pavilion overlooking the Neva and the embankments of Vasilievsky Island – the nearest that a Soviet choreographer could get to writing works of pure dance.[12]

Yakobson's approach had something in common with what Frederick Ashton was doing at the same time in London – broad burlesque character dances alternating with sometimes epicene lyricism – a resemblance derived from the indebtedness of both to the Ballets Russes. But Yakobson employed more variation in pace, including bravura running lifts, and occasionally turned to a more sculptural treatment of the body, as in a pas-de-trois for three brawny male 'statues' in *Choreographic Miniatures*.[13] For the local public, too, his ballets were not only statuesque but racy, more adventurously erotic than the canons of Soviet art usually permitted.[14]

In the event, the association with the Kirov was to be short, and Yakobson's more adventurous works did not remain in repertoire. *Novellas of Love* (to music by Ravel), and a ballet based on the Leningrad playwright Evgeny Shvarts's fantasies, *Wonderland*, vanished from the Kirov altogether, leaving Prokofiev's *Cinderella* and *Romeo and Juliet* as the only ballets of recent date. It was the warhorses of the nineteenth-century repertoire – *Raimonda, La Bayadère*, and, of course, the famous trilogy scored by Tchaikovsky, *Swan Lake, Sleeping Beauty*, and *The Nutcracker* – which made up the Kirov's fighting battalions.

Like other classical art forms, ballets underwent adaptation in the Soviet period, sometimes of a wide-ranging kind. An example is Oleg Vinogradov's 1971 staging of *La Précaution inutile* (1789, better-known to British audiences in the Ashton version, *La Fille mal gardée*). Vinogradov deliberately eschewed the familiar score by Peter Ludwig Hertel used for Petipa's staging of 1885 and later revivals. Instead, he decided to use Ferdinand Hérold's version of 1828, itself an adaptation of the medley of folk tunes used for the original production. The basis of the score was exiguous rehearsal notes used at the Mariinsky in the nineteenth century, which required extensive reconstruction by the leader of the Kirov orchestra. The choreography had to be 'recomposed from scratch, relying on the traditions of pre-romantic and romantic ballet' – though not so much so as to seem excessively 'stylised', 'in the manner of porcelain, tapestries, or engravings' (which would have been a step too far towards the traditions of Diaghilev).[15] Vinogradov's staging of *Coppélia* was an equally adventurous exercise in historical purism.[16] Yet his innovations – unlike, say, those in Yury Grigorovich's 1969 version of *Swan Lake* for the Bol'shoi Ballet – did not draw attention to their own existence.[17] Thus, Leningrad ballet resembled the 'restored' (that is, reconstructed) architecture of the same period, and it too came to symbolise the concern for meticulous preservation of pre-Soviet material peculiar to the city. It was not just choreography but dance technique that stood out. The Leningrad balletic style, epitomised by Ulanova, signified restraint, allusiveness, and in a technical sense, a particular liquidity of the upper body that dancers retained wherever they later worked.[18]

Conservatism of this kind of course characterises classical art forms wherever they are practised. But in other European countries, institutions with a custodial role are generally located in capital cities and represent 'national' traditions (the Royal Ballets of London and Copenhagen, the Vienna State Opera and Vienna Philharmonic, the Ballet national de Paris, are obvious cases in point). In asserting the *national* validity of a *local* tradition, the performing arts in Leningrad were, in this context, unique. At the same time, this did not preclude innovation. Leonid Yakobson moved on from occasional work at the Kirov to form his own company, developing the non-narrative line in work such as the light-hearted *Exercise XX*.[19] Boris Eifman, who began working at the Kirov Theatre in 1971 when he was only twenty-five, was to become perhaps the leading exponent of modern ballet in the Soviet Union. But his stay in academic ballet lasted only six years, and his own company, the 'New Theatre', polarised local opinion (like the work of Maurice Béjart or Roland Petit in the West): either he was a bracing and radical force, or alternatively, a crass vulgarian, a disturbingly provincial artist who should not have been unleashed on the home of true ballet.[20]

No other art form had quite the authority of the ballet in its claims to this custodial role. The radical past of Leningrad opera – exemplified by Shostakovich's *Lady Macbeth of Mtsensk*, also premiered at MALEGOT – was passed over in tactful silence. In the performances of the nineteenth-century repertoire, whether national (*Ivan Susanin, Boris Godunov*) or Western (Verdi, Puccini, Bellini), the city could not challenge the Bol'shoi's national dominance. There was no 'Leningrad school' of vocal technique to compare with Vaganova's contribution to dance.[21] Significantly it was ballet, rather than opera, in which the foremost Leningrad conductor, Evgeny Mravinsky, specialised when he was conducting at GATOB (1932–38). So far as the concert repertoire was concerned, local orchestras such as the Leningrad Philharmonic of course sensed a particular allegiance to Shostakovich and Tchaikovsky, but the programmes they played embraced the national and international canon: Mravinsky's work with the Philharmonic included Bach, Beethoven, Bruckner, Sibelius, Brahms, and Schubert among others.[22] Ravil' Martynov, a pupil of Mravinsky's who had inherited the master's attachment to a kind of negative capability (nothing to interfere with the music), was to become a noted interpreter of Mahler.[23]

Yet, in the context of worldwide musical culture, it was less what got played that was characteristic than what was not, and in particular the almost total absence from the programme of twentieth-century music by non-Russian composers – a fact one might attribute to anxieties about performers' rights, except that the Soviet Union did not sign the International Copyright Convention until 1973. However, the personality of the local orchestras was not characterised only in negative terms. There was also a special 'Leningrad sound', depending on the exceptional polish and meticulousness of the realisation, and on a performing style that was at once lush and disciplined. Mravinsky described this at one remove in a birthday tribute to Shostakovich:

> This *masking of feeling* sometimes baffles listeners and gives them an entirely misleading impression of Shostakovich's supposed lack of emotionalism. In actual fact, deep lyrical feelings are concealed in his music, feelings

6.3 Ravil' Martynov (left) conducting a rehearsal in the Leningrad Kapella, 1986. On the right is the tenor Yury Marusin.

> that are carefully preserved from the coarse gaze, the careless touch. They are not put on show; you have to track them down; and when you do, you cannot fail to prize their elevation, their purity, and their self-contained power.[24]

Shostakovich himself at first found Mravinsky's approach, in rehearsal, unduly finicking, before coming to trust the conductor's expertise and even, on occasion, accepting editorial suggestions from him.[25] Mravinsky was indeed, as one commentator put it, a master of 'inner temperament'.[26] On the other hand, Yury Temirkanov, though a pupil of Mravinsky, belonged to a different and more explicitly Romantic tradition; but in his performances too, the personality of the players came through.

If ballet and music could be called the quintessential Leningrad art forms, local artists established distinguished traditions in other arts as well. The city had its own studio, Lenfilm, one of whose directors, Grigory Kozintsev (1905–73), was responsible for two internationally recognised masterpieces of the post-Stalin era, *Hamlet* (1964) and *King Lear* (1970). The other elder statesmen at Lenfilm were of lesser stature. The best-known of them, Joseph Heifetz, who died in 1995 at the age of ninety, was primarily a miracle of longevity, though he was a competent craftsman, and *Married for the First Time* (1979) was a plain and affecting tale about a put-upon single mother who eventually found true happiness by leaving the city and taking up with a lonely bachelor in the countryside. But in the late 1960s, a remarkable group of younger directors began working at the studio, including Vitaly Mel'nikov (born in 1928), Viktor Sokolov (also born in 1928), and most particularly Il'ya Averbakh (1934–96) and Dinara Asanova (1942–85).

All four worked in an impromptu, studiedly artless manner that was indebted not just to Italian neo-realism but to the documentary film traditions that were a Leningrad speciality. A customary strategy, as in Mel'nikov's *Mother's Gone and Got Married* (1969), was to begin with a group scene into which narrative was introduced only gradually.[27] For instance, *Mother's Gone and Got Married* opened with footage of women restorers working on a structure in the centre of the city, busy with trowels and hods on the scaffolding. Averbakh's medical drama *Degree of Risk* (1968) began from an extensive sequence of a child patient being given treatment, with the camera following the trolley down a corridor and then panning round the concentrated faces of the doctors as the operation got underway.[28] Documentary style was pushed to its limits in Asanova's extraordinary debut film, *The Woodpecker Never Gets Headaches* (1974), which depicted a situation (a teenage boy with a passion for playing the drums), rather than an elaborated plot. One long sequence consisted of a performance by a 'vocal-instrumental ensemble' at a local culture club, and another of an extended improvisation on drums by the protagonist himself.

Focus on everyday detail, sometimes raised to the level of still life by an aestheticising mise-en-scène, but not always, acted as a kind of shared handwriting. A metacinematic approach was also characteristic. In Averbakh's *The Personal Life of Valentin Kuzyaev* (1966) (co-directed with Igor' Maslennikov), the opening scene was shot as though by the camera belonging to a TV film crew, concealed in a display column for advertisements, that the viewer glimpsed at the beginning. The music playing on the soundtrack in the first scene turned out later to be the theme tune of the broadcast that the camera crew had been creating. At the same time, the fact that Averbakh and Maslennikov did not choreograph their actors at all, repeatedly filming them from behind, stood in striking contrast to the techniques used by the TV crew at the end of the film, where vox-pops were groomed to say what was expected, and to sing the right responses in the chorus to a morally uplifting song ('"Do we want to go to the moon?" "Yes!" – "Do we find life boring?" "No!"'). The film thus mounted a double challenge to contemporary film aesthetics: because it was artful, and because it was spontaneous.

In Mel'nikov's *Mother's Gone and Got Married*, the black-and-white sequence at the beginning showing women restorers placidly working[29] acted like a clip from an official documentary; a sequence in colour with the women in their underwear out on the roof sunbathing presented an obvious aesthetic, as well as thematic, contrast. The general principles of intertextual play were pushed to the limits in Averbakh's *Voice* (1982), which focused on a production team engaged in creating the soundtrack for a film. In the film they were working on, the woman star was herself regularly shown taking photographs, and at one point she appeared, with her camera, in an inset film-within-a-film, taking the number of different refracting lenses to three.

Something else shared by this remarkable group of directors was their interest in the landscape of the city. Piter is a particularly cinegenic place, something that emerges even from the webcam footage on internet weather sites, with its hypnotic rooftop shots and glimpses of streetlife in real time.[30] However, directors based there have often chosen to set films elsewhere – as in the case of Kozintsev, Heifetz, or more recently Alexander Sokurov. The cinematic tradition of the late 1960s and 1970s, on the other hand, was locality-obsessed to an extent that could be matched in no other art form.

That said, the different directors each had their own idiosyncratic approach to the urban landscape. There was no unified 'Leningrad text'. For her part, Dinara Asanova had a preference for marginal settings. *The Woodpecker Never Gets Headaches* was filmed in an area of Krestovsky Island that was so remote and wild-looking that it was hard to associate it with Leningrad. *My Wife's Left Me*, mainly shot in Asanova's own cheerless and dilapidated 1930s flat, used as its anchorage in the external world a park with a recognisably 'Piter' character that could have been more or less anywhere in the city.[31] In some films by other directors, though, Leningrad topography was pivotal. *Mother's Gone and Got Married* moved between the centre (where the heroine and her sister worked) and the inchoate expanses of Grazhdanka. *Valentin Kuzyaev* began on Nevsky prospekt, then moved to Kuzyaev's room in what looked like a courtyard off ulitsa Nekrasova; it took in shots through a café window down on to Suvorovsky prospekt as well as a day trip to Leningrad's dacha surroundings. The most complex set of city scenes was in Sokolov's *Mixed Sunshine and Rain* (1967), another film of desultory action, following two boys on a day of skipped school. The local streets and courtyards were as much a part of the film as the uneasy relationship between the swot and the perpetual bottom-marker of the class, and the film provided a whole 'encyclopaedia of Leningrad life', from the back streets of Kolomna to the expanses of Nevsky, from the bleak interior of a classroom with its Venetian window to a stand-up café and cinema at Moscow Gates.

While none of these films had the wide appeal of Georgy Daneliya's *The Autumn Marathon* (1979), their glimpses of the city landscape were more subtle than his glimpses of the Moika, and they were shaped by an insider's intimacy. When settings that would have been recognised by any tourist were on show – as in a scene at Peter and Paul Fortress in *Mother's Gone and Got Married* – then so, too, were tourists, a neat local in-joke.

In visual arts, the intimate eye was also ubiquitous. Easel-painting was deeply preoccupied with the local landscape (as in the many oil studies of city scenes perpetually assorted with puddles and rain-clouds). Sometimes an unusual viewpoint might be chosen, as in Arseny Semyonov's *A Spring Day* (1959), a schematic rendition of trucks progressing along a street of nineteenth-century buildings towards the embankment seen from high up.[32] If easel-painting was provincial not just in terms of its subject-matter but in terms of its national standing as well, in the graphic arts and photography, particularly, Leningrad official artists could hold their own.[33] Even photo-advertising and photo-journalism were often not just technically assured but imaginative: the work of one of the rare women photographers, Galina Lisyutich, included large numbers of elegant publicity photographs, but also stunning on-set shots of landmark productions such as Aleksei German's *Twenty Days Without War* (1976) and Sergei Mikaelyan's *The Widows* (1976).[34]

6.4 On the set of Sergei Mikaelyan's *The Widows*, 1976.

The 'Leningrad school' in painting was strongly linear, with a muted colour palette, recognisable not just because it evoked corners of the city landscape but through its laconic, self-contained manner of presenting familiar things.[35] Characteristically 'local' was also the tradition of artist's books, particularly involving collaborations between visual and verbal creators: Mikhail Karasik's *The Leningrad Literary Underground* (2003) presented eight little booklets inside a replica matchbox, echoing the classic Piter emphasis on concealed treasures and meanings, while *The Affirmer of the Avant-Garde* (2011) paid tribute to the severe architectural modernism of the Cultural Revolution.

The traditions of the Leningrad dramatic theatre were individual too. Certainly, this art form did not have the national pre-eminence of the ballet. Before 1917, Moscow had a more diverse theatrical culture than St Petersburg, and its status as capital enhanced this advantage. There was no Petrograd or Leningrad director in the 1920s or 1930s that could rival such live forces as Meyerhold, Vakhtangov, or Tairov, with the possible exception of Nikolai Evreinov, whose emigration to Paris meant that he could not be claimed publicly as an influence even after 'formalist theatre' had once again become respectable in the 1960s. Even patriotic Leningraders acknowledged, in the late Soviet period, that theatrical life in Moscow was 'livelier and more dynamic' than in Piter.[36]

In the post-Stalin era, some of the most radical work in the Soviet theatre was being done by directors outside Russia altogether, such as Robert Sturua at the Shota Rustaveli theatre in Tbilisi, or Juozas Miltinis, director of the Panevėžys Drama Theatre in the Lithuanian provincial town of that name, whose productions became famous throughout the Soviet Union.[37] Lighting, sets, staging, costumes, make-up, and acting styles were more adventurous than those of many leading Russian troupes. By contrast, the cultural repression of the late 1940s (whose side effects included the dismissal from his post as director of the Comedy Theatre of Nikolai Akimov, then the city's leading talent) had left Leningrad theatres looking staid and depleted. But from the late 1950s onwards, the scene became far more diverse. A leader in the transformation was Georgy Tovstonogov (1915–89), whose work was to achieve national and international renown.

## The Story of a Director

Tovstonogov began directing in 1934, and in the post-war years worked at the Lensovet Theatre and the Pushkin Theatre, two of the leading venues in the city. His 1955 production of Vsevolod Vishnevsky's revolutionary drama *Optimistic Tragedy*, created for the Pushkin Theatre, was one of the major cultural events of the era. The setting for the action was explicitly denoted as Leningrad, giving the piece local immediacy, and viewers were excited by the spare, expressive nature of the staging, its total lack of 'dry academicism'.[38]

Tovstonogov's move to the Bol'shoi Drama Theatre (BDT), shortly after *Optimistic Tragedy* was premiered, was the start of a truly extraordinary run of productions. Outwardly, the theatre's repertoire was much the same as that of many Soviet theatres of the day, founded primarily on realist work by dramatists from the late nineteenth century and from the Soviet period, and also on new plays by Soviet dramatists. Occasionally, work by international contemporary writers made its way through: a hit of the late 1950s was the Brazilian dramatist Guilherme Figureido's *The Fox and the Grapes*, first staged in 1957; in 1966, John Steinbeck's *Of Mice and Men* created a sensation. All the same, it was Russian material that made the greatest impact.[39]

Like other important directors of the day, notably Anatoly Efros and Yury Lyubimov, Tovstonogov did not confine himself to the extant dramatic repertoire. Adaptations of prose were an enormously important part of the theatre's output, helped by the work of Dina Shvarts, the tireless head of the literature department. Indeed, the two productions which did most to make BDT nationally and internationally famous – *The Idiot* (1957) and *The Story of a Horse* (1975) – were creative reworkings of prose texts, by Dostoevsky and Tolstoy respectively. Working with adaptations allowed scope for idiosyncratic, director-led productions that were not subject to the immediate accusation of having betrayed the intentions of a dramatist from the national literary canon. This likely also explains the marginal place, in Tovstonogov's work, of Shakespeare and Chekhov, the two most obviously 'safe' choices for any Soviet dramatist.[40]

The task of turning BDT into a showcase for idiosyncratic theatrical brilliance may have been helped by the fact that it, like another leading theatre of the post-Stalin era, the Lensovet, was specifically a Soviet (as opposed to Petersburg) institution. The theatre had been built in 1879, but had no permanent troupe before the revolution. From 1920, however, it became the home of the 'Petrograd Communal Theatres' movement, organised by M. F. Andreeva, and with a programme that at first focused on 'forward-thinking' work by classic writers such as Schiller, Shakespeare, Goldoni, Molière, and Beaumarchais. By the late 1920s, work by Soviet dramatists was also being shown (in 1925–7, the most popular play was A. N. Tolstoy and A. N. Shchegolev's *The Empress's Conspiracy*, which was seen by over 30,000 people in April 1925 alone; at this period, the theatre also premiered Evgeny Zamyatin's adaptation of Leskov's *The Flea*).[41] The theatre paid its dues to ideological issues of the day with productions of plays such as Boris Lavrenev's *Enemies* (premiered in the 1928–9 season), which explored the theme of class vigilance through the story of two brothers, one of whom betrayed the Soviet cause, and Viktor Gusev's *Glory* (1935), a verse drama celebrating the

Komsomol contribution to the building of socialism. After the War, 'military-patriotic plays' were at first the order of the day.[42]

By the early 1950s, BDT was, by general consensus, in the doldrums, and Tovstonogov had a free hand to do as he liked with the company. His first action on being appointed director was to warn the notoriously difficult troupe, 'You won't eat *me*,' and to send 30 of them packing.[43] Those who remained had to submit to a regime that combined charm and ruthlessness. Work organisation had a strongly hierarchical character, not just because Tovstonogov himself occupied a position of enlightened despotism (though always welcoming input from the cast at rehearsals), but because the lead actors were paid considerably more and had more authority. They belonged to the theatre's artistic council, and had a consultative role at auditions and play readings.[44] However, young actors, if they proved themselves (the auditioning process was ferocious), could rapidly work their way into favour. Indeed Tovstonogov (contrary to the practices obtaining at, say, the Moscow Arts Theatre, where a particular cast might inhabit the roles of a play for a decade or more) liked to keep actors guessing about castings: in the case of *The Idiot*, he rehearsed another actor for the starring role before, unexpectedly for everyone but himself, picking the eventual lead, Innokenty Smoktunovsky, who made his name with the part.[45]

Tovstonogov's writings on drama, with their references to the 'civic commitment' vital for the director and other pompous abstractions, give little immediate sense of why people fought to get to BDT, travelling to the theatre from right across the Soviet Union.[46] There is the usual ritual obeisance to Stanislavsky, who since the late 1930s and the rout of 'formalism' in theatrical performance had been considered the founding father of the Soviet theatre. At the same time, Tovstonogov's expression of allegiance to Stanislavsky was, in terms of nuance, innovative. He emphasised that the great director was a living theatrical force, not a classic from the distant past: his legacy included not just wisdom but also 'crafty humour'.[47]

The lack of concrete detail in Tovstonogov's discussion of his canonical predecessor pointed to the fact that he was actually evoking not Stanislavsky but 'Stanislavsky', a legitimating brand name for his own strongly-held views on how plays should be staged. In fact, the historical legacy that shaped him included figures less congenial to Soviet academic theatre. *Optimistic Tragedy*, for instance, had been the subject of a famous 'formalist' production by Aleksandr Tairov (1933), giving the play a strong association with alternative Soviet theatrical traditions.[48] But Tovstonogov was not remotely pious towards the 'formalist' past. The sets used for *Optimistic Tragedy* softened the severe geometrism of the 1933 production: there were life-size models of the stone lions outside the Senate, and a projection of the Admiralty's spire was used as background.[49] And Tovstonogov's directing style was not concept-driven (as in the case of Meyerhold's famous stagings of the 1920s, such as *Woe to Wit* and *The Government Inspector*); it was concerned with the incidentals of perception and behaviour.

However, Tovstonogov's work was also very different from the canonical traditions of method acting as showcased by the Moscow Arts Theatre. As he himself noted, he saw no division between 'psychological' and 'stylised' theatre.[50] Whether staging classics or new plays, he put far more emphasis on the actors' physicality than was conventionally the case in the Soviet theatre. The performance photographs from *Of Mice and Men* show the lead actress stretched out on her male co-star's lap, head touching the floor; a close tactile relationship was built up between the male characters also.[51]

At rehearsals, Tovstonogov did not require actors to 'think their way' into a role, but to apply themselves to gesture with maximal concentration: out of movement came insight into psychology, both for players and audience. Innokenty Smoktunovsky, the actor who played Myshkin, remembered that he got the 'key' to the role when he noticed a person whose entire body-language conveyed the sense that they were living in a different world; only later did he find out that the person concerned was a severe epileptic. Smoktunovsky's notes taken down in rehearsals fuse emotional and physical commentaries. Of Myshkin's reaction to seeing Nastas'ya Filippovna, he observed: 'He's shocked by the encounter. Flabbergasted. He freezes to the spot when he sees her. Total

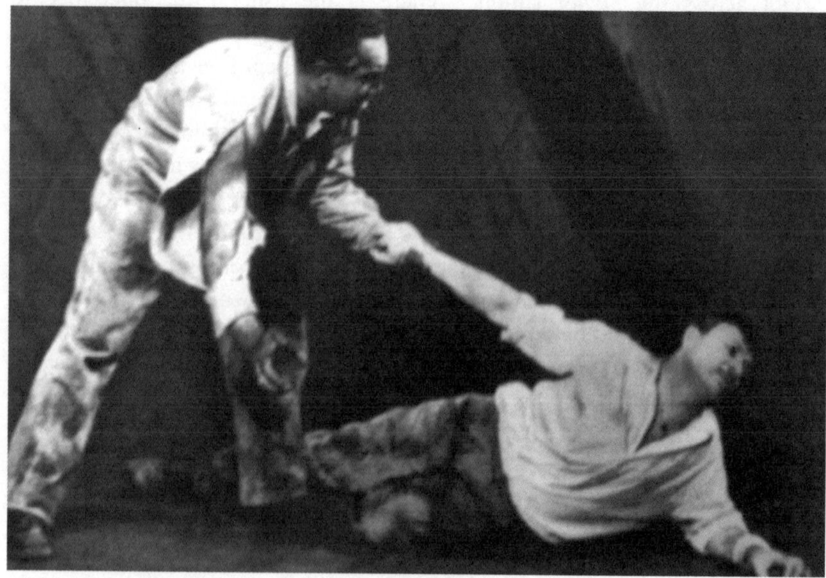

6.5 A 1961 performance at the BDT of *With Unbowed Heads*, adapted from Nathan Douglas (Nedrick Young) and Harold Smith's *The Defiant Ones*.

lockjaw.'[52] Psychological insight and gesture were understood to go hand-in-hand.

Alongside visuals, crucial to Tovstonogov's work was the sound environment of the productions – including not just naturalistic noises, such as the flushing lavatory and crying baby in Alfred Jarry's *The Sixth Floor*, first staged in 1957, but also specially composed or arranged incidental music. This was not performed as interludes, hived off from the main action; it was used to counterpoint the dialogue, bringing with it the 'sharp rhythms' that Tovstonogov considered essential to the staging.[53]

Such non-verbal elements were especially important in *The Story of a Horse*, premiered in 1975. The show was based on Tolstoy's first-person narrative of a piebald gelding, Strider, who looks back over his life of adventure and exploitation.[54] Unlike John Dexter's production of Peter Shaffer's *Equus* in London two years earlier, the costumes included no horse masks or hoof details.[55] While rudimentary leather strapping was used to suggest bridles and harness, the 'equine' elements came almost entirely from the gestures used by the actors: pawing the air, tossing the head or looking sideways on, presenting a foot – hoof – to have it picked out. Once again, rhythm prevailed over literalism.

The central elements of the staging were evolved by Mark Rozovsky, who had been developing the play for the studio theatre at BDT when Tovstonogov took over. However, Tovstonogov not only set his seal of approval on the production, getting it transferred to the main auditorium, but also introduced various changes to the staging, and himself rehearsed the actors in the fine detail of voice and movement.[56] The result, according to an inspired review by the leading drama critic David Zolotnitsky, was something extraordinary: less 'drama' than *deistvo*, a word more often used for spectacle and pageantry, as in classical tragedy, medieval mystery plays, or the symbolist dramas of the early twentieth century.[57]

BDT was not, by contemporary international standards, a particularly radical theatre. The 'fourth wall' convention remained; the pared-down style of sets (hopsack drop-curtains, wooden steps, rough-hewn benches) was transferred from one production to another. The repertoire was far more 'Soviet' than at Lyubimov's Taganka Theatre in Moscow, which, by the 1980s, was producing adaptations of Bulgakov, and where productions also had a much stronger whiff of the counter-culture.[58]

But Tovstonogov pushed to their limits the dominant academic traditions of Leningrad theatre. Both he and his actors did their best to avoid falling into comfortable stereotyping. If the director quite often used actors whom the audience did not know, 'who didn't have a whole train of previous roles floating behind them', the actors themselves eschewed habit.[59] In a culture where every detail of casting and staging had to be agreed with the authorities, the commitment to uncertainty carried a high level of risk. And many of the productions were themselves controversial. Griboedov's Chatsky, the hero of *Woe from Wit*, represented in the Soviet schoolroom as a founding hero of radical politics, was in the BDT's portrayal fragile, socially inept, guileless (the actor cast in this role, Sergei Yursky, was only twenty-seven at the time when the premiere took place in 1964), and, from the point of view of looks, no Adonis. An uproar resulted, with letters to the paper condemning Tovstonogov's approach.[60] From the early 1970s, under the withering eye of Grigory Romanov, Tovstonogov's life became increasingly difficult. The theatre never had its generous funding withdrawn or reduced, and public acclaim was unabated, but director and actors came under growing pressure from the censorship. Yursky, in particular, was reduced to the status of persona non grata.[61]

## Stagers and Studios

Another star of the Leningrad theatre who found himself in the paradoxical situation of a popular favourite who was constantly chivvied by the watchdogs of Soviet society was the comedian Arkady Raikin, performer of satirical sketches about Soviet everyday life.[62] Raikin had warm personal relations with no less a person than Brezhnev (he had also been admired by Stalin) and was a favourite with members of the establishment lower down (the young secret police officer Vladimir Putin's first date with his future wife Lyudmila was a show by Raikin).[63] This did not, however, soothe the concerns of Leningrad censorship officials, who rigorously policed the content of his shows.

As in Tovstonogov's case, the risks that Raikin took were both calculated and real. His sketches guyed the self-revealing inarticulacy of *homo sovieticus*: the plumber who vacillated between the mangled polysyllables of what he called 'putting it scientifically' and earthy references to 'taps what'uss leaking out the side', or the factory director who confided, 'Don't do no work myself, so why should you neither'. Other targets were those who thought themselves superior to everyone else: the silver-haired Leningrad intellectual, with his references to artistic periodicals of the fin-de-siècle ('not that *you* will have heard of them, of course'); or the Caucasian wheeler-dealer who boasted of having 'got hold of something what's deficit'. 'You know no one else has got it. You're the only one what has.' But if these were figures that might have been found in the official magazine *Krokodil*, Raikin sometimes sailed closer to the wind, as in a sketch of a tipsy boss bumbling away in Soviet rhetoric.[64] In the context of Soviet comedy his work was truly liberating, the inspiration for a host of talented successors, including Mikhail Zhvanetsky, who worked with Raikin at the Theatre of Miniatures from 1964, and the comic duo Roman Kartsev and Viktor Il'chenko.

The extent to which Tovstonogov, and indeed Raikin, could be considered specifically Leningrad phenomena is questionable. TV broadcasts brought their work to a far wider audience than one city. Both were adopted citizens of Piter, born in Tiflis and Riga respectively, and both led the nomadic life of the successful performer. Raikin's claims to deep patriotism had the ring of perhaps unintentional irony: 'Whenever, along with the other passengers, I leave the "Red Arrow" to the sounds of "The Hymn of a Great City" and walk on to the platform of the station in Leningrad, I feel as though I were at last home after some particularly long-drawn-out tour.'[65]

Yet Raikin, in his way, kept alive the quintessentially Petersburg tradition of cabaret, whose last surviving pre-revolutionary exponent, Aleksandr Vertinsky, had died in 1957, on the cusp of the new age.[66] His characters from Soviet life bore as much relation to the sketches of the elegant humorous magazine *Satirikon*, published in the early twentieth century, and to the music-hall acts of that era, as to the pages of *Krokodil*.[67] His humour was primarily verbal: plumbers were comical because of the way that they talked about dripping taps. And perhaps the most characteristic local feature was exactly this emphasis on language. In his memoirs, Raikin spoke nostalgically of the performances he had seen in the Aleksandrinka (later the Pushkin Theatre) back in the 1920s: 'exemplary in their meticulous attitude to the word on stage'.[68] It was, Ol'ga Egoshina remembered, the vocal effects that stayed with the spectator of Tovstonogov's productions too: 'not so much words and speeches, but the intonation, the timbre of the voice, the brittleness of the phrasing and the breathing in between words.'[69] In theatre as in music or ballet, it was this highly refined, fragile, and rather calculated manner of performing that was associated with the city.

If styles of performance tended to be constrained, so did the buildings Leningrad artists performed in. The post-Stalin years did witness the construction of two major new venues: the Theatre of Young Viewers on Pioneer Square, designed by Aleksandr Zhuk and opened in 1962, and the October Concert Hall, the work of the same architect, completed in 1966.[70] However, the majority of the city's resorts of culture were old buildings – indeed, in many cases, architectural monuments. Four – the Kirov, the Malyi, BDT, and the Pushkin (Aleksandrinsky) Theatre – were former court theatres. The Philharmonic occupied the pillared hall which had once housed the Assembly of the Gentry and Nobility; the Lensovet Theatre inhabited the former Merchants' Club, which immediately before the Revolution had been a gaming hall. The traditions of the house bulked large; in some theatres (the Malyi and BDT, for instance), they were showcased in museums, and everywhere walls were hung with photographs of performances long past. Such stately auditoriums were not conducive to improvisation.

The most adventurous work was often done by non-professional theatres: trainee directors and actors studying at one of the city's arts institutes, or indeed, the theatre studio of Leningrad State University, where Andrei Tolubeev

6.6 The artistes' foyer at BDT, 1979. Note the photographs of luminaries from the theatre's past hanging on the walls, including Alexander Blok and Maxim Gorky.

(1945–2008), later to be a lead actor at BDT, made his debut in a production of Peter Weiss's *Marat-Sade*.[71] The 'studio theatre' movement had been most dynamic in the 1920s, before a rigid division between 'professional' and 'amateur' performance was imposed on artistic production.[72] But the studios, now with an 'amateur club' role, continued working into the post-war years as well, and the emphasis on grassroots activism in the Khrushchev years gave them a significant boost. Despite increasing control after 1968, they were an important force in the late Soviet period too, sometimes producing work that would not have been permitted on the professional stage, and winning faithful audiences for their experimental production values.[73]

Even when alternative theatre started asserting itself more, academic theatre still kept to its former paths. There were few real signs of crossover between different theatrical traditions: the ingrained tendency to look down on work by 'dilettantes' and 'amateurs' was strong.[74] One permanent theatre that did have a 'studio' feel, however, was the Leningrad Regional Theatre on ulitsa Rubinshteina.[75] Despite its modest title, the building of the former Trinity Theatre (from the street's pre-revolutionary name) had a distinguished history of association with small, dynamic companies going back to the Theatre of Revolutionary Youth (TRAM) in the 1920s.[76] It entered a new phase of creativity in 1973, when Efim Padve, an associate of Tovstonogov's, took over as the artistic director. Padve generously promoted the work of others, including Lev Dodin, who began to stage productions in 1973, when he was still in his late 20s, and who replaced Padve as artistic director in 1983.

Dodin's work was far more radically 'formalist' than anything seen in Leningrad for decades. Ensemble work dispensed with any vestige of the star system; type-casting, alive and well in the academic theatre, was thrown to the winds; positively gymnastic feats were required from the actors, as they flung themselves across the stage or suddenly emerged from beyond – the use of all the different geometrical planes was Dodin's hallmark. In *Gaudeamus* (1990), based on the Moscow writer Sergei Kaledin's stark account of life in a military 'construction battalion' (where recruits not considered suitable for conscription into the regular army served time doing building projects, enduring squalor and bullying), heads popped from orifices in the stage floor as well as the wings, and figures swung on ropes across the arena.[77] While the subject-matter here was pure glasnost, the impact of Dodin's work long preceded political change. His productions of two spectacles with a rural setting, *Brothers and Sisters*, based on stories by the Leningrad 'village prose' writer Fyodor Abramov, and *Live and Remember*, by Valentin Rasputin, were widely admired for their harsh and uncompromising lyricism.[78] With the death of Tovstonogov in 1989, Dodin became the premier director in Leningrad, on a par with figures such as Yury Lyubimov and Anatoly Efros in Moscow. At the same time, the whole tenor of his work, with scenic effects and body dynamics uppermost, went against the accepted emphasis on language in performance. The rise of Dodin also spelled the decline of 'Leningrad traditions' in the theatre, as they had formerly been understood.

## 'It Was Simply the Done Thing to Go'

Leningrad theatre traditions lay as much in the eye of the audience as in the intonational and gestural repertoire of the performer. There was a widespread if not universal belief that being a city-dweller in a full sense meant taking an interest in culture – and not just architecture and the Hermitage, but the performing arts as well. Incomers rapidly assimilated. A complaint from a group of African students to the City Committee of the Communist Party in 1963 recorded that 'Mali and Somali students are subject to harassment and unjustified insults from the side of Soviet citizens, and because of this cannot visit theatres, the cinema, take part in shows, visit restaurants and cafés, or walk the streets of the city.'[79] The order was significant.

At the same time, if performances fell below the standards expected, Leningraders were trenchant. Official reviewing often hedged its bets, but in private people spoke directly. Even the prophets of the stage were not spared. Anatoly Naiman grudgingly conceded that Tovstonogov's production of *The*

*Idiot* was the only show he had seen that he had not found terminally boring.[80] But Lev Lurie remembered that his circle, while idolising the Polish director Jerzy Grotowski, did not rate Tovstonogov at all.[81] Tatiana Doronina, one of the BDT's lead actresses from the late 1950s until 1983, when she left for the Moscow Arts, had, as one female member of the Leningrad intelligentsia put it, 'all the presence of some young chit off the factory floor'.[82] Even the world-famous musical theatres had their detractors. 'Getting tickets for the Kirov was a big hassle, and there was no point in going to the Malyi,' one man remembered. 'It was shocking. The singers were off-key, the dancers moved round the stage as if they couldn't be bothered. Just dismal.'[83] Another connoisseur was equally rude about opera in the Kirov: 'Clouds of dust were coming off the scenery, and the singers were stuck round on the stage like street bollards.'[84] This was not just a question of retrospect: in a poem about the theatre by Aleksandr Kushner first published in 1986, the key words were also 'boredom' and 'dust'.[85]

At a more elevated level, Brodsky's 1976 poem addressed to his fellow exile Mikhail Baryshnikov characterised, with ironic negligence, the Kirov as a fortuitously preserved bastion of local history. Here, he and the rest of Leningrad society might 'press our bums' into seats of 'imperial soft plush', while gazing across the moat of the orchestra pit at a beauty who was definitely not to be 'lain with'. Life had not changed since the only thing exploding into the air was one of Pavlova's leaps.[86] A couple of decades later, Vladimir Gandel'sman was to recall a performance of *Woe from Wit* at BDT back in the early 1960s less for its own properties (the 'monkey tricks' of corpulent, melodramatically panting actresses were dismissively evoked) than because of its associations with a personal drama: 'Will you prefer him at the leavers' ball?'[87] For Andrei Bitov, the ballet was a tautology precisely because it was so much at home, an egregious exemplification of Petersburg's phantasmic theatricality.[88]

This is not to say that the entire city was gripped by begrudgerism. Leningrad had its elite of immensely knowledgeable 'melomanes', 'theatre types' (*teatraly*), and 'balletomanes'. The last had an encyclopaedic command of repertoire and dancers, and would attend a performance only if they knew that a favourite artist would be dancing a given role. On the whole, they eschewed partisanship. Ringing the box office to find out who was dancing was *comme il faut*, as was paying well over the odds to get a ticket for a night when a real star was appearing. People routinely applauded after a virtuoso display of dancing, even if this broke up the flow. But cheering loudly or screaming 'boo' would have been considered vulgar. Major performers had their 'groupies' who lavished money on bouquets and regarded them with devoted reverence, but the claques found at, say, La Scala were not part of the local scene.[89]

In any case, not everyone was, or wanted to be, an expert. For many, an enjoyable night out meant classical pops: *Carmen*, the *1812 Overture, Swan Lake*.[90] The arts had a social function as much as an intellectual one. 'It was

6.7 The scene outside the Bol'shoi Dramatic Theatre just before a performance, 1979. Some of the figures were certainly whispering, 'Might you have a spare ticket?'

simply the done thing to go,' one man remembered.[91] Like best-selling books, tickets to something thought to be worth watching were at once accessible and out of reach: easily affordable, but scarce. 'You could *buy* them easily, you just couldn't *get* them,' one man remembered, playing on the difference between *kupit'* and *dostat'*.[92] The most sought-after venues would be surrounded, during box-office hours and most particularly just before a performance, by people wanting to buy 'a spare ticket'.[93]

Anyone who had connections would use them to obtain at least a *kontramarka* (free pass), which allowed the person concerned to occupy unsold seats, or if there were none, a tip-up perch at the end of a row.[94] An impromptu strategy was to attempt to blag a ticket from the theatre administrator using any claim to entitlement one could possibly press (Westerners would be dispatched by Russian friends to the administrator's window to flash their passports and launch into a sob story: 'I'm only here for two weeks and I just must see this show, and please can I have four seats . . .').[95]

Trying to get round the difficulties could be part of the attraction: as with buying what you wanted, a successful hunt could be celebrated in anecdote (though so too could a disaster). If all else failed, you could resort to self-help of an illicit kind:

> You'd buy a season ticket, but then you'd want to go to concerts from another subscription cycle [*abonement*] as well. And so then you had to fake this big number on the ticket. So I'd use a razor, and then Indian ink or something to mark the number. [. . .] And then, once you were inside, you were home and dry. The climate in Leningrad is just so awful there are always seats going, someone will have taken ill and not come right at the last moment, and so [. . .] you just have to wait till the orchestra starts coming in, and then they shut the doors, and you can come and take any empty seat you fancy.

In the case of particularly popular concerts, when the police were called in to avoid a stampede, passing off an adulterated ticket was even easier, since the average policeman had little idea what a real one looked like, while the ushers would wave people past. Alternatively, one could simply float on the edge of a group and be confident that exact numbers of tickets and people were unlikely to be compared.[96]

However tickets were obtained, going to the theatre or a concert were ways of spending an enjoyable time in a city without too many diversions on offer. Even if the show was duff, it might be appealing in other ways. As Tat'yana Derviz remembered: 'In [Vsevolod Vishnevsky's] *Unforgettable 1919*, almost an entire act took place in an aristocratic salon that had miraculously survived the Revolution. You had the chance to see good-looking actors and actresses in good-looking costumes, and to hear hits of the day being sung, and the dialogue might have satirised the "counter-revolutionaries" in a very obvious way, but it was witty as well.'[97] For teenagers, an evening at the Leningrad Philharmonic was a good place for a date: not likely to worry your parents, but with a chance to snatch a kiss in private behind the red curtains at the side of the auditorium.[98] Indeed, asking someone out to the theatre was an accepted method of paying courtship indirectly.[99]

Whatever one's purpose, the discreetly charming rituals, from coat-checking to the consumption of sweet Soviet 'champagne' and smoked-salmon open sandwiches in the buffet, to the conspiratorial strut around the foyer looking to see who else was there, had an enduring appeal. And while the occasional spectator might write to the paper in disgust over the production, the majority of those attending had different priorities. In the comment books at BDT, the standard cause for complaint was not a glitch in the production or an actor giving a below-par performance (though the theatre's day-book indicates that such were not unknown), but the fact that someone's seat was uncomfortable or restricted-view, or that the ushers had refused entry to only-slightly-latecomers at the beginning or after an interval.[100] The phrasing of these complaints made clear that the way in which many saw their visit to the theatre was as 'leisure' (*otdykh*), and they took great exception to anything which interfered with that end.[101]

This did not mean that people were uninterested in what they were watching. Programme substitutions were a cause of disaffection, little better than not getting tickets at all.[102] People naturally went out with the intention of seeing something specific. But unlike some European cities, such as Vienna, Leningrad had no seasonal subscription system at theatres (as opposed to concert halls), so people went along on impulse – often prompted by word-of-mouth.[103] Upcoming cultural events were not systematically advertised, but news would quickly get round. Anything out of the ordinary – exhibitions of US or European art, showings of contemporary Western films, *gastroli* by foreign companies, a visit by an artiste from abroad – generated a surge of interest.[104]

The high-water-mark for tours by foreign artists, as one would expect, was the Thaw years, at which point even the official press was at least cautiously approving. When the Sadler's Wells Opera visited with Britten productions in 1964, a *Leningradskaya pravda* reviewer criticised *The Turn of the Screw* for its 'impossibly odd and archaic' subject ('we thought operas with ghosts in them had gone out with the era of Boieldieu's *La Dame blanche*'), but admired *Peter Grimes* and *The Rape of Lucretia*.[105]

Perhaps the biggest stir was created by exhibitions. As the Moscow writer Vladimir Soloukhin, later to become a leader of the literary nationalist movement, observed, a show of US architecture at the Academy of Arts in 1965 was the talk of the town:

> When I mentioned the exhibition to a friend, a Leningrad painter, he said straight away that really, I was completely out of touch, people had been talking about nothing else all week. I was about to belt off to the University Embankment and make up for lost time, but my friend said it was almost impossible to get in. People were queuing for five or six hours and there were police everywhere, and you couldn't get near the building.[106]

Soloukhin got in only because the friend took pity on him and handed over a free pass. He found that indeed the Academy was cut off by a double line of policemen, and inside were torrents of visitors eddying round the young Americans who acted as guides. Judging by the quantities of exhibition catalogues that were disappearing (it was handed out free to anyone who made it through), around 8000 people a day were visiting, and of course, as Soloukhin observed, the hidden circulation of the catalogue would have been many times higher.[107] Yury Luchinsky, born in 1952, remembered that the buildings on exhibition had looked like 'something from Mars' to the contemporary Leningrad eye, and that the other American exhibitions of the day, including graphic art (held at the Russian Museum in 1963), had been just as sensational.[108] The level of interest was a source of considerable anxiety to the authorities who – as with the famous American exhibition in Moscow in 1959 – organised propagandists to ask awkward questions, report back on public reactions, and write critical comments in the visitors' books.[109]

### Art Below the Line

The background to the enthusiasm for these exhibitions of 'capitalist art' was that even Leningraders with conventional tastes often found official Soviet ones dull. In 1960, the writer Anatoly Belinsky (whose dream was to join the Writers' Union) wrote to his wife that, while considering a show of contemporary British paintings 'awful filth', he had not at all enjoyed the 'Soviet Russia' exhibition ('It was amazingly mediocre. All these identical welders, milkmaids, pictures called "Youth" and "The Female Swimmer", and all so grey'). With major paintings by the Impressionists and Post-Impressionists hanging in the Hermitage, some Leningraders could not avoid noticing how hidebound the stars of the local Union of Artists were.[110]

By the 1970s, a fully-fledged alternative art scene was starting to emerge. Scandalous successes were common, helped by the intrusion of the police who, as an eyewitness ironically remembered, 'made mediocre exhibitions a big success' by their attempts to suppress these. With space in galleries and exhibition halls hard to fix up, one strategy was to hang pictures in a studio or private living space (the so-called 'apartment exhibitions').[111] 'Apartment concerts' (*kvartirniki*) were a fixture on the alternative music circuit, since official venues mainly played *estrada* (Soviet popular music), not rock, and the authorities' attempts to sanction certain rock groups as 'vocal-instrumental ensembles' were met in some circles with contempt. On the rare occasions when a performer with a serious following was allowed to give a public concert, there was space for only a fraction of those who might have wished to go along.[112]

From the early 1970s, as official venues became less hospitable to work by artists and musicians who were not members of a 'creative union', some devoted all their energies to the underground. Yet there was no absolute division between 'official' and 'unofficial'. Individual artists maintained a liminal existence. If some painters and photographers never even considered doing work that might have passed muster for exhibition or publication, others produced different types of work to diverse ends. The photographer Leonid Bogdanov, for example, led a completely above-board photographers' club at the Food Industries Palace of Culture, and his own work included lyrical scenes of the

Summer Garden that were in no respect subversive. But he also photographed the flotsam and jetsam of late socialist urban life. A teetering drunk swaps gazes with a watchful Alsatian; people queue outside a beer-bar, faces formless and puffy with years of alcohol abuse; on a decayed public building, a dusty, broken clock will never point the way to the bright future.[113] Artists and musicians all had to learn their skills somewhere, and while some simply relied on friendship networks, others got support from the clubs attached to palaces and houses of culture, at least in the initial stages.[114]

Avant-garde painters also occupied a kind of liminal space. Some had taken their first steps as members of official art clubs for children. Timur Novikov, for instance, had trained in a club at the Hermitage, and his earliest work includes paintings of the city in the manner of painters such as Baturin, setting the cross-hatching of black branches and fences against a classically yellow sky. However, by the early 1980s Novikov was introducing radical distortions of foreshortening into his Leningrad panoramas (as in *Leningrad View* of 1982, or *Palace Square*, painted a year later, where the Admiralty inclines one shoulder towards St Isaac's Cathedral).[115] Moving still further away from local canons, he became (like his friend Sergei 'Afrika' Bugaev) a notable exponent of alternative representational techniques, for example embroidery and appliqué. While the practice of collage itself has been claimed as a specifically Leningrad/Petersburg avant-garde feature,[116] the different orientations among non-official artists (expressionism of different kinds, the production of work using 'found objects', ironic recycling of Soviet traditions, to name only a few) make generalising according to place of origin more or less meaningless. Yet the studiedly negligent representational techniques in use and their 'impudently cack-handed' air were particularly offensive in the Academy of Art's home city, with its limited local history of avant-garde production even in the early modernist era.[117] The independence of immediate context was one of the 'scandalous' features of unofficial work.

A milestone in the development of the ambiguous counter-culture – held on sufferance, but not suppressed – was Klub-81, set up in March 1981. The moving spirit behind this (at least from inside alternative culture) was Gena Zaitsev, a member of the so-called 'system', or network of 'hangouts' (*tusovki*).[118] However, like the artists' association The Comradeship of Experimental Visual Arts (TEZI), the impetus depended also on the fact that the local administrators of official culture were prepared to lend a modest level of support to the endeavours: just as the painters were now allowed to hold exhibitions in state premises, so the rock musicians found shelter in a legitimate cultural enterprise, the hall of the Dostoevsky Museum. The trade-off was that musicians appearing here had to accept the patronising designation of 'amateur' performers – a title usually associated with folk-dancing collectives and balalaika players. Ticket sales were forbidden, as was advertising. In a short time, local groups such as 'Aquarium',

'Alisa', 'Strange Games', and 'Secret', to name only a few of the most famous, had begun making a huge impact on audiences at and beyond the clubs. Some of the musicians involved, particularly Boris Grebenshchikov, Sergei Kuryokhin, and Viktor Tsoi, rapidly acquired a reputation across the Soviet Union.[119]

Student theatres and professional associations also provided at least a temporary haven for unorthodox performers. For instance, one Leningrader born in the late 1960s remembered seeing Maksim Leonidov, later lead singer with the beat band 'Secret', perform as Elvis Presley during his graduation show in 1983. Word soon ran round about the parody 'All-Stars' line-up, and the student revue became the hottest ticket in the city.[120] The House of Scholars on Palace Embankment regularly used to have concerts and readings, also very well attended, and not just by bona fide scholars, but by their relations, friends, and assorted connections.[121] There were entire art forms that stood on the boundary between acceptable and unacceptable, such as jazz, pervaded by a whiff of the illicit since attacks on it as a 'bourgeois' art form in the 1930s; however, leading Leningrad musicians, such as the composer and performer David Goloshchokin and the band-leader Iosif Vainshtein, not only gave public performances but also released the occasional recording with the state label, Melodiya; Kvadrat ('Square') club in the Kirov Palace of Culture on Vasilievsky offered regular concerts, some adventurous.[122] In the glasnost years, Goloshchokin was to open the State Philharmonia of Jazz Music, an institution that brought jazz into the fold of Leningrad academic institutions, a development that was specific not just in terms of the history of Soviet jazz, but of the art form's history internationally.[123] In fact, Leningrad jazz fans were as likely to admire Alban Berg as the Beatles; the scene graded into avant-garde classical at one end, and rock at the other.[124]

## The Vagaries of Leningrad Taste

Not everyone in Leningrad was interested in 'alternative' arts, or indeed in artistic innovation. Writing to ask the Directorate of Culture's permission to drop the Hungarian playwright István Örkény's *Tóték* (*The Toth Family*) from the repertoire, the theatre's director observed in 1975, 'The genre and staging proved too complex for our audience, which is simply not used to the grotesque in its sharpest forms'.[125] There was no city-wide template of taste. Taking pride in the fact that Leningrad theatre was wonderful did not necessarily prompt an inclination to watch any, or all, productions; if there were jazz fans for whom good performances and interesting recordings were like gold dust, there were other people for whom even the semi-clandestine character of jazz did not make it palatable.[126] There were Leningraders who were convinced they had no ear for music, and there were others, in particular men, who found concerts dull and the ballet ridiculous.[127]

As in any other country, social and educational status had considerable weight, but the relationship between these and involvement in the arts was not always clear-cut. There were well-educated individuals who had no time for high culture.[128] On the other hand, some working-class Leningraders were enthusiasts, as suggested by a complaint sent to the Ministry of Culture in 1957. In it, a cab driver alleged that a party of would-be passengers had subjected him to 'afensive behaviour' (sic: *oskarblenie*) when he refused to take them all home (they were drunk and there were too many of them to fit in his cab, he said). The interesting detail is that the driver immediately recognised his antagonists as actors from the Pushkin Theatre, and used his knowledge of drama to make the actors look small. 'And a scene took place that was like something out of V. Vishnevsky's *Optimistic Tragedy*, only it was happening on the corner of Nevsky and Sadovaya ul. [. . .] A taxi driver feels hurt and injured that in a wonderful collective like our Leningrad Theatre of the Name of Pushkin, there are people who besmirch the noble calling of actor by their day-to-day behaviour.'[129]

Just as Leningraders of all social backgrounds were almost certain to be taken to a museum at some point during their school career, so a collective visit to some cultural event was a pretty well universal experience. Young children might attend a performance at one of Leningrad's puppet theatres or the circus, while older ones might find themselves at the Theatre of Young Viewers (TYuZ), or indeed the Kirov or BDT.[130] The state distribution system not only provided for such educational visits, but also made block allocations of tickets to workplaces, including factories.[131] But as with other areas of the deficit economy, what was easily available was not always valued. Organised trips were regarded with suspicion – a way of dumping tickets that no one would have wanted otherwise.[132] They turned what might have been a pleasurable evening into *obyazalovka* (a tedious obligation). On the other hand, factory workers did not have the connections to 'get hold of' tickets, in the way that people working in the field of culture did, or indeed school teachers, if the children of leading actors happened to be in their class.[133] More importantly, going to these events was not part of the culture.[134] Often, working-class people only remember going to the theatre as children, and even then what they saw did not necessarily make much impression on them.[135]

Leningrad, though, also had its less cerebral venues. The Musical Comedy Theatre, whose repertoire consisted of Soviet and international operetta, was one of the favourite venues in the city despite being off the itineraries of foreign tourists. In 1963, it had annual ticket sales of 493,700, coming second only to the Kirov with 608,000 – but the Musical Comedy Theatre was less than half the Kirov's size, seating 750 as against 1609.[136] Like the London theatres that could boast, 'We Never Closed', the Musical Comedy Theatre had an exceptional war record: its staff had not been evacuated, and during the Blockade they had staged more than 1000 performances.[137] This was not just the stuff of pompous official commemoration. Performances were remembered by siege survivors with warmth and appreciation: how, as they sat in their overcoats and felt boots (strictly not allowed in any theatre or concert hall in normal times), Nikolai Yanet, the company's lead singer and wartime artistic director, and his wife, Nina Pel'tser, rushed about the stage in scanty evening dress, somehow managing to keep everyone's buoyancy up.[138] But the theatre's capacity audiences were not inspired simply by sentimental memories: the programmes of light-hearted Soviet operettas (Dunaevsky's *The Golden Valley*, Listov's *The Sebastopol Waltz*), plus classics of the Western repertoire (including Offenbach and Strauss), and, from the early 1970s, also musicals, attracted audiences who would have been daunted by grand opera.[139]

Soviet operettas and *myuzikli* were on the cusp between the musical theatre in a strict sense and what in Russian tradition was known as *estrada*, variety. In the 1970s and 1980s, this turned, at its top end, into a high-gloss commercial product, dominated by Moscow-based artistes such as Alla Pugacheva, with her super-size curves, ochre mane, and insatiable taste for glitter.[140] However, there were also humbler venues which offered live *estrada*, including the many palaces of culture and factory clubs across the city. The Kirov Factory, for instance, had a prize-winning brass band that offered classical 'easy listening' alongside medleys of war songs, and favourites from the Russian nineteenth-century repertoire, as well as *The March of the Red Putilov Workers*. There was also an active amateur dramatic society with a programme of melodramas and comedies.[141] Such clubs were not attended exclusively by manual workers; they attracted an audience drawn from all over the district.[142] All the same, to some, even culture clubs could seem out of reach. In 1962, a report to the Secret Department of the City Committee of the Communist Party indicated that workers thought the costs of visiting not just theatres, but also youth cafés and palaces of culture, were unduly high: 'In order to spend their free evenings in a cultured way, young people have to pay, and to pay a lot as well. It's not easy to get into a hobby circle either, which is why young people hang round on the streets.'[143]

Tickets for the cinema, on the other hand, cost less, and seeing a film was also more 'democratic' in the sense that there were venues all over the city, including the new suburbs.[144]

'Cinema was cheap, mass-market. You could discuss all the films. Everyone always watched the same thing. Any rate, if it was a new film, then almost everyone would know about it,' remembered a woman born in 1937. Examples of such hit films were Vladimir Basov's *Battle on the Road* (1961), based on Galina Nikolaeva's novel of Stalin-era factory life in the Urals, and setting romantic entanglements against the demands of production and the stresses of the industrialisation drive, or the same director's *Silence*, focusing on political

I Decorative wrought iron river anchor and plasterwork sea anchor in the archway at the entrance to the Admiralty, 2012.

II The main hangar in the Tram Museum, Tram Park no. 62, Vasilievsky Island, September 2010. Visible are tram cars from the 1940s.

III Flyover for trams, Nevsky district, April 2011. The trams dream of a bright future.

IV Factory yard, Vyborg Side, 2010.

V New Holland, the former wharf and warehouse area (used in the late Tsarist period as a naval prison), October 2011. The archway was beloved of twentieth-century artists, but by the late Soviet period the entire site was in decay. It is now being reclaimed as an arts centre.

VI 'Leningrad Selection' patisseries, 2004.

VII The Eliseev Stores after reopening in March 2012. The giant palm in the centre was the cause of some controversy (see Chapter 5).

VIII 'Leningrad' sprats on a Lomonosov Factory plate, June 2011.

IX Fruit kiosk, ul. Chaikovskogo, April 2010. Note the Soviet-era loudspeakers on the wall, used for playing martial music and the like. The security camera is, of course, a modern addition.

X Apraksin dvor, still stubbornly resistant to 'improvement', 2012. Signs advertise 'accessories' and 'Turkish knitwear'.

XI Fans celebrate a second goal by Zenit, on the way to beating TsSKA-Moscow, 14 April 2012. To the left of the monitor is the dome of St Catherine's Church on Vasilievsky Island, enclosed in scaffolding.

XII Perambulating on the Griboedov Canal, April 2012. Boots, scarf, and dogwear to match.

XIII The garden of a pansionat in Repino, 2005.

XIV A haul of freshly-gathered mushrooms on the veranda of a dacha in the south-west of Leningrad province, 2008.

XV The seventeenth-century wooden church in the formerly important village of Soginitsy, Podporozh'e district, about 300 kilometres north-east of St Petersburg, September 2012. There are now more locals in the cemetery than in the surrounding houses.

XVI On the Tikhvinka River, in the city of Tikhvin (215 kilometres east of St Petersburg), looking towards the Monastery of the Dormition, June 2012. The childhood home of the composer Nikolai Rimsky-Korsakov is about 100 metres to the right of the fishermen, just out of shot.

XVII Piskaryovka Cemetery, October 2011, featuring the marker for the common grave from 1942 – the worst period of the Blockade.

6.8 The 'Baltic' cinema, 1952. This well-known cinema (originally built as the 'Forum' in the 1910s, reconstructed during the Stalin years, and demolished in the post-Soviet era to make way for expensive apartments) not only reflected the rise and fall of Leningrad cinema-going, but itself had a role in film, since it was one of the places where the philandering lecturer in *Autumn Marathon* met his mistress.

repression in the post-war years.[145] In 1968, another of Basov's films, *The Shield and the Sword*, shot to popularity, and to this day the film remains one of the most memorable for older Leningraders.[146] By the 1970s, on the other hand, film hits tended to be made of softer stuff: Georgy Yungval'd-Khil'kevich's *D'Artagnan and the Three Musketeers* (1978), for example, was an enjoyable romp based on Dumas, one of the country's favourite writers.[147]

In fact, 'everyone always watched the same thing' was inaccurate. The very accessibility of film led to differentiation of taste, a process that became all the more marked when Soviet studios began producing films specifically geared to a mass market in the 1970s.[148] Such *kassovye fil'my* (thrillers and comedies) were the staple fare of working-class audiences, along with Bollywood; art films were much less of a draw.[149] The cream of the intelligentsia, on the other hand, would visit The House of Cinematographers to watch Antonioni or Louis Malle, not deterred by the high thin voiceover in which an elderly lady who must have learned her foreign languages at Smolnyi Institute for Daughters of the Nobility rendered the dialogue for the monoglot.[150] Bergman was a cult figure in Leningrad, as he was all over Europe; Italian neo-realism was also much admired.[151]

One did not necessarily need an entrée to an exclusive club to watch foreign films. The Spartak cinema was 'an oasis of culture' back in the pre-perestroika days, where you could watch Fellini, Zeffirelli, or Godard. 'There were big queues, but you got through quickly, and you could always get in. And the tickets were really cheap. [. . .] We went there nearly as often as we went into work.'[152] Among this public, interest in Soviet films tended to be limited to arthouse masterpieces such as Kozintsev's film adaptations of Shakespeare, or the films of Andrei Tarkovsky, or of the Armenian director Sergei Paradzhanov (generally films from the Caucasus were more or less guaranteed an admiring audience). That said, venues such as the Kirov Palace of Culture also sometimes offered Western films, and there was also an intelligentsia audience for Soviet comedies. Taglines from Leonid Gaidai's light-hearted thriller *The Diamond Hand* (1968), with Svetlana Svetlichnaya as a Soviet glamourpuss in an Ursula Andress bikini, became part of late Soviet folklore. The innocent cliché *Khorosho sidim!* ('Nice party, eh?') acquired a permanent ironic coloration after being intoned by one of the participants in a scene of masterly social embarrassment from *Autumn Marathon*.[153]

*Autumn Marathon* was a case where a film's success at least partly depended on its local setting. But if films *about* Leningrad appealed to the local public, there was no sense in which they necessarily preferred films *made in* the city. Mass appeal and local specificity were in a relation to each other that, while not antagonistic, was not necessarily complementary. In the world of sport too, there was no inevitable association between popularity and geographical immediacy. The single sport which had been well developed before 1917, horse racing, had no base in late Soviet Leningrad at all.[154] The local football teams – Dinamo and Zenit, Automobilist, and, until 1962, Admiralteyets – all had their loyal followings, but none of them was outstanding at national level (Zenit, the best of an unimpressive bunch, was Soviet champion just once, in 1944). None was firmly identified as the city 'brand'.[155] As in other Soviet cities, ice hockey and basketball were at least as appealing to locals as football. Spartak, the leading basketball team, had a fairly modest history during the first eighteen years of its existence, but in 1953, the team came out victorious in the All-Soviet Spartak Competition, and in the 1958 season, it was admitted to the Premier Division. In the 1970s came its era of glory: between 1970 and 1978, it was champion of the Soviet Union once (in 1975), and runner-up no less than six times. Victor in the USSR Cup in 1978, it also took home the Cup of Cups in 1973 and 1975. Over the decade, Spartak was to supply around a dozen members of national teams, including the 1972 Olympic championship team, which was led by the formidably lanky Aleksandr Belov, scorer of the winning 'golden basket'. Unusually in the male-dominated world of competitive team games, the women's basketball side was just as successful, also dominating nationally and internationally throughout the 1970s.[156]

At the same time, with TV becoming far and away the most influential form of mass entertainment, local teams started to face competition from those promoted to national audiences on the small screen. Many Leningraders, like people all over the Soviet Union, were primarily excited by the achievements of the national sides, the ultimate heroes being those who had brought home gold medals from the Olympics.[157] Once they had 'all-Soviet' status, stars tended to lose their local connections, disappearing to 'central' (i.e. Moscow) clubs and becoming part of a nationwide pantheon. The impact of TV on the status of entertainers was comparable. Arkady Raikin, made lastingly famous by the medium, was also the last Leningrad star to enjoy a dominant position courtesy of television.[158]

## Perestroika Visits the Movies

The glasnost era at first gave a huge boost to cultural life in Leningrad. Theatres, concert halls, and cinemas were suddenly packed. 'Do you know how perestroika started for me? With Abuladze's film *Repentance*, released in 1984,' recalled a woman born in 1970.[159] An equally striking film dating from the same year, Aleksei German's carnivalesque drama about a 1930s police investigator, *My Friend Ivan Lapshin*, which was made (although not set) in Leningrad, was also to become a landmark of perestroika, drawing back an intelligentsia audience that had largely deserted the Soviet cinema.[160] In 1987, Leningrad TV (Channel 5) began broadcasting *600 Seconds*, a magazine-format excursion into investigative journalism that was without parallel in Soviet television history, and hard to match in the history of any other medium either. Combining criticism of the authorities with grisly footage of 'true crimes', the programme made no pretence at objectivity, but was compulsively watchable; it rapidly began attracting massive audiences.[161] In 1990, Stanislav Govorukhin's documentary film using the same presenter, Aleksandr Nevzorov, *We Can't Live Like This*, capitalised on some of the success of the series in order to make a similar plea for social change on the large screen.

The glasnost period was also a breakthrough in the theatre. In particular, the deregulation of public assembly and demise of cultural censorship brought a surge in activity by studio groups. Like 'informal' institutions generally, studio theatres now had a legitimate right to existence; they could apply for their own premises, advertise their shows, and admit the general public without hindrance. Theatre-goers reacted with enthusiasm to the chance to see performances of avant-garde classics, or of new plays, or adventurous stagings of familiar ones. Suddenly, Leningraders were confronted – mostly to their approval – with productions that dispensed with the traditional players and audience divide. Even a drama on a 'safe' topic such as the Decembrist Rebellion in 1825 was likely to be realised boldly:

> It begins in the foyer, where heroes of the past appear before the spectators by candlelight, and a song about life's long and difficult roads draws us into the atmosphere of those distant dramatic events. The actors do not attempt to metamorphose into concrete historical figures, do not try to convince us that what we see on stage is the 'real' Senate Square or rooms in the Winter Palace, or faraway settlement in Siberia (all the more since there is no stage as such – things are all happening right next to the spectators).[162]

Now it had become a compliment to say, as a *Leningradskaya pravda* journalist did in 1988, that a production had a 'genuine studio theatre character'.[163] At the end of 1989, there were over 160 active studio groups in Leningrad.[164] Some, such as Akhe and Formal'nyi teatr (the Formalist Theatre), were closer to performance arts than to conventional theatre; the latter staged improvised events ('rituals' and 'initiations'), while the former presented 'illustrations' of notable new-wave literary texts, such as Sasha Sokolov's *A School for Fools*.[165]

But the euphoria did not last. Enthusiasm for new forms of expression was soon offset by anxiety about economic crisis. By 1990, cultural institutions, like state institutions of all kinds, were fighting for survival as state funding collapsed. Every practical step was beset with difficulty – even transferring money for essential equipment turned into a nightmare as bank accounts were frozen and orders got stuck at the starting point.[166] Yet the leading Leningrad cultural institutions, like the city's famous museums, were 'brands' in a way that educational institutions and hospitals, and indeed studio theatres, were not. Klub-81, for instance, folded quickly: 'Why cram into a 500-seater hall when you can see "Aquarium" at the Jubilee Stadium?' one former habitué remembered.[167] On the other hand, the Kirov Theatre, renamed Mariinsky in 1992, flourished under its exceptionally energetic director, Valery Gergiev. Gergiev adeptly followed Western precedent in forging sponsorship deals and arranging foreign tours; a double tariff for locals and foreigners, with the latter paying prices 100 per cent higher (the Mariinsky was the only theatre in Russia to operate such an arrangement), generated a significant premium on ticket revenue.

The late 1990s and 2000s saw a proliferation of commercial troupes with the words 'St Petersburg' and 'ballet' in their titles, some with tenuous links to the city and equally dubious claims to artistic lustre. But the city's most famous ballet survived remarkably well, helped partly by the conservatism of its dancers. In 1995, Farouk Ruzimatov explained to a US journalist why he had decided to return after spending time at the American Ballet Theatre: 'In New York there were individual opportunities for me, but I did not feel connected to a tradition. I did not have a base or foundation under me. At the Kirov we have three layers of dancers: beginners or juniors, dependable and talented professionals, and experts or masters with experience and dedication. This gives the theater the ability to grow into the future.'[168]

Unlike most other major companies, including, by the 2000s, the Bol'shoi, the Mariinsky almost never featured guest stars, and its own school remained the place where most artists were trained. Post-Soviet leading dancers, particularly Ulyan'ya Lopatkina, a ballerina with the sterling combination of virtuosic technique and lyricism of line, were as impressive as those of earlier generations.[169] Certainly the new financial, as well as symbolic, importance of international tours meant that opportunities to watch the leading dancers in their home city were limited to gala occasions such as the relentlessly promoted 'Stars of the White Nights' festival in the early summer. But there were compensations since, unlike earlier directors of the theatre, Valery Gergiev was himself more attached to opera than ballet.

If there was a lack of recent non-Russian repertoire (perhaps a side-effect of royalty payments),[170] the Russian repertoire had become more adventurous, with the first performances in the auditorium of such local creations as Shostakovich's *The Nose*, a revival of the original version of *A Life for the Tsar* (now with its royalist title restored), and outings for some masterpieces of early twentieth-century repertoire such as *The City of Kitezh* and *The Golden Cockerel*. In ballet, the company became one of the few licensed by the Balanchine estate to perform the works of the master, and also housed the Russian premiere of Aleksei Ratmansky's ballet *Anna Karenina*, originally written for the Danish Royal Ballet. At the same time, it was still the classic ballets of the nineteenth century, such as *Raimonda* and *The Nutcracker*, which dominated the programmes. The main difference from the past was that Soviet-era ballets were seldom revived, a rare exception being the Shostakovich/Igor' Bel'sky *Leningrad Symphony*, though this was generally performed only on the ritual date of 22 June, the anniversary of the start of the war. Of Yakobson's ballets, only the blockbusters – *Shurale* and *Spartak* – remained in the Mariinsky's lists.[171]

This conservatism was in a sense fortunate: new-style productions tended to be not so much daring as misguided. In 2005 came the premiere of Dmitry Chernyakov's version of *Tristan and Isolde*, set among what seemed to be the German or Russian new rich. A diminutive, scrawny Tristan (huddled in a gabardine raincoat) and a vast, beehive-haired Isolde declared undying love in the chromium-embellished state-room of a billionaire's yacht.[172] As a disaffected local opera-lover complained, 'There's this element of deliberate derision, if it's a Russian opera, Mussorgsky or Rimsky-Korsakov, then there just has to be some drunken character in battered runners, yes, really, a drunk in battered runners, and an overflowing refuse container or two – even if they're performing *The Snow Maiden*'.[173] Understandably, such handling of the classics did little to wean the Mariinsky Theatre's public away from their preferences for familiar works and production values.

Bold theatrics were, however, the order of the day at the former Malyi Theatre, now renamed the Mikhailovsky, once this reopened in 2007, having been elaborately restored at the expense of the successful businessman Vladimir Kekhman, its general director as well as the head of the JFC fruit importing company. The auditorium and lobbies, which had reached a perilous state, were returned to magnificence, and the funding that Kekhman was able to provide attracted major foreign artists, such as the Spanish choreographer Nacho Duato, to work at the theatre.[174] While the corps de ballet was not at the level of the Mariinsky's, the small orchestra sometimes performed with more panache.[175] Oleg Vinogradov, whose tenure at the Mariinsky had ended unhappily in 1997,[176] kept the standards of Petersburg classicism aloft, and the theatre had its own stars, particularly the ballerina Ekaterina Borchenko. Thanks to steep discounts on the ticket prices in the hour before curtain-up, and better conditions for the spectators, there was a larger proportion of locals in the audience than in the bigger and more famous house.[177] Some opinion-formers held that its repertoire and production values were more interesting than those at the Mariinsky, and certainly some of the stagings, with use of spectacular light effects and laser displays, were more assured.[178] In the autumn of 2011, it was announced that Natalya Osipova and Ivan Vasiliev, leading dancers at the Bolshoi, were to move to the Mikhailovsky, attracted not just by the prospect of better pay but by the chance to perform in new productions staged by Duato, and by a more flexible working regime and different relationship with the audience.[179]

Some of the mavericks of the Soviet theatre were also flourishing. Boris Eifman's dance spectaculars, such as *Red Giselle*, remained extremely commercial, and his profile in the city was raised by the construction of a theatre specially to house his company.[180] Lev Dodin's Malyi Theatre continued to produce striking productions – a version of Platonov's dystopian novel *Chevengur*, using the trademark device of shaven-headed figures popping out of raked backdrops, was one highlight of the mid-2000s. An impressive new theatre, a looming green-tiled fortress on Petrograd Side, all *moderne* arabesques, was built to house the Litsedei [Mask] Theatre, specialising in pantomime.[181] But Anton Adasinsky, probably the most innovative performance artist to come out of the late 1980s theatrical renaissance, moved his base to Dresden and visited St Petersburg only occasionally. 'It's all about money with us in Russia,' he complained to a journalist in 2009. 'Yes, we've got experience behind us, but that's all in the past. A museum of theatre – that's what we have.'[182] An expert in the history of the ballet, pondering the role of culture in the post-Soviet period, wondered in 2012 whether it was possible for art forms that were based on an expectation of hard work up to the level of self-immolation in return for levels of glamour that were contextually unique ('dancers were our Hollywood') to survive outside a society of authoritarian control and economic deficit.[183] While the halls of the Vaganova School looked much as they had since the early twentieth century, and the meticulous process of learning the classical steps survived as well, inside there was a sense of uncertainty: what point, said a member of staff, could there be in training, for free, dancers who would end up performing 'in some god-forsaken hole out in Austria or Slovakia'?[184]

For its part, the art scene was short of radical new names, with the greatest creativity expended less on individual works than on the orchestration of radical exhibitions, such as those set up by the Pro Arte group in the Peter and Paul Fortress: *Soviet Underwear* and *Cat Mania*, with material from the Museum of the History of St Petersburg's own collections, were particular crowd-pleasers, but the group also mounted more cerebral photo-installations that used the facture of the tunnel system inside the bastions to creepy effect.[185] Another striking space embowelled in the city's memory was the crypt of the Lutheran Church of St Peter and Paul on Nevsky prospekt. Within it remained, preserved for ever, the vast concrete shell of the swimming pool built inside the church during the Soviet period. Too hefty for destruction (which would have brought the entire building down), the colossal basin had simply been left, and

6.9 Part of a memorial complex to the Germans deported from Leningrad, doubling as an art gallery, in the crypt of the Lutheran Church of St Peter and Paul, Nevsky prospekt, October 2011.

the floor of the church raised to conceal it. Inside this double space of church and pool were naive paintings, some of vaguely religious content, others commemorating the deportation of Petersburg's Germans. Sometimes the remaining blank walls were used for temporary exhibitions.[186]

More conventional, though still striking, was the Loft-Etazhi conversion of a bread factory, a pleasant space in an international 'alternative' style of recycled wood, distressed surfaces, and mock-'street' graffiti, made remarkable mainly by its rooftop, quintessentially 'Piter', view and by the narrow staircase up which visitors mounted as though attending a clandestine 'apartment exhibition'.[187]

Another important arts centre, in the former warehouses at New Holland, was initatied in 2011, sponsored by Roman Abramovich and Daria Zhukova, and open in summer only. With its duck-boarding painted in tasteful grey, its (almost unused) cycle racks, its Frisbee zones, and its 'gastronomic market' at weekends, the space was (at least initially) more remarkable as an inner-city amenity in the style of 'New Amsterdam' (at jarring odds with the otherwise deprived area of dockland in which it stood) than as a showcase of live art.[188]

6.10 Art installation by Dmitry Tolitsyn in Loft-Proekt Etazhi, 2010.

6.11 The 'gastronomic market' at New Holland arts centre, September 2012.

The sense of 'Petersburg culture' was visibly altering. On the surface, city-dwellers, and above all recent incomers, still felt that they should adhere to the old attitudes. 'Kupchino's certainly not Petersburg! Those people wouldn't dream of buying a ticket to the Mariinsky or just walking down the Nevsky. Never. And that's a mass phenomenon,' snorted one local.[189] This sense that you only really had claims to belong if you took advantage of cultural opportunities was rapidly internalised by incomers as well: 'Well . . . I've never actually been to the theatre,' said one of our informants, before adding immediately, 'But don't write that down.'[190] Yet, as this example also suggested, prevailing ideals did not necessarily translate into reality.

There was more, these days, to do at home. TV lost much of its intellectual appeal after the end of the 1990s, but home entertainment (videos, DVDs, and in due course online streaming of recent films – illegal but unstoppable) was more and more absorbing.[191] There were plenty of attractions beyond one's home divan as well: rock and pop concerts, musicals, farces, and – for those who wished – even lifestyle courses (which had replaced 'Communist education' in many palaces of culture). You could, for example, attend series on relationships and on assertiveness training for women – but fashion and cooking events were just as attractive to the public.[192]

The profile of sporting events also altered radically, with the meteoric rise to national – and, from 2008, international – dominance of Zenit. Few Petersburgers were much bothered about the fairly haphazard progress of the national side, as the local club collected trophy after trophy. Some carped: 'Zenit is Gazprom money, and that's all. It's only the name that's left' – but matches brought the city to a complete standstill.[193] Cheers and whistles sounded far beyond the stadium; within it, displays like a nineteenth-century diorama of the Battle of Borodino (despite an official ban on fireworks) lit up the stand whenever the home side scored.[194] Local feeling during matches ran high. The team's relocation to the Petrovsky (formerly Lenin) Stadium placed it at the heart of the city. The Cathedrals of St Isaac and St Vladimir, and the spire of the Admiralty, rose above the top rim of the stands. Matches began with massed singing of the 'Zenit Hymn', an adaptation of the 1957 tribute to Leningrad, 'Evening Song':

City on the free Nevá,
All of us Zenit supporters are [. . .]
We're with you heart and soul
Though rain and wind may howl . . .[195]

Official banners on the home stands announced, 'It's a Capital City and it's the Best Team', and the supporters' chants harped on 'Piter' as well as the team's name. The city was not so much football-mad, as seized heart and soul by Zenit. As a sports correspondent put it, 'everyone who likes football supports Zenit'.[196] An especial draw for fans was the striker Andrei Arshavin, who briefly played in the UK for Arsenal before returning to his home club in 2012.[197] The effort in 2009–10 to create a second team, Dinamo, was rather like the official attempt to invent an opposition for United Russia: artificial, and unlikely to be effective.[198]

By the 2000s, football was posing a largely successful challenge to culture as the leisure pursuit with representative force in terms of local patriotism. (Other sports, such as basketball and volleyball, had receded into the 'specialist interest' category, and the clubs involved, however distinguished in the past, had to struggle to survive. Though different forms of popular music, taken together, probably had a bigger audience than sport, no individual group or trend had the same representative force.)[199] There was considerably more emotional energy expanded on Zenit's successes (or, conversely, hooliganish behaviour by Zenit fans, held to besmirch the traditions of the 'cultural capital') than there was about the quality of productions in the city's theatres. In 2008, an ugly incident when the Zenit fans unfurled a banner reading 'Yashin's dead, and so will Dynamo be' (referring to Lev Yashin, 1929–1990, the Soviet Union and Dynamo's most famous goalkeeper) generated miles of agonised journalism and online comment.[200] News about the classical arts, on the other hand, was now mainly the province of the Kul'tura TV channel, with its decidedly middle-aged air. Duato's adaptation of Petipa's *Sleeping Beauty*, for the Mikhailovsky, generated more controversy in Moscow and indeed Britain than it did in Petersburg.[201] Even the most remarkable figures of the 1960s and 1970s had been more or less forgotten. Leonid Yakobson's centenary in 2011 was marked by a single performance of *Choreographic Miniatures* in the Conservatoire, and ignored by Petersburg's leading theatres.[202]

Few creative artists regretted the Soviet past, when control over their professions had been intrusive. But some reluctantly conceded that culture had seemed more important. 'A special public used to go to orchestral concerts back then,' one leading musician remembered. He did not miss the groups from institutes and workplaces who had been 'driven there' and 'yawned through' the performances, but the experienced listeners who had once had the time and energy to go to the Philharmonic every day.[203] Former members of the old art underground were particularly inclined to wax nostalgic about the community spirit and romantic deviance of back then. 'It was a kind of brotherhood', the broadcaster Alexander Kan remembered.[204] The louche days gone by also had a significant afterlife in what one might call 'post-nostalgia': the attachment to vanished times among those not old enough to have experienced these directly.[205] By the 2000s, YouTube and RuTube clips were making footage of Viktor Tsoi, Boris Grebenshchikov, and Sergei Kuryokhin available to new generations.

The fact that Grebenshchikov was the only 1980s rock idol to have survived into the new century (in a physical sense, of course) underlined the feeling that a unique musical culture had disappeared.[206] The graves of Kuryokhin and Tsoi were turned into improvised shrines, with offerings brought by fans; 'Kamchatka', the boiler-house where Tsoi had once worked, became a full-scale people's museum. An entire era – or, rather, one specific aspect of it – was commemorated by an imaginary necropolis, a set of half-effaced traces of the past.[207]

So far as culture in the sense of the so-called legitimate theatre and classical music was concerned, a certain loss of national status was underway. There were now other cities with strong traditions of theatre and of artistic production generally – not just Moscow, but Perm', Ekaterinburg, Novosibirsk, and many others. 'Petersburg theatre' had lost the mystique once enjoyed by 'Leningrad theatre'. There were people from the provinces who contended, as they probably would not have done back in Soviet days, that the theatre was actually better where they had come from.[208] The vice-governor of Perm' from 2010, the theatre director Boris Milgram, was a unique example of a successful local politician who was also a creative artist, and the city's spending on the arts was on a lavish scale. Its government-backed bid to become cultural capital of Europe, unveiled to fanfares in 2012, suggested the scale of the city's ambitions.[209]

6.12 Inscriptions by fans on the wall outside the Viktor Tsoi bar-museum, Kamchatka, June 2012. Note the votive beer bottle.

Whether Petersburg remained the 'cultural capital' of its home country in anyone's eyes was, by the 2010s, debatable.[210] The importance of the designation had, of course, been partly an indication of secondariness in everything else. Now the local elite had the relocation of government agencies such as Gazprom and the Supreme Court to look forward to, not to speak of more representatives in the corridors of power than at any period since 1926 (indeed, arguably, since 1917). Ordinary Petersburgers were no longer so awestruck by the arts either. Many preferred to catch concerts or plays on the television.[211] Some of the flagship cinemas of the Soviet era – if they had survived at all – were now serving other (mainly commercial) purposes, and when the House of Film showed recent Russian and post-Soviet films, its halls were usually almost empty.[212] The Lenfilm studio itself, now more or less unused and in deep financial trouble, was left to stagger along until September 2012. At that point, the Minister of Culture, Vladimir Medinsky, imposed a new board of directors. The groups campaigning to save the studio immediately began to fissure. Since the studio's decaying territory occupied a substantial area just off the Kamennoostrovsky prospekt corridor, one of the city's prime real-estate zones, it was not clear in any case how viable the desire to preserve the historic studio – at any rate on its traditional site – might be.[213]

Even if people could be bothered to attend a cultural event, their attitude was not necessarily reverential. Whispering and even talking were common, and the stereotypical annoying cellphone conversation began, 'HI! CAN'T TALK NOW! I'M WATCHING A MOVIE'.[214] Even more than before, attending concert halls and theatres often amounted to a search for a good night out:

> We went to the BDT to see *Antigone*, but actually, what they had on was *Masquerade* with Tolubeev himself. I remember that, because it was an unusual set of people we were with. Usually, Lena and I would go along on our own and have a jolly good look at everyone in the auditorium, always, as well as looking at the stage – well, we were young unmarried girls at the time. [. . .] But on that occasion, there was a big group of us, there was my auntie, and this other lady, a friend, or rather no, another relation, a distant one, and getting on a bit too. [. . .] And we got great seats, all four of us together, and we were delighted with the show, we had such good seats. And in the interval, we went to the buffet and were thinking of having a café-cognac, only we decided not to.[215]

In this account, the performance hardly signified (even the substitution of another play was not a matter of moment, though the chance to see a famous actor was welcome). It was the people-watching, the company one went with, and not least the refreshments, that were the draw. Thus, for many people, cultural events still provided an excuse for an enjoyable get-together, rather than being an end in themselves.

At the same time, cultural events no longer had the social importance they had back in Soviet days, when the demand for 'hot tickets', like deficit foods, had been self-perpetuating. As a woman in her twenties recalled of her mother: 'She says that back when she was young, she used to go to anything cool [*prikol'no*]. Say some amazing exhibition turned up or whatever, she'd wait in this huge [queue] for tickets . . . in Moscow or whatever. [. . .] That was the whole fun of it, really. And now she can't be bothered.'[216]

Petersburgers often moaned about the expense of theatrical and musical events. Indeed, where Soviet tickets had cost maybe one or two per cent of an average wage, even the cheapest seats represented, by the late 1990s, about double that amount.[217] But admission to most events (concerts by world-famous artistes aside) still cost considerably less, both absolutely and proportionately, than tickets to top venues in the West. In any case, the traditional ways of getting in 'on the skive' (*nakhalyavu*) still often worked – for instance, turning up at the first interval and slipping into an empty seat. Often, the will to sit out the full programme was no longer there – 'We watched one act, and that was enough for us,' said a man who had dropped into the Mariinsky once, out of curiosity.[218] Performances were still often very long (three hours or more was not unusual, both in the theatre and in the musical theatre), but significant fractions of the public disappeared in the final interval, while curtain calls were taken to the staccato beat of people running by dozens to the cloakroom.

So far as the city-wide image of the Mariinsky went, it did not help that the theatre's excursions into architecture (despite much public discussion) should have been so inept. The brazen ugliness of the Mariinsky's new concert hall – whose interior felt like the inside of an imperfectly mashed banana – was at least in a relatively discreet position. The theatre's modern auditorium, as assertively banal as the green glass atrium of any new business centre, was a disaster of indifference to one of the city's handsomest squares.

All the same, with the classical arts less fashionable, they sometimes became less forbidding, as in the case of a young single mother from working-class roots who was prepared to watch the same play or ballet many times on end, 'and every time you find something new, you see it in a quite different way.'[219] While some Petersburgers no longer felt compelled to honour the traditions of the 'cultural capital', for others – including members of social groups that had not traditionally been in the catchment of spectatorship – visiting the theatre, the concert hall, and the opera house continued to be an essential part of their relationship with the city.[220]

And real enthusiasts remained. Whatever the cost, they were prepared to save up – as in the case of a woman who, living on a pittance in 1995, still managed to find the money for visits to the theatre, albeit in the very cheapest seats.[221] As another Petersburger put it, 'People who love the theatre will go along – even if they have to wear some old woollen dress and a darned cardigan.'[222] There were non-monetary ways of organising visits, too, as in the case of a woman who signed up as a duty doctor in theatres so as to take her granddaughter along.[223] In fact, classical art forms were left with the core audience of real enthusiasts, those whose interest had been driven by fashion having fallen away.[224] When the pianist Grigory Sokolov played at the Philharmonia in April 2012, the crush was indescribable, despite ticket prices of up to 200 dollars. Yet the audience was dominated by music-lovers rather than glitterati. Queuing for those holding 'entry only' tickets began outside the doors around an hour before the start time, with the 'Philharmonia old ladies' deftly using sharp elbows and tongues to make sure they got to the front. A week or so later, a performance by the Chicago Symphony Orchestra attracted an even bigger scrum.[225] There was a special quality of tangible, rapt silence at events of this calibre, among well-dressed younger people as well as the 'Philharmonia old ladies' – and the hall's decoration of Corinthian capitals and palmette frieze, offset by deep red curtains, also endured.

# 7

# From Nord to Saigon

*In my youth I lived in a café,*
*In my youth I lived in Saigon,*
*I was finished, had no one to love me,*
*Then it turned out you were the one.*
(Boris Grebenshchikov)[1]

In his essay 'Vanishing Petersburg', the writer Valery Popov paid lyrical tribute to the cafés of past days. The milk bar 'Leningrad', with its ice-creams and milk-shakes; the *sosiska* (wurst) outlet, 'where at lunchtime the mirrors on the wall were moist with steam rising from the tasty *chanakhi, solyanka, kharcho*';[2] the café Sever 'with its shaded lamps on each table – so intimate and cosy, with its elegant public, the celebrities of the day: lawyers, artists, artistes. And if you had something to celebrate, whether personal or a group event, then there was the Astoria or the Evropeiskaya.' In the post-Soviet era, on the other hand, 'you can walk down Nevsky from end to end and not recognise one thing, not find a single familiar, cosy spot to go into'. The 'most popular, cosy, familiar' places were precisely those that had vanished most quickly, with the many cellar cafés replaced by US fast-food chains, 'cowboy shops', and places selling sportswear. The nineteenth-century retro of, say, the café in what had once been Vol'f's bookshop was no compensation. 'At no historical era can there ever have been such smooth, white, totally featureless walls'.[3]

While Popov's favourite places had all belonged to the Leningrad period of Petersburg's history, the apparent anachronism in his title was deliberate. He was expressing a commonly held view among members of the older generations: 'Petersburg was far more like Petersburg when its name was still Leningrad'.[4]

This romantic view of the restaurants and cafés of Leningrad might have surprised a visitor from Paris or Vienna, or indeed Budapest, Warsaw or Prague, who visited them in the 1960s and 1970s of Popov's fond description.[5] Given its size, Leningrad was short of restaurants. In 1967, there were forty-one, in 1968 forty-two, and as late as 1988 only eighty-three right across the city, including ten in mainline stations.[6] Apart from a handful located in the hotels receiving foreign guests (by the 1970s fashionable places included the penthouse bar of the Hotel Leningrad as well as the time-honoured Astoria and Evropeiskaya), entry to which could be tricky,[7] there were only a few restaurants that locals considered top-flight. These included the Vostochnyi (Oriental), open till 1964; the Sadko, which replaced this; the Moskva; and the sole remaining pre-revolutionary institution, the Metropole, which, alone among top restaurants, still had something resembling 'Petersburg' décor.[8] To an outsider, even the city's most elegant restaurants had a downtrodden look. *Servis* was usually in abeyance.[9]

'Petersburg cuisine' was also scarce to the vanishing point. It is doubtful whether it had much existed even before the revolution, when the menus of leading restaurants, as well as the tables of elite households, were dominated by Western European, particularly French and German, dishes.[10] In the Soviet period, restaurants were subject to the same nationwide standardisation that affected catering everywhere.[11] Menus were dominated by hors-d'oeuvres that could be prepared in advance, such as meat or tongue in aspic (*studen'*) and salads; entrées were usually fried meat – *shnitsel', antrekot, eskalop* – or fried fish (above all *sudak*, pike-perch, and *sig*, whitefish). While some restaurants did have their 'specials', these were not unique in a technical sense. 'Metropole, buns', for example, were no more than spheres of plain choux pastry filled with sweetened cream. The *kotleta* (patty or rissole) might come dressed in a local name such as 'Gatchina', but it was always made of minced meat or poultry and bread soaked in milk. Seasoning was often limited to salt, and perhaps a little pepper.

This hardly mattered to Leningraders, since the point of a restaurant visit was not to pore over a sequence of immaculately presented, exquisitely flavoured dishes, as in contemporary Paris or Tokyo, but to have a riotous time with no expense spared. Vadim Shefner's short story, 'A Palace for Three, or The Confessions of a Bachelor', depicted a visit thus:

> That evening, me and my friend got dressed up to the nines and took a taxi to the Kvinsisansa [Quintessence] Restaurant, where we ordered Gatchina *kotlety*, roast pheasant, a bottle of imported cognac Napoléon, a bottle of crème de cacao, a dozen bottles of beer and three dozen crawfish. Our table was right by the band, and four times in a row, sparing no expense, I got the musicians to play 'Ramona' – the tune reminded me of Lida.[12]

Shefner's vignette, though satirically exaggerated, did not distort reality. Evgeny Rein and his friends on the lash in the Rooftop (*Krysha*) restaurant at the Evropeiskaya ordered a feast that was not far different: 'various vodkas and cognacs and some fish delicacies – lamprey, eels, crayfish (done two ways, plain boiled and as a soup [. . .]). And for the mains – spit-roast sturgeon and sterlet biting their own tails'.[13]

Foreigners who visited top Soviet restaurants were usually amazed by the high prices and poor value, not realising that they would have needed to pay at least ten times more to enjoy the evening.[14] People went to restaurants to celebrate, not to have a quick meal or gaze into each other's eyes on a first date. As a visiting US graduate student commented, based on observations in the mid-1970s, 'A typical Soviet family never goes to a restaurant, except perhaps to give away their daughter in marriage [. . .] Military officers are, together with Georgian fruit salesmen and blue jeans black marketeers, among the few individuals who have enough disposable income to go to restaurants more than once or twice a year.'[15] This was an overstatement. As Rein's memories suggest, film-makers and journalists were also fairly regular visitors to restaurants, as were establishment writers and artists, successful architects, and other members of the prosperous 'creative intelligentsia'. The 'creative unions', such as the House of Journalists, the House of Actors, the House of Architects and House of Film, had their own restaurants, with good reputations.[16] But even for people who had the chance to dine out more than once in a lifetime, a restaurant meal definitely meant having a party.[17]

Like luxury foods, restaurants were inaccessible not so much economically as psychologically. Even students could afford such places, at least every now and again.[18] State pricing meant that the city's top venues were not necessarily more expensive, for special occasions, than any others.[19] But to eat regularly in such places would have seemed pretentious.[20] And dining out could be fraught with bad experiences – overcharging and rude service in particular.[21] Every year, many hundreds of complaints reached the city authorities about the public catering outlets across the city.[22] Many other victims, no doubt, suffered in silence. Obviously, it mattered more when the amount paid was significant – as it was likely to be, given that Leningrad was so short of pleasant, everyday restaurants.

The 1970s did see some development of the sector offering reasonable food at 'human prices'. An article published in *Leningradskaya pravda* in 1975 was able to make some recommendations, based on letters from readers, including a specialist fish restaurant called Dem'yanova ukha (The Blowout) on Petrograd Side.[23] But as *Leningradskaya pravda* insinuated, not all the new places were so successful. It was not elaborate names, such as 'The Hunting Lodge' or 'The Banks of the Neva', and not fancy signs 'or bright neon advertising', the author concluded. 'It's not even the interior decoration that makes a place like this command respect. It's comfort, a warm welcome, goodwill, excellent food and impeccable service that attract patrons.'[24] The article hardly needed to add that all these things were in desperately short supply.

Whatever restaurant one chose, bad or good, queues were endemic, and a long wait did not guarantee entry since doormen operated their own 'inside track' system for valued patrons, who would be let through without queuing whenever they chose to turn up.[25] Those grown rich on the shadow economy had money to splash around, and they made some places their own, particularly Elbrus on Ligovsky prospekt, a shrine of 'bandit music'. Baku on Sadovaya, and the floating restaurants The Sail and The Smelt, had a more mainstream public (the directors of furniture stores and so on), but here too, the music – ranging from Odessa street songs to Western rock – was more the point than the menu. The female public was –as someone who played in a restaurant band remembered – mainly made up of people who hung out with foreigners and black-market dealers – a genteel form of prostitution.[26]

## 'Coffee on Fire'

It was not Leningrad's restaurants so much as its cafés where everyday eating and socialising took place. The numbers of such places expanded hugely over the post-Stalin years, a Central Committee decree of 7 March 1967 ordering the improvement of Soviet 'social catering' acting as the watershed. In 1967, there were 55, in 1968, 76, and in 1988, 238, spread right across the city.[27]

The word *kafe* (*kafeterii* was also used more or less interchangeably)[28] could mean several things. It might be somewhere mainly offering tea, coffee, and sweet things – essentially, a patisserie. Pre-eminent among such *kafe* was Sever, known until the chauvinist 1940s as 'Café Nord', which served the superb pastries sold in the shop of the same name, as well as elegant open sandwiches, and other sophisticated delights:

7.1 Café-patisserie, 8 Nevsky prospekt, 1965.

> Back then you had to go down a few steps and walk through the entire shop, tormented by the sugary smell of the best pastries in the city ('it's from Nord'), and open a low door into the café itself. There were little tables with a layer of glass over green baize covers and lots of little china polar bears, mirrors, low ceilings.
>
> And the treats there! 'Coffee on Fire', for instance. It didn't actually taste all that nice, but it burned away merrily (there was a layer of spirits on top), and you had this sense of happiness bubbling over, quite unstoppable happy excitement.[29]

Moscow, Leningraders would boast, had nothing like the Sever, and they were right. Indeed, the city was definitely the café metropolis of the Russian Federation, meeting its match only in Baltic places such as Riga, Tallinn, and Tartu.[30]

The ice-cream café affectionately nicknamed 'Lyagushatnik' ('The Frog Pond' – because the seats were green), on the corner of Nevsky and ul. Sof'i Perovskoi (Malaya Konyushennaya), was another widely favoured spot from the early 1960s onwards.[31] Indeed, patisseries were the main guardians of a specific 'Leningrad style'. Alongside standard Soviet gâteaux such as the Prague, or 'Bird's Milk' marshmallow in chocolate, locals could eat treats such as 'pancake pastries', 'not ordinary cream horns, but layered envelopes of the thinnest crepes'.[32]

A second type of *kafe* offered quick meals. These were usually known by the name of the products they sold ('Cheburechnaya', dough envelopes with meat inside; 'Pyshechnaya', doughnuts; 'Shashlychnaya', kebabs; 'Pirozhkovaya', little pies) though there were also more imaginative names. Among those remembered as the best were Minutka (with pies, 'really tasty, amazing, for 22 kopecks you were in heaven'); the stand-up snack bar run by the Metropole restaurant, serving puff-pastry pies and chicken patties Kiev and Pozharski; the Universal café; the snack-bar in the House of Leningrad Trade; and the Lukomor'e and Pogrebok cafés on Vasilievsky Island.[33] Vladimir Uflyand's list of such places reads like a piece of free verse:

> The auto-café with drinks vending machines on the corner of Troitskaya [ul. Rubinsteina] and Nevsky. The snack bar at the Baltiiskaya Hotel. The *chanakhi* place on Zagorodnyi. The *shashlik* place on Raz"ezzhaya. The snack bars on Ligovka and the kiosks in the Moscow Station. The café and wine bar on the corner of Suvorovsky and Nevsky. [. . .] The ice cream place on Nadezhdinskaya (now Mayakovskogo), on the corner of Basseinaya (still called Nekrasova). [. . .] Vechernii restaurant [. . .] The 'U evreev' [At the Jews'] Restaurant. The Kavkazskii. The Sadko.[34]

A third variety of *kafe* was a café in the French sense of the word, somewhere that might offer snacks, but whose primary purpose was providing drinks. Such places might have an actual name (for example, 'Havana'), but might equally well be known generically as 'Kafe', 'Molochnoe kafe' (Milk Café), or 'Kafeterii'.[35]

Whatever type they belonged to, *kafe* offered more restricted menus than restaurants, and a range of beverages that did not include vodka (though tipples of a more refined sort, such as cocktails, might be on offer). Leningrad, like any other Soviet city, also had its canteens (*stolovye*) of varying quality, some (including student and boffin havens such as 'Vosmyor'ka' (Number 8) and 'Akademichka' on Vasilievsky Island) with their own distinctive character.[36] But it was the cafés which dominated social interaction in the late Soviet period.

This was not because of their appeal in aesthetic terms. Whatever their official category and name (or lack of the latter), they were generally decorated in a drab and, to the foreigner's eye, rather depressing, style. Colours were muddy, curtains drooped, and the already dim lighting was further reduced by missing or malfunctioning bulbs. The floors were often made of fake-marble composite that seemed to have a preliminary admixture of dirt running into the seams. In an attempt to enhance turnover, the *zabegalovka* system (run-in-and-grab) was customary. Here, no seating was offered, and customers were expected to stand at tall, usually rather wobbly, tables with tops of smeared plastic or steel. Cups were usually plain white china, forks and spoons low-grade aluminium that bent to the touch. The non-availability of knives was a foregone conclusion.[37]

Cafés were favoured not because they were better than home, but because they were different. They offered the chance to associate with a circle beyond the family, without censure on either side. This was especially important for the artistic bohemian. It was hard to seem counter-cultural when sitting at a table neatly set with doilies, while one's solicitous mama pressed tea and cakes on guests.[38] Even standing offered a different and in some respects more relaxed mode of life to the 'sitting' that was expected at family parties (it was easier to leave when you wanted). Coffee was a louche alternative to the respectable tea; as people delightedly pointed out, in Piter it had always been the proletarian drink of choice.[39]

As with English pubs of a similar generation, it was impossible to tell why people should favour one rather than another. But individual cafés did acquire their own following. For instance, a *chebureki* place on prospekt Maiorova (Voznesenskaya) was a hang-out for rockers.[40] Regulars would lift generic food outlets out of banality by giving them unofficial names. One student haunt on Vasilievsky Island was known as 'The Sphynx' (while the official canteen in Leningrad University's Philology Faculty, a cheap, cheerless place, was derisively nicknamed 'The Pit').[41] Often it was habit, or the mood of the moment, that generated loyalty to one 'greasy spoon' over another.

The food was certainly not the point – at best, it was likely to be cheap and satisfying. The nickname for one favourite café on ul. Rubinshteina was 'Gastritis',[42] revealing the expected level of cuisine. But if the food was unimportant, it was vital that a place served decent coffee. The appearance of the first Italian espresso machines created a sensation, and imposed new norms.[43] 'The Crack', a buffet in the side of the Astoria, which might in itself have been considered too 'bourgeois' by many intellectuals, was tolerated because the coffee was particularly good.[44] 'A double without sugar' became the rocket-fuel of post-Stalinist intellectual culture.[45] But still more important were the opportunities for contact with an expected, yet still unpredictable, social set. Far more than watering holes, cafés were meeting places, the sites for an obsessive 'chewing of the fat' that partly overlapped with, but was also quite different from, 'kitchen conversation'.

The fact that there was always a long wait in line if you visited a fashionable place was taken in good part. People were used to waiting, and it was less painful if the end in view was not a matter of life or death. In any case, 'a queue in a Soviet public catering outlet was like a table in a Paris café – the place for long, intense conversations.'[46] It was even somewhere you might meet the love of your life.[47] Food queues were tensely purposive, but the people waiting for service in cafés minded much less about when they reached the counter. The lack of seats did not stop people from hanging round for hours. Regulars would spend long sessions propped against a table, windowsill or wall. In restaurants, waiters were always chivvying clients, but in *kafe* you could do more or less what you liked. No one had the time to pester. In the standard cry of overworked assistants, 'There's lots of you, but only one of me'.

## 'Negative Freedom'

The intense flowering of the café in the post-Stalin era was partly fostered by official policy. In the 1960s, a drive began to popularise youth cafés, *molodyozhnye kafe*, which were supposed to have the double function of filling young people's time in a 'cultured' way and providing them with a venue where hard liquor was not on offer. The original vision for the 'youth café' was a kind of artistic salon open to the general public, rather than anywhere 'commercial'. Musical evenings and poetry readings were the thing. The programme at the café Rovesnik (Coeval) on Karl Marx prospekt included literary evenings, film showings, big band concerts, exhibitions of photography, and performances by guitar poets, as well as more conventional events of the kind often organised by Palaces of Culture (for example, Komsomol weddings, jubilee celebrations, and 'thematic evenings' of the 'Welcome to Spring' variety).[48]

It was not always easy to direct the activities that went on in 'youth cafés'. An exhibition of work by artist-poets Aleksandr Morev and Konstantin Kuz'minsky, accompanied by readings, at the Havana café in 1961 passed without incident.[49] But in 1963, the activities at the Buratino café were the subject of denunciatory comments in *Izvestiya*: how had certain poets 'contrived to read their filthy, vulgar verses' in this venue?[50] However, when this café switched in 1965 to somewhere dominated by loud music in a sub-Elvis Presley style, tobacco smoke, and people hanging round doing nothing very much, the authorities did not like that either.[51]

Despite official disapproval, various cafés did acquire a genuine cultural life. The Vostok ('East', after Yury Gagarin's spaceship), which operated from 1961 in the unlikely venue of the Catering Trade Union's Palace of Culture, became a well-liked song club, lasting into the post-Soviet era as a premier venue for bards.[52]

The 'youth café' on Malaya Sadovaya, especially favoured in the 1960s, was to lend its name to an entire school of poets, and there was also a 'poets' café' on ul. Poltavskaya.[53] But from the end of the 1960s, an apparently standard *zabegalovka* next to the Moskva restaurant was to become the main refuge of the counter-culture. This was the famous, or infamous, venue known – probably out of the desire to provoke – as 'Saigon'.[54]

'Saigon' was not just a place, it was an entire concept, an ideal, a constituent of the *Zeitgeist*. Mikhail Berg remembered it as an inalienable feature of 1970s

7.2 A montage of materials from the 'Vostok' club, 1960s.

and 1980s life, along with refuseniks, 'lectures on UFOs, unofficial exhibitions, boiler-rooms, samizdat, tamizdat, translations, the "voices" [Western radio stations]'.[55] It was a space where the imagination could run free. In the words of Anna Katsman, the first wife of Viktor Krivulin: 'We didn't live in Soviet Leningrad. The "Saigon" transported us to a different café, one more congenial to us in terms of atmosphere and interests – the "Wandering Dog". However, that cabaret, the famous haunt of Akhmatova, Mandelstam, Tamara Karsavina and the entire artistic bohemia of St Petersburg, had elegant hand-bills and programmes, as well as wall paintings by Sergei Sudeikin. In 'Saigon', on the other hand, 'the décor didn't matter. Actually, there simply wasn't any décor.'[56]

The very anonymity of the surroundings acted as stimulus to intellectual life. Tat'yana Bogomolova, who moved to Leningrad from the provincial south in the late 1960s to live miserably in a student hostel, remembered the transforming effect: 'Here was what I'd been looking for: freedom, the artist's life, the Bohemian life [. . .] After Maikop, the Saigon was another universe.'[57] A mixture of a university seminar, a drop-in centre, and a *tusovka* (youth hangout), Saigon was, by the mid-1970s, the single most famous alternative venue in the city and it retained its allure in later years as well, although the original habitués had by then moved on, declaring it had lost its cachet.[58]

If Leningrad cafés scarcely measured up to those of Paris or Vienna visually, the life lived in them was comparably intense. Indeed, perhaps more so, given that it was not customary just to sit in the corner with a book or newspaper, using a cup of coffee as the entrance fee to a kind of city-centre reading-room. If you went on your own, you were likely on the hunt for company, and would surely soon find it. The improvised character of the arrangements – no seats, no table service – was a help to this. Instead of being marooned at small tables, with oceans of social chill between them, people shared debatable territory. Speaking to your neighbour in the queue was easier and more 'natural' than it would have been to strike up conversation with someone at the next table. Yet, while the sense of public space as no-man's land was typically Soviet, Leningrad cafés were, in the context of the national culture, unique. In other Russian cities, people visited cafés, had their favourites, and even gave them nicknames, but nowhere else did a few special places have a comparable standing with the intelligentsia city-wide, and nowhere else were they a place of 'negative freedom' in this way.[59]

However 'alternative' their patrons, cafés had to observe convention in one respect: they closed at what, by beat standards, was an indecently early time. Like other Soviet cities, officially Leningrad had no night-life – 11 pm was the witching hour for cafés across the city, if they were open even that late. Only bars and restaurants in the leading hotels serving foreigners had a 'late shift', and they were beyond reach for most Leningraders. Those wanting to prolong the evening had to move on – perhaps to some dim archway to buy vodka from a street tout (an illegal, but tolerated, practice), or perhaps to someone's flat nearby (or first to the one place, and then the other).[60]

In such late-night places, the chat also flowed. Not necessarily to the exclusion of everything else: Joseph Brodsky and his friends, for example, were fond not only of literary argument, but of paper games, particularly comic verse improvisations.[61] But many Leningrad sets inclined more to weighty political and philosophical discussion. In the 1970s, these blossomed into regular, if clandestine, seminars, often of a self-consciously 'dissident' character.[62]

## Conversations Outdoors

Talk did not have to happen indoors. The city also had areas locally favoured for short, pleasurable strolls of the kind referred to by the special verb *gulyat'*, meaning both to walk as a leisure activity, and to go on the razzle – though the latter was strictly discouraged by Leningrad's formidable public-order regulations, which banned not just public drinking, bathing in unsanctioned places, 'damage to architectural monuments and other such structures', but the riding of motorbikes and scooters 'causing noise that might disturb the peace of the citizenry', and even loud singing.[63] The result was enforced decorum even in side streets, let alone in the premier spaces of the city.

First among these was, of course, Nevsky prospekt, favoured even in Soviet times as a place of social display. The post-revolutionary years had seen the democratisation of this formerly elegant street, and it was perambulated by a motley crowd, from indigents up to groups dressed for an evening out. In the 1960s, the more fashionable 'sunny' or south-facing side between Liteinyi and ploshchad' Vosstaniya was familiarly known, among young Bohemians, as Brodvei (Broadway) or Brod, and used as a place to converge.[64] The nickname vanished with this generation, but the preference for the place survived.

The prominence of Nevsky was assured by its uniqueness. There simply was no other comparable street for strolling, nowhere else you could be certain of meeting someone you knew, and probably more than once.[65] Nevsky combined the Champs Elysées *and* the Grands Boulevards, the Kudamm *and* Unter den Linden, Oxford Street, Piccadilly, *and* the Strand. (The boulevardisation of various streets in the Soviet period, such as Bol'shoi prospekt on Vasilievsky Island, or Ligovka and ul. Zhelyabova near Nevsky, had no impact on this situation.)[66] While this was a mark of Leningrad's provincialism (recalling the *passagio* of small Italian, Greek, or, indeed, Russian cities), foreign visitors in the Soviet era remarked that the city did have an unusual elegance: 'It is surprising to find anywhere in Russia so many well-dressed and attractive women as you can now see on the Nevsky Prospekt,' Ronald Hingley observed in 1961.[67]

Parks had a secondary role as strolling places. These, and 'square gardens' (*skvery*) in the city centre were favoured among adults more for sitting or meeting your date[68] than for strolling, though children would regularly be brought to take the air. The Central Park of Culture and Rest on Elagin Island was for outdoor recreation, such as boating, and taking part in outdoor festivals. It was tricky to get to: the nearest metro station, Chernaya rechka (opened only in 1982), was at least half an hour away on foot. On ordinary days, the park was often more or less empty, though in summer the proximity to Stone Island, a place of elegant 'rest homes' for the city's elite (retired actors among others), might mean that one came across a group of spry septuagenarians doing their exercises to piped music (a sight that the city's alternative intelligentsia, rather puritanically, regarded as 'fascist').[69]

The Central Park of Culture and Rest had reached its heyday in the Stalin era. As historicism became more influential, the whole idea of the 'culture park' began to be questioned. In 1982, the provision of fairground rides in the park at Tsarskoe Selo and Pavlovsk become the subject of a national debate. The ideal was now a 'reserve' (*zapovednik*), rather than a place where people could ride helter-skelters and dodgems, or, worse, behave as though they were in 'a wood', plucking the place bare of lily-of-the-valley in spring.[70]

The city's historic cemeteries also attracted strollers.[71] They appealed not just for lack of other green spaces in some areas (for instance, the central section of Vasilievsky Island, or parts of the Okhta), but – at least to some of the public – because control here was lax. In the pre-revolutionary period, when parks were guarded by armed warders, cemeteries were a traditional strolling place for members of the 'lower orders', who would not have been admitted elsewhere.[72] In the Soviet era, cemetery staff, who did not do much even to combat vandalism and theft, seldom interfered with visitors who wanted to use cemeteries as a form of more or less unregulated public space; to drink or play card games, for instance.[73] But these were extreme activities and generally people used cemeteries for quieter pursuits – airing a baby or small children, or conversing as they walked round with friends. Increasingly popular, too, as interest in pre-revolutionary history developed, was the purposive stroll taking in some notable area with literary or cultural associations, such as Vyacheslav Ivanov's 'tower' overlooking the Tauride Garden.[74]

Activities outdoors were limited by the city's notoriously vile weather, which daunted even locals.[75] During the brief heatwaves, the city's outdoor spaces would fill up with people eating ice-cream, sipping soda-water,[76] *kvas*, or Pepsi, or sitting on the artificial beach by the Peter and Paul Fortress, a rare refuge for sunbathers, to soak up the feeble rays. In the long winter months, on the other hand, cafés offered a refuge from the cold and damp, as well as from crowded domestic spaces.

## Champagne and 'Gut-Rot'

For many intellectuals, certainly of the younger generations, avid conversation – whether inside or outside – was the primary manifestation of 'Leningrad culture'. But *tusovki* (hangouts) were not just an intelligentsia preoccupation, though few from the working classes went to cafés.[77] As a senior worker at the Twenty-Second Congress Metal Factory said in 1976, meeting up at home was the thing. On a recent evening, 'we gathered with our wives and had a sing-song to the guitar.' The person concerned was a brigade leader and a Hero of Soviet Labour, and the occasion being celebrated was the award of some medals to members of the brigade. But even so, the club was not for them. 'There's no tradition of doing it like that, and anyway, we know from bitter experience how pompous and stiff occasions like that sometimes are.' The journalist's response was to suggest a trip to a café serving only tea, but she did not seem to have convinced even herself that this would have been a likely alternative.[78]

The intellectual and political tastes of different groups might vary, as well as the places where they met up, but there was one form of leisure activity that was common to all of them – drinking. With narcotic use extremely rare even in the bohemian intelligentsia until at least the early 1980s, alcohol was the drug of choice.[79] Alongside Uflyand's list of cafés was a considerably more serious list of bars:

> The 'Uzbek Wines' bar on the corner of Basseinaya and Znamenskaya. That was a place Sergei [Dovlatov] didn't just go to when he happened to be passing. The café Buratino on Znamenskaya: Dovlatov and I went there just the once. The Medved' [Bear] beer-bar on Potemkinskaya; we went there quite a lot more than just the once. [. . .] That bar called 'Volga' or 'Volna' [The Wave] on the corner of Kirochnaya and Voskresenskaya. We were always in such a hurry to get inside that we never took the name in [. . .] The wine bar on Panteleimonovskaya. The wine bar on the corner of Ital'yanskaya and Sadovaya (obviously).[80]

A comment by the writer Lev Lurie about once walking from Malaya Okhta to Kanonersky Island in fourteen hours – a distance that a determined pedestrian could cover in three, or at most four – gives a good indication of how often temptation was encountered along the way.[81]

Like cafés, bars had sub-types. The *ryumochnaya* sold spirits by the glass, the *pivnoi bar* or *pivnoi laryok*, beer from the keg, while the *razliv* or *razlivukha* was a winebar. In the last case, the English rendering should not give the wrong impression. Such places were a touch more genteel than *ryumochnye* and *pivnye*, and had their own etiquette, but mainly to do with round-buying and strategies for borrowing money to fund the next glass. Wine was sold by the

7.3 The Zhiguli beer-bar, 1979. The beaten-metal panelling was super-modish at that time.

measure, alongside cognac and Soviet champagne (and indeed Soviet champagne cocktails, with an admixture of local mineral water as well as wine and spirits, for the more pretentious).[82] But this was definitely not a question of fine vintages. *Razlivukhi* had the gloom and fug – if not the curlicued stucco, red plush, and engraved mirrors – of a Victorian gin palace on an outer London high street. The liquid served, familiarly known as 'gut-rot' (*gniloe*), was not designed for the delicate palate ('don't sniff it – you'll puke', advised a graduate of the system).[83]

Sipping was not customary either, and no one referred coyly to suns behind yardarms, 'opening time', or what in pretentious circles before 1917 was known as 'the curfew hour' (*komendantskii chas*). If you felt like drinking and alcohol was not on the menu (as in many cafés), you brought your own: to adapt the famous saying about work and pay under socialism, 'we pretend not to drink and they pretend not to see us'.[84] Leningraders drank when they felt like it, from early in the day till late, and right through the night if they happened to be so inclined. As Gleb Gorbovsky wrote:

They drank vodka, drank mixtures,
drank to see the depths,
and on the unwashed window
the moon rubbed its bare arse.[85]

In his cups, Gorbovsky could shock even friends from the avant-garde – once threatening to piss over other passengers on a trolleybus who had somehow piqued him.[86] Drink could also provide the licence for social criticism that would not have been tolerated had someone been sober (here one key case was Ol'ga Berggol'ts, responsible for remarkably brave vodka-fuelled comments throughout the post-war era).[87] But there were also many less famous people who boozed on a professional scale. It was common to begin at fifteen or sixteen, sometimes younger, since the rules about selling alcohol to young people, introduced in the late 1950s, were widely ignored.[88] By student days, drinking was *de rigueur*. As Nikita Alekseev put it in his story 'Chronicles of Piter':

> In the 1960s and 1970s, drinking amounted to an entire lifestyle – compare the 'bachelor feasts' and duelling of Pushkin and his friends from the Guards. If you were studying literature and didn't drink, you got treated like a leper. The only valid excuse was a serious interest in sport. But then, the University isn't the Lesgaft Sports Institute, is it? So everyone drank. Turning up dead drunk to a lecture was totally out of order. But if you barely sat out the first class of the day with a dreadful hangover, and then slunk off to the Andreevsky Market, where they sold beer straight from the cask and a herring roe sandwich to go with it – that was completely normal.[89]

Hard liquor was for serious drinking, and people usually embarked on it later in the day – usually, but not always.[90] Beer was only reclassified as 'alcohol' in 2012, and was the usual 'hair of the dog', with people's moods turning from grim to cheerful as they downed a glass (unless the beer ran out, a frequent minor disaster).[91] Even Leningrad pigeons were seldom sober – they hung round beer-bars waiting for people to blow froth off their freshly poured half-litres.[92]

It was standard for Western commentators of the day (such as Hedrick Smith, in his bestseller *The Russians*, 1976) to assume that Soviet citizens swilled down vodka in search of oblivion.[93] Drinking, though, was a more complex activity than that. While connoisseurship of the 'first growth' kind was ruled out, people did discriminate between different tipples; fortified wines such as Kagor were often preferred to vodka, let alone the eaux de cologne that Venedikt Erofeev's alter ego Venichka had gulped on his way from Moscow to Petushki. But *Moscow-Petushki* (1973) was a cult book in Leningrad too, and here also people drank to generate an alternative metaphysical state. In the words of Lev Losev: 'I owe everything worthwhile in myself to vodka. Vodka was the catalyser of spiritual liberation, it opened up doors to interesting bits of your subconscious, and it also helped you stop being afraid – of other people, of the authorities.'[94] Above all, it facilitated the crucial involvement in talk: 'People never got drunk, not to the dead drunk stage. It was a way of making conversation flow. People behaved themselves, you understand. I never saw any drunken fights, rows, scenes.'[95]

Such social facilitation was not available to everyone. Leningrad drinking was male-dominated (Ol'ga Berggol'ts's extravagant drinking was both exceptional and the source of disapproval).[96] Women might quaff round the table at home, and occasionally be invited for a drink in some more or less decent watering-hole, but they were not part of regular company:

> If there were women round [. . .] they soon ended up acting like men. And the women who did hang round, well they'd attract silent disapproval. Or even not silent. So when a man happened to be doing something with his girlfriend or his wife, well who cares which, and he wanted to drop by and spend some time with the lads, she'd go shopping or something like that. And he'd spend a bit of time with his mates, and then go and meet up with her. Because taking a decent woman somewhere like that was considered dead indecent.[97]

Or alternatively, such 'decent women' could choose to sit out the wait in a different sort of place, for example somewhere selling ice-cream or cakes, where their respectability would not be in question. When they did drink, women generally stuck to 'ladies' drinks' such as table wine and cognac rather than vodka. Only the boldest free spirits expanded their repertoire to include 'booze' of any description.[98]

Within their own lights, drinking dens were subtly different. For instance, one near the entrance to the city zoo, known as 'The Monkey' or 'The Elephant', was considered an 'intellectual' place, for reasons most obvious to its frequenters.[99] But intellectuals also drank from beer kiosks at the side of the road, on station platforms, below bridges, and on building sites (which offered shelter from prying eyes as well as the weather). In any of these places, one's neighbours might be 'surgeons, actors, deputies of the Supreme Soviet', but they might also be workmen in overalls.[100] Under courtyard arches and in cellar bars, on the slush-covered steps of basement vodka shops, an identifiably Leningrad style of drinking prevailed: grimy, uncompromising, but with a certain ascetic dedication, an indubitable literary resonance. It was easy, swigging vodka from blurry, ribbed tumblers, to imagine yourself back in the days of Dostoevsky.

## Retro and Co-ops

But not all Leningraders were enraptured by Dostoevsky, and, as interest in a glamorised version of the city's past rose, the city's cafés and bars became the object of distaste among some. A journalist writing in 1980 complained: 'Should not the more prestigious Leningrad cafés have, instead of numbers, real Russian names, worthy of our glorious city? And should we not start with our well-loved "Frog Pond"? Can we really not find a name that would link the place with the history of Nevsky Prospekt, with its architectural harmony?'[101]

Certainly, passéism could still attract suspicion. A journalist writing in 1980 saw a retro-style bar in Frankfurt-am-Main as a sad symptom of the worn-out capitalist values that socialist countries had surpassed.[102] There was a highly specific, officially favoured, 'Leningrad manner', running to decorative schemes with a so-called 'White Nights' colour palette that had no recognisable connections to the interiors favoured in historic Petersburg.[103] But a certain discreet revivalism was beginning to work through. In 1984, the interiors of the Siberian Trading Bank, no. 46 Nevsky prospekt, which was home to the more elegant branch of the Café Sever, were elaborately restored under the supervision of the Monuments Department, with the participation of planners and master builders from East Germany. The reopened café rapidly became one of Leningrad's most fashionable spots.[104]

When another famous place, the former Vol'f bookshop on Nevsky, was turned into a literary café, the brash modernism of the refit was found offensive, not exciting. What had happened to the tapestries of 'Pushkin's Petersburg' and the murals based on his poems, the lamp-stands, table-lamps, and chairs modelled on 1830s prototypes? asked *Leningradskaya panorama* in 1985. 'Unfortunately, almost nothing from the original plans widely discussed in 1982 has survived. And instead we see all sorts of things you'd never have found in a café back then – such as the metal trees passing as lamp-stands on the ground floor.'[105]

7.4 The Literary Café, 1985.

As with historical purism generally, such criticisms were soon overtaken by cultural change. The arrival of the co-operative movement transformed the service sector. While some new places harked back to the NEP era in terms of their names at least – for instance, 'Retro' on Petrograd side, or the 'Natsional'' on prospekt Nauki[106] – others had little or no sense of local history. One much-publicised arrival was a branch of the famous 'Lagidze Waters' café in Tbilisi, a bastion in its time of the Georgian modernist movement, but not exactly indigenous to this part of the world.[107] The new co-operatives – some of which traded in hard currency only – were beyond the reach of many, but it did not take long for Leningrad institutions to start disappearing. As early as April 1988, one former *ryumochnaya* on ul. Bronnitskaya had become a modernised café with (oh horror) a non-smoking policy.[108]

These events were the early manifestations of what in due course became a pattern. The Saigon was closed down in the late 1980s for reconstruction as a larger and slicker café – 100 covers were planned – but died on the operating table and was replaced by a shop selling bathroom equipment.[109] The Saigon's parent, the Moskva, also disappeared. With the arrival of 'savage capitalism', a wave of privatisation began.[110] The racketeers and mafiosi who had always made up the majority clientele of certain restaurants became the dominant public in most places.[111] New restaurants opened, often providing patrons with floor-shows along with the traditional bands and banquets, blurring into the genre of nightclub, which was also booming at the time.[112]

## 'Aristocratic Cuisine since 1874'

While the 'Al Capone' style faded with the disappearance into the background of organised crime, the restaurant scene had changed for good. The top end of the market was now dominated by what purported to be a revival of Petersburg traditions. Tsar, on Sadovaya, a favourite with 'suits' from the business world, had 'chairs with royal monograms and ermine covers, and crazy prices'.[113] Palkin, round the corner on Nevsky prospekt, advertised itself as offering 'aristocratic cuisine since 1874', though in fact the restaurant of that name had closed in 1925, and the premises were occupied during the Soviet period by a cinema. The menu offered such 'authentic Petersburg' delights as salad leaves and goat's cheese, Kamchatka crab with avocado, wild Chilean seabass, marbled meat grilled on volcanic lava, cream of mascarpone with chocolate, and citrus cheesecake. But as the prices suggested (over 200 dollars for 30 grams of caviar with blini on the side), the point was to spend money, rather than enjoy a rarefied taste sensation (so far, tradition still held).

Palkin's was the most meretricious updating of a nineteenth-century restaurant brand, but other places played on the past too: 'At Prince Golitsyn's', 'The Assembly of the Nobility', or 'Elena Molokhovets' Dream', which offered comparably anonymous international fusion food (marinated venison with *sauce verte*, terrine of salmon) under the banner of the queen of Russian cookbook writers.[114] If all else failed, as in the case of a venue called simply 'Restoran" ' (Ресторанъ), the presence of the hard sign at the end of the word, abolished in 1918, indicated an adherence to time-honoured values.[115]

'Soviet restaurants', in the sense of museums of Soviet kitsch, did exist, but seldom prospered. An example on the Fontanka, where the main reminders of the past were worn copies of five-year plan novels, closed in the early 2000s after a few inert years, its space absorbed by the much more popular café next door, offering mixed Russian and Uzbek food in a slightly rustic, pronouncedly 'cosy', interior. The restaurants from before 1991 that did not vanish altogether were transformed, leaving only the name as a link with the past. The fish restaurant Dem'yanova ukha was still going strong in the 2000s, but a reporter for a local paper commented approvingly in 2003 that the only 'Soviet' touch in the place was neatly quartered paper napkins.[116] The Metropole reopened in 2010 as a 'Belgian brasserie' and micro-brewery, with nothing but the interiors (which predated the Soviet period in any case) to recall the past.

The menus, on the other hand, were more conservative. Despite the fancy names and design values (starched damask or, conversely, handsome undyed linen cloths, sparkling glasses and flatware), the top restaurants had little sense of local tradition.[117] It was typical for a flamboyant title – 'The Tenderness of Sister Teresa', say – to conceal a mass-catering standard from back in the Brezhnev days (here, 'salad of beetroot with prunes').[118] Many professional chefs had received their training back in the old days, and had retained the mindset: 100 portions of exactly 120 grams each.[119] In a certain would-be elegant, and extremely expensive, 'Petersburg-style' restaurant, one party of locals was dismayed by the mediocre food (including rubbery blini that weren't a patch on the ones in a leading local fast-food chain) and appalling service. As they were leaving, the waiter 'bawled across the entire room – which, I should say, was almost full – "I let you have a cup of tea for nothing and then you leave me 100 roubles!" ' Someone else, visiting a similar place, wondered how an establishment boasting a pre-revolutionary aristocratic title could serve such ordinary food. 'Even on a city dump, they wouldn't consider lasagne a main course.'[120]

In the circumstances, it was not surprising that the clientele often consisted mainly of visitors to the city and occasional locals looking for a special night out – a conjunction of interests that led, on one occasion, to a close encounter between a senior Orthodox churchman, being entertained by an academic after a talk, and a welcoming party for the pop star Bryan Ferry, complete with assorted micro-skirted groupies.[121] By the late 1990s, the city had acquired a cohort of 'family restaurants', but even these were sometimes subject to strange confusion about their role, as in the case of a mock-Ukrainian place on Five

Corners whose fifth anniversary celebrations in 2004 included not just a quiz and a floor show, but also an unadvertised striptease.[122] The Soviet idea that customers were a burden died hard. In 2013, the waitress in a Kolomna restaurant, dancing attendance on three tables of fleshy young businessmen with younger female companions, tossed her dyed black hair and snapped, as I ordered soup, a salad and potato cakes, 'If you want all that food, you're going to have to wait.' The 'business lunch', advertised as available from noon until four, had 'completely sold out' by two o'clock; the 'Lenten salad' contained slices of calf's tongue. As the gaps between the arrivals of my orders stretched to infinity, a constant flow of spirits and dishes was carried to the other tables, where expenditure of time for the sake of it was the order of the day.[123]

## Chez Jules and 'The Rusty Horseshoe'

For most permanent residents of the city, the reliable choice continued to be a *kafe*. In the early 1990s, pleasant ones were still thin on the ground and, as in the Soviet period, hotels sometimes filled the gap: when the Hotel de l'Europe opened a patisserie shop in 1994, this made the front pages of local newspapers.[124] But a few years later, places were starting to proliferate. Down Nevsky, the public lavatories once located in basements (a refuge for black-marketeers and even drug dealers back in Soviet days) disappeared, many replaced by cafés. It was not just the 'cosiest places in the city' that were forced out by the new order.[125]

Some Soviet-era places had survived in more or less unreconstructed form – for instance, the chebureki bar on Voznesensky. But more often, references to the past were of a secondary kind. The title *ryumochnaya* or *pivnoi bar* was sometimes used for a newly-opened place offering cheap drinks (see figure 7.5).

The main link with the past was in social practices – the primary function of visiting was to get drunk quickly.[126] Drinkers shared the historic local indifference to what was now called *dizain*. But the 'retro' style was the expression of inertia – how else did you decorate a bar? – rather than planning. It was mainly eating places favoured by foreigners that espoused 'Soviet junk shop chic'; in places frequented by Russians with strivings for elegance, *Western* retro was preferred.[127] On the whole, a 'ye olde Russian' name indicated that the staff were probably from somewhere further to the east, as in a place called 'The Barrel' serving, alongside *kvas*, tomato salad whose excellence betrayed the Uzbek origins of its cooks, or the 'Rusty Horseshoe Tavern', where a Tatar influence was clear in the high quality of the *chebureki* and courtesy of the staff.[128] The name of one place, 'Vereshchagin', was witty given that it was furnished in a mixture of *kilim* rugs and samovars, with a seven-string guitar on one wall, and that the painter Vasily Vereshchagin painted many famous views of Central Asia during the tsarist colonial era.[129]

7.5 A retro *ryumochnaya* opposite the Leningrad Metal Factory, photographed in 2010. The 'retro', however, goes only so far: note the sign advertising mobile phone top-ups.

The de-Sovietisation of most public catering in St Petersburg was striking. In Moscow, enduring public institutions such as the former Lenin Library tended, as late as the 2010s, to offer their customers unreconstructed canteen food: grated carrot salads; spreading dun-coloured dollops of stew or soup; cloudy crimson glasses of compote. In Petersburg, by this point, the microwave had ejected aluminium vats and ladles from most such outlets. Sometimes this fact was out in the open – one selected an airline-style tub from a counter and waited while it was heated up. Sometimes the process of confection would be veiled by a screen, with only a ping to give things away.

There were exceptions to this push for modernity. On Bol'shaya Konyushennaya remained a media-celebrated doughnut outlet, where the dish was still prepared to the original recipe in Soviet catering manuals; service, too, was authentically brusque.[130] A less famous (but considerably more appealing) survival was the place simply called Cheburechnaya on the sixth line of Vasilievsky Island, which now provided its visitors with such luxuries as metal Vienna chairs and even knives, but whose menu of slow-seethed stews, as well

7.6 Interior of the 'Barrel' café, with glass of kvas, 2011.

as the eponymous dough pouches, had not altered.[131] A café in the Academy of Sciences Library offered food of a kind that one could have eaten in the 1970s (though only in the dining-room of a top institution or a Party department) – salads, soups, and schnitzels cooked to order. The queues, too, were long. But there was nothing self-consciously revivalist in this, and people did not eat there because they wanted to steep themselves in the past. It was just that the meals were 'tasty'. What mattered was that the food should be fresh, simply prepared, inexpensive, and within the range of familiar flavour associations. Adventurous aromas were neither expected nor desired.[132]

Certainly, fast-food outlets run by chains had proliferated. By 2010, there were forty-two branches of McDonalds, including a dozen in the heart of the old city.[133] Other foreign chains (for example, Sbarro and Pizza Hut) and Moscow ones (including Yolki-palki) had also made their mark. Sushi (rumoured to be among Vladimir Putin's favourite foods) was ubiquitous. International and national café groups, such as Coffee House, Shokoladnitsa (The Chocolate Pot) and Ideal'naya chashka (The Ideal Cup), had also moved in, with Starbucks poised for arrival at the start of the 2010s.[134] The Moscow bakery chain Volkonsky, with loaves and croissants 'uniting the best of French, Ukrainian, and Russian tradition', had become a favourite place for ladies whose handbags weighed more than they did (particularly the branch near one end of Kamennoostrovsky prospekt).

But there were also local chains – for instance Koshkin dom (The Cat's House, named after a famous children's play by Samuil Marshak and Elizaveta Vasilieva). More importantly, there were many one-off places with a genuine local feel, from an organic bakery near the Admiralty to a loosely French 'corner café' not far from the Blockade Museum.[135] For the most part locals, particularly the middle-aged, were set in their ways, and designer sandwiches and salads (widespread in Moscow) were in much less demand than the traditional 'set lunch' of salad, soup, and a meat course, followed by tea.[136]

The city retained its love of patisseries. The 'Sladkoezhka' (Sweet Tooth) cafés offered bizarre flight-of-fancy cakes to commission (such as one for the 'No. 103 Building Company', showing a newly-constructed housing estate, roofed in fondant icing), and in season, paschal loaves (*kulichi*), 'blessed for your convenience on Good Friday'. But they also had primly elegant fruit tarts, meringues, babas and choux buns. The extent to which the company had succeeded in 'reviving the art of Petersburg pastry-making' (as its advertising claimed) might be questionable, but the products were delicious and well-liked.[137]

With the proliferation of alternatives, queues had nearly vanished. If one place was full, you simply went elsewhere. In other ways, too, things were more relaxed than in the past. Opening hours were more generous. 'From Noon till the Last Guest Leaves' was a ubiquitous promise, and many places operated till at least midnight. In most cafés and bars in the centre, women could now order a drink without any sense of disapproval from staff or patrons.[138] Prices in 'tourist Petersburg' were quite high, but you could still go somewhere like a bakery, or the refectory of the Alexander Nevsky Monastery, and eat for remarkably little.[139] There was usually no pressure to keep ordering – these places were more in the Viennese than the Paris or London tradition.[140] In summer, strollers, who in the past had needed a camel's resistance to hunger, thirst, and the need to take 'comfort breaks', could call in at a pavement café or park kiosk.[141] 'Life has become better, life has become more fun,' the musician Evgeny Drapkin remarked, parodying Stalin's famous declaration in 1935. However, Drapkin also added, 'But there's something missing.'[142]

## 'Looking Really Good'

What was 'missing' was the 'club' role of cafés. No longer did a handful of places dominate anyone and everyone's list of where it was worth going. Many people now had a favourite café of their own. The place in the House of Books, with its superb view of Nevsky, was far too expensive for most locals, charging the same for a couple of coffees as two three-course lunches with drinks would have cost in most mid-price places.[143] More 'democratic' (in the sense of accessible) was the café in another bookstore, the central branch of Bukvoed, hard by ploshchad' Vosstaniya.[144] However, more out-of-the-way places were often favoured – often somewhere round the corner from work, useful for quick lunches or occasional celebrations, referred to affectionately as a *kafeshka*.[145]

The relationship between eating out and the rest of one's life had altered too. Some people visited cafés more than they had in the past.[146] But the café had become a subordinate part of existence: a place you went from home, rather than home being somewhere you retreated to when the café had closed.[147] Where the intellectual cafés of the 1960s and 1970s had emerged spontaneously, attempts to revivify the tradition were now self-conscious, such as a project in 2004 to set up a 'science café' with British Council sponsorship in Cafemax on Nevsky prospekt.[148] In the past, people had more time to sit round in cafés, and fewer appealing ways of spending it. Now, leisure hours had dwindled because so many were doing more than one job; long sessions were ruled out.[149]

There was also far more competition in terms of alternatives to the café. Particularly among young people, a full-scale 'going out' culture had developed. Petersburg clubbing was not as developed as in some other European cities, but there were plenty of places, from the mainstream (such as Fish fabrique), to the snobby (the members-only Absinth Club, at 40–60 dollars and upwards per person), to the specialised (Central Station, with go-go boys and drag queen contests), to the gauche (Money Honey, for wannabee cowboys, and Purga (The Blizzard), 'where every night is New Year's Eve . . .').[150] By the 2000s, some self-consciously downbeat places had also opened – for instance, Dacha next to the Duma building, offering a well-used and cosy look, or the neighbouring Fidel. In both, having a good time was a great deal more important than posing.[151]

But an ethos of display was widespread. In 1998, a poll of Petersburg school-leavers indicated that 'looking really good' was considered the second most important thing in life, after 'good health'.[152] This attitude persisted into the following decades. The middle-aged not only had less time, but less disposable income too, paying household bills while stay-at-home teenagers and twenty-somethings lashed out on new clothes, mobile telephones, and MP3-players, and often cars on credit as well.[153] Members of the younger generations were now likely to go on the town as much as their resources allowed.[154] And night-life as a theme ran through the new popular culture. The group 'Today Tonight' played on this not just in terms of its name, but by making hoarse tributes to an after-hours transgressive culture. A YouTube clip, 'Between Luxury and Anguish' (2008), showed a young woman spinning between members of the group under the impassive eyes of male and female police officers.[155]

The hedonism of the post-Soviet generations was the subject of much anxious debate, both in the press and in ordinary conversation.[156] According to figures from 2005, 40 per cent of the population aged 14 to 20 had tried drugs, as opposed to 20 per cent in Russia as a whole; certainly, people who reached their late teens at the end of the 1980s and later took glue-sniffing just as casually as drinking.[157] Attitudes to sexual activity had also changed: by the late 1990s, 'we all just wanted to lose our virginity as soon as possible'.[158] No more were long city walks the standard means of courting, as they had been in Joseph Brodsky's day, when, as he remembered, 'it would make an astronomical sum if we were charged for mileage'.[159]

But promenading continued, particularly along Nevsky. As in other post-Soviet places, many young women preferred the 'glamour look'.[160] Back in the Soviet period, visits to the hairdresser and beauty salon had been not just possible but expected. 'Women here wouldn't even take out the rubbish without their make-up on,' reminisced a professional beautician.[161] Now, glossy magazines gave the old ethos a global twist, and also promoted a much more sexualised body culture than would have been considered appropriate in the past. The old 'healthy living' ethos was replaced by dieting, Planet Fitness, and the suntan parlour. With the price of imported clothes and make-up boosted by duty, people who cared about their appearance wanted impact for their money.[162] Glamour also advertised one's distance from manual work – not just of the professional kind, but the daily grind of goods-schlepping and scrubbing that had been the lot of Soviet women. Stratospheric heels made the distinction between promenading and mere 'walking' obvious (for men, the equivalent footwear of perambulatory distinction was a shoe in tender leather with an exaggeratedly pointed toe, or a studiedly non-utilitarian trainer).

Still, professionals insisted that Petersburg style was, compared with Moscow, discreet: people did not necessarily wear *all* the gold chains they owned at once; labels such as Versace were considered *de trop*.[163] In the 1990s, the New Russian in a 'raspberry-coloured jacket' was a figure of local mythology, and people avoided anything outré into the 2000s.[164] Often, ingenuity was expended on the elaborate straightening and colouring of hair, rather than the selection of bought garments. Sometimes there would be city-wide crazes: fashion gumboots, say – tartan, flowered, paisley, or leopard-spotted – or 'those idiot fur gilets, just everyone was buying them'.[165] But there were also more self-conscious fashion-followers, with the borrowed word *hipster* used for figures who would have fitted into the Williamsburg or Hoxton scene, their clothes radically contoured and negligently seamed and their boots a parody of those once worn in the now closed factories.[166]

7.7 CultuRRe-Space (Prostranstvo kul'tuRRy), a gallery for young designers, June 2011.

The middle-aged, on the other hand, continued to favour the sober colours and restrained styles of the Soviet past, though Soviet-era garments, such as heavy wool overcoats, had been replaced by the global clichés of quilted nylon or waterproof crease-resistant outerwear. There were many young people who went for a downbeat sportswear look as well.

If Nevsky was given over to different uniforms, people who eschewed banality of dress might appear more or less anywhere in the city, and just as suddenly melt away: a passer-by braving filthy Liteinyi Bridge in a champagne-coloured coat and pale grey scarf; a girl in kingfisher-blue sequined platforms and puffball skirt on Furshtadtskaya; a scarlet and black multi-layered chiffon dress in the drab surroundings of the Hotel St Petersburg.[167] Given the prevailing restraint, appearances of this kind were as startling as the sudden sight of a loud, laughing mouth full of gold teeth in the back of a silent trolleybus load.[168] In the older generation, particularly, local style of a certain kind was typified by women in trim, dark winter coats and fawn scarves, whose need for colour was usually satisfied by the extravagant all-in-ones in which they dressed their lap-dogs.[169]

Perhaps the traditional self-control of Petersburgers, as well as their disinclination to like what they were supposed to, also explained the artificiality of the pedestrian zones off Nevsky.[170] In these well-tended corrals, pavement art was also of a strictly commercial kind, with lurches into fantasy reserved for other parts of the city. In March 2008, two concrete globes on Kutuzov Embankment introduced by the city authorities as an anti-parking device were painted bright yellow, and turned into the giant breasts of a heathen goddess made of snow, with a scattering of earth for her pubic hair.[171] Graffiti artists also regularly subverted the city administration's efforts to order the city landscape, covering entire walls with swirling vignettes in livid colours, and providing unsolicited commentaries on the hideous copies of famous Russian paintings suspended by the Russian Museum along the Griboedov Canal.[172] Attempts by the authorities to 'tame' the genre by setting aside specific areas (such as the approaches to Apraksin Market or back courtyards round the Pushkinskaya 10 arts centre) were at best partly successful.

The shift in the preferred types of promenading completely transformed some areas. By the end of the 1990s, the sculptures of the Soviet era had gone from Elagin and Stone Islands, and at weekends Elagin was packed with families making use of the nearby Krestovsky Island metro stop (next to which was a year-round funfair). Stone Island, on the other hand, had respite from fast traffic only at weekends, but was not much used for walks as public transport was poor and its increasingly obvious status as a high-end residential area was daunting. In the 1990s and 2000s, one of the favourite spots for crowds of young people to gather from evening onwards was the Field of Mars, once the august venue for official ceremonies. Standing on the blocks commemorating the undying heroism of the revolutionary fallen, they played their guitars and shouted their songs. School-leavers thronged in graduation finery, photographing each other with the Eternal Flame as backdrop. Such activities colonised a formerly sacred memory space and also a place that, in the late Soviet period, had been mainly used, on ordinary days, for taking out children.[173] Sometimes crusts of vomit on heroes' gravestones pointed to the dislocation in values.[174] (See figure 7.8.)

These social changes were not a post-Soviet development pure and simple. Already by 1987, Leningrad's public order regulations had been revised to prohibit 'the wearing of symbols, attributes and other items or representations contrary to the norms of morality and decency, or which represent a threat to the health and life of the citizenry', and 'the use in public places of perfumes and other chemical substances or medical preparations without prescription, and with the aim of inducing alcoholic or other forms of intoxication', as well as the on-street sale of alcohol to the under-21s.[175] But though the ways that young people passed their time did not shift radically with the demise of Soviet power, there was a tendency to associate them, retrospectively, with that

7.8 Young people using the memorial on the Champs de Mars as a 'hangout' (*tusovka*), 2010. To add to the irony, the inscription reads, 'NOT VICTIMS BUT HEROES'.

enormous change. This in turn became a major cause of nostalgia among the middle-aged. Even at the time, Soviet cafés, in their very drabness, could be the source of poetic inspiration – as evoked in Nonna Slepakova's 'Peterhof' ('Your cooled coffee looked from its white cup/Into the damp morning with a mid-brown eye').[176] After privatisation, outright sentimentality became the rule, with Valery Popov's memories being a particular case in point.

But there is no arguing with a lament. Popov's primary aim was in any case not so much to suggest that things actually *were* better back in Soviet days as to give voice to a sense of insecurity. When you are no longer sure you are getting the best, your self-confidence disappears. Being able to sit in any café you like is a poor substitute for knowing that you and your friends regularly visit the only one in the city that is worth going to. Alongside this sense of affront, very important in a city so attached to exclusivity, people also gave voice to a view held by many in post-Soviet culture, independent of place: there was more sense of companionship back then. The post-Soviet generations had no cause to miss the café discussions they had never experienced, or link the rise of cosiness at home with the disappearance of *uyut* everywhere else. Admiration for the Saigon as an icon of alternative culture, among those not born when it existed, did not create a feeling that things were now 'worse'. Their elders, however, were left to bewail the demise of the beloved meeting places and vivid social contact of the past, and to seek lost pleasures in memoirs, on Kul'tura TV channel, and on the internet.

# 8

# The Twenty-Seventh Kilometre

*Lost in the dunes we took from the Chukhna*
*was the plywood settlement, where a single sneeze*
*would bring a telegram from Sweden – 'Bless you!'*
(Joseph Brodsky)[1]

By no means all Leningraders were keen to range outside their city. The world over the country's borders was inaccessible for most, and travel within the Soviet Union – to what Leningraders thought of as 'the provinces' – lacked appeal.[2] Many had spent immense efforts to escape a small town or distant city and reach Leningrad.[3] In any case, it was sometimes difficult to get leave: Aleksei Gonchukov, despite holding a position as a political activist at the Kirov Factory, was able to take his first holiday only in May 1940, at the age of 35.[4] Often, travel was the prerogative of those 'on command' – that is, voyaging on business.[5]

From the late 1950s, the situation began to change. Holiday time increased, and opportunities to stay in 'houses of rest' proliferated.[6] In 1970, the Kirov Factory completed work on an enormous guest house complex, White Nights ('like a vast ship'), at Sochi.[7] 'The South' in a broad sense – the Ukraine, the Caucasus, the Krasnodar area – became a much-favoured destination for tourist trips.[8] The resorts of the Black Sea, above all Koktebel', had the kind of cachet that had once drawn Petersburgers to Biarritz.[9]

Leisure travel round the provinces of inland Russia also became popular in the 1970s, but mainly to historic places, particularly the medieval cities beginning to be promoted as 'the Golden Ring', such as Rostov, Yaroslavl', Vladimir, and Suzdal'.[10] Moving beyond this network of resorts and accepted tourist destinations was the prerogative of specific subcultures. Travellers had to be prepared to rough it – no hotels or places to eat, quite possibly nowhere even to buy food.[11] This did not mean that going 'off-map' was intrinsically subversive. Since the 1930s, there had been official backing for the *turisty* or 'hikers', whose exploration of remote areas was seen as useful to Soviet power (there was overlap here with geological and ethnographic expeditions, a professional, but at the same time informal, type of travel).[12] At the same time 'savage', or

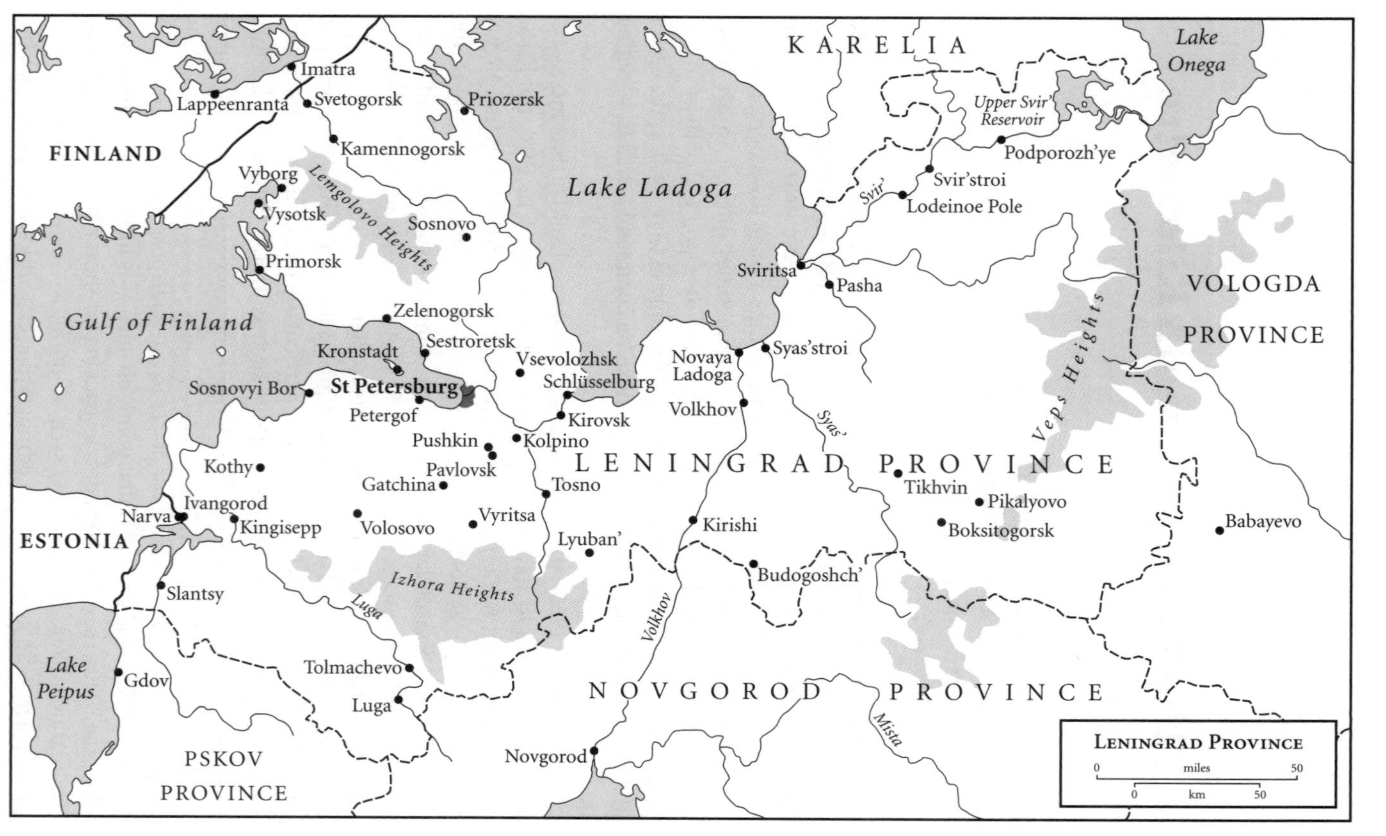

LENINGRAD PROVINCE
0
miles
50
0
km
50
KARELIA
Lake Onega
Upper Svir' Reservoir
Podporozh'ye
Svir'stroi
Svir'
Lodeinoe Pole
FINLAND
Imatra
Lappeenranta
Svetogorsk
Priozersk
Kamennogorsk
Vyborg
Vysotsk
Lemgolovo Heights
Sosnovo
Primorsk
Lake Ladoga
Sviritsa
Pasha
VOLOGDA PROVINCE
Veps Heights
Gulf of Finland
Zelenogorsk
Sestroretsk
Kronstadt
Vsevolozhsk
Novaya Ladoga
Syas'stroi
Sosnovyi Bor
St Petersburg
Schlüsselburg
Petergof
Volkhov
Kirovsk
Syas'
Pushkin
Kolpino
Pavlovsk
LENINGRAD PROVINCE
Kothy
Gatchina
Tosno
Tikhvin
Pikalyovo
Ivangorod
Narva
Kingisepp
Volosovo
Vyritsa
Kirishi
Boksitogorsk
Babayevo
ESTONIA
Lyuban'
Budogoshch'
Slantsy
Izhora Heights
Luga
Volkhov
Lake Peipus
Gdov
Tolmachevo
NOVGOROD PROVINCE
Luga
Mista
Novgorod
PSKOV PROVINCE

unplanned, travelling could carry the scent of liberty with it – both metaphysically ('the freedom of the mountains'), and practically (sharing a tent with one's boyfriend or girlfriend was common).[13] For the hippy *sistema*, going on the road was a way of life, just as it was for social marginals such as *bomzhi* (those 'without fixed address'), or abandoned children.[14] Unofficial works of art paid tribute to unsanctioned travel, as in Gennady Prikhod'ko's 'Pagan Cycle' (1972–82), in which his travelling companion, and later wife, posed nude against the rugged landscape of the northern wilderness.[15]

Much commoner was travel within the immediate hinterland of Leningrad. Between 1927 and 1944, the city had been the administrative centre of a vast territory comprising more than 350,000 square kilometres, and stretching from the Estonian and Finnish borders in the West to the western border of what is now Vologda province. Post-war reforms reduced Leningrad province to a comparatively modest slice of land less than a quarter that extent, and more or less cognate with the pre-1917 St Petersburg province, though also including districts to the west that had once been part of Finland, and lands to the east that had originally belonged to Novgorod province.[16] However, even the diminished province was more than four times the size of Wales, and to negotiate its west-east sprawl along the Gulf of Finland would have taken an entire day's hard travelling. And the nature of road and rail connections meant that Novgorod, for instance, was closer to Leningrad than some places that were administratively tied to the city; there were direct trains to Vologda, but only local buses to, say, Old and New Ladoga. Across the entire North-West, population centres were under the more or less direct sway of Leningrad.

The city's grip on the region meant that it was routine for officials to move from posts in Leningrad to posts in provincial centres, such as Pskov or Vologda, and the same process sometimes happened in reverse.[17] As a city-state and the much-mythologised home of medieval Russian democracy, the centre of counter-factual speculation about what might have happened to Russia had Moscow not emerged as its capital, Novgorod enjoyed sentimental favour with the Leningrad intellectual opposition. Obvious parallels were drawn.[18] But most of all, the hinterland was, for settled Leningraders, a place for mass exodus during the summer months – to the dacha settlements that clustered round the Gulf of Finland and pushed far down south into former field and forest zones. In July and August, the city population dwindled as noticeably as in Paris or Madrid; in May, June, and the first half of September, the place emptied at weekends. Already well established before 1917, the dacha culture was more entrenched in Leningrad than anywhere else in Soviet Russia.[19]

The social divide between these temporary migrants and those actually living in rural areas was sharp. It could be sensed already in the transport taking people out of and into the city. The local trains, *elektrichki*, with their dark-green 1940s rolling stock, were often packed to the doors, and sometimes beyond. 'In Leningrad', Ronald Hingley reported in 1961, 'I saw a train steam out with large numbers of people clinging to the roof. Was this permitted? "No, but it is a hot day." '[20] Even when empty, local trains were uninviting, with their wooden benches, draughty windows, and constant whiff of cigarette smoke from the airlocks at the ends of the carriages. Despite journey times often running two, three, or even four or five hours, they had no lavatories. Chilly in winter, in summer they hissed like kettles. Passengers were often grimy and tattered, some boozing openly; rowdy sing-songs were the order of the day. Late in the evenings, *elektrichki* became – particularly in the 1990s – positively dangerous.[21] Fares were low compared with city transport, though still too high for some users. When prices went up in 1998, the numbers of tickets sold fell by 60 per cent immediately and 75–80 per cent in the long run.[22] This did not necessarily mean a commensurate fall in the numbers of passengers, since riding 'like a hare' on the *elektrichka* was a time-honoured practice.[23] All the same, places with *elektrichka* services fell into the first category of rural outposts: the vast majority were served by country buses, wandering infrequently through villages at a rate of perhaps 30 kilometres an hour.

8.1 Interior of an *elektrichka*, 2011.

## The Outer Borders

The *elektrichka* did not just take people out to 'the periphery'; it also brought people in – often for shopping. There was a favourite riddle in the Soviet period: 'What's long and green and smells of sausage? The train from Leningrad.'[24] The city's many institutes also made it a favoured destination for incoming students.[25] Piter might have lost its role as imperial capital, but it continued to suck population into the workforce and to gobble territory for housing and amenity use. Already in the 1940s, housing was being built in areas that had formerly been villages – Avtovo, for example – and summer settlements (Udel'naya). In the 1960s and 1970s, population rose not just in the new suburbs, but in areas on the city fringes, such as Pargolovo (to the north) and Ligovo (to the south). The state of things could not remain unrecognised by the city administration for ever, and gradually districts formerly outside the city limits were brought under its control.[26]

The territorial expansion of Leningrad and St Petersburg still lagged behind its expansion in terms of population. Even in the late twentieth century, the city covered less than a fifth the area of Moscow within the outer ring-road, and less than an eighth of the area of Paris or London, though these cities were only twice the size in terms of population. As a local politician pointed out in 2003, the area of St Petersburg was comparable with that of Saratov, which had a population of only 850,000. His proposed solution was to create a 'Big Petersburg' measuring 1100 square kilometres, to be separated administratively from the surrounding Leningrad province.[27]

But this could have solved the problem only temporarily, given the relentless pressure at the city's borders. Despite the rigid controls on planning and migrancy in the Soviet days, the boundaries were porous. In places, urban life came to a juddering halt. The high-rise blocks round the city rim stood next to wooden houses, or wasteland blending into forest. There were and are also historic areas where the same sudden rupture of the urban fabric could be found. Walking through the former Transfiguration Cemetery, which holds the memorial to the victims of Bloody Sunday,[28] you suddenly shift from tarmac paths lined so thickly with graves it is hardly possible to squeeze between them to open, empty bogland where reeds and rushes sprout from virulent green patches of stagnation – the primal landscape of the Neva delta.[29] Small towns and cities have tangible boundaries – city walls, or simply the last row of houses before the fields begin; in big cities, the boundaries within districts can be as important, or more important, than the dividing line with the outside world.[30]

This sense of spatial dislocation becoming temporal dislocation was captured in Gennady Grigor'ev's poem 'Losing My Way', where 'Leningrad' reverts to its former self:

OK, if I'd
got lost in foreign parts,
where you can't move without a guidebook.
OK, if I'd
mixed up the floor
in the high-rise city of Chicago.

But – in Leningrad?!
God, it's so dark.
Here was a square, but now it's bog, not square.

And not a single window lighted,
And not one taxi, or a policeman.
How the pines moan and how the river roars!
I'm coming to the sandy rift.
What time is it? How long until
Liteinaya
Perspective is cut through?[31]

A quintessentially modern, 'Soviet' experience became the prompt for memories of the city's origins, before one of the oldest streets even existed.

The sense of bewilderment in Grigor'ev's poem articulated an emotion many visitors to the city's periphery shared, both before and after the 1991 divide. With large numbers of strangers living on the doorstep, social relations changed. In Kolomyagi, on the northern outskirts, cottage-owners complained to a visiting journalist in 2005 that, when the new blocks appeared, they had suddenly needed to acquire padlocks.[32] Some parts of Pargolovo, a former dacha area to the north of the city, were overlooked by public transport planners (inhabitants were faced with a hike of up to five kilometres to reach the nearest bus stop). The residents of the once independent settlement of Turf Bog (Torfyanoe) found that bureaucrats did not know how to document their birthplace on identity papers, so that they had to endure the anomaly of being registered as having been born in two places.[33]

The boundary of the city was porous in the other direction as well. New arrivals from the countryside might bring their habits and attitudes with them. Until the 1940s, it was common for people in working-class areas to keep small livestock, such as poultry, a practice that revived again in the early 1990s as supplies in the shops dried up.[34] By the start of the twenty-first century, animal husbandry was more of a curiosity, but patches of it still flourished, as in the case of a woman working in an experimental market garden on ul. Baikova, next to Sosnovka Park, who was the proud owner of eight goats.[35] Even now, there was regular contact between recent incomers and the countryside, both because they would go back to their home village for the summer, and because food supplies would be sent from there.[36] Of course, such rural incomers were not exclusively from the Leningrad province itself, or even from the North-West. But Piter had always been the natural destiny of people from these areas, and in many cases continued to be even after political and economic dominance had shifted to Moscow.[37]

## The Hinterland

In the Soviet era, coverage of the province in official publications tended to be upbeat. Already in 1932, it was reported, literacy had stood at 90 per cent (oral history would suggest that functional literacy was considerably lower, even in the late Soviet period).[38] 'Directed' descriptions by locals were of this order too. Typical was an essay by a sixteen-year-old schoolgirl published in the anthology *In Our Leningrad* (1961), and looking forward to the bright future of a settlement there:

> The resort of Roshchino is no longer the basic settlement that it was back in the 1960s.
>
> Around the little town, many Pioneer camps and health sanatoria are clustered. They are situated in picturesque places; on the banks of lakes, in pinewoods, where the air is fresh and pure. When you go on a walk in the woods, you luxuriate in the beauty of nature, in the pine-scented air.
>
> The whole town is drowning in greenery. The schoolchildren of Roshchino have been busying themselves with planting trees. The fragile young saplings are now tall slender trees, standing along the road like a green wall.
>
> The little houses that once filled the town are long gone; now big multi-storey blocks stand everywhere. The material they are made of is easy to handle; houses like that are made of sections. In two or three days, they are ready.
>
> A big Pioneer Palace has been built for the schoolchildren, and they spend all their free time here. A theatre and many cinemas have been built for the residents of Roshchino.[39]

Ol'ga Berggol'ts's 1971 memoir *Daylight Stars* recalled the impact of travelling, in the 1920s, past the Volkhovstroi Hydro-Electric Power Station (begun before the Soviet period, but regarded as a key achievement of the post-revolutionary era), and seeing how 'light is made out of the waterfall'.[40]

Occasionally, official sources put forward a different picture. In 1967, *Leningradskaya pravda* reported on a state farm where the supply conditions were dire. The canteen was hardly ever open, and in any case, locals could not afford it, so they would take packages of home food to work, but even obtaining that was not easy as the local shop sold nothing except vodka (available in any quantity at any time). Even onions, macaroni, and salt herring were nowhere to be had. In small towns, conditions were sometimes reported to be almost as bad.[41]

In private, inhabitants of the province complained about many other things as well. Dairy-workers had no sanitary facilities or even basins, and milk spoilt because the creamery closed before the evening milking was done; consumer goods were desperately scarce, and there were shortages of products such as sausages and soft drinks; wages were low, particularly for women workers; animal feed was in short supply; and transport links were terrible. People did not necessarily even live in a healthier environment, given that some of the industries out in the backlands, such as cellulose production, were highly pollutant.[42]

Local administrators were more rough than ready. Party activists organising 'patronage to the village' by major Leningrad cultural institutions were taken aback by colleagues who could not be bothered with cultural work, and thought that Impressionist art was 'anti-Soviet'.[43] Getting around was difficult – to reach even the centre of some districts took over six hours from the big city.[44] Certainly, the complaints on their own tell only part of the story – many members of the older generation were sharply aware that conditions in the province were far better than in earlier decades.[45] But migration to Piter was an inexorable fact of life. Between 1959 and 1989, the population of village dwellers dropped by 50 per cent.[46]

The hinterland was also deprived in terms of official memory. In places, Russian settlement went back much further than it did in the immediate environs of Petersburg. Of the 254 architectural monuments listed in 1944, all were constructed in the 1800s or earlier.[47] Even in its post-war configuration, the province included large numbers of important monuments, among them the fortress of Oreshek and the former city, now village, of Old Ladoga. Administratively within the city limits, but functionally autonomous, were the palaces of Pushkin (Tsarskoe Selo), Pavlovsk, and Petrodvorets (Peterhof), among the most lavish post-war restoration projects in the entire Soviet Union.[48] The settlements around the palaces, though much less elegant than they had been before 1917, were still eminently desirable places to live, with green space surrounding traditional streets.

Not all historic buildings, though, received this degree of care. The palaces at Oranienbaum, relatively little damaged during the war, started getting attention more than five decades after the Tsarskoe Selo-Pushkin complex. In the 1980s, the Great Men'shikov Palace was still in use as a military institute; the pavilions at the ends of the building were covered in scaffolding, and the park was in a semi-ruinous condition.[49]

8.2 Street in Oranienbaum, 1985.

8.3 Great Men'shikov Palace, Oranienbaum, 1985.

Further away from the city, preservation was still more sporadic. In the post-war years, no one would have advocated razing a medieval monastery, as had been proposed in 1932 for the Kirillovo-Belozersk and Valdai-Iversky Monasteries and Ferapontovo and Goritsky Convents.[50] From the late 1940s, efforts were made to protect the major complexes of ecclesiastical buildings, and to repulse the efforts of local collective farm managements to use listed churches as places to store tractors and repair machinery.[51]

But only a few of the province's many buildings were official monuments, and caring even for those was highly problematic given the distances involved and the difficulty of access. Of the fifty-seven churches listed in 1950, eleven were completely destroyed or in ruination by the start of the twenty-first century: some had been deliberately demolished, others had burned down, and a few had simply collapsed.[52] Churches, particularly wooden ones, were vulnerable to theft (sometimes carried out with the direct connivance of the local authorities), to fire, to natural disasters, and to the passage of time.[53] Among the listed churches in Leningrad province, only two were used for worship, reducing the likelihood that local communities would have an investment in protecting them.[54] The response of the cultural authorities to the fragility of these places was to organise expeditions by staff at Leningrad museums, who had the mandate to remove any items of artistic or historic value they happened to locate. However, this was also a way of asset-stripping local memory, as was clear from the protests of local congregations when their treasured icons happened to be removed.[55] As late as the 2010s, the state of the sixteenth-century Convent of the Presentation in Tikhvin – with its main churches bare of paint and plaster and crumbling under their tin roofs, and the Cathedral of the Nativity of the Virgin still arranged as a children's gym – indicated the likely fate of even major historical buildings under Soviet power.[56] Even in Old Ladoga – a tourist attraction since the late Soviet period – the twelfth-century cathedral in the St Nicholas Monastery survived the decades only in battered condition. Not just a listed monument, it was also restored by a group from Leningrad State University in 1948, but this did not stop the local machine-tractor station from using it to house farm machinery.[57]

The problem might have been solved with more autonomy for the province's outputs. But support to on-the-ground preservation initiatives in outlying villages and small towns was limited, though sometimes metropolitan museums and institutes might extend a helping hand to enthusiasts for 'local studies', in line with the revival of the subject that was being promoted at national level.[58] Party administrators in Leningrad were equally suspicious of the rural population's capacity to act as appropriate custodians of recent memory. In 1978, a report to the Regional Committee of the Communist Party listed twenty-two commemorative structures, including numerous war memorials, which had been illicitly built by collective farm and small town administrations over the

8.4 St Nicholas Cathedral, Old Ladoga, September 2012.

previous two years. For instance, in Rakh'ya settlement, Vsevolozhsky district, a stele had been placed to honour locals who had died in the Great Patriotic War. The aesthetics left much to be desired: 'The architectural conceptualisation and the memorial inscriptions have not been carried out to a satisfactory standard.' A more serious violation had taken place in Vyborg district. A bust to Hero of the Soviet Union P. V. Kondrat'ev had been commissioned by the local soviet, though such busts were supposed to be put up 'only by decree of the Supreme Soviet, and only in order to honour double heroes of the Soviet Union in their actual birthplace.'[59]

Such 'memory management' reflected the patronising attitude to rural outposts that was characteristic of the Soviet elite across the country.[60] But the Leningrad region had its own peculiar historical sensitivities. This was territory whose 'Russian' character needed to be emphasised, given that substantial tracts had been seized from Finland during the 'Winter War' of 1939–40. Intensive resettlement in the post-war years had provided formerly Finnish areas with a Russian population, and some settlements had been renamed ('Zelenogorsk' from 'Terijoki', for example). The inhabitants of the villages had often been shipped in from far afield and had little in common with each other (places of origin ran from traditional northern Russian villages to Mordovia).[61] The first generations to arrive were conscious of living on alien land: people still remember today how in their childhood they would explore the abandoned Finnish farms, so neat, well-built, and comfortable.[62] In the eastern part of Leningrad province, there were also substantial communities of Finno-Ugric ethnic groups, such as the Veps, but their presence went largely unrecognised in the post-war years.[63]

Underlining the Leningrad region's Russian heritage was also important given that large areas of it, unlike the city itself, had been under German occupation, and exposed to propaganda that sought to create disaffection with the Soviet order.[64] Yet the 1960s and 1970s were also a period when rural outposts and small towns were undergoing radical modernisation, acquiring their own ranks of concrete high-rises, tarmac roads, 'daily life' centres, and the other conveniences of late Soviet existence.[65] 'Traditions' were celebrated, but they were also called into question.

An example of the complicated identity brought by modernisation was Tikhvin, historically the home of one of Russia's most famous icons, housed in the Monastery of the Dormition, a centre for pilgrims from across Russia. The icon of the Tikhvin Mother of God disappeared during the brief German occupation. In the late Soviet period, just one of the monastery's churches, the so-called 'Little Porch' (Krylechko) (built by N. L. Benois in 1861–63 in order to protect a wall painting that was venerated locally), was open for worship. Yet in many respects the town, up to the mid-1960s, remained much as it had been before 1917. With over 1000 houses at the end of the nineteenth century and a population of 6630, Tikhvin had been quite big and prosperous by pre-revolutionary standards, just as (with around 16,000) it was, by Soviet measures, small and remote.[66] The war left the place with its major monuments damaged, but the occupation was brief, and new houses were built during the post-war years in traditional style. Many of the handsome two-storey houses once lived in by merchants survived. Tiffs between the parish priest and his flock (in 1965 parishioners complained that the priest had 'in front of everyone grabbed and taken over to the left side' an icon whose position was in dispute) barely acknowledged the Soviet world at all.[67]

From the mid-1960s, however, Tikhvin began to be transformed into an industrial town. The arrival of the Kirov Factory's annexe, a major tractor plant, tripled the population in a few years (in 1975, it was just over 48,000).[68] Almost half the inhabitants were young Komsomols who had come in when the plant was opened. As a photo-reportage of 1980 put it, 'The town is the factory, and the factory is the town'.[69] While the old monuments spoke of the dominance of Novgorod, the new ones celebrated Leningrad: an important complex of war memorials commemorated evacuees from the city who had been killed around Tikhvin. The town's own war honours were longer in coming – it received its medal for heroism only in 1974.[70]

In the case of some places in Leningrad province, the description 'the town is the factory' was literally true. Kolpino, on the fringes of the city, was entirely dominated by the enormous Izhorsky Works, founded in 1722, and one of Russia's largest machine-building operations. In character, it was somewhere between a provincial town and a remote suburb; with its own historic buildings and distinctive atmosphere, it was dependent on the city for facilities until well into the twenty-first century.[71] Boksitogorsk (founded in 1929 as a mining and processing settlement) represented industrial development of a different era. A town from 1950, it belonged historically to the category of 'settlement', and had few distinguishing features.

Though many 'settlements' were monotowns, such places were created not just by industrialisation but by the new collectivising drives of the Khrushchev and Brezhnev eras, as populations were moved from 'futureless villages' to local centres.[72] Yet what Russian geographers have termed 'rurbanisation' – the incursion of urban values into the countryside[73] – was not supported by transformation of the infrastructure. Sanitation was non-existent, and even electricity supplies erratic. All of this increased the push for people to travel from the region's fringes to its dominating centre – a process accelerated (as was the case all over rural Europe of the day) by modernisation in the villages, as television and consumer goods brought a sense of what the world beyond could actually offer.

## Summer Visitors

Acquiring a seasonal dwelling outside the city was a great deal less trouble than relocating to an urban area, and it became easier over time as well. In the 1940s and 1950s, permanent access to a second home was an unusual privilege, granted exclusively to members of the elite. The resorts on the Gulf of Finland such as Zelenogorsk (Terijoki), Repino (Kuokkola), and Komarovo (Kellomäki) were enclaves of *kazyonnye dachi* (state dachas) allocated on a grace-and-favour basis to Party and city officials, members of the Academy of Sciences and the 'creative unions' (Union of Writers, Architects, etc.), and other leading figures in the local hierarchy. But humbler individuals were able to rent somewhere, whether from a city bigwig or, more likely, a local who wanted to make a little summer money.[74]

The situation was transformed during the 1960s and 1970s, when there was large-scale development of the so-called 'garden settlements', *sadovodstva*, an initiative originally set up in the late 1940s.[75] These were communities of small plots (most often 'six hundredths', i.e. 0.06 of a hectare, or around a tenth of an acre).[76] The plots were primarily meant to be used for vegetable-growing, but a wooden dwelling of strictly controlled size might be erected. Local regulations in Leningrad limited the acceptable dimensions of this hut-style structure to one storey of 25 square metres in area (with attic accommodation permitted under the eaves, though this could not be heated, and a veranda). The entire building could be a maximum of 6.5 metres in height.[77] The purpose was to stop the 'garden settlements' becoming permanent residences, which also explained the prohibition on heating and insulating one's little house for winter use.

Despite the obstacles, there was a boom in out-of-town dwellings. Across the Russian Federation, the 40,000 members of garden settlements in 1950 had swelled to 3 million in 1970, and 8.5 million by 1990.[78] By 1990, almost a quarter of families in St Petersburg had a garden plot, including both settlements and allotments (less than a tenth that number owned a dacha).[79] The *sadovodstva* attracted the scorn of some. The geographer Boris Rodoman described them as 'slum peripolises' (*trushchobnye sverkhgoroda*).[80] Leningraders of the older generations denied them the title of dacha at all. In the words of the poet Nonna Slepakova, typical was a 'little house/With a tatty roof/A meagre garden/And a gnarled tree'.[81]

But growth was inexorable, pegged only – or so city-dwellers felt – by obstructiveness on the part of local administrations. In December 1989, *Vechernii Leningrad* reported that, despite a 25-per-cent rise in the numbers of garden plots since the start of 1986, there were still about one third fewer plots than were needed to satisfy the demand of Leningraders for an exurban bolt-hole. While there was perhaps genuine cause for anxiety over the beavers of Gatchina district (allegedly threatened by new building), in certain other districts the slow expansion was down to foot-dragging by local officials.[82] Behind this discussion could be seen the erosion of the hegemony of agriculture that had obtained in the Soviet period.

Soviet planners saw the presence of city-dwellers in the countryside instrumentally. It was beneficial if people enjoyed a healthy vacation, and took their children into the fresh air; the exurban settlements (it was rumoured) were also intended as possible places of refuge in case of nuclear war.[83] But the primary purpose of moving people out seasonally was to grow more food. Right up to the end of Soviet power, large numbers of people were forcibly dispatched in summer and early autumn to the countryside in order to help with lifting potatoes, picking cabbages, and other types of harvesting.[84] Seasonal conscription of this kind was organised through educational institutions, starting with the top classes of secondary schools and continuing through all tertiary institutions, and through workplaces. It was considered to be of moral benefit (encouraging participation in 'collective values'), and attempting to elude participation was seen as shirking. As with any forced labour, the main ways of making things palatable were camaraderie (joking, smoking, and drinking together made life easier to bear), and – for those without much in the way of brawn – a nifty move into any non-agricultural job that presented itself.[85]

The authorities also attempted to manage how people spent their time on their private exurban plots, in terms of proscription if nothing else. The managements of garden settlements were empowered to take measures against people who broke the rules and built dwellings of non-regulation size and shape, and against those whose plots were not in good order. What got built was relatively easy to regulate; forcing people to grow vegetables was more problematic. An obvious incentive to production would have been to allow people to sell the produce they grew, but making money out of your dacha was considered bourgeois and rapacious.[86] Public opinion, as revealed by a frank survey published by *Komsomol'skaya pravda*, was divided: some people held that the state should support those living on garden settlements by buying up their produce, others were vehemently opposed to the entire system as 'selfish', while yet another group would not hear a word against garden settlements.[87]

In any case, people's relationship with their dacha could not be decreed. For some, there was a true sense of bonding with the soil. In 1997, Vladimir Sidorov (who had spent his entire life living in a city) remembered 'the most extraordinary day of his life':

> the day when he, sixty already, first set foot on his own little plot near the village of Pupyshevo. He took off his shoes and stood barefoot on the soil, his own soil, bare earth with nothing growing on it, with boot marks all over it, a mess, but there was such a sense of life coming from it that he immediately felt a great responsibility for its fate. It was not only him that needed to live, the soil did too. Would his fumbling spadework do it harm?[88]

But not all Leningraders had this sort of direct relationship with the soil. The stubborn nature of the terrain – much of the Leningrad region was composed of bog – meant that gardening was very hard work. This was not a place for the burgeoning gardens of Ukraine or the Moscow area, as luxuriant as illustrations in medieval books of hours. Often, plots consisted of trees, and perhaps a few fruit bushes (particularly hardy natives such as sea buckthorn, rowan, or chokeberry).[89] For many, land was valuable because a house could be put up on it; 'vegetable growing' was a dead letter. The very process of building the house could be a major part of the attraction, though like any construction project, it took effort and ingenuity. One woman remembered having to take the planks she had found on a city dump, along with a sack of potatoes and her own baby, three kilometres from the nearest station, there being no bus, a task achieved by packing the lot on a wheelbarrow.[90]

Dachas in the democratised sense, little wooden boltholes inhabited by individuals and individual families, were now a fact of life. A complaint sent to

VOOPIiK in 1984 that the fringes of the Constantine Park at Strel'na were under attack from illegal dacha-building made clear the inexorable rise of demand for plots.[91] Increasingly, dacha ownership became, like car ownership, a mark of belonging to respectable society – indeed, the two were connected, since transporting the family and the clobber needed for a summer's stay was difficult without a car, while car ownership gave access to the new 'garden plot' areas that were hard to reach by rail.[92] Even those without dachas were likely to cluster in dacha areas when they took trips beyond Leningrad, since these were the ones best served by public transport.[93]

### 'When the Strawberries are Ripe'

Despite the different types of dwelling – rented, government, and privately-owned – dacha life had certain unifying traditions. Not everyone enjoyed the dacha,[94] but most people did, and certainly most of those brought up in Leningrad, for whom staying out of town was encrusted with happy childhood memories. The dacha offered urban children much more space and time to do what they liked, as a man whose family holidayed at his grandfather's official dacha in the 1950s and 1960s remembered:

> I used to spend every summer in Solnechnoe settlement, right next to Beloostrov here. My granddad was an old Bolshevik, and so they gave him a dacha, a government dacha. And that's where I spent my childhood, I had lots of dacha friends. I was one of the leaders, we used to play Cossacks and Robbers, build hideouts made of grass and twigs . . . We'd run into the grounds of the rest home on the shore of the Gulf of Finland, we'd go to the woods and collect mushrooms, not that I was very good at that, I didn't like them, but I loved collecting berries. [. . .] We'd swim, lie in the sun . . . That's how I remember childhood.[95]

There was a firm belief that children should spend all of the summer at the dacha, but adults would expect to spend long periods there too – especially if they were from a 'moveable' profession, such as teachers.[96] The dacha was a place to catch up with relations you had little time to see day to day, as well as somewhere to spend relaxed days with close family. Friends might arrive to stay for days, or simply drop in for the afternoon, since the town was never far away.[97] Here, you had only the neighbours you chose on the other side of the partition wall. The fact that a dacha cost money also meant that your neighbours in the next houses along were likely to be solvent and sober – in other words, the kind of people you were happy to know.[98] Where neighbours in city flats often did their best to avoid each other, dacha neighbours would babysit each other's children, drink tea together, and chat about the weather over the palisade fence.[99]

8.5 A divan on a glassed-in dacha veranda, 2002.

The nature of dacha settlements themselves also threw people on their own resources. Nothing was provided in the way of professionalised entertainment. There were no organised beaches with deck-chairs and cafés, even if there happened to be a lake, river, or sea-front nearby (at most there might be a shack selling drinks, some kind of prepared meat or fish, and salads), no go-kart tracks, seldom even a tennis court. 'Touring bases' or pensions might offer facilities such as mini-golf and swings to their residents, but these were off-limits to dacha-dwellers. You could not hire motor-boats or water-skis. So, quiet swims or stints of fishing, depending on tastes, alternated with reading, sun-bathing, lying in hammocks, or most often, sitting round talking. The end of the season usually brought foraging for mushrooms and berries, followed by frenetic stints of putting food by.[100] Otherwise, cooking was very basic, the ritual dish being *shashlyk* – marinaded and barbecued kebabs – one of the few culinary endeavours on which the average paterfamilias was ready to embark.

None of this bored people. It offered a reassuring sameness and comfort in the face of city life that was becoming, even before 1991, increasingly frantic, noisy, and stressful. There were more and less 'prestigious' dacha settlements, running from inland 'garden settlements' at one end to the resorts of the 'Northern Riviera' at the other, above all Repino and Komarovo, where Party leaders, the Academy of Sciences and cultural institutions had their official compounds.[101] But even here, things were low key. People who wanted a 'prestige' holiday chose somewhere else, such as a southern resort. The point of coming to the dacha was to dress down (even jeans were too smart), to live surrounded by comfortable things that had got past the stage when they could decently be used in the city, and to stop worrying.[102] This was the antithesis of 'Petersburg style', of self-conscious collecting. The old things here had accreted fortuitously, exported from the city when they had got too old-fashioned or battered for respectable use. Decade-old dented pans, patched sheets, and scratched cupboards were typical, but so too was a working samovar that ran on charcoal, a barbecue, and other solid tokens of sociability.[103]

The association of the dacha with family traditions made it a favoured site for celebrations, such as birthday parties:

> Every year, in the summer, round about 9 July, which is Mama's birthday, we'd all gather, us and all our friends, they'd drive over and bring sleeping bags, sometimes even tents, put them up on our plot, and we'd always spend two days drinking and celebrating. And that's just when the strawberries are ripe, so everyone would come to eat strawberries and kebabs.[104]

Dacha-dwellers also often turned the opening up of the dacha at the start of summer into a celebration:

> And so on 9 May, when it was a bit warmer, or a bit later, around the end of May and the start of June, the first night we spent out on the plot, we'd buy a bottle or two of wine, red, usually, that was Mama's favourite, and make some food to go with it, and my parents would sit themselves down at the dacha at the end of the day, switch on the TV, have a drink or two and plan what we were going to do over the summer. That 'ritual', so to speak, was more or less a complete fixture.[105]

Such family festivals marked the fact that a dacha, unlike a city flat, was *one's own*, used over the decades, and passed down through the generations. Even official dachas often had this 'family' resonance, since access rights could be inherited. And looking over the accretions of belongings, people had the sense of an entire family history in its connections with this treasured place. In many ways, the dacha was more 'home' than your rented flat in Leningrad.

### Finnish Houses and 'Bandit Baronial'

This apparently settled landscape was soon hit, like the rest of Soviet society, by the reverberations of change. The opening of borders in the Gorbachev years gave Leningraders the chance, for the first time, to travel at will – though acquiring a foreign passport still required effort, and getting hold of foreign currency even more so (the legal method, using a bureau-de-change in the Hotel Leningrad, meant queuing for many hours).[106]

In the early days, the main prompt to foreign travel was curiosity, and the likely destinations major cities in Europe, Israel, and America. With resources tight, people's first choice was often to go to places where they had relations or friends. In the course of the 1990s, however, a package holiday market opened up. Petersburgers were eager to desert the city's mist and damp for guaranteed sunshine. Now that the 'sun holiday' resorts of the former Soviet south had become more difficult and expensive to reach (because of rises in fares and the introduction of visa regimes in most of the territory bordering the Black Sea), there was a boom in travel to Mediterranean resorts, particularly in Turkey, Greece, and Cyprus, but also in Egypt, Israel, Thailand, Africa, and the Gulf. With the help of a last-minute 'hot deal' (*goryashchaya putyovka*), it could be cheaper to stay, and to eat out, than it was in Russia.[107]

On the other hand, the purchase of summer homes abroad was relatively rare. The exodus north (including to the historic monasteries of Solovki and Varlaam) rivalled the exodus south.[108] Certainly, 'houses of rest', now cast on to a commercial footing, sometimes struggled if the management could not afford to give them 'Euro-repairs'. Block-bookings from conferences and pensioners on trips sponsored by social services were the likeliest day-to-day business; some formerly exclusive places now looked distinctly decayed. The dacha, on the other hand, retained its hold. The popularity of Finland among moneyed northwesterners was explained by the fact that buying a summer-house there offered not just ecologically attractive conditions, but also the opportunity to recreate the nearest possible thing to the dacha experience.[109] The dacha's appeal lay not just in tradition, but because a close destination maximised the amount of time that could be spent in the given place; and in any case, buying abroad required self-assurance, both legal and linguistic.

Marketisation had also, in principle, made it much easier to acquire a bolt-hole in the city's vicinity. Gone were the restrictive regulations, the assessment of whether people 'deserved' their second home. The circumstances also changed for those who already had somewhere to go. Many availed themselves of the opportunity to privatise their tiny plots, and sometimes of the opportunity to acquire more land and the new freedom in terms of what they could build.[110] With dachas of the classic kind, owned by the local administration or by institutions such as the Academy of Sciences or the Union of Writers, the situation was more complicated. In 1989, some of these were taken over for collective use, but the long-term trend was to privatisation as well.[111]

One result was a boom in exurban building, with sites and structures proliferating as owners of larger holdings in settlements sold off tracts of land.[112] Another was the construction of much more ambitious dwellings. Even the most opulent Soviet-era dacha paled before the edifices that began to mushroom from the early 1990s. Particularly favoured was a kind of 'bandit baronial' – turreted mansions in brick, strait-laced parodies of the style used by rich dacha-builders around 1900, such as Countess Maria Kleinmichel, the owner of one of the most prominent summer mansions on Stone Island. Some aimed even higher. One rich businessman put a version of the Catherine Palace at Tsarskoe Selo on his site out at Vyritsa, near Gatchina. Looking, on the outside, a little like a cross between the original and a ceramic teapot, with the gilded dome of a chapel jutting from one end, it reportedly had a 14-metre ceiling in the grand hall, marble walls, and brocade window-treatments. A rival plutocrat commissioned himself an imitation of the cascades at Peterhof.[113] Not all houses were on this scale, or even purpose-built – 'Finnish houses' constructed from prefabricated sections were also common. But almost all were larger and taller than anything built before, clustering like pedigree guinea pigs among house mice.

Inside, these newbuilds were splendidly appointed. Forty-metre-square living rooms with German stoves and hardwood floors, Italian lighting, and Scandinavian triple-glazed picture windows were the norm. Keeping somewhere like this safe in the winter required year-round live-in staff, so there

8.6 A 'bandit baronial', June 2010.

would be a separate garage with staff flat.[114] Even smaller houses often had all-weather insulation, and if not full sanitation, at least an indoor 'ecological toilet', obviating the traditional trip to 'outside conveniences' in the shape of a wooden hut with earth closet at the edge of the plot. Yet, while the rash of new building was typical of dacha settlements all over the Soviet Union, local heritage meant that the structures did not seem as alien as those clustering round provincial towns, or, indeed, Moscow. You could hardly live in Petersburg and not be aware that at the turn of the twentieth century, 'dacha' had often meant a substantial villa (as in the dacha of Grand Duke Boris Vasilievich, constructed by Scott in the manner of Hampstead Garden Suburb, and kitted out by Maple of Tottenham Court Road).[115] But if not 'alien', the new dwellings were definitely 'vulgar' – and intrusive, too, as they pressed against the boundary fences of neighbours' plots.

## New Topographies

Dacha life started to stratify in topographical, as well as sociological, terms. The most fashionable places, such as Repino and Komarovo, were also the most favoured spots for new building (despite legislation making the coastal area a protected zone). Though nothing could clean up the sea (where only dogs, children, and the hardiest pensioners swam), the price of land sky-rocketed. By 1992, lots in this area were selling for 600,000–800,000 roubles (60,000–80,000 dollars), more than a good-sized flat in the city.[116] By the 2000s, Komarovo had acquired an enormous sea-front restaurant; arrivals were greeted by a vast poster showing a scarlet Hummer. 'Modesty does not enhance life,' the caption announced.[117] Under pressure from newbuild, the dachas of the past began to disappear. While the Borman dacha in Komarovo was safe-guarded by its use as an out-of-town residence for the city governor, others were vulnerable. Numerous stately old wooden villas fell victim to summary demolition.[118]

The appeal of the leading Soviet resorts was partly practical. These places had a more reliable electricity supply, full piped water rather than simply the outside tap that was the norm in a garden settlement, sanitation, and – by the 2010s – even mains gas supply. Plots were also larger than in garden settlements, so that there was more space to expand. But the draw of these places was also, as with fashionable city districts, a function of cultural inertia. They were prestigious after 1991 because they had been exclusive before.

For the moderately affluent, accessible garden plot settlements – those along the lines to Priozersk and Vyborg, for instance – represented an alternative to the fantastically expensive 'St Petersburg riviera' out at Repino. According to word of mouth, the most luxurious dwellings towards the end of the line were built by people from Vyborg, but these settlements were well-liked among

St Petersburgers too. The result was energetic building in these places, with multi-gabled villas rising next to the simple boxes of the past.[119]

But privatisation was not just an engine of development. Not everyone understood how to navigate the labyrinth of the land registry system, and obtaining legal title often defeated those who could not afford the services of an agent. Many settlements decayed into a precarious condition. Self-managing from 1991, few had administrations that were competent to run local services such as electricity: often, community action extended only as far as getting a watchman.[120] The most ambitious and affluent usually deserted the shelter of the co-op, and remaining members were often unsure about how to capitalise on the public funding that was available for local development.[121]

In settlements with extensive new building, modest, Soviet-era wooden dachas hung on, since the most many people could afford was to carry out running repairs, and perhaps also to provide their summer homes with slightly more modern sanitation. Often, owners would do at least part of the work themselves – or members of the family would.[122] Even those with money sometimes preferred to build in the old style, though the houses might be solider and more spacious – with maybe an extra bedroom downstairs and a study upstairs. Meanwhile, the owners of traditional dachas held on to social distinction where they could. It was considerably easier to buy a building site in a prestigious area of the northern coastline than to acquire a plot in Komarovo cemetery, long used as an alternative burial place by the Leningrad intelligentsia, where official tombs to distinguished writers, artists and musicians – less pompous than those in city cemeteries – stood next to simple rustic wooden crosses.[123]

Dacha life, too, largely continued on its time-honoured tracks. The new rich might hang round indoors by their billiard tables, or drive out for an overpriced meal.[124] But the usual round of fishing, berry-picking, swimming, barbecues, and chat continued for others, though perhaps with some new possessions – such as sun-loungers, grills, and picnic baskets – on show, and wine boxes alongside the vodka at parties. Gardening was still generally desultory, but strimmers to tame the bog and meadow grass had become common all the same.[125] Given the established history of seeing Leningrad dachas as primarily a place for relaxation, the ambivalence about what dachas were *for* that emerged in, say, central Russia was not much in evidence here.[126]

## Further Homes

However they chose to spend their time once there, office workers and professionals considered the trip to the dacha an inalienable right. Local government departments and even many private companies worked at 'tickover rate' from the start of the May holidays until the schools returned on 1 September.

Expecting to find anyone at work much after lunchtime on a Friday was optimistic; Monday morning was no better.[127] In Moscow, people shortened their weekends as life became more frenetic; in Petersburg, they tended to adapt work to the demands of dacha life, as in the case of a building company that worked on city sites in the winter and dacha construction in the summer.[128]

Another kind of exurban settlement was putting down roots as well. From 1987, city-dwellers were able to buy a house in a village. At first, significant restrictions obtained – people could only make a purchase if they (as an individual or a family) did not already have a dacha or access to a state dacha, and were not a member of a dacha or garden co-operative. The construction of outbuildings was allowed, but the new villagers had to cultivate the land, or it would be removed. In 1988, settlement in rural territory outside villages was allowed as well – with a much larger maximum size than in the garden settlements (up to 60 square metres).[129] Though collective and state farms retained the right of refusal, and priority was given to organisations rather than private buyers, the 1990s and 2000s saw a rise in currency for the village option. The relative cheapness of old houses (a few hundred dollars, as opposed to many thousands for even garden huts in the most prestigious areas), and the unspoiled beauty of the countryside – particularly as former farmland went back to nature – were a major draw, offsetting the long distances that had to be travelled, the need for a car, and the exigencies of life in very remote areas (most produce had to be grown, or brought in by the carload).[130] By the 2010s, the exurban incursion, combined with dropping rural populations, had transformed some villages into the kind of summer-only settlements typical of northern Scandinavian countries. The traditional rural population had simply disappeared.[131]

However, the vast majority of city-dwellers still stuck to the areas immediately round cities. Wealthy St Petersburgers were not interested in doing up manor houses of the kind falling down all over the place in Leningrad province and other parts of the North-West.[132] But they did want attractive views. Already by 1992, Sergei Gorbatenko, the head of UGIOP, lamented the host of 'vast hideous "*kottedzhi*"' that were springing up in places such as the banks of the Slavyanka River in the palace park at Pavlovsk.[133] While this did not lead to the construction of housing estates within sight of the windows of the Catherine Palace, there was a surge of new one-off mansions in faux baroque style around the fringes of the former royal estates. Above all, the stretch between Strel'nya (where the elaborate reconstruction of the 'presidential palace' was completed in 2003) and Peterhof became a parade of luxurious dwellings for the new rich.

With all-weather housing becoming increasingly widespread, and the controls of the Soviet era removed (or unenforceable),[134] it was only a matter of time before St Petersburg started to acquire something resembling the 'suburbs' of Western Europe or North America. As in Moscow, the engine for exurban growth was not necessarily the fact that city-dwellers themselves wanted to move out. Outlying areas were still mostly served by slow roads and even slower trains. As of 2010, it took 45 minutes to reach Vyborg if you used the Allegro express to Helsinki, but over two hours on the *elektrichka*. Riding most local trains was still a testing experience. As the deputy director of the local railway system explained, the introduction of toilets and padded seats had to be suspended after only two days; passengers had simply wrecked them. The main virtue of the system remained its cheapness.[135]

The suburbs acted as a way in for new arrivals to Petersburg who could not afford to live in the city itself, rather than as a mainstream alternative to city life for people who had already established themselves there.[136] At the same time, there was also a constituency of city-dwellers, particularly pensioners, for whom moving out to the dacha was an attractive option. You could let out your city flat and live on the income, and make a little money on the side by selling your produce.[137] For younger people, it could be a hard choice between 'earn enough for somewhere decent in town, or shove off to the sticks' – with the latter preferable to 'having neighbours who don't always make it to the toilet on time'.[138] And so far as the moneyed population went, the increasing availability of well-constructed separate houses with their own gardens was starting to be a draw.[139]

By the late 2000s, even places around 100 kilometres out were beginning to be affected by the outward ripple. In Siverskaya, for instance, rather a deprived settlement, where vandalism and theft were common, outsiders were starting to buy up land and to push through electric cables, hoping for site potential.[140] During the 2010s, sites in the middle distance were worth around three times less than those in the prized resort area, but at least twice as much as those more than 100 kilometres out. On offer were increasing numbers of houses in estates, as well as one-off dwellings.[141] These places usually had at least the potential for year-round living, though how many people actually inhabited them month on month is hard to say. But the slogan, 'Improve Your Living Conditions and Remain a Petersburger!' had compelling force.[142] (See figure 8.7.)

### Living in the Province: 'Footnote 3'

For the province's indigenous inhabitants, things looked different. In Russia generally, privatisation tore apart the structure of industrial enterprises and state farms that had formerly held the economy together, and provided employment to the vast majority of adults. Within a decade, the percentage of those employed had dropped by nearly 50 per cent.[143] The effects of marketisation seem to have been less devastating in Leningrad region than in some other parts of Russia: in 2010, unemployment was running, by official figures, at just over 5 per cent.[144] However, rising numbers of cars and falling numbers of

8.7 Advertisement for 'Tokari-Lend', Garant Developers, 2012.

clubs pointed to the decline of local facilities and local communities, the population was becoming age-heavy, and new building was dropping.[145] Crime in St Petersburg's hinterland, like Moscow's, was high.[146] A gulf also opened up between the western and eastern parts of the province – the former was far more populous and urbanised – and between the immediate boundaries of Piter and the less accessible areas 70 to 140 kilometres further out.[147] By the early 1990s, the 'exchange' columns of St Petersburg newspapers included not just city apartments, but also advertisements from the owners of houses in outlying villages desperate to move to Piter, or, failing that, to suburban settlements such as Pavlovsk.[148] Between 1995 and 2005, the overall population dropped by more than 40,000, and between 2005 and 2010, by more than 15,000.[149]

As city-dwellers saw it, the *oblast'* resonated with hopeless anomie. The *reductio ad absurdum* of this attitude to the hinterland was the pseudonymously-published *The New Radishchev*, by a certain 'A. Sen'kin-Tolstyi'. This modern parody of Alexander Radishchev's *Journey from Petersburg to Moscow* showed a population enserfed, not by landowners, but by drink. In one episode, the male inhabitants of two villages, disoriented by thick smoke, were unable to find their way back and ended up involuntarily swapping homes. The end results were harmonious, however. The men soon found themselves jobs and bed partners; as for the women, the narrator remarked, it was a matter of indifference which particular drunkard they happened to be saddled with. 'Footnote 3', cited on almost every page, motivated this or that case of strange behaviour as determined by 'alcoholic intoxication'.[150]

8.8 Fresh from the bird factory: 'Select Quails' Eggs' supplied by Lenoblptitseprom (Lenprovbirdind), 2010.

This Flann O'Brien-ish picture ('Sen'kin' was an admirer of Irish prose) had some foundation in reality. As collective farms disintegrated, some inhabitants of the 'ragwort belt' sank into alcoholically-fuelled despair.[151] By 2010, only about 10 per cent of the adult population was employed full-time in agriculture.[152] Part-timing was still common: at the start of the 2010s, there were over 200,000 small-scale farms, as opposed to 6314 medium-sized enterprises, and 217 large ones.[153] But the general trend of agricultural production was downwards.[154] Yet some rural farmers were able to benefit from the market in the city for fresh produce (while grain production fell in the 1990s and 2000s, production of vegetables climbed).[155] Milk and meat production were buoyant, with occasional excursions into exotic areas, such as rabbit- or ostrich-breeding, and even peacock-rearing.[156] (Quail farming was quite widespread, with the eggs in particular a staple in many middle-range supermarkets.)

Gradually, produce from the North-West started to have a more prominent retail presence. In 2012, the medium-size producers (*fermery*) began direct-selling online – though at a price.[157]As in rural Russia generally, it was less stagnation than adaptability that was on show.[158]

The province's industries also managed to sustain at least modest levels of development, particularly in areas such as car manufacturing, food production, and paper milling. At the same time, the major initiatives were backed by foreign companies, such as Ford and Philip Morris, with local support mostly at the level of 'development plans'.[159] This of course made the area vulnerable to disinvestment by multinationals in search of maximum profits, not to speak of troubled industrial relations, such as plagued the Ford plant in Vsevolozhsk.[160] A case that made national and international headlines was the unrest in Pikalyovo, whose inhabitants blocked the highway outside the city as a protest against the threatened closure in 2009 of three gravel works owned by Basel Cement, Metakhim, and Pikalyovo Cement, employing 4500 of the town's 25,000 population.[161] Some parts of the province were as economically deprived as anywhere in the North-West. On the border with Karelia, hydro-electric power stations were a memorial to the brave aspirations of Soviet power. But towns such as Lodeinoe Pole and Podporozh'e, with their closed factories and the broken dreams of an unwanted and unfinished estate of 'town houses', spoke of a culture where, in the words of a local priest, 'there's no work and all the young people are leaving'. The wooden villages along unmade roads in what had once been the Olonetsk government were now mostly inhabited seasonally; locals whose roots went back generations were in crumbling 'Khrushchev slums', and mostly glad enough of the easier living conditions.[162]

Yet, by the standards of non-metropolitan Russia, particularly outside the fertile 'grain belt' areas, let alone rural areas internationally, Leningrad province was reasonably prosperous.[163] It helped that even outlying areas could expect some influx of visitors over the summer months.[164] Main roads were of remarkably high quality, and by the start of the 2010s, there was talk of substantial structural funding – which (if one chose to see things optimistically) had the prospect of transforming the local economy, as happened with EU grants in a comparable area of northern Europe, the West of Ireland, in the 1970s and 1980s. Considerable efforts were also being made to assert regional diversity, with places all over the province rediscovering their distant past, alongside (or rather than) their Soviet heritage. Tikhvin, for example, once more became a centre of pilgrimage. Its famous icon of the Mother of God was returned in 2004 by Archbishop John Garklavs of Chicago, into whose possession it had come after the German retreat from the Soviet Union.[165]

The town's official website dwelled in detail on the place's history up to the late sixteenth century, its role as the birthplace of Rimsky-Korsakov, and the fact that a decisive victory in the Great Patriotic War had taken place not far away. The industrial development in which Soviet newspapers had taken such pride was not mentioned at all.[166] While several plants (including a railway wagon building enterprise) and an IKEA furniture factory remained in production, the tourist literature focused mainly on the 'holy places' of the district, and the local museum (once championing Soviet progress) now celebrated the

8.9 Soviet-era Tikhvin, June 2012.

lives of Tikhvin's solid citizenry during the nineteenth century. When I visited in June 2012, the monastic vistas in the centre looked much as they might have done through the 'Imperial Realist' lens of Sergei Prokudin-Gorsky, the pioneering colour photographer who produced a stunningly beautiful celebration of the tsar's lands as a gift for Nicholas II. Cows wandered along the streets leading out into green open land with a gentle roll to it. The most prestigious new building (such as the 'Coaching Inn' (Podvor'e) hotel just off the main street) also harped on traditional themes. But if all this was a textbook example of pre-revolutionary provincial revivalism, the clusters of determinedly mendicant alcoholics, and the grimy concrete blocks set out along thoroughfares that were literally nameless, pulled in a different direction.[167]

Whatever spin one chose to put on provincial life, things were tangibly changing. Above all, food-growing was increasingly dominated by agribusiness. If individual plots had produced substantial amounts in the 1990s, by the 2000s production had dropped back, and in 2010 all sectors apart from potato-growing were dominated by large farms. One of the most familiar features of the countryside was the 'bird factory', for the battery rearing of chickens or other poultry.[168] But, of course, none of this fitted conventional ideas of attractive countryside, thus further exacerbating the rural–urban divide.

City-dwellers preferred to simplify – and usually in a negative direction. In general urban usage, the word 'village' suggested a benighted hell-hole, rather than a bucolic paradise.[169] Even those more favourably inclined would romanticise only at a distance. A professional singer whose first job was taking part in concerts at a village club enthused about the cultural provision: 'Imagine! You've spent the day working in the pig-sty and milking cows, and then you come home for a wash and go to the club – to a concert!' Then, practically in the next sentence, she announced, 'But of course, *I* didn't want to stay there – I wanted a higher education, and especially since I was good. I was talented.'[170] In 2012, Danila Kotsyubinsky, a leading ideologist of regional self-assertion, put forward the idea of simply hiving off the west part of the province, which in practice, he argued, constituted a 'Greater St Petersburg'. He pointed out that even maps for motorists usually omitted the eastern part of the province, which from the point of view of city-dwellers was beyond the known world. If reintegrated with Karelia, Novgorod, and Vologda, these territories might, he felt, lose their historical inferiority complex and have greater freedom for economic development. The fact that they would then be as remote from the centre of anywhere else was not raised as an issue.[171]

Interestingly, the main internet reaction to this article was from commentators pointing out that many places in the west and south of the province were 'dumps' as well.[172] Even the nearer settlements were regarded with

8.10 Petersburgers' view of the likely behaviour of those from the sticks: a warning notice in the women's lavatory at Novodevichy Convent, 2010.

condescension. A woman from Kolpino who studied in St Petersburg recalled the hiss that fellow students let out when finding where she was from: 'Some of them even asked whether we still had wooden houses there.'[173]

While parts of the Leningrad hinterland were very remote, the place had never enjoyed the mythic appeal of 'the true North' – Novgorod, the Onega area, Vologda, or Archangel. When Russian ethnographers went 'to the people' in the nineteenth and early twentieth centuries, it was to these areas that they travelled.[174] Their successors, such as the Leningrad archaeographer Alexander Malyshev (1910–76), continued to work in this area.[175] Leningrad's leading writer of 'village prose', Fyodor Abramov (1920–83), was a northerner, and his work evoked the Archangel rural world in which he had grown up. There was a tradition of romanticising the 'sad Finnish landscape' of the dacha places round Piter, such as Komarovo.[176] The conifers and beaches of the area round the Gulf, and the flowering gardens round dachas, were staple presences in the work of late nineteenth- and early twentieth-century painters such as Shishkin, Serov, and Benois, whom the Leningrad intelligentsia knew well.[177] From the hazy fringes of the gulf, Piter itself could seem alien, the Neva 'a shining blade' that 'ripped the city down the seam'.[178] However, the same pines and water, heath and boggy scrub, where they lacked familiarity and cultural associations, were simply boring.

In a sense, the immediate rural surroundings of Piter were culturally invisible. The natural world was not picturesque, Russian peasant traditions were in abeyance, and work had long been mechanised. Since the 1920s, activists from the city had done their best to fight traditional holidays and customs, which were held to impede the course of progress.[179] In the late Soviet and post-Soviet period, it was generally assumed that the local culture had been thoroughly urbanised. *Rhymes of Leningrad Province*,[180] a set of prints in raw-naïf style by the Mit'ki artist Andrei Filippov, harped on unhappy love that was likely to end in knife-fights or abortions, drinking, and desperation.

On the other hand, those searching for 'authentic' folk culture were likely to be disappointed. One response (as in other parts of Russia) was the attempt to revive rural traditions with an injection of grant-sponsored quaintness: in the town of Lodeinoe Pole, for instance, a 'White Mushroom' festival, involving displays of berries, cooking, and local crafts (as well as, of course, mushrooms), was held in September to 'support and stimulate the creative activity of the local inhabitants'.[181] Government programmes aimed to seek out and sustain the culture of minorities – some decades after other government programmes had more or less successfully effaced that culture to begin with. Nevertheless, the fact that people now talked about their non-Russian past was a major change: 'My father never told me he was Veps by background,' one young woman in her 30s told me, 'or rather, not until I started working at the local museum.'[182]

8.11 Andrei Filippov, 'Let Me Dance on Your Territory' (from the *Rhymes of Leningrad Province* series): a village femme fatale in fishnet tights bewails her problems with her two lovers, who lie stabbed in pools of blood in the background, while cows caper and churches tumble.

A different stance to the issue of disappearing local lore was taken by the actor-singer Igor' Rasteryaev, whose ballad 'Combine Harvesters' (2010) evoked not traditional peasants, but the 'rurbanised' proletariat:

> Far away from big cities and towns,
> Where no expensive boutiques can be found,
> People are of a different kind,
> And singers pay them no mind.
>
> There are no TV serials about them at all,
> They're not compatible with digital,
> You won't find them on FB or the Net
> They give nobody cause for regret.
>
> They're young, but they don't go to college,
> Lenta and Okei are beyond their knowledge.

They've never got a solarium tan,
And a sushi bar is outside their ken.

They've no posh furniture in their halls,
They think that Emo's a load of balls,
They don't sit in chats, go online:
They go harvesting in their combines.[183]

If the subject of Rasteryaev's song was the country-dweller, its anticipated audience was not. His anti-urban and anti-globalisation philippic was aimed precisely at those who visited 'expensive boutiques' and sat glued to their smartphones.

In a predictable paradox, a video-clip of 'Combine Harvesters' went viral in the summer of 2010, making Rasteryaev a celebrity with the internet generations.[184] For them, as for Rasteryaev himself, the countryside was a place of temporary habitation at best, not somewhere that realistically might be the scene of an alternative existence. Striking, to a British observer, was the complete indifference of most dacha-dwellers to the natural world around them: I have never met a Petersburger who enjoyed bird-watching or botanising. A joke goes round that a certain well-read and highly intelligent literary scholar once confused the rear end of a cow, seen at a distance, with a magpie; I have met people who were surprised to hear that you could find rats outside the city. This is partly to do with a widespread contempt for amateur anything (the words 'amateur' and 'dilettante' have a hostile ring). But it also comes from a certain world-view. Rural life is precious where it is a haven for alternative human experience. Fishing may be a classic activity, and hunting for some, but observing animal behaviour is not. And in any case, the province still has large areas of forest, where the issue, for outsiders, is to avoid being totally overwhelmed rather than to admire the survival of plants and creatures specific to that locality.[185]

The presence of so many relatively well-off and culturally distinctive temporary visitors from the city in rural areas has brought its own stresses, particularly in the buffer zone between the resort areas that immediately surrounded Petersburg and the agricultural belt proper, which lay roughly 70 kilometres outside the city. In Chekhov's classic story, 'Dacha Folk', tension blew up between villagers and summer visitors because the former kept driving their animals in to the latter's plots. While this source of conflict was ended by factory farming (from the mid twentieth century, cows and pigs lived year-round in intensive units), villagers were still inclined to think of dacha-dwellers as 'rich', and hence fair game.[186] After the collapse of the Soviet Union, pilfering from second homes reached epidemic proportions, and those departing summer residences for the winter that were located within easy reach of a former collective farm had to hide or take with them everything likely to prove attractive to thieves – which included not just televisions and computer equipment, but knives and forks, highly valued because their scrap-metal value held out the lure of a drinking binge.[187] Leaving your city dwelling unoccupied also carried risks, as the summer season was a peak time for adventitious burglars.[188] Nothing, though, could stop the outward drive of city-dwellers, keen to quit the loud and dusty city in search of green space – but mostly not, if they could help it, to settle there for long.[189]

# 9

# The Last Journey

*The graves of Ivan Bunin, Nabokov, [Joseph] Brodsky, Viktor Nekrasov, [Sergei] Dovlatov, Roman Jakobson and thousands of other big guns of the Russian language lie peacefully in lovely clean Western cemeteries. There's no risk they'll one day get covered in tarmac – as might well happen in Russia.*
(Vladimir Uflyand)[1]

Sooner or later, every inhabitant of Piter had to trace a city-wide trajectory over which he or she had no control: to one of the city's cemeteries. If he or she died at home, traditional Orthodox practice was to call a priest to minister both before and after the final moments, and to lead the procession carrying the body when it was taken from its final dwelling-place (the so-called *vynos*, or removal). With or without a priest, the removal was invariably a solemn ritual: it was customary for neighbours to emerge from their homes to pay their last respects, though visitors from the provinces in the late Soviet and post-Soviet periods noted that in Piter this practice had disappeared.[2] However, the fact that websites instructing relations on how to arrange funerals still felt it necessary, as late as the 2000s, to caution against some traditions – for instance, the banning of the carrying of the coffin by near relations of the deceased – indicated the tenacity of these.[3]

Of course, if someone did not die at home, religious and folk procedures would be effaced by medical ones. Some hospital morgues were former chapels – for instance the graceful domed structure belonging to the First Medical Institute (the former Peter and Paul Hospital) on the banks of the Karpovka opposite the Botanic Gardens – but after the separation of church and state in 1918, they lost their original role.[4]

In the Soviet period, a great deal of energy was put into the creation of alternative, secular rituals – particularly in the 1920s and again from the late 1950s. Leningrad was an important centre of this movement, not just in the case of workplace festivals such as the 'Initiation into the Working Class', but in the case of the threshold rituals of private life. City officials were proud of their role in pioneering the 'Palaces of Marriage' that began offering couples a less Spartan wedding rite from the late 1950s onwards, and also promoted baby-naming rituals at which the newborn was presented with a 'Born in Leningrad' medal.[5] But when it came to funerals, Soviet 'party-planners' were less exuberant. This was not just because of the increasing tendency in this modern society, as in many others, to see death as a private experience whose emotional impact was not supposed to go beyond the narrow family circle.[6] It was also because there was something embarrassingly un-Soviet about physical demise – a sullying of the bright future, so to speak. The dozens of books and brochures published to manage Soviet 'new traditions' in the Khrushchev and Brezhnev eras became terse when they arrived at the final threshold ritual in a Soviet citizen's existence;[7] the institutions openly known as 'funeral bureaux' before 1917 were now veiled by the term 'ritual services'.

The instruction accompanying the 1918 Decree on the Separation of Church and State had explicitly banned religious rites, including funerals, from all public places except religious buildings.[8] However, 'red funerals' – one of the new rites of the 1920s – were not revived in the post-Stalin era.[9] The standard way of honouring the dead was the local equivalent of a secular memorial service, the *grazhdanskaya panikhida* [civic funeral]. Leningrad rites of this kind were no different from the generally obtaining Soviet norms. They might incidentally be held in a magnificent room (if, say, the deceased had been a member of an Academy of Sciences institute), but the ritual always boiled down to two elements: wreaths and speeches. The latter were invariably in strict pecking order: first the director, 'and then, say, the trade union boss. . . Friends? Right at the end.'[10] The rituals of interment were equally sketchy: perhaps a band to play a funeral march or two, if the mourners could afford it, but otherwise awkward silence and standing around.

Cemeteries, too, could be Spartan – though here one should draw a distinction between the cemeteries with an official commemorative function, and those that merely happened to be used for interments. Before 1917, some cemeteries were more exclusive than others in a social sense – with the various burial grounds at the Alexander Nevsky Monastery and Novodevichy Convent preferred by the bereaved beau monde.[11] But there was no attempt to create anything resembling a 'national pantheon', even if prominent figures from public life were likely to have particularly impressive graves. Mainly, how people were commemorated depended on what their families could afford – though in an ominous foreshadowing of the future, the most notorious political criminals, such as the Decembrist rebels, were buried in unmarked graves after their executions.[12] And the location of the cemeteries was to a large extent practically driven – with new burial grounds created on the outskirts as the city expanded around the turn of 1900.[13]

This picture changed in the Soviet era, which saw a drive to create new graveyards fit for heroes within, or in place of, established burial grounds. Of these, by far the most important, in the last years of Soviet power, was the memorial complex at Piskaryovka Cemetery.

The effort to commemorate those who had died in the Blockade began almost immediately after the war had ended, but at first, plans were for a whole series of monuments in the various sites where burials had taken place, including Decembrists' Island as well as a series of official cemeteries. A great deal of argument then ensued about exactly what form the monuments should have: an article in Leningrad's architectural journal commented acidly in 1946 that many of the projects put forward in a competition for commemorative ideas had lacked the necessary grandeur, resembling merely 'what one might find on an allotment'.[14] Later, large-scale commemoration in most Blockade burial grounds was shelved, and efforts concentrated in just two places. A decree of Lensovet passed on 25 December 1956 that was generally aimed at regularisation of the city's burial places anticipated the construction, on the Piskaryovka and Serafimovskoe Cemeteries, of monuments 'to the warriors of the Red Army and Leningraders who died in the defence of the city'.[15]

Part of the Serafimovskoe Cemetery (thought to shelter at least 100,000 dead) was reconstructed as green space offsetting a memorial colonnade against which figures of Leningrad workers stand like reinterpretations of caryatids; work was completed in early 1965.[16] The Piskaryovka Cemetery, on the other hand, became the site of a far more extensive and ambitious memorial park, including a whole variety of monuments as well as landscaping of the natural setting on a grand scale. Creating the cemetery required extensive work not just on the site itself, but on the entire district. A suitably resonant approach was laid out in the form of a major thoroughfare, prospekt Nepokoryonnykh (Avenue of the Unsubdued), a wide boulevard that swept past the gates of the sonorously named 'Memorial Cemetery', and which also provided space for the large numbers of tour-buses bringing visitors to the complex. In a classic Soviet memory stand-off, reconstruction of the district required the removal of a memorial of another kind – the Trinity Church at Lesnaya, the only local Orthodox place of worship that had remained open through the Stalin years, but which was demolished in 1967.[17]

Completed in 1960, from 1961 the Piskaryovka Memorial Cemetery served as an obligatory stop on the itinerary of every tourist, and ritual visits were paid by local factory delegations and other manifestations of the Soviet rational collective on all and any possible occasions.[18] Albums and guidebooks immediately listed it among the city's most important sites.[19] As a brochure put it in 1967, 'Which Soviet person does not want to visit? Which of our foreign friends shuns this most sacred of names?'[20] Clearly, a monumental complex on this scale needed to satisfy establishment expectations of propriety, and much in the way that Piskaryovka was realised was thoroughly conventional.[21] V. V. Isaeva and R. K. Taurit's 'Motherland' statue, towering over the neatly-tended graves, espoused the routine symbolism of late Soviet war commemoration.[22] Yet the walls behind it were inscribed with lines from the poet Ol'ga Berggol'ts, whose steadfast presence in the city and many radio broadcasts had made her the voice of the Blockade, but who had also made herself a thorn in the side of the Leningrad Party authorities.[23] And with its neo-classical pavilions at the entrance and its massing of grass, water, and trees, the landscape of the cemetery followed the traditions of local park architecture as adopted in the Soviet period – not least, the Victory Parks created during the late 1940s and early 1950s. Like the original Soviet memorial to the fallen on the Champs de Mars, it was perpetually open, with a vista from the street that gave first place to the 'eternal flame'.[24] Undemonstratively moving, with its enormous burial mounds labelled simply by year, the cemetery was – above all on ordinary days, without celebrities, wreaths, and brass bands – a dignified, if perforce hardly adequate, memorial to the many hundreds of thousands who lay there.[25]

## Pantheons and 'Isolated Graves'

Like any other city, Leningrad also had its cemeteries and necropolises for those who had died in peacetime – gardens of remembrance to the ordinary, as

9.1 Piskaryovka Cemetery, October 2011.

well as the extraordinary, dead. So far as official culture was concerned, it was definitely the latter that were given priority. A picture-book published in 1962 to showcase the Piskaryovka Cemetery referred to the place as 'a necropolis for mass burials'.[26] This was, in Soviet terms, an oxymoron, since practices distinguished scrupulously between those worthy of afterlife in a 'necropolis' and the last resting place of those of lesser significance.

From the start of the Soviet period, it was customary to place the graves of Soviet officials in a separate section of the cemetery. A pioneering example of this practice was the so-called 'Communist Square' in the Alexander Nevsky Monastery, where graves with red stars brandished an alternative symbolism right up against the crosses of the Christian dead. A slightly later, but logically inseparable, practice was to relocate the graves of the pre-revolutionary foundational saints of Soviet power to special enclosures, claiming them for the new order. In the late 1930s, a section of the Volkovo Cemetery, Literatorskie mostki [Literary Paths], began being transformed into a pantheon to political figures (including different members of the Ul'yanov family, such as Lenin's sister Mar'ya) and famous writers. The site – like the analogous memorial cemeteries at the Alexander Nevsky Monastery, the Lazarevskoe and Tikhvinskoe – was managed by the Museum of City Sculpture, founded in 1935.[27]

In preparation for the reconstruction of Volkovo Cemetery, a Lensovet order of 28 September 1938 ordered citizens whose relatives' graves were 'subject to liquidation' to apply within two weeks for transference of their remains to a different cemetery. Unclaimed graves would be demolished.[28] In 1940, a list of the famous dead whom the Museum staff wished to have transferred was drawn up: it included, for example, the writer Ivan Goncharov, Pushkin's friend and confidant Anton Del'vig, the painter Boris Kustodiev, the architect Konstantin Ton, and the poet Alexander Blok.[29] This process continued in later years and decades.[30] As other cemeteries were closed, reduced in size, or declined into neglect, so more and more tombs that were considered of historic or artistic interest were moved to the 'museum' cemeteries.[31] The process of moving burial grounds from city centres and of landscaping ones where burial had long ceased was international.[32] However, the Soviet case was unusual both because of the characteristic peremptoriness with which the 'ordinary dead' were treated, and because of the gulf between this and the handling of remains that were considered important. While the Decree on the Separation of Church and State in 1918 had explicitly stipulated that those providing religious funerals were not to provide different categories of service depending on the status of the person being buried, Soviet practice itself drew a firm line between the unimportant and the important.[33]

The reserves of the city, in which famous people lay next to other famous people, were more like outdoor museums than 'cemeteries' in the ordinary sense. Monuments as well as graves might lack an authentic connection with their new site: if major figures' tombs had been lost, or used an insufficiently dignified style, new ones would be erected.[34] The sense of post-mortem historical propriety ignored the likely wishes of the departed in other ways as well. The famous might find themselves sundered from their loved ones, and placed cheek by jowl with a literary enemy; two writers of radically different political orientations, Apollon Grigoriev and Vissarion Belinsky, were within what could only be described as spitting distance in the 'Literary Paths'.[35] Suitably distinguished Soviet citizens were also ensconced in the official pantheons, sometimes in considerably more opulent tombs than the more famous nineteenth-century figures surrounding them.

This exquisite care for the famous dead did not extend to what were usually described in official documents as 'the graves of isolated citizens' (*mogily otdel'nykh grazhdan*). The very word 'isolated' ('individual' in the sense of 'abnormal') had a negative flavour, as in the 'isolated problems' from which Soviet society was supposed to suffer.[36] Tenants of these 'isolated graves', which were (in a process of circular reasoning) held to lack 'artistic' or 'historic' interest, faced summary reburial as cemeteries were closed or reconstructed.

9.2 Grave of the worker writer Aleksei Chapygin (born in northern Russia, 1870, and lucky enough to die a natural death in 1937, despite his connections with the Proletkult organisation), 'Literary Paths', Volkovo Cemetery, 2012.

As a Lensovet order of 1 December 1939 put it, 'The eastern section of the Transfiguration Cemetery in Volodarsky District is to be liquidated. Volodarsky District Soviet is to notify interested citizens about the transfer of bodies buried on this part of the cemetery to another place.'[37] Few relatives of the dead had the political capital to dispute such a move, or to make choices about final resting places of any kind. In 1940, a descendant of the Stasov family was able to intimidate Lensovet officials into at least giving consideration to her plan to have her husband transferred from Volkovo Cemetery into the family vault.[38] But it was more usual for family members of those buried to be given short shrift, even when a grave had disappeared without their knowledge, as sometimes happened when a memorial cemetery was expanding. Curt letters telling relations that the burden of proof lay with them, or even denying the grave had ever existed, were the rule. 'If you have documentation of ownership in your possession, we can allow you to reconstruct the grave of Lebedev, your father, but without the cross and scallop-shell that originally decorated it,' one woman was flatly informed in 1968.[39]

Any eye-catching memorial was likely to be recycled, as shown by a mishap that overcame the memorial belonging to Count Sergei Witte, architect of economic modernisation under Alexander III and Nicholas II, in 1964:

> Members of the Ancillary Post of Party and Soviet Control at the Museum of City Sculpture received notification that the gravestone in polished granite belonging to the famous Russian statesman Count S. Yu. Witte had been discovered to be missing from the Necropolis of the Eighteenth Century [at Alexander Nevsky Monastery]. After an investigation by the staff of the Post, the gravestone of S. Yu. Witte (measuring 145 cm by 73 cm) was discovered in the works yard of the Necropolis, which is used by restorers. The inscription turned out to have been effaced, and the gravestone had been repolished, apparently so that it could be reused for another grave.
>
> Nearby in the works yard was lying a gravestone of unknown origin with an inscription in German which was in the process of being prepared for work to transform it for reuse.
>
> We recommend that the Directorate [of the Museum of City Sculpture] should investigate the affair of Count S. Yu. Witte's gravestone and call those responsible to account. We consider that Count Witte's gravestone should have its inscription recarved and should be returned to its place. The chains on the railings round the grave, which were broken when the gravestone was removed, should be repaired.[40]

The incident led to a ban on works other than restoration in the Necropolis of the Eighteenth Century. But it is notable that the investigators were not in the least concerned about the origins or fate of the gravestone inscribed in German that they also discovered in the works yard. Recycling 'isolated' grave markers was perfectly in order. There are persistent – and perhaps justified – rumours that quite large sections of the handsome granite cladding round major Soviet public buildings, including the headquarters of the NKVD, consisted of recycled gravestones.[41] Certainly, the grave-markers in Leningrad's many 'liquidated' cemeteries were used as paving for streets in the centre of the city.[42]

Beyond the pantheons that counted as official monuments, dilapidation was pervasive. In 1971, a Fellow of the Institute of Historical Research at the Academy of Sciences wrote to the Directorate of the Institute to report that, while the grave of the poet Nikolai Nekrasov at the Novodevichy Cemetery was in reasonably good condition, 'the cemetery surrounding it is in such a dire state that the sight of it is extremely depressing'.[43] Thus, 'isolated' graves could attract attention where they lowered the status of graves where famous people lay. All the same, substantial restoration work was not carried out, and in the following decades the cemetery still housed statues with heads lopped off, battered cenotaphs, and family vaults whose floors opened to reveal the edges of crumbling stone caskets.[44]

9.3 Funerary vault in the Novodevichy Cemetery, 2010.

At the Smolensk Cemetery, too, physical destruction – in this case blamed on vandalism – was rife. In 1962, the head of the City Directorate of Culture wrote to the local District Committee of the Communist Party:

> On the façades of the houses facing the cemetery are swear-words written in oil paint, in letters a metre high. Dozens of monuments are being destroyed by rowdies and vandals, and what is more, it is not just the graves of isolated citizens that are being desecrated, but war graves, and also the graves of outstanding figures placed under state protection by the Decree of the Council of Ministers of the RSFSR passed on 30 August 1960.[45]

The phrasing conveyed the order of priorities, with 'isolated citizens' once more ranked below 'outstanding figures'. But while officials might make symbolic stands on behalf of the latter, the will to finance proper supervision was lacking. Grave-diggers and other cemetery maintenance staff were one of the most morally intractable subcultures of Russian Soviet cities. They were more concerned to extort payments from the bereaved than to act as cemetery guardians.[46] In the circumstances, only three categories of memorial were likely to be in good condition – those of the extremely famous dead, those of the war dead, and those of 'isolated citizens' whose families regularly visited their own commemorative spot, or who were prepared to pay someone else to tend it.

Even the most assiduous visitors were not proof against another Soviet practice – the reuse of memorial territories for urban development.[47] As a Lenproekt proposal of 1978 put it, the implacable search for building sites made this process unavoidable: 'Empty sites for building are vanishing fast, which makes it essential to seek out reserves of land for constructing apartments and buildings necessary for the development of different areas of the city economy. For this reason, it is sometimes necessary to redeploy part of a cemetery or to completely demolish old closed cemeteries, with reburial of the remains pertaining to graves that are visited in the active cemeteries of the city.'[48] Of the city's twenty-five civilian cemeteries, only six were still fully active; eight were partially closed (including several pre-revolutionary cemeteries, such as the Serafimovskoe and Porokhovoe); the remaining eleven were completely closed, most of them more than twenty-five years previously.[49] These redundant cemeteries, it was decided, should be diverted to other uses.

Part of the background to this was the advocacy of cremation as a rational alternative to burial, a process that began in the 1920s (Leningrad was the first Soviet city to acquire a cremation facility), but which was stepped up in the post-Stalin era with the founding of a modern crematorium.[50] A document of 1967 anticipated the creation of this new facility on 143 hectares of land in the northern reaches of the city between the Okhta Gulf and Ruch'i, then still a rural area (some of the land was to be reclaimed from a state farm).[51] The work was commissioned from a leading architect, D. S. Gol'dgor, in collaboration with N. M. Zakhar'ina, Yu. I. Zemtsov, and A. S. Konstantinov. Completed in 1973, the crematorium was extensively landscaped and finished with an elegant stone facing; it held several different 'memorial halls', as well as offices and departments where funeral accoutrements could be purchased. The site had great symbolic resonance, located as it was only 4 or 5 kilometres from the Piskaryovka Cemetery; everything was done to emphasise the fact that cremation was now the practice that cultivated Leningraders were certain to favour.[52]

Cemeteries, on the other hand, were considered 'backward', to be effaced as soon as might be practicable. In the past, shut ones had sometimes been swallowed up by new developments (as had happened with the Mitrofanovskoe Cemetery and the Vyborg Side Catholic Cemetery in the 1930s). In 1978, this fate was proposed for some – for example, the Smolenskoe Armenian Cemetery – though in this case, arrangements were to be made to transfer graves to one of the open cemeteries (and 'architecturally interesting' tombs to one of the memorial cemeteries elsewhere in the city).[53] In other cases, the procedure was to be different: it was now 'permissible' to reconstruct these cemeteries 'as parks or gardens'.[54] A case in point was the Smolenskoe Orthodox Cemetery. Here, architecturally or historically interesting graves would be moved into a 'necropolis' on the original site, along with any graves that were still being visited, allowing most of the cemetery grounds to be reconstructed. The lack of local amenities would therefore be rectified: 'In the central area of Vasilievsky Island is a whole group of closed cemeteries [. . .] while the surrounding residential areas do not have enough green space for general use'.[55]

In point of fact, these reconstructions never got off the ground.[56] There continued to be three alternatives for historic cemeteries: total disappearance; complete restructuring, 'museum' style; or survival in a reduced and neglected condition.

Even in dilapidation, cemeteries did not lose their sacral significance for many visitors. Cremation continued to inspire scruples, even among the religiously indifferent. It cannot have helped that there were persistent rumours about corpses half-incinerated in the kilns of a brick factory during the Blockade, when official facilities for the disposal of remains could no longer cope.[57] The columbaria (*kolumbarii*) for the deposit of ashes were placed in marginal zones of cemeteries and had the uninviting look of celestial mailrooms.[58] Superficially, burial zones were Sovietised. Most new monuments took the form of plain headstones, sometimes decorated with photographs, as well as emblems such as the Soviet star. Sometimes, the grave of a notability would be embellished by an elaborate sculpture of the departed, replacing the tradition of allegorical figures such as angels or mourners.[59] But visitors still commemorated the dead in time-honoured ways, visiting to plant flowers and to picnic beside graves (enclosures often contained wooden benches) as they might have done in a village graveyard. Commemoration practices sometimes had an explicitly religious tinge. On several of the city's older cemeteries – the Volkovo, Serafimovskoe, Smolenskoe, Transfiguration, Okhta, Shuvalovo – there was a working church. But bizarre forms of folk Orthodoxy also flourished, to the disapproval of the church hierarchy.

In 1951, it came to the attention of Metropolitan Grigory that local cults had developed at a funerary chapel in the Smolenskoe Cemetery dedicated to 'the Blessed Anna'. 'Thereupon followed more, and now completely legendary, discoveries of graves: of the "Forty Martyrs", "Mother Blessed Xenia", and many others. A well has been dug out from which "holy water" is emerging.' In Bogoslovskoe Cemetery, 'a grave supposedly of John of Kronstadt has been discovered'. (The grave of John of Kronstadt was in fact in the former St John Convent on the Karpovka Embankment.)[60] Metropolitan Grigory went on to discourage local priests from supporting 'superstitious' practices of this kind by conducting burial services at the shrines, and required that they should attempt to dissuade their flocks from participating in them.[61] But such practices did not die out. When the Chapel of the Blessed Xenia in the Smolenskoe Cemetery was closed in 1962, folk cults in the saint's memory continued; the return of the building to the Russian Orthodox Church in 1983 was a recognition of their quasi-legitimacy.[62]

The city authorities did what they could to discourage burial. The paperwork was wearing and funeral goods – starting with coffins – expensive in proportionate terms and, more important, hard to get hold of.[63] If the crematorium was new building at its most opulent, the Southern Cemetery, out beyond the city's southern fringes on the way to Krasnoe Selo, was an aggressively secular and strictly functional space. Organisationally, it was limited to a couple of hangars at the entrance, covered in pale-grey blocks: there were no gates, no approach avenues, and the tracks inside the cemeteries were thickly lined by miniature plots. It had the relationship to traditional cemeteries of the new 'garden settlements' to established dacha areas. Above all, it had no prayer houses – and this was deliberate. Harassment of Jews and Muslims who wished to bury their dead in traditional ways was yet more widespread than harassment of the Orthodox.[64] Their historic cemeteries were in particularly poor repair, even by Soviet standards, and hardly impacted on the city's consciousness. Certainly, Joseph Brodsky's 'The Jewish Cemetery Roundabout Leningrad' recalled the place where 'lawyers, traders, musicians, and revolutionaries' lay:

> remembering nowt,
> nor forgetting it either,
> behind a squinting fence of rotten plywood
> four miles from where the tramlines run out.[65]

9.4 Ruined grave enclosure in the Jewish Cemetery, 2010.

However, this early poem was one that Brodsky was later reluctant to reprint, as though artistic imperfection matched infelicitous commemoration.

## Cemetery Cults and Slow Decay

As the Soviet system unravelled, the practices associated with honouring the dead changed significantly. The celebration of the Millennium of the Christianisation of Russia in 1988 was a watershed for church-state relations, and in 1992 freedom of conscience became a matter of official statute. Orthodox funeral services and commemorative rituals, such as paying for an *akathistos* to be said in memory of the dead, surged in popularity, and the list of available 'ritual services' expanded. Those who had the money could avail themselves of VIP facilities – a white sarcophagus, say, or, if they preferred, a 'Toronto' or 'Delaware' coffin to see off the loved one in approved North American style.[66] But commemoration at the stage beyond the funeral continued to be marked by a divide between the famous and the ordinary. Leading Petersburg politicians, for instance, were laid to rest in a new pantheon, in the Nikol'skoe

Cemetery in the Alexander Nevsky Monastery, which had all the pomp and ceremony of such Soviet memorial gardens of the elite as the Novodevichy Cemetery in Moscow.

War cemeteries continued to be well maintained. Grass might grow out of the monument to the victims of Bloody Sunday in the former Cemetery of the Transfiguration, but Piskaryovka's lawns were smooth and its roses clipped, with tender bushes along the street frontage hulled in cloth the colour of old blood to keep them safe for winter.[67] Yet the new political order, while creating some new pantheons and honouring an established memorial cemetery, did also create, or to be more accurate sponsor the creation of, its very own 'necropolis of the masses'.

The marginal status of monuments to the Terror in central St Petersburg was counterbalanced by the development of a site on the edges of the city. Levashovskaya pustosh' (Levashovo Waste) was a stretch of moorland used by the NKVD and MGB for the mass burial of executed political prisoners, at least 19,000 of whom were secretly committed to the earth on the spot. The decision to create a memorial complex on the site went back to 1989; the first attempts to landscape the cemetery began in 1990, and construction of memorials in 1992. Apart from a brief period in 1996, no municipal funding was offered, and the voluntary groups and individuals doing the work had a high degree of freedom about the style of monument to build.[68] By the 2000s, Levashovo had become a remarkably diverse and moving place of commemoration, including not just official monuments (raised by individuals as well as representatives of national groups such as Germans, Norwegians, and Poles, as well as Russian and Soviet official agencies and community groups), but private ones. Inside the aggressively green fence dating from its secret-police days, a softer green, grey, and dun forest landscape opened up. Sometimes people's relatives had placed a tablet against a tree, allowing the natural environment itself to carry the function of memorialisation; sometimes conventional grave-markers had been used. A small museum held documents about, and mementos of, those buried outside. Absent from both museum and burial ground was any attempt to make some of the dead seem more important than others – in contradistinction to standard practice in Soviet cemeteries.

Pluralism also developed energetically in the city's mainstream cemeteries. Over the late 1980s and early 1990s, more and more Christian symbolism began appearing. On many graves, crosses replaced headstones, or Soviet emblems such as red stars. In some places, notably the Nikol'skoe Cemetery at the Alexander Nevsky Monastery, funerary chapels began to be decorated with impromptu wall paintings, carried out in bright commercial gloss. One chapel became a shrine dedicated to the memory of the last Tsar, Nicholas II, and his family, canonised as martyrs by the Russian Orthodox Church Abroad in 1981 (see figure 9.6).[69]

Cults grew up around individual monuments in other cemeteries, too – for example, the tomb of Anna Vershinina in the Novodevichy Cemetery. Almost

9.5 Memorial to Leningrader Gen-Si-U, born 1885, executed 1938, in Levashovo.

nothing is known about the life of Vershinina, the wife of a general who died in 1914, aged 56, at the spa town of Essentuki, but she seems to have been an unremarkable member of the upper class of her day. The visitors bringing flowers, candles, and messages to the tomb were inspired by the striking sculpture of Christ that decorated it, rather than by attachment to the tomb's inhabitant. The starting point for attachment to the place was, in fact, an attack by vandals on the statue in 1989, after which it rapidly became the focus of rumours and pilgrimages.[70]

By the end of the decade, 'voluntaristic' commemoration of this kind had died down, though the graves of popular political leaders, such as Anatoly Sobchak and Galina Starovoitova, regularly bore spontaneous tributes. Memorialisation of individuals in St Petersburg cemeteries was generally restrained. There were no equivalents of the luxurious full-length portraits of 'businessmen' complete with Mercedes keys (and usually with the inscription, 'tragically slain') in Moscow's Vagankovo cemetery.[71] Since official supervision of cemeteries continued to be haphazard, the main task for grieving relatives was to maintain graves in acceptable condition, rather than to try and build the

9.6 'Awaken, Russia': wall painting of Tsar Nicholas II and Tsaritsa Alexandra in the Nikol'skoe Cemetery, photographed in 1996. The painting has since been destroyed.

Taj Mahal over them.[72] As Nonna Slepakova wrote in a dignified poem of 1995, keeping up a grave meant making 'senseless payments' in order to honour 'an eternity no use to anyone'.[73] Modern cemeteries in particular were extremely simple, and, by the 2010s, there were even 'virtual cemeteries' allowing people to commemorate relations exactly as they wanted.[74] Indeed, the city administration's response to the problems of maintenance was to shift responsibility on to those to whom the graves belonged. On 25 February 2005, owners were offered a choice of clearing up graves themselves or paying for this to be done.[75] Municipal finance was directed in the first instance at developing and maintaining active cemeteries – 2.5 billion roubles was diverted to this purpose from the city budget in 2008.[76] Historic cemeteries were a much lower priority, and poor repair was still the rule.[77]

Once again, closed cemeteries, and particularly those which had already been despoiled in the Soviet era, came under threat. In 1997 came a proposal to redevelop the entire area once covered by the Mitrofanovskoe Cemetery to form a business and residential area called 'Izmailovsky View'. A decade later, the plan was dusted down and given official approval by the Government of St Petersburg. The cemetery was to be built over, and graves of historic interest were to be displayed in a specially laid out memorial section, with lawns. This announcement provoked mass protests and the formation of the 'Mitrofanovskoe Society', whose founder-members were the descendants of the hundreds of thousands of Petersburgers buried in the cemetery.[78] With reference to federal legislation stipulating that cemeteries might only be replaced by parks, the Society campaigned for the conservation of the former cemetery territory, and memorialisation of the sites that had once been churches. Mandated in 2009 to present a report on the site to the State Inspectorate of Monuments, its members carried out archival searches and archaeological work in the effort to trace the cemetery's history. According to their estimates, over 300,000 burials had taken place on the site, so that reburial would be practically impossible. Searches also turned up a substantial fragment of a pillar from one of the destroyed churches, suggesting that arguments from archaeology might also be advanced. But as of 2013, it was unclear what the outcome of the tussle would be.[79]

Another reason for the subsidence of individual commemoration in historic cemeteries, apart from the diversion of energies to other things, was that the Russian Orthodox Church, as part of its far more assertive role in society generally, had begun to lay claim to the process of commemorating the dead. While it was difficult to stop private individuals remembering their own relatives in the way that they wanted, or to impede fringe cults, new burials started to have a much more regimented look.[80] In order to direct the commemorative zeal of believers along the right paths, clergy themselves assiduously promoted forms of local memory that they considered appropriate.

The most striking example of this was the official church sponsorship of the cult of Xenia of Petersburg. In contradistinction to their attitudes in the Soviet period, members of the church hierarchy did all they could to encourage mass devotion to 'Mother Xenia'. In 1988, Xenia was canonised, and the church – restored, repainted, and reopened the previous year – became the pristine centrepiece of entire battlements of stands holding petitions, candles, and religious brochures; at weekends and holidays, hundreds of people waited in line to enter the chapel. St Xenia was soon one of the best-loved saints in post-Soviet Russia, receiving hundreds of letters annually with prayers for her intercession in cases of sickness and personal tragedy. The correspondence was encouraged by articles in official church newspapers, pointing to the efficacy of devotion to the saint.[81] While the cult reached far beyond Petersburg itself, Xenia's links with the city were vital in establishing reverence for her there.

The striving of the Russian Orthodox clergy to attain custodianship of memory was not limited to Xenia's legacy. Nor was it limited to Orthodox tradition as strictly defined (for example, the commemoration of the Orthodox priests and faithful who suffered political repression in the years of Soviet power, the subjects of an important memorial complex at the Alexander Nevsky Monastery). By the twenty-first century, churchmen were attempting to exercise influence over other kinds of memorialisation as well. Father Vyacheslav Kharinov, at the Church of the Mother of God Joy of Those who Grieve on ul. Shpalernaya, became the co-ordinator of a project that aimed to exhume, identify, and ceremonially rebury the remains of soldiers fallen at the Leningrad Front during the defence of the city in 1941–44. 'Eternal memory,' he observed, 'is a phenomenon specific to consciousness within the Church.'[82]

Father Vladimir Sorokin at the Prince Vladimir Cathedral was leading a project with even broader aims – the commemoration of every single victim of political repression in Leningrad during Soviet times. This involved the compilation of a Book of Remembrance in which the relations of the dead could ask for the names of those they had lost to be inscribed. 'We want to create a database with a selection of names, so that people are able to remember their own history,' Father Vladimir said in 2009. He pointed to the Orthodox tradition of regular commemoration of the dead, on 'Parents' Saturdays', for example, as an illustration of why national memory was best protected by the Church. Those on the list included much-decorated war veterans, but also many ordinary people: victims of the Blockade, as well as others suggested by visitors to the Cathedral ('bring us your relations, we'll include them'). 'It's my dream that there's a Book of Remembrance like that in every church, whether it's Catholic, or Orthodox, or Baptist, whichever you want, and in every museum and school,' Father Vladimir commented.[83]

Both these schemes were – by design, at least – inclusive, without restriction in terms of the beliefs or faith of those commemorated. Indeed, Father Vyacheslav emphasised that German remains also deserved reburial, and initiated a scheme for handing these over to the German authorities so that they could be repatriated. At the same time, the day-to-day commemorative practices of the Orthodox Church were restrictive: it was common for those wishing to request that prayers be said in memory of the dear departed to be informed that those so commemorated must be christened adherents of the Orthodox faith.[84]

Another issue was that not everyone being remembered would have welcomed Orthodox commemoration. After all, the victims of politics and war in Leningrad included fervent atheists, not to speak of Baptists, Lutherans, Catholics, Jews, and Muslims. Orthodox imagery did mark a firm break with the Soviet past, something that many felt to be necessary when remembering the victims of Soviet power. But such imagery was potentially divisive in a multinational and secular society, and the more it was presented as universal in significance, the more that potential for divisiveness was likely to grow. No one objected to an Orthodox presence in places of mass remembrance, such as Levashovskaya pustosh', where a bell hanging from a small wooden belfry topped with the Orthodox cross was traditionally rung by those leaving the cemetery. But there was concern that this should not make marginal the suffering of the non-Orthodox victims of the Terror. The proportions among the repressed of people who officially held Polish, Finnish, Norwegian, and Jewish nationality were much higher than the proportions of these groups in the local population at the time, while the faiths of the judicially murdered were multiple, including radical atheism, Buddhism, Judaism, and Islam, as well as denominations across the Christian spectrum. Too great an emphasis on the 'national church' risked further enactment of repression, this time of a symbolic kind.[85]

Far less change had taken place in the cemeteries for the war dead. A few graves (for instance, in the Cemetery of the Victims of 9 January 1905) now bore an Orthodox cross, but there was no high-level religious commemoration. At Piskaryovka, the scene was unchanged. In 2007, a local news agency reported that there had been damage to some of the trees and mounds (the cemetery was still used for 'sub-burials', or further interments in established plots); but the defects were rapidly made good once more.[86]

The cemeteries for the 'isolated dead', on the other hand, remained much as they had always been. Certainly, 1992 saw the construction of an Orthodox Chapel on the Southern Cemetery; in 2008, the Northern Cemetery acquired a church bearing the name of the Church of the Dormition that had once stood on the site. But mainly, these places still consisted of tightly packed rows of graves, with minimum infrastructure provided. Public transport was in abeyance: the enormous Southern Cemetery, where hundreds of thousands lay buried, was served by just two bus routes running at long intervals.[87] It was hard to get water in order to tend plants and preserve cut flowers, the main paths were poorly maintained and the small ones so overgrown that people had to walk over graves to reach those of their relatives. The cemetery's beautiful location – overlooked by the Pulkovo Heights which briefly interrupt the largely flat country round Leningrad – might have prompted imaginative landscaping, but none had been attempted. Into the 2010s, the Southern Cemetery remained a basic burial ground with no architectural pretensions whatever.[88] For many, it was a grim place. 'The land is so wet that they only dig the grave when you turn up with the coffin,' one man remembered. 'They bring in a bulldozer, with the mourners standing right there. It's awful.'[89]

Yet relatives tried to make up for the authorities' deficiencies. They made great efforts to visit on important anniversaries, jolting out in buses from outlying metro stops,[90] passing the Parmezan [sic] Pizza house, the car part stores, and the outlets for cheap clothes in Brezhnev-era high-rise buildings, through the belt of wooden houses that in the Soviet period would have been pulled down but had somehow managed to hang on, and then the pink and ochre towers of post-Soviet newbuild, the enormous discount warehouses, and the elephantine sheds of inward-investment industry. Here, at a car-park surrounded by the sellers of desperately colourful wreaths, was the start of an often confusing effort to find one's own plot, perhaps changed out of all recognition by new graves round it. An hourly shuttle-bus service took people to the furthest limits, some 3 kilometres from the gates. But the majority of people – on regular days, overwhelmingly middle-aged and elderly women, some with sulky, embarrassed youngsters in tow – would set off themselves at a

9.7 Author visiting a grave in the Southern Cemetery, 2012.

swinging trudge, a flower or two in one hand, past the more opulent graves near the entrance (for instance an entire family group embellished with gilded twirls and vases holding immortelles in retina-searing orange nylon), eyes scanning for the familiar spot.[91] Still, at least in this weather, there was the beauty of the trees, and likely also snow, to offset the open land – and none of the mud that plagued visitors at other times.

To visit the crematorium, on the other hand, you got a regular and well-appointed bus from near ploshchad' Muzhestva that made its stately way up prospekt Nepokoryonnykh. On the square itself, a sign saying '1945' struggled with the usual ever-changing feed of ads for credit and new apartments, but the avenue itself took you on a trip back into the Soviet era. A couple of neon-lit Western-style bars at the end of the avenue made little impact on the panorama; a small wooden Orthodox chapel in Piskaryovka Park was almost unnoticeable. Past the beautiful stands of birch and pine in the park, and past the ever-open grounds of Piskaryovka Cemetery, over the railway line and down under the motorway, you emerged at the entranceway of the crematorium, which still impresses, at least at a distance, as one of the city's finest modern buildings. The landscaping on the entrance avenue wittily associates the ranks of columbaria with a line of benches that takes its tone from traditional graveyard furnishing. Two long stone-faced walls flank a broad staircase of low steps: as you approach, all you can see above it is sky. The crematorium chimney faintly echoes a traditional belfry – but Italian, rather than Russian; the roof of the 'medium mourning hall' rises to an elegant pyramid, inset with skylights like tears.

Yet the bus you travel in both to and from the crematorium is completely empty. The ranks of columbaria up the avenue have no remains in them. One or two figures distantly cross the park as you approach the steps, but there is no one up on the terrace either, or in the 'large mourning hall', or in the closed café or the offices. The massing of green plants, crimson upholstery, and pale wood is in the best Soviet taste, but there is no public to appreciate it; an indicator with a space for 'Today's Ritual Events' carries nothing but a picture of the crematorium itself. It is hard to escape the sense that what you are visiting is not so much a memorial to the dead as to a certain defunct vision of the city; to a vanished, would-be orderly world that had no room for the graves of 'isolated citizens'.

9.8 View of the columbaria by the main avenue of the Leningrad Crematorium, with the smoke-stack behind. Photographed in 2012.

10

# Afterword

After 1956, the integrated and homogeneous narrative of national development propounded in the Stalin years was replaced by a whole variety of different memory practices and 'memory communities'. In Leningrad, workers and engineers at the Kirov Factory, regulars at the Saigon, the frequenters of wine-bars, the regular public at the BDT and the Philharmonia (to name only a few of the different city circles) all had their own sense of what was 'essential' about city life, their own pantheons of local heroes (dead or alive), and their own familiar spots. Individual lives might cross all these different zones and more. A researcher for the Academy of Sciences might be in the same friendship group as a bohemian poet or artist, a scientist or doctor might collect antiques, an engineer search for material on local history in his or her spare time.

The background to remembrance was rapid change to the material fabric of the city as new districts rose on the city peripheries, often inhabited by highly articulate individuals, whose search for local belonging was precipitated by their geographically marginal location. The pressures increased after 1991, as the vanishing of state socialism brought a new sense of empowerment for those with the financial resources to choose where they wanted to live, but also swept away job security and the serenity of the city's beloved cultural institutions. Under pressure from the city administration's determination to 'Europeanise', street markets and kiosks were edged out by by super- and hypermarkets. Foods people had queued for hours to buy had become banal staples; the once cheap local *koryushka* was now a 'regional speciality'. The *kafeterii* of the past, with their high steel tables and punishing lack of seats, were replaced by global villages of cafés and bars, often thronged with single people using laptops rather than clusters of poets and philosophers talking in queues. There was *komfort* and there was *servis*, though those who remembered the old days tended to feel 'something was missing'.

What people saw as crucial about the city had also altered. By the 2000s, a shared love of football, or popular music in its different forms, welded at least as many people together as concerts, the theatre, or even the ballet. This was symptomatic of a wider process of displacement, as the cultural weight moved from manufacturing and cultural production to business, from strolling down Nevsky as a counter-cultural gesture to 'outskirts patriotism'.

The changes were not simply about becoming 'more local' (or, conversely, less); they were also about different ways of defining the local. As had happened over the decades before, things, phenomena, and events that were slippery and unstable came to be perceived as enduring. Just as local patriotism had often fixated, in the past, on buildings that had been multiply reconstructed as symbols of the city's inalienable character, now a football team entirely re-invented in recent years became a symbol of stubborn continuity. For some living in the city, its main appeal was as the home of techno, or raves, or indeed drug use[1] – the point was to *escape* the past.

Yet a negative reaction to heritage was still a recognition of the power of heritage. And in fact, new practices often ensconced themselves in historic spaces. Until the city authorities intervened, favourite places for raves included the historic fortresses round the city (particularly Oreshek, and the chain of fortified islands near Kronstadt).[2] While the protests against election-rigging on 10 December 2011 were relegated by official fiat to Pionerskaya ploshchad', a spot that had no associations with political unrest in earlier eras, the unsanctioned protests of March 2012 focused on places that did have such

10.1 Protest meeting on St Isaac's Square, 5 March 2012.

10.2 'Zenit are the Champions', graffito (since removed) under Liteinyi Bridge, October 2011.

associations – St Isaac's Square and ploshchad' Vosstaniya.[3] And at protests in September 2012, marchers chanted 'This is our city!' and carried banners excoriating the 'ruination' of Petersburg, the venality of the Committee on State Property (KUGI), and the proposed relocation of the historic Military-Medical Academy.[4]

The choice of one football-mad graffitist for a tribute to Zenit in 2011 was nothing less than the granite underpinnings of the Liteinyi Bridge – one symbol of the city challenging another.

People fretted about how things had changed and the old spirit had gone, how the city was full of 'people who want a twenty-year mortgage, a Ford Focus on credit, send the wife on holiday to Turkey and hang a fur coat on her, and pack off the kids to wherever, and then, God forgive me, go and screw some tarts in a brothel'.[5] But such outbursts also indicated how many Petersburgers still felt that adherence to the city's traditional association with higher values should define their lives.

Looking in detail at how a concrete place changed as state socialism receded, with the specific and the non-specific constantly in play, raises questions about the overall cultural context. As the critic and cultural historian Stanislav Savitsky argues, treatments of 'Russianness' overall tend to end up as celebrations (or denigrations) of 'ethnographic exoticism'. The regional view is valuable not because one can substitute one form of particularism for another, but because it allows one to grasp how chaotically diverse recent Russian culture was and is.[6] Equally, confronting the many differences of life in a single place raises important questions about the value, in overall defining terms, of the words 'post-Soviet' and 'post-socialist', not to speak of 'Soviet'. Leningrad and its citizens were both typical of the broader culture and not – and in this they were, paradoxically, typical. To achieve individuality was in some respects to defy Soviet culture's rigid norms, yet individuality was also what those norms, by the post-Stalin era, themselves anticipated. As the script of El'dar Ryazanov's hugely popular 1976 film comedy, *The Irony of Fate*, written by the director and Emil' Braginsky, put it:

> In the olden days, when someone fetched up in a town or city they didn't know, they felt lonely and lost. Everything was strange: alien houses, alien streets, alien life.
>
> All that's changed now. Someone fetches up in a town they don't know, they feel right at home: all the houses, the streets, the life are exactly the same. They long ago stopped building to individual plans, now everything is pattern-book.
>
> In the past, in one place you'd find St Isaac's Cathedral, in another the Bol'shoi Theatre, in another the Odessa Steps. Now every town has a cinema called Cosmos, built to a pattern-book design, in which you can watch a pattern-book film.
>
> There's not too much variety in street names either. Which city doesn't have a Pervaya Zagorodnaya [First Backwoods Street], Vtoraya Proletarskaya [Second Proletarian Street], Tret'ya Fabrichnaya [Third Factory Street] . . . Pervaya Parkovaya ulitsa [First Park Street], Vtoraya Sadovaya [Second Garden Street], Tret'ya ulitsa Stroitelei [Third Street of the Builders] . . .? Lovely, isn't it . . .?[7]

It was not just 'fate' that was ironic in the film. But at the same time, Ryazanov and Braginsky's sarcasm was softened by the fact that in *The Irony of Fate*, standardisation was the engine of romance. Only because one Soviet street looked completely like another, independent of location, did the Moscow hero manage to meet up with the Leningrad heroine when he let himself into her flat (which had the identical number, and stood on an identically named street) thinking it was his own. The film conveyed the sense that individuality could be generated not *in spite* of standardisation, but *as a result* of this.

The Soviet apartment is sometimes seen in retrospect as simply a kind of drab box, a mass-produced unit. The sociologist Lev Gudkov has gone so far as to attribute standard thinking to the influence of pattern-book dwellings.[8]

Westerners also have tended to see these spaces as uniform, and by extension the Soviet (and indeed socialist) city, with minimum differentiation in terms of districts and zones, and a socially mixed population evenly spread over the entire area.[9] But the leeway available for the creation of a specific self, inflected by family connections, was wide. Both in their homes, and in spaces beyond – courtyards, streets, workplaces, cafés and theatres – people also developed and enacted a sense of themselves as the bearers of 'Leningrad' traditions. While the sense of pride was sometimes questionable in its exclusivity, it generated self-belief that was vital to survival.[10]

Thus, the question of what got remembered and forgotten was not reducible to the construction of apologias for totalitarianism, or the deliberate effacement of politically sensitive material. Indeed, it was often the *personal* past – and its material traces, such as family objects and private graves, written records – that most easily made the transition from 'treasure' to 'rubbish'.[11] It was the everyday pain of poverty and shortage, rather than the grand narratives of persecution, that was difficult to voice.[12] The phrase, 'That's enough about sad things', was used to cut off recollections before they became embarrassing.[13] Experience of this kind became meaningful only in the context of moral narratives of collective experience – as a way of lamenting the disjunctive effects of 'shock therapy', for instance.[14] However, remembering more positive experiences could be equally difficult, compromised as this process was by the association between happiness and political conformity in Soviet propaganda.[15]

Yet 'mundane memory', whether articulated or not, remained inescapable. As they shopped in the Eliseev Stores or ate at the Café Nord or the Metropole, people simultaneously underwent symbolic encounters with the economic and social structures of a particular era, and concrete experiences of a given place. Those brought up in Leningrad or Petersburg mentally compared particular landscapes or individual spaces with their memories of these at earlier times, while incomers attempted to reconcile their lives in this new city with levels of experience that were spatially as well as temporally distinct.

An extended look at this varied and sophisticated place makes one cautious about using the word 'Soviet' in a monolithic sense. By extension the fluid and elusive, as well as wide-ranging, memory practices associated with Leningrad culture challenge the tendency among Western commentators to emphasise the Russian relationship with the past as somehow always inadequate, a tendency that returns us to Pyotr Chaadaev's famous lament, in his First Philosophical Letter of 1836, about how his country had no monuments or memory, and in effect no history at all.[16] As a place shaped by the intricate and wayward processes of remembrance and forgetfulness, Leningrad-Petersburg shows us how the memory and reality of cultures usually seen as 'other' can be reconstructed only by 'unlearning what we think we know';[17] by suspending judgement and listening to the past, with all its many and contrary voices.

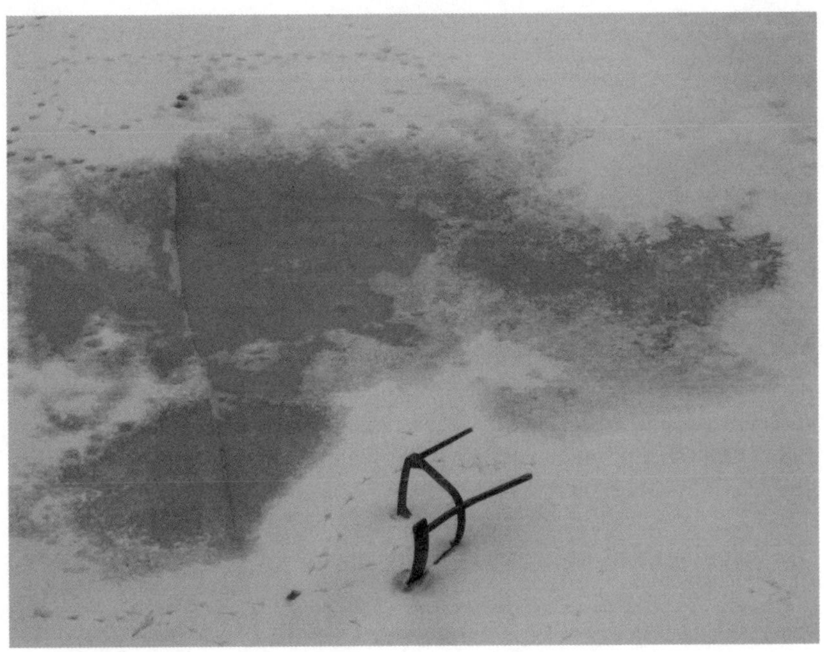

10.3 A chair finds its last resting place in the ice of the Bol'shaya Nevka, 2011.

# Abbreviations and Conventions

Transliteration is in a modified form of British Standard ('Yakovlev', etc.), with exceptions made in the main text for the names of individuals that have a different established form (Likhachev not Likhachov; Lurie not Lur'e). For books and other printed materials published in Leningrad and St Petersburg, the place of publication is omitted.

The following abbreviations are used throughout:

### Interviews

For the AHRC-funded project, 'National Identity in Russia', interviews are coded 'Oxf/AHRC SPb', with a date identifier (07 for 2007, etc.), a recording number (e.g. PF1) and the interviewer's initials (AB = Andy Byford, AK = Alexandra Kasatkina, ANK = Anna Kushkova, AP = Alexandra Piir, CK = Catriona Kelly, EG = Evgeniya Gulyaeva, IN = Irina Nazarova, MS = Marina Samsonova, NG = Natalia Galetkina, VM = Veronika Makarova). Interviews for the Leverhulme-funded project, 'Childhood in Russia' (carried out by Alexandra Piir), are coded 'Oxf/AHRC SPb', with a date identifier and a recording number. For further information about the project, and a detailed informant list, see www.ehrc.ox.ac.uk/lifehistory.

### Publications

*BILGS*: *Byulleten' ispolnitel'nogo komiteta Leningradskogo gorodskogo soveta deputatov trudyashchikhsya.*
*ESP*: *Entsiklopediya Sankt-Peterburga*, ed. A. V. Kobak et al. (www.encspb.ru).
*L*: *Leningrad.*
*LP*: *Leningradskaya pravda.*
*LPan*: *Leningradskaya panorama.*
*M*: *Moskva* [*Moscow*].
*MR*: *Moi raion.* The different numbers for different districts are given as follows: *K* = Kalininsky; *O* = Islands; *Ts* = Central; *V* = Vyborg Side; *VO* = Vasilievsky Island.

*NV*: *Nevskoe vremya*.
*NY*: *New York*.
OL: refers to chapters in Catriona Kelly, *Remembering St Petersburg*, online publication forthcoming (http://oxford.academia.edu/CatrionaKelly).
*PD*: *Peterburgskii dnevnik*.
*SAL*: *Stroitel'stvo i arkhitektury Leningrada*.
*SPbK*: *Sankt-Peterburgskii kur'er*.
*VechL*: *Vechernii Leningrad*.
*VechP*: *Vechernii Peterburg*.

## Archives, Museums and Libraries

AM: Arkhiv Memoriala [Archive of Memorial, St Petersburg].
AMKZ: Arkhiv Muzeya Kirovskogo zavoda [Archive of the Kirov Factory Museum].
ASPbE: Arkhiv Sankt-Peterburgskoi eparkhii [Archive of the St Petersburg Eparchy].
BAN: Biblioteka Akademii Nauk [Library of the Academy of Sciences, St Petersburg].
FN: author's field notes.
GA RF: Gosudarstvennyi arkhiv Rossiiskoi Federatsii [State Archive of the Russian Federation].
GMISPb.: Gosudarstvennyi muzei istorii Sankt-Peterburga [State Museum of St Petersburg].
NA UGIOP: Nauchnyi arkhiv Upravleniya Gosudarstvennoi inspektsii okhrany pamyatnikov [Scholarly Archive of the Board of Management of the State Inspectorate for the Preservation of Monuments, St Petersburg].
RGANI: Rossiiskii gosudarstvennyi arkhiv noveishei istorii [Russian State Archive of Recent History, Moscow].
RGB: Rossiiskaya gosudarstvennaya biblioteka [State Russian Library, former Lenin Library, Moscow].
RNB: Rossiiskaya natsional'naya biblioteka [National Russian Library, former Public Library, St Petersburg].
TsGA-SPb.: Tsentral'nyi gosudarstvennyi arkhiv Sankt-Peterburga [Central State Archive of St Petersburg].
TsGAIPD-SPb.: Tsentral'nyi gosudarstvennyi arkhiv istoriko-politicheskikh dokumentov Sankt-Peterburga [Central State Archive of Historico-Political Documents, St Petersburg].
TsGAKFFD-SPb.: Tsentral'nyi gosudarstvennyi arkhiv kino- foto- fonodokumentov Sankt-Peterburga [State Archive of Film, Photographic, and Phonographic Documents, St Petersburg].
TsGALI-SPb.: Tsentral'nyi gosudarstvennyi arkhiv literatury i iskusstva Sankt-Peterburga [Central State Archive of Literature and Art, St Petersburg].

TsGANTD-SPb.: Tsentral'nyi gosudarstvennyi arkhiv nauchno-tekhnicheskoi dokumentatsii Sankt-Peterburga [Central State Archive of Scientific and Technical Documentation, St Petersburg].

# Notes

### Introduction: City Panorama

1. Gurevich. Cf. Oxf/AHRC UK-08 PF39 AB.
2. See particularly David King's fascinating photo-essay, *The Commissar Vanishes*.
3. This sounds like a legend, but in fact, the copies of the second edition of the *Great Soviet Encyclopedia* in Oxford libraries include this article – pasted inside the covers of the volume concerned. In Russian libraries such as RNB it is neatly inserted into the binding (in BAN the entire volume is missing). On this and comparable episodes, see also Dewhirst and Farrell.
4. In Margaret MacMillan's recent dossier of deceit, *The Uses and Abuses of History*, Russia is accorded a prominent place, which is reasonable enough at one level, but ignores the protests against official 'history management' by Russians themselves: see e.g. Koposov. On the problems of researching the 'Great Patriotic War', see Merridale, *Ivan's War*.
5. See e.g. Khapaeva; Etkind; Jones, 'Memories of Terror'. The examination of post-totalitarian memory in Russia and the Soviet Union developed later than Holocaust memory studies and was strongly influenced by these; here, on the other hand, I am following the lead of Alon Confino and Peter Fritzsche, who as long ago as 2002, in *The Work of Memory*, suggested the need to go beyond the fixation on guilt and suppression. Another factor left out of the count is the way in which memory of traumatic events may itself modulate: see esp. Novick on the Holocaust.
6. Jersild, Applebaum, Snyder etc.
7. See e.g. Verdery, *The Political Lives*; Crowley; Bassin, Ely and Stockdale. For an excellent treatment of the architectural erasure in Russian history, see Schönle.
8. Vail', *Genii mesta*.
9. Though the image is rather dated: for instance, what the sociologist Vadim Volkov termed 'violent entrepreneurs' had their heyday in the 1990s and early 2000s; many have now 'gone legit' and are mainly to be seen climbing from their Hummers on the way to some fashionable restaurant. See V. Volkov, *Violent Entrepreneurs*, and the updated Russian-language edition, *Silovoe predprinimatel'stvo*. Now one can find, say, a mobile telephone network making jokes about 'hard men' (an MTS ad in 2012 showed a muscly shaven-headed man with and without dark glasses: 'You needn't be scared of mobile Internet with us!') – a sure sign that the days of real fear are past.
10. This joke has had a healthy post-Soviet afterlife: see e.g. the anti-patriotic site www.wayoffool.org/news/news%7B%7Ds-prazdnikom-dorogoe-khuetechestvo-s-dnem-rossii.html. For a persuasive analytical treatment of this condition, see Sergei Oushakine, *The Patriotism of Despair: Nation, War, and Loss in Russia* (Ithaca, NY, 2009).
11. 'A ne zrya li Leningrad v Sankt-Peterburg pereimenovali?', post from July 2001, http://forum.ixbt.com/post.cgi?id=print:34:553
12. *NV* 15 June 1991, p. 1.
13. There is an enormous literature on the Blockade. Yarov's *Blokadnaya etika* is an important recent analysis based on documents. Two of the best recent sources in English are Bidlack and Lomagin's anthology, and Anna Reid's narrative history, based on documents and memoirs.
14. Natal'ya Kosmarskaya, contribution to Forum 12, *Forum for Anthropology and Culture* 7 (2011).
15. On the early history of the alterations to ploshchad' Vosstaniya, see Lebina and Izmozik; on the later history, and on the equally conservative history of street renaming, [OL Chapter 2].
16. On the invisibility of statues, see particularly Yampolsky.
17. Brodsky, 'Pochti elegiya', *Stikhotvoreniya i poemy*, 1, p. 68.
18. That said, I would of course not deny or belittle the role of monuments, and more broadly the official institutions of memory (including museums, guidebooks, albums), as well as literature and

the academic study of history, on the inhabitants of cities – and particularly on those who are highly educated. Originally, this study was supposed to cover *both* these institutions, and the institutions of 'mundane memory' (with two parts titled 'Making History' and 'Living with History'). However, the sheer size of the result made it essential to unjoin the twins, and I have presented the 'Making History' section as a separate book, *Remembering St Petersburg*. Where necessary, sections of this text are referred to here as [OL Chapter 1] etc., in square brackets.

19. Paul Connerton, *How Societies Remember* (Cambridge, UK, 1989).
20. This is worth emphasising, given that the situation in Western countries in the post-war era could be slightly different. See, for example, the entry for 20 July 1969 from a British teenager's diary (published by the author, Dinah Hall, in the letters column of the *Guardian*, 5 January 2013): 'I went to [the] arts centre (by myself!) in yellow cords and blouse. Ian was there but he didn't speak to me. Got rhyme put in my handbag from someone who's apparently got a crush on me. It's Nicholas I think. UGH. Man landed on moon.'
21. Oxf/AHRC SPb-11 PF3 NG. For a well-practised story of surviving the Blockade as a child, see Oxf/AHRC UK-08 PF22 AB.
22. Some find the term over-familiar, but it is useful where one is referring to long-term characteristics of city life; I have therefore regularly used it here.
23. My thanks to Marina Samsonova for pointing this out to me.
24. Granin, 'Dom na Fontanke', *SS v 5 tomakh*, 3, p. 166.
25. For a further discussion, see my 'The Leningrad Affair'; [OL Chapter 1].
26. The delay was almost certainly a result of the period of national mourning that followed Stalin's death on 5 March 1953, though I have not come across any documentation that concretely states the reasons. Some albums evidently designed for the Jubilee were quietly published a year late, in 1954.
27. See e.g. *Leningrad: Khudozhestvennye pamyatniki*, ed. Shvarts, though a strategic Kirov quotation played for caution, 299–300. More detail on topics such as guidebooks, architectural preservation, and the museums of St Petersburg is provided in material that I had to cut from the printed version of this book for space reasons, and available on www.mod-langs.ox.ac.uk/russian/nationalism/piter/htm. [OL Chapter 1] addresses the master narratives of Petersburg, such as 'Leningrad Communism', [OL Chapter 2] monuments and street names (some of this material is included in Chapter 9 below), [OL Chapter 3] the heritage preservation movement, and [OL Chapter 4] museums.
28. 'Protokol zasedaniya Uchenogo soveta GIOPa Glav. APU Lengorispolkoma', 10 January 1966, TsGANTD-SPb, 386/1-1/13/1.
29. See Basina, *Puteshestvie po Leningradu* (1979). On learning how to take visitors round the city as a popular exercise in foreign-language classes, I am indebted to the participants in the Urban Anthropology Seminar, European University, St Petersburg, for sharing their memories with me.
30. Oxf/AHRC SPb-07 PF3 CK. *Bloknot agitatora* did indeed carry many items on streets and buildings from the late 1950s.
31. Boris Ivanov, 'Po tu storonu ofitsial'nosti', *Sochineniya* 2, p. 426.
32. See Vladimir N. Toporov, *Peterburgskii tekst*; Bitov, *Pushkinskii dom*; Brodsky, 'Pochti elegiya', etc.
33. Belova's larger-than-life personality is described, mostly affectionately, in *Vospominaniya o L. N. Belovoi*, ed. M. D. Yakovleva, I. M. Karuseva (2004).
34. On Western city museums, see e.g. Francis Sheppard, *The Treasury of London's Past: An Historical Account of the Museum of London and its Predecessors, the Guildhall Museum and the London Museum* (London, 1991).
35. *Gospodin oformitel'*, directed by Oleg Teptsov, is still, judging by the enormous number of sites with copies of it, a hugely popular film.
36. I recall hearing both these stories, sometimes presented as fact, and sometimes not, in 1981.
37. Olga Edelman, 'Protsess Iosifa Brodskogo', *Novyi Mir* no. 1 (2007), http://magazines.russ.ru/novyi_mi/2007/1/ei11.html. For a gripping first-hand account of struggling with the authorities, see Kostsinsky. A more detailed account of Leningrad politics is given in [OL Chapter 1].
38. Likhachev, 'Ansambli Leningrada'. This is worth emphasising because of the widespread tendency to assert the inviolability of the city landscape. 'The St Petersburg urban landscape was still intact, resembling an animated nineteenth-century painting, rather than a modern metropolis' (Glikin; cf. Ruble, 85).
39. See [OL Chapter 4].
40. Likhachev, 'Chetvertoe izmerenie'. This was a response to the Chief Architect of Leningrad, who argued that outside the Kremlin, contemporary style should rule. See [OL Chapter 3].

41. There are some exceptions – for example, the Finland Station (P. A. Ashastin, N. V. Baranov, Ya. N. Lukin, completed in 1960), or the sports hall of the Railway Institute on Kronverksky prospekt (I. S. Trofimenkov, G. S. Levin, V. F. Khrushchev, 1975–79) – but they are rare.
42. Letters from V. I. Petropavlovsky to N. A. Belova, TsGALI-SPb 405/1/112/14–21.
43. Compare the figures in *Itogi Vsesoyuznoi perepisi 1959 g.*, 1: 30 (table 6), which gives the 1959 figure as 2,899,955 (or 96 per cent of the 1939 figure), and *Itogi vsesoyuznoi perepisi naseleniya 1979 g.*, 1: 45 (table 6), which gives the figure as 4,578,548.
44. This phrase often comes up in interviews: see e.g. Oxf/AHRC-SPb-08 PF-54 IN; Oxf/AHRC-SPb-07 PF 1 A K; Oxf/AHRC SPb-08 PF-45 IN (taking a more critical view of the term than is typical); Oxf/AHRC Evp-07 PF-2 IN, etc.
45. See Chapter 2.
46. According to *Narodnoe khozyaistvo goroda Leningrada. Statisticheskii sbornik* (M, 1957), p. 7, the population of Leningrad increased from 1,614,000 in 1926 to 3,015,100 in 1939. The 1926 figure represented an artificially low population level, as a result of outflow during the Revolution and Civil War (by 1910, the population of St Petersburg had already reached 1,905,600), but even so, the population influx was dramatic. On post-war population levels, see e.g. Ruble, Vakser, Elizabeth White, Peeling.
47. Cf. the collection ed. Beaumont and Dart on different practices in Western city life – though the engagement with public space is the focus there.
48. For the crooner Mark Bernes's rendition of the song, illustrated with splendid 1960s photographs of Leningrad, see www.youtube.com/watch?v=WjT5GzPBiQ0.
49. Granin, *Leningradskii katalog*, 8–10.
50. Asta Vonderau puts the situation nicely: 'In contrast to their standardised form, the functions and significances of things in Eastern Europe were varied and wondrous' (p. 130). By this she means above all the capacity of their owners to adapt and modify them, both imaginatively and practically. See also the two studies of material anthropology by Miller.
51. Slepakova, 'Snesennyi dom', *Stikhotvoreniya i poemy*, p. 121; 'Byt moikh vremen', ibid., pp. 222–3.
52. Dovlatov, *Chemodan*. The placing *en valeur* of everyday objects is comparable with the processes in other post-socialist countries, as recognised, for instance, by Berdahl; Boym, *The Future*; Pachenkov; Todorova and Gille. However, the commercialisation of objects found in East Germany (the manufacture of reproduction objects etc., see Berdahl), is not characteristic of Russia, where authenticity matters (see Roman Abramov, 'Chto takoe nostal'giya'). Another inspiration in writing this book has been the object-pervaded accounts of St Petersburg by writers from an earlier period where materiality had discursive weight, for example Sergei Gornyi (1925) and S. V. Svetlov (1892).
53. The sociologist Boris Gladarev also emphasises the highly concrete character of St Petersburg city identity.
54. Rogers, *The Old Faith*, p. 28. Cf. his reference to 'tacking between' fact-filled history and 'quiet, dialogic, and embodied historical consciousness', ibid., pp. 298–9. Rogers's own book is a virtuoso illustration of this dynamic, as is the article by Sergei Alymov, '"Perestroika" in the Russian Provinces'.
55. Here I am distancing myself from the 'Whiggist' position adopted by Hobsbawm and Ranger. Particularly prominent in encouraging the study of how communities define tradition is Michael Herzfeld: see for example, *The Body Impolitic*. Among anthropologists, an ancillary movement to this 'localising' of traditions has been a localisation of the concept of 'modernisation', which, as Bruce M. Knauff has pointed out (in his Introduction to *Critically Modern*), 'the power of becoming modern is contested and mediated through alter-native [sic: i.e. "other" + native] guises'. On the positive force of myth, see also Yerushalmi. I have learned much from the sophisticated study of social memory in Ireland by Beiner, and from Raphael Samuel's robust defence of popular views of history.
56. Yerushalmi, *Zakhor*.
57. As Irina Paperno, for instance, has demonstrated in 'Dreams of Terror' and *Stories of the Soviet Experience*, which illustrate the vital role in views of the past played by nebulous testimony such as people's recollections of dreams.
58. The 'Petersburg text' of foreign visitors would be an interesting subject for detailed study. There is a good introduction to its conventions, as well as some excellent extracts, in Cross.
59. Ibid., xii. For more about the local 'aversion to walking', see Chapter 1.
60. Cf. the stand taken against the 'postcard' appreciation in Dragomoshchenko, 'Peterburg na polyakh'.
61. Smirnov, *Genezis*, p. 219 (a riposte to Peter Sloterdijk's understanding of the city as 'transparent'). Cf. Tokareva's interview with Andrei Bitov, where he describes the post-Soviet city as 'like a stage

set of a stage set, practically a mirage. It's morally and physically exhausted to the point of no return, and that's become its new self [oblik]'.

62. Artem'ev talks (in a typical local paradox) about the *liberality* with which the city allows people into such *hidden* places. Burlak discusses the hidden city, e.g. the lives of the local cats. It is interesting that the photographer Andrei Chezhin, on the other hand, chose precisely to photograph the city's landmarks, rather than its back courtyards, as a radical gesture: see the interview with him on the Pushkinskaya 10 site, www.p-10.ru/. The role of the city's courtyards is discussed in Chapter 3.
63. On secret love, see e.g. the depiction of a melancholy unresolved affair between the heroine and an older man she meets regularly at metro stations in Boym, *Ninochka*. An important form of secret knowledge closely associated with the city is mathematics – from Avdotya Izmailova-Golitsyna (known as 'Princesse Minuit') in the 1820s, who evolved her own theories of higher mathematics, but was understood by no mathematicians of her time (or later ones), to the waywardly brilliant Grigory Perel'man in the 2000s.
64. On the early history, see particularly Healey. Homosexuality was legalised in the Russian Federation in 1993, but even in the early twenty-first century the homosexual scene (known in slang as *tema*, from the hippy term *sistema*) was still fraught, as indicated by the vote at the Petersburg's Legislative Assembly to ban 'propaganda for homosexuality' in November 2011, preceding the national ban by more than a year.
65. On these, see the documentation from 1960 in TsGA 7384/36/587/1–48.
66. As described by Aleksandr Zapesotsky, who worked in such an institute: 'Lev Gumilev: lektor ot Boga', in *Lev Nikolaevich Gumilev*, 2, pp. 90–5. The many 'numbered' or 'regime' factories were more of an open secret: everyone knew where the Kirov Factory was and that it made tanks as well as tractors, though the munitions production lines were shrouded in mystery.
67. Maramzin, pp. 11–12.
68. Quoted in Bechtolsheim, p. 446.
69. Krivulin, *Okhota*, p. 55.
70. Almedingen, p. 38.
71. Take, say, the reference to leaving the 'Viennese Quack' and his followers 'to jog on, in their third-class carriage of thought, through the police state of sexual myth' (*Speak, Memory*, p. 230). Akhmatova's conversations with Lidiya Chukovskaya also contain many examples of this mania for ranking.
72. Lotman, 'Simvolika Peterburga' (1984).
73. Both emotions are expressed in SPbAG AKF Bologoe-01 PF1. Cf. the comment from a recent émigré that Muscovites and Petersburgers are considerably less friendly than people from other places when it comes to socialising with other Russians: Oxf/AHRC UK-08 PF52 AB.
74. Interview with I. S. Kon by Aleksandr Zapesotsky, *University Magazine* [produced by the SPb Gumanitarnyi universitet profsoyuzov], no. 11–12 (2004), p. 44.
75. Nikolai Rubtsov, letter to V. I. Safonov, March 1960, http://rubtsov.id.ru/biographia/chronics.htm (last accessed 29 August 2010). I have corrected the name 'Diosphenes', an obvious slip.
76. E. Mokrushina, 'Kuplyu propisku', *MR-K* 15 October 2004, p. 5. Registration then cost 1800 roubles, and citizenship only 800. Legal registration was also expensive and difficult: see Oxf/AHRC SPb-11 PF15 EI (this informant was paying 1500 roubles a month, or about 50 dollars, for the bureaucracy).
77. www.liveinternet.ru/community/petersburg/post87580989/.
78. Sobchak, p. 9. Cf. Naiman, *Poeziya*, p. 104, referring to local attitudes as 'vulnerable and arrogant' (towards Muscovites particularly). Even passing visitors have sometimes recognised this: see e.g. Rau, p. 13: a ticket seller at the Mariinsky had told her group that it was not worth buying tickets for *Swan Lake* as it was 'some company from Novgorod', showing 'that special Leningrad arrogance that we were soon to recognise'.
79. As in the case of the film director Il'ya Averbakh, who had impeccable Petersburg antecedents and stood out in artistic circles for his formal good manners, but whose considerable talent was matched by his hauteur: see Mikhail Petrov, 'Fenomen Averbakha', *Zvezda* 1 (2006), http://magazines.russ.ru/zvezda/2006/1/pe13.html.
80. P. I. Kapitsa, 'Eto bylo tak', *Neva* 5 (1988), p. 140.
81. This might be a biographical background to the interesting contention of Katerina Clark that Moscow as new capital was 'Peterbourgeoisée' in the 1930s: see her 'Pétersbourg et Moscou dans la Russie des années 1930', in Bérard (ed.), *Saint-Pétersbourg*, pp. 79–85.
82. On the history of departures from the city, see e.g. Smirnov, *Deistvuyushchie litsa*, pp. 17–18.
83. An entertaining recent contribution to this genre is Ol'ga Lukas, *Porebrik iz bordyurnogo kamnya* (2011), where Muscovites with their perpetual designer sunglasses and iPods stood opposed to

St Petersburgers in bedraggled top hats. A city ruled by the twin muses of Depression and Excursion, Petersburg was a place where even boasting had to be done in the tone of the dying fall.

84. Viktor Toporov, in his *Dvoinoe dno* (aptly subtitled 'Confessions of a Scandal-Maker'), p. 202, duly mocks these perceptions. Refined humour is traditionally identified in, say, the comedian Arkady Raikin (on whom see further in Chapter 6). Another nice example is the poet Dmitry Bobyshev's joke: 'How many angels can you get on the needle [spire] of Peter and Paul Fortress? – There's one there already' (*Ya zdes'*, p. 57).
85. An exemplary treatment of the impact of status on consumption is Zakharova, *S'habiller*.
86. I have expanded on these distinctions in, for example, Chapter 5.
87. Dovlatov, *Chemodan*. Joseph Brodsky's poetry also regularly assailed the canons of refinement: cf. Dovlatov's remembered aphorism, 'Only tailors have good taste' (*Solo na IBM*, www.sergeidovlatov.com/books/zap_kn.html).
88. From a round-up of replies to a questionnaire, 'Lyubimyi gorod', *Leninskie iskry* 17 July 1965, p. 1.
89. The interesting collection ed. Nivat, *Les sites de la mémoire russe*, likewise focuses (in the first volume, at any rate, the only one to appear before this book was published) on 'official' memory sites: museums, churches, 'pagan' (sic) sacred places, libraries, cities, etc.
90. See e.g. the list of *pamyatnye i znakovye mesta* (memory-rich and significant places) on the site of the action group Zhivoi Gorod, which includes, for example, the Eliseev Stores, the Saigon cafeteria, but also various generic snack bars and bookshops that happened to acquire a following (www.save-spb.ru/page/announce/znakoe_mesto.html). Even the city administration has recognised some such places: see e.g. the 2008 list of 16 'memory places' that were to be enshrined in the 'Red Book' (by analogy with the international lists of endangered species): 'V Krasnuyu knigu pamyatnykh mest Peterburga vneseno vsego 16 nazavanii', 26 February 2008. www.gazeta.spb.ru/26465-0/.
91. Exactly this sort of issue figured largely at the meetings of the co-operative to which I belong that I attended in April 2008, January 2010, etc. As well as Certeau, I have been influenced here by anthropologists and cultural geographers such as Michael Herzfeld and Edward Soja, and by books such as Karl Schlögel, *Moskau lessen*, as well as the excellent corpus of work by anthropologists on post-Soviet and post-socialist reality: see e.g. Humphrey; Rogers, 'Postsocialisms'; Patico; Rivkin-Fish; Fehérváry; Rausing.
92. Among influential studies of globalisation and its impact on the urban environment is Massey. See also Dixon, 'Gazprom versus the Skyline'; and [OL Chapter 3]. I have some reservations about the suitability of recent 'globalisation' paradigms to Russian cities, but discussions of modern Western cities such as Sharon Zukin's books are helpful in suggesting ways of interpretation that one can at least react against. Stronger direct influences are the writings of German urbanists such as Karl Schlögel.
93. A. Sobchak, *Iz Leningrada v Peterburg*, p. 7. This ignores the Parisians who detest Haussmann's work: see e.g. Hazan.
94. There is a good account of this in Elena Hellberg-Hirn, *Imperial Imprints: Post-Soviet St Petersburg* (Helsinki, 2003).
95. Pers. obs., 2011–2012.
96. See e.g. Volkov, *Istoriya kul'tury SPb.*; George and George.
97. See Bibliography. Excellent studies of pre-revolutionary Petersburg culture include Buckler; Steinberg; Kolonitsky, *Tragicheskaya erotica*. On early twentieth-century history see also Clark, *Petersburg*; Schlögel, *Petersburg*; and several of the essays in Schlögel, Schenk, and Ackeret. On the social composition of the city, see also the essays collected in Vikhavainen [=Vihavainen]. My analysis of the period in question has also been enriched by the work of scholars studying the post-Stalin era and present day in a general sense, such as Polly Jones, Susan Reid, Juliane Fürst, Sergei Zhuk, Mark B. Smith, and Steven Harris, Hilary Pilkington, Caroline Humphrey, Bruce Grant, Olga Shevchenko, and many others.
98. Two of Lebina's books, *Obyvatel' i reformy* and *Peterburg sovetskii*, have been particularly useful for the discussion here.
99. Among recent examples of autobiography on which I draw directly in this book are those by Mikhail German, Boris Ivanov, Dmitry Bobyshev, Joseph Brodsky, and Lev Losev. Cases of displaced autobiography include Boym, *Common Places*, sections of which are based on the writer's childhood experiences of life in a communal flat, and her *The Future of Nostalgia*. Yurchak, *Everything Was Forever*, gives expression to the author's own position as a member of 'the last Soviet generation' and to the experiences of his friendship group. The excellent analytical sections of these books are directed more at the exploration of Soviet and post-Soviet culture generally than at the specificities of local life.

100. For 'Petersburg nostalgia', see esp. Boym, *The Future of Nostalgia*. Hellberg-Hirn takes a slightly different tack, offering an accessible introduction to post-Soviet St Petersburg.
101. Andrei Khrzhanovsky, *Poltory komnaty* (2008). In *The Future of Nostalgia*, Boym distinguishes between 'reflective nostalgia' and 'restorative nostalgia', seeing the latter as essentially an artefact of the political elite, while the former is characteristic of creative artists. However, this neat binary oversimplifies the situation with all sorts of different types of 'cultural text', from internet sites to films such as Valery Todorovsky's *Stilyagi* (2008), as well as commercial artefacts and official festivals, taking a celebratory view of the Soviet material past.
102. German, *Slozhnoe proshedshee*.
103. The regional theme in late Soviet and post-Soviet culture has generally been addressed with reference to smaller places. See e.g. Petro; Akhmetova and Lur'e; Watts; Donovan. For an overall discussion of regionalisation from the point of view of economic geography, see the work of Tatiana Nefedova. For a discussion of the cultural dimensions of regionalisation, see *Glubinnaya Rossiya: 2000–2002*. Regional feeling was one of the themes of the 2011 election: for example, United Russia used the slogan, 'Vote Petersburg!' for its election posters and leaflets, and included interviews with well-known local figures in the latter (see e.g. *Vyberi Peterburg* October 2011, pp. 17–23).
104. For 'ripping down the seams', see Oxf/AHRC SPb-11 PF4 NG (man b. 1962). An interesting general study of the discourse of post-Soviet crisis (with an argument that this is usually intertwined with commitment to self-reliance) is Shevchenko. See also Alymov; Rogers, 'Postsocialisms'. Industrial decline is discussed in more detail in Chapter 4 below. The undoubted fact that some people lived reasonably well under Soviet power is, in retrospect, sometimes presented as a systemic norm: i.e., only the idle and disorganised could not afford a decent flat, a car, a satisfying job, etc. For claims of this kind, see e.g. Aleksandr Lavrov, '"Deti Pobedy"'. Oushakine, *The Patriotism of Despair* is an excellent general study of defensive self-perception in the post-Soviet era. For work on the new St Petersburg see e.g. the special issue of the *International Journal of Urban and Regional Research* 3 (1997) dedicated to the city; Salmi; Rosa Vihavainen; and the publications of the Centre for Independent Sociological Research (Tsentr nezavisimykh sotsiologicheskikh issledovany) (www.cisr.ru/).
105. The complexity of these cultural processes has been repeatedly emphasised in discussions of the recent past in former socialist countries: see e.g. Velikonja.
106. For a detailed discussion of crime as local myth and as concrete experience see [OL Chapter 1]. Volkov's *Violent Entrepreneurs* is the most important academic study of Petersburg crime at this period.
107. Velikonja gives a useful typology of reactions: rejection of the past; amnesia; revisionism ('the culture of death' etc.); nostalgia. Combinations of these reactions are of course also possible, indeed likely.
108. For the argument that social dislocation fostered the emergence of personal autonomy, see Shevchenko, *Crisis and the Everyday*.
109. See [OL Chapter 1].
110. Stone Island was the main inner-city recreation area for the Party elite, including 'houses of rest' for top officials. Not all were accommodated in pre-revolutionary buildings: the KGB had a slick facility with narrow windows and expensive cladding, like an opulent ochre-brown pillbox.
111. Memories of 1991 would deserve detailed treatment in their own right. Maybe it is because my perception of history has been formed by reading *War and Peace* as a child that I tend to assume that 'authentic' eye-witness testimony is desultory. Many recollections of August 1991 are more upbeat, and not only when people remember actually doing things (printing leaflets, for example – Nikolai Vakhtin, pers. inf.) but the Palace Square meeting itself. See e.g. Melikhov.
112. For a short history of the Library, see Polina Vakhtina, 'La Bibliothèque publique de Saint-Pétersbourg' in Nivat (ed.), *Les sites*, vol. 1, pp. 667–83.

### 1 Moscow Station and Palace Bridge

1. Slepakova, Prazdnichnyi put', *Stikhotvoreniya i poemy*, p. 84.
2. As commemorated in Ol'ga Forsh's fictionalised memoir, *Sumasshedshii korabl'* (1931).
3. The *Krasin* was in fact British-built, by the Armstrong Company in Newcastle in 1916, and saw service during the Russian Civil War on the side of the interventionists under her original name *Svyatogorsk*. She was purchased by the Soviet government in 1921. See the display in the Museum of the Arctic and Antarctic.
4. See, for example, Blok's 'In late autumn from the harbour' ('Pozdnei osen'yu iz gavani', 1909).

5. For example, 'The End of a Marvellous Era' ('Konets prekrasnoi epokhi', 1969), *Stikhotvoreniya i poemy*, 1, p. 288. Brodsky's drawings were on show in the Russian National Library, December 2010.
6. Yu. M. Lotman, letter to B. A. Uspensky, 29 April 1981, *Perepiska*, p. 385.
7. One might compare the proliferation of retired ships and marine hardware down the embankments of the Thames, now that the wharves have been turned into flats, restaurants, and hotels.
8. There was a municipal yacht club, and also one attached to the Kirov Factory, but these were strictly collective ventures, along with the sailing trips organised by the Pioneer and Komsomol movement.
9. *Nash gorod Leningrad*, p. 47, claimed that there were sea routes out of Leningrad to 400 different ports, but given that most were cruise ships serving multiple destinations, this translates into a relatively small number of actual routes (perhaps 50–60).
10. See, for example, Daniil Granin's recollections of sailing round Europe on the *Rossiya* with a group of prominent writers in 1956 ('Avtobiografiya', *SS v 5 tomakh* 1, p. 11), or the memories of a trip on the *Baltika* to Scandinavia of Steblin-Kamensky (pp. 66–84).
11. The 'marine façade' first became a concern of planners in 1947 (as discussed by Ruble, *Leningrad*, p. 51), but the realisation of the project took another twenty years. On the prestige of the area, see Chapter 3 below.
12. www.mfspb.ru/index.php?lang=ru.
13. One might contrast the local identity of Sebastopol, which had a pronouncedly naval flavour: see Qualls, esp. pp. 131–42.
14. See e.g. Oxf/AHRC SPb-10 PF8 MS, and the detailed discussion in Chapter 5 below.
15. On affection for the navy, see e.g. Joseph Brodsky, *Less Than One*, pp. 466–7.
16. Nikolai Rubtsov, 'V okeane', http://rubtsov.id.ru/. Leningrad also had its tradition of seafaring novels: for example, the writer Viktor Konetsky (1929–2002), born in the city, was one of the most prominent producers of 'sea dog' prose in this period (as Vitaly Bianki was in the 1920s and 1930s). (On Konetsky, see www.baltkon.ru/.) However, these writers did not so much evoke Leningrad specifically as 'Northern waters' more generally.
17. Occasional press items did get published: see e.g. V. Bezbrezhnyi, 'Zavod na Fabrichnom ostrove', *LP* 28 January 1971, p. 4, or V. N. Bereslavsky, 'Vremya bol'skhikh peremen', *LPan* 1 (1984), pp. 6–8 (on the history of the Nevsky zavod im. Lenina). But these referred to the city's *traditions* of military ship-building, rather than what was going on in the present. Generally, studies of the city's industry referred only to tanker-building and floating-fish-factory production: see e.g. *Nash gorod Leningrad*, p. 27, and *Leningradskaya promyshlennost'*, pp. 48–74.
18. I recall from personal observation that in the 1980s there was an extraordinary festive atmosphere down at these embankments in July and August, with people strolling by the lighted decks of the vessels, and sailors passing up and down staring out at the passing crowds. On the shashlyk bars, pers. inf. from man b. early 1960s.
19. My thanks to an informant who lived in Estonia in the 1960s and 1970s for this reminiscence.
20. On the Stalin era canal-building behind this legendary status, see Karl Schlögel, 'Eine Stadt am Meer. Die Eröffnung des Moskwa-Wolga-Kanals', in his *Terror und Traum*.
21. By 2011, the cobbling had mostly gone, but the military air remained.
22. For the orders to construct these monuments, see 'O sooruzhenii v Sankt-Peterburge pamyatnikov: Rasporyazhenie Mera Sankt-Peterburga ot 28 Marta 1996 g. No. 268-r', Memorial Archive. On the curious figurehead-style structure on the point of Petrovskaya Embankment, see [OL Chapter 2]. Others included one on the ploshchad' Baltiiskikh yung, Vasilievsky Island, and the Novodevichy Cemetery.
23. In 2010, the turnover of the St Petersburg cargo port was 58 million tonnes, according to figures from the Association of Sea Ports of the Russian Federation (www.morport.com/rus/publications/document1142.shtml). Novorossiisk handled just over 117 million tonnes, and the RF's no. 3 port, Vostochnyi, around 35 million tonnes (ibid.).
24. For instance, by 2005 Shanghai's cargo volume stood at more than 460 million metric tonnes (http://geo.1september.ru/articlef.php?ID=200600113); by 2009, this had reached 505 million metric tonnes (www.aapa-ports.org/industry/content.cfm?ItemNumber=900&navItemNumber=551). As the information on the American Association of Port Authorities' site points out (ibid.), there are many possible comparators of port size, including shipping tonnage, value of cargo, traffic flow (e.g. number of containers handled), and revenue, as well as cargo volume. However, St Petersburg could clearly not count as a world leader by any index.
25. For instance, in 2008, London handled about 52 million tonnes, and in 2009, 45 million tonnes (see http://travel.uk.msn.com/news/articles.aspx?cp-documentid=154291486).

26. See further in Chapter 4.
27. In merchant shipping, privatisation raised all kinds of issues about pay, conditions of work, and rights, which was addressed by the model statute, 'Ob osobennostyakh regulirovaniya truda moryakov', passed at the Eighteenth Plenary Session of the Interparliamentary Assembly of CIS States, 24 November 2001. See http://arhiv.inpravo.ru/data/base637/text637v152i228.htm.
28. Nataliya Tolstaya's short story 'V ramkakh dvizheniya', *Zvezda* 10 (1999), pp. 9–12, depicted a one-off cruise on a clipper to Scandinavia, one of a series of 'freebies' for city officials and their connections.
29. Anastasiya Gavrielova, 'Ot yakorya vse otreklis' ', *MR (VO)* 20 August 2004, p. 4.
30. See the credit sequence. The viewer who knows St Petersburg watches the film with an uneasy sense of estranged vision: the rooftop sequences look 'right', as do the trams – but then a steep hilly street, a detail impossible in the Petersburg landscape, comes into view. In our interview with him (Oxf/AHRC SPb-11 PF18), Sokurov confirmed the Lisbon setting.
31. Irina Znamenskaya, 'Damba ili amba?' (2 March 2007), www.apn-spb.ru/publications/article543.htm (accessed 30 August 2010) refers to the situation as 'an ecological Chernobyl'.
32. Smol'noe was the site of the so-called 'aeroplane affair', the first attempted hijacking in the Soviet Union. In 1970, a group led by some Leningrad Jews who had been refused permission to emigrate collectively bought tickets for all the seats in a small plane, intending to force the pilot to land in Stockholm. However, their plan came to the ears of the authorities, and they were arrested before boarding. The two leaders of the group were condemned to death, but the sentence was commuted after an international outcry. An interesting account of the case, which was a landmark in the history of Jewish emigration, is given by one of the lawyers for the defence, Semyon Ariya, in 'Samoletnoe delo', *Vechernyaya Moskva*, 17 January 2002.
33. Edmonds, *Russian Vistas*, p. 38.
34. *Nash gorod Leningrad*, p. 52.
35. See e.g. O. K. Petrov, 'Vsegda na perednem krae', *Stroitel'stvo i arkhitektura Leningrada* 5 (1975), p. 27. In 2009, Pulkovo-1 was placed on the list of the only 20 works of Soviet architecture from 1957–1987 that the Union of Architects deemed to merit preservation: see www.online812.ru/2009/05/25/006/. On the architecture of Pulkovo-1, see also Yu. I. Kurbatov, *Petrograd. Leningrad. Sankt-Peterburg. Arkhitekturno-gradostroitel'nye uroki* (2008), p. 140.
36. Tat'yana Nikitina, 'Zemnye zaboty aviatorov', *LPan* 1 (1992), pp. 7–8.
37. Cf. F. A. Belinskaya's letter to her husband Anatoly, 1 August 1964: 'In Oryol, they told me in the public information office there are almost always no tickets to Leningrad ("Try the Mother and Child Room, they might have them there.") To Moscow, I had a free choice of trains.' (Belinsky, *Pis'ma proshlogo veka*, p. 479).
38. Tamara Zibunova, 'Tartu v 1960-e', http://zibunova.narod.ru/zibmtartu.htm.
39. In 1990, I travelled to Tartu and back from Leningrad, a trip of around six hours, in these conditions; another minus was that 'comfort breaks' were of unpredictable frequency and duration. 'On the other hand, the drivers also allowed themselves various unscheduled stops at every village between Narva and Tartu in order to drop off girlfriends, visit relatives and check on the availability of scarce goods' (CK, letter home, May 1990).
40. For instance, in spring 2011, the company 'Business-Visit' was advertising a round-trip fare of 2500 roubles on 'comfortable tourist-class buses', www.b-v.ru/text/0322.html.
41. Pers. obs., December 2010. In the summer, buses to resort towns would also be used by tourists, but in the winter migrant labour and students are the likeliest market.
42. *Avtostop* was never forbidden or even discouraged, and as road traffic increased, opportunities proliferated. See Shchepanskaya, *Kul'tura dorogi*.
43. For example, a woman b. 1945 recollected that in the Soviet period, she and her family had used the train even for travelling to Central Asia (Oxf/AHRC SPb-10 PF2 MS). For the importance of the railway as recognised by an official source, see 'Oktyabr'skaya zheleznaya doroga' in *Tekhnicheskii zheleznodorozhnyi slovar'*, available online, http://dic.academic.ru/dic.nsf/railway/1701/О К Т Я Б Р Ь С К А Я.
44. As, for example, in the case of Metropolitan Nikodim (see the material on his time of office in the biography by Archimandrite Avgustin (Nikitin), *Tserkov' plenennaya*, pp. 86–102). The 'Red Arrow' first ran in 1931, and originally took nearly 10 hours, leaving at 1.30 a.m.; in the late Soviet period, departure was always on the dot of midnight, followed by equally punctual arrival at 8.30. See 'Krasnaya strela', *ESP*.
45. In the Soviet period, there was an elaborate system of more and less prestigious trains (the former more comfortable as well as faster, and linking major population centres). The number of so-called *firmennye poezda*, or 'brand-name trains', increased in the post-Soviet era, and by the late 2000s

some overnight trains on the Moscow–St Petersburg route had been provided with 'luxury' carriages; most other *firmennye poezda* had new carriages that were of significantly higher quality than the old ones. Slower trains went on running with the old rolling stock. Prices reflected the differences in comfort and convenience, with 'luxury' (two-berth sleeping car) accommodation costing about twice as much as *kupeinoe* (four-berth couchette), four times as much as a *platskarta*, and more than ten times the cost of an ordinary seat (in 2010, according to the Rossiiskie zheleznye dorogi site (rzd.ru), the figures were approximately 4000, 2000, 1000 and 385 roubles). For comments on the different trains, see a blog of 10 October 2007, leanelle.livejournal.com/137514.html), 'The "Nikolaevskii Express" is wonderful, I'd love to travel like that all the time, only thing is it arrives a bit early. But best not ever use the train on the Murmansk–Moscow route. They start getting you out of your berth 2 hours early, i.e. at 5 a.m . . . '. On the introduction of the first 'new-generation' high-speed train (between Helsinki and St Petersburg), see Yuliya Galkina, 'Putin sygral "Allegro"', *Sankt-Peterburgskii kur'er*, 22 December 2010, p. 3; on the 'Sapsan' (high-speed Moscow–Petersburg train), http://sapsan.su/.

46. According to *ESP* (keyword 'Krasnaya strela'), this practice began in 1965. Here, the music is said to be played on departure; in my experience, it is also always played on arrival.
47. The majority of stations lay on suburban lines, at the bottom of the city's transport hierarchy (see Chapter 8). A sense of the importance of the railway to city life is given also by an account of the miniature line for children (MOZhD, the Youth Railway): see Igor' Kopaisov, 'Vospominaniya o detstve', http://railways.id.ru/memoirs/001.html. MOZhD's stations were stocked with chocolate, ice-cream, lemonade, and pies, and some had facilities for table tennis.
48. In 1978, the termini serving long-distance trains were Moskovskii, Finlyandskii, Vitebskii, and Varshavskii vokzaly (see 'Raspisanie poezdov dal'nego sledovaniya na leto 1978 goda', *LP* 7 June 1978, p. 4). On the history of the stations, see in particular Frolov; on their cultural meaning, Frithjof Benjamin Schenk, 'Bahnhöfe: Stadttore der Moderne', in Schlögel, Schenk, and Markus Ackeret (eds), *Sankt-Petersburg*.
49. Oksana Boiko, 'Vokzal dlya dachnikov i revolyutsionerov', *NV* 12 February 2000, p. 1; http://mkmagazin.almanacwhf.ru/venicle/n_293.htm. Last accessed 30 December 2010.
50. RGANI 5/ 34/60/27. In fact the costs had to be reduced after the Transport Ministry did not come up with its contribution, and Lenoblkom had to get a million roubles from the Central Committee, which was duly agreed (see ibid., l, p. 28).
51. Internet sources refer to plans to transform the station into a museum along the lines of the Quai d'Orsay in Paris, but nothing had happened at the time of writing. In February 2013, the outbuildings were the centre of a conflict between radical preservationists and the police: see the TV discussion, http://vk.com/feed?z=video-45764_164221061%2F6807e25ecc6b51d44f.
52. B. G. Metlitsky, 'Sokhranim staryi vokzal', *LPan* 12 (1986), p. 33.
53. Piryutko, 'Mezhdu Leningradom i Peterburgom', p. 465.
54. On the background to the change – the source of self-congratulation on Anatoly Sobchak's part, but fiercely opposed by Communists – see [OL Chapter 2].
55. On antique trains, see Yu. L. Il'in, 'Parovozy-eksponaty', *LPan* 7 (1987), pp. 30–1. On hypermodern ones, Andrei Potapenko, 'Sled "Sokola" na Moskovskom trakte', *NV* 27 January 1995, p. 3 (on a high-speed train intended to do the Moscow–St Petersburg run in 147 minutes, and a futuristic new design for the Moscow Station).
56. An issue not considered here, however, is the rising losses on some lines in the northwest. As of 2011, winter timetables to Arkhangel'sk, for instance, had reduced numbers of trains to two-to-three weekly, rather than a daily service. At the same time, increased costs were making train travel quite expensive (the summer 2012 prices of a return to Moscow in sleeper class were well over 300 dollars), threatening the future of the system.
57. Corsini, *Caviar for Breakfast*, p. 13, pp. 15–16. The procedure of singling out foreign visitors, even if travelling within the Soviet Union, continued up to the late 1980s and the abolition of internal visas. I can recall myself the embarrassment of an internal flight back to Voronezh (where I was a student in 1980–81) from Leningrad. 'To Voronezh! One *inturist*!' shouted the hostess accompanying me, as the other hundred or so passengers resolutely affected uninterest.
58. In my recollection a 'green channel/red channel' system, with optional completion of a customs declaration, was introduced in 2003.
59. See the article on the *zastavy* by I. A. Bogdanov, *ESP*.
60. The cult of the border guard began during the 1930s (as I have discussed in *Children's World*, Ch. 3, it was particularly thoroughly propagandised among Soviet children). It continued to be of great importance later. For example, a big illustrated compendium on the city published in 1961 carried a piece by one Lt-Col Sidorov (co-authored with Mikhail Slonimsky), 'Pogranichnik' (The Border

Guard) (*U nas v Leningrade*, pp. 198–204), which expounded the virtues of the breed: 'Constant watchfulness, everlasting tension, intense awareness of any stranger, hunger, cold – all this has become customary both for children and for adults.' There followed anecdotes about spy-catching, and about the border-guards' skill in being able to distinguish 'absent-minded travellers on business trips' who really had forgotten their papers from lying aliens. Fundamental was a Sherlock Holmesian eye for detail, such as unusual amounts of dirt on boots (meaning a long walk before joining the train), etc. In 1994, the border guards' own newspaper, *Pogranichnik: gazeta Severo-Zapada*, regularly carried similar tales of bravery and resourcefulness on duty (see e.g. 'Bditel'nost' – nashe oruzhie', *Pogranichnik* 19 February 1994, p. 1; 'Passazhir passazhiram – rozn' ', ibid., 28 March 1994, p. 1).

61. See e.g. Lev Losev's account of how a customs officer, 'with ill-concealed sadistic glee, after a look at our coughing, sneezing, temperature-ridden children, removed all the medicines we had for them', *Meandr*, p. 260. The experience of leaving also generated legends about the successful evasion of surveillance – grand pianos transported in pieces, precious stamps wrapped in condoms and held inside a person's cheek, hamster-style, dollars burned before leaving home and retrieved abroad because the owners had listed their numbers (Viktor Toporov, *Dvoinoe dno*, p. 355).
62. This I can say from personal experience. It was only when I started to come and go regularly in the late 1990s that my friends decided an *otval'naya* might be dispensable; it is still customary to see people off.
63. See http://mbla.livejournal.com/695305.html (posted on 1 November 2010). Whether true or not, this view of things has symbolic weight.
64. *Chelnoki*, 'shuttlers' importing goods for market trading, made heavy use of the airport, particularly for flights to and from Helsinki, and ordinary travellers stuffed their luggage with goods as well (pers. obs.).
65. As in a Leningrad anecdote: a man goes to the Universitetskaya embankment and turns in various directions to test out the echo, yelling 'Blyadi, blyadi, blyadi!' [Whores, whores, whores!]. From Vasilievsky Island, the Vyborg Side, Petrogradka etc. comes the answer 'Di-di-di' [the last syllable of the word]. From the Moscow Station, he hears a shout: 'I-dyom!' [Here we come!] (pers. inf.). Igor' Stoma, '"Zona" pod kryshei', *LPan* 6 (1992), p. 9, reports that the station and 'BAN' (the tram stop just outside it) were favoured haunts of prostitutes in the 1980s. See also German Gurevich, 'Vospominaniya', www.gergur.ru/work/220/ (on a misunderstanding when a female friend of his was sitting chewing a pie at the Moscow Station and a man approached and said, 'How much?' 'Ten.' 'That's a lot!' 'Yes, but for a meat one.' 'Stupid bitch!' he snorted and walked off. Only then did she realise what kind of 'goods' he was actually interested in).
66. Igor' Stoma, '"Zona" pod kryshei', *LPan* 6 (1992), pp. 7–10.
67. Even in the late 1990s pickpockets were widespread (pers. obs.).
68. The existence of these offices was an interesting paradox in a society where freedom of information was definitely not part of the culture. In the post-Soviet era, these official services vanished (however, personal details were easy to get hold of through the internet, and might also be purchased on CD-Roms at metro stations).
69. Yuliya Dmitrieva, 'Na Moskovskom vokzale budet, kak v Evrope', *NevV* 7 September 1995, p. 4, describes the new ticket hall at the Finland Station (sic) set up by the Finnish company Klausen, Finland. This was the first place in Russia to have numbered queues. Moscow Station was to have a similar facility later. (As of the 2010s, the Finland Station facility was still working, and in superb order, as was the streamlined, spotless waiting-room for the Helsinki trains alongside. But Moscow Station was yet to acquire anything of this order.)
70. On the 'Europeanisation' of the station as an official ideal, see Sirotinina, 'The Moscow Station', pp. 7–11.
71. Petrov-Vodkin, 'O "Mire iskusstva": Otryvki iz vospominanii' (1929), in *Prostranstvo Evklida*, p. 673.
72. German, *Slozhnoe proshedshee*, p. 621: 'After my trips to Paris I had grown sick of our dead expanses, the stuccoed façades that are so beautiful in the distance and as crude as cardboard close to, the peeling pine-stumps of the mansions and palaces, the portals of the once splendid shops, filled either with endless queues or a gloomy, reeking void, the expression of fearful exhaustion on all the faces.'
73. Dmitry Mukhin, 'Mgnoven'ya', unpublished text, c. 2007. First words emphasised in original. My thanks to the author and Irina Nazarova for supplying a copy of this text. Of course, the internet can now help with avoiding this kind of disorientation: see e.g. the information site 'Khochu v Piter!', http://hochuvpiter.ru/. On the other hand, access to online resources in the provinces is still limited, and in any case people often take culture shock for granted – it is part of the migration experience.

74. Nina Savushkina, 'Dver' v zastoi', *Zarubezhnye zapiski* 16 (2008), http://magazines.russ.ru/zz/2008/16/sa4-pr.html. See also the video and comments on http://hovan.livejournal.com/100855.html. The official name for the place is 'Dorozhnoe' (approximately, 'The Wayfarer'): see ibid.
75. In 2005, an enterprising small business was offering to steer motorists from outside the city round the centre (avoiding traffic jams) at a cost of 500 roubles a time (or 350 on weekdays). D. Litvintsev, 'Lotsmany gorodskikh dorog', MR 28 January 2005, p. 4 – another example of how the 'personal touch' was preferred to the map.
76. This presents not just the banal challenge of deciding whether the numbers will run up one side and down the other, or with even numbers down one side and odd down the other, but the fact that numbers may be set back in a courtyard, and that odd and even numbers may well be significantly out of kilter (so that, say, no. 5 is opposite no. 16, or no. 23 opposite no. 4, and so on). For this reason, modern street signage includes number ranges on corners.
77. *Arkhitekturnye pamyatniki Leningrada* (1979). (See also illustration.) Non-availability of to-scale maps was a function of the obsession with security. Even a transport route map proposed by Lenizdat in 1965 fell foul of the military authorities: TsGAIPD-SPb. 24/137/20/2.
78. By the start of the 2010s, the authorities had (not before time!) introduced a kiosk offering fixed-price trips. But it was not always manned.
79. Oxf/AHRC SPb-07 PF32 IN. Cf. the account of making a first trip as a child in Oxf/AHRC SPb-11 PF6 EI.
80. Cf. Dmitry Likhachev's recollections of the city's vanished boat traffic in his *Vospominaniya*: see e.g. 1, p. 51.
81. For an affectionate reminiscence of these, see Oxf/AHRC SPb-11 PF4 NG.
82. On the first electric trams, see Yu. L'vov, 'Na tramvae po l'du Nevy', *Peterburgskie magistrali* 4 (6409), 7 April 2010, p. 8. I owe the information about short cuts across the ice to an informant born in 1920, who regularly crossed that way in the post-war years.
83. The Paris figures are available on the site of the Laboratoire centrale des Ponts et Chaussées (www.lcpc.fr/en/sources/paris/index.dml). The others are my own calculations, from maps.
84. Krivulin, *Okhota na mamonta*, p. 333.
85. For the date, see Lidiya Petrovna Bulankova of the Dom tvorchestva yunykh (formerly the Dvorets pionerov), Anna Snezhina, 'Kak "Sekret" "Avroru" pobedil', Sankt-Peterburgskie vedomosti, 18 June 2010. www.spbvedomosti.ru/article.htm?id=10267242@SV_Articles.
86. Lidiya Petrovna Bulankova of the Pioneer Palace, Anna Snezhina, 'Kak "Sekret" "Avroru" pobedil', Sankt-Peterburgskie vedomosti, 18 June 2010. www.spbvedomosti.ru/article.htm?id=10267242@SV_Articles.
87. Snezhina, 'Kak "Sekret" "Avroru" pobedil'.
88. In 1950, Grin was labelled a 'bourgeois cosmopolitan', and his works were not reprinted till the Thaw era. According to the catalogue of the RNB, 4 editions of *Red Sails* appeared in the 1950s, 3 in the 1960s, around 15 in the 1970s, and over 30 in the 1980s. The story was also adapted as a play and a *feeriya* (magic show). In 1961, it became a successful film.
89. Anastasiya Gavrielova, '"Gremikha", i "Ekaterina" do navigatsii ne dozhili' MR(V) 3 June 2005, p. 5.
90. This is of course not the only route, but happens to be one that I did myself when attending a post-conference party in 2008.
91. 'Spravka o vypolnenii postanovleniya byuro Leningradskogo Obkoma KPSS ot 25/IV-1967 goda . . .', TsGAIPD-SPb. 24/102/31/5. These floating restaurants soon acquired quite a louche reputation: see Chapter 7 below.
92. The cost was 150 roubles a trip, then more than 6 times the cost of the metro or a bus: see *MR(V)* 21 October 2005, p. 6. These vehicles were rather elusive, too, with a vestigial timetable and a chronic shortage of seating, as well as a short season.
93. FN, June 2011, September 2011, October 2011.
94. Sometimes in quite an aggressive sense, as in the case of a *sukhogruz* (barge) that ran into one of the piers of Volodarsky Bridge on 28 October 2010.
95. FN June 2011.
96. The fun, for a Leningrad audience, lay partly in the fact that the hero evidently lived on Vyborg Side, and his mistress in the centre – so that he would have had a choice of many different bridges to get back (and in any case, he always used the metro).
97. Aleksandr Medvedev, 'Zerkala komnaty smekha: Leningradskii plakat 1980-kh', www.advertology.ru/article32112.htm. Medvedkin's image, unlike the postcard, uses the bridge to frame the city's industrial landscape, not its famous sights.

98. This was and is a popular occupation even in winter: cf. 'O podlednom love', *MR (Vas)* 6 February 2004, p. 6, a reader's letter complaining about fishermen getting themselves into difficulties after a drop too many and having to call out the emergency services.
99. Pers. inf.
100. Not Obvodnyi Canal, though, an irredeemably proletarian location, which there were plans in the Soviet era to fill in and transform into a motorway (Piir and Zhukovsky, 'Skorostnaya magistral' na Obvodnom kanale'). Cf. Sobchak's plans to do this (cited in 'Introduction: City Panorama' here, p. 16).
101. Lidiya Chukovskaya, diary entry of 8 February 1940. *Zapiski* 1, p. 79.
102. German, *Slozhnoe proshedshee,* p. 256). Plans for the metro in fact went back far longer than this – to 1889 – and were seriously revived in the 1910s: see Enakiev, *Zadachi preobrazovaniya S-Peterburga*, pp. 48–9.
103. The original plan in Leningrad had been to rebuild the church and use it as the entrance to the station. But it was not replaced after being demolished in 1940 – no doubt because of the intervention of the war. The booth is sometimes referred to as a kind of hapless parody of the church (see e.g. Antonov and Kobak, *Svyatyni Peterburga*), but was in a style that had become widespread in Moscow (see e.g. Kalanchovskaya ploshchad' by the three main Moscow railway stations), so simply fitted a pattern-book of how to build in sites where the station was supposed to be 'a feature'. For an interesting discussion of the Moscow metro's affinities with religious architecture, see Jenks, 'A Metro on the Mount'.
104. See e.g. 'Proekty stantsii metro', *LP* 5 January 1957, p. 4.
105. 'Proekty stantsii'.
106. Denis Sadovsky, 'Mify Piterskoi podzemki', *MR-V* 16 September 2005, 4. This article both undermines legends about hidden tunnels and reinforces them, alluding to a tunnel between 'strategic objects' in the city.
107. 'Chto proizoshlo vchera v metro?' *LP* 13 Nov. 1969, p. 4.
108. Lev Golovanchik, 'Transportnaya blokada', *NV* 17 October 1995, p. 1.
109. A. Oreshkin, 'Kak «Sennaya" stalo ubiitsei', *Smena* 15 June 1999, p. 1.
110. Oxf/AHRC SPb-11 PF13 EI (the station was Parnas, in the northern suburbs).
111. For instance, in 1971 the Chairman of the Vyborgsky raikom requested that completion of the section running between ploshchad' Lenina and Akademicheskaya should be brought forward, but this was refused on financial grounds (TsGAIPD-SPb. 25/108/12/20). In fact, this was one of the trickiest stretches of building in the city, because of an underground water-course (which was later to break into the tunnelling, see above).
112. See the material on http://spb.metro.ru/history.html.
113. Nadezhda Kulikova, 'Metro k porogu vashego doma', *MR-Ts* 5 September 2003, p. 5.
114. See e.g. Enakiev, *Zadachi.*
115. The central function of the railway belt has always been for goods transport. See TsGAIPD-SPb.25/108/12/20, where in 1971 a representative of the Gorkom explains to the chairman of the Vyborg raikom that the rail network in his area could not be used to relieve pressure on ground transport while the metro was completed because it was needed for freight, and there was no money to upgrade the line in any case.
116. There is a large literature on the symbolic force of the Moscow metro: see particularly the two articles by Ryklin, and Jenks, 'Metro on the Mount'.
117. This was a persistent feature. In 2010 the line formerly running from ulitsa Dybenko to Komendantskii prospekt was chopped in half, with the eastern part turned into another north–south line, running past Volkovo Cemetery.
118. On the appeal of the suburbs, see also Chapter 3.
119. The code is reproduced in the online forum for fans of the metro at http://metro.nwd.ru/download/file.php?id=11970&sid=3fb833f40ce545f552d120fb3dc0ccbc&mode=view. See also *BILGS* 22 (1957), pp. 6–7.
120. Based on my memories of using it as a student in the 1970s and 1980s.
121. The head was my own. FN, March 2009.
122. See *Leningradskii tramvai* (6 January 1965), p. 3.
123. On public transport behaviour, especially dealing with the extraordinarily small amount of space available, see Voz'yanov, '"Proizvodstvo passazhirov"'.
124. This was also an excuse for practising verbs of motion, a notoriously tricky area for learners (pers. obs.).
125. K. Logachev, 'O tom, kto vas obsluzhivaet: Voditel' tramvaya', *LP* 17 September 1975, p. 3. Cf. *Leningradskii tramvai, passim.*

126. See the staff newspaper *Leningradskii tramvai*, passim. Of course, there were also hortatory pieces about self-improvement: see e.g. M. Plotnikov, 'S khalturoi mirit'sya nel'zya', *Leningradskii tramvai*, 26 May 1965, p. 3; 'Kak nado rabotat'' (*Leningradskii tramvai*, 4 September 1965, p. 3).
127. German, *Slozhnoe proshedshee*, 41–3. The same picture is given in a guidebook to Petrograd of 1915: Moskvich, *Petrograd i ego okrestnosti*, p. 10: 'Truth to tell, there are many drawbacks to the St Petersburg tram.' So packed were they it was difficult to sit down. 'People shove and kick each other to the sound of groans from old ladies, moans from the elderly and infirm and so on.' The only plus was that travelling was very cheap. According to Enakiev, *Zadachi*, p. 51, there were already over 115 million tram passengers in 1911, roughly 45 per cent of them travelling on the Finland–Baltic Railway Stations link.
128. New introductions included the LM-57, LM-68, and KTM-5M3, all of which are on show at the Muzei gorodskogo elektricheskogo transporta in St Petersburg (see below). However, 1940s models such as the LM-LP-47 and LM-LP-49 remained in service into the 1970s, according to the museum's display. Cf. Oxf/AHRC SPb-07 PF13, 14 SA (woman b. 1950), 'And I used to get the no. 6 tram, and you know what kind of tram that was? Wooden, a sort of *amerikanka*. I experienced that. It had all these wooden benches facing each other, and those hand-grips, and a conductor . . .'
129. *Proekt razmeshcheniya zhilishchnogo*, supplement 'Dorogi i inzhinerno-transportnye sooruzheniya', p. 6 (on the Grazhdanskii and Tikhoretskii prospekt areas of Vyborgsky district). This document remarked that rapid construction of a metro station was 'essential' (ibid.), but in fact one was only finished in 1978.
130. 'Pravila pol'zovaniya tramvaem v gor. Leningrade' (15 August 1957), *BILGS* 16 (1957), pp. 11–13.
131. *Nash gorod Leningrad*, pp. 59, 52, 54.
132. N. Nikiforova', 'Vospominaniya o traditsiyakh', *VL* 24 October 1989, p. 1 (on the loss of routes in the late 1970s). On the loss of routes later on, see 'Tramvainaya stolitsa teryaet marshruty', *NV* 29 November 2000, p. 1. Sadovaya temporarily lost its trams that same year, during road repairs: O. Boiko, 'Sadovaya ostanetsya bez tramvaya', *NV* 17 November 2000, p. 1.
133. Nikiforova', 'Vospominaniya o traditsiyakh', p. 1.
134. An extreme case of this was reported by Lev Golovanchik, 'O vrede i pol'ze zhestkogo kontrolya', *NevV* 10 January 1995, p. 5. Five hefty men had tossed a man with no ticket out of the back door of a bus in the late evening. He had fallen on the pavement, and was lucky to escape serious injury. On the other hand, the piece also quoted an inspector's report that he was sworn at and assaulted by a drunk, and the police would do nothing.
135. Golovanchik, 'O vrede', reported that at the start of 1995, 500 out of a total of 530 inspectors worked part-time and were not prepared to wear a uniform – a situation that obviously encouraged personation. Once conductors were introduced, there was some discussion about phasing them out again – see e.g. *MR Ts* 12 (2004), p. 3 – since the initial shock effect had not been compensated, in the long term, by revenue increases. In the event, they disappeared only on some suburban bus routes (e.g. on Vasilievsky Island).
136. In 2005, *Moi raion* reported that 50 per cent of tram routes were scheduled to be shut down by 2006. The trams at that point were carrying about 700 passengers a day on routes out to Vasilievsky Island, as opposed to 12,000 passengers carried on *marshrutki* (Natal'ya Tikhonova, 'Tramvai popali pod sokrashchenie', *MR(V)* 11 November 2005, p. 4).
137. FN June 2008. The driver called out 'Voz'mite gazetki!' as people climbed on board.
138. As reported by the guide on my visit to the Tram Museum, Sept. 2010 (FN).
139. In Western European cities, trams regularly manage 12–13 km per hour; in St Petersburg, 4–5 km per hour is standard. Interview with the guide at the Tram Museum, Sept. 2010 (FN).
140. Ibid.
141. Mansur Arifulin, '"Vspomnim vsekh poimenno"', *Peterburgskie magistrali* (the official newspaper of Gorelektrotrans), no. 4 (6409), 7 April 2010, p. 1. The newspaper regularly carried such items.
142. In fact, there are substantial networks in other Russian cities, and colonies of 'tram fans' in many other places too. See Voz'yanov, 'Tramvainye fanaty'.
143. Among secondary studies of the modernist preoccupation with the tram are Timenchik; Tapp.
144. R. Mandel'shtam, 'Alyi tramvai', *Blue Lagoon*, 1, p. 133.
145. Viktor Krivulin, 'Kryl'ya bezdomnosti', dukhovnyi i dukhovoi', *Okhota na mamonta*, p. 186.
146. Telephone interview with the director, FN, September 2010.
147. K. I. Aleksandrov, 'Nash staryi drug tramvai', *LPan* 1 (1987), pp. 13–14.
148. Tat'yana Alekseeva, '"Slony" i "golovasochki" v tramvainom parke', *Vech P* 7 October 2000, p. 1.
149. 'Loshadi pridut pozzhe', *MR (VO)* 29 October 2004, p. 1.
150. As indicated by the labels at the Tram Museum.

151. *Peterburgskii tramvai: istoriya.*
152. The figure given for the number of drivers is actually '114', but this has to be a typo.
153. Man b. 1967: Oxf/AHRC SPb-08 SA PF18. The other form of transport with 'nostalgia value' was the trolleybus. A poll organised by the Rosbalt news site on 25 April 2011 produced a majority vote in favour of retaining this form of transport. Almost 10 per cent of trolleybus supporters chose the option 'because our grannies rode them too' (www.rosbalt.ru/poll/446/results/).
154. The electric transport newspaper, *Peterburgskie magistrali*, still presented a cheerful image, but the mood at the top level of the city administration was hardening. In autumn 2010 there were proposals to remove the tramlines down Kronverksky prospekt, which would abolish one of the city's oldest routes, though this proposal was deferred by Valentina Matvienko after protests from local residents. In the following months, the attitudes to public transport at the top level of the city administration became more proactive: at the end of 2011, work began on tram and public transport 'corridors' down Sadovaya and Kronverksky, and for the first time statements were made about the need to discourage car use. Elena Bespalova, 'Na tramvae – s veterkom', *SPK* 1–7 September 2011, p. 4. On the other hand, by this point the Tram Museum had come under threat from developers: see 'Tramvainyi park zhdet svoego prigovora', *Metro* 13 June 2011, p. 15. Increasingly, it was suburban routes (with new rolling stock introduced) where the future was seen to lie; by April 2013, some even had Wi-Fi (FN).
155. Pers. obs., see also Oxf/AHRC SPb 10 PF8 MS. Admittedly, the metro was not problem-free: in 1990, passengers were having to travel in gloom because of a shortage of light-bulbs: 'Mrak v metro', *LPan* 6 (1990), p. 11.
156. Viktor Morozkin, 'Metro: Rezerv na iskhode', *LPan* 10 (1991), pp. 6–7.
157. This is based on my own recollections, confirmed by Sergei Tachaev, 'Appetit ukhodit pri vide edy', *NevV* 1 May 1992, p.1.
158. The name *tezhka* (apparently based on the T-prefix for the municipal buses, as opposed to the K-prefix for commercial ones) was said by a St Petersburg contributor to the lingvo.ru forum in August 2005 (http://forum.lingvo.ru/actualthread.aspx?tid=30461) to have edged out the word *marshrutka*, but I have personally much more often heard the latter term in use (while those using *tezhka* have been older people). All the other contributors to the lingvo.ru forum also agreed that *marshrutka* was commoner.
159. *Nash gorod Leningrad*, p. 56.
160. See the excellent article on 'Marshrutnoe taksi' in the Russian version of Wikipedia. A fascinating snapshot of the practices associated with running and using marshrutki in the late 1990s is offered in Humphrey, 'Sovereignty and Ways of Life'.
161. A pun on GAZ (Gorky Automobile Factory) and the animal, whose long-legged elegance is, however, a far cry from these boxy vehicles.
162. Pers. obs.
163. FN, August 2008; FN, March 2009.
164. FN, 11 April 2009. 'To f . . . with them!' represents the fact that she said, 'Seichas popov na kh' (pronouncing only the first letter of the obscene oath).
165. Pers. inf. from St Petersburger, January 2005.
166. Email to CK, 26 August 2010 [English in original].
167. In theory, marshrutki were quite strictly regulated – from 2007, drivers were supposed to halt only at official stops – but in practice, they stopped more or less on request, except on bridges.
168. Oxf/AHRC SPb-08 PF52 IN. Notably, even the liberal local paper *Moi raion* tended to take the passengers' side (mainly, no doubt, because they were more likely to be among its readers). See e.g. Margarita Chernetsova, 'Voditeli marshrutok lyubyat ne vsyakie den'gi', *MR (K)*, 27 August 2004, p. 3, complaining that drivers were sometimes refusing to change 500 and 1000 rouble notes. The head of the depot described the practice as regrettable, though understandable, given the high levels of forgery of such notes and the fact that drivers did not carry devices to test them.
169. www.gazeta.spb.ru/37700-0/.
170. www.rg.ru/2008/01/21/reg-szapad/crashes.html. These figures put Petersburg in fourth place across the Russian Federation in terms of road accidents, and Leningrad region third. According to official traffic police statistics (www.avtodeti.ru/?t=88&s=278), there were 233,809 accidents and 33,308 deaths across the Russian Federation in 2007, meaning that over 5 per cent of accidents took place in the region.
171. In 1910, George Dobson, long-term correspondent for *The Times*, recalled that when trams were first introduced, the drivers were intoxicated by the potential of speed, so that emergency stops were necessary and the passengers got thrown off their feet constantly. 'The casualties and confusion resulting from this innovation led to another novel arrangement, which had never before

been seen in systematic operation on Russian streets – namely, the regulation of the traffic by the police', which in turn led to constant conflict between police and drivers (*St Petersburg Painted*, pp. 115–16). On the Soviet period, see below.

172. Natal'ya Tikhonova, '"Gazeli" obrecheny na vymiranie', *MR(V)*, 26 August 2005, pp. 1, 4.
173. In FN August 2008, I observed 'the bus is more solemn than the [original Gazel'-style] marshrutka because you pay at the door and don't have to pass the change along and people can get up and announce stops to the driver' (as opposed to yelling out their destination from the back). This difference was observable later as well.
174. Oxf/AHRC SPb-11 PF27 MS.
175. V. M. Tarasenko, 'Taksa dlya taksista – den', provedennyi s taksistom', *LPan* 8 (1985), pp. 19–20, was a sympathetic account of a day spent going round the city with a taxi driver. Cf. the case described in Chapter 6 (about a taxi driver's dispute with some actors, ending in a victory for the former). For a scandal, see 'Khapugam ne mesto za rulem!', *LP* 16 February 1965, p. 4.
176. See e.g. Gal'perin, *Russkii variant*, in *Most cherez Letu*, p. 518, where one character suggests buying from a driver, and another is horrified: 'They'll take a tenner off you!'
177. Lev Godovanchik, '"Moskvich" pokoryaet gorodskoe taksi', *NevV* 27 January 1995, p. 3.
178. *Smena* 20 June 1998, p. 1, reported that a second taxi driver had been killed in one week in SPb., and stated that taxi firm heads had claimed this was typical, with 1–2 being murdered every week.
179. As noted earlier, the airport route was especially risky – I recall being warned about this in 1992 or 1993. Occasionally, bandit drivers surfaced in later years as well – though normally when people hailed cabs on the street. On 12 March 2008, there were news reports (see e.g. www.gazeta.spb.ru/29695-0/) about an Azerbaijani taxi driver who was cruising St Petersburg picking up fares who looked the worse for wear, then offering them coffee, buying some at a wayside stall and doctoring it with psychotropic drugs. The grounds for suspicion were a description from one victim who managed to get home and remember what the driver looked like, and also the discovery of a cache of medicines in the boot. An Oxford colleague was attacked by a driver in 2007, and dumped in Pargolovo park, on the northern outskirts.
180. Personal obs. The same was true of moonlighting private drivers.
181. The pronoun 'he' is used advisedly: I have never come across a female taxi driver, or a male dispatcher.
182. B. A. Romanov, letter to E. A. Kusheva, 21 May 1946, *Perepiska 1940–1957 gg.*, p. 23.
183. For the general background of motorisation across the USSR, see the excellent study by Siegelbaum, *Cars for Comrades*.
184. See e.g. Gennady Gerasimov, 'Amerikanskoe chudovishche – avtomobil' ', *LP* 6 September 1970, p. 3. Ruble, *Leningrad*, observed (p. 66): 'Except for Moscow and the largest cities of the People's Republic of China, no other urban center of comparable size has experienced such immense territorial expansion without reliance on the private automobile.'
185. See the secret figures in 'Statisticheskii byulleten' no. 13 (134): Kapital'noe stroitel'stvo: Blizhaishie pokazateli po avtomobil'nomu, zheleznodorozhnomu, morskomu, rechnomu transportu i svyazi', TsGAIPD-SPb. 25/91/103/113.
186. I. Lisochkin, 'Glavnyi dokument voditelya', *LP* 28 April 1976, p. 3. These changes were said here to have followed the USSR's ratification of the European Treaty on Transport in 1968.
187. See the good discussion in Siegelbaum, *Cars for Comrades*.
188. Thubron, *Among the Russians*, p. 74.
189. *St Petersburg Painted*, p. 119. Cf. V. Lapin, *Zvuki i zapakhi Sankt-Peterburga* (St Petersburg, 2007).
190. A. Dudarev, 'Uvazhaite tishinu!' *LP* 16 September 1966, p. 3.
191. V. Arendarenko, 'Na krutykh virazhakh', *LP* 25 June 1975, p. 2.
192. On dachas as an index of middle-classness, see Lovell, *Summerfolk*. My own *Children's World*, Chapter 12, includes a discussion about the prestige of special language-teaching and other 'profile' schools.
193. At times, certainly, it was so seen in Leningrad: see e.g. the 'typical workers' questions' from 1962 asking why car and dacha owners were not made to pay taxes on their possessions: 'After all, everyone knows that these people are making money on the side and they keep getting richer and richer' (TsGAIPD-SPb. 25/89/66/20).
194. I have myself participated in, observed, or heard about all these different types of transaction.
195. Personal obs.
196. Across the Russian Federation the number of cars sold rose by more than 120 per cent between 2001 and 2008 (http://autoconsultant.com.ua/russiannews/view/2901/). By comparison, between 1980–2000, overall road traffic in the UK increased by 71 per cent (www.statistics.gov.uk).

197. Ol'ga Nikonova, 'Most Aleksandra Nevskogo ustal. Smertel'no', *NevV* 5 July 1995, p. 2: 11,000 vehicles an hour were then said to be crossing the bridge, which had started to decay as early as 1982, when part of the cantilevering fell into the river. Lev Golovanchik, 'Tri nedeli blokady', *NevV* 7 March 1995, p. 2, reported that conditions were so bad on ul. Bol'sheozerskaya that bus drivers would not use it and so Primorsky raion was cut off. The article was illustrated with a picture of a Mercedes up to its wheel-rims in water. Tat'yana Ryabinina, 'Proverka na dorogakh [. . .]', *Smena* 21 January 1998, p. 5, referred to the 'avral'no-khaoticheskii sposob' ['crash-chaos method'] of roadmending, i.e. the habit of repairing large numbers of roads at one go (a 'method' that remained in force in the two following decades as well).
198. Elaborate schemes for underground parking either came to nothing or were much delayed. For instance, a report of such a scheme from the late 1990s was hopelessly optimistic (Andrei Lyubimov, 'Dvortsovaya ploshchad' stanet mnogoetazhnoi', *Smena* 2 March 1999, p. 1). Something resembling this scheme was implemented only in 2008, the best part of a decade later. It was common for 'entrepreneurs' to take advantage of drivers' desperation. Natal'ya Tikhonova, 'Dokhodnoe mesto kontroliruyut moshenniki', *MR(V)* 3 June 2005, p. 3, reported that a courtyard on ploshchad' Vosstaniya had been cordoned off and turned into a pay-only parking lot, though the people running it had no right to do this. I observed a similar phenomenon outside the Oktyabr'skaya Hotel when I stayed there in the late 1990s, and it was happening outside the Mariinsky Theatre in 2003–2007 as well.
199. 'Osobennosti natsional'noi erotiki', *MR(V)* 27 May 2005, p. 6. (I can't confirm or deny this myself, but I can say that when I was sitting in a friend's car on Nevsky in 2003, he was handed a leaflet that turned out to advertise the services of an *hotel de passe*.)
200. For newspaper discussion of all this, see e.g. Vladimir Strugatsky, 'Kak probit' peterburgskie "probki"?' *Smena* 3 February 1994, p. 5 (on the need for automated traffic lights and a ring road along Leninskii prospekt, pr. Slavy, Volodarskii Bridge, etc., and a ban on heavy goods traffic in the centre); Marina Bogdanova, 'Gruzovik ili koshelek', *MR (Ts)* 4 May 2003, p. 4 (on the use of Lieutenant Shmidt Bridge by heavy traffic from the customs terminal on Vasilievsky Island); Marina Bogdanova, 'Nas spaset beg po krugu', *MR (Ts)* 4 April 2003, p. 5 (drivers' sceptical reactions to the introduction of further one-way restrictions, including one person's comment that people would just not observe the rules); Natal'ya Tikhonova, 'Tsentr goroda spasut ot mashin', *MR(V)* 29 July 2005, p. 5. (Plans to close Nevsky to traffic, make parking pay-only, introduce 'intelligent' traffic lights.) The 'Vopros-otvet' section, *NV* 13 April 2010, p. 8, reported the imminent introduction of one-way traffic on Lines 10–13 of Vasilievsky Island. For a good discussion of motoring hell in Moscow, see Argenbright.
201. Oxf/AHRC SPb-08 PF47 IN (man b. 1972, builder).
202. On the drivers' rights groups, see Lonkila. The most acrimonious struggles have been over garage buildings, rights to which the nationwide drivers' association, VAO (the Russian equivalent of the AA), was relatively active in defending until 2007, when the then president was murdered (ibid.).
203. On promenading, see Chapter 7.
204. *Sumerki Saigona*, p. 262. On the Saigon café, see Chapter 7.
205. Maiya Borisova, 'Esli vam ne ko spekhu', *Interesnee peshkom* (2003), p. 6. See also http://lib.1september.ru/2006/14/15.htm.
206. On the pollution anxiety, see Oxf/AHRC SPb-11 PF1 EI.
207. For instance, a survey of ploshchad' Vosstaniya in 1932 taken over the course of 18 hours established that about 1500 trams and 2700 motor-vehicles, as well as approximately 350 horse-drawn vehicles, passed through. Over the course of the year, there were 181 accidents (70 *neschastnykh sluchaev* and 111 *avarii*). TsGA-SPb. 7384/33/163/8; ibid., p. 154.
208. My thanks to Victoria Donovan who, when living in a flat nearby in 2008, sometimes passed the mangled remains, for this information.
209. See the report 'Pogibla doch' mera Sochi', 22 July 2007, http://vz.ru/society/2007/7/22/95746.html. Later it emerged that carriages are officially banned from the embankments. The driver seems to have misjudged the bridge over the Winter Culvert (Zimnyaya kanava) and lost control of the car.
210. FN 25 June 2008; pers. obs. A regular cyclist reported to me in June 2012 (FN) that she had also had a driver crash into her deliberately.
211. As shown by overheard comments on 21 December 2010, as the whole of Bol'shoi prospekt on Vasilievsky Island was brought to a halt by a convoy of blue-light-carrying official cars.
212. See e.g. the Piter-TV report of 2 April 2012 (http://piter.tv/event/Magistral_neprerivnogo_/). During building, residents of the district (I can speak from personal experience) had to put up with building racket and flying dirt, but on the other hand, the compensation was that in summer

2012 Finlyandsky prospekt and the Sampson Bridge were turned into an impromptu pedestrian zone – alas only temporarily (FN June 2012).

213. Aleksandra Kozlova, 'Vmesto vetkhogo zhil'ya postroyat parkingi', *Metro* 7 March 2012, p. 16.
214. For instance, the memoirs of Princess Sof'ya Volkonskaya (*The Way of Bitterness*) vividly recollect walking across Petersburg after the Revolution.
215. Enakiev, *Zadachi*, p. 41. It is hard to think of a carriage accident in a British novel as famous as *Crime and Punishment*, although Charlotte M. Yonge's *Pillars of the House* is an example from Victorian children's fiction.
216. Pers. obs.
217. See e.g. Asya Karmanova, 'Polis ot sosulek', *PD*, 13 December 2010; Yuliya Galkina, 'Pod ekovatnym odeyalom', *SPbK*, 22 December 2010, p. 3 (on a plan to use special insulation so that the icicles do not form). December and January 2009–2010 were not particularly cold, but there were unusual amounts of snow, leading to build-up of ice on roofs and deaths of workers brought in to clear this. Many victims of falling icicles were hospitalised. In January 2011, a six-year-old boy was killed by a falling 'icick' described as the size of a door (www.gazeta.spb.ru/436179-0/), after which there were attempts to prosecute the building's administration, and a drive to clear them from roofs city-wide. See e.g. 'Finskii otvet sosul'kam', *Peterburgskii dnevnik*, 7 February 2011, p. 10, and, on the problems of dangerously snowy and icy pavements, 'Ne ubrali – kto vinovat?', ibid., p. 10. See [OL Chapter 1].
218. Compare the young man who used to pound the pavements to get away from his parents as a teenager in the 2000s: 'You stick the music in your ears and start tearing through the kilometres' (Oxf/AHRC SPb-11 PF4 EI).
219. Cyclists actually on the road, by contrast, were very rare birds, with expressions that suggested awareness of their 'endangered species' status. Cf. Oxf/AHRC SPb-11 PF20 EI, a summer cyclist who talks about it as 'an extreme activity'.
220. FN, March 2009.
221. Elena Shvarts, 'Avtomobil'noe', *Sochineniya* 1, p. 333.
222. Pers. obs.
223. For the Las Vegas analogy, see Glikin; interview with the artist Andrei Filippov, Oxf/AHRC SPb-10 PF4 MS.
224. See further in Chapter 3.

## 2 Making a Home on the Neva

1. Ginzburg, 'Zapisnye knizhki 1950-kh – 1960-kh gg.', *Zapisnye knizhki*, p. 234.
2. See e.g. Thornycroft – where the beautifully decorated apartment in a historic building formerly owned by the British expert on Russian art and picture dealer, John Stuart, is featured, or Cerwinske; and cf. Fallowell's description as 'a city not of houses but of palatial blocks' (p. 12).
3. Devyatova and Kurennoi. The standard length of timber beams (between 2–3⅓ sazhens, i.e. 4.3–7.1 metres, with 3 sazhens, or 6.4 metres, the most common) acted as a factor limiting space: by the start of the twentieth century, the standard ceiling height had dropped from 3.3 to 2.8 metres. In 1900, just under 50 per cent of homes had sanitation, and 60 per cent a piped water supply (ibid.).
4. On the courtyards, see Chapter 7 below. The word *dokhodnyi dom* literally means 'building for income' (cf. the German *Mietskaserne*).
5. E. Yukhneva, *Peterburgskie dokhodnye doma*.
6. Prokofiev sketched it in a letter to his father – see his *Avtobiografiya*, pp. 152–3.
7. Likhachev, *Vospominaniya*, 1, p. 70.
8. On the development of the *cour d'honneur*, see Piir, 'What is a Courtyard For?', p. 314; for a description and plan of an apartment building with such a courtyard, the K. V. Markov house, see Kirikov, *Pamyatniki arkhitektury*, p. 435.
9. *Petrograd. Statisticheskie dannye, 1916*, p. 5; *Statisticheskii spravochnik*, pp. 38–9.
10. For material on the Anichkov Palace, in parts of whose buildings staff were accommodated, see TsGALI-SPb. 72/1/3/3–6.
11. Both these buildings survive today, the former as the Museum Apartment of Sergei Kirov (http://kirovmuseum.ru/), the latter as apartments mostly inhabited by the descendants of the original residents. The Museum Apartment of I. S. Pavlov (the famous physiologist) gives a sense of how prominent academics lived in the early Soviet era: see www.museum.ru/m125. Obertreis also emphasises the exclusivity of separate apartments in pre-war Leningrad: *Tränen*, p. 287.

12. Bitov, *Pushkinskii dom*, pp. 16–17. The successful writer Yury German also lived in a separate flat with his family (see the memoir by his son, Mikhail German, 19–20).
13. On the *doma-kommuny*, see Obertreis, pp. 343–60.
14. See the intriguing oral history by Anne Nivat, *La Maison haute*.
15. For instance, the block known as 'The Nest of Gentry' on Petrovsky Embankment (see also Chapter 4).
16. *Konkurs na sostavlenie*, pp. 3–5. The brochure also invited tenders for the construction of a model hostel, with rooms of 10–12 square metres (for single people) and 16 square metres (for couples), a canteen with 70 places, a reading room, a 'red corner', and an office.
17. See the Lensoviet decree, 'O merakh po uluchsheniyu kommunal'no-bytovogo i kul'turnogo obsluzhivaniya prozhivaniya v obshchezhityakh Leningrada', 16 March 1970, *BILGS* 8 (1970), pp. 3–8.
18. According to Vasil'eva, *The Young People of Leningrad*, p. 167, approx. 75 per cent of 20–29-year-old incomers lived in hostels, rented private rooms, or a share of privately rented rooms. It took 10–15 years for the difference from locally-born Leningraders to level out. On illegal settlement, see 'O merakh po uluchsheniyu', p. 4. 'Obshchezhitiya: istochnik pravonarushenii ili . . . [sic]', *Leningradskaya militsiya*, 31 March 1990, p. 3, reported of the fourth storey of the SOKZ hostel on ul. Sestoretskaya, 2, that none of the families living there now had any connections with the construction industry, and that in any case the building was not certified for human habitation at all.
19. 'Stenogramma besedy s vospitatelyami obshchezhitii na temu: "Ideino-politicheskaya i kul'turno-massovaya rabota s prozhivayushchimi v obshchezhitiyakh' (1970), TsGAIPD-SPb. 25/ 102/126/21. The picture was much the same in a newspaper story of the same date, 'Obshchezhitie: kakim emu byt'?', *LP* 26 May 1970, p. 2. See also 'Obshchezhitie – tvoi dom, ty – ego khozyain', *Kirovets* 28 March 1967, p. 2, which commends some inhabitants for making their own light-fittings etc., but also complains about mess. On the other hand, if one compares all this with Aleksei Gonchukov's chronicle of Leningrad life (see Chapter 4), it is clear that conditions had improved significantly since the 1940s.
20. The decree and non-compliance with it are discussed in 'O merakh po uluchsheniyu', pp. 3–4. For a later report of insanitary conditions: 'Obshchezhitiya: istochnik', p. 3.
21. For example, in the popular militia (DND) reports, where hostels are noted as a problem: see e.g. TsGAIPD-SPb. 25/ 99/ 47/7, which states that in the last 3 months of 1965 more than 2000 students had been picked up across the city in a drunken condition. Figures from the glasnost era indicate that in 1989, 1600 crimes were committed by the inhabitants of *obshchezhitiya* (1063 individuals were involved), including 39 murders, 196 thefts of state property, 180 burglaries (*grabezhi*), 1032 drinking offences and 273 cases of petty hooliganism ('Obshchezhitiya: istochnik', p. 3). However, cases like this were in a sense self-fulfilling, because hostels were seen as a problem and therefore regularly raided.
22. 'Ob organizatsii vospitatel'noi raboty so studentami prozhivayushchimi v obshchezhitiyakh vuzov Leningrada' (1967), TsGAIPD-SPb. 25/ 99/47/ passim. On l. 8 of this file it is reported that 90 per cent of hostels were, at best, in a 'satisfactory' condition from the hygiene point of view.
23. Letter to V. I. Safonov, March 1960, http://rubtsov.id.ru/.
24. See e.g. 'O pravilakh vnutrennego rasporyadka dlya rabochikh obshchezhitii koechnogo tipa predpriyatii, uchrezhdenii i organizatsii gorodskogo khozyaistva', 10 November 1957, *BILGS* 23 (1957), p. 5.
25. Based on personal observation in hostels during the late 1970s and 1980s.
26. Oxf/AHRC SPb-08 PF51 IN.
27. This was done in the hostel where I lived in Voronezh for ten months in 1980–1981, for example, though in the Leningrad State University hostel no. 10 and the Polytechnic hostel, where I spent short visits in 1981 and in 1979 respectively, partitioning of space was not attempted (possibly supervision by the hostel authorities was stricter – technically, moving the furniture around was a breach of the rules).
28. Vyacheslav Rezvov, 'Obshchezhitie: rok ili nadezhda?', *Vech P* 1 May 2000, p. 1. Rezvov was a *limitchik*, one of a population of incomers granted limited settlement rights in order to fill vacancies at factories and institutes (see further in Chapter 4).
29. See e.g. L. Robinson, *An American in Leningrad*.
30. On renting a 'corner', see e.g. Oxf/AHRC SPb-10 PF5 MS (woman b. 1940, family arrived in 1948).
31. Homeless adults and children did not sleep on the streets, given that it was usually too cold and they were likely to be rounded up. Sources of artificial warmth, such as (in the 1920s and 1930s) tar boilers and at later periods pedestrian subways (the so-called 'tubes' in the middle of Nevsky

prospekt) and the tunnels carrying central heating pipes, were favoured. On the pre-war decades, see e.g. T. E. Segalov, 'Deti-brodyagi: Opyt kharakteristiki', *Pravo i zhizn'* 7–8 (1925), pp. 84–9; pp. 9–10 (1925), pp. 89–95; on the later period, www.hippy.ru/saygon.htm (the 'tubes'); on central heating pipes, informant b. 1950, pers. inf. 2010. Another possibility, building sites, where one could build shelters with planks etc., is mentioned in Oxf/AHRC SPb-11 PF9 EI.

32. Shchepanskaya, *Sistema*, pp. 68–72. The words *flet* and *skvot* are, of course, borrowings from English – cf. *shuzy* (shoes), *aizy* (eyes), *batl* or *botl* (bottle), and many others. Rozhansky's word-list of hippy slang lists around 100 terms of English origin.
33. Ol'ga Nikonova, 'Ya molyu Boga za vsekh . . .', *NV* 3 July 1995, p. 4.
34. Hostels being privatised illegally: see e.g. Irina Baglinova, 'V Peterburge – 600 tysyach "krepostnykh"', *NV* 12 May 1995, p. 5. 'V Petrogradskom raione rasselyat 7 obshchezhitii', fontanka.ru 19 May 2007, www.fontanka.ru/2007/05/19/006/, revealed that – unknown to Governor Matvienko – the whole of Sernyi Island was privatised back in the 1990s.
35. The study with the broadest historical and informational range is Gerasimova, *Sovetskaya kommunal'naya kvartira kak sotsial'nyi institut*, which addresses the entire political, social, and legal framework of the communal apartment and changes to its status at different periods. Utekhin, *Ocherki*, is an interesting study of the daily life of the kommunalka in the late Soviet and post-Soviet period. Boym's *Common Places* includes a chapter on the communal apartment, largely based on personal experience. See also the useful 'virtual museum' set up by Il'ya Utekhin and Nancy Ries, www.kommunalka.spb.ru. The fact that the poor reputation of the kommunalka is more an indication of the cultural leverage of its inhabitants than of objectively appalling conditions is indicated also by the findings of a Soviet sociologist in 1975 (Vasil'eva, *The Young People of Leningrad*, 26): 'The entire complex of material and living conditions is more favorable among families with a higher socio-occupational level – living conditions are better, and there is more often a home library and a work area for the pupil (a desk, a storage area for school materials, toys, and so on).' This was irrespective of whether the families concerned lived in communal or separate apartments.
36. Woman b. Leningrad, 1931, CKQ Oxf-03 PF2.
37. Pers. inf. 2004.
38. Utekhin, *Ocherki*, p. 27.
39. On hygiene, see Utekhin, Chapter 4.
40. The extent to which tenants' possessions were 'present' in the kitchen might vary according to the specific relations between them. As Gerasimova points out (p. 18), in later decades of Soviet power people who had spent years living together as neighbours often established a high degree of trust, and might keep pieces of furniture etc. in the kitchen. There are photographs of such arrangements on www.kommunalka.spb.ru.
41. Utekhin, *Ocherki*, p. 31.
42. On playing in the corridor, see Kelly, *Children's World*, Chapter 11. At the same time, the corridor could seem, when a child was on its own, a threatening, alien space, especially after dark: see Oxf/Lev SPb-03 PF14 AP.
43. Oxf/Lev SPb-03 PF 26 (man b. 1960). Cf. Oxf/Lev SPb-02 PF 14 (woman b. 1969), recalling the two divans (one for the parents, one for the children) in the 27-square-metre room that her family lived in until the mid-1980s. Oxf/Lev SPb-03 PF 28 (man b. 1972) recalled that his own child's bed was behind a *shkaf*.
44. For example, the informant in Oxf/Lev SPb-03 PF14 recalled her family's ownership of a 'large colour' TV.
45. On alcoholic drinks, see Oxf/Lev SPb-02 PF6 (women b. 1908 and 1931): 'There was always a carafe of *vino* [literally, "wine", but often used to mean "vodka", as opposed to *sukhoe vino*, "dry wine", for the kind made of grapes] on the sideboard.' The role of the *servant* is extensively discussed by Boym, *Common Places*, and Utekhin, *Ocherki*.
46. This is based on personal observation: bookcases are too obvious a possession to get mentioned by informants or Russian commentators. In Soviet days they were usually of a standard sort: a wooden unit large enough to hold a single row of books, with glass sliding doors. These could be stacked to form a multi-tiered bookcase. The shelves might also be used for displays of other objects, as in the *servant*.
47. See e.g. Oxf/Lev SPb-03 PF24 (man b. 1960).
48. Conditions were considerably better than in the rented rooms described in George Orwell's famous *Down and Out in Paris and London* (1933). On Berlin, see Geist and Kürvers; on Glasgow, Worsdall.
49. An example was the writer Mikhail Zoshchenko, whose short stories about Leningrad, such as 'Cats and People' or 'The Bathhouse', immortalised 1920s and 1930s communal life.

50. Alexander Werth, *Leningrad*, p. 36.
51. For example, sources such as the diaries of Lidiya Chukovskaya (*Zapiski ob Anne Akhmatovoi*) or the diaries of Ol'ga Berggol'ts (*Ol'ga: Zapretnyi dnevnik*) are primarily concerned with the constraints on intellectual and emotional freedom that went with communal living. The unpublished memoir-chronicle of Aleksei Gonchukov (see Chapter 4) takes a very positive view of life in the communal apartment, while complaining constantly about shortage of money, the dishonesty of the factory administration, and so on.
52. Retrospective accounts, e.g. Utekhin's *Ocherki kommunal'nogo byta*, tend to represent informants' recollections of communitarianism as pure nostalgia, but evidence such as diaries would suggest things are not quite so simple.
53. As expressed, for example, in Boym, *Common Places*.
54. P. Bobchenok, 'Kakie kvartiry nam nuzhny?', *LP* 30 June 1970, p. 2. The 1990 figures were given in a highly critical series about the work of the different district soviets running in *Vechernii Leningrad* in January, February, and March 1990, 'Vse ispolnilos' v srok?'. For a district profile, see also Tomchin, *Razvitie Peterburga*; L. I. Raikova, 'Rezervy starogo fonda', *LPan* 5 (1988), pp. 12–13 (as late as 1988, Smol'ninskii district had a full 77 per cent of its population in communal apartments).
55. See e.g. the comments by D. S. Gol'dgor at a Lenproekt meeting in 1957 (TsGANTD-SPb. 36/ 1-1/ 216/18): 'We want to settle the 27 square metre two-room apartments with just one family in each, but it won't work out that way.' Bobchenok, 'Kakie kvartiry', also records the practice of settling multi-room flats with several families; see also V. L. Ruzhzhe, N. I. Eliseeva, T. S. Kadibur, 'Kogda babushka ryadom', *Naselenie Leningrada*, p. 82: up to 40 per cent of flats had been settled communally 'in isolated years' (code for 'fairly often').
56. P. Pozdnyakov's article, 'Kakie kvartiry nuzhny leningradtsam?', *Stroitel'nyi rabochii* 15 February 1961, p. 3, refers to the need to match flat sizes to the population's needs (here, three and four room flats are suggested).
57. Catrell, pp. 135–6. In practice, these prices were quite high for some people: cf. Oxf/AHRC SPb-07 PF10 SA. But a more important disincentive was that those applying for a place in a co-operative had to satisfy the same deficiency-of-living-space conditions as those applying for a state flat. If one shared a very large room in a *kommunalka*, one was ineligible. Cf. Oxf/AHRC SPb-11 PF19 MS: 'We wanted to get on the co-operative queue, but they wouldn't let us'; Oxf/AHRC SPb-08 PF51 IN.
58. A Decree of Lengorispolkom on 26 October 1963 pointed to the disappointingly slow pace of co-operative building and decreed that from 1 January 1964, such co-operatives would be formed 'on the intercession [*po khodataistvu*] of enterprises, organisations, and institutions': TsGALI-SPb. 105/1/1483/163–165; ibid. l.178.
59. This process of reconstruction began to be reported in the press in the early 1960s, at first because of anxiety that perfectly good building materials were being wasted: *LP* 28 May 1963, p. 2: 'Den'gi na svalku'. Later, as interest in heritage rose, there was also indignation that historic interiors were being lost. However, a Lensovet order of 7 April 1969 merely specified that items of architectural interest should be transferred to the Museum of the City of Leningrad: *BILGS* no. 8 (1969), pp. 2–3. The reconstructions also suffered from similar problems of hasty and sometimes shoddy building to the newbuild of the era: see the item in *LP*, 21 August 1964, p. 3, 'Iz remonta v remont. Reid L-skoi pravdy'. For a more upbeat view of the process (the centre is not a museum, etc.), see L. Burak and R. Mishkovsky, 'Novoe v starykh kvartalakh', *LP* 26 December 1968, p. 2.
60. Boym, *Common Places*, is a good illustration of the imaginative associations.
61. Krivulin, p. 47. On this milieu, see also Skobkina; *Sumerki Saigona*.
62. See [OL Chapter 1]. The last decades of the twentieth century saw an upsurge of literary interest in the *kommunalka*, beginning with texts such as Katerli, *Sennaya ploshchad'*, and extending to literary memoirs (e.g. Krivulin, *Okhota*, Boym, *Common Places*).
63. This attitude persisted into the post-Soviet period: see e.g. Oxf/AHRC SPb-11 PF8 EI (living in a communal flat means you can take off whenever you like).
64. The concept of *uyut* was not invented at this period. It started to become important as part of the mid-1930s drive to emphasise to Soviet citizens that the Revolution had also brought them prosperity in a material sense. There is a large secondary literature dealing with this subject: see e.g. Fitzpatrick, *Everyday Stalinism*; Gronow; Kettering; Glushchenko. On *uyut* in the 1960s, see Susan Reid, 'Communist Comfort'. The precise evolution of the concept over time is an interesting question. The 'National Corpus of the Russian Language' cites examples where *uyut* was used ironically in the 1920s and 1930s, or at the very least juxtaposed with the 'high struggle' of life (see e.g. the quotation from A. R. Belyaev's *Prodavets vozdukha*, 1929); such examples disappear in the selection

of later materials. On the other hand, the bias of this source is towards literature, rather than journalism, so its evidence is not conclusive.

65. See M. Luchutenkov, 'Kvartiry – dostoinym', *LP* 7 May 1969, p. 2; and the many similar reports in the local press, e.g. 'Kvartaly shaguyut dal'she', *LP* 12 March 1967, p. 2. A. Andreev, 'Ritm – 23 kvartiry v den' ', *LP* 24 January 1968, p. 1; V. Zakhar'ko, Yu Sovolinsky, 'Vosemnadtsat' kilometrov novoselii', *LP* 19 February 1969, p. 2, etc.
66. Edmonds, p. 41.
67. On the 1960s, see K. Fetisova, M. Shitov, 'O domakh, v kotorykh my zhivem', *LP* 23 January 1963, p. 3; A. Klyushin, 'nachal'nik Gosarkhstroi-kontrol'; 'Vash novyi dom: O nekotorykh problemakh kachestva stroitel'stva', *LP* 23 December 1966, p. 2; N. Roslyakov, 'Pochemu kvartiry pustuyut?', *LP* 21 July 1967, p. 4. See also Lebina and Chistikov, p. 177.
68. *BILGS* 8 (1982), p. 5.
69. 'Etot kovarnyi styk', *LPan* 3 (1986), pp. 18–20. Co-operative blocks had some of the disadvantages of other newbuild – services, particularly telephone connections, might be slow to arrive – but the quality of finish was generally better in co-operative blocks than ordinary state ones.
70. Edmonds, *Russian Vistas*, p. 41.
71. The minimalism of Western social architecture at this period has its defenders, too: see e.g. Hathersley, who contrasts this period approvingly with the would-be cheery post-modernism of more recent decades.
72. 'Stenograficheskii otchet Sektsii arkhitektury Tekhnicheskogo soveta Leningradskogo gosudarstvennogo proektnogo instituta "Lenproekt", 5 marta 1957 g.', TsGANTD-SPb. 36/1-1/216/11–12.
73. Novye Cheremushki, the most famous of the newbuild districts across the Soviet Union, was the subject of a comic opera by Shostakovich (*Moskva-Cheremushki*, 1958).
74. 'Stenograficheskii otchet zasedaniya Sektsii arkhitektury Tekhnicheskogo soveta Leningradskogo gosudarstvennogo proektnogo instituta "Lenproekt", 9 oktyabrya 1957', TsGANTD-SPb. 36/1-1/234/32.
75. 'Stenograficheskii otchet zasedaniya Sektsii arkhitektury Tekhnicheskogo soveta Leningradskogo gosudarstvennogo proektnogo instituta "Lenproekt", 4 aprelya 1961 g.', TsGANTD-SPb. 36/1–2/488/25. The word 'artist's impression' translates as 'plakat', which usually means 'poster', but here clearly refers to a mock-up of the apartment interior.
76. 'Stenograficheskii otchet plenarnogo zasedaniya Tekhnicheskogo soveta Leningradskogo gosudarstvennogo proektnogo institute "Lenproekt", 2 marta 1961 g.', TsGANTD-SPb., 36/1-2/482/45.
77. Zakhar'ko and Sovolinsky, 'Vosemnadtsat' kilometrov novoselii', reported that the latest buildings had been improved by ironing out the mistakes of the past – for example, entrance halls (*prikhozhie*) and kitchens were larger.
78. V. Poltorak, V. Konovalov, 'Leningradskaya kvartira: kak sdelat' ee luchshe?', *Leningradskii rabochii*, 27 January 1973, pp. 10–11.
79. See e.g. V. Poltorak, V. Konovalov, 'V Moskvu za opytom', *Leningradskii rabochii*, 17 March 1973, p. 3.
80. For a discussion of the *novosel'e*, see Reid, ' "Happy Housewarming!" '.
81. For nostalgia about food among St Petersburg informants, see Kushkova, 'Surviving in the Time of Deficit'. On the widespread preference for what is seen as '*nash*' ('ours', i.e. native Russian), see Caldwell, 'The Taste of Nationalism'.
82. Oxf/AHRC SPb-10 PF2 MS (woman b. 1945).
83. Oxf/Lev SPb-07 PF2 AK: woman b. Leningrad, 1977.
84. For the name, see Lebina and Chistikov, p. 180.
85. M. Luchutenkov, 'Kvartiry – dostoinym', *LP* 7 May 1969, p. 2.
86. Cf. the recollection of one informant that her family lived in a room with a 'four metre' ceiling (Oxf/Lev SPb-02 PF14): while probably exaggerated, this is typical. Blocks built in the 1970s and 1980s had higher ceilings (2.8 metres was standard). Once again, one should bear in mind that 2.4 metres was a normal height for new apartment blocks and houses in Western cities of the period too (and still is).
87. This storage, typically, included built-in cupboards, *antresoli* (overhead storage next to the kitchen), a 'cold cupboard' (*kholodnyi shkaf*) in the kitchen, used as a kind of larder for storing food, and so on (pers. obs.).
88. See e.g. S. Birman, 'Zdes' rozhdaetsya mebel' ', *LP* 7 January 1965, p. 4.
89. See e.g. T. Duraeva, 'Dom, o kotorom zabotilsya ZHEK', *Leningradskii rabochii* 6 June 1980, p. 5 (in the context here of district administrations 'acquiring' pipes by means best known to themselves). On this principle in the socialist economy generally, see Verdery, *What Was Socialism*.
90. FN April 2012.

91. Here and below, I base my comments on personal observation during visits to Leningrad in the late 1970s and 1980s, which I have cross-checked with the sets of local films such as *The Red Arrow*, *Monologue*, *Mother's Gone and Got Married*, *His Wife's Left Him*, etc.
92. On the 'black, white, grey' considered to be chic in the 1960s West, see Baudrillard, *The System of Objects*, p. 31.
93. See e.g. B. Vakhramev and A. I. Chudovsky, 'Kakaya nuzhna mebel'?', *Leningradskii stroitel'* 15 December 1973, pp. 10–11, which featured the new mass-produced (*tipovaya*) furniture that had become available, e.g. open wall-units (*vetrennye stenki*).
94. See the interesting discussion in Collier, *Post-Soviet Social*, esp. pp. 100–2, 202–44.
95. Oxf/Lev SPb-07 PF2 AK: Anna L., b. 1977, father official in factory and Party member, mother accountant.
96. Few of the informants interviewed for our St Petersburg project can easily identify any 'family heirlooms'. Of course, the term itself has a daunting resonance, suggesting the assimilation of personal possessions to the memorial items discussed in Chapter 9.
97. See e.g. Oxf/AHRC SPb.-10 PF10 NG (woman b. 1937): '. . . For a long time this hob stood in the kitchen [. . .] we used to keep warm by burning coal. It saved our lives during the Blockade, because we burned chairs in it, and furniture, and even books.' Oxf/AHRC SPb-12 PF44 MS (man b. 1975, a fifth-generation St Petersburger): only the piano and some drawings survived; etc.
98. See e.g. Oxf/AHRC SPb-10 PF5 MS (woman b. 1940, describing her father's attitude).
99. Granin, *Leningradskii katalog*, p.21.
100. Oxf/AHRC GB-08 CK PF1.
101. When the father of a friend of mine took home old furniture that was being cleared out of his workplace in the 1970s, his colleagues were astonished that he might be interested in 'junk' (*barakhlo*) of that kind. (Pers. inf.) Cf. Viktor Krivulin's comments: 'In the rooms, furniture of some kind had remained behind from the last tenants, which had got more and more rickety and was reaching the point of no return – wardrobes with cracked mirrors, high-backed armchairs with holes in them, real nests of bed-bugs, couches from the brave dawn of the twentieth century with shreds of silk twill still clinging to them' (*Okhota*, p. 48).
102. As Vera Ziltinkevich [Tolz] has remembered of Dmitry Likhachev, her grandfather: when her parents began collecting antique furniture, he ranted that this was 'petit-bourgeois, shameful, unworthy!' (*Dmitry Likhachev i ego epokha*, p. 38).
103. For instance, an informant b. 1944 remembers a military decoration belonging to her grandfather: Oxf/AHRC SPb-07 PF1 SA; another informant, b. 1984, remembers silver flatware (Oxf/AHRC SPb-08 PF43). However, contrast an informant's recollection that things such as jewellery were sold after the War in order to buy food during the severe shortages of 1946–47: Oxf/AHRC SPb-07 PF8 SA.
104. Oxf/AHRC SPb.-08 PF51 (man from Sestroretsk, b. 1944. The informant jokingly refers to the question of family relics as 'a trade secret').
105. Oxf/AHRC SPb.-07 PF1 IN (man b. 1938). While a collector would have made efforts to find out something about the history of the clock, for most people such an object is just 'old'. Interestingly, native Leningraders (like this man) do not differ from people who originally lived elsewhere: take the following case: 'There were these tablecloths, for instance, snow-white with flowers on, poppies, and rugs, there was this black rug with pink flowers. Then later, it was used too as a covering for cabbage. [. . .] Yes, the rug as well. When we were pickling cabbage and all that, we used it as a covering, it was all old stuff, and so it wasn't specially valued . . .': Oxf/AHRC SPb.-07 PF1 AK (woman b. 1951). Cf. Oxf/AHRC SPb.-10 PF2 MS (woman b. 1945, Gorky province [now Nizhny-Novgorod province]): the informant recollects a beautiful embroidered cloth, and then comments 'it may be in the dacha somewhere now').
106. Vlasov, pp. 32–4.
107. On reconstruction, see above. In practice, family apartments with old features were likely to be those that had been converted back in the 1920s or 1930s.
108. Cf. Krivulin's dismissive comment, 'Ordinary petit-bourgeois cosiness [*meshchansky uyut*] was achieved by the expenditure of monstrous efforts' (*Okhota*, p. 48). On the history of the term *meshchanstvo*, see Boym, *Common Places*; Kelly, *Refining Russia*, ch. 3. In the early 1980s, Thubron (p. 79) encountered the after-effects of this allergy to *uyut* without offering any explanation for it: 'The living room was monopolized by two huge beds raised on blocks of wood. The curtains were gossamer thin. Heavy furniture stood about, its drawers crammed with worn blankets, pillows, books. A budgerigar perched dumb in a cage. There were no carpets, no ornaments, no pretence at decoration at all. The Russian aesthetic sense seemed to have died with Lucia's ancestors.'

109. For comments on porcelain as a 'site of memory', mainly from the point of view of systematic collectors, see M. Boubtichikova, 'La mémoire de la porcelaine russe', in Nivat (ed.), *Les sites*, vol. 1, 343–51.
110. In my own flat, I inherited from the previous owners a collection of Carpathian pottery, and also some items of Georgian ceramics etc. dating from the 1980s.
111. Shefner, *Skazki dlya umnykh*, p. 260. Shefner's character could not think of anything better for his kitchen than 'golden primuses' and 'lots of tables made of Karelian birch' – once again, an ennoblement of the *kommunalka*.
112. Here and below, the generalisations come from first-hand observation.
113. The practice of assigning extra space for professional purposes to artists, academics, etc., went back to the 1920s. See Obertreis, *Tränen*, p. 198.
114. The word *pochetnaya gramota* is used for a certificate of congratulation or illuminated address of the kind given to prize-winners, etc.
115. Granin, *Kerogaz i vse drugie*, p. 80.
116. See e.g. Oxf/AHRC SPb.-08 PF36 IN (man b. 1980). For an analysis of the social function of the album, see Boitsova, *Lyubitel'skaya fotografiya*, section 2.
117. On the 'editorial' side of amateur photography in a political sense, see Figes; Sarkizova and Shevchenko. I have myself seen family albums with wedding photographs etc. halved.
118. This is now the Museum of Anna Akhmatova in the Fontannyi dom.
119. Such reproductions, along with old maps, were a hit of the transitional era.
120. On collecting the classics, particularly *podpisnye izdaniya* (subscription editions, which were scarce and therefore regarded as important status symbols), see Lovell, *The Russian Reading Revolution*.
121. As I pointed out in Chapter 3, it is notable that many of the leading specialists in local history, for example, Dmitry Likhachev, leader of the Leningrad preservationist movement, and Alexander Panchenko, lived in modern areas of the city.
122. Fridman. A comparable picture of a Moscow kitchen places emphasis on food storage as well as talk: Ries, pp. 10–11.
123. Ivan Goncharov's sketch, 'Moi slugi', on the trials of a hard-working civil servant with severe staff problems forced to resort to the *kharchevnya* at intervals, gives one view of this. In Belinsky's sketch of Moscow and Petersburg, the pervasiveness of eating-out is a signifying feature of the new capital.
124. As described at length in CKQ-Oxf-03 PF2.
125. See Kushkova, 'V tsentre stola'; Kelly, 'Leningradskaya kukhnya'.
126. See Alexander Werth, *Leningrad*, p. 25. Minogi are a dark peat-brown in colour, with a rubbery texture and a sharp yet greasy flavour that to the taste of some outsiders (such as my husband) is reminiscent of chest lubricant. I personally find them more intriguing than delicious.
127. *Koryushka* (*Osmerus eperlanus*), known in English as smelt, rainbow smelt, or sparling, 'occurs in the Baltic, round the British Isles and in the Bay of Biscay. It tolerates water of low salinity; indeed there are some landlocked freshwater populations' (A. Davidson, p. 48). It is known for its distinctive and pleasant smell (which most people think resembles cucumbers). It is popular in Normandy (where smelt are found in the mouth of the Seine) and the Netherlands as well as Russia.
128. Oxf/AHRC-SPb-08 PF-51 IN. The informant is making a joke here, since 'a *koryushka* from Sestroretsk', as he explained at the start of the interview, was a generic term for somebody from the place, 'because you mostly get that fish here, it smells of it everywhere'.
129. It was, obviously, much easier to keep a pet in a separate apartment, though communal tenants were permitted to have one if the other tenants agreed (*BILGS* 13 (1982), 8–10). The main difficulty was the food, though both dogs and cats survived surprisingly well on porridge oats during the deficit era.
130. Slepakova, 'Poslednie minuty', *Stikhotvoreniya i poemy*, 141.
131. http://gorlanova-eu.livejournal.com/29724.html (8 May 2011).
132. For a cynical view of the festival – 'we have all these wonderful festivals for instance Koryushka day, when loads of fat, sweaty, moustachioed men with their shirts off go down to the neva and swill beer all day piss on the monuments and decimate the entire fish population after which they rush round merrily blowing bubbles and flying kites' – see blog entry, 2 August 2010, http://mayte-one.livejournal.com/13275.html?thread=69595.
133. On the cheapness of this fish in the Soviet period, see 'Koryushka – rybka piterskoi natsional'nosti', www.gazeta.lv/story/3844.html. On the *Prazdnik koryushki*, see http://rus.ruvr.ru/2010/05/15/7879324.html. Another blogger contended the main symbol of Petersburg was the rat, though the

*koryushka* was the fish symbol: http://vaino78.livejournal.com/6884.html (28 July 2010). See also 21 July 2010 blog (http://aou.livejournal.com/312240.html).

134. In June 2012, the glossy magazine provided free on the cruise ship *Princess Anastasia* included a number of recipes from top restaurants. The variation between them consisted in whether you seasoned the flour before or after coating the fish, and which oil you fried it in (FN).
135. The term literally means something like *specialité de la maison*, i.e. a dish that you might find in a restaurant or delicatessen.
136. Fussing over the fact that some *firmennoe blyudo* has not turned out as well as usual is typical: see e.g. FN January 2011.
137. From an informal interview with a contact born in the 1940s, St Petersburg, FN January 2010. See also the descriptions in Ries.
138. *Ukhazhivanie* also means paying court to someone (as a prelude to the formation of a marital or sexual relationship): in other words, it covers a range running from 'paying compliments', 'flirting', to what small ads call 'Lead To Relationship'. The ambiguity is nicely captured in the children's stories by Viktor Dragunsky, *Deniskiny rasskazy*, where the parents sometimes fall out rather spectacularly after one thinks the other has been crossing an invisible borderline in the practice of *ukhazhivanie*.
139. This would likely be a prized possession: see e.g. Oxf/AHRC SPb-07 PF10 SA: 'We had a "Sarma" fridge, wonderful machine, it hung on the wall, and opened like this [*demonstrates*]. It lasted for hundreds of years – till granny Lena dived in there with a knife to scrape a chicken off the bottom of the freezer compartment.'
140. See e.g. Shtern, *Brodsky*, p. 50: Evgeny Rein's mother, having baked a *vatrushka* [curd cheese tart] specially so that he could entertain Shtern, whom he was desultorily courting, left it in the kitchen with a note: 'I've baked this masterpiece for your lovely lady. In return you're to take the filth bucket out for the next two weeks without a squeak of complaint, and to go and buy potatoes.'
141. This was another reason for the predominance of salads as a festival food.
142. This is based on personal observation in the 1980s.
143. 'Vy – vladelets kvartiry', *VL* 12 April 1991, p. 2, referred to the long delay; O. Slobozhan, 'Den' v "osnovnom"', *VL* 27 April 1991, p. 1, stated that the reform was nearing completion. The first advertisements for the sale of rooms appeared in *VL* on 29 April.
144. According to the *Zhilishchnyi kodeks RF* [2004] Article 3, p 1 'The dwelling is inalienable'. Article 3.2 stated, 'No one has the right to enter a dwelling without the consent of the citizens living in it on a legal footing except in the circumstances anticipated in this Code or in other instruments of Federal law, or on the basis of a decision made by a court of law.' Article 30.3 read: 'The owner of a dwelling bears the burden of upkeep of the given dwelling, and, if the dwelling is an apartment, of the common property of the owners of the premises in the given apartment block' (including the 'common parts' of the communal flat). Article 32, on the other hand, assigned the authorities wide-ranging powers of compulsory purchase (according to point 1, 'A dwelling may be removed from its owner by purchase in connection with the removal of the relevant site for state or municipal needs'. Though it added, 'such purchase is carried forward only with the agreement of the owner,' point 10 (added in 2006) decreed that, if a block was declared 'in dangerous condition' and was not knocked down, then its site would be confiscated, and so would the individual dwellings. In practice, evictions of those living in blocks who had privatised their homes were quite widespread (see e.g. 'V Peterburge iz avariinogo doma vyselili ocherednykh zhil'tsov', 3 September 2007, www.rosinvest.com/news/325307/).
145. *Zhilishchnyi kodeks RF* [2004], articles 25–6, pp. 17–18.
146. R. Vihavainen, pp. 73–78, 129–31, provides an extensive discussion of all this. The press in the 1990s and 2000s carried frequent reports of scams – speculators who obtained a legal transfer of ownership in return for a fictional title to another property – and about the plight of non-owner-occupiers: see e.g. Narime Karapetyan, 'Izgoi velikogo goroda', *NevV* 20 August 1993 1 (on tramps, numbering up to 50,000); 'V Petrogradskom raione rasselyat 7 obshchezhitii', fontanka.ru 19 May 2007, www.fontanka.ru/2007/05/19/006/, etc.
147. See Rosa Vihavainen, p. 72.
148. In the early 1980s, from my own recollections, a cassette recorder of the kind that cost about 30 dollars in the West was worth around 250 roubles, or more than double the average monthly salary. On these items, see also Chapter 5 below.
149. Tat'yana Derviz (p. 159) recalled how her mother was overwhelmed by the quality of some Latvian furniture that she saw when on holiday there, and quickly arranged to have some sent back home.

150. This furniture can be observed in the various generic furniture shops of the city, e.g. Adamant, or individual ones, e.g. Ikea, Ligne Roset, etc.
151. For instance, the builders who renovated my own apartment threw out most of the Soviet-era items, though these things included a couple of pieces of 1970s Finnish furniture, once highly prized, that I had been hoping to keep. It was generally pensioners who were reluctant to throw out 'perfectly good' pieces from the old days. (Pers. obs.)
152. The authoritative National Corpus of the Russian Language ('Natsional'nyi korpus russkogo yazyka', http://ruscorpora.ru) includes citations for this term going back to 1996.
153. Among the glitziest new blocks were ul. Shpalernaya, 60 (an enormous glass structure built by 'St Petersburg Renaissance'), the 'Zelenyi ostrov' (Green Island) development on Konstantinovsky prospekt, 26, Krestovsky Island (where a 4-room apartment was selling for 2 million dollars in March 2011, see www.mirkvartir.ru/18677917/), and the Mont Blanc tower on Vyborg Side. All these had individual provision of services such as water and gas, air conditioning, underfloor garages, and round-the-clock security. On reconstruction, see e.g. Vika Uzdina, 'V starykh stenakh novye kvartiry', *Smena* 9 September 1993, p. 5. A woman whom I encountered on a plane journey from St Petersburg to London and who was married to a prosperous businessman was extremely proud of the fact that her building in the prestigious area round the Tauride Gardens was a completely new imitation of St Petersburg *style moderne*, which she had furnished with reproduction Jugendstil furniture from Vienna.
154. I have observed this in several completely unconnected families from the relatively well-off intelligentsia in Petersburg.
155. *Domovodstvo*, pp. 12–15, 22–3.
156. FN, September 2009. (Woman b. early 1960s.)
157. *Domovodstvo*, p. 13.
158. For a more extensive discussion of the rise of collecting and antiques, see [OL Chapter 4].
159. See e.g. the site of a St Petersburg company offering all sorts of 'kitchen corners', from plain wooden benches to padded: www.slavico.ru/category/katalogh/kukhnia/kukhonnyie-ugholki. On the other hand, stools retained their popularity (more practical in smaller kitchens), as did divans (which could be used as an extra bed if necessary).
160. All three images appeared in a 2009 post by the blogger zoe_dorogaya, http://zoe-dorogaya.livejournal.com/246159.html.
161. Cf. Vera Zilitinkevich (Tolz's) recollection that D. S. Likhachev, in his last years, acquired *style empire* armchairs with turquoise upholstery, and liked to sit on these when doing TV interviews: *Dmitry Likhachev i ego epokha*, p. 38. I have noted among more affluent and Western-oriented younger Russians a penchant for objects such as enamel signs, old clocks, carved bread-boxes and so on.
162. Perhaps the most remarkable case is the observation in the advertisement for the 2-million-dollar duplex apartment on Krestovskii Island, www.mirkvartir.ru/18677917/, that 'the functional and decorative elements contribute to the creation of *uyut* in the apartment'. This apartment, interestingly, had a kitchen-dining room rather than a separate space for eating.
163. http://forum.mr-spb.ru/showthread.php?t=11011.
164. This might sound obvious, but as Kate Fox points out in *Watching the English*, 'cosy' is a taboo word for the English upper middle classes and above; their houses (the word 'home' also being considered vulgar) tend to combine faded elegance with conditions that are sometimes chilly, damp, and decidedly *un*comfortable.
165. Ira and Galya, 'Muzei durnogo vkusa', *Leninskie iskry*, 3 April 1965, p. 3. Another contributor to the same discussion, Ol'ga Sal'man, aged about 13, remarked that a plethora of ornaments was in bad taste and symptomatic of a love of the 'pretty-pretty' (*krasiven'koe*), not of beauty (ibid.). See also Kelly, *Refining Russia*, ch. 6.
166. On the series, see 'Nasledniki po krivoi' (no author given), *Kommersant*, 24 December 2004, www.kommersant.ru/doc/536051/print.
167. An example is a black porcelain mug with St Isaac's Cathedral in gilding that I was given in 2009: on the underneath of the box it was packed in was MADE IN CHINA in very small print.
168. In my own flat, a porcelain angel is in uneasy balance with another friend's donation of a 'house spirit' (*domovoi*) figurine, grinning evilly under its hairy brows. Since various appalling problems with the electricity when this creature first arrived, I feel an irrational need to keep it supplied with vodka libations; either this or the presence of the angel means that comparable disasters have been avoided since.
169. Oxf/Lev SPb-11 PF13 MS (woman b. 1989). Where Bachelard's concept of the 'poetics of space' in the home emphasises dreaming rather than memory, I associate the home, rather, with memory in a specific and selective sense.

### 3 'The Hermitage and My Own Front Door'

1. Quoted by Rau, *My Russian Journey*, p. 39.
2. Nepomnyashchy, pp. 7–53; quotations p. 27, p. 29.
3. For a discussion of the book's impact, see Paperno, *Chernyshevsky and the Age of Realism*.
4. 'Stenograficheskii otchet zasedaniya tekhnicheskogo soveta', 1 August 1961, TsGANTD-SPb. 36/1-2/ 514/20-1.
5. Ol'ga Berggol'ts, 'Mezhdunarodnyi prospekt' (1946–63), *Izbrannye proizvedeniya*, p. 355.
6. See e.g. N. V. Baranov, 'General'nyi plan razvitiya Leningrada' in *Leningrad* (1943), pp. 69–72, and my 'Socialist Churches'.
7. *Leningrad: Vidy goroda.*
8. On the block ('the Nest of Gentlefolk'), see also below, and Chapter 4.
9. TsGANTD-SPb. 36/1-4/44/28-9.
10. See e.g. O. K. Petrov, 'Vsegda na perednem krae', *LPan* 5 (1975), p. 27, which uses the phrase about the Jubilee Palace of Sport, an immense modern drum dwarfing the eighteenth-century Prince Vladimir Cathedral behind it. Cf. Zh. M. Verzhbitsky, 'Organichnoe vsegda sovremenno', *LPan* 8 (1975), pp. 5–7, where O. B. Golynkin and Ya. D. Bolotin's *dom byta* on ul. Sedova, a glass and concrete box in the manner of Corbusier, is named as 'organic'.
11. Pers. obs. For concern about authenticity in the colours of architectural monuments, see e.g. the document from 1927 at NA UGIOP f. 8/2 l. (Andreevskii sobor), l.36 (my thanks to Alexandra Piir for this reference).
12. 'Problemy, mneniya, spory. Kupchino – eto Leningrad?', *Stroitel'stvo i arkhitektura* 1 (1970), pp. 21–2.
13. Oxf/Lev SPb-11 PF13 MS (woman b. 1989).
14. 'Putin oproverg zakrytie Voenno-Meditsinskoi Akademii', *Vzglyad*, 25 September 2012, www.vz.ru/news/2012/9/25/599741.html/ The Academy is the focus of enormous pride (civilians who are able use its hospital and obstetrics facilities), and there was considerable local anxiety that its expertise would simply be lost if it was reformed (see e.g. FN January 2013).
15. See Chapter 1. Apart from Kirov on ulitsa Krasnykh Zor', other leading Party and Lensovet officials were based on Kronversky (prospekt im. Gor'kogo), as well as, of course, the Lensovet building; flagship new buildings included the House of Specialists on Malyi prospekt, the Dom politkatorzhan on pl. Revolyutsii (Troitskaya), and ul. Lenina housed many prominent members of the local intelligentsia.
16. Before the Revolution, brass plates often carried residents' names on the doors, and a few survived into the new era, but this custom, widespread in Europe generally, did not pass into Soviet practice. On the 'concrete walls, painted dark green to the level of a theoretical dado rail', see Fallowell, p. 9.
17. As noted in [Chapter 1 OL], the use of the term *paradnaya* is often taken as a marker of 'Petersburg' as opposed to 'Moscow' speech, but it is often incomers or outsiders who are most insistent on using it. For example, when I published a version of the present chapter as an article, the title (in Russian, 'Ermitazh i rodnoi pod"ezd'), which quotes a Petersburg informant verbatim, was altered by the editors of the (non-St Petersburg) journal in which it appeared to 'Ermitazh i *rodnaya paradnaya*'. For decayed splendour, see the striking description by Alexander Werth quoted in Chapter 2, p. 70.
18. For the official understanding of the *dvornik*'s function, see e.g. Sotnikov, *Obraztsovyi gorod*, p. 110.
19. Some did survive. See Oxf/AHRC SPb-11 PF5 MS (woman b. 1940): the informant's father worked in this role during the 1950s. In Oxf/AHRC SPb-11 PF4 NG the informant (b. 1962) recalls that his mother worked as a *dvornik* when he was a child, carrying out the vast 20-litre vats of food waste on each landing, clearing snow, etc. One of my informants, born in the late 1950s, stressed the fact that she and her family of well-educated professionals had certainly never cleaned staircases, etc. anywhere: there was a yardman for that.
20. See e.g. Avdeev, pp. 22–31.
21. Official regulations relating to the courtyards and street frontages of blocks were strict: no unregulated building of sheds, etc. was allowed, and tenants were not supposed to hang washing, carpets, etc. on balconies placed on the 'external façades' (see e.g. 'Ob utverzhdenii "Pravil uborki ulichnogo i dvorovykh territorii Leningrada i ego prigorodov', *BILGS* 16 (1972), pp. 7–16). But the 'human factor' was still key. On 'horizontal surveillance' by older women in particular, see Piir, 'What is a Courtyard For?'.
22. See e.g. Oxf/AHRC SPb-11 PF4 NG, where the informant says that relations were good, but that people did not visit each other's homes. Most other informants (e.g. Oxf/AHRC SPb-11 PF12 EI)

were considerably less positive: 'Neighbours never come to make social contact, they just come and complain'. On the other hand, Salmi, pp. 141–64, produces a different picture, with neighbours quite frequently relied on for help – though still regarded without much warmth.

23. On neighbours and privacy (including the noise argument), see the discussion by Steven Harris.
24. Such leakage might well provoke a furious visit or telephone call to the supposed perpetrator of the outrage. For instance, in spring 2010 I was woken at about 5 a.m. by a woman screaming down the telephone, 'It's leaking from your toilet into our toilet!' This was a physical impossibility, since my flat is situated above a so-called *tekhnichesky etazh* (a space for central heating pipes etc.), with a restaurant below that. However, only when she discovered that I lived in a completely different house on a different street did she stop fulminating and ring off – without apology. [FN March 2010]
25. See e.g. the complaint in a reader's letter to *MR-V*, 4 April 2003, p. 6, that it had been impossible to get neighbours to agree to pay for locks on a *pod"ezd* at no. 4 Kamennoostrovsky, since most tenants were 'birds of passage'. My own co-operative regularly posts in the *pod"ezd* lists of persistent defaulters on utilities, some of whom owe 5–6 months of back charges, the equivalent of hundreds of dollars: on this phenomenon, see also Rosa Vihavainen, pp. 140–8. In 2012, legislation was altered to allow eviction on defaulters of more than three months' duration.
26. Groups of young people who organised frequent parties (*tusovki*) might behave like this. The flat on ul. Rubinshteina that I rented at intervals in 2003–2005 had a front door that was contested territory between the respectable middle-aged, posting notices about the need to keep it closed, and younger people, leaving it open. See further below.
27. By the 2010s, the vast majority of *pod"ezdy* did have barriers to entry – in the form of press-button panels if nothing else – but it took around twenty years for this process to happen.
28. *Zhilishchnyi kodeks Rossiiskoi Federatsii* [2004], articles 135–52. See also the detailed discussion in Rosa Vihavainen, esp. pp. 86–97. The 2005 housing reform also provided for management by residents as individuals, or by a management company; however, in St Petersburg, 54 per cent of houses were managed by TSZh (as opposed to 2.6 per cent across Russia generally); but only half had selected a type of management by 2007 (ibid., p. 99). Vihavainen also points to a recent revival of staircase councils (ibid., p. 117).
29. For instance, in a house on prospekt Dobrolyubova in the late 2000s, residents had the *pod"ezdy* restored, including replacing the handsome mirrors contemporary with the *style moderne* building (FN January 2008).
30. This is true, for example, of my own block.
31. Pers. obs.
32. The stink of the *pod"ezd* is often the main identifier in talk about it – see, for example, Oxf/AHRC SPb-08 PF43 IN.
33. Notice in hallway, ul. Rubinshteina, 2004. Cf. Oxf/AHRC SPb-11 PF4 EI: the informant hates coming back to find someone shooting up, or blood all over the hallway.
34. Factory workers, schoolteachers, and schoolchildren left early, unless on the 'second shift' (which started in the afternoon), but many members of the intelligentsia had at least a partly 'free timetable', going in to work some days and not others.
35. Pers. obs.
36. See Kelly, 'City Texts'.
37. Mikhail Lur'e, 'Graffery'; 'Subkul'tura grafferov'.
38. See Bushnell.
39. Cf. the comment from a woman living on Ital'yanskaya ul., 'I'd have those artists thrashed,' after a student and two schoolgirls were caught doing artwork nearby. Attempts to confine graffiti to licit spaces (a courtyard off Nevsky, a wall on Ligovsky, and the courtyard of Apraksin dvor) were evidently having limited success (Natal'ya Tikhonova, 'Na skam'yu pozora – za isporchennye skameiki', *MR (V)* 27 March 2009, p. 2).
40. Smyth, *Three Cities in Russia*, 1:192, p. 190. Among the most famous literary descriptions of the courtyard is Dostoevsky's *Poor Folk* (1845).
41. *St Petersburg Painted*, p. 138.
42. B. M. Kirikov, 'Peterburgskie dvory', *LPan* 8 (1988), pp. 37–8.
43. In the Soviet period, some multi-storey garages were constructed in Leningrad, but the only alternative to the street for the majority of car owners was a *garazh-boks* (a steel lockup) (see e.g. the decision of Lengorispolkom to allow Raduga, Oktyabr'sky and Neva garage co-ops to build garages for *invalidy* in kvartaly 2, 17 and next to tyre repair works: 3 November 1986, *BILGS* 2 (1987), p. 15). As the references to *invalidy* indicates, access to co-operative garages (and still more to state garages) was extremely limited, with certain categories of people (e.g. the disabled, war veterans)

given priority. Claims had to be re-registered annually, and only car owners were entitled to renew the lease (though registering a car in the name of someone who was entitled to a garage, but did not actually drive it, offered a possible dodge). (Pers. inf., June 2010). These rules remained in force in the post-Soviet period, while at the same time the pool of garages contracted: for example, in 2005, 300,000 *garazhi-boksy* were demolished, despite the opposition of the drivers' association (Artemy Aleksandrov, 'Trista tysyach mashin vygonyayut na ulitsu', *MR(V)* 19 August 2005, 1, p. 4). This naturally increased pressure for the construction of alternative garage accommodation. Another complicating factor was the lack of any official requirement for new housing development to offer car parking, so that only elite blocks did this (usually in the form of 'warm [heated] garages' on a separate floor of the block).

44. Such initiatives began in the 1920s and 1930s (particularly the years of the so-called 'Cultural Revolution', 1928–32), and were revived again in the 1960s. See e.g. 'O nekotorykh novykh formakh organizatsii vospitatel'noi raboty sredi trudyashchikhsya po mestu zhitel'stva v Moskve i Leningrade' (1961), RGANI 5/ 34/ 95/36-54; the material in TsGAIPD-SPb. 25/89/120/1-70 (1962, e.g. 'Predlozheniya po kul'turno-massovoi rabote sredi naseleniya', ll. 1–7, on making flowerbeds in courtyards on Moskovskii prospekt, etc.): Avdeev, *Zhilishchnoe khozyaistvo Leningrada*, pp. 22–4.
45. Piir, 'What is a Courtyard For?', *passim*.
46. Oxf/Lev SPb-03 PF24 AP. This kind of situation persisted later too: see e.g. Oxf/Lev SPb-11 PF13 MS (woman b. 1989).
47. Cf. an incident reported to me about how a woman living in the Vasilievsky Island area of the city discovered that her neighbours had purposely buried the car in snow in order to make the point that it was not parked where it should be. When this strategy did not deter her, a vociferous delegation arrived to argue the case directly (FN January 2010).
48. The movement to 'ennoble' courtyards was first alluded to in the late 1980s. As reported by N. Kozhevnikova, 'Dvor – kak sad?', *VL* 21 November 1988, p. 2, in 1986, residents of Moskovsky raion started organising a voluntary drive to tidy up yards (through the removal of rubbish, installation of benches, plantings, etc.). The municipal drive to clean up yards was a feature of Valentina Matvienko's period of office. The effects were noticeable in some places (e.g. the area round Tavrichesky sad, on the doorstep of the city administration), and haphazard in others. As late as the early 2010s, many yards were still bleak stretches of tarmac, and some (e.g. the yard of the House of Specialists on Lesnoi prospekt) scattered with rubbish and seamed with cracks and potholes.
49. Aleksandr Oreshkin, 'Luchsche khoroshii dvornik tselyi god, chem subbotnik vesnoi', *Smena* 20 May 1998, p. 1. The *subbotnik* (from *subbota*, 'Saturday') came into use in the early Soviet period for a 'voluntary' (though to all intents and purposes unavoidable) session of cleaning up at a workplace, dwelling house, or public place.
50. A general discussion, 'Lenin bez brevna, ili Antropologiya sovetskogo subbotnika', started by Mikhail Alekseevsky in 2007, with commentators from Moscow, Petersburg, and elsewhere, many in their 30s or younger, turned up a largely ironic view of this social institution. To quote one participant: 'I've hated *subbotniki* since I was a child, like other manifestations of the Soviet spirit pure and simple' (http://alekseevsky.livejournal.com/166208.html). However, a completely different view emerges in Oxf/AHRC SPb-11 PF4 NG, where an older informant (aged about 50) lyrically recalls the *subbotniki*: 'It felt like a holiday. Music was playing through loudspeakers. People would clear the spaces round their blocks, clear up the rubbish.'
51. Averbakh and Maslennikov's *The Private Life of Kuzyaev Valentin* (1966) has a vignette of a women playing her accordion at the window; in later decades, the speakers of a hi-fi might be put on the window to achieve the same effect.
52. Some of the discussions of this phenomenon, to be observed in Moscow too, have a 'moral panic' dimension. In fact, children are still to be seen out playing war games etc. in some yards (e.g. my own). But in middle-class families, it is now the norm not to let children out, something characteristic only of certain families in the past.
53. Elena Shvarts, 'The Dump', trans. Catriona Kelly, from *Paradise: Selected Poems* (Newcastle: Bloodaxe Books, 1999), p. 25.
54. Boris Khersonsky, 'Komendantsky chas' (2010), ЂКрещатикї 2010, p. 4. My thanks to Gerry Smith for this reference.
55. See, for example, the assurance of a Lenproekt architect-planner in 1957 that the design of the new *tipovye doma* was organised so that residents would not have to carry their rubbish along the street; 'Zasedanie arkhitekturnoi sektsii Tekhnicheskogo soveta instituta', 5 March 1957, TsGANTD-SPb.36/1-1/ 216/6. Traditionally, carrying out the bucket of refuse was men's work (see Chapter 5), another indication of its non-gentility. Being seen carrying refuse if one is female, therefore, is

tantamount to indicating publicly that there is no man about the house (or that he is too drunk, idle, or shameless to do it).

56. There is an excellent discussion of this in Osorina, *Sekretnyi mir detei*. For a typical reader's letter complaining about the dump, see 'Khotim vstretit' prazdnik v blagoustroennom, chistom dvore', *MR-V* 4 April 2003, p. 6.
57. Building materials and anthologies of folk epics – the latter neatly laid out by a skip on Vasilievsky Island, a notably academic area of the city – pers. obs. On clothes, see Astvatsaturov, *Skuns-Kamera*, p. 168 (adults boasting about possessions are like children showing off their privates during the nursery school 'quiet hour': 'do you really think he wants to tell you [. . .] about the sweater that dossers will be trying on by the rubbish tip inside the year?'). See also Yu. Dmitrieva, 'Cheburechnaya v koridore', *NevV* 27 December 1995, p. 1; 'Pochemu my perestali lyubit' dvornikov' (vox pop), *NevV* 18 November 2000, p. 1, which records a man who had lived in Finland complaining, 'The only people who sort rubbish here are tramps.'
58. On picking up antiques on the dump, see Chapter 2.
59. Pers. obs. See also Fig. 3.11.
60. As pointed out in Natal'ya Tikhonova, 'Kto otvetit za musor?', *MR-Ts*, 25 July 2004, p. 5.
61. Lina Zernova, 'Peterburg mozhet prevratit'sya v avtomobil'noe kladbishche', *Smena* 25 February 1998, p. 5 recorded that recycling centres were completely overwhelmed; a Swiss student had counted 150 rusting heaps while walking round the city (and then, presumably, given up the count).
62. Tuan, *Space and Place*, p. 170.
63. Soja, *Thirdspace*, pp. 285–309.
64. The 'thread' of *Tishe!* was in fact the repeated mending of an enormous hole in the road, but this insight dawned on the viewer only gradually, so the first impression was desultory scenes: a shy boy awkwardly steers a bouquet along to meet his girlfriend; people put up umbrellas and remove their jackets depending on weather; an old lady hushes her dog (giving the title of the film). Whichever way, the film is a delight to watch and in its quirky originality stood out from the standard line of tributes for the tercentenary.
65. In ordinary practice, *mikroraion* was and is simply a geographical subdivision, with branch offices of the local administration, etc. In the 1960s, the word briefly had a utopian meaning as a kind of crucible of Soviet civilisation and imagined community of a kind like the reformed 'courtyard', but on a much larger scale. On this, see particularly Mark B. Smith, *Property of Communists*, pp. 116–21. As Smith himself acknowledges, it is not clear how much the reports about such drives in the press were simply propaganda artefact; certainly, I have come across material about civilising initiatives only on a smaller scale (see above).
66. Yu. Yulin, 'V novykh raionakh Peterburga eshche deistvuyut prezhnie administratory', *Smena* 22 March 1994, p. 3.
67. A possible exception here is Nevsky district, which has a large concentration of factories, but 'industrial zones' inspire distaste in the social elite wherever they happen to be located (see below).
68. I have heard this said, for instance, by a friend in her 60s who has lived since she was born on what she stoutly refuses to call 'Vas'ka'. 'Petrogradka' is considered respectable by larger numbers of people, though I have heard this usage criticised too.
69. The poet Elena Shvarts lived for some time in this area, and commemorated it in her poetry.
70. For a rare discussion of this, see Gubin, Lur'e, and Poroshin, *Real'nyi Peterburg*.
71. Such museums included the Nevskaya zastava, founded in 1967 (www.museum.ru/m197), and the Narvskaya zastava museum, founded in 1990 (http://narvskaya-zastava.ru/main/). Local schools also had museums: for example, the Museum of the Arctic in School no. 336 on ul. Sedova, founded in 1969 (http://my-sedovo.narod.ru/MUZEI_336.html).
72. Cf. Oxf/AHRC SPb-11 PF4 NG (man b. 1961, working class, family lived at the prestigious end of the Moika).
73. Interestingly, before the revolution, it was number of rooms and not apartment size that was specified in advertisements: see Yukhneva, *Peterburgskie dokhodnye doma*, p. 111.
74. The first case: pers. inf., 2003. This person himself was born in a provincial town remote from Leningrad, another indication that affective identity and objective identity often differ. For the opposite ('Rzhevka was the only option that suited'), see Oxf/AHRC SPb-11 PF20 EI.
75. See the materials from the BDT in TsGALI-SPb. 268/3/697 (correspondence from 1986) and d. 720 (correspondence from 1989).
76. The process was evoked in Yuri Trifonov's famous short story about Moscow, 'The Exchange' (1969), and worked the same way in Leningrad as it did everywhere else. By 1986, the Leningrad branch of the state agency handling these deals had processed over 120,000 applications (with

many thousands more carried out unofficially, since this method was quicker) ('Kak obmenyat' kvartiru', *LPan* 4 (1986), pp. 19–20, an interview with V. F. Fedorov, the head of Goszhilobmen). Alongside straightforward swaps, there were also *mnogoetazhnye* ('multi-step') exchanges, which naturally got very complicated (cf. house-buyers' chains in market economies). A local snag was the horrendous slowness of bureaucratic departments (particularly the housing office in a given block and the passport office) in processing paperwork, and their capricious insistence on multiple certification, etc. On this, see the article in *Literaturnaya gazeta* by G. Silina, 7 July 1982, and the responses to it by the Leningrad Party authorities (which described the article as 'one-sided', a back-handed admission that its conclusions were largely correct). TsGAIPD-SPb. 24/ 191/16/35-8.

77. *Zakroite vorota, duet sil'no!* (FN September 2008). The joke reflected the reality that the Narva Gates were regularly vandalised. See the Museum of City Sculpture report from 1964, TsGALI-SPb. 405/1/102/54.
78. This was also often true at later stages as well. See e.g. the album of 'local' photographs included in *Peterburg kak kino*, where Kupchino is the only 'dormitory suburb', with a rather defensive essay by Ivan Chechot as introduction.
79. Bitov, *Pushkinskii dom*, p. 58. Emphasis original.
80. The official zoning policy was set out in Makhrovskaya, *Rekonstruktsiya zhilykh raionov Leningrada*, pp. 5–14. In Zone III, with a preponderance of industrial enterprises, there were no building restrictions of any kind. This source recognises that insanitary conditions and noise pollution were issues in these zones (p. 11). For the Slepakova quotation, 'krome snega, ne bylo prirody', see her 'Prazdnichnyi put' ', *Stikhotovreniya i poemy*, p. 85.
81. Kolker, 'Parkhatogo mogila ispravit'.
82. Cf. the evidence on districts in Vasil'eva, *The Young People of Leningrad*. While noting (p. 19), 'In our discussion the city is regarded as a unified, integral territory, and the differences that exist between individual zones of the city and among schools are not taken into account', Vasil'eva also observed, 'However, these differences are rather important.' She was able to adduce that the basic 'centre/periphery' dichotomy was nuanced by parental occupation and educational level: 88 per cent of children of parents with secondary education only, and living in the centre, had visited museums, but only 73 per cent of those living in outer areas. However, the figures for children of parents with higher education were 89 and 83 per cent respectively (ibid.).
83. Viktor Tsoi, 'Dal'she deistovat' budem my' (from the film, *The End of the Holidays* [*Konets kanikul*], 1986).
84. Elena Shvarts, 'Novostroiki', *Sochineniya*, 1.46.
85. Cf. the exchange in Dovlatov, *Zona* (1982) (www.sergeidovlatov.com/books/): ' "Are you from Piter?" "From Okhta." "In headquarters they tell this story. Major Berezhnoi arrived at Ropcha. The sentry don't let him in. Berezhnoi he goes, 'I'm from headquarters!' And the sentry, he goes, 'And I'm from Ligovka!' " '.
86. Oxf/AHRC SPb-08 PF25 IN (Interview with woman b. 1941, working-class background). Cf. Oxf/ Lev SPb-03 PF24B AP (man b. 1960, working-class background). Having described how extensive fighting took place between different courtyards ('people went to do each other over [. . .] into strange courtyards [. . .] to stop them doing raids on our territory, our garbage tips'), the informant agreed that similar fighting took place district to district ('Yes, that happened too. Something would happen, and we'd go and set things to rights'); and the discussion of the 'Krestovsky hoodlums' and 'Krestovsky mob', Oxf/AHRC SPb-07 PF17 IN (man b. 1929, Leningrad, working-class background and occupation).
87. *NV* 10 December 1992, 5; *NV* 17 December 1992, p. 5.
88. It could work the other way round, too – once such districts became prestigious, people persuaded themselves they liked high ceilings. See e.g. Oxf/AHRC SPb-11 PF7 EI, in which the informant (b. 1985) recalls that he hated 'those dreadful high ceilings' as a child.
89. Gubin, Lur'e, Poroshin, *Real'nyi Peterburg*, pp. 226–31. Cf. the real estate site 'Ya khochu' www.advecs.com/projects/elite/.
90. In the *Almanach de St Pétersbourg* (1910), the beau-monde was densely settled round the Winter Palace (Dvortsovaya naberezhnaya, Millionaya) and Senate Square to its west (Galernaya, the English Embankment) and the northern end of Liteinyi to its east (Sergievskaya, Furshtatskaya, Preobrazhenskaya, Zhukovskaya).
91. Cf. the presence on Gubin, Lur'e and Poroshin's list of 4 Petrovskaya Embankment ('The Nest of Gentlefolk', see Chapter 4), and Brezhnev-era housing on Nalichnaya, also constructed for Party and city administration high-ups. The informant in Oxf/AHRC SPb-11 PF6 EI recalls renting a duplex in this area (on Morskoi prospekt) after he and his friends stole a load of industrial silver in 1990.

92. By 2008, according to realtors' sites, apartments in the most favoured developments here cost around 12,000 dollars a square metre (about twice the cost of apartments in the Tauride Garden area), and in 2011, 15,000. As for Stone Island, where housing was not on public sale and building was not officially allowed, it was now the favoured place for the private residences of local politicians, referred to regularly as 'the Petersburg Rublyovka' – from an exceptionally exclusive area of suburban Moscow.
93. All of this emerged from interviews – Udel'naya in particular was very often named as the place where people would most like to live.
94. Tomchin, p. 11.
95. In 2007, I talked to a woman working in the cloakroom of BAN whose building opposite the Yusupov Garden, occupied by elderly people who had lived there for decades and had all bought their own rooms, was being forcibly cleared to make way for a hotel (FN Sept 2007). For the joke, see Oxf/AHRC SPb-11 PF6 EI.
96. See e.g. Oxf/AHRC SPb-11 PF9 EI (man b. 1987, who rented space in his friends' kitchen). Oxf/AHRC SPb-11 PF18 EI describes a whole series of peregrinations, caused by nasty neighbours or landlords who did not have the right to let, or unpleasant conditions such as stinking old furniture. On living in a *skvot*, see ibid.
97. On the negative attitudes of post-Soviet Russians to mortgages, see particularly Zavisca. The reluctance to take up mortgages can be contrasted with the lively market in small loans (on which see Chapter 5).
98. Yuri N., b. 1938, Leningrad, intelligentsia background, higher education, Oxf/AHRC SPb-07 PF3 IN. On the *zaplevannost'* and *bezobrazie* of Nevsky, see ibid. PF1. Cf. Yuliya S., b. 1968, Leningrad, working-class background, higher education, Oxf/AHRC SPb-07 PF16 IN; Oxf/AHRC SPb-11 PF17 EI (woman b. 1981).
99. Zukin's *Naked City* has, in fact, questioned the association with reference to New York, pointing out that the traditional neighbourhoods that Jacobs saw as the model were the homes of homogeneous, settled communities, so that they were a poor 'control' for the housing projects.
100. 'Chuvak v maike svoego raiona – eto kruto', *MR (V)* 2 June 2005, p. 4. Stogov's best-known work, for instance, the novel *Macho Men Don't Cry*, is set in grimier parts of the old centre, proving once again the split between imagination and practicality.
101. Astvatsurov, *Skuns-kamera*, p. 11.
102. See further in Chapter 8.
103. See e.g. the work of Nikolai Bondar' in *Peterburg kak kino*.
104. For a fuller discussion, see Kelly, '"V podlive otrazhaetsya salyut"'.
105. N. Yamakova, 'Rastut goroda', *Stikhi v Peterburge: 21 vek*, pp. 461–2. For an example of a Central Asian visual artist also inspired by the 'anonymous' spaces of so-called 'dormitory districts', see Skakov, 'A Tribute to Otherness'.
106. Sergei Stratanovsky, 'Tak ukhodit zemlya, ot kotoroi rozhdayutsya bogi', in *Stikhi*.
107. On the attempts to preserve this structure, see the discussions in GIOP during 1967, TsGANTD-SPb. 386/ 1-1/31/88.
108. The asylum itself is not ordinarily open to the public, but the church, behind its high perimeter wall, can be visited (FN September 2012).
109. See e.g. Gusentsova and Dobrynina. A particularly impressive example of local studies is *Lesnoi: ischeznuvshii mir*, on the Lesnoi prospekt enclave, where several generations of some notable intelligentsia families, such as the Kobaks, have lived since pre-revolutionary days.
110. For an excellent discussion of this phenomenon in the context of Moscows Zaryad'e district, site of the enormous and ugly Rossiya Hotel (built in the Brezhnev era and now demolished), see Kupriyanov and Sadovnikova.
111. Sindalovsky's books are actually mentioned in Oxf/AHRC SPb-07 PF19B. While speaking rudely about the author's achievements, the informant still leans heavily on his work. For a more mystical, not to say bizarre, view of the city see an 'astrological guide' (Leonidova, *Peterburg astrologicheskii*), which claims that, for instance, those born under Libra are happiest in the area around the Summer Garden and ul. Chaikovskogo, and that Virgo are likely to flourish on Vasilievsky Island.
112. See e.g. the two collections of such essays published in the late 1990s, *Moya Petrogradskaya storona*. There were some schools in the pre-war Soviet Union where 'local knowledge' was imparted, but study at earlier periods was of an abstract kind – surveying the local roads and courtyards, counting, and perhaps also manufacturing, road-signs, etc.
113. 'Chuvak v maike'.

114. Oxf/AHRC SPb-11 PF24 MS. *Nespal'nyi raion* (e.g. issue of October 2011). In 2013, the district planned an international arts festival to celebrate local history (my thanks to the Irish artist Gareth Kennedy, one of those involved, for the information). It should be said that other districts' official periodicals were less lively – see e.g. *Slavyanka*, a freesheet for Nevsky district (www.nslav.spb.ru, issue of 17 December 2010).
115. For the Vasilievsky Island idea (the currency's name puns on Vasyuki, a town on the Volga that Il'ya Il'f and Evgeny Petrov's trickster figure Ostap Bender said would become the capital of the USSR, and then the world), see Oxf/AHRC SPb-10 PF4 MS. The informant traced the idea back to the perestroika era.
116. The newspaper also has a Moscow edition.
117. For the figures, see http://dimagubin.livejournal.com/36351.html. According to TSN Gallup Media, the figures were 769,200 circulation and a print run of 435,000 (October 2006–Februrary 2007). www.mr-spb.ru/companynews/2007/03/20/news_13.html.
118. 'Where do people in love arrange to meet in newbuild districts? By the metro, by the shopping centre. It would be more romantic to meet by the monument to Kindness and Goodness or the sculpture of Cupid. But statues are generally found only in the centre, and the dormitory suburbs lead a bleak life, with no beautiful stone things. "The districts are built outside Petersburg traditions, where street sculpture has evolved over centuries,' says Anatoly Dema, the chair of the Department of Sculpture and Plastic Arts at the Academy of Industrial Arts"' (T. Morozova, 'Spal'nye raiony stradayut ot bezkul'turya', *MR (Ts)*, 3 July 2008; www.mr-spb.ru/story/top/story_4420.html).
119. Shown to me by Yuri Nikolaev, an artist living locally, September 2008.
120. Tat'yana Zimbuli, 'Raionnye ekspeditsii', in the forum 'Emotsional'nye novosti Peterburga', 5 October 2007, www.wmos.ru/piter. One of my informants, living in the same district, an incomer from Pskov province, was very enthusiastic about this area, because it allowed rapid exit into beautiful woodland round a former country estate (FN September 2006). So the search for beauty can be rewarded.
121. Oxf/AHRC SPb-11 PF20 EI. This is brought out also by the essay on Kupchino and photographs of it in *Peterburg kak kino*.
122. Oxf/AHRC SPb-07 PF43 IN.
123. SPb-07 PF1 AK (woman b. 1951).
124. Sergei Petrashov (school No. 75, SPb.), writing in *Moya Petrogradskaya storona* (1998), p. 236.
125. An interesting study of naming patterns in the late Soviet period is V. F. Lu're, *Mikrotoponimika*. However, quite a number of the names given here are extremely fanciful (e.g., 'the Big Top with a flag' for the Frunzensky District Committee of the Communist Party), as commentators on the internet have frequently pointed out (see e.g. http://spb-projects.ru/forum/viewtopic.php?t=1545&sid=edfb2c8df850a81e9044c7773f1a812d).
126. Whether the developers of this self-described elite clubhouse in Kupchino knew about the David Lynch resonance is debatable: they were probably simply referring to the height of the building, as in the hills called the 'Twin Peaks' outside San Francisco. See the official site at www.clubdom.ru/house/. Interestingly, the new monuments have mostly not been nicknamed either – there is no equivalent to Dublin's 'floozie in a Jacuzzi' (the popular title for a pretentious statue of Anna Livia Pluribelle).
127. A rare exception is the obelisk on ploshchad' Vosstaniya that eventually (in 1985) replaced the statue of Alexander III, known locally as 'The Impotent's Dream' (see [OL Chapter 2]). However, this is not a piece of original wit: at least three monuments in Moscow, not to speak of many elsewhere, are known by this title (see e.g. www.gramota.ru/slovari/argo/53_7056), as well as the now dismantled monument to the discoverers of Siberia in Irkutsk, etc.
128. See e.g. Oxf/AHRC SPb-07 PF20 IN ('Three Idiots'), Oxf/AHRC SPb-11 PF4 EI ('Gribanal').
129. Gubin, Lur'e, Poroshin, *Real'nyi Peterburg*, p. 176. Cf. one of the 'You're from Petersburg if . . .' characteristics: 'You're from Piter, if . . . on hearing the words "Kupchino", "Devyatkino", and "Prospekt Veteranov", you break out into a cold sweat' (http://citroens-club.ru/forum/lofiversion/index.php/t9329-0.html).
130. Woman b. 1975. Oxf/AHRC SPb-07 PF15 IN. Cf. Oxf/AHRC SPb-07 PF3 SA.
131. Man b. 1975. Oxf/AHRC SPb-07 PF10 IN. The opinion about sewage in Obvodnyi may well be accurate, but the canal is hardly unique in that: pollution in other water-courses, in particular the Fontanka, has been a regular source of complaint since the 1960s (see [OL Chapter 1]).
132. Andrei N., b. 1961, intelligentsia background, professional ed. Interviewed by Irina Nazarova. Oxf/AHRC SPb-07 PF 19 IN.

133. On Krestovsky Island, Oxf/AHRC SPb-11 PF5 EI; on prospekt Kosmonavtov, Oxf/AHRC SPb-11 PF6 EI.
134. For the localisation according to streets, see Sergei Stratanovsky (on ul. Shkalina near the Narva Gates), writing in *Peterburg kak kino*, p. 225. For alcoholics and the 'micro-climate', see Oxf/ AHRC SPb-11 PF20 EI.
135. Oxf/AHRC SPb-08 PF43 IN (woman b. 1984, raised in Leningrad, intelligentsia background, higher education, graduate student).
136. I owe the information about the Sergievsky gorodok case to Lyubov' Osinkina, a local resident. On the Lomonosovskaya case (which united local people angered by the disappearance of an amenity, church activists, and those lobbying to preserve historical cemeteries, and which, after a great deal of publicity, was unexpectedly resolved by the death of the chairman of the company of developers), see 'Net tochechnoi zastroike! – Zashchitniki skvera na st. metro "Lomonosovskaia" proveli miting, http://community.livejournal.com/zastrojke_net/43280.html (5 July 2008, accessed 8 July 2008). See www.restate.ru/material/53257.html for a report on the campaign as of August 2008. Later materials can be found in the blog entry of 10 March 2010 by Nikolai Lavrent'ev and Ivan Puchkov, http://forestier.livejournal.com/82236.html. Cf. the material on protests by residents of Lakhtinskaya ul. on Petrogradskaya storona at http://community.livejournal.com/ zastrojke_net/42512.html (accessed 5 July 2008).
137. Churches vary a good deal, and the strongest sense of community is often in churches in outlying districts, e.g. the Church of the Resurrection on ul. Dvinskaya, or the former Putilovsky zavod church in Narva District, the Church of St Anna Kashinskaya on Bol'shoi Sampsonievsky, etc. (pers. obs.).
138. E.g. *Nespal'nyi raion, Slavyanka* (see above).
139. This was even before discussion of the Georgian-Ossetian crisis began generating thousands of responses in August 2008. It should be said also that *Moi raion* was then functioning as a source of independent city-wide news and comment, rather than of 'parish pump' information: for example, an editorial published on 21 August 2008 was highly critical of alleged disinformation on the official site of the RF's Ministry of Defence.
140. *Muzei – anti-muzei. Diskussiya* (Borey Art Center, 1995), p. 6.
141. The area also known as Peski, close to the junction of Nevsky prospekt and Suvorovsky prospekt.
142. Interview with man b. 1977 (vocational education), Oxf/AHRC SPb-07 SA PF3A.
143. Nadezhda, contribution to 'Severnyi Peterburg', 25 April 2009, www.forum.aroundspb.ru/index. php?t—sg&th=6168&goto=63445#msg_63445.
144. As discussed in Osorina, *Sekretnyi mir detei*.
145. Oxf/AHRC SPb-07 PF28 IN (man b. 1979). Soon afterwards, the informant states that the only new area that has a positive resonance is prospekt Bol'shevikov, because his wife used to live there.
146. This likely explains the enthusiasm of younger people for the centre ('I don't want all that green stuff', etc.: see e.g. Oxf/AHRC SPb-11 PF4 EI), as opposed to their elders' preference for the outskirts. For an interesting account of shifting attitudes – from a dislike and fear of the centre as a child to a hatred of the new areas – see Oxf/Lev SPb-11 PF7 EI.
147. This was not necessarily the case in the Soviet period, when people living in new districts sometimes had to go on a bus-ride to buy food. See e.g. Oxf/AHRC SPb-11 PF7 EI.
148. Oxf/AHRC SPb-07 PF1 AK.
149. Oxf/AHRC SPb-08 PF44 IN (man b. 1983).
150. The closure of former 'through courtyards' is a regular topic in the news reports and correspondence columns of local newspapers. See e.g. D. Livintsev, 'Zapertye v sobstvennom dome', *MR(V)*, 2005, 18 February, p. 4; 'Pis'mo ot Galiny M.', *MR (V)* 24 June 2005, 9; 'Pis'mo ot zhitelya Petrogradskoi storony', *MR (V)*, 5 August 2005, 9.
151. Oxf/AHRC SPb-07 PF1 AK.

## 4 Initiation into the Working Class

1. Elena Shvarts, 'Detskii sad cherez tridtsat' let', *Sochineniya* 1, p. 234.
2. The memoirs, 'Gonchukov Aleksei Andreevich. Moya zhizn' i rabota. Vospominaniya (Kirovskii zavod)', are held in the archives of the Institute of the History of the Party of the Leningrad Regional Committee of the Communist Party (Institut istorii partii Leningradskogo obkoma KPSS), TsGAIPD 4000/18/ d. 333, d. 334, d. 335. All further references are in the format Gonchukov 333.2 [file no. followed by folio] etc.
3. In terms of social background, Gonchukov came from the *meshchanstvo*, or urban lower class (here and below the information comes from his memoirs).

4. Later, Gonchukov generally recorded his children's affairs when related to broader social themes, e.g. his disappointment in what he considered his son's ne'er-do-well behaviour in dropping out of his institute (334.57), 'Igor' has in essence become an enemy for himself and the family, and all means of dealing with an enemy are good ones.' The year 1954 saw him fretting about his daughter's bad marks at school (335.15). On his and his wife's twenty-eighth wedding anniversary in 1959 (335.73), he declared the results of their marriage 'not bad' (*itogi neplokhie*): their son was now a fourth-year student and their daughter had qualified as a medical orderly.
5. Gonchukov 333.83, 333.129, 333.149.
6. Gonchukov 335.5, 334.34, 334.9, 334.55.
7. Similarly, on 6 June 1953 Gonchukov had written to the factory committee that in 1948, contrary to press reports, 'the factory produced no tractors whatever', 335.7.
8. Gonchukov 335.14. A quotation from the Fourth Dream of Vera Pavlovna, in the novel *What is to Be Done?* (1862) (Chapter XVI Section 11), which became a textbook citation in the Soviet period.
9. Gonchukov 335.30.
10. Gonchukov 335.83.
11. Gonchukov 335.70. The term that Gonchukov uses, *gordynya*, is used in Russian Orthodox tradition to refer to the sin of pride. Clearly, no ironic undertones are meant, but the phrase 'puffed up with pride' is meant to capture what an educated Russian reader would see as slightly inept phrasing.
12. See [OL Introduction].
13. Gonchukov 335.6. The original verse (from Pushkin's 'Epistle to Chaadaev', usually dated to 1818) adapted by Gonchukov reads: 'Comrade, have faith: she will arise/The star of captivating happiness/Russia will awaken from sleep/And on the shards of autocracy/Others will scratch our names.' It was a favourite text in Soviet anthologies and textbooks. (See Baiburin and Piir.)
14. This is spelled out in capitals on the first page: 'I expect to conclude IN TIME FOR THE FIFTIETH ANNIVERSARY OF SOVIET POWER' (333.1).
15. See Vail' and Genis, *1960-e*, pp. 105, 192, 200–201.
16. 'Stenogramma soveshchaniya direktorov tekstil'nykh predpriyatii v otdele legkoi promyshlennosti obkoma KPSS', 24 November 1960, TsGAIPD 24/137/107/ l. 4, l. 15, l. 27, etc.
17. 'Zapiska o kharaktere voprosov i nastroenii trudyashchikhsya', signed Zazersky (undated – assigned by the archivist to 1962), TsGAIPD 25/89/66/ l. 14, l. 13.
18. Gurevich, 'Aktivno uchastvuet v obshchestvennoi zhizni', from his 'Vospominaniya'.
19. For instance, in 1962 there was an extensive programme of anti-religious activities at Leningrad's factories: see 'Spravka o sostoyanii nauchno-ateisticheskoi propagandy v Vyborgskom raione g. Leningrada', TsGAIPD 25/89/122/ ll. 33–34, l. 40. In the same year, lectures at the Kotlyakov Factory touched on the situation in China, the Leningrad metro, the US lifestyle, etc. ('Zapiska o kharaktere voprosov', TsGAIPD 25/89/66/19).
20. 'Spravka o rabote partiinoi gruppy po uluchsheniyu kachestva vypuskaemoi produktsii na II uchastke II tkatskogo proizvodstva Fabriki "Rabochii"' (1972), TsGAIPD-SPb. 25/108/83/46.
21. Oxf/AHRC SPb-10 PF5 MS. See also I. Sidorov, 'Stat' baltiitsem', *Smena*, 5 January 1980, p. 2, which sets out the biography of Yurka Tyunaev, who hated metal-working at school but loves making components after a friend persuaded him to sign up at the PTU.
22. 'Zapiska o kharaktere voprosov', TsGAIPD-SPb. 25/89/66/11–19.
23. TsGAIPD-SPb. 24/159/2 ll. 2-32, ll. 52–9.
24. It was customary in Soviet sources to distinguish between 'material' and 'moral' 'stimuli for labour' (see Rogers, *The Old Faith and the Russian Land*, p. 125), but in fact the two were densely intertwined.
25. TsGAIPD-SPb. 25/108/49/63.
26. *Narodnoe khozyaistvo SSSR v 1972 g. Statisticheskii ezhegodnik* (M., 1972), p. 473.
27. The online 'Natsional'nyi korpus russkogo yazyka' has citations for a sardonic use of 'philanthropy' in a work setting from Pavel Bazhov (*Ocherki. Ural'skie byli*, 1923–1924), Il'ya Il'f and Evgeny Petrov, *Odnoetazhnaya Amerika* (1936), Yury German, *Dorogoi moi chelovek* (1961), etc. This tradition followed an established pattern among pre-revolutionary Russian intellectuals, as exemplified by the protagonist of Chekhov's story 'A Doctor's Case-Notes' (1898).
28. As argued by Simon Clarke, 'Privatization and the Development of Capitalism in Russia', *New Left Review* 1/196 (1992), www.newleftreview.org/?view=1691: 'Any profits which remained to the enterprise, once it had met its obligations, were not appropriated as capital, but were generally spent on improving the working and social conditions of the labour collective.'
29. The pre-revolutionary term *gorodok*, literally 'small town', for a factory territory such as the Nobelevsky gorodok on Vyborg Side, encapsulated this status.

30. On the policy of agglutination, see Vakser. On its effects, see e.g. Patryshev, 'Rodnoi zavod'. Patryshev, who worked in the IT department of the Leningrad Mechanical Factory (LMZ) from 1974, found himself, after the Twenty-Second Congress Factory was absorbed into LMZ, moved to new premises on ul. Sedova in a completely different district (Nevsky and not Vyborgsky), and constructed to a far lower standard.
31. 'Stenogramma besedy s vospitatelyami na temu, "Ideino-politicheskaya i kul'turno-massovaya rabota s prozhivayushchimi v obshchezhitiyakh"' (1970), TsGAIPD-SPb. 25/102/126/31.
32. Oxf/AHRC SPb-10 PF5 MS. The Kirov Factory Museum contains a booklet with the text of this ceremony, dating from the 1970s.
33. For a persuasive discussion of this, see Kondratieva.
34. Cf. Clarke's emphasis on the division between 'the underlying contradiction between the role of the collective labourer as direct producer and the role of the collective labourer as object of exploitation' ('Privatization and the Development of Capitalism in Russia').
35. Oxf/AHRC SPb-08 PF51 IN, p. 11–13: man b. 1944, working-class background. Extract edited to remove interviewer's responses.
36. See, for instance, Oxf/AHRC SPb-11 PF5 MS.
37. Basic pay was known as *zarplata* (*zarabotnaya plata*), or 'payment for work', or in white-collar professions, *oklad*. The first term was Soviet, the second pre-revolutionary.
38. The discussion, 'Stenogramma besedy s vospitatelyami obshchezhitii', revealed some very primitive conditions in factory hostels (on this see also Chapter 2), but at least people were now accommodated in hostels. On the machinery, see e.g. TsGAIPD 25/108/12/15 (the Worker textile factory had acquired equipment from Czechoslovakia and the GDR in the late 1960s).
39. 'Stenogramma besedy s vospitatelyami obshchezhitii', TsGAIPD 25/102/126/26.
40. 'Stenogramma besedy', l. 27.
41. See e.g. 'Stenogramma besedy', *passim*.
42. As the technical school teacher Lev Korotkin put it in 1984, the inaccessibility of Moscow made people 'descend on Leningrad in vast numbers' (*vot i valyat v Leningrad*), but turnover was very high ('SSSR, rabochii klass vos'midesyatykh godov').
43. Oxf/AHRC SPb-10 PF3 NG.
44. Boris Khodorovsky, 'Na Kirovskom zavode', *Smena* 20 February 1999, p. 3. Material housed in the AMKZ indicates that other anniversaries were regularly celebrated too – for example, the tenth anniversary of the founding of the 'Garden Settlement', the subject of a special album (1958).
45. See Chapter 1.
46. Based on visits to the museum in 2010 and 2012; see also E. N. Koriechenko, 'Muzei istorii i tekhniki OAO 'Kirovskii zavod', AMKZ.
47. Oxf/AHRC SPb-10 PF5 MS.
48. See e.g. T. Maslova, 'Pervaya zarplata', *Prazdniki, rozhdennye zhiznyu* (Yaroslavl', 1980), pp. 108–10. Both types of ritual were performed at the Kirov Factory, as indicated by materials in the Museum and articles in *Kirovets* (see e.g. V. Kuz'min, 'Novye trudovye knigi', *Kirovets*, 8 January 1975, p. 4).
49. V. N. Bereslavsky, 'Vremya bol'shikh peremen', *LPan* 1 (1984), pp. 6–8. See also 'Nasledniki: rasskaz o rabochei dinastii', *LP* 5 December 1970, p. 2.
50. Oxf/AHRC-SPb 10 PF5 MS, and the Kirov Factory museum display.
51. It was also common for model factory workers to be selected as the subjects of jubilees when these were celebrated in district Palaces of Culture etc. For example, in 1967 Frunze raikom selected as the first honorands in the area Maria and Petr Osipovich; the latter had worked at the Karl Marx Factory for 32 years, while the former 'had devoted much effort to productive labour, the upbringing of her daughter, and now her ten-year-old granddaughter Olya'. 'Spravka o vnedrenii v byt novykh sovetskikh obryadov' (1969), TsGAIPD 25/102/58/1.
52. See O. V. Kalacheva, 'Den' rozhdeniya: prazdnichnoe ustroistvo i osnovnye znacheniya', in *Problemy sotsial'nogo i gumanitarnogo znaniya*, ed. N. V. Vakhtin et al. (2000), 399–422.
53. O. Barabashev, 'Za krasnyi byt', *Yunyi proletarii*, 1 (1924), pp. 4–7.
54. See e.g. the spread, 'Sovremennyi Leningrad' in *Petrograd* 5 (1924) (interlacing the whole number): 'The First Shift', 'Late for the Hooter', 'Four a.m. in the Harbour', 'Working Holidays'.
55. This of course continued into the 1960s and 1970s as well. For example, in 1967 (to commemorate the 50th anniversary of the October Revolution), the Svetlana, Karl Marx, and Il'ich works were each awarded 'perpetual custody of the memorial banners of the Central Committee of the USSR, Presidium of the Supreme Soviet, the Soviet of Ministers of the USSR, and the All-Union Soviet of Trade Unions'. Lesser factories were awarded banners of lesser significance (TsGAIPD-SPb. 25/99/76/35).

56. 'In view of the fact that red christenings have reached epidemic proportions, they should be organised less often,' recommended a speaker at a meeting of raikom representatives in 1924. Another speaker thought they should be 'brought into an organised channel' (*organizovannoe ruslo*) (TsGA-SPb. 1001/9/10/29).
57. Borodkin, p. 80.
58. On the break with traditional family ties, see e.g. Kelly, *Comrade Pavlik*; on the Stalin cult, e.g. Balázs Apor, Jan Behrends, Polly Jones, and E. Arvon Rees (eds), *The Leader Cult in Communist Dictatorships: Stalin and the Eastern Bloc* (Basingstoke, 2004); Jan Plamper, *The Stalin Cult: A Study of the Alchemy of Power* (New Haven, 2012).
59. For example, the informant in Oxf/AHRC SPb-10 PF5 MS, though later a great patriot of the Kirov, originally moved there because she had been sent to work outside Leningrad, despite being married and having a small baby. On being allowed to remain in Leningrad as a reward for good study, see Oxf/AHRC UK-08 PF22 AB.
60. The practice of recruiting employees who did not already have a registration in Leningrad became widespread in the 1960s, and persisted into the 1970s and later, despite official attempts to crack down. For instance, in 1970 Lensovet issued strictures against passport violations by enterprises and institutes, but in 1972 further violations were reported: one director of an institute had used the student quota in order to recruit cleaners, and there were other offences by the head of a building trust and so on. The response by Lensovet – to forbid use of the *limit* by violators – indicates how entrenched the system had become. 'O narusheniyakh pasportnoi sistemy v Leningrade,' *BILGS* 11 (1972), pp. 6–7.
61. An augmentation of this is the system of actual 'marriages of convenience' to stay in the city – i.e. marrying someone who had a *propiska*, which is widely talked about (though, as with bribery, people don't admit to having done this themselves).
62. See Shcherba. On the conditions, see the discussion of the Kirov Factory below.
63. See the detailed report to the State Committee of the Council of Ministers, 17 May 1966, TsGAIPD 24/136/99/4–5.
64. TsGAIPD-SPb. 25/108/12/1.
65. The cement shortage was passed on to the Party authorities, and reported to the Gorkom (TsGAIPD-SPb. 25/108/12/1). Reconstructing the backdoors wheeler-dealing is more difficult, though a sense of the negotiating style is given by the complaint of a Lensovet official in 1991 that Anatoly Sobchak was 'too soft' in dealing with factory directors who had stymied a scheme of selling scrap abroad in order to raise funds for food products by hiking up the prices they wanted to charge Lensovet for the scrap. The former mayor, Khodyrev, 'would have sorted all this out long ago. He'd have got the directors together and said, "Look, mates, you see how things are." And if he'd had to, he'd have put the screws on.' (S. Vital'ev, 'Myaso skvoz' "zheleznyi zanaves"', *VL* 4 January 1991, p. 1.) For a general discussion of wheeler-dealing in the former Soviet bloc, see Katherine Verdery, *What Was Socialism, and What Comes Next?* (Princeton, NJ, 1996). Paul Gregory, 'Productivity, Slack, and Time Theft in the Soviet Economy,' in Millar (ed.), *Politics, Work, and Daily Life*, pp. 241–75, reported that around 40 per cent of Soviet Interview Project respondents recalled regular or occasional problems with supplies, and nearly 60 per cent regular or occasional problems with absenteeism.
66. Vadim Shefner, 'Dvorets na troikh, ili priznanie kholostyaka,' in his *Skazki dlya umnykh*, p. 236.
67. Cf. the informant b. 1931 quoted in Baiburin and Piir, p. 176: 'I was head of a section then, and I'd be allocated a hundred and twenty litres of ethylene a month. It was no problem to siphon off a couple to take' (i.e. along to the demonstration).
68. L. Ivankin, 'Kriminal'nye "khobbi"', *LP* 18 January 1976, p. 2. The engineer's peccadillo was discovered when he got drunk and was unable to help deliver a set that was on order. Cases of theft from the workplace are also mentioned in V. Strakhov, '"Melkaya" krazha,' *LP* 18 July 1968, p. 2.
69. As remembered by a friend of mine born in the early 1950s.
70. Here I follow the argument of Smolyak (based on materials for Perm'). She points out that the actions of *nesuny* ['takers-out,' petty thieves] have become encrusted with retrospective mythology, making the true extent difficult to compute, but certainly there is a mismatch between the mere handful of cases subject to disciplinary procedures and people's memories that 'everyone' was involved in these practices.
71. Oxf/AHRC SPb-07 PF7 SA (woman b. 1961). Time theft and other breaches of labour discipline are among the best researched areas of Soviet work history. See e.g. Filtzer, *Soviet Workers and Destalinization*.
72. S. Utkin, 'P'yanaya dorozhka k stanku,' *Smena* 17 May 1980, p. 2.
73. Utkin, 'P'yanaya dorozhka.'

74. The Kirov Factory's newspaper, *Kirovets*, ran a series called 'The Culprits Behind the Interruptions in Production' ['Vinovniki sryvov'] in January and February 1970 (see e.g. 27 January, p. 1, 13 February, p. 1). But this was exceptional, as were the lively cartoons directed against outré dress in the 1960s (see Chapter 5).
75. See e.g. Oxf/AHRC SPb-07 PF25 IN (this person regularly received an extra month's summer leave because of working very hard over the winter).
76. Examples from Gurevich, 'Vospominaniya'.
77. Patryshev, 'Rodnoi zavod', describes this process with one of his workmates.
78. For instance, in museums and archives, the Chief Curator (*glavnyi khranitel'*) is to this day the only person with ultimate jurisdiction over the materials in his or her care. (Pers. obs.)
79. Ibid.
80. On houses of rest, see the album in AMKZ on the 'White Nights' pension in Sochi, and the discussion in Oxf/AHRC SPb-10 PF5 MS; on *kommandirovki*, Patryshev, 'Rodnoi zavod'. Priority in hotel bookings was given to 'the commanded', so in practice it was almost impossible to stay in a decent hotel without the official chit (*kommandirovochnoe udostoverenie*).
81. See e.g. Oxf/AHRC SPb-10 PF5 MS; Oxf/AHRC SPb-07 PF7 SA.
82. As mentioned by Patryshev.
83. TsGAIPD-SPb. 25/91/103/175–7.
84. See the study by Glowka for a detailed account of these reforms.
85. The most notorious part of the vocational education system was the 'polytechnic schools' (PTU), which offered a general education with some work training to those whose marks were not good enough to qualify for the top classes in secondary schools. A former Leningrad teacher who emigrated to the West in the early 1980s gave a horrific picture of these: pupils received little useful training, quickly became cynical about factory work when they saw their elders drunk on the job, and spent their leisure time drinking, smoking, having drunken sex, fighting, and vandalising their hostels. (See ' 'SSSR, rabochii klass vos'midesyatykh godov', *passim*). Our informants remember weak pupils at Leningrad schools being tormented by teachers with 'the PTU's coming to get you!' (see e.g. Oxf/Lev SPb-03 PF24). Even official discussions, behind closed doors, admitted these schools were problematic: see e.g. the report of a plenary session of the Leningrad City Committee of the Komsomol held in 1969, TSGAIPD-SPb. K-881/17/4/27. Graduates' recollections are generally quite negative too (e.g. Oxf/Lev SPb-03 PF24; however, a much more positive view is given in Oxf/Lev SPb-03 PF29). Many working-class young people were in any case frustrated with study by their late teens: see e.g. the recollections by a woman b. 1969 about her brother, who after dropping out of driving courses eventually got fixed up with a job in his father's factory, where he was able to fulfil his dream of working as a driver (Oxf/Lev SPb-03 PF14).
86. See the transcript of an informative programme on the local TV-5 station, presented by Lev Lurie: www.5-tv.ru/video/502760/.
87. Our interviews with Leningraders in the Oxf/Lev and Oxf/AHRC series point to an overwhelming correlation between social background and educational advantage. For a study of a characteristic Leningrad special school (once a pre-revolutionary *gimnaziya*, classical high school), see Pashkova, which also makes clear that compulsory stints of work experience in factories were no help at all in making manual work seem appealing (pp. 253–4).
88. There is a substantial literature on the city administration in the Soviet period: see e.g. Catrell; Ruble.
89. In the pre-war decades, the city administration had less of a Party colouration, because of the leading role of 'bourgeois specialists' (for instance, planners). I have explored this side of Leningrad life in 'Socialist Churches'.
90. German Gurevich recalled that at Lenenergoremont, the administration kept ideological effort to a minimum. Most people working there did not even take part in demonstrations, as the director had cunningly secured a prominent place in the procession for the enterprise's representatives, so that their delegation made more of an impact than its size deserved. Items in *Kirovets* sometimes pointed to slackness in ideological work: see e.g. the reader's letter published on 9 January 1957, p. 2, which complained that the 'red corner' meant for political discussions was only being used for smoking and playing dominos.
91. Alexander Zinoviev, *Gomo sovetikus* (1986), www.zinoviev.ru/ru/zinoviev/zinoviev-homo-sovieticus.pdf.
92. TsGANTD-SPb. 36/1-1/310/57.
93. This is partly based on personal observation, supported by the sets of Soviet-era films, such as Igor' Sheshukov's *The Red Arrow*, which includes numerous scenes set in offices. See also S. Birman, 'Zdes' rozhdaetsya mebel' ', *LP* 7 January 1965, p. 4, which pictures furniture designs.

94. Some of these impressive instruments survive, for instance, in AMKZ. On the *vertushka*, see Alena Ledeneva, 'Trust and Security: The Workings of *vertushka*', paper presented at the 'Trust and Distrust in Russian Culture' conference, UCL, February 2012.
95. Kuraev, 'Belyi polotnyannyi'.
96. On contacts with the bureaucracy, see e.g. Oxf/AHRC SPb-11 PF31 MS (man b. 1940 recalls how he had 'at least eight visits' from officials when he began working, because they found his unusual surname suspect).
97. See the report of 24 March 1961, TsGAIPD 24/123/25/1–8.
98. 'Zasedaniya Tekhnicheskogo soveta NII Lenproekt', 11 April 1961, TsGANTD-SPb. 36/1-1/490/4–14.
99. On the liking of officials for this area, see Gubin, Lur'e, Poroshin, p. 231, and the discussion in Chapter 3 above.
100. Logan Robinson, *An American in Leningrad*, p. 163.
101. On food, see Chapter 9; on dachas, Chapter 12. A Moscow friend of mine (born in the early 1930s) who spent the war years in Kazan' and Tashkent remembered that the families of academicians evacuated from Leningrad lived in a style she had never seen, with separate, spacious flats, and in one case a nursery for the children and a nursemaid (*bonna*) (pers. inf.). The diaries of the artist Anna Ostroumova-Lebedeva, wife of a famous chemist, show this sphere from the inside – regular trips to Torgsin and to take the air at Detskoe Selo, a maid, the use of a car . . . (OR RNB 606/51, 52).
102. As in the case of Leonid Kuznetsov, mentioned by Bereslavsky, 'Vremya bol'shikh peremen'.
103. See Aleksandr Lavrov, '"Deti Pobedy"', which records that the author entered the Institute of Applied Chemistry in 1971 on a salary of 100 roubles, but three years later was receiving 145 roubles; in 1978, after he finished his candidate's dissertation, he had another rise (to 185 roubles), and by 1980 (after promotion to senior researcher) he earned 280 roubles, increased to 300 in 1981. Bonuses paid for the completion of projects and so on regularly boosted this too. A comparable account is given in Oxf/AHRC UK-08 PF22 AB (as a docent – roughly, senior lecturer or associate professor – this person got 320 roubles).
104. For instance, the Academic Council of the Institute of the History of Material Culture was revived in 1955 (see Piotrovsky, *Stranitsy moei zhizni*, p. 276).
105. There is a large literature on this issue, including, for example, Graham; Mikhail Robinson, *Sud'by akademicheskoi elity*.
106. As argued by Yarov, *Konformizm v sovetskoi Rossii*. In some cases, accommodation was prompted by the assumption (in retrospect naïve) that one's intellectual concerns were above politics – cf. the case of P. P. Veiner discussed in [OL Chapter 3].
107. Ginzburg, 'Zapisi 1943–1945 gg.' in her *Prokhodyashchie kharaktery*, pp. 139–47.
108. For example, there was much opposition from academics to the plan to reform university admissions criteria so as to give priority to those who had done a period of manual work. See Glowka.
109. See Oxf/AHRC SPb-07 PF10 ANK, also Oxf/AHRC SPb-08 PF46 IN. An informant of mine was 'let go' from his institute when he failed to show sufficient enthusiasm for 'socially useful work' (FN April 2012).
110. Oxf/AHRC SPb-07 PF3 CK.
111. See the account by F. A. Belinskaya of her efforts to get the administrators in her laboratory to agree that she could purchase a grinder made of jasper for her work in chemistry; they insisted a ceramic one would be fine. (Letter to Anatoly Belinsky, 24 November 1954: *Pis'ma proshlogo veka*, p. 193. On 28 November 1954, 'my boss agreed' [ibid., p. 197], but on 18 June 1955, she was still without it [p. 319]).
112. The use of *mat* appears to have been rare in these circles, though museum directors, whose role was only partly academic, sometimes used it. One of my informants remembered that L. N. Belova, when he declined the position of director of one of the museum's dependent exhibitions, responded indignantly: 'I've seen plenty of dickheads [*mudaki*] in my time, but it's the first time I've seen a dickhead like you' (Oxf/AHRC SPb-09 PF4 CK).
113. Piotrovsky, *Stranitsy moei zhizni*, p. 253. However, he also noted that M. I. Artamonov had a completely different style (ibid., p. 279).
114. On the stuffiness, see German, *Slozhnoe proshedshee*. For a recent study of the intellectual stagnation that set in after the anti-Semitic purges of the late 1940s, see Druzhinin.
115. For a recent study of an academic dynasty, see Korzun and Kolevatov.
116. A. Golovtsov, 'Leningrad – LETI – shestidesyatye', http://hepd.pnpi.spb.ru/hepd/red/golovtsov_page/proza/Leningrad.htm. The humiliation ritual, which Golovtsov only heard about since he did all he could to avoid it, involved being beaten on the bare buttocks with spoons.

117. For an approving account of the 'aristocratic' character of local scholars, contrasted with the 'oikishness' of recent incomers ('they were straight from the plough'), see Oxf/AHRC UK-08 PF60 AB.
118. See e.g. Viktor Toporov, *Dvoinoe dno: zapiski skandalista*, p. 141.
119. These comments are based on personal observation of the Tartu Russian Department, which I visited in 1990. For a general intellectual history of Lotman and his circle, see Waldstein. For memoirs of student life, see Oxf/AHRC UK-08 PF49 AB; Tamara Zibunova, 'Tartu v shestedesyatye', www.pseudology.org/Dovlatov/Podrugi/Zibunova/Tartu_60_1.htm.
120. 'Stenogramma soveshchaniya propagandistov i zamestitelei sekretarei partiinykh organizatsii uchrezhdenii literatury i iskusstva g. Leningrada po teme: "O perspektivakh sovershenstvovaniya partiinogo obrazovaniya tvorcheskoi intelligentsii"', 18 November 1971, TsGAIPD 24/145/12, l. 13, l. 15, l. 8.
121. For example, this was allegedly the case with Arkady Raikin's Theatre of Miniatures, as reported in Kirill Narbutov, Aleksandr Mikhailov, 'Raikin: Korol' i shut strany sovetov' (2011), www.1tv.ru/documentary/fi7288/fd201110231220.
122. See the records of auditions at BDT: e.g. 'Protokoly zasedanii Khudozhestvennogo soveta teatra, 2 marta – 26 dekabrya 1972 g.', TsGALI-SPb. 268/3/521, e.g. ll. 3–6. This material also makes clear that plays were judged primarily on their emotional impact and scenic qualities.
123. Lyudmila Putilova in *Teatr Leonida Yakobsona*, p. 143. On the other hand, one of our informants recalled that the film director, Gleb Panfilov, was just difficult full stop: he would approve publicity photographs one day and then reject them the next, and on location, was given to calling on his staff at any time he felt like, though often they were billeted some distance away in lodgings, while he had more convenient and prestigious accommodation in a pension (FN, June 2012).
124. Likhachev, *Vospominaniya*, pp. 313–24. A scene in Il'ya Averbakh's film *Monologue*, as the hero is taken to task for pursuing his own research line, also gives a good idea of the procedures, though in this case the 'working over' ends with a show of benevolence, which was far from inevitable.
125. In *Ruf' Zernova*, pp. 52–3. However, Koroleva was later to suffer the reverse side of this magnificence, when she was sacked for an unsanctioned meeting with a foreigner and defended by none of the august scholars who worked at Pushkin House (ibid.).
126. Pers. obs.
127. This point is made wittily by Richard Stites in 'Crowded on the Edge of Vastness' in Jeremy Smith (ed.), *Beyond the Limits*, pp. 260–2. It is particularly strikingly exemplified by the Institute of the History of Material Culture, which is housed in a masterpiece of 'eclectic' design not far from the Winter Palace.
128. On 'sitting' see Chapter 2, and also Dale Pesmen, *Russia and Soul* (Ithaca, NY, 2000), pp. 171–88.
129. Bonuses paid for the completion of research projects usually amounted to about 25 per cent of the basic salary (see Lavrov, '"Deti Pobedy"').
130. Tat'yana Shchepanskaya, contribution to 'Forum 10: Dialogue in the Academic World', *Forum for Anthropology and Culture* 6 (2009), p. 300.
131. For both sides of the coin, see the comments by Lev Klein, 'Obuchenie arkheologii'. The intense process of study with a leading specialist is also described by Frantsuzov.
132. See particularly Shlapentokh.
133. For a discussion of this performative attitude to privateness and publicness, see Manyulov.
134. On the *kapustnik*, see e.g. Oxf/AHRC SPb-07 PF10 SA. The example of an in-joke (from Leningrad State University in 1990) is given in Mikhail Lur'e, 'Sadistic Verse', p. 361. On birthday parties, see e.g. Oxf/AHRC GB-08 PF1 CK (the informant worked for many years in the Hermitage). A general study of birthday parties, focusing on the intelligentsia, is Kalacheva. On corporate humour of this kind – with a specific focus on the parodic transformation of Soviet discourse – see the excellent discussion in Yurchak, *Everything Was Forever*, pp. 259–64.
135. Applicants for exit visas were sacked as a matter of course, leading to long-term hardship for those whose applications were turned down (the 'refuseniks', in US parlance, or those 'trapped [literally, "sitting"] in a state of refusal', to translate the local term literally). Part of the procedure for obtaining an exit visa required near relations to grant permission for the departure; if they did so, they were then themselves subject to reprisals. For example, the distinguished eighteenth-century scholar Il'ya Zakharovich Serman was sacked from Pushkin House Institute of Russian Literature in 1976 for sanctioning his daughter Nina's emigration to Israel (see *Ruf' Zernova*; http://xviii.pushkinskijdom.ru/Default.aspx?tabid=4910).
136. Kolker, 'Moi kochegarki'.
137. Cf. Nielsen's comments on work as primarily a legitimating activity for many.
138. Kolker, 'Moi kochegarki'.

139. See e.g. Oxf/AHRC-SPb-07 PF14 (woman b. 1975); Oxf/AHRC-SPb-07 PF 4 IN (woman b. 1969), Oxf/AHRC-SPb-07 PF 23 IN (woman b. 1931).
140. 'Interlude: Vitya', in Nielsen.
141. As recalled by a professional taxi driver, b. 1958, in Oxf/AHRC SPb-11 PF27 MS.
142. On private tutors and home abortions, personal inf.
143. M. P. Tubli, 'Defitsit pri izobilii. Kakim byt' Leningradskomu farforu?', *LPan* 7 (1985), pp. 12–14.
144. For a highly critical account of co-operatives, see Sergei Sobolev, 'Biznes pod nadezhnoi kryshei', *LPan* no. 1 (1990), pp. 9–11; this alleges that their main function was reselling the goods produced by state enterprises at hiked-up prices, under a ridiculously favourable tax regime.
145. Nefedova, Polyan, Treivish, *Gorod i derevnya*, table 2.3.3 (2.5 per cent in 1996, compared with 5 per cent in 1970). On the general situation of labour politics at this period, see Filtzer, *Soviet Workers and the Collapse of Perestroika*; Clarke (ed.), *Conflict and Change*; Clarke, *Making Ends Meet*.
146. See 'Promyshlennost' Leningrad i Leningradskogo ekonomicheskogo raiona za 1959–1963 gg.' April 1964, TsGAIPD-SPb. 25/91/103/13–20. It is characteristic of the city's culture of secrecy that even though this list was classified (the brochure is marked 'Secret. To be returned', and is a numbered copy), it does not include defence production.
147. See the example on display in the Kirov Factory Museum.
148. Natal'ya Ipatova, 'Promyshlennost' Peterburga', *Smena* 20 January 1994, p. 3, recorded that silk production dropped in 1993 by 82.6 per cent and cotton production by 54 per cent.
149. See Yury Zvyagin, 'V Smol'nom predlagayut vykup', *Rossiiskaya gazeta*, 4 October 2004, www.rg.ru/2004/10/04/peterburg.html.
150. FN, June 2008.
151. Other initiatives were often temporary. The former 'Red Triangle' rubber factory was briefly used by the 'Art-Vokzal' club in 2007–9 (see www.afisha.ru/spb/club/14093/), but the club then folded. On 27–30 October 2011, 'Fragments of the Unseen City', an installation/performance, and featuring members of the Institut für Raumexperimente, was held on the territory of the former 'Red Flag' factory on Petrogradka (email circular from the Urban Anthropology seminar, 25 October 2011).
152. See Shtiglits's account of her own career, Oxf/AHRC-SPb-08 PF3 AP.
153. Ibid.
154. Svyatoslav Tarasenko, 'Rasselenie Obvodnogo: vse khotyat, nikto ne mozhet', *Metro* 8 June 2012, p. 5.
155. See e.g. the Urban3 site (http://urban3p.ru/objects/?region_id=15), which includes material on Petersburg, and various pages on Live Journal (e.g. http://periskop.livejournal.com/381409.html).
156. Other spaces that opened in the early 2010s were Taiga, on Palace Embankment (in a decayed mansion), and 'Chetvert' (i.e. 'Quartier') on pereulok Pirogova, also in an enormous former elite dwelling house (FN April 2013).
157. www.gidropriborstroi.ru.
158. Pers. obs.
159. The Admiralty Wharves, one of the largest ship-building operations in the RF, was run by the state until 2008: see www.admship.ru. According to the entry in the business directory www.spb-business.ru/, the company is now largely supported by commercial orders and is increasingly involved in civilian ship-building.
160. Marina Vashchilo, 'Rozhdeno konkurentsiei', *LPan* 11 (1991), pp. 4–6.
161. www.fdo-skorohod.ru/company/history/.
162. http://motor.ru/news/2011/10/19/spb/.
163. For an example of local opinion, see FN April 2012. Given the extent of controls on the press, local and central, establishing which view is right is currently more or less impossible.
164. V. Kulikov, 'Pamyati Alekseya Gavrilovicha Romanova', *Kirovets* 2 August 2010, p. 3; 'Predstavlenie nagrazhdeniyu potchtennym diplomom ili ob"yavleniyu blagodarnosti Zakonodatel'nym sobraniem Sankt-Peterburga': www.assembly.spb.ru/manage/page/priem/1_deputat.htm?tid=633200038&nd=706116948; the citation for T. A. Markova quoted here is given as an example.
165. On the Kirov, see my interview with a former engineer (FN September 2010).
166. www.gergur.ru/work/214.
167. Oxf/AHRC SPb-10 PF5 MF.
168. 'Pravila ob ocherednykh i dopolnitel'nykh otpuskakh. Izdany na osnovanii Postanovleniya SNK SSSR ot 2 fevralya 1930 g.', with amendments to 1936, http://base.consultant.ru/cons/cgi/online.cgi?req=doc;base=LAW;n=53448;fld=134;dst=100028.

169. On the weakness of the union movement, see e.g. Evgeny Valov, 'Naskol'ko nezavisimy profsoyuzy v Rossii?', *Golos Baikala* 2 May 2012, http://голосбайкала.рф/blog/2012/05/02.
170. As in the case with Okhta, for example (pers. obs.).
171. Yuri Zvyagin, 'V Smol'nom predlagayut vykup', 4 October 2004, www.rg.ru/2004/10/04/peterburg.html.
172. The redevelopment of New Holland was delayed by the financial crisis of 2008, causing the original plan for restructuring by Norman Foster to be abandoned. However, in 2011 the redevelopment project was raised again, this time with extensive consultation about what should be done with the site (it was open to the public for a considerable period in the summers of 2011 and 2012: see Chapter 6).
173. See the discussion by Shmulyar.
174. Pers. inf., 2009.
175. Informal interview, FN, Jan. 2012.
176. Stanyukovich, p. 88.
177. Pers. inf.
178. L. Robinson, p. 52.
179. Oxf/AHRC SPb-11 PF24 MS. I have heard this kind of comment about other places as well – lecturers never wanting to answer questions because they were off for a cup of coffee with a colleague, or not having time to mark work because they were in love . . .
180. See the information on the University's website, www.herzen.spb.ru, and Oxf/AHRC SPb-11 PF28 MS.
181. Oxf/AHRC SPb-11 PF24 MS.
182. The example with which I am most familiar is the European University, St Petersburg. The Higher School of Economics, and Smol'nyi College at Leningrad State University, also base teaching on Western models. On the original plans for the founding of the European University announced by Sobchak see M. Sedykh, 'Evropeiskii universitet – v Leningrade', *VL* 17 May 1991, p. 1.
183. *Kto est' kto v Sankt-Peterburge* (2006) gives numerous case histories, such as the former lecturer at the Institute for Further Qualifications in Industry who now runs an ISP, or the telephone engineer who has a communications company. Andrei Rogachev, one of the few St Petersburg businessmen to make the Forbes Rich List, worked at the Institute of Oceanography before founding an ecological instruments co-operative in the late 1980s (see www.anticompromat.org/milliardery/ruforbes09.html).
184. On Perel'man, see Gessen, *Perfect Rigour*.
185. See e.g. CKQ-M-04 PF7.
186. Not everyone was so high-minded. There were persistent rumours that you could buy your way into certain institutes, and buy your results when there (one man alleged that the cost in some places was a 10-pack of CDs: Oxf/AHRC SPb-08 PF47 IN). But other sources said the contrary. Cf. the discussion on http://wellcoman.ru/?ForumView&ID=3798912 about whether you can get into different places with bribes: the teachers at the State University, says one participant, are too well-paid to care.
187. A case in point was Yury Molchanov (b. 1952), director of foreign relations at Leningrad State University, who founded the company InterLink in 1991, and became one of the city's leading businessmen and, in due course, political figures. See further below.
188. Volkov, *Violent Entrepreneurs*, profiles the typical 1990s bandit businessman as someone with a practical bent, and often an interest in athletics.
189. Oxf/AHRC UK-08 PF80 AB.
190. G. Zelenin, 'Ni shagu bez vzyatki' (interview with Boris Khvoles), *VL* 21 June 1991, p. 2.
191. As in the case discussed by Nielsen.
192. Oxf/AHRC SPb-07 PF 20 IN (man builder b. 1960).
193. Among the many people who have voiced this view to me was a successful Petersburg businesswoman in her late 40s (running a catering company employing around 700 people) who complained that her time for her family was very limited, and contrasted this with the big family celebrations of the past. FN, March 2012.
194. On non-working wives, see e.g. Oxf/AHRC SPb-10 PF3 MS, Oxf/AHRC SPb-11 PF23 MS.
195. TsGAIPD, f. 24, op. 191, d. 16, l. 35 – in the context of a passport returned by a person's husband in the course of a flat exchange.
196. This is well argued by Stites, 'Crowded on the Edge of Vastness', pp. 262–9.
197. See e.g. Oxf/AHRC SPb-07 PF7 SA: a woman b. 1961 described how she first of all enjoyed working for a publisher's that involved lots of travelling and social events, and then started to find it a drain.

198. For an example of the last, see Oxf/AHRC SPb-11 PF19 MS. See also the comments by Jennifer Patico (216–17) about how her teacher informants were starting to move out of the profession, which they had previously seen as 'safe', by the 2000s.
199. Cf., on the first count, a reminiscence of being passed over for head of section, and not paid enough, at a medical insurance company (man b. 1979, doctor): Oxf/AHRC SPb-07 PF28 IN; on the second – relocation without warning – see Oxf/AHRC SPb-07 PF17 SA (woman b. 1980).
200. Both these two comments are based on observations by Western businessmen with experience of working in St Petersburg.
201. See 'Studentam ne platyat za rabotu!', *NV* 13 April 2010, p. 8. Interestingly, complaints on shopping websites also include allegations that payment has not been forthcoming: see e.g. the May 2012 materials on www.spr.ru/otzyvy/velikolukskiy-myasokombinat-1003065.html.
202. I have repeatedly been warned by St Petersburgers that 'any agreement should be in writing' (which comes as no surprise when, for instance, building work is involved, but more so when one is organising a meal for a conference, say). This type of binary paper-exchange has replaced the one-sided provision of a *spravka*, or 'chit', which governed business relations in the Soviet period.
203. As indicated by Shmulyar's cohort of young managers.
204. See the report in *Metro*, 10 April 2013, p. 8. This came shortly after government measures aiming to tie people more tightly to their dwelling-places, an indication of the contradictory policies of economic liberalisation and political dirigisme that typified the Putin years.
205. See, for instance, Oxf/AHRC SPb-07 PF43 IN, where a woman born in the mid-1980s recalls that she was the first child in her generation to enjoy Kindersurprise chocolates because her aunt, an artist, used to earn good money selling Russian dolls at the informal art markets.
206. Compare the diagnosis of 'waiting around' as characteristic of post-Soviet reality generally in Lars Højer and Morten Axel Pedersen, *Urban Hunters: Dealing and Dreaming in Times of Transition* (New Haven, 2013).
207. Aleksandr Yankevich, 'Perekovka cheloveka v torgovogo agenta', *Smena* 5 February 1999, p. 1. As Yankevich pointed out, such advertisements violated the law, which stipulated that pay and conditions must be clearly specified, but similar small ads could be seen in metro carriages and on walls in the 2000s and 2010s.
208. On 12 May 2012, there were nearly 3000 positions going under 'Sales', and over 1500 in the category 'First jobs and jobs for students', as against 1705 in manufacturing, and 1319 in construction (www.jobs.ru, St Petersburg page).
209. One reason behind high turnover was that many or most students now needed to work alongside studying: see e.g. Oxf/AHRC SPb-11 PF2 EI.
210. See Pachenkov, Solov'eva, and Kudryavtseva. Judging by a later visit (FN September 2012), this assessment still holds.
211. For micro-studies of those professions, see Patico (teaching) and Rivkin-Fish (medicine).
212. Pers. inf., 2011.
213. This depends partly on the definition of 'punctual', of course, but my own experience suggests that fifteen minutes after the official start of work is, in Petersburg workplaces, simply not interpreted as 'late', i.e. that there is a wider margin of tolerance.
214. I have found myself that paying people a generous flat salary for some particular job is less effective than a lower flat rate, accompanied by incentive payments for specific services or activities.
215. Valentina Matvienko was elected governor in 2003; after resigning her post in 2006, she was then appointed by President Putin to serve a second term, thus enacting the transition from elected leader to presidential appointee. Even colleagues of Sobchak's who were also committed to reform found the mayor egotistical and reluctant to consult. See Oxf/AHRC SPb-11 PF29 MS (interview with Aleksandr Belyaev, Chairman of Lensovet in the transitional period).
216. See the biographies in *Kto est' kto v Sankt-Peterburge*.
217. See his official biography on http://gov.spb.ru/gov/admin/molchanov, and also the supplementary information on http://news.yandex.ru/people/tjul1panov_vadim.html.
218. The reluctance to make decisions that might be disapproved higher up the line is quite common in private companies as well, as is remarked by Western businessmen working in the city (pers. inf.). But it is only in departments of the city bureaucracy that the Soviet-era model of the workplace as primarily somewhere for social contact and where profitable time is reduced to the minimum is more or less exactly replicated.
219. Dina Kachalova, 'Poteryannoe utro', *MR* 6 February 2004, p. 6. Cf. *MR(V)* 23 September 2005, p. 5 (a reader's letter on OVIR).

220. '"Mama, eto nasha ochered'!"', *MR(V)* 22 July 2005, p. 3, reported that a mother and son who were selling places in the land registry (FRS) queue were making 10,000–50,000 roubles a day, at 2500 roubles per person. At this period, the offices of notaries (e.g., the vast practice on ul. Vosstaniya) were also offering to obtain registration, at a significantly lower cost (pers. obs.). In the circumstances, the introduction of 'unitary document centres' (*edinye tsentry dokumentov*), where Petersburgers could pay a fee in order to have their applications processed efficiently by the municipal authorities, was a rational and welcome step, at least among those who could afford the costs (around 30 dollars for a medical certificate to get a driving licence or permit to sail a small boat, for instance), though even they were subject to queues at peak times (such as passport renewals before the summer holidays).
221. Oxf/AHRC SPb-07 PF30 IN (woman b. 1956).
222. 'Kak Matvienko v polikliniku zvonila', 1 March 2011, www.fontanka.ru/2011/03/01/046/.
223. As in the comments from US Embassy staff that emerged into the public eye through the Wikileaks scandals: see the coverage in the *Guardian*, 1 December 2010.
224. '"Vzyatki davali i davat' budem!"', *MR(V)* 22 July 2005, p. 9. Between 2001 and 2005, the call-up average had risen by over 400 per cent.
225. As observed in June 2010.
226. FN Jan. 2012.
227. This came out very strongly in our interviews with migrant workers: see e.g. Oxf/AHRC SPb-08 PF56 IN; Oxf/AHRC SPb-08 PF42 IN; Oxf/AHRC SPb-08 PF5 EG.
228. See e.g. Oxf/AHRC-SPb-07 PF 1 AK, where the informant laments the necessity of taking officials 'a token of your esteem' (*pochest'*).
229. The sums expended on bribery in connection with military service rose between 2001 and 2005 by over 400 per cent, which partly, no doubt, reflects the rising sums demanded, but certainly also the larger numbers of such bribes on offer ('"Vzyatki davali i davat' budem!"', p. 9).
230. Certainly, our informants mainly attributed such practices to others: see e.g. Oxf/AHRC SPb-11 PF13, where the informant reports rumours that admissions to her university were on the basis of bribes, but also denies that is how she herself got in. See also the highly critical article about how Mariya Kumarina-Barsukova, whose father, Vladimir, leader of the 'Tambov gang' sent down for fourteen years in 2009, enjoyed the full support of a leading figure at St Petersburg State University, where she was a paying student in the Faculty of Law. As the article delicately put it, this person 'has the reputation of someone who one can always make a deal with' ('Praskov'ya Pshenichnaya', 'Glamurnaya doch' Vladimira Kumarina-Barsukova ne otvechaet za otsa', http://versia-na-neve.livejournal.com/107201.html).
231. See e.g. Ledeneva, *Russia's Economy of Favours* and her *How Russia Really Works*.
232. The persistence of the bonus as simultaneously a reward and an entitlement would appear from the outside to be a factor in the institutionalisation of 'self-interested giving', but within Russian work culture, a bonus is definitely not the same thing as a 'bribe' (just as cards and presents to colleagues are not 'bribes', but tokens of esteem).
233. For a good discussion of the subtleties of gift-giving, see Patico. A particularly interesting observation is that several of her informants who came from a small-town background saw gift-giving to doctors etc. as an oddity – something characteristic of big-city anonymity (p. 191).
234. Pers. inf. from a professional building contractor, 2006.
235. I was told about this dodge with reference to another city in northwestern Russia, but the people discussing it saw it as a universal practice (FN September 2012).
236. Artemy Aleksandrov, 'Vzyatki chinovniku otrazhayutsya na karmane pokupatelya', *MR(V)*, 2 September 2005, p. 5.
237. The technique, as described to me by a victim of the scam, was for someone in a large expensive car (e.g. a bullet-proofed BMW SUV) to cause a low-level collision, then blame the person they had run into and start demanding large sums for repairs. The role of the police was to instruct the driver to move the car (so that the insurance marshals could not be called, ruling out a claim) and to support the aggressors' view of the incident.
238. www.zakon.gov.spb.ru/hot_line.
239. I heard of a case where such a list was produced by a government inspector in 2005; those dealing with the person concerned were indignant, but still provided the goods, special 'Thirty-Three Cows' brand milk, bottles of Johnny Walker Black Label whisky, etc.
240. E.g. FN September 2008. Five years later, my work in the Academy of Sciences Library was pleasantly disrupted by the sounds of an Old New Year celebration in the staff cubby-hole of the room where I was working, with present-swapping and degustation of baking. A couple of hours later, the ordinary tea-break disturbed the temporary silence (FN January 2013).

241. FN April 2013.
242. Exceptions have come when riding public transport, for instance where I paid an official 'to buy the ticket for me' when changing boats, rather than risk missing onward transport by taking a trip to the ticket office 200 metres away (FN September 2011), or changed my mind about where I wanted to get off a train (FN September 2012), and paid a small 'fine' to the guard for overriding.
243. There is no space here to discuss the interesting issue of how 'self-interested giving' is nuanced according to social characteristics, such as gender. I have the sense that men are more likely than women to be expected to 'come up with the goods' (as with gratuities in British culture). For instance, my husband, on his first ever visit to Russia in 1988, and speaking almost no Russian, was asked by the receptionist in the Moscow hotel where we were staying to purchase a scarf from the Beriozka hard currency shop across the lobby – this in return for releasing our passports, which we needed to visit friends in the British Embassy. A seasoned traveller in the Middle East since student days, he found this request perfectly normal and was surprised by my outraged reaction when I found out what had happened.
244. One element of municipal leverage was in the low level of land that had been privatised, allowing local administrations discretion in the assignation of tenure and in the calculation of cadastral value. See Pyle, 'The Ownership of Industrial Land in Russian Cities'.
245. Oxf/AHRC-SPb-07 PF43 IN (woman b. 1984).
246. Oxf/AHRC SPb-07 PF39 IN (man b. 1980).
247. Ibid. I have altered 'district committee' (of the Communist Party), an obvious slip of the tongue, to 'district soviet': complaining to a local Party cell about the behaviour of higher Party authority would have been pointless.
248. See www.rosyama.ru. The comparable site www.rospil.info offers the opportunity to moan about administrative abuses.
249. Compare the astute observation of Kate Fox in *Watching the English* that the constant cry of 'typical!' both criticises and accepts inefficient and irrational practices.
250. I have quite often come across such researchers directly, or noted their entries in the user ledgers of St Petersburg's archives (e.g. FN October 2011).
251. *Peterburg – istoriya torgovli*; Baryshnikova.
252. A notable victim of this strategy was the Institute of History of Arts, in St Isaac's Square, which fought off an attempt by Moscow-based businessmen to take over the building in the early 2000s. See also Chapter 3.
253. Observed on many occasions as I walked past. In 2010, however, another operator took over, and personal clutter was minimised.
254. www.rosbalt.ru/poll/436/results/. There were 62 per cent in favour of the siesta, 18 per cent in favour of the feria, 14 per cent in favour of tapas, 2 per cent in favour of the corrida. That said, a businessman with experience of working in both capitals denied that there was a significant difference in work culture – but he came from a provincial town, so from a group that is motivated to succeed whatever the environment (FN September 2012).

## 5 Eliseev and Aprashka

1. Joseph Brodsky, 'Samson, domashnii kot', *Stikhotvoreniya i poemy*, 2, p. 302.
2. See e.g. 'Kakim byt' Nevskomu prospektu?', *LP* 5 December 1965, p. 2. Here, the suggestion of no shops at all came from a reader, but the official plans included reducing the number of shops and increasing the number of cultural institutions on the street. This idea was raised again by D. S. Likhachev in the late 1980s: see e.g. 'Otvetstvennaya zadacha Leningradtsev', *LPan* 7 (1988), p. 3.
3. Katerli, 'Sennaya ploshchad'', Ch. 1, p. 5. The story was first published abroad, in *Glagol* no. 3 (1981).
4. The first Leningrad supermarkets were opened in 1954, and there were ninety by the autumn of 1956 (Lebina and Chistikov, p. 231). Stores were still being opened in the late 1960s: see e.g. 'Krupneishii v strane', *LP* 22 January 1967, p. 2, on one on ul. Marshala Govorova. But in the following decade, development went into reverse: by 1980, there were only thirty, exclusively in outlying areas of the city, such as Kupchino (*Gorodskaya vlast'*, p. 423). Problems with packaging goods (see Lebina, Chistikov, 231) as well as anxieties about monitoring purchase levels seem to have been at the root of this. Levels of theft (known tactfully as 'disappearance') were, perhaps surprisingly, not significantly higher in self-service stores – or at any rate, those selling clothing etc. (see the Gosplan document of 1969, 'O normakh poter' dlya promtovarnykh magazinov samoobsluzhivaniya', TsGAIPD 25/102/ 31/28–9).

5. Sergei Dovlatov, 'Eto neperevodimoe slovo "khamstvo"', *SS*, vol. 4, www.sergeidovlatov.com/books/etoneper.html. In the original, the 'wheedling tone' is conveyed by using all possible and impossible words in the diminutive form. For a complaint about a shop assistant who was keeping sausages under the counter, see TsGAIPD-SPb. 24/165/62/4.
6. I. Ivanova, 'Vdol' po ulitse Schastlivoi . . .', *VL* 5 January 1990, p. 2.
7. Oxf/AHRC SPb-08 PF46 ANK.
8. Oxf/AHRC-SPb-07 PF 5 IN (woman b. 1969). She recalled this of the Gorbachev era, but exotic fruits, such as mandarins and bananas, were the subject of long queues in the late 1970s and early 1980s too (pers. obs.).
9. On the social uses of the queue, see Bogdanov, 'The Queue as Narrative'.
10. This is based on personal memories. There seem to have been some exceptions: for instance, one of our informants recalled that on Krestovsky Island life was green, quiet, and pleasant, and the shops civilised: 'You go out of doors and it's quiet everywhere, culture. You visit a shop, everything's laid out neatly, it's all nice and clean, all of it, and you turn up, you come in, you take what you like.' But he also remembered that the place stood out against the 'noise and grime' of the centre. Oxf/AHRC-SPb-07 PF 17 IN, man b. 1929, working-class background. Of course, all this was 'naturalised' for a lot of people too, so that they were resigned to shops like this, but transfixed by better ones. For instance, a woman born in 1938 recalled of living in Cuba in the 1960s: 'The shops – I'd never even imagined shops could be like that, you know? At first, we used just to go on trips to those diplomatic stores where we had the right to acquire things, for the sheer pleasure of it' (Oxf/AHRC-SPb-07 PF 21 IN).
11. Anon., 'Letnyaya torgovlya', *LP* 26 April 1976, p. 2. The article also reported that trade school students were being asked to help out during a shortage of regular workers. Cf. 'Pochemu v magazinakh ne khvataet moloka?' (*LP* 24 June 1966, p. 2), explaining milk shortages by insufficiency of glassware and milk under-production. Cafés had been using condensed milk. 'Posle prazdnikov', *LP* 15 May 1969, p. 3, gives an idea of the holiday situation. As the article tactfully put it, 'The holidays were slightly put in shadow by hiccups in the supply' (caused by a run on milk, problems in the delivery system, the late arrival of early cabbage, generating unexpected demand for sauerkraut, and so on). Readers were promised that things should be sorted out in a few days. Among 'worker questions' in 1975 were worries about why it was impossible to buy caviar, fish, and onions (TsGAIPD-SPb. 24/159/2/53).
12. For example, a report from the Gorkom to Aleksei Kosygin, then Chairman of the Council of Ministers of the USSR, filed on 6 March 1969 reported that there was a 7000-tonne shortfall in the meat needed to make sausage in Leningrad at that point: TsGAIPD-SPb. 25/102/31/2.
13. For instance, in 1976, *LP* assured its readers that Leningrad was not in fact going to be assigned to a lower category of food supply: 'Letnyaya torgovlya', *LP* 26 April 1976, p. 2.
14. Mikhail Mittseev, who arrived in Leningrad as one of a group of twelve students from Sverdlovsk in February 1952, recalled ('Moya pervaya vstrecha') that he and the others would visit the shops on Nevsky simply to gaze at their contents – the Eliseev Stores in particular. 'The abundance that we witnessed seemed like a fairy-tale compared with hungry Sverdlovsk'. Three decades later, in Voronezh, where I spent a year as a student in 1980–1, there was meat and full-fat butter on sale only at the collective farm market; milk and sour cream frequently disappeared from state shops over the winter. See also *Peterburg: istoriya torgovli*, 2, p. 134: 'As a centre of the defence industry, ship-building above all, Leningrad enjoyed superior norms of supply, which is why average levels of meat consumption reached over 100 kg a year at their peak'. This statement is based on the annual *Narodnoe khozyaistvo*, so one has to be wary of taking it too much on trust (published tables of consumption were a way of advertising the regime's success in providing Soviet workers with what they needed), but oral history also acknowledges the relatively good conditions in the city (see below). The relatively high levels of supply in Leningrad are confirmed in personal reminiscences as well: see e.g. 'Mestnyi mudrets', 28 January 2010, http://bolshoyforum.org/forum/index.php?topic=52625.2100 (in Togliatti, on the other hand, everything except milk and bread was on ration cards by 1981, ibid.).
15. My thanks to Kirill Maslinsky for this information.
16. A salad of chopped cabbage and other ingredients (e.g. carrots, or sometimes apples and/or berries) with a sweetened oil and vinegar dressing, left to stand.
17. Oxf/AHRC SPb-07 PF13, 14 SA.
18. FN, June 2012.
19. Oxf/AHRC PF13 IN (woman b. 1935, working-class background).
20. My thanks to Ekaterina Golynkina for the identification. On the joke and for a description of the shop, see also Ekaterina Glikman, 'Dovlatov – v dosku' (20 September 2007), www.novayagazeta.ru/society/34012.html.

21. As remembered by a woman born in the early 1960s (FN, April 2011). Cf. http://clubs.ya.ru/4611686018427408897/replies.xml?item_no=2253 (post of 11 February 2011).
22. Metter, *Izbrannoe*, p. 57.
23. Oxf/Lev SPb-02 PF 9.
24. Oxf/AHRC SPb-07 PF8 SA. On the other hand, shortages of ordinary foodstuffs were known in the 1950s. See e.g. F. A. Belinskaya's letter to her husband, 6 December 1954: 'Lena suggested going out to Peterhof or Sestoretsk for butter [. . .] someone had said there were no queues. So we went to Peterhof. We left at noon and didn't get back till six. No butter in sight, of course, and they looked at us as though we were crazy when we asked about it' (6 December 1954, Belinsky, p. 205).
25. Interview with man b. 1957, Oxf/AHRC-SPb-07. PF10-ANK. Cf. the comments of Anna Kushkova in 'Surviving in the Time of Deficit'.
26. Oxf/AHRC-SPb-08-PF48-ANK (woman b. 1930).
27. A point made in *Peterburg – istoriya torgovli*: see e.g. 2, p. 67 on beers, 2, p. 139 on milk products. By far the largest section of the book (2, 191–245) is on *konditerskie*. An interesting exception to the generally locality-free marketing was cigarettes: local Leningrad brands included 'Oktyabr' and 'Peter I'. See Vadim Sharapov, 'Chto my kurili', http://society.presscom.org/other/20743.html (last accessed 29 October 2010). At the same time, no Leningrad cigarettes had the appeal to demanding consumers of Western or even Bulgarian ones.
28. 'Mestnyi mudrets' on forum 'Kakim v deistvitel'nosti byl SSSR?', recalled that schoolchildren ate jelly dragees on ordinary days, but 'dreamed' of more luxurious sweets such as 'Queen of Spades' and 'Leningrad': http://bolshoyforum.org/forum/index.php?topic=52625.2100, 28 January 2010. On Fabrika Krupskoi, see www.meronq.com/threads/4439 (comment from St Petersburg, 11 August 2009); on the Café Sever (Nord), see Chapter 7.
29. A. I. Kucher, 'Teplo gostepriimnogo "Severa"', *LPan* 4 (1986), pp. 21–2; idem, 'Vostochnye sladosti po-leningradski', *LPan* 3 (1987), pp. 15–16.
30. Kushkova, 'Surviving'.
31. Oxf/AHRC SPb-08 PF28 ANK; Oxf/AHRC SPb-08 PF17.
32. FN April 2013.
33. Kushkova, 'Surviving'.
34. On mustard shortages, see Oxf/AHRC SPb-08 PF28 ANK, and cf. Logan Robinson, p. 137. On the shortages generally, see Derviz, pp. 37–40.
35. See Kelly, 'Roskosh' ili neobkhodimost''.
36. On *vybrasyvat'/vykidyvat'*, see Oxf/AHRC SPb-08 PF46 ANK (woman b. 1969). These terms were generic-Soviet, rather than Leningrad-specific, and derive from the vocabulary of rationing.
37. TsGAIPD-SPb. 24/165/62/1-8.
38. Oxf/AHRC SPb-08 PF31 ANK (woman b. 1933, from intelligentsia background, worker in scientific institute).
39. See Oxf/AHRC SPb-07-08 PF1-50 ANK. Guava puree is mentioned in Oxf/AHRC SPb-07 PF11 ANK, referring to the 1980s.
40. Oxf/AHRC SPb-08 PF31 ANK. In this particular case, the recipient of the gift chose to return it, but not everyone would have been so self-denying.
41. On raffles etc. see e.g. Oxf/AHRC SPb-07 PF8 ANK.
42. Cf. the condemnation of price-hiking during a food shortage, 'Letnyaya torgovlya', *LP* 26 April 1976, p. 2. This also promised that price controls on green vegetables would be imposed, though in practice, these would certainly have been unenforceable.
43. 'Kto kogo', *Rezets* 29 (1924), p. 3–4.
44. On Raikin, see Oxf/AHRC SPb-07 PF1 ANK. I recall such stories myself, and accounts are also found in our project interviews: see e.g. Oxf/AHRC SPb-07 PF10 ANK; Oxf/AHRC SPb-07 PF11 ANK. In fact, food, 'leaked' (*kapalo*) at many different levels before it reached shops as well: anyone who headed a workshop (*tsekh*) in a factory would have ample opportunity to siphon off the goods that were produced there, and the raw materials that were used in the production process (see SPb-07 PF10 ANK, and also Chapter 4).
45. SPb-07 PF10 ANK.
46. A good discussion of these is Ledeneva, *Russia's Economy of Favours*.
47. Przhepyurko, 'Leningradskie prikoly'. As Przhepyurko remembered, he himself visited Gostinyi dvor and purchased items such as a big enamel tub for washing nappies etc., a folding Czech high chair, large quantities of baby clothes, and mohair knitting wool so that his wife could make herself a hat, as well as a 'Leningrad' light metre for photography, 'which was really hard to get back then'. On arriving in Dnepropetrovsk, a Leningrader in his compartment helped unload all the stuff, and

Przhepyurko then helped *him* with work contacts in Dnepropetrovsk – a nice thumbnail sketch of informal relations.

48. On the use of guards, see e.g. Oxf/Lev SPb-03 PF28B (man b. 1972): 'we always used to meet the parcel'. An overnight train was quicker than the post, more reliable, and there were also no prohibitions on what could be sent (foodstuffs – along with poisonous snakes, explosives, and ammunition – were subject to restrictions in the postal service, as notices displayed in the 1980s used to advertise).
49. Oxf/AHRC PF8A IN, p. 11. *Chebureki* are fried dough parcels with chopped meat inside (see Chapter 7).
50. Krivulin, *Okhota*, p. 6. The *semerka*, made between 1971 and 2012, was a four-door family Lada, the most popular car ever built under Soviet power: http://topgearworld.ucoz.ru/news/poslednjaja_semerka/2012-06-16-6.
51. *St Petersburg Painted*, pp. 99–100.
52. On beards and 'trousers outrageous to society', see Boris Ivanov, 'Po tu storonu ofitsial'nosti', *Sochineniya* 2, p. 426; on missing one's own wedding, Shtern, *Leaving Leningrad*, pp. 79–80. Yurchak convincingly argues that such principled self-distancing from official norms was not universal; however, it was a notable feature of Leningrad dissident and quasi-dissident circles, as I can attest from personal observation. The long list of taboo objects included anything red, but especially red carnations; the Palace of Marriages and other formal occasions; luxurious clothing or household ornaments, etc. Indeed, tastes in these circles were decidedly 'Bolshevik' (as opposed to Stalinist or late Soviet), though direct imitation of this precedent was certainly not the intention. Naïve questions about whether someone owned or did something taboo are greeted by 'Da ty chto?' [What're you on?]
53. One of the best was on the corner of Nevsky and ul. Gertsena (Bol'shaya Morskaya) (see Alekseev), another on Liteinyi prospekt (www.save-spb.ru/page/announce/znakoe_mesto.html).
54. 'Proshlo 20 let: Leningradskie "svyatyni" ', *MR (Ostrova)* 9 September 2011, pp. 6–7.
55. I remember being told about the market in 1981. An attempt by the police to crack down on this had limited success; when the police arrived with Alsatians, the dealers scurried into some concrete pipes piled up for laying, and it died down for a while before reviving.
56. On *magnitizdat* see G. Smith, *Songs to Seven Strings*. An indication of the scarcity of popular music was that recordings by the Soviet bards Vysotsky and Okudzhava were available only in the hard-currency *beriozki* (pers. obs.). For a discussion of 'rock on the bones' (invented in Leningrad), see Hufen.
57. I remember noticing this in his flat when I visited in summer 1985. Its presence was rather paradoxical, given that Krivulin spent most of the evening decrying the decadence and materialism of the West.
58. See e.g. I. Zakhoroshko, 'Kak odevat'sya molodomu uchitelyu?', *LP* 12 February 1965, p. 4, which shows formal wear such as a blouse and pinafore, or a suit.
59. Oxf/AHRC SPb-07 PF13, 14 SA, woman b. 1950.
60. On Soviet underwear, see Gurova.
61. Arkady and Boris Strugatsky, *Ponedel'nik nachinaetsya v subbotu* (1965), http://lib.ru/STRUGACKIE/ponedelx.txt. My thanks to Muireann Maguire for suggesting this source.
62. See 'Dzhazmen provel v muzee master-klass "Leningradskie stilyagi" ', Gazeta.ru, 12 February 2009, www.gazeta.spb.ru/123322-0/. On the movement generally, see Fürst.
63. Oxf/AHRC PF13 SA, woman b. 1950. See also the picture-story, 'Khimiya v odezhde', *Kirovets* 24 April 1964, p. 2, about a fashion-show involving all-synthetic clothes.
64. http://community.livejournal.com/ru_politics/21403817.html (last accessed 22 October 2010).
65. *Sumerki Saigona*, p. 386.
66. See e.g. Lev Lur'e, 'Kak Nevskii prospekt', p. 213. Yurchak (196–7) has aptly described jeans as 'a signifier of the imaginary West' as well as a garment.
67. I recall that the guide working for Sputnik, the Komsomol travel agency that organised my own first-ever trip to Leningrad in 1979, was never out of jeans the entire month of the visit.
68. Mikhail Veller, 'Koshelek', first published in *Khochu byt' dvornikom* (1983): see http://lib.ru/WELLER/purse.txt.
69. 'Dlya vas, molodye', *Smena* 17 July 1970, p. 3. There were also pictures of a lumpy suit for a man.
70. Igor' Bogdanov, *Leningradskii leksikon*, p. 251.
71. On the *bolon'ka*, see ibid. On the other items, see fig. 5.4. These comments also come from personal observation. Platform boots, for instance, arrived later than in Western Europe and the fashion lasted correspondingly longer.
72. As I remember being asked about my own petrol-blue character shoes in the 1980s. A get-up of an old royal blue Viyella dressing gown of my father's (knee-length), which I wore alternately with red

leather ankle boots and with ditto in white canvas, and a large Naf-Naf canvas beach bag with brightly-coloured post-Matisse flowers, attracted disapproval for other reasons – it made it far, far too obvious that I was a foreigner. Interestingly, in the 1950s such clothes had been more familiar to the Leningrad bohemia: see Gorbovsky, *Ostyvshie sledy*, p. 239, which describes how he and Viktor Buzinov processed down Bol'shoi prospekt, Vasilievsky Island, dressed in women's hats, with aces of diamonds (traditionally sewn on prison gear) appliquéd on their jackets, and 'large patches on our trousers –meant to provoke, because in those post-war years, long before hippies and jeans, people were terribly embarrassed by such things.' For a mother's outraged recollection of how her son came back home in the 1970s wearing 'jeans off someone's grimy arse', see Oxf/AHRC SPb-07 PF25 IN (woman b. 1941).

73. Begun in 1908 under the direction of E. F. Virrikh (but using ideas from other architects who had taken part in the competition to select a project for the store), the building was not in fact completed until after the Revolution. See e.g. Kirikov, *Arkhitektura Peterburgskogo moderna*.
74. The architects were by E. I. and L. S. Katonin, E. M. Sokolov, and K. L. Ioganson. There is a large literature on the prospekt: see e.g. Busyreva, *Lev Il'in*; Yu. I. Kurbatov, *Petrograd. Leningrad. Sankt-Peterburg*.
75. Vadim Lur'e, *Mikrotoponimika*, includes 3 shops under the name *steklyashka*, as well as 5 cafés. The term *steklyashka* is used generically in Oxf/AHRC SPb-09 PF-54 IN.
76. Here there is a major difference from the consumer culture of other socialist countries, such as Czechoslovakia, on which see Bren.
77. See e.g. Oxf/AHRC SPb-08 PF46 AK (woman b. 1969, recalling the 1980s): 'on the top gallery of the first floor there were always these queues – it was this gallery, the first floor, yes, where they . . . always used to sell [*vybrasyvat*] all kinds of deficit goods.' In retrospect, Gostinyi dvor is sometimes remembered with affection: cf. Oxf/AHRC SPb-07 PF5 SA: 'We loved that shop, it was such fun having a look round, I'm walking on, and on, and then suddenly a door opens and there are boots inside. Just like that: bang, and I'm: Oh! And I end up second in line.'
78. See the interview with a woman b. 1935, Oxf/AHRC PF13A IN.
79. Oxf/AHRC PF13A IN. For a considerably more detailed and thorough account of shopping practices in Leningrad, with reference to a survey of 500 families, see Zakharova, *S'habiller*.
80. Oxf/AHRC SPb-07 PF4 SA.
81. See e.g. Oxf/AHRC SPb-08 PF46 ANK.
82. Thubron (p. 91) reports being told by a member of a Leningrad dissident circle that there were 'more than twenty-six rouble millionaires whose wealth derived from underground business'.
83. Veller, 'Legenda o rodonachal'nike fartsovki Fime Bleishitse', *Legendy o Nevskom prospekte*, pp. 8–48.
84. Corsini, p. 21.
85. As I remember myself.
86. TsGAIPD-SPb. K-881/20/59/1-30. Incomplete figures for 1978 (see TsGAIPD-SPb. K-881/21/27, 28, passim) stood at 3410 cases of 'pestering foreigners' and 7200 of unauthorised street trading.
87. See Oxf/AHRC SPb-07 PF5 SA, remembering a visit to one of these: 'It was interesting: she had her entire room crammed with all sorts of junk, just pick out what you'd like. [*Laughs*]. And the prices were kind of crazy of course, but we did buy stuff there, people would sell stuff on. I didn't buy things on the street myself, but you could do it, no trouble. It was by Gostinka [Gostinnyi dvor], that gallery there – Perinnaya liniya [Feather Row], they would all be standing there, and you could buy from them.'
88. For disapproving comments about *fartsovshchiki* see e.g. AHRC SPb-08 PF18 SA (man b. 1967), and cf. Yurchak, pp. 202–3. A comparable case of 'commodity laundering' would be drug supply in the West at this era – many people who used cannabis at parties would have been horrified by the thought of buying from a dealer.
89. Unfortunately, it turned out the zip was faulty, requiring emergency surgery when the couple celebrated his demob by enjoying a little too much beer and then a drunken grope (http://hepd.pnpi.spb.ru/hepd/red/golovtsov_page/proza/Leningrad.htm, accessed 7 December 2008).
90. See Gorsuch, *All This is Your World*.
91. Oxf/AHRC SPb-07 PF10 SA. A more satisfactory relation was the husband who brought his wife back an entire roll of Crimplene from Germany in 1978: see the post by xaxachu, 12 January 2009, http://community.livejournal.com/costume_history/317534.html?thread=2399070.
92. Oxf/AHRC SPb-11 PF28 MS. The shop also served workers in the docks and shipping offices (ibid.).
93. On certificate roubles, see Oxf/AHRC SPb-07 PF6 (woman b. 1961, father physicist): her dress for her school-leavers' ball ('cornflower blue, with spots [. . .] a beautiful dress') was made from material bought in a certificate rouble shop. I remember myself being taken to the *beryozka* and instructed to purchase goods – mainly cigarettes, whisky, and scarce books.

94. As recollected by Yury Luchinsky (b. 1952), 18 June 2011, http://retro-piter.livejournal.com/350609.html (last accessed 8 August 2011).
95. 'Russkii sapozhok', *Smena* 17 November 1965. On the Pepsi franchise, see Sonne, 'Cold War Consumption'. There is an informative article on Soyuz Apollon (made in the USSR in the American style and generally available only on the black market) on the Russian Wikipedia.
96. Man in his 60s, FN, March 2008. 'Cough mixture' translates *apteka*, a generic term for anything from the pharmacy. That said, Soyuz Apollon did not go down a bomb either: in the words of a friend (email 4 October 2012), 'I remember very vividly the Soyuz Apollon and anticipation of having the real American stuff and disappointment when it turned out to be quite disgusting.'
97. Oxf/AHRC-SPb-07 PF 9 IN.
98. Oxf/AHRC SPb-07 PF13 SA. Cf. Oxf/AHRC SPb-07 PF17 IN (on Czechoslovak shoes).
99. On buying an East German jacket in the *komissionnaya*, woman b. late 1950s.
100. On the shampoo, see Oxf/AHRC SPb-07 PF13 SA; on the toothpaste, Logan Robinson, pp. 122–4. The salesgirl was keeping this under the counter for favoured customers, but the cashier assumed a foreigner would want the 'better' stuff, so Robinson ended up with the Bulgarian by mistake. He was mystified by its popularity, since he found it quite awful, but friends explained that scarcity made it seem desirable – a classic example of 'deficit mentality'. The lead department stores and 'brand shops' (*firmennye magaziny*), of which there were quite a number (see *Spisok abonentov LTS* 1988), used to be the main outlets for stuff of this kind.
101. For example, Oxf/AHRC SPb-07 PF33 IN, on how the informant's grandmother would only tolerate one brand of hand-cream, *Balet* [Ballet], which was manufactured (or so she believed) in Leningrad.
102. Pokshishevskaya argues that this style – characterised by restrained elegance and a witty use of visual puns – developed in the 1960s.
103. For newspaper coverage of fashions, see e.g. 'Mody edut v Leiptsig', *LP* 20 July 1969, p. 4. For the rumours, see e.g. Igor' Bogdanov, *Leningradskii leksikon*, p. 154.
104. For a good scholarly discussion of Leningrad fashion, see Zakharova, 'Fabriquer'. There is a lively popular discussion in Igor' Bogdanov, *Leningradskii leksikon*, pp. 176–82.
105. Gardimer, 'Kartinki' (she also mentions an *atel'e* for men in Apraksin dvor). The tenor Gerard Vasiliev always used to order his tail coats from Leningradsky dom modelei: see http://she-kitt.narod.ru/gerard.html. Another extremely prestigious *atel'e* was the venue selling underwear and nightwear made of knitted silk at 12 Nevsky prospekt, popularly known as 'Death to Husbands' (because of its elegance and cost). See Lebina and Chistikov, p. 222. On actresses as models of fashion for the Soviet population at large, see Zakharova, 'Dior in Moscow'.
106. Cf. the recollections of Anna Ostroumova-Lebedeva's great-niece Anna Grigor'eva, p. 142: 'She took great care of her appearance and dress, and was extremely offended with Sinitsyn, the photographer, when he made her look like an ordinary babushka in a portrait he did of her. [. . .] Unfortunately, the directors of a 1980 film for TV missed this point about Anna Petrovna; they obviously had today's grannies in mind. The film was a travesty. They showed her in a headscarf, though Anna Petrovna never wore such things; even during the Blockade, she always wore a beret.' Fallowell recollects meeting a lady who typified 'the aristocrat circa 1930' with her 'dove-grey cloaklike coat' and scarf fastened at the neck with a brooch.
107. Derviz, *Ryadom s bol'shoi istoriei*, p. 59.
108. The characters concerned were from a working-class family, which legitimated an episode that might otherwise have been understood as championing 'petit-bourgeois' values. Instead, it signified 'how well the proletariat live now!'
109. FN April 2011. For one of our informants, it was hats with veils that were more characteristic: Oxf/AHRC SPb-11 PF17 EI.
110. Passport interview, Oxf/AHRC SPb-07 PF5 DT.
111. Oxf/AHRC SPb-07 PF13 SA.
112. Boris Vakhtin, 'Dublenka', in *Portret neznakomtsa*, PAGES.
113. http://lib.ru/WELLER/purse.txt, last accessed 18 October 2010.
114. Following Karl Marx, whose picture turned up on a newspaper at the bottom of Dovlatov's suitcase, this was a demonstration of the 'theory of surplus value' in action. A readership that had been made to study dialectical materialism did not need the point laboured.
115. 'Sokhranit' velikii gorod. "Kruglyi stol" zhurnala Leningradskoi panoramy', *LPan* 9 (1988), p. 6.
116. See e.g. S. Sobolev, 'Biznes pod nadezhnoi kryshei (Komsomol i perestroika)', *LPan* 1 (1990), pp. 9–11.

117. As I recall myself from visits in 1988–90. Before the co-operative era, the few shops that were not simply numbered ('Household Goods Shop no. 14' etc.) had standard names with a Soviet patriotic resonance, such as Horizon, Sputnik, Youth, etc.
118. *VL* 10 January 1990, p. 1.
119. Karnaukhov, 'Pokhorony edy'. Caroline Humphrey has pointed out that the term 'rationing' is a confusingly generic description of a set of retail controls that included coupons, cards, orders, and coupon orders (and, one could add, informal controls by shop assistants too). See *The Unmaking of Soviet Life*, pp. 17–18.
120. G. Markonya, 'Nas ne provedesh'!', *Vechernii Leningrad*, 12 January 1990, p. 3.
121. Karnaukhov, 'Pokhorony edy'.
122. FN January 2009.
123. V. Kokosov, 'Est' li mafiya v Leningrade?', *Vechernii Leningrad*, 16 March 1990, p. 2.
124. The sociologist Vadim Volkov has described this as the first phase of 'silovik entrepreneurship': see his *Silovoe predprinimatel'stvo*.
125. 'You'd buy vodka you didn't need, but you had the coupon. Since it was an excellent kind of . . . coinage. For instance, if a plumber turned up . . .' (Oxf/AHRC SPb-08 PF44 ANK).
126. Oxf/AHRC SPb-07 PF17 ANK.
127. A. Shtompel', 'Delo – tabak', *Leningradskaya militsiya* 8 September 1990, p. 2.
128. Irina Dantsig, 'Chei-nibud' uzh blizok chas', *NevV* 16 March 1991, p. 4.
129. Aleksandr Lebedev, 'Turetskie trusiki dlya proletariata', *NV* 23 February 1991, p. 3. At the end of 1990, a drive began at city-wide level to sell scrap metal on the Western market and use the cash to buy food products. See S. Vital'ev, 'Myaso svoz' "zheleznyi zanaves"', *VL* 4 January 1991, p. 1. Success was, however, hampered by the foot-dragging of the Central Committee (worried about the sale of 'strategic materials' abroad). When the deal eventually was agreed, the food products never in fact materialised, because by then market liberalisation was already in train, bringing to an end the system of state supply. On this sequel, see the interview with Aleksandr Belyaev at www.svobodanews.ru/content/article/1990526.html.
130. 'Plokhoi khoroshii Novyi god', *NV* 1 January 1992, p. 1.
131. August 1991 prices: CK, letter home, 18 August 1991; 1992 prices: *NV* 4 January 1992, p. 1.
132. Pers. inf., 1992.
133. Sergei Tachaev, 'Appetit ukhodit pri vide edy', *NevV* 1 May 1992, p. 1.
134. 'Detishkam na odezhonku', *NevV* 11 August 1992, p. 3.
135. Sergei Tachaev, 'Tseny – uzhe "svinskie"', *Nevskoe vremya* 6 January 1995, p. 2.
136. See e.g. http://charity.lfond.spb.ru/miloserdie/; www.spb-hamburg.de/index_rus.php?show=2.
137. For a general discussion, see Igor' Karlinsky, 'Ot miloserdiya do blagotvoritel'nosti – put' dlinoyu v dvenadtsat' let', *Pchela* 16 (1998), www.pchela.ru/podshiv/16/path.htm. For 'dog sausage', see Oxf/AHRC SPb-11 PF18 MS. The problems continued later as well. According to Aleksandra Yankevich, 'Tamozhnya ne daet pokurit', *Smena* 5 March 1999, p. 1, over 50 per cent of humanitarian aid ended up being sold in shops, and customs were understandably resentful when tax-free cigarettes were sold without duty being paid.
138. Oxf/AHRC-SPb-09 PF-58 IN.
139. A. Zhelnina, 'Sennaya ploshchad' – "chrevo" ili litso Peterburga?', www.urban-club.ru/?p=35. See also www.dimo.spb.ru/reference/sennaya-ploschad (a 2005 memoir by a man who spent his childhood living locally). I recall a visit in December 1988, when little seemed to have changed since the 1860s: a dirty and depressed air was pervasive. Cf. descriptions of the place as 'scary' in the past in Oxf/AHRC SPb-11 PF16 MS (woman b. 1949), and as the 'nightmare maw of Petersburg' (Oxf/AHRC SPb-07 PF5 IN, woman b. 1967). For pictures of the market during the war, see http://exponline.livejournal.com/147961.html.
140. One domestic premises survived as late as 2005 (korpus 15). The 5 families there shared 11 rooms, and were quite pleased with their accommodation (400 metres of living space, and a corridor 50 metres long), if not with the proximity of the market, where they refused to shop on principle. 'We're completely sick of it.' Anastasiya Gabrielova, 'Moi adres – ne dom i ne ulitsa', *MR* 18 March 2005, p. 4.
141. See the mayoral decree of 6 August 1991, No. 209, at http://lawru.info/base27/part5/d27ru5120.htm.
142. Alla Borisova, 'Pochem zamok, babulya?', *NevV* 3 October 1992, p. 3. The article also reported that grannies would buy ten-packs of cigarettes and then sell them on individually next to metro stations, a form of secondary trading that remained popular into the 2000s.
143. Sergei Arten'ev, 'Apraksin dvor: "chtoby tovary prodavali pravdivo"', *NevV* 22 July 1995, p. 8.
144. Oxf/AHRC-SPb-07 PF 47 IN.
145. Borisova, 'Pochem zamok'; Arten'ev, 'Apraksin dvor'.

146. 'Neprofil'nye aktivy', 22 June 2010, http://v-s-demin.livejournal.com/474717.html.
147. Cf. the analysis of tensions between the local and global in trading at this period generally in Humphrey, 'Traders, "Disorder", and Citizenship Regimes'.
148. Kalugin, *Rynki Peterburga*, see esp. pp. 69–92. This accords with observations about the situation in other post-Soviet cities as well: on Moscow, for example, see Humphrey, *The Unmaking*, pp. 48–50.
149. Tat'yana Fedorchenko, 'Ne pokupaite vodku s tarakanom!', *NevV* 11 July 1993, p. 7; Nonna Tsai, 'Ne vse parizhskie dukhi iz Parizha', *NevV* 15 July 1992, p. 5; Nelli Efimova, 'Gzhel' – boites' poddelok', *NV* 24 February 1995, p. 2; N. Kolenko, 'Podpol'noi byvaet ne tol'ko vodka, no i moloko', *Smena* 14 March 1998, p. 2. Reporting of this kind persisted into the next decade as well, despite increased penal tariffs imposing up to a two-year gaol sentence: see e.g. '"Pierre Carden" s Maloi Arnautskoi' (unsigned), *MR(V)* 24 June 2005, p. 6. For anxieties about deception as a general phenomenon of Soviet life during transition, see Humphrey, *The Unmaking*, 52–6; on Petersburg, Patico, pp. 117–25.
150. Pers. inf.
151. In July 2007, a young Muscovite woman published her mother's culinary diary of 1991–92 (http://asena.livejournal.com/219536.html). Among the comments was a reminiscence from a Leningrad woman, then a schoolgirl, about how her parents had kept body and soul together by private enterprise: her father, an engineer, and his workmates had produced TV remote control devices using materials available in their factory, while her mother made work gloves at home. This allowed the purchase of tinned ham and Chinese smoked chicken sausages. Later, the family kept chickens and rabbits. Somehow, they managed to buy sugar, and 'the stocks of matches we laid up then have only just run out'.
152. Oxf/AHRC-SPb-07 PF 9 IN.
153. Dmitry Yakimov, 'Sennaya ploshchad' do i posle', www.dimo.spb.ru/reference/sennaya-ploschad.
154. Cf. Asta Vonderau's discussion of how the early 1990s was a time remembered with great enthusiasm by her 'new Latvian' informants.
155. 'Tovar kupit' – ne pole pereiti', *NevV* 10 July 1993, p. 2.
156. Those who lived well above average at this point included academics (local included) on foreign grants, since once again a small figure by Western standards was worth very large sums locally. (Pers. obs.)
157. The 'New Russians' were the butt of jokes throughout the 1990s, mostly harping on the combination of new-found wealth and ignorance. 'A New Russian goes into the shop at the Alexander Nevsky Monastery, whacks down a roll of bills, and asks for a cross. "I wanna gold 'un. A big 'un. The biggest you've got." An enormous pectoral crucifix is carefully extracted from its cabinet and shown to him. "Well, the size is OK. But can you get that gymnast off the front for me?"' 'A New Russian is shown his recently-arrived baby in the hospital. "Three-five", says the nurse. [i.e. three and a half kilos]. He gets out his wallet and hands over three and a half thousand . . .' (told to me by a woman in her sixties in 1996).
158. When living out at Udel'naya in August 1996, I regularly used a food market by the metro station. As well as booths, there was also an area where people back from visiting the woods on the *elektrichka* would sell mushrooms and berries. After a raid by OMON, these sellers disappeared. In 1998, they were no longer present at all.
159. No doubt, part of the background to this was shaped by the business interests of local chain-store magnates. This sort of issue is difficult to document, but it is notable that the kiosks opposite the Finland Station were right next door to a branch of 'Pyaterochka' supermarket. Since the kiosks went, a new shopping centre has also been constructed on the other side of the road, outside the metro station.
160. FN September 2012. See also the discussion in Pachenkov, Solov'eva, and Kudryavtseva.
161. As indicated by the boxes it is displayed in at e.g. Kuznetsky Market. Some produce – such as superb Armenian tomatoes sold by an elderly lady – is still imported from the former Soviet Union, but strictly seasonally. On the decline of markets across Russia generally, see 'Otechestvennye rynki ischezayut' (no author given), *Metro* 5 March 2012, p. 13: this reported that 270 open markets, or around 9 per cent of the total number across Russia, had closed or been remodelled in the course of 2011.
162. www.apraksinagency.spb.ru/objects/info.php.
163. Beginning with the arcade simply known as Passazh, on Nevsky prospekt, which was put up in 1846–48 by R. A. Zhelyazevich on land owned by Count a. I. Essen-Stenbok-Fermor. See http://pda.gov.spb.ru/culture/culture_history/arcitecture/arch_ensemble/nevsky/passage. (last accessed 18 Oct. 2010).
164. In 2010, the shop in my own block was taken over by one company, having formerly been run by another. I noticed the difference only when my discount card was contemptuously refused by the

cashier. On closer scrutiny, it turned out that the stock was slightly better, and the Suchard Milka cow was gone, but a number of the staff still worked there and the overall layout etc. was almost identical.

165. See, for example, the report on 'Bal'tinfo', 18 November 2012: www.baltinfo.ru/2012/11/18/Stikhiinyi-miting-u-universama-Narodnyi-sobral-250-vozmuschennykh-zhitelei-317988.
166. See the store's own website, www.rucompany.ru/company.php?id_company=1380 on its recent history. For the description, FN September 2012.
167. 'Kafe razmestitsya v pomeshcheniyakh Eliseevskogo magazina v Peterburge', RIA-Novosti, 15 September 2010, www.rian.ru/society/20100915/275939415.html (last accessed 14 October 2010).
168. For newspaper coverage, see e.g. Natal'ya Skipacheva, '"Eliseevskii" otkryvaet dveri', *Metro* 5 March 2012, p. 18. It should be said that the café in the middle at least provided a smell of coffee as drink, if not of the ground substance.
169. On *otbornoe*, see e.g. B. B. Piotrovsky's recollections of the Abrikosov grocery, 'which displayed select fresh fruit, Algerian dates in a package with Arabs on the front, Capitain biscuits in a tin showing a French officer, fragrant dried fruit and different types of chocolate' (p. 11). In May 2011, the National Corpus of the Russian Language (www.ruscorpora.ru) included 2 citations of the word *elitnyi* up to and including 1988, and 85 for 1995 onwards. Soviet-era citations for *elita* include *zasrannaya elita* ('beshitten elite', Yuri Daniel', 1966), *elita zavisti* ('the elite of envy', I. A. Il'in, 1952), etc.
170. FN March 2005.
171. See fig. 5.14.
172. Oxf/AHRC-SPb-07 PF 5 IN.
173. Oxf/AHRC SPb-07 PF48 IN.
174. See e.g. the comment by an informant born in 1968, 'If you used to get rudeness every step of the way in those shops, now things have gone through some kind of perestroika' (Oxf/AHRC-SPb-07 PF 16). Galina Kolesova, 'Kak ya primeryala dzhinsy', *Smena* 30 July 1994, p. 5, describes calling at all the most expensive clothing shops in town and encountering the entire spectrum of reactions – from those who rushed for the next size to those who didn't interrupt their conversation to look at her at all. The situation was similarly unpredictable in later years as well. See e.g. the complaint on a consumer website about staff who refused to show a shopper a second chandelier when she took a dislike to the first one on close inspection ('we expect customers here to buy anything we get down from the ceiling'): post of 5 May 2004 on http://cinik.ru/. More recently, the site http://szo.spr.ru/ has carried large numbers of complaints, though more often about the quality of goods than about the behaviour of sales staff.
175. There is no mystery to this: I have watched assistants unload their float at the start of the day, which typically consists of one example of every type of note in circulation. Until sufficient customers have paid in small change (responding to the familiar cry of 'Please get small money ready!') there simply is no change to hand. A different question, of course, is why the floats are so small . . .
176. FN January 2012.
177. On kettles by credit, see the internet discussion, www.bank-klient.ru/banki-forum/showthread.php?t=44. I have also heard of people doing this from pers. inf.
178. Sergeev, 'Pishchevaya promyshlennost'', pp. 44–6, indicates that in 1995 grain production stood at less than 70 per cent of the 1990 level, while meat production had fallen from 10.1 million tonnes to just under 5.8 million tonnes, milk from 55.7 million tonnes to just over 39.2 million, and so on. The quantities produced then rose slightly up to 2008, at which point a new economic crisis generated another drop.
179. Pers. obs.
180. I have heard claims, for instance, that only one particular brand of aspirin (German, at a premium price) is reliable.
181. Lyudmila Kadilova, 'Dnevnik pensionerki: Est', pit' i odevat'sya na 3383 rublya v mesyats', *Izvestiya* 8 July 2008 (www.izvestia.ru/obshestvo/article3118176). Graphs at the end of the article show that the 'survival minimum' (*prozhitochnyi minimum*) rose steadily between 2000 and 2007, but pensions kept pace only in 2002 and 2004–06.
182. Oxf/AHRC SPb-09 PF9 SA.
183. The rapid turnover of food stores was, by the early 2010s, becoming a noticeable feature of some areas, with certain shops surviving only a few months.
184. In one case I know of, an émigré Leningrader who came to Britain in the 1970s was driven into nervous collapse by the task of dealing with supermarkets; in another, I remember spending hours going round shops in Oxford (not one of the world's consumer centres) with a friend who rejected dozens of options for clothes and cosmetics. Precious hard currency had to be spent on something that was *exactly right*.
185. See Marina Alekseeva, 'Pokupat'-to pokupat'. No gde?', *Vech P* 13 July 2000, pp. 1–2.

186. Bagdat Tumalaev, 'Lyubite klubniku? Pol'zuetes' kontrol'nymi vesami' *MR(V)* 10 June 2005, p. 2.
187. I was caught by this myself near the Finland Station (in an informal market-row later 'cleaned up' by the city authorities) in 2008. The bibulous appearance of said granny should have alerted me.
188. I overheard a loud complaint to this effect from a member of staff in an archive I was visiting in March 2011.
189. Again, anxiety about 'naturalness' was common in other post-Soviet cities as well. See the discussion in Caldwell, 'Domesticating the French Fry'. On fakes, see e.g. '"Pierre Carden" s Maloi Arnautskoi' (unsigned), *MR(V)* 24 June 2005, p. 6. The builders who worked for me in 2005–6 were all extremely wary of *kontrfakt* – taps with well-known German labels actually made in China, etc.
190. The industrialisation of the Soviet food industry is discussed, for example, in Glushchenko, *Obshchepit*.
191. The Soviet recipe for mayonnaise was based on a US precedent, and contained dried egg, spirit vinegar, commercially-produced mustard, etc. See Kelly (as Kelli), 'Leningradskaya kukhnya'.
192. I was given some 'jellied fruits' in December 2010 that looked spectacular, but turned out to be made entirely from coloured and flavoured syrup, plus agar gum. It should be said that the introduction of compulsory E-numbers under EU-wide legislation from the late 1980s onwards (see www.foodlaw.rdg.ac.uk/additive.htm) had a similar shock effect on many people in Britain, who were not used to the detailed declaration of ingredients, which had been compulsory in Germany for much longer.
193. This change took place at the start of the 2010s (pers. obs.).
194. Sergeev, 'Pishchevaya promyshlennost'', pp. 44–5. These figures are for the Russian Federation generally, but observation of supermarket shelves and purchasing patterns would suggest that Petersburg habits conform to these wider patterns.
195. See e.g. A. Davllitsarov, 'Nas zadushit ne dollar, a import', *Smena* 28 August 1998, p. 1; O. Podmoskovnaya, 'Vernem "doktorskuyu" na russkii buterbrod', *Smena* 29 August 1998, p. 2.
196. I have watched this process happen when shopping with people of the older generation.
197. Plate VII. On the preference for 'local' produce, see also Patico, p. 119.
198. See also Oxf/AHRC UK-08 PF11 AB: a woman living in London praises the quality of Petersburg pel'meni and red caviar.
199. Irina Ozerskaya, 'Novost' No. 1 – kolbasa – eto zakuska', *NevV* 17 October 1992, p. 1.
200. Yuliya Ivanova, 'Eta elegantnaya "Bolshevichka"', *NevV* 14 January 1995, p. 2.
201. FN September 2010.
202. That said, by the end of the 2000s Russian clothes of good quality started to become available at reasonable prices, a fact reflected in people's buying patterns.
203. The shop concerned is 'Lend', where I have made frequent visits since 2003.
204. See e.g. the shops along ulitsa Sedova in the 2010s. A rare example of a shop on Nevsky that still looks much as it did back in Soviet days – apart from computerised tills, a mobile phone top-up machine, and designer lighting – is the Bulochnaya (bread and cake shop) on the corner of Malaya Sadovaya.
205. See the official site of the agency, www.apraksinagency.spb.ru/objects/info.php.
206. 'Glavstroi nameren ustroit' Koven-Garden v Apraksinom dvore', 22 October 2008, www.restate.ru/material/53431.html. There was a long history of fantasising about cultural uses for Aprashka. In 1991, 'Subbota' studio theatre had attempted to get space there (Yu. Shipilova, S. Yaroshetsky, '"Subbota" nadeetsja na ponedel'nik', *VL* 18 May 1991, p. 1).
207. Natal'ya Tikhonova, 'Apraksin dvor obnesut zaborom', *Moi raion* 5 November 2009, www.mr7.ru/news/society/story_20024.html.
208. www.restate.ru/material/107769.html.
209. www.mr7.ru/news/society/story_20024.html. Cf. the claim by a blogger, Sergei Utkin, that Aprashka is the most criminal market in Petersburg and all the police are in the pay of the criminals: 22 October 2010, http://don-ald.livejournal.com/494997.html?thread=2005653.
210. 'Apraksin dvor nachali osvobozhdat' ot arendatorov', 16 October 2008, www.restate.ru.
211. www.mr7.ru/news/society/story_20024.html. Another commentator here described the market as 'an infected organ [. . .] most people are there illegally, not many of them are Russian citizens either [*rossiyane*].'
212. www.mr7.ru/news/society/story_20024.html. Another contributor stated that she would not have been able to afford winter boots for her children if she hadn't bought them there (ibid.). As put by a man in his 50s: 'The whole city goes there' (FN June 2006). Cf. the comment that, when you've got no money, *sekondkhend* and markets are the only option: Off LifE, 20 October 2010, http://ani-viva.livejournal.com/18921.html.

## 6 Theatre Street

1. Losev, 'Pokuda Mel'pomena i Evterpa', *Znamya* 11 (1989). Cf. Gandel'sman, 'Teatr', in *Novye rifmy*.
2. Among those who left for Moscow in the 1930s were A. N. Tolstoy, Veniamin Kaverin, Osip Mandelstam, and the leading children's writers Kornei Chukovsky and Samuil Marshak. Among prominent Leningraders who moved to Moscow in the late Soviet period were Evgeny Rein, Anatoly Naiman, Andrei Bitov, and Vasily Aksenov (though the departure of Aksenov, as someone who had merely studied in the city, did not have the same resonance).
3. Khentova, *Shostakovich v Petrograde-Leningrade*.
4. Vaganova, *Osnovy klassicheskogo tantsa*. The biographies in *Peterburgskii balet 1903–2003* indicate that even in the late twentieth century, the leading ballerinas were only two or three generations away from Vaganova herself (for instance, Lopatkina was taught by Dudinskaya, who was a pupil of Vaganova's, while Diana Vishynova's teacher Kovalyova was taught by Kamkova, another pupil of Vaganova's, and so on).
5. http://balletschool.perm.ru/about/.
6. These were simply the most famous cases: in 1976, for example, Kaleriya Fedicheva (Nureyev's partner in fig. 6.1 here) followed his example, and left the Soviet Union for the West.
7. The recent biography of Nureyev by Kavanagh makes this point about Nureyev's relative lack of credentials. On the other famous defectors of this period, see Makarova, Smakov, and Makarova, *A Dance Autobiography*; Baryshnikov and Swope, *Baryshnikov at Work*.
8. TsGAIPD-SPb. 25/108/12/65-6; cf. the observation on l. 72 that work on the film *A Pilot of the First Class* was advancing.
9. See the discussion in Stern; Ezrahi, *Swans in the Kremlin*, Chapter 2.
10. On this ballet, see [OL Introduction].
11. Pressure increased significantly after the passing of an official Central Committee decree in 1957 ordaining greater political and social relevance in the ballet. For a detailed discussion of the paradoxes of ballet's standing during the Thaw, see Ezrahi, Chapters 3 and 4.
12. The ballet was filmed in 1960 by Mikhail Sheinin for Lenfil'm (see http://video.yandex.ru/users/alekx2016/view/3418/# for background information and a link to the film).
13. For a discussion of the nature of Yakobson's work, with performance photographs, see Demidov, 'Improvizatsii Leonida Yakobsona'. There are more extensive discussions in *Leonid Yakobson: tvorcheskii put' baletmeistera*, and Dobrovol'skaya, *Baletmeister Leonid Yakobson*.
14. My thanks to Ol'ga Kuznetsova for making this point to me. FN, June 2012.
15. Vinogradov, pp. 88–9.
16. Ibid., pp. 93–6.
17. On the history of ballet adaptations generally, see Scholl, *From Petipa to Balanchine*, particularly Ch. 7.
18. On the 'Leningrad' characteristics of Ulanova, see e.g. I. Rudenko, 'Sensatsiya XX veka', *Komsomol'skaya pravda*, 8 January 1980, p. 4.
19. See the materials in *Teatr Leonida Yakobsona*.
20. This was less characteristic of the generally positive Soviet press coverage (as recorded by a 65th birthday exhibition on Eifman held at TsGALI-SPb. in 2011) than of the intellectual ballet-going public, or at least a section of it. While some St Petersburgers have assured me they could never stand Eifman, others speak enthusiastically about his work as a high point of their theatrical experiences.
21. Galina Vishnevskaya's affectionate memoirs of her Leningrad teacher include much material on her remarkable flat, but nothing on the local features of the training.
22. For a knowledgeable Moscow friend of mine, it was Mravinsky's range which above all made him stand out as a conductor (FN May 2012).
23. 'Umer Ravil' Martynov', *Kommersant* 10 November 2004, www.kommersant.ru/Doc/523511.
24. Mravinsky, 'Tridtsat' let s muzykoi Shostakovicha' (1966).
25. Ibid.
26. Vladimir Kin, 'Legenda Mravinskogo', *Novoe russkoe slovo*, 7–8 November 1983, www.mravinsky.org/pages/rems.htm.
27. This film, as well as all the others mentioned, was made available on YouTube by Lenfilm Studio in 2011.
28. Averbakh had himself trained as a medical student before moving to cinema, so first-hand knowledge came in handy here.
29. In tune with the 'documentary' feeling of the film, a real building under restoration was used as a location for the shooting.

30. Particularly wonderful webcam footage is available on www.yr.no/place/Russia/St.%C2%A0 Petersburg/Saint-Petersburg/.
31. On the setting for *The Woodpecker*, see the remarks by the cameraman, Dmitry Dolinin, in *Peterburg kak kino*, p. 360.
32. There is an excellent selection of such 'official' art in Sergei Ivanov, *Neizvestnyi sotsrealizm*. See also the associated site, www.leningradartist.com/right_r.html.
33. On photography, see particularly Nikitin, *Optimizm pamyati*. Most secondary discussion of the visual arts deals with an earlier period: see e.g. Kaganov; for comments on the work of the etcher D. I. Mitrokhin (1883–1973), see Barskova, 'The Fluid Margins', pp. 297–9. The Karl Bulla Museum on Nevsky prospekt and Rosfoto on Bol'shaya Morskaya both mount exhibitions by local photographers; the superiority of this art form (and graphics) to most locally-produced art in other medias was also extremely evident at the retrospective exhibition in the Manège in January 2013, 'Peterburg – 20-letie', which included some work from the Soviet period too.
34. My thanks to Galina Vladimirovna Lisyutich for sharing her memories and photo-archive with me (FN June 2012).
35. This is manifested in the work of Anna Ostroumova-Lebedeva, for example, or Aleksandr Baturin (1914–2003) (see *Geometriya prirody*, and http://inutero.ru/).
36. Arkady Raikin, *Bez grima*, p. 33.
37. On the latter, see V. Zabarauskas, 'Mil'tinis', in *Portrety rezhisserov*, pp. 45–79.
38. See e.g. the review by Valentin Pluchek, 'Ispytanie vremeni', *VL* 19 December 1955, p. 3. The production was awarded a Lenin Prize in 1958.
39. Starosel'skaya, *Tovstonogov*, offers a lively insider's account of the director's life, focusing on his work at BDT. For a detailed list of productions up to 1967, see Tovstonogov, *O professii rezhissera*.
40. There was a highly specific 'mass market' interpretation of Shakespeare that emphasised the 'democratic' resonance of his works and their proto-realist status, and this cramped directorial styles from the late 1930s onwards.
41. On the history of the BDT building (which, confusingly, was originally known as the Malyi [Small], rather than the Bol'shoi [Big], Theatre, a title that in the Soviet period was used for the former Mikhailovsky) and of the 'Petrograd Communal Theatres', see the note to *opis'* 3.1 of TsGALI-SPb. f. 268, ll. 1-2. In the first two decades of its existence, BDT was studiedly agitational: see ibid., l. 3. For details of the repertoire and viewing figures (Zamyatin's *The Flea* was the second most popular play in 1926–27 after *The Empress's Conspiracy*, being seen by 33,471 people in 30 performances), see TsGALI-SPb. 268/1/25/1-35.
42. On *Vragi*, see TsGALI-SPb. 268/1/31/8-16; on *Slava* and the post-war repertoire, ibid. 268/3.1/4, passim.
43. This episode has been described repeatedly. See e.g. Starosel'skaya, *Tovstonogov*, p. 140.
44. As is clear from the BDT materials in TsGALI-SPb., f. 268: see e.g. 'Kniga ucheta Tvorcheskogo sostava teatra i ispolnitelei po spektaklyam sezona 1971–72 gg.', ibid. 268/3/510/ 9-11, which makes clear that the leading actor, Evgeny Lebedev, earned nearly 4 times as much as the 10 actors at the bottom of the pay hierarchy, most of whom were also junior in terms of age. However, the lower pay categories also included some actors who were senior by birth date, but were evidently playing bit parts. Yuri Gal'perin's novel, *Russkii variant*, includes a sketch of a Leningrad actor whose life is blighted by always playing secondary roles (*Most cherez Letu*, pp. 313–587).
45. Starosel'skaya, *Tovstonogov*, p. 154. The original actor was Panteleimon Krymov. In later years, certainly, Tovstonogov seems to have gone over to more conventional methods: actors would stick with roles for several years, and the death or non-availability of a given actor was sometimes put forward to the city administration's Directorate of Culture as grounds for shelving a given production altogether. For a review of Smoktunovsky's performance ('truly one of the most notable successes on the Leningrad stage in recent times'), see K. Kulikova, 'Novaya vstrecha s geroem Dostoevskogo', *LP* 21 February 1958, p. 3.
46. See e.g. *O professii rezhissera* (and the later reprint, *Zerkalo stseny*).
47. '[. . .] udivitel'nyi splav mudrosti i lukavogo yumora' (see the article, 'Vremya Stanislavskogo' (1963), first published in *Izvestiya* and reprinted in *O professii rezhissera*, pp. 19–29; this quotation p. 26).
48. For a discussion of the production, see Starosel'skaya, *Tovstonogov*, pp. 126–37.
49. See the performance photographs in *O professii rezhissera*, between pp. 208–9.
50. Starosel'skaya, *Tovstonogov*, p. 298.
51. See the performance photographs in *O professii rezhissera*, between pp. 328–9.
52. Egoshina, *Akterskie tetradi*, p. 33. On Smoktunovsky's encounter with the epileptic, see Starosel'skaya.

53. For the sound effects, see the daily report sheets on performances at BDT, 1957, TsGALI-SPb. 268/3.1/67, and ibid., d. 68; e.g. 268/3/67/9 ob., ibid. l. 38 ob. These sheets also indicate the meticulous attention of the producers to minute details: for instance, the register in 1957 recorded an irritable complaint that the stage hands in one production had provided yellow, rather than red, lemonade to stand in for wine, and on another that the (live) cat had appeared without the ribbon round its neck. See ibid. l. 46 ob. (cat), ibid. d. 68, l. 12 (wine). On the rhythms, see Smoktunovsky's note on a rehearsal of *Idiot*: 'The rhythms must be sharp' (quoted in Egoshina, *Akterskie tetradi*, p. 28).
54. Tolstoy's story (in full *Kholstomer: istoriya loshadi*) was first published in 1886.
55. The striking wire-effect horse-head masks and leather hoof-boots for *Equus*, designed by John Napier, can be seen on the website of the National Theatre at *www.nationaltheatre.org.uk/download.php?id=1776*.
56. As is clear from *Georgy Tovstonogov repetiruet i uchit*, pp. 431–532.
57. David Zolotnitsky, 'Deistvo o Kholstomere', *Smena* 19 December 1975, 4. An informant of mine who remembered disliking the production a great deal when he saw it in the theatre's latter years still recalled the shock effect of seeing Lebedev, the lead actor, more familiar as a figure in Soviet realist dramas, playing the put-upon horse – a casting that threw Lebedev's portrayals of Soviet protagonists into satirical relief, turning them also into helpless drudges (FN January 2012).
58. On the Taganka, see Birgit Beumers, *Yuri Lyubimov at the Taganka Theatre, 1964–1994* (Amsterdam, 1997).
59. For example, when *Idiot* had been in repertory for a few years, Smoktunovsky wrote to a friend advising against seeing the production, as he felt that his performance was already beset with clichés (*shtampy*): see Egoshina, *Akterskie tetradi*, p. 51.
60. Starosel'skaya, p. 208.
61. Starosel'skaya, pp. 231–63.
62. This was brought out well by Kirill Narbutov and Aleksandr Mikhailov's TV biography made to commemorate the comedian's centenary in September 2011: 'Raikin: Korol' i shut strany sovetov', www.1tv.ru/documentary/fi7288/fd201110231220.
63. On the Putin date, see 'Putinskii Peterburg: ekskursiya s istorikom L'vom Lur'e', *Kommersant* 1 October 2012, www.kommersant.ru/doc/2029604.
64. Arkady Raikin, 'Miniatyury' (1964), http://video.mail.ru/list/32151/238/2742.html.
65. Raikin, *Bez grima*, p. 33.
66. See Vertinsky, *Zapiski russkogo P'ero*; Raikin, *Bez grima*, etc. Truman Capote's *The Muses are Heard* includes an acid sketch of Vertinsky and his wife (under a garbled name); allegedly, while she was obsessed with attempting to buy Western clothes from the visiting US troupe, Vertinsky was simply self-obsessed.
67. The material from musical halls is preserved in *Polnyi sbornik libretto dlya grammofona* (5 issues: 1905–07).
68. Raikin, *Bez grima*, p. 105.
69. Egoshina, *Akterskie tetradi*, p. 50.
70. The Youth Theatre is one of the city's more successful public buildings; the October Concert Hall, on the other hand, ineptly massed at the front and with a rear and side that were evidently not meant to be seen (unlike the disconcertingly shiny front façades), has limitations in its own right, as well as being totally wrong for the site.
71. See Oxf/AHRC-SPb-10 PF4 MS; AHRC SPb-08 PF18 SA.
72. See Mally, *Revolutionary Acts*.
73. See the good general discussion (mainly with reference to Moscow, though with a little on Leningrad as well) in Constanzo, 'Reclaiming the Stage'.
74. Costanzo, 'Reclaiming', makes the point that even studio audiences and performers saw themselves as stigmatised by the label of amateurism, though qualities such as 'sincerity' could be held to make up for lack of polish.
75. Another small theatre with quite an adventurous repertoire was the Leningrad Regional Theatre on Liteinyi (now the Theatre on the Liteinyi), where one of our informants recalls being impressed by Yakov Khamarmer's staging of *One Flew Over the Cuckoo's Nest*: Oxf/AHRC SPb-07 PF2 IN.
76. On TRAM, see e.g. Bogemskaya et al. (eds), *Samodeyatel'noe khudozhestvennoe tvorchestvo v SSSR*, pp. 146–53; Mally, *Revolutionary Acts*.
77. Based on my memories of seeing the production in London in 1990.
78. Shevtsova; see also Dodin, *Repetitsii p'esy* and *Puteshestvie bez kontsa*.
79. Memo sent by the Secret Department, Special Sector, of the Leningrad Gorkom to the Central Committee of the CPSU etc., TsGAIPD-SPb. 25/ 91/59/29-32.

80. Naiman, *Poeziya i nepravda*, p. 137.
81. Lur'e, 'Kak Nevskii prospekt'.
82. Oxf/Lev SPb-07 PF25 IN (woman b. 1941).
83. Oxf/AHRC SPb-10 PF3 NG. One way to get tickets was through the workplace, but this did not always work terribly well: 'Net li lichnogo biletika?', *LP* 28 January 1968, p. 3, reported that people were sometimes coerced into taking tickets they did not want, while at other times, those selling did not manage to get rid of many tickets.
84. Oxf/AHRC SPb-07 PF28 IN (man b. 1979, reporting his father's memories).
85. 'Teatr, teatr! Kak skuchno mne lyubit'/Tebya' (Kushner, *Dnevnye sni*, p. 5).
86. I. Brodsky, 'Klassicheskii balet est' zamok krasoty', *Stikhotvoreniya i poemy*, 1.362.
87. Gandel'sman, 'Teatr'.
88. Bitov, 'Kniga puteshestvii', p. 133.
89. As an expert on the ballet has put it, opinions were expressed fiercely in the theatre lobbies, but making a song and dance at the performance was not on: 'all performances were doomed to succeed', as far as the obligatory polite applause went (Oxf/AHRC SPb-12 PF13 CK). For the pre-revolutionary tradition of theatrical *Schwärmerei*, see Fishzon, 'Confessions'.
90. This is true of the post-Soviet era too: see e.g. Oxf/Lev SPb-07 PF38 IN (man b. 1979); Oxf/AHRC-SPb-07 PF 29 (woman b. 1969).
91. Oxf/AHRC SPb-08 PF54 IN (b. 1937, lived in Leningrad from 1963).
92. Oxf/AHRC SPb-07 PF3 IN (man b. 1938, Leningrad, intelligentsia background).
93. See e.g. Oxf/AHRC-Evp-07 PF-2 IN, where the informant (b. 1937 and from Evpatoriya on the Black Sea) recalls how a woman she knew in Leningrad, who had been their neighbour when living in evacuation, made enormous efforts to get the informant's daughter theatre tickets when the latter visited Leningrad in the mid-1960s: 'I'd never bother on my own account, but I stood for hours asking, "Might you by any chance have a ticket" [*biletik*, the diminutive conveying a wheedling tone], I schlepped round all the theatres . . .'
94. See e.g. the recollections in a blog by Tanya (no surname given), b. 1948, about how she counted on this method of getting in to a concert by the popular Spanish songster Raphael when he visited Leningrad in 1970 (in fact, she ended up acting as his official translator) (http://age60.ru/PRINT-f10-t529.html).
95. I remember being sent to do this myself in 1981, for what turned out to be a dreadfully tedious production of Chekhov's *Ivanov*, brought by the Moscow Arts Theatre on a visit to Leningrad. Not only was the administrator almost always able to provide spare tickets, but they were handed over for nothing. Such discretionary allocations were a bone of contention in the local press and in complaints from members of the public: see e.g. TsGALI-SPb 268/3/561/17, where in response to representations from *LP* in 1975, the theatre's director explained the system thus: 'In the realization of tickets left over after reservations have been made, the management gives priority to artistes visiting Leningrad for study trips, to directors and other creative workers visiting our city, to residents of distant areas of the country, to BAM and KAMAZ workers.'
96. Oxf/AHRC GB-08 PF1 CK (woman b. 1931, intelligentsia background); FN April 2012.
97. Derviz, *Ryadom s bol'shoi istoriei*, p. 273.
98. As reported by a woman b. 1947, FN September 2010.
99. See e.g. Oxf/Lev SPb-08 PF58 IN (the informant recalled how when a middle-aged male acquaintance made such an invitation, she retorted, 'Why not ask your wife out to the theatre?').
100. See 'Kniga zhalob i predlozhenii' (1943–1960), TsGALI-SPb. 268/3/158, passim.
101. Ibid., l. 5, l. 30, l. 39, etc.
102. 'Kniga zhalob', l. 38, l. 45.
103. Except in the case of school parties, who were obviously condemned to what was thought to be good for them, and those who had been unlucky with ticket fixers (see above). In Vienna, by contrast, people would turn up to performances because their subscription had come round (in the words of a woman I overhead in 1978, 'I can't stand this opera [Gottfried von Einem's indeed very dreary musical setting of Dürrenmatt's *The Visit*], and I've seen it once already, but you see I have an *Abonnement* . . .').
104. See e.g. Oxf/AHRC SPb-07 PF8 IN (man b. 1975, on a US film festival in 1985, 'vse, konechno, tam kupirovalos").
105. *LP*, 30 September 1964, p. 4. See also *The Muses are Heard*, Capote's famous memoir of a 1956 tour with *Porgy and Bess*.
106. 'Pis'ma iz russkogo muzeya', http://rus-sky.com/gosudarstvo/solouhin/letters.htm.
107. Soloukhin, 'Pis'ma iz russkogo muzeya', ibid. The basis for the statistic is presumably that Soloukhin asked the young woman giving out copies how many were being handed out a day.

108. http://retro-piter.livejournal.com/350609.html.
109. See e.g. 'Informatsiya Oktyabr'skogo RK KPSS o dezhurstve propagandistskoi gruppy na vystavke "Obrazovanie SShA"', 30 July 1969, TsGAIPD-SPb. 25/102/58/40-43. On the 'kitchen exhibition', see Reid, 'Who Will Beat Whom?'.
110. Belinsky, *Pis'ma proshlogo veka*, pp. 436–7. Belinsky also remarked on seeing 'a show of works by French Impressionists and others – Matisse, Picasso, Monet, Corot, Renois, Gauguin' hanging near the British artists.
111. See e.g. Skobkina, p. 6. For a first-hand description from nearer the time, see Robinson, *An American in Leningrad*, pp. 208–14 (on an exhibition in Dresdenskaya ul., with photographs). *Post-Soviet Art and Architecture*, ed. Yurasovsky and Ovenden, includes some remarks on individual figures, e.g. Timur Novikov.
112. On the alternative music scene, see particularly McMichael, '"After All, You're a Rock and Roll Star"'; Oxf/AHRC SPb-07 PF27 IN (on the difficulties of getting tickets to a concert by Bulat Okudzhava).
113. *Leningradskii fotoandergraund*, 143–69. Photography was the art form where the boundaries between 'unofficial' and 'official' were most permeable. Cameras and film were readily available (artists' materials, on the other hand, were supposed to be supplied only to registered art students and members of 'creative unions', and musical instruments were relatively expensive and scarce). There was considerable concern in official quarters to maximise accessibility: for instance, an article by B. Barsov published in *Smena* (15 December 1982) about the poor quality of work by developing laboratories (impeding the unparalleled popularity of photography, which was being encouraged by shows, competitions, the manufacture of albums etc.) led to an investigation by the Regional Committee of the Communist Party (TsGAIPD-SPb. 24/191/16/130-1).
114. The majority of the photographers featured in *Leningradskii fotoandergraund* received training at such clubs, and, in some cases, elsewhere. Grigory Prikhod'ko, for instance, was the graduate of a course in photography for 'employees at the managerial level' (*rukovodyashchie rabotniki*, p. 36), and Boris Kudryakov had attended photography school. Ol'ga Korsunova had been taught photography by Boris Smelov, but this background was less typical.
115. See the reproductions on www.timurnovikov.ru.
116. For example, by Olesia Turkhina and Viktor Mazin, writing in *Post-Soviet Art and Architecture*, p. 83.
117. Stanislav Savitsky has pointed to the resemblance between the style of some 1980s artists and 'outsider' or 'children's' art: see his 'Prazdnik svobody' in *Vzglyad*, p. 163. See ibid. for the phrase 'impudently cack-handed'. Novikov was to coin the title 'New Academy of Allsorts Art' (later 'New Academy of Fine Arts') for his initiatives in 1985, but this did not signify neo-academicism in terms of artistic production.
118. The *tusovka* as a cultural phenomenon (the term means 'a group', and also the physical space when it meets up, and its practices) has been defined by Tat'yana Shchepanskaya as 'a communicative milieu': see her *Sistema*, pp. 43–47; Yurchak, *Everything Was Forever*, pp. 146–8, discusses the *tusovka* more narrowly, in the context of underground music.
119. In the case of Grebenshchikov and 'Aquarium', the breakthrough came a little earlier – with his scandalous performance at an official rock concert in Tbilisi in 1980. On the Leningrad musical underground, see Kan, 'Leningradskii rok-klub', and McMichael, '"After All, You're a Rock and Roll Star"'.
120. Oxf/AHRC SPb-07 PF5 SA.
121. Oxf/AHRC SPb-07 PF5 SA (the informant's mother was a member of the House of Scholars).
122. For example, Goloshchokin's *Vremena goda* was released in 1974, *Dzhazovye kompozitsii* in 1979, and he was also represented on the compilation albums *Dzhaz-ansambli Leningrada* (1980) and *Kollazh. Dzhazovye pianisty Leningrada* (1987). See the 'Jazz-Info' site, http://info-jazz.ru/community/jazzmen/?action=show&id=52. An informative memoir of the local scene is Kan, *Poka ne nachalsya jazz.*
123. On the history of the Philharmonia, see www.jazz-hall.spb.ru/history.html.
124. See Kan, *Poka ne nachalsya jazz.*
125. TsGALI-SPb. 268/ 3/561/15. Cf. the letter from an indignant spectator in 1960 complaining that BDT had commissioned work from *stilyagi* [beatniks] (TsGALI-SPb., 268/3/159/30), and conversely, the letter from an army officer in 1961: 'I can't find words to describe my delight and gratitude to the people who created such a patriotic and true-to life production!' (TsGALI-SPb 268/3/131/2).
126. The informant in Oxf/AHRC SPb-07 PF35 IN recalls attending a Goloshchokin concert where large numbers of people simply walked out. For contrasting, enthusiastic comments about the musician's work from the post-Soviet period, see Oxf/AHRC SPb-07 PF 44 IN.

127. 'No ear for music': see Oxf/AHRC-SPb-07 PF 46, man b. 1931; intolerance of concerts and ballet: Oxf/AHRC SPb-07 PF7 IN, man b. 1975.
128. As in the case of Oxf/AHRC SPb-07 PF46 (the informant here not only had higher education, but had ancestors from the pre-revolutionary social elite, merchants and gentry), and Oxf/AHRC SPb-07 PF7 IN (mother a geologist).
129. I. S. Shavrov, 'Zhaloba', 11 March 1957, TsGALI 105/1/586/22; on the result, see the reply to Shavrov from the Upravlenie kul'tury, 29 March 1957, ibid., l. 21.
130. See e.g. Oxf/AHRC SPb-11 PF4A NG (man b. 1962, working-class background), who recalled the puppet theatre, the circus, and BDT. On TYuZ, see Oxf/AHRC SPb-08 PF11A IN, woman b. 1973, Leningrad, intelligentsia parents; though not much liking the theatre on the whole, she remembered *Bambi* there with great affection.
131. For evidence of how the distribution system worked, see the letter sent by the management of BDT to *Leningradskaya pravda*, 16 May 1975 (evidently in answer to a complaint in a reader's letter), which stated that 280 tickets at every performance went for sale at factories in outlying districts of the city, and 420–450 were distributed in response to group bookings. War invalids and Heroes of the USSR and Heroes of Soviet Labour, as well as deputies of the Supreme Soviet, diplomats, and the 'Intourist' agency for foreign tourists, were also given priority. Kiosks across the city got 430 tickets, and 140–170 were retained by the theatre for direct sale, with priority given to visiting theatrical professionals from the USSR and abroad and to workers on the BAM and KAMAZ projects. 'Unfortunately, we cannot keep pace with demand, and many Leningraders have to leave the theatre disappointed.' (TsGALI-SPb. 268/3/561/17).
132. See e.g. Oxf/AHRC SPb-10 PF10 MS (on a school-teacher who was deputed to circulate tickets and kept foisting them on her neighbours' children – this in the mid-1980s).
133. On this see the account by a teacher (b. 1952), Oxf/Lev SPb-08 PF58 IN.
134. Katerina Gerasimova and Sof'ya Chuikina, in 'Ot kapitalisticheskogo Peterburga k sotsialisticheskomu Leningradu: Izmenenie sotsial'no-prostranstvennoi struktury goroda v 30-e gody', in Vikhavainen [=Vihavainen] (ed.), *Normy i tsennosti*, pp. 27–74, argue that working-class Leningraders didn't go to cultural events in the 1930s either.
135. Oxf/AHRC SPb-11 PF4A NG, recalled that the class had been passed 'unsold tickets'. While this person could remember the names of circus stars, they recalled nothing concrete of anything seen in the theatre; Oxf/AHRC-SPb-07 PF-50 IN, woman b. 1982, Sestroretsk, only remembered going as a child.
136. For the sales, see the brochure of classified statistics on health, education, culture and science in Leningrad during 1963, published in June 1964, TsGAIPD-SPb. 25/91/103/73 ob. Other figures included 478,500 for the Pushkin (Aleksandrinskii) Theatre (seating capacity 946), and 466,700 for the BDT (seating capacity 1116). For the seating information, http://rossteatr.ru.
137. See www.rosteatr.ru/ru/search.aspx?org=209. The theatre was in fact closed for just over a month (25 January–4 March 1942), while the power in the city was completely down (http://leningrad-pobeda.ru/iskusstvo-blokadnogo-leningrada/4/).
138. Oxf/AHRC-SPb-11 PF14 MS. Woman b. 1927, Uzbekistan, went to school and studied in Leningrad. Nina Pel'tser's name has been supplied by me (the informant had forgotten it).
139. See material on http://rossteatr.ru; for recollections from a working-class man b. 1929 who used to enjoy going there, see Oxf/AHRC-SPb-07 PF17 IN.
140. For work on *estrada* in English, see e.g. Stites, *Russian Popular Culture*, and the trilogy of books by David MacFadyen: *Songs for Fat People*, *Red Stars*, and *Estrada?!*
141. See the material in the KMA.
142. For instance, the informant in Oxf/AHRC SPb-07 PF13 SA (woman b. 1950, intelligentsia background) remembered attending the club at the Maxim Gorky paper mills on the corner of Ural'skaya and Zheleznovodskaya: 'the whole of Zheleznya [the area round Zheleznovodskaya] used to go there'.
143. TsGAIPD-SPb. 25/89/66/14. A study of worker budgets from 1963 indicated that the lowest spend (apart from rent, at 9 roubles a month) out of the average household income of 841.3 roubles was 13.8 roubles on theatre and cinema tickets. In comparison, 21.5 roubles went on 'relaxation and hygiene' (i.e. trips to the *banya*, hairdresser, sport), and 36.4 on alcohol. 'Itogi obsledovaniya lichnykh byudzhetov semei rabochikh promyshlennosti Leningrada', TsGAIPD-SPb. 24/91/103/37. Low participation in 'cultured leisure' was observable in working-class districts during the 1930s as well (see Chuikina and Gerasimova, 'Ot kapitalisticheskogo Peterburga').
144. See e.g. Oxf/AHRC SPb-11 PF10 MS, in which the informant (b. 1939, Leningrad, from a working-class background) indignantly criticises the term *spal'nyi raion* ('a dormitory area'), on the grounds that there was plenty to do: 'They built cinemas. People went to the cinema.' Oxf/

AHRC SPb-10 PF1 NG recalls a number of the cinemas: Oktyabr' and Avrora, on the Nevsky, but also various ones in the Moskovsky prospekt area, where she lived: Zenit, Znamya, Kosmonavt.

145. Oxf/AHRC SPb-10 PF1 NG.
146. Oxf/Lev SPb-03 PF16 (woman b. 1969, working-class background). The film is also an acknowledged favourite of Vladimir Putin's.
147. For reminiscences of this film, see Oxf/AHRC SPb-07 PF14 SA (woman b. 1950, Leningrad).
148. See 'Soviet and Russian Blockbuster Films'.
149. On Indian films in the USSR, see Rajagopalan.
150. Pers. obs., 1981. For the outsider, this generated a kind of Brechtian alienation effect, all the more so when scenes of erotic passion ('Oh, mon amour! Baise-moi tout de suite!') were glossed in this voice of otherworldly detachment. On the House of Cinematographers, see also Oxf/AHRC SPb-12 PF12 CK.
151. I remember being told in 1981 by a friend who would never willingly have watched a Soviet film that Andrei Tarkovsky, for instance, was not a patch on Bergman. On neo-realism, see e.g. Oxf/AHRC SPb-07 PF14 SA (woman b. 1950, Leningrad) (in this particular case, Vittorio de Sica's 1964 drama *Matrimonio all'italiana*, starring Marcello Mastroianni and Sophia Loren).
152. Oxf/AHRC-SPb-07 PF 5 IN.
153. The impact of *Brilliantovaya ruka* as a vision of glamour is discussed in Gurova, *Sovetskoe nizhnee bel'e*, pp. 102–3; on *Osennii marofon*, see Nikolai Vakhtin, 'On Certain Peculiarities in the Act of Communication', *Forum for Anthropology and Culture* 2 (2005), p. 214.
154. The Leningrad Hippodrome was closed down in 1947, and the site later used for the Theatre of the Young Viewer. For a memoir of the hippodrome in the 1920s (as a haunt of depravity), see Vladimir Polyakov, 'Moya sto devyanostaya shkola', http://fb2.booksgid.com/content/53/vladimir-polyakov-moya-sto-devyanostaya-shkola/31.html.
155. The relatively low official standing of the teams is suggested by the fact that in 1966 they were the subject of a misuse-of-funds investigation, because players had been retained on full pay who were not taking part in a tour, and Zenit was overspending on players' food by a rouble per lunch: see the report in TsGAIPD 24/136/71/1-3.
156. www.bc-spartak.ru/about/history. In 2011, plans were formed to set up a 'Basketball Hall of Fame' in St Petersburg, commemorating, for example, Natal'ya Zakharova, captain of the women's team at the 1976 Olympics: see www.baltinfo.ru/2011/12/15/V-Peterburge-poyavitsya-Zal-slavy-piterskogo-basketbola-247652. The Leningrad volleyball team Avtomobilist (known as Spartak until 1969) was also extremely successful: www.vcavtomobilist.ru/history.php. For excellent accounts of Soviet spectator sports generally at this period, see Robert Edelman, *Serious Fun: Spectator Sport in the USSR* (New York, 1993), and his *Spartak Moscow: A History of the People's Team in the Workers' State* (Ithaca, NY, 2009).
157. The gymnasts were, for example, honoured in the official publication *10 pyatiletok Leningrada*, pp. 368–9.
158. Firsov, *Televidenie glazami sotsiologa*, pp. 108–14, estimated that in 1967, over 85 per cent of the Leningrad population owned a TV (as opposed to only 50 per cent in 1962). This figure showed no significant variation for social status or educational levels (university professors were just as likely to have TVs as were manual workers). The most popular programmes in Leningrad were films (i.e. TV showings of cinefilms), followed by KVN, a kind of 'have a go' competition in which teams responded to challenges of daring and initiative, different types of estrada act, and TV serials. Considerably lower down came concerts and broadcasts of drama (i.e., the genres in which Leningrad as 'cultural capital' traditionally specialised). Least popular of all were programmes of local news (see ibid., pp. 126–30).
159. Oxf/AHRC SPb-07 PF41 IN (woman b. 1970).
160. I recall first seeing this film in 1985, with Leningrad friends who had certainly never suggested setting foot inside a cinema before.
161. In March 1993, during the political tension preceding Boris Yeltsin's stand-off at the White House in Moscow, the programme was pulled (see the contemporary news report from www.kommersant.ru/doc/43017), and never returned to the airwaves.
162. K. Klyuevskaya, 'V Pushkine – prem'era', *LP*, 1 January 1988, p. 3. By the standards of the time, this was tame. For instance, in 1988 one studio theatre's production included a scene where one of the characters spat the contents of his mouth, containing chewed black bread with raspberry jam, over the head of a Lenin bust. (My thanks to Judy Pallot for this recollection.)
163. Klyuevskaya, 'V Pushkine – prem'era'.
164. Beumers, *Pop Culture Russia!*, p. 142.

165. On the history of these groups, see their sites: www.akhe.ru/rus/about.html; http://formalnyteatr.ru/category/teatr/. My thanks also to Alina Kravchenko for reminiscences about them.
166. See the correspondence in the files of BDT about efforts to import parts for the stage lighting in 1993: TsGALI-SPb. 268/3/745/14.
167. Kan, 'Leningradskii rok-klub'.
168. Jack Walker, 'Farouk Ruzimatov, an Interview' (1995), www.kirov.com/stories/farouk/walker3.html.
169. As Ol'ga Kuznetsova has put it, other ballerinas may dance the role with glitter, but only Lopatkina sends shivers down your spine (FN, June 2012).
170. This may also explain why only early works by Stravinsky seem to be safely ensconced on the programme.
171. Yakobson's experimental later work was revived at the start of the 1990s (see 'Khronika 1990 g.', *NLO* no. 84 (2007), http://magazines.russ.ru/nlo/2007/84/ia3.html), but thereafter vanished from view.
172. Description based on my own visit, FN, June 2010.
173. Man b. 1980, lecturer in history in institute of higher education, Oxf/AHRC-SPb-07 36 PF IN. The correlative was an equally stereotypical portrayal of foreigners, as in a version of Tchaikovsky's *Mazeppa* where the Russians resembled heroes of the Socialist Realist era, while the Poles, vulgarly resplendent in scarlet and black evening dress and too much jewellery, circulated at an event that had the look of a particularly self-indulgent halt on the EU gravy train. (FN 2006: see also the press coverage at www.smotr.ru/2006/nemoskva/2006_mariinsky_mazepa.htm).
174. Not that Petersburgers were grateful for this largesse; instead, they regularly made fun of 'that banana merchant', and snobbishly claimed he would never fit in, Oxf/AHRC-SPb-08 PF49 IN. I have several times been told by locals who have never visited the place that it is entirely frequented by people with cloth ears who simply think that one should be seen there.
175. In my experience, musical standards at the Mariinsky are unpredictable. A concert performance in October 2011, conducted by Gergiev, was mainly held together by terrific playing from the pianist Daniil Trifonov in Tchaikovsky's First Piano Concerto; the orchestra's rendition of Stravinsky was insecure in terms of ensemble and intonation (FN).
176. Vinogradov presented his side of the story, a long and murky narrative involving a foreign sponsor and attempts at extortion by two leading dancers, followed by accusations that Vinogradov and A. F. Mal'kov, the Mariinsky's theatre director, had been engaging in bribery, in an interview some years ago (Anon, '"Mne sledovalo uiti srazu posle prikhoda Gergieva"', *Izvestiya* 17 September 2007, http://izvestia.ru/news/328812). As Vinogradov points out, he and the other accused, the Mariinsky's assistant director, A. F. Mal'kov, were cleared of all charges after a police investigation.
177. Bringing home the issue about the theatre as a 'good night out', one of our informants asked why you should spend 100 dollars on a bottle of champagne in the Mariinsky and then have to stand holding the bottle and glasses with nowhere to put it (Oxf/AHRC SPb-11 PF24 MS).
178. Based on visits in 2009, 2010, 2011, and 2012. See Lev Lur'e, *Putevoditel*, p. 339, for the opinion that 'ballet's official home is now the [former] Maly'.
179. See 'Osipova i Vasil'ev prishli v Mikhailovsky ne za den'gami – glava teatra', 24 November 2011, http://ria.ru/culture/20111124/496829308.html (accessed 29 November 2011).
180. Oxf/AHRC SPb-08 PF49 IN (woman b. 1956 would like a ticket to any of his productions as a gift, though normally only stooping to Nureyev re-runs on TV).
181. In 2013, however, the theatre's presence became the focus of an unholy row with the building's new lessees, with accusations and counter-accusations flying around. As I completed this book, it was unclear whether Litsedei would remain.
182. 'Teatr Derevo otprazdnuet yubilei svoego osnovatelya spektaklyami v Peterburge' (24 April 2009), http://gazeta.spb.ru/144687-0/.
183. Oxf/AHRC SPb-12 PF13 CK. This informant remembered, for instance, seeing a teacher at the Vaganova School who was coaching a pas-de-deux give the female dancer a hard slap in order to make her negotiate a tricky leap into her partner's arms: only through pain could the fear of pain be overcome.
184. FN, September 2012.
185. Savitsky, *Vzglyad*, gives extensive coverage to the art show scene: see e.g. pp. 157–61. On Pro Arte, see also [OL Chapter 4].
186. Visit, FN, October 2011.
187. Several visits, e.g. October 2011 (FN).
188. FN September 2012.

189. Oxf/AHRC SPb-11 PF19 MS (woman b. Leningrad, 1970, intelligentsia background).
190. Oxf/AHRC SPb-05 PF56 IN.
191. A good deal of this activity is in clear breach of international copyright law, but Russian companies have usually accepted the inevitable.
192. For relationship counselling etc., see Oxf/AHRC SPb-11 PF9 EI. Culinary events include displays by the popular radio chef Ilya Lazerson, presenter of 'Culinary First Aid' on a local station, and fashion events the workshop organised by Snob magazine at the Benois School in February 2011 (FN).
193. FN Sept. 2008. See also Oxf/AHRC SPb-11 PF35 MS.
194. Based on personal observation: FN April 2012.
195. The text is widely available on the internet. For its history (it was composed as an anthem for the Soviet-era club in 1980), see Aleksei Antipov, 'Pesnya nad vol'noi Nevoi', *Nash Zenit* no. 16 (414), 30 April–6 May 2007, p. 9. www.fc-zenit.ru/data/media/pdf/archive/414/414.pdf.
196. FN, April 2012.
197. Arshavin has his own website: www.arshavin.eu/ru/index.php, including treacly items about his family life with Yuliya and the kiddies, some written by the lady herself.
198. See, for example, the rather unconvincing page-spread promoting Dinamo, *MR(Vyb)* 26 March 2010, p. 11, including interviews with one fan who recalls thinking in the Soviet period that Dinamo was 'the real thing', a former footballer who lamented the 'poor memory' of Russian football, and an ex-footballer turned priest now working as a chaplain for 'Zenit' who said he would be happy to help other clubs in the future (meaning, presumably, when his temporal, rather than spiritual, contract expired). Like Petrotrest, the city's third team, Dinamo has had to settle for only moderate success even at regional level in the meantime.
199. Spartak, as of 2012, was still reasonably successful, with a basketball complex planned for Krestovsky Island, but two other basketball teams, St Petersburg Lions and Dynamo, both folded in short order. On the former, see Mariya Kravchenko, 'Basketbol. Sankt-Peterburg Laions', www.sport-express.ru/newspaper/2000-07-12/7_4/. Part of the problem is a dearth of local sponsorship: for example, 'Avtomobilist' volleyball team were doing quite well until 2005, when their local sponsor, Baltika, was forced to pull out because of a ban on beer advertising. Since then they have been relegated to regional significance only. See www.vcavtomobilist.ru/history.php. So far as the popular music scene is concerned, I am going by comments from interviews and social websites: for instance, while the singer-songwriter Yury Shevchuk (who moved to Leningrad in 1985 and whose group DDT then became a fixture on the local scene) is still a crucial figure for some, others find his socially critical work (secret policemen at their luxurious dachas etc.) too crude for their tastes.
200. See e.g. www.vremya.ru/2008/214/11/217332.html; http://russianews.ru/freetime/19504/. It should be said that racist slurs by Zenit supporters do not attract this level of intense interest.
201. See the review in *Kommersant*, 'Sueta vokrug kanona', 20 December 2011 (http://kommersant.ru/doc/1841886, and Luke Jennings, 'Who's Pulling the Strings in Russia's Ballet Revolution?', *Observer* 1 January 2012, www.guardian.co.uk/stage/2012/jan/01/mikhailovsky-ballet-bolshoi.
202. As pointed out by Nina Alovert, 'Sankt-Peterburg: kontsert, posvyashchennyi pamyati khoreografa', http://kommersant.russian-bazaar.com/ru/doc/1841886content/4782.htm. Even the Leonid Yakobson Theatre had only two of his works in repertoire, *Spartacus* and an evening of miniatures: www.yacobsonballet.ru/.
203. Oxf/AHRC SPb-12 PF36 MS (musician, b. 1948).
204. Kan, 'Leningradskii rok-klub'.
205. See particularly Oxf/AHRC SPb-12 PF44 MS, where a man b. 1975 who organised apartment concerts in the 2000s and 2010s remarks that he was not old enough to have attended a Soviet-era *kvartirnik*, but wishes he had been.
206. There was a high casualty rate among avant-garde artists generally; Boris Smelov and Timur Novikov were others to die an untimely death. But unlike the musicians, they did not become the subject of posthumous cults.
207. In 2006, the boiler-house museum was spared from demolition by Valentina Matvienko, and by the twentieth anniversary of Tsoi's death his cult had enough establishment appeal to be featured in the Transaero company magazine. What would have been Tsoi's fiftieth birthday in June 2012 was commemorated by an exhibition of blown-up glossy portrait photographs down Malaya Sadovaya. But all of this was quite separate from the initiatives organised by fans themselves.
208. For instance, a woman from Minsk (b. 1978), intelligentsia background, Oxf/AHRC-SPb-07 PF 38 IN. Even in smaller towns in the North-West, people have lost the automatic deference that Leningrad once exerted: see, for example, SPbAG AKF NE PF7, 8, 18, 23, 57, with informants split

between saying that Petersburg is the most beautiful city they know and they always go there for, say, the theatre, and saying that they are no longer interested.

209. See the coverage in *Rossiiskaya gazeta*, 11 May 2012, www.rg.ru/2012/05/11/reg-pfo/perm-ofis-anons.html, and also the Vkontakte page,
210. The title was challenged, for example, in a widely-debated article by Lev Lur'e, 'Petrodegradatsiya', *Kommersant*, 17 December 2012, http://kommersant.ru/doc/2087160.
211. See e.g. Oxf/AHRC SPb-11 PF36 MS.
212. I have repeatedly observed the dearth of audiences for post-Soviet films on visits to the House of Film, most recently to Vladimir Mirzoev's *Boris Godunov* in 2012. For a photograph of the former Sputnik cinema, see fig. 5.16.
213. For a report on the situation, see Igor' Karasev, 'Prinyata kontseptsiya po "Lenfil'mu"', *Metro*, 12 Sept. 2012, pp. 1–2. As of the end of 2012, the situation was still not resolved.
214. On litter, see Oxf/AHRC SPb-07 PF28 IN (man b. 1979). The material about loud talking and mobile telephone conversations comes from my own participant observation.
215. Oxf/AHRC-SPb-07 PF 34 (woman b. 1975, settlement outside Leningrad, working-class single mother).
216. Oxf/AHRC SPb-08 PF43 IN (woman b. 1984).
217. An interesting discussion of this is http://blog.fontanka.ru/posts/86925/ (posts from November 2011): complaints about high prices in the Mariinsky were countered by stories about how to get cheap tickets, and ripostes that only idiot tourists or those who wanted to 'act the toff' [*probivat' ponty*] would visit the place anyway. At the same time, our apartment organiser informant talks about cost as a real deterrent: people would attend no more than one concert, film, or play a week in the 2010s (Oxf/AHRC SPb-12 PF44 MS).
218. Oxf/AHRC SPb-08 PF45 IN (man b. 1987), electrician.
219. Oxf/AHRC SPb-07 PF6IN (woman b. Leningrad, 1986).
220. Cf. the comments made by a young woman sitting next to me in the Mikhailovsky Theatre in 2010, who had brought her daughter to Dvořák's *Rusalka*, and said enthusiastically how much they'd enjoyed it. She added that they always assumed that 'opera isn't for us', but the production, with its striking laser effects and imaginative costumes and staging, had convinced them otherwise. One should not exaggerate this effect – contrast, for instance, Oxf/AHRC-SPb-07 PF 31 IN, in which a young man from working-class roots talks about his marked preference for blues and jazz to classical music. However, in the past, audiences tended to be split between spectators on factory outings who sat rigid with indifference and boredom, Soviet plutocrats who were simply there because tickets were scarce, and a narrow in-group of experienced art-lovers. Now, audiences are not so obviously divided by social status in terms of appreciation, which is certainly a positive development.
221. Oxf/AHRC SPb-07 PF33 IN (woman b. 1958, southern Russia, moved to military settlement outside Leningrad, c. 1980).
222. Oxf/AHRC SPb-07 PF35 IN.
223. Oxf/Lev SPb-11 PF13 MS (woman b. 1989).
224. This was still more the case with films, given that projection facilities in cinemas were often far from top-class, which made staying in with a DVD or online streaming an attractive alternative. See e.g. Oxf/AHRC-SPb-07 PF 16 IN (woman b. 1968, Leningrad, working-class background, now works in business).
225. FN, April 2012.

## 7 From Nord to Saigon

1. Freely adapted from Grebenshchikov, 'Bud' dlya menya kak banka' (www.mirpoezylit.ru/books/5339/247/).
2. *Chanakhi, solyanka*, and *kharcho* are all hearty meat dishes of a soup-stew consistency, and became staples of Soviet mass catering: *solyanka* is traditionally Russian, and flavoured mainly with pickles, while the first and the third are adaptations of spicy Georgian originals (cf. Viennese appropriations of Hungarian *gulyás*).
3. Popov, *Zapomnite nas takimi*, pp. 172–3.
4. Said in 1992 by a friend of mine born in the late 1950s.
5. Following the anthropologist Paul Manning's study of Tiflis in the early twentieth century (see Bibliography), one might describe the typical Leningrad place as a 'café peripheral' – having cafés was essential to the city's claims to be modern, yet there were fears they did not measure up.

6. For the 1967 and 1968 figures, see 'Spravka o vypolnenii postanovleniya byuro Leningradskogo Obkoma KPSS ot 25/IV-1967 goda "O zadachakh partiinykh organizatsii Leningrada i oblasti po dal'neishemu uluchsheniyu i razvitiyu obshchestvennogo pitaniya v sootvetstvii s postanovleniem TsK KPSS i Soveta Ministrov SSSR ot 7/III-1967 g.', TsGAIPD-SPb. 25/102/31/5; *Spisok abonentov LGTS* (1988).
7. Getting admitted to an Intourist hotel was a complicated business, since all visitors were required to show their passports at the door. Foreigners were allowed in without further ado, but locals had to demonstrate a 'right' to be in the hotel and might well fall under suspicion of black-market trading etc. While the prices were not necessarily higher than elsewhere in the city, this cordon sanitaire acted as a deterrent to many. One of our informants who did remember going to such places got in because she worked as a tour guide (Oxf/AHRC SPb-11 PF35 MS).
8. See e.g. the comments of Yury Petrovich in *Sumerki Saigona*, ed. Valieva, p. 310. The Metropole, however, was considered a rung or so below the others by some: see e.g. the comments by Lev Lur'e, quoted in Kseniya Poteeva, Egor Elkin, 'Metropol' otkrylsya s novoi nachinkoi', 27 April 2010 (www.fontanka.ru/2010/04/27/108/). It may possibly have been the presence of a private hall for Party bigwigs with a 'Regional Committee table' that generated snobbery.
9. Some of our informants (e.g. Oxf/AHRC SPb-10 PF7 MS, Oxf/AHRC SPb-07 PF6 SA) were also distinctly unflattering about the endless queues in restaurants and cafés, the abiding smell of dreary food, and so on. The many positive memories, as I discuss below, are related to the company not the fare.
10. Already in the 1790s, Georgi (p. 444) observed that the elite of St Petersburg generally ate French food, with the exception of some token dishes such as *kut'ya* [frumenty], *kulebyaka* [fish pie], *botvin'ya* [beet leaf soup], *kisel'* [fruit compote thickened with potato flour], *shchi* [cabbage soup] etc. The habit of serving *zakuski* with vodka was also universal (ibid., p. 445). Note also the bias towards French food in the collection of recipes from the Durnovo household in the 1850s (Lotman and Pogosyan). Professor Piazzi Smyth, Astronomer Royal for Scotland, was generally very enthusiastic about St Petersburg (which he visited in the 1850s), but noted that his furnished rooms had attached 'a bad and costly imitation of a Paris restaurant' (vol. 1, p. 193).
11. Cf. the comments of Pamela Davidson, 'When I asked a chef in Tallinn what her best and most typically Estonian recipes were, she produced a mammoth book put out in the 1950s by the Ministry of Trade for all catering establishments in the Soviet Union (complete with tables of quantities for 100 people) and started enumerating the standard fish dishes to be found in every Soviet restaurant, such as the inevitable Ryba Po-Pol'ski [fish, Polish style], a sad combination of fish with hard-boiled egg on top' ('Recipes from the Soviet Union', p. 341).
12. Vadim Shefner, 'Dvorets na troikh: Priznanie kholostyaka', *Skazki dlya umnykh*, p. 274.
13. Rein, *Mne skuchno bez Dovlatova*, p. 81. Poteeva and Elkin, 'Metropol otkrylsya' (see n. 8 above), mentions a former military translator going on the razzle in the Metropole during the 1980s, with money earned in the Middle East.
14. Corsini, *Caviar for Breakfast*, p. 20, is a typical example of a tourist missing the point: 'It wasn't an especially complicated meal but the waiter, a bald toothless old man, took his own good time serving it. Between courses he would vanish into the back regions for a half-hour at a stretch. The poor man was eighty, we learned. He should have been enjoying the retirement he deserved at his age. But there seems to be a labour shortage in the Soviet Union, especially in unskilled workers, and waiters' jobs go begging.' Why give up a prestigious job, such as working in the Astoria, with so many deficit items within ready reach, and the promise of tips too? Foreigners' bewilderment at bad service was because they hadn't built up a relationship with a waiter who would 'see them right' if they saw him right. For an account of such a relationship, see Rein, *Mne skuchno bez Dovlatova*, pp. 81–4.
15. Robinson, *An American in Leningrad*, pp. 138, 150. According to Poteeva and Elkin, 'Metropol' otkrylsya' (see n. 8 above), that restaurant was particularly popular with military types.
16. See e.g. Oxf/AHRC SPb-11 PF35 (mentioning the House of Actors and the House of Architects). As of the 2010s, the House of Actors still offered good versions of Soviet restaurant classics (red caviar and blini etc.) at moderate prices, in a hall with beautiful plasterwork. (FN June 2012, April 2013).
17. Cf. Yury Petrovich in Valieva (ed.), *Sumerki Saigona*: 'If you had plenty of money you'd visit a big restaurant in a big group, if you had a bit less, you'd visit a middle-sized one with a smaller group . . . and so on. If you had no money at all, you'd go to a park. Whichever way, there was always the feeling money was a bit tight.' Smirnov, *Deistvuyushchie litsa*, p. 21, recalls ordering meatballs and vodka 'on tick' in the Vostochnyi, with one's student record book [*zachetnaya kniga*] as security. Viktor Toporov, *Dvoinoe dno*, p. 103, recalls that in the 1960s, 'When we had a bit of money, we'd go to the Metropol''.

18. Zhores Alferov (a physicist originally from Minsk) recalled that in the 1940s, when he was a student, he ate regularly at the 'Rooftop' restaurant of the Evropeiskaya (Aleksandr Zapesotsky, 'Interv'yu s Z. I. Alfedovym', *University Magazine*, pp. 11–12 (2004), p. 31). By the 1960s, a grant would not have gone far (certainly in the evening), but such restaurants could be visited as a treat.
19. One of my informants recalled organising a wedding reception in the Evropeiskaya because it didn't cost any more than anywhere else, but was significantly better (this was in the early 1970s).
20. The analogy in, say, London would be that tea in a leading hotel would not necessarily cost more than a fairly mediocre lunch somewhere else, but eating it every day would be, to a native of the city, distinctly odd.
21. V. Smirnov, 'Vecher v restorane', *LP* 7 February 1975, p. 2, gave some eye-stretching examples: in one case, two manual workers who went to a restaurant had been presented with a series of excessive bills, the first overcharging them by 100 per cent; when they paid the last one (which was still for too much), they got insulted. The Karyushka Restaurant had 'lost' a banquet booking and hiked the final bill up 78.60 roubles (then a substantial sum). The Nevsky Restaurant (one of the city's premier venues) was a hive of corruption; the Moskva (ditto) had cases of poor service. Complaints were dealt with, in one restaurant, by a crafty system of 'double accounting' that had the customers write in one book, while another, virginally blank, was forwarded to the local administration.
22. For example, in 1966 there were 973 complaints; in 1967, 860; and in 1968, 844, of which 283, 220, and 193 respectively were aimed at the quality of the meal. 'Spravka o vypolnenii', l. 13 (the number of covers across the city was 233,666 in 1967 and 265,192 in 1968). Customer service experts in 2000s Britain reckoned that for every person who complained, twenty-five others were dissatisfied; if applied to Leningrad, this would suggest quite formidable levels of dissatisfaction.
23. The name is derived from Ivan Krylov's poem, about how the over-assiduous host Dem'yan forces his guests to eat far more than they wish of the delicious fish soup at his table.
24. The restaurants named, Fregat, Okolitse, Dem'yanova ukha, Volkhov and Primorsky, were all in outlying areas of the city. Smirnov, 'Vecher v restorane'.
25. On queuing, see Oxf/AHRC SPb-11 PF18 MS: 'You couldn't get into the "Nevsky", you couldn't get into the "Universal"', as for the "Moskva" – there were queues everywhere. And even the plain little cafés, the ones some way out, on Petrograd Side – you couldn't even get into those if it was a Friday or Saturday'.
26. See the interesting accounts by Evgeny Drapkin (2003), http://arkasha-severnij.narod.ru/minesd-zaza.html, and Vladimir Lavrov (2004), 'Ot El'brusa do Baku', www.blat.dp.ua/legenda/lavrov.htm. On this type of popular music generally, see Hufen.
27. For the 1967 and 1968 figures, see 'Spravka o vypolnenii', l. 5; *Spisok abonentov LGTS* (1988).
28. *Kafe* was the broader term: while a *kafeterii* never had table service, a *kafe* sometimes did, but on the other hand, a self-service place might be called either one or the other.
29. German, *Slozhnoe proshedshee*, p. 71.
30. As suggested by the fond memories of Tartu by Georgy Levinton in idem and Nikolai Vakhtin, 'Ot redaktorov', p. 11.
31. See e.g. Tat'yana Nikol'skaya in *Sumerki "Saigona"*, p. 17 (she and her friends preferred the cocktails to the ice-cream); Oxf/AHRC SPb-11 PF7 EI; Oxf/AHRC GB-08 CK PF2. A more repressive line was taken in Yu. Orokhvatsky, 'Kafe nachinaetsya s imeni', *Smena*, 2 July 1980, p. 2, which remarked that the café was so called because of the 'swamp green of its furniture, walls, light-fittings and mats', and that the place was rather short of choice in ice-creams. It served a drink called 'Privet' [Hi!], but this had an ironic effect, as the beverage was strangely bitter. Other cafés mentioned in memoirs etc. include 'Dessert', 'The café on Konyushennaya', and 'Spartacus' (Nina Savchenkova in *Muzei – anti-muzei*, p. 8).
32. German, *Slozhnoe proshedshee*, p. 71. Sweets and patisseries (*konditerskie izdeliya*) are extensively discussed in *Peterburg: istoriya torgovli*, 2, pp. 191–245.
33. Minutka, Metropol', DLT. and Universal, all Oxf/AHRC SPb-07 PF9 SA; Lukomor'e cafe on VO. V. Smirnov, 'Vecher v restorane', *LP* 7 February 1975, p. 2. On the Pogrebok, see Oxf/AHRC SPb-07 PF1 IN. The two most popular places selling doughnuts were next to the Moscow Station and close by the House of Leningrad Trade: FN February 2011; Oxf/AHRC-07 PF9 SA; Oxf/AHRC SPb-11 PF18 MS.
34. V. Uflyand, 'Otmetki na karte Peterburga', *"Esli Bog poshlet mne chitatelei"* (St Petersburg: Blits, 1999), p. 67. The places named were numbers 6–11, 15, 17, 27, 34–6 of a list of places associated with Sergei Dovlatov.
35. In 1988, there were 108 cafés in the city with names, 45 with no names, around 80 ice-cream cafés, and five *kafeterii*. *Spisok abonentov LGTS* (1988).

36. On the 'Vos'myorka' and 'Akademichka', see Olesya Guk and Daniil Dugaev, 'Akademichka', *Pchela* 6 (1996), www.pchela.ru/podshiv/6/academ.htm.
37. Based on my own memories of Leningrad cafés in the 1970s and 1980s.
38. Cf. Anna Katsman, Viktor Krivulin's first wife, on the home life of his parents (Valieva (ed.), *Sumerki Saigona*, p. 262): their flat 'was well-looked after, with heavy crimson curtains at the many windows of the main room, French-polished furniture and crystal in the display cabinets' (in dissident and Bohemian circles, these things were signifiers of 'petit-bourgeois' tastes). This point is made also by L. Lur'e, 'Kak Nevskii prospekt', p. 212.
39. I remember being told this about coffee in the 1980s; displays at the Museum of the History of Leningrad had a coffee urn rather than a samovar. Coffee also appealed because there was no requirement to eat with it; on the other hand, tea without food was disapprovingly known as 'naked tea' (see Davidson, 'Food and Community'). It should be said that the lack of seats did not appeal to everyone: cf. the dismissal of Soviet-era cafés, 'there was nowhere to sit', by woman b. 1945 (Oxf/AHRC SPb-10 PF4 MS), or the description of feeling constantly under pressure to order something (Oxf/AHRC-SPb-07 35 PF IN) (woman b. 1961).
40. http://rock.ru/forum/index.php?topic=27924.80.
41. My thanks to Marina Samsonova for the memories of 'Yama'. (Nina Savchenkova, in *Muzei – antimuzei*, p. 8, talks about the process by which cafés became *metaphors*.)
42. See Aleksandr Vyal'tsev in Valieva (ed.), *Sumerki Saigona*, p. 510.
43. See e.g. Skobkina, pp. 86–7
44. In 2008, some of the artists who had once visited 'the Crack' organised a special exhibition, 'Svet i sumerki shchelei', named in honour of the place, by then long vanished. 'The Crack' was also favoured for a nip of cognac.
45. Vakhtin, 'Malen'kii dvoinoi'.
46. German, p. 631.
47. As recounted in Oxf/AHRC UK-08 PF62 (the queue in question being in the buffet of the State Public Library, now RNB).
48. See the memoir of Efim Marikhbein, 'Vremya, otpusti na vremya!' (2010), www.proza.ru/2010/01/15/1575. On the 'youth cafe' movement generally, see Tsipursky.
49. Zinaida Partis, 'Eto ya pomnyu', http://posev.ru/files/articles/2006/ne_6065.htm.
50. N. Kosareva, 'Byt' tribunom ne tol'ko v stikhakh!', *Izvestiya*, 23 May 1963, p. 3. The article – whose author was then First Secretary of the Dzerzhinsky raikom KPSS – also denounced Viktor Sosnora and others 'for stuffing the heads of young people with their dubious, formalist verses'.
51. Yu. Golubensky, 'Ot "Gavana" do "Fantazii": Zametki o molodezhnykh kafe', *Smena* 25 February 1965, p. 3.
52. See the description by a regular, the photographer Galina Lisyutich, who first met Vysotsky there in 1969. Oxf/AHRC SPb-12 PF12 CK; and also the transcript of the TV programme led by Lev Lur'e, 'Klub "Vostok"', 7 February 2009, www.5-tv.ru/programs/broadcast/503149/.
53. 'Nevskii prospekt do i posle'. The café on ul. Poltavskaya and its regulars are described in Partis.
54. Various explanations for the nickname are bandied about; one common one is that an outraged policeman, viewing the scene before him, exclaimed: 'What's all this here? Are you trying to organise your own Saigon or something?' (Toporov, *Dvoinoe dno*, p. 115). However, a likelier reason for the name may lie in the fact that the Soviet authorities constantly harped on the Vietnam War as a shameful instance of American imperialism. In the counter-culture, this type of official evaluation was inverted, and it was natural to wish to identify with the South Vietnamese, the 'bourgeois lackeys of imperialist aggression', rather than the North Vietnamese (and with the Israelis against the Palestinians, etc.). Interestingly, another 'alternative' hangout was known as 'Ulster', presumably because the place was also associated with rebellion (on the name, see V. Lur'e, *Mikrotoponimika*; for a description of 'Ulster' as 'a popular bohemian hangout/nondescript coffee shop', see the post by the writer Mikhail Iossel, Facebook, 28 December 2012.
55. See Scabon, response to Mikhail Berg, 21 May 2009, http://mikhail-berg.livejournal.com/4554.html?thread=14794.
56. Valieva (ed.), *Sumerki Saigona*, p. 261.
57. Tat'yana Bogomolova in *Sumerki Saigona*, p. 295.
58. There is an enormous literature on Saigon. Besides Valieva's indispensable anthology, *Sumerki Saigona*, see Elena Zdravomyslova, 'Leningradskii Saigon: prostranstvo negativnoi svobody', *NLO* 100 (2009), http://magazines.russ.ru/nlo/2009/100/el47.html; 'Nevskii prospekt do i posle'; Boym, *The Future*; Toporov, *Dvoinoe dno*, pp. 116–36; etc.
59. For the phrase 'negative freedom', see Zdravomyslova. In Voronezh (where I lived from 1980–1), one 'milk café' was called 'The Dumb Knight', after Pushkin's 'Little Tragedy', because it was used as

a meeting-place by the profoundly deaf, who used to meet up and have conversations in sign-language. There were various canteens and cafés that had better reputations than others. But there was no one place that had the kind of central role of Saigon, Malaya Sadovaya, Lyagushatnik, etc.

60. Zinaida Partis, 'Eto ya pomnyu', talks about the switch to flats around 11 pm: http://posev.ru/files/articles/2006/ne_6065.htm.
61. Shtern, 'Epistolyarnye i drugie igry', *Brodsky: Osya, Iosif, Joseph*, pp. 94–101. See also Sergei Vasil'ev in Valieva (ed.), *Sumerki Saigona*, p. 441, parodies of official 'Dokladnaya zapiska' about which buildings are to be retained and which demolished.
62. For example, the home seminars and forums and poetry readings organised by the '37' group. See Zitzewitz, 'The "Religious Renaissance" of the 1970s'; Yuri Kolker, 'V storonu Khodasevicha', http://yuri-kolker-up-to-date.narod.ru/prose/my_boiler_rooms.htm.
63. Lists of such rules appeared annually. In 1970, for example, citizens were forbidden to perform 'loud music, song, and other noise that disturbs the peace of the citizenry in streets and courtyards between 11 pm and 7 am'; by 1972, such noise was forbidden at all times of day. See *BILGS* 20 (1970), p. 16; ibid., p. 21 (1972), p. 14. For further sets of such regulations, see e.g. *BILGS* 16 (1982), pp. 17–19.
64. See e.g. the discussion on http://vkontakte.ru/topic-998865_21434274. The borrowing *Brodvei* was a pun on the Russian verb *brodit'* (to wander), and was standard in the youth culture of other cities as well.
65. See e.g. Smirnov, *Deistvuyushchie litsa*, p. 17: 'You go down the street and exchange a few words with the friends you encounter along the way, and you catch up on all the important news in the city – not the kind of thing you'd ever hear on the radio.'
66. Nor were the pre-revolutionary boulevards, such as Konnogvardeisky [Profsoyuzov] much favoured for strolling, probably because there were few cafés and so on here.
67. Hingley, *Under Soviet Skins*, p. 14.
68. Some had the reputation of cruising places too, particularly 'Kat'kin sad' [the Catherine Garden] next to the Pushkin [Aleksandrinsky] Theatre. The translation 'square gardens' ennobles the *skver*, which was usually just a patch of grass between buildings, often replacing bombed-out structures in the post-war era as part of the policy of 'greening' the city.
69. I remember a comment of this kind from a friend in 1985.
70. The debate was started by Z. Gorchakova's article, 'Pavlovskie karuseli', published in *Sovetskaya Rossiya* on 7 July 1982. As a result, the Upravlenie kul'tury hastened to assure the Leningrad Regional Committee of the CP that plans to turn the park into a reserve were already in train (for the cutting and response, see TsGAIPD 24/191/16/25-6).
71. See e.g. Oxf/AHRC SPb-07 PF 12 (man b. 1977).
72. Almedingen, p. 173, recalls seeing a notice banning 'lower ranks of the army and navy', as well as dogs and beggars, from the Summer Garden. In Nadezhda Teffi's 1910 story 'Walled Up' [Za stenoi], a mistress taunts her cook for 'walking out' in a cemetery.
73. See, for example, the report from 1963 on what had been going on in 1962 and 1963 at the Smolenskoe Cemetery: TsGALI 105/1/1502/39.
74. I remember being taken to this in the 1980s. The building still exists, but the area round it has been rendered unrecognisable by new building. This kind of purposive strolling acquired its own guide-books in the post-Soviet era: see e.g. Izmozik.
75. 'In the Nevsky delta, the weather most of the year is really horrible, and so walking with your friends out of doors isn't much fun' (Lev Lur'e, 'Kak Nevskii prospekt', p. 212). Slush (especially when mixed with crude salt) also takes a terrible toll on footwear, which in the Soviet period was hard to get, and thereafter very expensive.
76. Nielsen has a nice discussion of the 'gasified water' of the Soviet period, complete with illustration of one of the machines (one kopeck for plain, three for water with syrup).
77. Cf. the declaration of a working-class informant (b. 1944) that 'I'd rather take my own food with me than go to one of those [i.e. a café]' (though his wife did visit) (Oxf/AHRC SPb-08 PF-51 IN). Oxf/AHRC SPb-11 PF4 NG recalls going to the *pyshechnaya* on ul. Zhelyabova (now B. Konyushennaya).
78. O. Kolesova, 'Gde vstrechaemsya segodnya? Problemy klubnoi raboty', *LP* 20 October 1976, p. 3. Cf. the recollection of a working-class informant b. 1929 that people would not have gone to a café or restaurant even to celebrate a wedding (Oxf/AHRC-SPb-07 PF17).
79. On the replacement of alcohol by drugs, see e.g. Zdravomyslova, 'Leningradskii "Saigon"'. Sokolov's 1989 guide for Leningrad temperance workers has valuable material on the ethnography of social drinking in the late Soviet era.
80. Uflyand, 'Otmetki', p. 69. Viktor Toporov, *Dvoinoe dno*, p. 116, mentions the Ol'ster on Nevsky most, and the bar in the Oktabr'skaya Hotel.

81. Lur'e, *Putevoditel'*, p. 7.
82. On the manufacture and consumption of Soviet champagne, see Konstantin Bogdanov, 'Sovetskoe shampanskoe: prazdnichnaya istoriya', *Antropologicheskii forum* 16 (2012), pp. 367–78.
83. Alekseev, 'Piterskie khroniki'. Even newspaper reports acknowledged that bars were usually dives: see e.g. S. Aleksashin, 'V bare posle urokov', *Smena* 21 March 1980, p. 2, which includes a vivid description of the 'Khmel'' [meaning Hop, but also 'a tipsy condition'] on Ligovsky prospekt.
84. For instance, Lev Losev (*Meandr*, p. 157) recalled how he and his father celebrated Losev's son's birth 'in the folk style – we went to a milk bar on Vladimirskaya ploshchad' with a quarter-bottle of vodka, doing the pouring under the table'.
85. 'Gleb Gorbovsky', in Kuzminsky and Kovalev (eds), *The Blue Lagoon Anthology*, p. 430.
86. Ibid., p. 426. Gorbovsky totally gave up drinking in the mid-1970s and has since adopted a very critical attitude to his alcoholic past, and to what he sees as the taboo hanging over excessive drinking in Russia generally: *Ostyvshie sledy*, pp. 76–7.
87. See the discussion in Hodgson, *Voicing*, pp. 29–31.
88. Aleksashin, 'V bare posle urokov', included vox pops with young people saying they never had any trouble getting served in cocktail bars and cafés, their preferred venues. Youth cafés served alcohol, and a waitress at one of these simply shrugged when asked why she did not require ID. On 17 May 1980, the deputy director of the canteens trust, Kuibyshev district, reported in *Smena* (p. 3) that measures had been taken: the director of *Vostok* café had been sacked and *Khmel'* (a particularly unsalubrious beer-bar on Ligovka) closed for redecoration. However, this certainly did not get to the root of the problem.
89. Alekseev, 'Piterskie khroniki'.
90. See e.g. Uflyand, 'Pogovorit' o literature', *"Esli Bog poshlet . . ."*, pp. 104–10. As for 'not always', I can remember taking a bottle of gin to some friends when I arrived in Leningrad in 1988, having not visited for a couple of years; it was immediately (at 10 in the morning) opened to celebrate.
91. As portrayed in Gal'perin, *Russkii variant*, in his *Most cherez Letu*, pp. 354–5. At later stages, barmen might serve *razbavon*, or watered-down beer – unpleasant, but better than nothing (ibid., p. 359).
92. So at least I was assured by a veteran of such places.
93. Hedrick Smith, *The Russians* (London, 1976), p. 155. 'They know no moderation. Once the vodka bottle is uncorked, it must be finished. There is no such thing as putting it back on the shelf, a notion that amuses Russians whenever a Westerner mentions the idea. Russians drink to obliterate themselves, to blot out the tedium of life, to warm themselves from the chilling winters, and they eagerly embrace the escapism it [drinking] offers.' For the wider meaning of drinking, see also Pesmen, pp. 170–88.
94. Losev, *Sobrannoe*, p. 551. As Gerry Smith has reminded me, Losev is playing on a famous saw of Maxim Gorky's: 'I owe everything worthwhile in myself to books'.
95. Oxf/AHRC SPb-11 PF3 NG.
96. See Hodgson, *Voicing*, pp. 29–30, which points out that a man who drank as much as Berggol'ts would have excited a very different reaction. The poet Elena Shvarts, another flamboyant female drinker (see below), also attracted disapproval, for similar reasons.
97. Ibid.
98. As in the case of Elena Shvarts, who 'would drink anything; she tended to refer to any alcoholic drink as *vypivon* [booze]' (Gerry Smith, email. July 2012).
99. Ibid. In general, wine bars such as the *razliv* described by Alekseev were a cut above *ryumochnye* and beer-bars (though the last could be used by anyone 'the morning after').
100. Oxf/AHRC SPb-11 PF3 NG. Cf. the post-Soviet recollection in Oxf/AHRC SPb-11 PF6 EI of seeing two total bums walking along effing and blinding, and suddenly hearing the words 'Mucius Scaevola', something he considered a real Petersburg experience.
101. Orokhvatsky, 'Kafe nachinaetsya s imeni', p. 2.
102. For instance, L. Emel'yanenko, 'Rogatki na molodezhnoi ulitse', *Smena* 24 August 1980, p. 3, was ironic about a style of retro bar in Frankfurt: it represented the worn-out system that socialists were trying to change. Restylings in Leningrad were superior because they were up-to-date. Indeed, shiny wood veneer and beaten metal were typical, as can be seen in the library of the European University, St Petersburg (formerly the canteen of the Institute of Labour Protection, and a rare surviving interior from this period).
103. This involved dark blue, silver, and gold, and can still be seen, for instance, in the tiling on the outside of the Hotel Leningrad, though the interiors have been remodelled. A lighting scheme with this palette was proposed in 1975 for Nevsky: see 'Ogni bol'shogo goroda', *LP* 9 April 1975,

p. 3. It was also used in shops: see e.g. V. I. Zhukovsky, 'Obnovlyaetsya knizhnyi salon', *LPan* 4 (1987), p. 52 – on such a scheme for the 'Leningrad' bookshop on Nevsky.

104. A. I. Kucher, 'Teplo gostepriimnogo "Severa" ', *LPan* 4 (1986), pp. 21–2.
105. V. I. Gribanov, 'Vlast' pamyatnogo mesta', *LPan* 7 (1985), pp. 27–9.
106. V. Barmin, 'Lanch v Natsionale', *VL* 4 January 1991, p. 1.
107. See the report in *LP* 16 July 1988, p. 4. To be more accurate, this was a repackaging, since the café had previously been known as 'Mineral Waters and Juices', and had sold much the same (my thanks to Nikolai Vakhtin for this information). Another early arrival was Pizza Express, whose second branch was opened in early 1991: see *VL* 16 February 1991, p. 2. On the Georgian original Lagidze, see Manning.
108. (Author not credited) 'Brosaem kurit', ili Kak v nashem gorode proshel pervyi den' bez nikotina', *Vechernii Leningrad*, 8 April 1988, p. 3.
109. On the planned transformation, see 'Pyat' voprosov', *LPan* 8 (1991), p. 11. On the bathroom shop, see 'Saigon: Oskolki istorii', www.hippy.ru/saygon.htm.
110. For instance, on 23 November 1994, the Baku, the Hotel Leningrad, the restaurant at the Finland Station, and numerous *stolovye* were privatised: http://lawrussia.ru/texts/legal_185/doc185a728x381.htm.
111. On this process, see e.g. Poteeva and Elkin, 'Metropol' otkrylsya'.
112. For an account of some of the clubs, see the article by a visiting American using the Nabokovian name 'Ada Trikster', 'Peterburgskie nait-kluby: inaya real'nost', *Smena*, 22 January 1994, p. 3; 29 January 1994, p. 6. The art club Borei on Liteinyi was, the writer had been told, the only place where there was still literary life to be seen. The individual places were unimpressive. Saturn on Sadovaya, for instance, was upmarket but stuffy. Wild Side at Narvskaya metro station was filled with tobacco fug and as claustrophic as the Cabinet of Doctor Caligari. In short, the scene was as dismal as in Mexico, with the only point of interest the sense of history being made.
113. Oxf/AHRC SPb-11 PF35 MS. This informant said that she had a voucher for 5000 roubles (around 200 dollars) to eat there, but 'that's really nothing'.
114. www.restoclub.ru/site/all/main/229/. To be fair, the menu also had some more traditional fare, for instance, jellied meat with horseradish, but Molokhovets would scarcely have recognised the 'mangos' etc. on offer.
115. For a discussion of the general significance of the hard sign as signifying 'traditional quality', see Baiburin, 'Ъ'.
116. 'Razgovory o ede', *MR* 1 August 2003, p. 9.
117. A more interesting retro venture, from the gastronomic point of view, was 'Erivan' (from the old spelling of the Armenian capital) on the Fontanka, presenting a refined menu of food with a distinctive national slant.
118. For mockery of the name, see 'Blyudo v tumane', *MR* 1 August 2003, p. 9. A more endearing case is the 'Afishka' (Handbill) Café on Mokhovaya, next to the Theatre Academy, where an ordinary cabbage salad might be called *Summerfolk* (literally The Dacha Dwellers, but from the title of Gorky's play), and a plate of banal pelmeni *The Three Sisters* (Oxf/AHRC SPb-07 PF28 IN, man b. 1979, Leningrad).
119. As acknowledged by a professional chef: Oxf/AHRC SPb-11 PF18 MS.
120. www.allcafe.info/guide/posts/3/ (3 November 2007).
121. As recounted by the academic in question, January 2003.
122. FN, June 2004.
123. FN, April 2013.
124. On the lack of cafés, Oxf/AHRC SPb-08 PF47 IN, p. 3: Andrei S., b. 1972, Ukraine, WB, builder. On the patisserie at the Evropeiskaya, see 'U sostoyatel'nykh sladkoezhek – prazdnik zhivota', *Smena* 7 July 1994, p. 1.
125. O. Boiko, 'Cherez dva mesyatsa tsentr mozhet okazat'sya bez tualetov', *NevV* 26 October 2000, pp. 1, 2. (The toilets were in fact replaced by Paris-style coin-operated booths in some places, but more often by supervised kiosks and by all kinds of temporary fixtures, including not just official toilet cabins, but also disused buses – there is one such on Universitetskaya naberezhnaya, and another in Aleksandrovsky park – and other such eccentricities.)
126. There is a cluster of such places on Kondrat'evsky prospekt, next to the Leningrad Metal-Working Factory (LMZ). In 2008, some women appealed to the local administration to intervene because their husbands were drinking their wages in these places – the modern touch being that the bars now offered credit, so that they were able to drink money they did not actually have. See the newsletter 'Finlyandsky okrug', www.finokrug.spb.ru/papers/92008.pdf (accessed 8 January 2011).

127. In the first category was, for example, 'Idiot' on the Moika (also favoured by returning émigrés: see Oxf/AHRC UK-08 PF80 AB); on the other, Dom byta on Raz"ezzhaya, which, despite its Soviet name, had 1960s furniture from London (www.the-village.ru/village/all-village/spb/105625-novoe-mesto-kafe-bar-dom-byta).
128. The former is on Millionnaya (a survival of the co-operative era, by the look of things), while the latter is on Troitsky prospekt.
129. FN, Dec. 2012.
130. FN, October 2011. For the media celebration, see e.g. 'Proshlo 20 let', a list of Leningrad 'sacred places', *MR (Ostrova)* 9 September 2011, pp. 6–7.
131. FN June 2012. Extremely popular with students back in the 1970s, as the friend who took me there recalled (ibid.), the place is still regularly mentioned on the internet as a reliable cheap option.
132. The main flavourings used in post-Soviet catering, as in the Soviet era, are salt and pepper, and pot herbs such as onion and carrot, and perhaps also bay leaf. It is interesting that a woman working in the catering business named 'tastiness' as her criterion too: Oxf/AHRC SPb-11 PF35 MS.
133. www.mcdonalds.ru/base/search/?city_id=7. On the arrival of McDonalds in Moscow, see Caldwell, 'Domesticating the French Fry'.
134. On Starbucks, see www.lenta.ru/news/2009/01/22/starbucks/.
135. The organic bakery is Ovsyanka on Gorokhovaya, the French corner café (mainly French in terms of its retro photographs) Chez Jules on ul. Gangutskaya. One of our informants (Oxf/AHRC SPb-11 PF35 MS), the proprietor of a café close to 'Five Corners', emphasised that she wanted to run somewhere for 'friends, and the friends of friends', a place aimed at families and young 'creative people'. Many small places in St Petersburg have that kind of feel.
136. As noted by a local businesswoman with a middle-sized catering business: FN March 2012. There are some vegetarians among young Petersburgers, but almost none in the middle and older generations.
137. For pictures of the cakes, see www.spb-business.ru/show.php?directory=1281. Other observations – FN April 2010. Cf. Bushe (=Bouchée, after a popular kind of chocolate-topped sweet sponge with a cream filling), though this goes for more of an international middle-market chic distressed paint and designer lampshade look, and the cakes are sleeker too.
138. On the shock effect of seeing women in cafés in the 1990s out drinking on their own – and not slappers either, normal women enjoying a glass of cognac, see Oxf/AHRC SPb-11 PF3 NG.
139. Near Lomonosovskaya metro station, for example, a bakery offered a slice of freshly-made pie with savoury or sweet fillings and a drink for about 70 roubles, or 2 dollars (FN April 2011).
140. This point is made by Oxf/AHRC SPb-07 PF35 IN (woman b. 1961); she in fact claimed that in St Petersburg one did not need to order at all, which may be pushing it, but certainly service was often very laid back or lackadaisical, depending on one's point of view.
141. A rather comical illustration of the Soviet disapproval of refreshments was the effort made by VOOPIiK's board in 1971 to try and regulate provisioning in the Summer Garden's Kofeinyi domik, the pavilion constructed (as its name suggested) for the serving of coffee. The preservationists reluctantly agreed that a 'limited assortment' of snacks etc. might be made available, but not including alcoholic drinks, justifying this by the need to preserve the monument: TsGALI-SPb. 229/1/50/37-8.
142. http://arkasha-severnij.narod.ru/minesdzaza.htm.
143. In October 2011, I paid over 40 dollars for a herb tea, a coffee, and a single portion of strudel.
144. Based on visits in 2010 and 2011.
145. Oxf/AHRC SPb-07 PF34 IN, p. 9 (woman b. 1975, Tikhvin district) – on Staronevsky, in this case. Oxf/AHRC SPb-07 PF 44 IN: kafe Bukvoed a 'cult place'. For *kafeshka*, see e.g. FN April 2010 (a man inviting a friend, 'we can drop in to this little *kafeshka* where quite a few boozing sessions have gone on'). This is more likely in the centre than the outlying areas, where, as one of our informants put it, 'everything's in those malls, those glass things' (Oxf/AHRC SPb-10 PF8 MS).
146. See e.g. Oxf/AHRC SPb-10 PF7 MS.
147. One explanation for this is surely the progressive marginalisation of the communal apartment: cf. the comment of one informant that 'the centre's kind of not lived in any more', just somewhere you would visit a café (Oxf/AHRC SPb-07 PF 4,5 A,B IN). That said, all-night cafés such as the one on Sennaya attract young people sitting with their laptops who look like refugees from nearby *kommunalki* (judging by a visit at 3 a.m. (FN June 2011), when a friend and I got caught on the wrong side of the Neva bridges).
148. Nadezhda Kulikova, 'Posporit' o nauke mozhno v bare', *MR(K)* 26 November 2004, p. 6.

149. One of our informants (man b. 1979) drew an interesting contrast between the hurried pace expected by most Russians in cafés and the more relaxed atmosphere in Paris: Oxf/AHRC-SPb-07 28 IN.
150. www.gotospb.ru/clubs.html (last accessed 18 October 2010). Among other places mentioned by informants were Stirki [The Laundry Room] and Cheshirskii kot [Cheshire Cat], described as 'underground clubs', the latter with 'far-out design' (Oxf/AHRC-SPb-08 PF-45).
151. See Oxf/AHRC SPb-11 PF13 EI for a reference to these places, which are also liked by my own students.
152. Vershlovsky, *Peterburgskaya shkola: Portret vypusnika*, p. 34. In 1993, 'looking good' had been only seventh, while 'someone to love' [lyubimyi chelovek'] fell from the second place it had occupied in 1993 to only seventh. 'Interesting work' and 'material well-being' had also risen in the list. The city also began acquiring image-makers. A leaflet given out at a fashion workshop organised by *Snob* magazine (FN February 2011) advertised makeovers such as '16 Ways to Plait Your Hair', 'Your Dream Come True: Colour Types and Colour Choices', 'Look Like a Cover Girl', 'Society Girls and Demi-Mondaines', 'It-Girls' (sic), and so on. On its site, the same place was advertising a two-day makeover service for 15,000 roubles (around 500 dollars), including a visit to a hairdresser and a makeup artist, with an optional extra charge of 5000 roubles for having your picture taken once transformed.
153. This comment is impressionistic, since so far as I have been able to find, census data does not include information about the numbers of young adults living at home.
154. *Peterburgskaya shkola: Portret vypusnika*, p. 43, established a correlation between how often school-leavers went out and what the family income was (the higher it was, the more they went out).
155. www.youtube.com/watch?v=kySalou451Q. Alongside this counter-cultural posing, the members of 'Segodnya noch'yu' are slickly dressed and the music is thoroughly commercial, marking a change in taste from the rock bands of the late Soviet era.
156. See e.g. Alla Borisova, 'Prochitala dnevnik docheri, a tam takoe . . .', *NV* 3 February 1995, p. 2, where an anxious mother reported that she had found material about parties, sex, and drugs in her daughter's private diary. See also Oxf/AHRC SPb 07 PF25 IN (a famous politician's daughter was in rehab etc.).
157. *Sotsial'naya istoriya Sankt-Peterburga*, p. 277, for the statistics; for recollections, see e.g. Oxf/AHRC SPb-07 PF12 IN; Oxf/AHRC-SPb-11 PF2 EI; Oxf/AHRC SPb 2011 PF14 EI.
158. Woman b. early 1980s, FN December 2010.
159. Brodsky, *Less Than One*, p. 27.
160. For a general discussion, see Goscilo and Strukov.
161. Oxf/AHRC SPb-11 PF23 MS. See also Ruf' Zernova's novella *Elizabeth Arden* (1978), *Vremya i my* 58 (1979), www.vtoraya-literatura.com/publ_191.html.
162. This was typical of 'post-Soviet space' generally: on Lithuania, see Vonderau.
163. Oxf/AHRC SPb-11 PF23 MS (chains), Oxf/AHRC SPb-11 PF25 MS (labels).
164. On the importance of the 'raspberry-coloured jacket' in identifying New Russians, see the extensive discussion in Patico.
165. On boots, pers. obs. (2010–11), and see also Oxf/AHRC SPb-11 PF15 EI; on gilets, Oxf/AHRC SPb-11 PF13 EI.
166. For the word, see Oxf/AHRC SPb-11 PF4 EI; for a description (artists in sweaters ten sizes too large, keds, and bird's nest hair), Oxf/AHRC SPb-11 PF13 EI. The informant in Oxf/AHRC SPb-11 PF5 EI (man b. 1976) was critical of the informality of dress on Nevsky: this was beachwear, and not 'Petersburg style'. This attitude was widespread in Soviet Leningrad too. A Muscovite assesses Petersburg dress as less 'polished' than Moscow (Oxf/AHRC SPb-11 PF8 EI); a fashion professional comments that the city is less obsessed with brands and bling (Oxf/AHRC SPb-11 PF25 MS).
167. FN, June 2010.
168. As spotted in March 2004.
169. Among particularly eye-catching dog outfits in October 2011, for instance, were a peacock blue and crimson combo worthy of Elvis Presley, a scarlet ski suit, and a sleek black onesie, all worn by preening dachshunds.
170. In the early 1990s, several streets off Nevsky, including Karetnaya, were pedestrianised, as well as 6-ya liniya of Vasilievsky Island (see O. Boiko, 'S 6-i liniei spravilis' za 6 let', *NV* 28 December 2000, p. 3). There were plans to take this policy further (e.g. to close Bol'shoi prospekt on Petrogradka to traffic: O. Boiko, 'Bol'shie peremeny na Bol'shom prospekte', *NV* 20 December 2000, p. 1; p. 2). However, at this stage pedestrianisation stopped.

171. FN March 2008.
172. For a fuller discussion of graffiti, see Kelly, 'City Texts'.
173. See the interviews with Nikolai Vakhtin in *Nomen est omen*. See also Oxf/AHRC SPb-11 PF4 NG.
174. I found such traces on the gravestone of the forgotten boy hero Kotya Mgebrov in October 2011 (FN).
175. *BILGS* 16 (1987), pp. 8–9. In 1983, there were 118 minors under medical observation after they had been found inhaling 'aromatic substances', as opposed to 9 on criminal charges for drug abuse: TsGAIPD, 24/196/14/96.
176. Nonna Slepakova, 'Petergof' (1959/1997), in her *Izbrannoe*, vol. 1 (SPb., 2006), p. 91. Cf. Kushner, 'V kafe', *Pryamaya rech'*, p. 78, which describes an encounter with a figure from the Soviet demimonde in a 'packed cafe with its hollow echo', and leaking windows.

## 8 The Twenty-Seventh Kilometre

1. Joseph Brodsky, 'Kelomäki', *Stikhovoreniya i poemy*, 1.412. 'Chukhna' is an abusive Russian term for the Finns (cf. Kraut or Frog in English).
2. See e.g. Oxf/AHRC SPb-07 PF11 IN: woman b. 1972 says she is only interested in visiting Moscow and Murmansk. Duty visits to family in provincial 'nowhere' were, of course, not to be avoided, however: see e.g. Oxf/Lev SPb-03 PF14.
3. See e.g. SPbAG AKF Bologoe-01 PF1. A common motif among people living in the Russian or former Soviet provinces is how much their locality did for the city: see e.g. the comments by Russian informants born in Latvia about how the place kept Piter supplied with food: Oxf/AHRC UK-08 PF69 AB.
4. TsGAIPD-SPb. 4000/18/ 333/113. For more on Gonchukov, see Chapter Four.
5. This remained true in the late Soviet period as well: e.g. Oxf/AHRC UK-08 PF22 AB, though such travel could also be enjoyable (as recollected here).
6. On the general background of Soviet leisure travel, see Gorsuch, *All This Is Your World*; Koenker and Gorsuch (eds), *Turizm*, and also Koenker, 'Whose Right to Rest?' For a discussion of Soviet-era holiday and work travel as offering opportunities for sexual dalliance (based on interviews with St Petersburgers), see Anna Rotkirch, 'Traveling Maidens and Men with Parallel Lives – Journeys as Private Space During Late Socialism', in Jeremy Smith (ed.), *Beyond the Limits*, pp. 131–49.
7. 'Pansionat dlya kirovtsev', *Kirovets* 3 July 1970, p. 2.
8. *Turisticheskie marshruty po SSSR*, published by the Leningrad Province Council on Tourism and Excusions in 1970, listed among possible destinations an air fare to Tbilisi at 130 roubles, and a three-week trip to Central Asia at 180 roubles (about double the average monthly wage), as well as steamer trips to Perm' or Rostov at 110–200 roubles for 3 weeks, a trip to Kizhi wooden architecture museum for 2 days at 68 roubles, and so on.
9. On Koktebel', see e.g. Oxf/AHRC SPb-07 PF1 SA; Oxf/AHRC-SPb-07 PF43 IN.
10. An informant of mine born in the late 1950s recalled that her mother became interested in making trips of this kind, taking her daughter along, in c. 1973 (pers. inf., 2005). Interestingly, the promotion of the 'Golden Ring' as a brand appears to have started in Leningrad, with the publication in 1974 of an album of glossy photographs under that title by the 'Avrora' publishers (see RNB catalogue).
11. Friends who visited Svanetia in the 1980s reported at the time that the local shopkeeper in the mountain village where they were staying at first refused to sell them anything, because she had lost the official price-list: after much argument, she consented to accept triple the going rate for a packet of Hungarian luncheon meat (all that was available in the shop, and ironically enough, then a chronically short delicacy in Leningrad) (email, 10 November 2012).
12. In the Soviet period, the assumption that 'real' folklore should show no traces of modern contamination tended to leave visitors to Leningrad province disappointed. For an entertaining account of hopelessly attempting to find traces of dialect in a village where the locals had nurtured their superb command of literary Russian on library books, see Volkomorov, *Legendy filfaka*.
13. On *turisty* generally, see the discussion in Gorsuch and Koenker (eds), *Turizm*. For a first-hand account by a Leningrader, see Il'in, *Ispoved' kochevnika*. The role of geological expeditions is extensively explored in Kuz'minsky and Kovalev's commentaries in *The Blue Lagoon Anthology of Modern Russian Poetry*.

14. A very broad discussion of attitudes to travel, including this period, is Shchepanskaya, *Kul'tura dorogi*. The phenomenon of abandoned children has been extensively discussed only for the 1920s (see e.g. Alan Ball, *And Now My Soul is Hardened* (Berkeley, CA, 1994); Caroli, *L'Enfance abandonnée et déliquente dans la Russie soviétique, 1918–1937* (Paris, 2004)). After the war and immediate post-war years, the numbers of such children declined, but the problem never went away completely: some material is given in Chapter 8 of my *Children's World*.
15. The pictures are reproduced in *Leningradskii fotoandergraund*; see also www.arteria.ru/photomarathon/left10.htm.
16. This simplifies a complex process of territorial reassignation, beginning as early as 1929 when twenty-three districts were ceded to the Western Region.
17. During the 'Leningrad Affair', this pattern of movement became part of the *corpus delicti*, with officials in Pskov who had previously served in Leningrad getting sucked into the maelstrom. Some of those involved were later to remember the special 'Leningrad spirit' they brought with them to the provinces: see *Leningradskoe delo*.
18. See e.g. Krivulin, *Okhota na mamonta*, p. 69: 'The history of the relationship between Petrograd-Leningrad and Moscow is strikingly similar to the history of the sacking of His Lordship Great Novgorod, "pro-Western" and prosperous, by Moscow [in the sixteenth century]'.
19. The most authoritative discussion of this is Lovell, *Summerfolk*.
20. Hingley, p. 20.
21. In 1995, the ethnographer and folklorist Larisa Ivleva was raped and murdered by a gang of youths at an *elektrichka* station outside St Petersburg when on her way back from visiting a friend in hospital (pers. inf.). For a recent case where a drunk attacked a passenger with a broken bottle, see 'Muzhchina provedet v kolonii 6 let za popytku ubiistva v elektrichke', Balt-Info 4 February 2011, www.baltinfo.ru/2011/02/04/Peterburzhetc-provedet-v-kolonii-6-let-za-popytku-ubiistva-v-elektrichke-186428.
22. Oksana Boiko, 'Vokzal dlya dachnikov i revolyutsionerov', *NV* 12 February 2000, p. 1.
23. For reports of fare-dodging on *elektrichki*, see e.g. *Smena* 26 February 1999, p. 1. 'Lipovye kontrolery protiv lipovykh passazhirov' – people who used to work for the railways had kept their identity cards and posed as ticket inspectors, then kept the fines. But a bigger problem was the sheer numbers of passengers who did not bother with tickets – 1,300,000 in 1998. Anastasiya Gavrielova, 'Solidol zaitsam ne pomekha', *MR(K)* 27 August 2004, p. 3, reported that the attempt to stop cheats by greasing gates at the Finland Station with solidol (a heavy-duty lubricant) had not worked.
24. This riddle was told in provincial places about Moscow as well: see Donovan; Raleigh.
25. See e.g. Oxf/AHRC SPb-10 PF4 MS (woman b. 1945); Oxf/AHRC-UK-08 PF32 AB (woman b. 1960s); Oxf/AHRC UK-07 PF11 AB (woman b. Perm', 1966 – on her father), etc.
26. In 1963, Ugritsk, Volodarsky, Lakhta, Ligovo, Rybatskoe and part of Pargolovo were absorbed, and in 1973, Krasnoe Selo, Gorelovo, Mozhaisky, and Toriki (*Leningrad i Leningradskaya oblast' v tsifrakh*, p. 17).
27. Tomchin, p. 27. Tomchin's calculation subtracted from the official area of the city (600 km) the area covered by the stretch of the Gulf of Finland between the city proper and Kronstadt, leaving 200 km.
28. The Soviet-era name was the Cemetery to the Victims of 9 January 1905, to commemorate the event when Russian government troops opened fire on a large crowd of peaceful protesters, led by Father Gapon, who had been intending to present a petition to Tsar Nicholas II at the Winter Palace. The cemetery lies to the south-east of Petersburg.
29. The sense of the primal bog everywhere was also mentioned by one of our informants, who found the city sometimes so oppressive it made him want to drink (Oxf/AHRC-SPb-07 PF 44 IN). This common sensation of inexplicable depression is more often rationalised by the weather.
30. Hamilton, 'Spatial Structure in East European Cities', in French and Hamilton (eds), *The Socialist City*, p. 237, claimed that socialist cities were distinctive because of having clear boundaries with the surrounding world: 'the socialist city contains no suburbs – only high-rise flats to the very edge of the urban area'. However, he immediately conceded, 'In reality, vestiges of suburbs may remain as village-relict features, illegal "wild settlements", or limited but legal "new class" villa development'.
31. *Russkie stikhi 1950–2000*, 2.378. One interpretation of this poem, by Natal'ya Pereverzentseva in her essay 'Chasy ostanovilis', *Zinziver* 2 (4), 2009 (www.zinziver.ru/14(2)2009/autor.php?id_pub=886), sees it as apocalyptic, but it can be so only in a loose sense, since it is devoid of traditional symbolism.
32. Daniil Litvintsev, 'Gorod nachinaetsya cherez dorogu', *MR(V)* 28 January 2005, p. 5.

33. On the bus stop issue, see *MR(V)* 30 September 2005, p. 6 (reader's letter); on the toponyms issue, Daniil Litvintsev, 'Poselok, kotorogo net ni na odnoi karte', *MR(V)*, 11 March 2005, p. 2.
34. On livestock keeping in the early Soviet period, see e.g. Tsendrovskaya.
35. Irina Sankina, 'Kozlinnaya idilliya v cherte goroda', *MR(K)* 20 August 2004, p. 4. There was also some experimental vegetable-growing on roofs from the late 1990s onwards: see Aleksei Oreshkin, 'Kryshi Peterburga obrosli pomidorami', *Smena* 28 April 1998, p. 1.
36. See e.g. Oxf/Lev SPb-11 PF13 MS (woman b. 1989).
37. For a case of an incomer from Vologda, see Oxf/AHRC SPb-07 PF32 IN (man b. 1983).
38. For the statistic, see TsGAIPD-SPb. 24/ 8/463/36 (from a document on the radiofication of Leningrad province compiled in 1937; the figures for this were also very optimistic). For the oral history, see the interviews carried out by Ekaterina Mel'nikova, Oksana Filicheva, and Veronika Makarova in Leningrad and Novgorod provinces during 2004 and 2005 with informants born in the 1920s to the 1940s (Oxf/Lev V-04, PF1-25 and V-05, PF1-14).
39. Galina Smirnova, 'Kakim budet Roshchino', *U nas v Leningrade*, p. 59.
40. Berggol'ts, *Dnevnye zvezdy*, p. 24.
41. F. Vishnyakov, 'Obed v uzelkakh', *LP* 26 May 1967, p. 2; cf. 'Gde poobedat'?' (a reader's complaint about how Ivangorod had only one *stolovaya*), *LP* 10 November 1971, p. 2.
42. See the questions to activists (1975) collected in TsGAIPD-SPb. 24/159/5/1-12. See also the information about readers' complaints to local newspapers, TsGAIPD-SPb. 24/159/6/1-123.
43. 'Soveshchanie s gruppoi sekretarei raikomov KPSS po voprosam kul'turnogo shefstva nad selom', 4 October 1971, TsGAIPD-SPb. 24/145/26/ 7.
44. As in the case of Boksitogorsk district: 'Soveshchanie s gruppoi sekretarei gorkomov KPSS po voprosam kul'turnogo shefstva nad selom', 18 October 1971, TsGAIPD-SPb. 24/145/26/30.
45. It is interesting to note that less than 10 per cent of the 3000 letters sent to the Kingisepp local newspaper in 1975 were complaints, with much higher numbers of notes on events of local importance etc. TsGAIPD-SPb. 24/159/6/69-73.
46. M. A. Sobol', 'Gde zhit' khorosho? Problemy razvitiya regiona', *LPan* 2 (1992), pp. 5–6.
47. 'Svedeniya ob ushcherbe, prichinennom pamyatnikam arkhitektury', 11 July 1944–4 December 1944. TsGANTD-SPb 388/1-1/2/1-20.
48. See Maddox; Kedrinsky, Kolotov, Medersky, and Raskin, *Letopis' vozrozhdeniya*. For similar material, see e.g. Tret'yakova, and the transcript of a broadcast on Ekho Moskvy-Peterburg: www.echomsk.spb.ru/content/prog/default.asp?shmode=3&idprog=1220&ida=81938. Before the war, the picture was different, with some of the palaces used as Houses of Rest and the general condition parlous: see the 1939 Narkompros reports in GA RF 259/37/296/6-8.
49. The first phase of restoration at Oranienbaum – allowing the reopening of a few staterooms in the Great Men'shikov Palace and the Chinese Palace – was completed in September 2011. The interior work had been completed to an extremely high standard, and this was the first case of a palace complex where decoration and furnishings of the mid nineteenth century had been left in place, rather than stripped back to the 'optimal date' (FN September 2011).
50. Shkarovsky, *Sankt-Peterburgskaya eparkhiya*, p. 150. Ferapontovo, whose Cathedral of the Nativity of the Virgin contains one of the most beautiful cycles of medieval religious painting anywhere, created by Dionisy and his sons in 1502, became a UNESCO World Heritage Site in 2000.
51. In 1948, the Leningrad Province Department of Architecture was involved in a stand-off with the Volkhovo Machine-Tractor Station (MTS) about the fate of the former Nikol'sky Cathedral in Old Ladoga, which the MTS was using as a repair workshop for farm machinery, having removed the padlock placed there by the Department. The conflict was mediated by the Volkhovo District Soviet, which suggested the MTS be allowed to do only non-intrusive repairs (without using heat etc.): TsGANTD-SPb. 388/1-1/115/13-16.
52. Figures based on a comparison of 'Spisok pamyatnikov arkhitektury religioznogo kul'ta po Leningradskoi oblasti, sostoyashchikh na uchete na 1/1-50 goda', TsGA-SPb 9620/2/7/77 (my thanks to Alexandra Piir for copying this material), and Bertash (ed.), *Zemlya Nevskaya pravoslavnaya*, passim. A stunning photographic record of the decay in the northwest generally (particularly Archangel and Vologda provinces) is Davies, *Wooden Churches*.
53. On theft with the connivance of the local authorities, see the petition sent on 8 January 1964 by the Church Council of St George's Church at Lozhgolovo in Kingisepp district, reporting that the church had been plundered of icons, communion vessels, etc., by a party of workman acting on the orders of the chairman of the village soviet and an official from the executive committee of Kingisepp district soviet: ASPbE 1/24/43/207.
54. See the lists from 1962 in ASPbE 1/26 (2)/21/1-39.

55. For an example of such a mandate, see ASPbE 1/26 (2)/19/229. For a protest by a church congregation (of the Church of the Dormition in Olonetsk in 1963), see ASPbE 1/24/43/96.
56. FN, June 2012.
57. For the exchange between GIOP, LGU, and the Leningrad province board of agricultural management, see TsGANTD-SPb 388/1-1/115/13.
58. For instance, in the late 1950s, initiatives to organise archaeological work in the area round Tikhvin were supported by professional archaeologists; the artefacts discovered by schoolchildren on the resulting expeditions are now the core of the Tikhvin Museum of Local Studies (visit to the museum, FN, June 2012).
59. 'Spravka o narusheniyakh mestnymi organizatsiyami poryadka vypolneniya rabot po pamyatnikam istorii i kul'tury v raionakh i gorodakh Leningradskoi oblasti (z 1976-1977 gg.)', TsGAIPD-SPb. 24/170/ 32/31.
60. Such urban condescension towards the rural hinterland has recently been vigorously addressed in Rogers, *The Old Faith and the Russian Land*. For the persistence of the assumption among Petersburgers that large cities 'play a mediating and civilising role, pulling the less developed periphery up to the contemporary level of development', see Guelman. People from smaller places do not always see the situation like that: see e.g. an interview with a woman b. 1990 from a village in Vologda province, recorded by D. K. Tuminas, A. A. Chechik, and Yu. Yu. Marinicheva (6 July 2011) (code С Я м 24–177), in which the informant expresses disappointment with the standards of accommodation and food on a recent visit to St Petersburg. (My thanks to Irina Nazarova for access to this material.)
61. See e.g. Oxf/Lev V-04 PF15. Another of our interviewees, brought up in Karelia, remembered attending a formerly Finnish school which was, by Soviet standards, extraordinarily well-equipped, but which, after four years of use under the new order, had turned into a 'pigsty' (Oxf/Lev V-04 PF24A). For an extensive discussion of local identity and the resonance of migration, see Melnikova, 'Svoya chuzhaya', and the collection of ethnographical material, *Granitsa i lyudi*.
62. See our interviews in rural Karelia, Oxf/Lev V-04 PF1-24. Cf. Oxf/AHRC SPb-10 PF10 MS (in this case, the person moved to the settlement as an adult, and the Finnish houses were still lived in).
63. As discussed by the staff at the Tikhvin Local Studies Museum, FN June 2012.
64. For example, the occupiers – as in other areas of Soviet Russia – had encouraged the Orthodox Church to reopen church buildings: see Shkarovsky, *Tserkov' zovet k zashchite Rodiny*. This was one factor behind Stalin's concordat with the church in 1943.
65. See e.g. A. I. Il'in, 'Raion bol'shikh vozmozhnostei', *LPan* 1 (1984), pp. 17–20 (on Gatchina); 'Sluzhba byta – sel'skim truzhenikam', *LPan* 1 (1984), pp. 40–1 (on Gatchina and Luga districts). There is good discussion of Tikhvin's history in Golubchikov's introduction to his geographical study of Leningrad province.
66. On the population figures in the late nineteenth and early twentieth centuries, see the entry in the Brockhaus-Efron *Entsiklopedicheskii slovar'*; on the figure in the 1960s, see Golubchikov.
67. ASPbE 1/7/236/58-9 (petition of 1965 from the parishioners of the Krylechko Church to the Metropolitan of Leningrad).
68. See the article on Tikhvin in the *BSE*, edn. 3.
69. 'Gorod – eto zavod. Zavod – eto gorod', *Smena*, 18 January 1980, pp. 1–3.
70. *BSE* edn. 3. For discussions of how expansion affected the self-perception of locals, see the articles by Kuleshov.
71. See the description in Oxf/AHRC SPb-11 PF13 EI. The informant was brought up in Kolpino, and the daughter of two workers at the Izhorsky Works. As she put it, it was only after Valentina Matvienko's 'Let's Develop Kolpino' drive that locals stopped having to go to Petersburg to do their shopping.
72. A case in point here was Mel'nikovo, in Karelia.
73. Nefedova, Polyan, and Treivish, *Gorod i derevnya*, p. 383.
74. Lovell, *Summerfolk*, pp. 169–78. This practice continued into later eras as well: see Sergei Tachaev, 'Munitsipial'nye dachi: smena vyvesok dlya vladel'tsev', *NV* 3 March 1993, p. 1.
75. For example, the Kirov Factory's settlement was begun in 1948. Vegetable-growing by the citizenry had been presented as a desirable contribution to the local economy for many years before that: see e.g. *Peterburgskoe ogorodnichestvo*, published in 1921. On the garden settlement generally, see Lovell, *Summerfolk*, pp. 190–7, and the articles by Kasatkina.
76. Sometimes, allocations were bigger: Oxf/AHRC SPb-07 PF4 SA recalls that her father, as an army veteran, was given 12 *sotok*.

77. 'Reshenie Ispolkoma Lenoblsoveta i Lengorsoveta ot 23/29 aprelya 1985 g. No. 253/190', *BILGS* no. 13 (1985), implementing the Decree of the Council of Ministers of the USSR, 29 December 1984. Outbuildings for animals such as hens and rabbits were also allowed.
78. Nefedova, Polyan, and Treivish, *Gorod i derevnya*, p. 385.
79. Ibid, p. 387.
80. B. B. Rodoman in *Problemy zemlepol'zovaniya* (Moscow, 1993), cited in Nefedova, Polyan, and Treivish, *Gorod i derevnya*, p. 386.
81. Slepakova, 'Dachnaya zona', *Stikhotvoreniya i poemy*, p. 247.
82. 'Kak poluchit' shest' sotok', *VL* 9 December 1989, p. 2.
83. According to a comment made by the historian Vladimir Lapin at the 'Konstruiruya sovetskoe' conference, European University, St Petersburg, April 2010.
84. Nefedova, Polyan, and Treivish, *Gorod i derevnya*, p. 384: around 300,000 people took part in such forced labour across the Russian Federation in 1989. There is an excoriating description of the process – everyone overworked and short of food, but doing their best to muddle through – in Volkomorov's otherwise cheery collection of stories about the Leningrad State University Philological Faculty, *Legendy Filfaka*. Volkomorov was understandably vindictive about the glasnost-era maudlin repentance by the Faculty's organiser of these boot camps.
85. Pashkova, p. 255; and pers. inf. One informant, for instance, recalled that she and a couple of other lightly-built women immediately volunteered for work in the collective farm kitchen (CKQ-Ox-04 PF12).
86. For example, articles published in the Sestroretsk local paper criticised money-making: 'Chastushka na kurorte', *Leningradskaya zdravnitsa* (the Sestroretsk local paper) 15 July 1960, p. 3, satirised someone who made a packet on rabbits and strawberries and then didn't want to have to pay taxes on his earnings; 'Torgovaya kontora Nakhamkina i Ko.' (*Leningradskaya zdravnitsa*, 30 December 1960, p. 3) denounced a man with a Leningrad registration who had been building up houses and capital in Sestroretsk.
87. 'Otdacha ot dachi', *Komsomol'skaya pravda*, 21 September 1980, p. 2. The attitude that the dacha was 'not for us' or somehow 'bourgeois' comes up in oral history too: see e.g. Oxf/AHRC SPb-10 PF4 MS.
88. No author given, 'K zemle kovylyaet doroga', *Dachnaya zhizn'* 1 (1997), p. 19. This side of dacha life is extensively discussed, in relation to materials from Moscow and Tver', by Caldwell, *Dacha Idylls*.
89. Here is an important difference from the dacha typology outlined by Caldwell, *Dacha Idylls*.
90. Oxf/AHRC-SPb-07 PF 1 AK. Cf. Oxf/AHRC-SPb-07 PF 3 IN ('Well, if you've taken a plot on, that brings obligations with it – you just have to build on it'). This informant also took pride in having built 'almost all of the place with my own hands'.
91. TsGALI-SPb. 229/1/540/18-20. Another kind of marginal land was also widely used – the sites of the battles that took place on this territory during the Second World War, where helmets and bones lay close to, or indeed scattered on, the surface of the ground. See e.g. Oxf/AHRC SPb-11 PF19 MS (in this case, the informant's dacha was next to the Sinyavskie Marshes). This was never mentioned in the Soviet period, which must have increased the unpleasant shock to those stumbling across war remains right by their dachas.
92. This binary relationship is also emphasised in Lovell, *Summerfolk*.
93. For a reference to going on picnics because you had no dacha, see e.g. Oxf/AHRC SPb-10 PF2 MS. There was also an intermediate arrangement – renting a room (AHRC SPb-08 PF18 SA).
94. See e.g. Oxf/Lev SPb-07 PF33 IN (woman b. 1958, Krasnodar).
95. Oxf/Lev SPb-07 PF26 IN (man b. 1947).
96. On teachers, see e.g. Oxf/AHRC SPb-07 PF 11 IN. Obviously, academics (particularly in the humanities) came into this category too, as did most people in intelligentsia professions, who could take a month off without trouble. In one case, an informant remembered that her mother would travel backwards and forwards to the city, leaving food in the mornings, as the neighbour would be there to keep an eye, and the land was fenced anyway (Oxf/Lev SPb-09 PF58 IN), but this arrangement was unusual. Normally at least one relation would be there with the children all the time.
97. While a second home too close to the city would not be regarded as a dacha (cf. one woman's doubts about whether her own place, within the outer ring road, would qualify, Oxf/AHRC SPb-10 PF8 MS), most settlements were not more than two hours' journey away – at least until the increased traffic flow of the late 1990s made getting out of the city much slower.
98. In the post-Soviet period, once control of settlements had ebbed, this was not always the case: I have come across several instances of people living next to alcoholics or drug users, and issues such as newbuild and fencing could also be contentious. But prior to the late 1980s, the threat of summary eviction acted as a regulator.

99. The role of the dacha as a place for social contact is emphasised by Vera Zhirmunskaya-Astvatsaturova, 'V shumnom dome teti Runi', *Ruf' Zernova*, pp. 93–5, which describes, for instance, how the family would deliberately go to a more distant beach so they could see friends.
100. A whole advice literature deals with this, including seasonal comments in ordinary newspapers (e.g. 'Sovety byvalogo gribnika', *Nevskoe vremya* 30 September 2000, p. 5), and specialist magazines such as *Dachnaya zhizn'*, *Lyubimaya dacha*, and *Priusadebnoe khoziaistvo*. These have now been supplemented by websites such as dom-dacha.info, dachi.ru, etc.
101. One of the stories told about the Party leader Grigory Romanov was that his son-in-law had set up fountains at the Obkom dacha in Komarovo and cut off the entire water supply for that section of the settlement (Toporov, *Dvoinoe dno*, p. 397). On the development of the Gulf of Finland resorts, see 'Etapy severnoi riv'ery', *LP* 5 June 1975, p. 4. The gamut was nicely suggested by an informant who commented: 'Heavens, I'd be delighted to live on Nevsky, if I had the chance, to have a dacha in Komarovo. But I'd be just as content with Novoladozhskaya ulitsa and a dacha – well, even Mshinskaya would suit me' (Oxf/AHRC SPb-08 PF54 IN). Mshinskaya is a settlement 109 kilometres south of Petersburg, in Luga district (generally, the territory to the south of the city is less prestigious for dacha areas). Cf. Oxf/AHRC-SPb-07 PF19 IN, where the informant sardonically points to his father's acceptance of a dacha way south of the city (despite being a factory director) as an indication of his unworldliness.
102. See e.g. Oxf/AHRC SPb-11 PF15, 'To say I dressed simply at the dacha was putting it mildly.' The interviewer observes that wearing jeans, as opposed to ancient tracksuit bottoms, would already have looked pretentious.
103. On old furniture at the dacha, see e.g. Oxf/AHRC SPb-07 PF10 SA. As often, what is mentioned here is just old, not antique – Soviet-era cabinets etc. In some circles, the dacha had another role as well – a discreet hiding place for things that it might have been dangerous to keep in a city flat, such as icons (see e.g. Oxf/AHRC SPb-11 PF21 MS), or – in dissident groups – 'subversive' books and manuscripts.
104. Oxf/AHRC SPb-07 PF2 AK (woman b. 1977).
105. Ibid.
106. There were also long queues at the consulates, particularly before branches were opened in Leningrad (in the 1960s, 1970s, and early 1980s, the only 'capitalist country' with a consulate was the USA).
107. For instance, in January 2012, online sites were offering seven-day trips to Egypt or Thailand at a day's notice for around 750 dollars a person all-in – less than the return air fares being offered for those dates.
108. On the popularity of these destinations, see 'Gde predpochitayut otdykhat' pitertsy?', *MR(V)* 12 August 2005, p. 9.
109. Cf. the many sites offering Russian buyers a dacha in Finland: www.findacha.ru/, www.datsha.com/rus/uutiset/280505.shtml, http://finvista.ru/, etc. The costs of a dacha in Finland, according to these sites, ranged from 50,000 euro to around 700,000 euro, and a site could be had for 10,000 euro and upwards, which made purchasing a summer house here significantly cheaper than a comparable dwelling in a popular area near St Petersburg, added to the fact that the infrastructure was better and one's house more secure when empty. On the other hand, even in a popular area such as Repino, a simple wooden house without sanitation somewhere distant from the centre could still be had for around 20,000 dollars in the 2010s (see e.g. the ad for a two-storey house on a river-bank at Repino, www.avito.ru, May 2011).
110. Regulation now depended on the whim of a particular garden settlement administration: see the answer to a reader's letter in *MR(VO)*, 16 June 2004, pointing out that there were now no general rules on membership dues, etc.
111. On the 1989 reform, see Tachaev, 'Munitsipial'nye dachi'. On the privatisation of former state dachas, ibid., and Lovell, *Summerfolk*, pp. 211–13.
112. In some cases, one or more members of an extended family that had jointly inherited a substantial holding would sell off part of the plot, a situation that could, obviously, lead to friction (FN June 2008).
113. See Tat'yana Likhanova, 'Chelovek, pokhozhii na Millera, stroit dvorets, pokhozhii na dvorets v Petergofe', *Novaya gazeta*, 13–16 August 2009, http://stomaster.livejournal.com/2095505.html.
114. FN Sept. 2007.
115. Margolis, *Tsarskosel'skii kottedzh*. Here I see a difference from the villa culture described in Caroline Humphrey's classic study of post-Soviet exurban culture, 'The Villas of the "New Russians": A Sketch in Consumption and Cultural Identity in Post-Soviet Landscapes', *The*

*Unmaking of Soviet Life*, pp. 175–201, which emphasises the bizarre relations of the new houses with their surroundings.

116. Filipp Urban, 'Auktsion ili attraktsion? Komu dostanetsya kottedzh v blizhnem prigorode i atel'e na Nevskom', *NV* 14 July 1992, p. 1. A salary of 150 roubles a month was still reasonably generous.
117. FN 1 July 2008. A pun was intended: the word for red (*krasnyi*) is etymologically connected with the word *ukrashat'* (to enhance, literally 'make beautiful').
118. See Maksim Kazinsky, 'Istoricheskie dachi v Komarove unichtozhayut', www.neva24.ru/a/2011/05/04/Istoricheskie_dachi_v_Komar. The story reported residents' fears that the early twentieth-century Shturman dacha, demolished in April, would soon be followed by the demolition of all the other buildings down its street in order to make room for a mini-hotel.
119. Visits, 2002, 2006, 2007, etc.
120. See the interesting discussion by Kasatkina, 'Sadovodcheskie nekommercheskie tovarishchestva'.
121. Ibid., and also Kasatkina, 'Kategoriya "sovetskoe"'.
122. Oxf/AHRC SPb-07 PF16 SA (man b. 1976 remembers helping his grandfather build his dacha). Conversely, the informant in Oxf/AHRC SPb-07 PF25 IN insists that she doesn't want a dacha because it would be too much work.
123. The cemetery also had its own historical literature: see e.g. Mel'nikov, Mozhenok, *Komarovskii nekropol'*. Comments based on several visits to the cemetery and on information from locals (e.g. FN, October 2011).
124. The practice of simply driving to the dacha for a few hours and driving back again, as described by Humphrey (*The Unmaking of Soviet Life*, p. 199) was not characteristic of St Petersburg's surrounding areas, if it ever was, but those rich enough to build substantial dachas tended to visit sporadically and to stick to the insides of their compounds.
125. FN September 2009. Caldwell, *Dacha Idylls*, p. 114, discusses the rise of the lawnmower, but in the rough conditions of Leningrad province dacha settlements the strimmer had more practical appeal.
126. See the discussion about competing discourses on dacha use in Kaluga province by Jane Zavisca, 'Contesting Capitalism at the Post-Soviet Dacha: The Meaning of Food Cultivation for Urban Russians', *Slavic Review* 62. 4 (2003), pp. 786–810.
127. Based on extensive personal experience.
128. The builders who worked for me in 2005–6 organised their activities like this. On adjustment of weekends in Moscow, see Caldwell, *Dacha Idylls*, p. 49.
129. S. Fedorova, 'Mozhno li kupit' dom v derevne?', *LP* 16 July 1988, p. 4. The legislation involved was a decree of the Executive Committee of the Leningrad Regional Soviet, 19 September 1987, 'On the Use of Empty Dwellings and Garden Plots in Rural Areas', and ditto of 5 March 1988, 'On Some Questions Relating to the Use of the Living Accommodation Stock and Garden Plots in Leningrad Region'. Even before this, there were cases where people owned village houses (see Oxf/AHRC GB-08 CK), but on the basis, presumably, of inheritance or customary law.
130. Pers. inf. By the 2010s, improved village houses were selling for more substantial sums (30,000–40,000 dollars): see www.avito.ru, but things were different if you picked up a disused house in a village.
131. On my visit to Tikhvin (FN, June 2012), I was told that it is now impossible to find dialect speakers and bearers of other traditional forms of culture in the villages in that area, and that members of the Veps community born in the post-war decades are monoglot in Russian.
132. The difficulties of doing this were formidable, since the places were usually in institutional hands, and had decayed completely over the Soviet period. Also, locals usually did not want outsiders moving in. Cf. the case of one of the Stroganov estates in Pskov province, where the boilerhouse handyman [*istopnik*] happily declared: 'Let it fall down. The main thing is that the bourjooi don't get hold of it' [«Ну и пусть развалится. Главное, чтоб буржуям не досталось»]. Dmitry Lovetsky, 'U grafskikh razvalin', *NV* 16 May 1992, p. 3. V. K. Dmitriev, *Leningradskaya oblast': Spravochnoe posobie po istorii kraya* (2010), lists 19 particularly important estate houses, of which 10 were wholly or partly collapsed, 2 were still in use as hospitals, and 4 were museums. A mere 3 were in private hands, and 2 of these were in commercial use (a hotel and 'house of rest'); restoration on the third was proceeding very slowly, though as of 2011 the place was inaccessible to the public behind a concrete fence (http://autotravel.ru/otklik.php/8871).
133. Sergei Gorbatenko, 'Kak spasti Lugovoi park?', *NV* 3 September 1992, p. 5. A *kottedzh* is not a 'cottage', but a substantial mansion.
134. On the attempts to regulate, such as the mayoral decree of 29 November 1993 setting up self-management committees, and the presidential decree of 27 June 1996 offering state funding, see 'O regulirovanii zemlepol'zovanii grazhdan', *Dachnaya zhizn'* 1 (1997), pp. 12–13. Some

inter-settlement co-operation survived from the Soviet period: e.g. the Peterburgsky (originally Leningradsky) Soyuz Sadovodov, founded 1986, supplied services to members such as legal advice and cost-price seeds and tools ('Peterburgsky Soyuz Sadovodov', *Dachnaya zhizn'* 1 (1997), pp. 26–7).

135. Svyatoslav Grigor'ev, 'Bilet mozhno budet kupit' cherez SMS' (interview with Vitaly Grigor'ev, pervyi zam gen direcktora OAO "Severo-Zapadnaya prigorodnaya passazhirskaya kompaniya"), *Metro* 30 March 2011, p. 6.
136. This is part of a nationwide problem: Nefedova, Polyan, Treivish, *Gorod i derevnya*, p. 388.
137. Cf. reader's letter in *NV*, 21 January 1995, p. 4, where a *korennaya peterburzhenka* writes to protest against the paper's campaign to stop people using shopping trolleys: how are she and other 'dirt poor elderly dacha folk' to bring back their produce? On growing vegetables in the 1990s (here for subsistence purposes), see also Oxf/AHRC UK-08 PF22 AB.
138. As put bluntly by a young woman then in her 20s, Oxf/AHRC SPb-08 PF43 IN.
139. See e.g. the seven-room *kottedzh* with sanitation and all-weather drive at Belostrov advertised on www.nedvizhimost.slando.spb.ru in May 2011 (selling for 27.5 million roubles, or a million dollars).
140. As recounted to me by a local resident working as a temporary coat check assistant in the Russian National Library (FN, August 2007).
141. For site prices, see http://spbzn.ru (June 2012); one-off dwellings, www.chance.ru/rubric/estate-region-house-sale; estate developments were regularly advertised in St Petersburg freesheets such as *Metro*, as well as on sites such as http://kupidom-spb.ru/default.aspx.
142. http://kupidom-spb.ru/default.aspx (June 2012).
143. According to 1991 figures cited by O'Brien et al., 86 per cent of adults across the Russian Federation were employed by the large enterprise in their area; in 2001, the figure was 46 per cent.
144. http://petrostat.gks.ru/lenobl/trud/2009/01aktiv_o.htm. The devastation of some parts of the countryside is discussed in Nefedova, *Sel'skaya Rossiya*. For a striking memoir of rural decline in Yaroslavl' province, see Mikhail Rumer-Zaraev, 'Anno Domini – Leto Gospodne', *Druzhba narodov* 1 (2006), http://magazines.russ.ru/druzhba/2006/1/ru7.html.
145. *Raiony leningradskoi oblasti*, pp. 19 (ageing population – 124 per cent of 1990 figures in 1994), 66 (car ownership: 76,100 in 1991 and 103,376 in 1995), 92–5 (falling numbers of libraries and clubs); *Leningradskaya oblast' 1994*, p. 9 (house-building had dropped from 808,100 new blocks in 1990 to 485,100 in 1994). These sources also point to high rates of infant mortality and divorce in some areas.
146. *Leningradskaya oblast' 1994*, p. 61.
147. Sobol', 'Gde zhit' khorosho?'; *Leningrad Province in the First Half of 2005*. Work by Russian economic geographers indicates that a dramatic drop in prosperity beyond the immediate boundaries of big cities is a pattern country-wide. See Nefedova, and also Aleksandr Trifonov, 'Rossiya raspadaet na chernye dyry', interview with Nefedova (19 April 2007, www.utro.ru/articles/2007/04/19/642334.shtml).
148. See e.g. the advertisement for 'wooden house in village beyond Pavlovsk, winter-proof, garden, plot of 15 sotki in exchange for separate one-room flat in St Petersburg, Pushkin or Pavlovsk, or one room [in a communal flat] by negotiation', *Smena* 6 January 1994, p. 7.
149. See the table on the site of the Federal Service of State Statistics, www.gks.ru/bgd/regl/B07_14s/IssWWW.exe/Stg/cz/02-08.htm, and http://petrostat.gks.ru/lenobl/naselenie/2010/01chisl_o.htm.
150. Sen'kin-Tolstyi, *Ferdinand, ili Novyi Radishchev*. The actual author of this wonderful book is widely assumed to be the distinguished historian Evgeny Anisimov.
151. When we were searching in a rural settlement in Leningrad province for informants born before the Second World War who could be interviewed for our project on childhood in Soviet Russia, it proved impossible to find men of the right generation: those who were not dead were hopeless drunks (email from Ekaterina Mel'nikova to CK, August 2003).
152. http://petrostat.gks.ru/lenobl/trud/2009/01aktiv_o.htm.
153. http://eng.lenobl.ru/economics/agriculture. This information is available only on the English-language version of the site, designed for potential investors.
154. *Leningrad Province in the First Half of 2005; Leningrad Province in the First Half of 2007.*
155. www.gks.ru/bgd/regl/B07_14s/IssWWW.exe/Stg/cz/02-08.htm.
156. See the individual sites for such enterprises, e.g. http://straus-spb.ru/ (ostrich and peacock farm).
157. See http://soyuzfermerov.ru/about/.
158. As argued by O'Brien et al., Pallot and Nefedova, Granberg, and others.
159. *Leningrad Province in the First Half of 2005.*

160. On a planned strike beginning 1 June 2012, see http://news2.ru/story/350654/ (filed on 16 May 2012). According to later reports, the strike was averted (www.vedomosti.ru/auto/news/1792549/spor_na_ford_zavershen, filed 29 May 2012).
161. See the news reports of the time, e.g. www.polit.ru/news/2009/06/05/jadina/. As Golubchikov points out (pp. 106–12), the most prosperous areas (typically for the country generally) are those where oil terminals etc. are located.
162. FN, September 2012. The unfinished 'luxury estate' is outside Podporozhye.
163. This point was made for the 1990s by Zimin and Bradshaw. In 2011, according to official government figures (www.gks.ru), the area had the third highest employment figures of any region in the Russian Federation bar Moscow and St Petersburg, though the rate of unemployment (at 4.4 per cent) was still significantly higher than in St Petersburg itself (1.9 per cent). The point about the relative prosperity, by international standards, of rural Russia generally, given the high standards of education and developed infrastructure, is made by O'Brien et al., p. 268.
164. An example of this effect is Luga, a district centre and the site of several factories (including a works for making crucibles), but most remarkable for its position in a popular area for holidaymakers.
165. On the return, see http://tikhvin.org/index.php?pcid=685&cid=1109.
166. http://tikhvin.org/region/histor2y.php. A more predictable silence related to the fact that Tikhvin itself was briefly under German occupation, though this episode was covered in the display of the local museum.
167. FN, June 2012. Houses in modern Tikhvin are numbered within 'microdistricts', and not by street. On the whole, the places that have benefited most from ecclesiastical and historical tourism are those closer to the city, for instance, Staraya Ladoga (the destination of many coach trips run out of St Petersburg) (FN, September 2012).
168. In 2010, large farms produced 92 per cent of the milk, 96.5 per cent of the meat, 60.7 per cent of the vegetables, though only 33.7 per cent of the potato yields across Leningrad province (my thanks to Judy Pallot for this information).
169. This is characteristic of Eastern Europe generally: see the remarks of Deema Kaneff on Bulgaria: 'Work, Identity, and Rural-Urban Relations' in Kaneff and Leonard, pp. 180–200, and *Who Owns the Past?*.
170. Oxf/AHRC UK-08 PF32.
171. See Kotsyubinsky. This article got Kotsyubinsky into trouble for so-called 'separatism', leading to threats to suspend his position at St Petersburg State University, though this was certainly more to do with the second strand of his argument – that St Petersburg should be given the status of a separate republic – than with his articulation of the idea of shedding the province's periphery. See Olesya Gerasimova.
172. www.rosbalt.ru/piter/2012/05/31/987259.html.
173. Oxf/AHRC SPb-11 PF13 EI.
174. See e.g. Aleksandr Gil'ferding, 'Olonetskaya guberniya i ee narodnye rapsody', preface to *Onezhskie byliny* (St Petersburg, 1873), p. xi.
175. As Gerry Smith has recalled (email, July 2012), 'Malyshev's (field)work aimed to recapture the pre-Petrine cultural heritage of the Russian North and North-West, with the distinct implication of a subsequent decline and fall; he was almost explicit about this when I used to talk with this remarkable man in the 1970s'.
176. See, for example, Lidiya Chukovskaya's reference in her diaries to 'a grey Finnish day, a grey sky, and dark noble evergreens to suit' (visit to Komarovo, 17 October 1963, *Zapiski* 3, p. 78).
177. For example, Shishkin, 'Fly Agaric Toadstools' (1879), 'Woad at Pargolovo' (1884), 'Misty Morning' (1885) (http://shishkin-art.ru/interactivgallery). Leningrad artists specialising in landscape scenes included Taisiya Afonina (1913–94), Vsevolod Bazhenov (1909–86), and many others. See www.leningradartist.com/index_r.html.
178. Kushner, 'Stikhi iz Strel'ni', *Pryamaya rech'*, p. 15.
179. There is an abundance of material of this kind in the files of TsGAIPD-SPb.: see e.g. f. 24 op. 2в, d. 1545, passim (reports from 1935 on the persistence of drunken parish holidays).
180. Filippov, *Chastushki Leningradskoi oblasti*.
181. www.lenoblinform.ru/?q=/taxonomy/term/95. 'White mushroom' is a literal translation of the Russian common name for *Boletus edulis*. For local festivals generally, see www.lentravel.ru/kalendar. This type of activity (often involving local houses of culture etc.) went back to the Soviet period, when there had even been plans to turn deserted villages into tourist centres and take visitors for sleigh rides, drinks of mead, and so on (Iu. M. Lobanov, 'Perspektivy razvitiia turizma v Leningradskoi oblasti', *Kraevedenie i turizm*, pp. 121–3).

182. FN, June 2012. In the local museum at Tikhvin, the staff pointed out the difficulties of retrieving the 'authentic culture' envisaged by federal programmes (ibid.).
183. www.igorrasteryaev.ru/page/page29.html.
184. The YouTube clip had over 4.5 million views by April 2013 (www.youtube.com/watch?v–dTMa1r_RR4); a remix on another link had over a million viewings. These could in principle have included young people from the villages, since there is 3G coverage over most of Leningrad province's inhabited areas: where Rasteryaev sees rural areas as primal, people actually living there complain that young people are obsessed with what their elders see as the electronic throw-away culture of the present (FN September 2012).
185. The writer Michael Viney, known for his work on rural Ireland, has often pointed out that the same attitude characterised the Irish (as opposed to the Anglo-Irish colonial settlers) until the very recent past. In similar vein, there were landowner nature-fanciers before 1917 (a famous example was Vladimir Nabokov, who mocked the typical ignorance of birds etc. in his *Speak, Memory!*).
186. Nefedova and Pallot, 'The Multiplicity', argue for increasing hostility to *dachniki* in the post-Soviet period, mainly because of the increase in numbers, though obviously this type of subjective shift is impossible to measure accurately.
187. This is a topic that I have discussed extensively with the owners of second homes. See e.g. Oxf/AHRC GB-08 CK PF1. For a written account, see e.g. Lyudmila Aleksandrova, 'Vladel'tsam shesti sotok nuzhny shchit i mech', VechP 3 March 2000, p. 1. One solution (as in the nineteenth century) was simply to transport household chattels with you: in September, metro carriages sprouted with ads offering van runs at 50 dollars a time (pers. obs.).
188. Margarita Golubova, 'Kak obespechit' kvartiru na dachnyi sezon', *MR(V)* 24 June 2005, 6.
189. Nefedova and Pallot, 'The Multiplicity', point out that the reluctance to settle long-term outside the city is characteristic of the Moscow area too, and trace this to the continuing issues with registration, as well as weak infrastructural development.

## 9 The Last Journey

1. Vladimir Uflyand, 'Orudie russkogo yazyka', *"Esli Bog poshlet mne chitatelei"*, p. 44.
2. Salmi.
3. See, for example, www.requiem.ru/rituals/vynos/ (the listing exclusively of Petersburg cemeteries on this site makes clear that it is local to St Petersburg).
4. The chapel was built in 1913–14 by D. A. Kryzhanovsky and A. P. Golitsyn. It is not included in Antonov and Kobak's *Svyatyni Peterburga*, but basic information is given on www.citywalls.ru/house17096.html.
5. *Pervyi v strane*. Comp. K. L. Emel'yanova (1964).
6. As argued notably by Philippe Ariès in *L'Homme devant la mort* (Paris, 1977).
7. See e.g. Borodkin; V. I. Brudny.
8. *Sbornik uzakonenii raboche-krest'yanskogo pravitel'stva* 62 (1918), article 685, p. 762.
9. On 'red funerals', see Anna Sokolova, 'Funerals without a Body: The Transformation of the Traditional Burial Rite', *Forum for Anthropology and Culture* 7 (2012), forthcoming.
10. FN, December 2012.
11. The handbook, *Peterburgskii nekropol'*, ed. V. I. Saitov (1912–13), gives a good grasp of this.
12. For a discussion of the whereabouts of the Decembrists' graves, see 'Zagadka mogily dekabristov', http://vsemzagadki.narod.ru/zagadki/zagadka_mogily_dekabristov.html.
13. For instance, the Preobrazhenskoe and Serafimovskoe cemeteries were both situated on the outskirts of the city.
14. A. V. Tvel'kmeier, 'Synov svoikh rodina ne zabudet, vragov ne prostit', *SA* June 1946, pp. 16–21.
15. BILGS 1 (1957), p. 6.
16. In 1946, plans had anticipated the construction of a figure of the Motherland at the Serafimovskoe Cemetery, and a plain obelisk at the Piskaryovka Cemetery: Tvel'kmeier. Evidently, the two plans were later amalgamated, though official brochures about the Piskaryovka Cemetery never mentioned this, suggesting instead that the architects had simply changed their minds. See Gennady Petrov, *Piskarevskoe kladbishche* (1967 and many subsequent editions), pp. 10–12.
17. The parishioners of the church protested vigorously after the demolition was announced, but their objections were unsuccessful: it is clear that Metropolitan Pimen of Leningrad well understood the ritual significance, in Soviet terms, of the church's location: writing to Patriarch Alexy in 1963, he emphasised that the church was being pulled down 'in view of the widening of the highway and the planned new construction along the route to the cemetery of victims of the Blockade, where a monument has been erected and an eternal flame lit' (ASPbE 1/7/122/61).

18. See the Lensovet decree of 22 April 1961, TsGANTD 36/1-1/453/41-6; for examples of official visits and ceremonies, see e.g. TsGAIPD-SPb. K-881/16/8/33 (on a 1966 ceremony as part of a local factory's birthday celebrations); TsGAIPD-SPb. 25/89/66/43 (on a 1962 visit by a delegation of Italian Communists). This tradition continued in later decades as well: even the celebrations of the Millennium of the Christianisation of Russia included a visit to Piskaryovka (see TsGA 2017/3/18/116-7). For an outline of the cemetery's importance (written in characteristically Soviet style, though of recent date), see the official website, http://pmemorial.ru/memorial.
19. An early example is the third edition of V. Shvarts, *Leningrad: Khudozhestvennye pamyatniki* (1966).
20. Petrov, *Piskarevskoe*, p. 4. Petrov also, no doubt concerned by the idea that this might seem a kind of freak show, emphasised the cemetery's distance from the ordinary tourist routes and its quietude and primary function as a place for *Leningraders* to visit.
21. For a good discussion on the planning and artistic aims of the Piskaryovskoe Cemetery, see Kirschenbaum. As is often pointed out, Leningrad's Blockade dead lay in many other cemeteries too, only one of which, the Serafimovskoe, had a memorial complex on any scale.
22. The memorial complex at Stalingrad employed closely comparable symbolism. See Scott W. Palmer, 'How Memory was Made: The Construction of the Memorial to the Heroes of the Battle of Stalingrad', *Russian Review* 68.3 (2009), pp. 373–407.
23. For a description of how Berggol'ts's own funeral was held in a hole-in-corner fashion, so that the numbers of those attending would be limited, when the service could have been held 'in the very heart of Leningrad, on Palace Square, under the shade of red flags and banners at half-mast, since Ol'ga Berggol'ts is a great daughter of our city, the first poet of blockaded Leningrad', see Fyodor Abramov, *Chem zhivem – kormimsya* (1986), p. 288.
24. It was only in 1956 that the Champs de Mars acquired an 'eternal flame', but this meant that it was the pioneering site in the city to have this characteristic late Soviet memorial feature. The 'twinning' of the two places was also emphasised by ceremonials that took place in both, as e.g. during visits by foreign delegations in 1975: TsGAIPD 24/159/16/36.
25. Here I disagree with Anna Reid's view, in *The Siege of Leningrad* (London, 2011), that Piskaryovka is an excessively formal and pronouncedly 'Soviet' place.
26. *Pamyatnik geroicheskim zashchitnikam Leningrada. Piskarevskoe memorial'noe kladbishche* (1962), p. 5.
27. For the date of founding, see TsGALI-SPb. 405/1/126/2. The Museum of City Sculpture's remit also extended to the management of some, though not all, the monumental sculpture in public places (e.g. the Narva Gates). Attempts to safeguard 'important' graves had begun significantly earlier. For example, in 1928, the staff of the Muzei goroda made efforts to remove the monuments to Nikolai Nekrasov, Apollon Maikov, and others; however, the application was refused. (TsGA-SPb. 3200/1/63/19-20: see Cherepnina and Shkarovsky, *Spravochnik po istorii*, pp. 26–7.)
28. *Byulleten' Leningradskogo soveta*, 28 September 1938.
29. TsGALI-SPb. 405/1/3/15.
30. For instance, in 1949 a further seventeen memorials were put up in 'Literary Paths', and in the Alexander Nevsky cemeteries, a number of monuments were erected, and one moved, with its contents, to a new site: TsGALI-SPb. 405/1/27/2. In 1957, various restoration works were carried out in these cemeteries: TsGALI-SPb. 405/1/53/17. For a detailed discussion of the reconstruction of cemeteries, see also Kobak and Piryutko.
31. See e.g. TsGALI-SPb. 405/1/78/10-14 ('Proekt pis'ma v OK KPSS: Nekropol' "Literaturnye mostki": kratkaya spravka', 28 October 1960); TsGALI-SPb. 405/1/141/21 (transfer of grave of Anna, Dostoevsky's second wife, in 1968).
32. As discussed by Howard Colvin, *Architecture and the After-Life* (New Haven, 1991).
33. The 1918 contract that had to be signed by users of religious buildings required them to perform over the dead 'religious rites that are identical for all' (*Sobranie uzakonenii i rasporyazhenii raboche-krest'yanskogo pravitel'stva* 62 (1918), article 685, point 9, p. 764).
34. For example, in 1940 it was noted that a 'cenotaph has been erected' to Aleksandr Radishchev, the famous radical writer, since his original tomb was lost (TsGALI-SPb. 405/1/3/15); in 1957, it was observed that the grave to the artist Dmitry Levitsky needed a new monument (TsGALI-SPb. 405/1/53/19), and that the tomb of the architect David Grimm (1823–98) should have a new inscription carved on it commemorating his son, German Grimm (1865–1942) (ibid., ll. 21–22). The tomb allocated to the Blok family, who had been moved from different sites (in the case of Lyubov' Dmitrievna Blok, an unmarked grave), had once belonged to a German baron (pers. inf.). For a detailed historical discussion of the fate of Leningrad's historic cemeteries, see Kobak and Piryutko, *Istoricheskie kladbishcha*.

35. As pointed out to me by a friend when we visited in May 1981.
36. For instance, a recent dictionary of political terminology cites the widespread phrase for political opponents as 'isolated comrades' ('*otdel'nye tovarishchi*'), who lay at the opposite pole from the invariably positive 'broad masses' ('*shirokie massy*'). The dictionary gives also 'isolated difficulties' ('*otdel'nye nedostatki*') and 'isolated mistakes' ('*otdel'nye oshibki*'). Gasan Guseinov, *DSP: materialy k russkomu slovaryu obshchestvenno-politicheskogo yazyka* (M., 2003), pp. 801–2. In a recent interpretation of Bulat Okudzhava's song, 'Belorusskii vokzal', Alexander Zholkovsky ['Otdel'nost', granitsa, razrezhennost'"] has shown how much effort has to be made to dwell on the word *otdel'nyi*, yet give this a positive colouration. (My thanks to Andrei Zorin for drawing my attention to this article.)
37. TsGA 7384/33/76/90.
38. TsGA-SPb. 7384/33/76/99.
39. TsGALI-SPb. 405/1/141/13 (for the original letter, see l. 11).
40. 'Pis'mo Direktoru MGS Belovoi N. A. ot Predsedatelya posta sodeistviya partiino-sovetskogo kontrolya D. Kuznets i chlenov posta Yudashevoi i A. Cherno', 6 October 1964, TsGALI-SPb. 405/1/102/32.
41. One of my informants swore that he went past the 'Big House' during restoration work, and saw that the granite slabs round the socle had inscriptions on them (pers. inf., 2008). Given that the St Sergius Cathedral was converted into an NKVD building, and completely remodelled, it, or its cemetery, may well have supplied raw materials for the NKVD headquarters.
42. Anna Lupal, 'Peshekhody gulyali po nadgrobiyam', *Metro* 30 March 2011, p. 3, reported that grave markers had been found during repairs of the roadway on Bol'shaya Konyushennaya in 2011, and quoted a construction worker as saying that 'all the black granite paving-stones' in the city were former grave markers.
43. TsGAIPD-SPb. 24/145/27/2, letter from N. N. Novikov, a senior fellow at the Leningrad Section of the Institute of History of the Academy of Sciences to the Directorate of the LS IHAS, 10 August 1971. Complaints of this kind are found in published sources too: see e.g. 'Reshenie Lengorsoveta o merakh po dal'neishemu blagoustroistvu gor. Leningrada' (25 December 1956), *BILGS* 1 (1957), p. 3: 'Many cemeteries are also in a dilapidated condition'.
44. Based on my own impressions of a visit in January 2010, when the cemetery was thick with snow, so that stumbling into a drift produced a sensation that one might be about to skid downwards into an open vault. The desolation had its own kind of lyricism, which has been best evoked by Gleb Gorbovsky in a passage on Novodevichy Cemetery from *Ostyvshie sledy*, pp. 104–5.
45. TsGALI-SPb. 105/1/1327/ 74.
46. The classic source on this for the late Soviet period is Sergei Kaledin's novella *The Humble Cemetery*, which portrays the Pyatnitskoe Cemetery in Moscow during the 1970s. Newspaper reports of the glasnost era indicate that the situation was comparable in Leningrad: see e.g. V. Dubkovsky, 'Rassledovanie . . . prekratit', *LP* 3 March 1988 (on how relatives were being made to pay for services that they were entitled to have for nothing). Even in the memorial graveyards, caretakers could have a rackety air: see the correspondence from 1968 in which a visitor to Literatorskie mostki complains that his son was bitten by the drunken caretaker's dog (he was offered an apology, but no compensation, for his son's ripped clothes) (TsGALI-SPb. 405/1/141/42-3).
47. There were cases where relatives' claims were simply ignored. For instance, according to formerly secret documents of 1933, when construction of an airstrip took place at Kronstadt over 2000 graves were obliterated, including 471 registered graves. The status of the latter was brushed aside: 'Although memorials, fences, railings etc. erected by private individuals are the legal property of those individuals, at present they are in poor condition, and the 471 registered graves are not maintained by the relatives at all, and it follows that the re-registration of the graves was carried out simply for form's sake and to delay the liquidation of the cemetery, whereas the relatives of the departed were obliged to maintain the memorials for twelve months' (the awkward phrasing follows the original) (TsGA 7384/2/20/96-96 ob.). It is possible that similar cases could be unearthed from later decades, if classified documents were made public.
48. TsGANTD-SPb. 386/3-2/51/3.
49. TsGANTD-SPb. 386/3-2/51/5-6.
50. On the first crematorium, opened on 14 December 1920, see M. Shkarovsky, 'Stroitel'stvo Petrogradskogo (Leningradskogo) krematoriya kak sredstvo bor'by s religiei', http://krotov.info/history/20/1920/1920krematory.htm; Lebina and Izmozik. On the general background to propaganda for cremation, see also Merridale, *Night of Stone*, ch. 2.
51. TsGANTD-SPb. 386/3-2/49/4-6.

52. Visit, December 2012. For a brief description of the architecture, see Lavrov, *1000 adresov v Sankt-Peterburge*, p. 345.
53. TsGANTD-SPb. 386/3-2/51/11. 'The Armenian-Gregorian Christian Cemetery, area 1 hectare, is to be completely transformed, with the burial of the remains of graves that are still visited in one of the active cemeteries of the city, while the valuable monuments and sepulchres are transported to one of the necropolis-parks.' The same fate was anticipated for the Malookhtenskoe and Kazanskoe Cemeteries. (In the margins, this passage has two question marks in pencil scrawled alongside it; possibly this scepticism is one reason why large-scale plans for reshaping did not go ahead.)
54. Ibid., l. 4.
55. Ibid., l. 10.
56. Nor was the work of transferring 'all graves of artistic and historical interest' to the necropolises brought to a conclusion, though this was said in 1968 to be in its final stages, to be completed in 1973: TsGALI-SPb. 405/1/141/62.
57. FN December 2012. The brick factory stood on the site of what is now the Moscow prospekt Victory Park, and is commemorated by a chapel and a secular memorial (FN January 2013). For a more decorous account of its operation, see 'Blokada', www.uhlib.ru/istorija/sankt_peterburg_istorija_v_predanijah_i_legendah/p29.php. During the Blockade, corpses were also stacked in streets, particularly what is now ul. Repina, but this was too aberrant a practice to inspire the same horror.
58. As, for example, in the Novodevich'e Cemetery and the Cemetery of the Martyrs of the 9 January. For the shudder inspired by cremation, see e.g. Mikhail Veller's story 'Krematorii', in which a widow discovers her deceased husband's suit for sale in the *komissionyi* shop on Apraksin dvor. The story sardonically juxtaposes the outwardly hygienic and well-ordered look of the crematorium and the cynicism of the staff within closed doors.
59. T. S. Tsar'kova, 'Memorial'nyi zhanr: obraztsy i podrazhaniya', in *Fenomen Peterburga*, p. 247, asserts that there was a special type of local grave marker in the nineteenth century – a miniature replica of The Bronze Horseman with an Orthodox cross on top, but Leningrad cemeteries did not have any locally specific emblems (unless one counts anchors for admirals, etc.)
60. In 1931, there had been a plan to move St John's remains so that his funerary chapel could be used as a dining room by the institute installed in the convent. However, the removal did not in fact take place, probably because of anxiety over possible protests from believers (Archpriest Ioann Ornatsky, arrested in 1936 on charges of counter-revolutionary activity, wrote to object to the planned move in 1932). (TsGA 1000/49/40/37-8).
61. 'O "svyatykh" mestakh na Smolenskom kladbishche i trebakh na mogile I. Kronshtadtskogo', Resolutsiya Mitropolita Grigoriya, 16 August 1951, Archive of the St Petersburg Eparchy, f. 1. op. 26 (3), d. 20, l. 40.
62. Bol'shakova, *Pod pokrovom*.
63. For this point generally in the Soviet context, see Kaledin, *Smirennoe kladbishche*.
64. See, for example, the report by the local Plenipotentiary for the Affairs of Religious Cults, G. S. Zharinov, in 1972 (TsGA-SPb. 2017/1/24/37-9) which stated that the ritual washing and laying-out facilities at the Muslim and Jewish burial grounds were to be transferred to the Southern Cemetery, a strategy that was certainly intended to discourage recourse to traditional burial practices (cf. the habit of assigning to believers churches that were far from the centre of Leningrad and hard to get to, in the hope that congregations would dwindle). The report makes clear that the Orthodox clergy had now adapted to the restrictions placed on their activities when it came to funerals, and clearly hoped for the same with other denominations.
65. Brodsky, 'Evreiskoe kladbishche okolo Leningrada', www.world-art.ru/lyric/lyric.php?id=7336. The poem does not appear in, for example, Lev Losev's edition of Brodsky's verse.
66. See www.funeralservice.ru/uslugi/vip-uslugi/.
67. Visit to the Cemetery of the Victims of 9 January 1905, September 2010; FN, October 2011, December 2012.
68. 'Martirolog: Levashovskaya pustosh, 1937–1938', *Vechernii Leningrad* 10 January 1990, p. 2; 'Prikaz Komiteta po potrebitel'skomu rynku', 17 January 2000 (Archive of Memorial); 'Khronologiya Levashovskogo mogil'nika' [2011] (ibid.), 'Proekt Postanovleniya o Levashovskom memorial'nom kladbishche' and the 'Istoricheskaya spravka' with it, February 2011 (ibid.); see also the information on the official municipal site, http://visz.nlr.ru/project/reg/peter.html.
69. These cults sprang up before the canonisation of the Imperial Family by the Russian Orthodox Church, which took place only in 2000.
70. See the detailed account by Elena Letenkova, '"I blazhen, kto ne soblaznitsya obo mne"', www.fontanka.ru/2007/06/18/030/.

71. Personal obs., 2003. On Moscow commemoration, see also Olga Matich, 'Uspeshnyi mafiozo – mertvyi mafiozo. Kul'tura pogrebal'nogo obryada', *Novoe literaturnoe obozrenie* 33 (1998), pp. 75–107; on comparable funerary pomp in the Far East, see Tobias Holzheimer, 'Le paradis des grands bandits: la culture de la mort violente en Extrême-Orient russe', www.ethnographiques.org.
72. On the deficiencies of individual supervision, see www.requiem.ru/publicism/boss/ (accessed 12 December 2009). Cf. the complaints about corrupt cemetery officials on http://spb.kp.ru/daily/24317/510317/ 27 June 2009.
73. Slepakova, 'Istoriya pamyatnika', *Stikhotvoreniya i poemy*, p. 106.
74. The main online 'virtual cemetery', www.rip.su/, includes numerous postings from Leningrad province and from Petersburg. For a discussion of these and of modern burial practices (with reference to the Vladimir countryside, but with more general application), see Sokolova. It should be said that a status division still persists in the virtual world: the 'Peterburgskii nekropol" site commemorates only the 'out of the ordinary' [*nezauryadnye*] dead, though potentially space here would surely be infinite, and in practice 'out of the ordinary' seems to extend to, say, engineers, if not members of the proletariat (http://spb-tombs-walkeru.narod.ru/walkeru/walkeru.htm).
75. Artemii Aleksandrov, 'Sotrudnikam piterskikh kladbishch pribavitsya raboty', *MR-V* 25 February 2005, p. 3.
76. www.kotlin.ru/news/2008/02/12/news_9715.html. Cf. www.rosbalt.ru/2008/12/04/547556.html (accessed 12 December 2009).
77. Cf. the undated text on www.requiem.ru/services/doc60/, which complains about the indifference of district administrations and *raionnye administratsii* and lack of *shefstva* from Akademiya Nauk; it claimed that finding graves of famous people in order to organise jubilee celebrations etc. was often impossible.
78. http://spb-mitrofan-society.org/ (accessed 1 November 2010).
79. Analogous conflicts were also taking place with reference to other former cemeteries, notably the Farforovskoe kladbishche at Lomonosovskaya: see e.g. http://spb-mitrofan-society.org/farfor_istor.php.
80. Based on personal observation in the inner-city cemeteries of St Petersburg, 2009–11.
81. Shtyrkov and Kormina.
82. See the interview with Father Vyacheslav on the church's website, www.bcex.ru/?page=0307. Accessed 1 November 2010. Svetlana Aksenova, 'Pravo na mogilu' (*Sotsial'noe bogoslovie*, 2009: see www.religare.ru/2_67693.html, accessed 30 April 2011). The quotation about 'eternal memory' is from the latter. In the church itself, a noticeboard displays materials about this project, including photographs, an article from *Zhurnal pravoslavnykh zhenshchin*, etc. (FN, January 2010).
83. Oxf/AHRC SPb-09 PF2 VM. See also Oxf/AHRC SPb-09 PF1 VM (interview with members of the congregation directly involved with compiling the Book of Remembrance). The word used was *pomyannik* (another traditional term is *sinodik*).
84. I have often seen notices of this kind myself in Orthodox churches, including those in St Petersburg.
85. In 2010–11, the proposal to construct an Orthodox church or chapel on the Levashovo site led to a polite but determined exchange of opinion. One side was primarily represented by A. Ya. Razumov, the head of the 'Vozvrashchennye imena' Centre', who argued that the general public regularly made comments in the vein, 'A church kind of seems to be missing' (*khrama vrode ne khvataet*), and on the other stood the representatives of Memorial, who held that the construction of a church on the actual cemetery site (as opposed to just outside it) would be intrusive, inappropriate in historical terms, and likely to precipitate demands for further creed-specific major structures (mosques, synagogues etc.) on the basis of 'parity of esteem'. See www.cogita.ru/intervyu/anatolii-razumov; www.cogita.ru/dokumenty/k-voprosu-o-vozvedenii-hrama-na-levashovskom-memorialnom-kladbische, and also the letters written by Irina Flige, Director of Memorial, to Metropolitan Vladimir of St Petersburg and Ladoga, Metropolitan Yuvenily, chairman of the Commission on Canonisation of the Moscow Patriarchate, and Patriarch Kirill (Memorial Archive). At the time of writing, the situation was still unresolved.
86. For the news report, see Mar'ya Tsygankova, 'Piskarevskoe kladbishche oskvernili "khozyaistvenniki"', www.fontanka.ru/2007/04/08/001/.
87. Visit, December 2012. See also www.funeralassociation.ru/ru/newspaper/new/0808/.
88. For the general landscaping etc., visit, December, 2012. For complaints about practical difficulties, see the feedback page operated by the management company running the cemetery, http://gmstar.ru/spb/1-241597-uzhnoe-kladbische.html.
89. FN December 2012.
90. The buses (and accompanying marshrutkas) run from Moskovskaya and prospekt Veteranov. In both cases, the stops are remote from the metro exit: after a good deal of searching, I found a taxi

driver who told me, without obvious humour, that the bus to the Southern Cemetery ran from 'the very last stop on the far side of the road'.

91. Visit, December 2012.

### Afterword

1. For the claim that St Petersburg is the main manufacturing centre for amphetamines etc., see Oxf/AHRC-SPb-09 PF-60 IN; on raves, see Oxf/AHRC-SPb-07 39 PF IN.
2. On the Kronstadt raves (which in recent years have transferred to the town itself), see http://caves.ru/threads/42064-форты-Кронштадта. On Oreshek, see '"Molodaya Gvardiya" provedet v zashchitu kreposti Oreshek aktsiyu "Reid protiv reidov"' (5 July 2007), http://saint-petersburg.ru/m/209888/molodaya_gwardiya_prowedet_w_zaschitu_kreposti_oresh.html.
3. For material on the protests, see http://rusrep.ru/article/2011/12/10/10december2; www.ridus.ru/news/14385/. Some of the protesters began the day by marching down Nevsky, but the primary historical associations of this space are with officially sanctioned parades, both before and after 1917, rather than with oppositional demonstrations. In 2012, the legislative assembly reacted with an outright ban on meetings in St Isaac's and Palace Squares, as well as Nevsky, attempting to deradicalise these places' memorial connotations.
4. FN September 2012.
5. Oxf/AHRC SPb-11 PF16 EI.
6. Savitsky, 'Svoe i nashe' in *Vzglyad na peterburgskoe iskusstvo*, pp. 3–5. In the words of the anthropologist Sergei Alymov ('"Perestroika in the Russian Provinces"', 'The issue is not about the construction of some kind of "ideal type" with a specific range of consistent characteristics, but rather about the analysis of the situational, intricately dependent, and plastic cultural practices of various groups of the population that have assimilated and used certain features of the (changing and fragmentary) Soviet culture.'
7. http://fictionbook.ru/author/yeldar_aleksandrovich_ryazanov/ironiya_sudbiy_ili_s_legkim_parom/read_online.html?
8. See e.g. Gudkov.
9. See, for example, French and Hamilton (eds), *The Socialist City*, especially French, 'The Individuality of the Soviet City' (by which is meant its peculiarity by Western standards in *lacking* individuality), pp. 73–104, and Hamilton, 'Spatial Structure in East European Cities', pp. 195–262. Such models are analytically convenient, but do not register the significant changes that came about in big cities through the rehousing policies of the 1960s and 1970s.
10. Lisa Kirschenbaum has, very reasonably, argued this for the Blockade era too. I am not certain, though, that there was a straightforward and direct transmission of this self-belief from one generation to another. Rather, distinct and unconnected groups of Leningraders/Petersburgers have nurtured it at different periods for different reasons – the city's war history, or its pre-1917 past, or its contemporary cultural life, and so on, usually with reference to an earlier group who held similar views.
11. See Chapter 2 and Chapter 6 here.
12. On the 'grand narratives of persecution', see, for example, the material on the 'Leningrad Affair' in [OL Chapter One]. The elision of personal deprivation from social memory has, of course, parallels in other cultures. 'The 1949 western "victory" produced by an Anglo-American airlift that overcame a total Soviet blockade of West Berlin depended on unruly Berliners continuing to practice the black marketeering and deal making that had enabled them to survive since the last months of the Second World War. True to the myths of everyday life, these same unruly Berliners retrospectively tended to explain their survival only in terms of the airlift, arguably to preserve their autonomy in a polarized international system that so circumscribed their lives (Paul Steege, Andrew Stuart Bergerson, Maureen Healy, Pamela E. Swett, 'The History of Everyday Life: A Second Chapter', *The Journal of Modern History* 80.2 (2008), pp. 358–78, this quote p. 370). Talking about personal hardship is bad manners also in other countries with a recent history of deprivation, not to speak of an incomparably more prosperous but also economically precarious present, for example, Ireland, Greece, and Italy.
13. In January 2012, a woman working in an archive where I was researching insisted that guided tours to cemeteries would be aesthetically unacceptable, as well as unethical (because they would trespass on the privacy of mourners) (FN).
14. I would agree with Olga Shevchenko's interpretation in *Crisis and the Everyday* that the 1990s were only one of many crisis periods (the existence of a pervasive sense of crisis is borne out by Nielsen's ethnography of Leningrad in the late 1970s and 1980s). But all the same, referring to the 'shock

therapy' era as something exceptional was common practice in the 2000s, particularly among those who were making an anti-liberal point (ordinary members of the public as well as politicians). (See e.g. FN March 2012.)

15. Baiburin and Piir's article, 'Happy Holidays', shows various informants negotiating this dilemma, as they recollect how state parades which they had to attend were actually enjoyable as well.
16. Alexander Chaadaev, 'Pervoe filosofskoe pis'mo', www.vehi.net/chaadaev/filpisma.html. The accusation of 'dysfunctional memory syndrome' is one of numerous critical clichés circulating about post-Soviet (and, more broadly, post-socialist) societies, such as the absence of 'civil society' and the 'market economy', which ignore the actual relations obtaining in such societies in favour of ideal models: see e.g. the comments by Christopher Hann in his introduction to *Postsocialism*, pp. 9–10, and the collection ed. Hann and Dunn, *Civil Society*; Humphrey, *The Unmaking of Soviet Life*. Once again I would emphasise that this is not intended to justify or condone the history of adjustment and erasure to history, as criticised by Khapaeva, Koposov, Schönle and others.
17. Stephen J. Collier (referring to the case of neo-liberal ideology), *Post-Soviet Social*, p. 12. Kevin M. F. Platt's study of the constantly modulating cultural roles of two Russian autocrats through time, *Terror and Greatness*, counsels informed agnosticism about whether there could ever be a wholly authoritative vision of the past that would be independent of the context in which understanding was shaped.

## Sources and their Uses

1. Alice A. Bauer, 'Guide for Interviewing Soviet Escapees', Harvard Interview Project, http://pds.lib.harvard.edu.
2. See, for example, Zemskov-Zuge, Voronina, and Utekhin; Meshcherina; Michina and Richards; Frisch, *A Shared Authority*. That said, as Vincent Crapanzano points out in *Tuhami*, the closed question/open question division is itself an academic abstraction: in practice, people will challenge 'closed' questions that contradict their views of life (and the results can be very informative), while sometimes being totally flummoxed by 'open' ones (not knowing what on earth to say in answer to something so global).
3. Paperno, *Stories of the Soviet Experience*, has convincingly argued for the impact of Lidiya Ginzburg's diaries on some online blogs, for instance (pp. 51–4).
4. See http://community.livejournal.com/costume_history/317534.html?thread=2399070. Social websites such as Vkontakte and Facebook, on the other hand, provide more collusive audiences for recollection (which probably explains their increasing popularity in the 2000s).
5. At a different level, the most up-to-date and reliable sources for official statistics (material on the demographics of Leningrad province, for instance) are now online, and there are excellent reference sources in other areas too, for example, the National Corpus of the Russian Language at www.ruscorpora.ru, most major nineteenth- and twentieth-century dictionaries, etc.
6. For reasons of space, newspaper articles and online items are generally not listed, though exceptions have been made for a few items of the first significance, such as D. S. Likhachev's articles in *Literaturnaya gazeta* and *LP* from 1965, and the online publications of the poet Yuri Kolker and others.

# Glossary and List of Major Place Names

Bol'shoi Sampsonievsky prospekt (Great Sampson Avenue, from the Cathedral of the Prophet Sampson, located on the street): runs from the Pirogov Embankment to the northern outskirts.

Dvortsovaya ploshchad' (Palace Square): fronts the Winter Palace (Hermitage).

Gorokhovaya ulitsa (Pea-Market Street): one of the city's three central radial avenues, along with Nevsky and Voznesensky prospekt.

Kamennoostrovsky prospekt (Stone Island Avenue): runs from Trinity Bridge to Kamenny ostrov (Stone Island); transformed into a street of elegant apartment blocks in the 1910s.

Kirovsky prospekt (Kirov Avenue): the name between 1934–91 of Kamennoostrovsky prospekt.

Lensovet: Leningrad City Soviet (the rough equivalent of a city council in the West); all important business was delegated to the Executive Committee (*ispolkom*). Subordinate to it were the district soviets (*raisovety*).

Marsovo pole (Champs de Mars/Field of Mars).

Mezhdunarodnyi prospekt (International Avenue): the name of Moskovsky prospekt between 1918–50.

Moskovsky prospekt (Moscow Avenue): runs from Sennaya south to ploshchad' Pobedy.

Nevsky prospekt (Neva Avenue): the central street in the city, known between 1918 and 1944 as prospekt 25 Oktyabrya (25 October Avenue, from the date of the October Revolution, 1917).

ploshchad' Lenina (Lenin Square): next to Finland Station.

ploshchad' Mira (Peace Square): the name of Sennaya ploshchad' from 1952–92.

ploshchad' Pobedy (Victory Square): major square to the south of the city centre, created in Srednyaya Rogatka district during the 1970s, as part of a vast war memorial complex.

ploshchad' Proletarskoi Diktatury (Square of the Dictatorship of the Proletariat): in front of Smol'nyi Cathedral.

ploshchad' Uritskogo (Uritsky Square): the name of Dvortsovaya ploshchad' from 1918–44.

ploshchad' Vosstaniya (Uprising Square), formerly Znamenskaya ploshchad' (Square of the Sign, from the Church of the Sign, demolished in 1940): lies half-way down Nevsky, next to the Moscow Station.

Poklonnaya Gora (Worship Hill): the highest point in the city, north of the centre; now a district of newbuild.

prospekt Maiorova: the name of Voznesensky prospekt from 1923–91.

prospekt Marksa (Marx Avenue): the name of Bol'shoi Sampsonievsky prospekt from 1918–91.

prospekt imeni Stalina (Stalin Avenue): the name of Moskovsky prospekt from 1950–56.

Regional Committee of the Communist Party (Oblkom KPSS): the most important organ of local administration, with jurisdiction over Lensovet as well as the lower-level party organs, the City Committee and the different District Committees.

Sadovaya ulitsa (Park Street): runs from Marsovo pole to Kolomna; known from 1918–44 as ulitsa 3 iyulya (3 July Street), in commemoration of the shooting of demonstrators on that date in 1917.

Sennaya ploshchad' (Haymarket): *see also* ploshchad' Mira; on Sadovaya ulitsa.

Stone Island (Kamenny ostrov) (between 1934–91, Kirov Island): an area of parks and summer homes to the north of the city centre.

Strelka: the 'point' of Vasilievsky Island, site of the city's most famous 'ensemble' of buildings, including the former Stock Exchange, the Kunstkamera, the former Customs House (now the Institute of Russian Literature of the Russian Academy of Sciences, or 'Pushkin House'), the Academy of Sciences, the original building of St Petersburg State University (the so-called 'Twelve Colleges'), etc.

ul. Dzerzhinskogo: the name of Gorokhovaya ulitsa from 1927–91 (in 1918–27 the street was known as Komissarovskaya).

ul. Krasnykh Zor' (Red Dawns Street): the name from 1918–34 of Kamennoostrovsky prospekt (except for the short section running across Kamenny ostrov).

Voznesensky prospekt (Ascension Avenue, from a church demolished in 1936): the third of three radial streets, along with Nevsky prospekt and Gorokhovaya, which define the topography of the city centre.

# Sources and their Uses

In the Soviet period, official commemorative practices were documented obsessively. Museums and bodies such as GIOP kept records of meetings, produced reports and statistical surveys, and in the case of museums, compiled lists of acquisitions [*spiski priobretenii*]. According to standard procedures, materials of this kind were also forwarded to the Party and local and central administrations (Lensovet, the Ministry of Culture), and, in due course, sent to the state archives. In total, many thousands of pages deal with 'monuments' of various kinds over the different decades of the post-Stalin era.

At the same time, this material is not easy to work with. In the Party archives particularly, documentation is scattered over numerous different sections of the administration – the Departments of Culture, Agitation and Propaganda, the General and Secret Departments. Subject indexes (if available at all) are far from complete, and the holdings themselves spotty and unpredictable. From the late 1960s, the records thin out radically. It would appear that many institutions were required to submit materials to the state archives on a rolling 25-year deadline (so that the last regular deposits took place in 1990). In the post-Soviet era, consignments have been made haphazardly, if at all. Large numbers of files from the late 1960s, 1970s and 1980s dealing with the state regulation of religious organisations were transferred from the Government of St Petersburg to TsGA in the late 2000s, but many other areas of administrative activity have not yet been deposited.

The result is that large numbers of documents remain with the institutions that produced them in the first place. These places all have their own archives, but the primary purpose of these is practical. Documentation is mainly used by employees, and by visitors with highly specific goals. Research of an abstract kind ('the history of museums in the post-Stalin era'), as opposed to efforts to find material about no. 42 Nevsky prospekt, or the Trinity Church at Lesnoi, is poorly understood and tends to provoke impatience and at times suspicion ('Call yourself a historian when you can't even tell me what you want to see!').

Much documentation from the recent past is still classified – particularly, but not exclusively, in the archives of the City Committee of the Communist Party, where materials on Lenin monuments may be bundled together with reports on bad behaviour by foreign students, orders of clothing for army officers, and corruption in the administration, all once and still counting as 'classified' material. In case of doubt, the instinct is to withhold.

Institutions may impose restrictions of their own: museums are reluctant to release detailed information about their holdings, such as lists of acquisitions (prompted by fear of theft); often, the minutes of meetings and other procedural materials (*deloproizvodstvo*) are not available (this is the case, for instance, in GIOP).

In any case, even if procedural documentation is abundant, dealing with it is not straightforward. Material of this kind, as Soviet historians have come to realise since the 1990s, records statements of intent, rather than testifying to action. It provides excellent evidence for the history of institutional conflicts and propaganda, but at best scanty support for the discussion of practices. We can learn which statues were built, but usually not how people reacted to them (except in extreme cases, such as when the objects constructed were vandalised); we can find out how many cafés there were, but not how they were used, and often not even what they had on the menu (as opposed to what they were supposed to serve).

For a sense of these elusive areas of memory-drenched city life, one has to turn to letters and diaries, memoirs and oral history, forms of recollection that often focus precisely on recollection of the everyday. These sources are also useful in that they provide particularly rich testimony to the workings of recollection. As Tolstoy argued in his essay, 'A Few Words about the Novel *War and Peace*', people start to adjust their memories almost immediately after something has happened; a field report is already much further from the scene of battle than a soldier's spontaneous comments when he re-enters the barracks. But if one is interested in memory to begin with, the likely interference of more recent events on perceptions, and the tendency of those who remember to engage in moralising narratives about 'then and now' – points that are often raised to question the historical value of recollection – become part of the analysis, rather than an obstacle to it. People's capacity to digress into lengthy family narratives (what I mentally labelled 'Uncle Yasha's poodle stories') and to zig-zag unpredictably between childhood and later phases of life, points to the ways in which views of the past influence the present, as well as vice versa.

While recording material for the Harvard Interview Project, researchers were supposed, in their relentless search for the 'typical' Soviet experience, to strip out anything 'irrelevant'. To quote the official project manual:

> The most effective method to prevent digression is to formulate questions as precisely as possible in order to restrict the range of information the respondent can give in answer to them. For example, a question such as 'What sort of problems did you have in getting supplies for your plant?' is

> an invitation to a general discourse on the nature of the Bolshevik regime. On the other hand, 'When you had difficulties getting supplies through regular channels, did you have connections in the Ministry who would help you out?' is more apt to get the data asked for, with little additional comment.

While interviewers were told not to interrupt, they were advised that 'shunting' and speeding-up questions were acceptable and necessary techniques.[1] More recent interviewing practice, on the other hand, emphasises the need to provide a sympathetic environment in which people can tell their life histories without this level of direct guidance: at most, interviews are semi-structured, and questions are generally open.[2] The interviews on which I draw here were wide-ranging discussions of people's relationship with the city, undercutting standard analytical categories such as 'personal' versus 'social' memory, and neat divisions into phases of life. This I have tried to reflect in my own narrative.

Another major source of information about how people reflect on the past is the ample material now available on the Russian internet. It would be naïve to see online forums and blogs as a kind of free space for spontaneous, unmediated recollection: reminiscence has its rules, and its paths of mediation here, as it does everywhere else.[3] But the internet is interesting because it shows how memory evolves through dialogue and confrontation: an innocent comment about how one remembers Crimplene as a luxury fabric back in the 1970s may produce a whole series of comments affirming or challenging the statement ('yes, I thought it was lovely back then'; 'if you thought that, it just showed what a diehard provincial you were').[4] And in addition to its usefulness as a source of 'live memory', the internet is also an unparalleled resource for more conventional types of material – not just memoirs and diaries but, as more and more academic institutions, archives, NGOs and societies build up their sites, for documentation, photographs, and entire treatises (often of very high quality) on local and national history. The copious 'online folklore' (sites such as 'You're a Real Petersburger If . . .'), and the local forums for gossip and exchange of information, have their own place in illustrating how city-dwellers, particularly of the younger generation, make sense of the world.[5]

As for my own recollections, from the early 2000s I have kept a diary of my visits to Petersburg, making entries several times a week (these are cited in the notes as FN). Using a lightweight digital camera (which appeals because using it is maximally unobtrusive), I have taken thousands of photographs as a separate and complementary record (where not otherwise credited, the photographs here are my own). I have drawn on my own archive (letters written from Leningrad in the Soviet period, old photographs) – though I wish I had been more systematic about documentation back then. In some cases, I have had to rely on pure recollections of things seen and heard, and have labelled these as 'pers. inf.' or 'pers. obs.', with a (necessarily approximate) date. Other people have kindly shared memory materials of their own, which are credited in the notes as well.

A further and important source for the illustrations is the material held in archives such as TsGAKFFD. Most of these images were originally taken for official agencies, such as LenTASS, with the result that they tend to be rather formal and related to the ideological concerns of the day. It is much easier to research, say, sport and public holidays than cafés, and posed publicity shots are much commoner in the theatre files than performance photographs. However, the rising interest in day-to-day living that was an important development in the post-Stalin era does mean that some more impromptu materials surface even here.

The bibliography that follows is not intended as an exhaustive survey of material about St Petersburg; I limit myself to the most important sources actually cited in my discussion.[6] However, it conveys the substance of the materials, in their variety and contradictoriness, that underlie the writing of my book, and also includes some of the many excellent earlier histories and scholarly evocations of Petersburg and Leningrad culture. As well as showing the paths taken so far, it will, I hope, act as a non-proscriptive guide to paths that might be taken in future.

# Select Bibliography


*Unpublished sources*

I have not given separate descriptions when archives hold relatively small collections of materials, grouped in a small number of generic *fondy* – e.g. ASPbE f. 1 'Correspondence of the Chancery of the Metropolitan' – the description of which is of little use in locating individual documents.

TsGA-SPb., f. 1001 (Administrativnyi otdel Petrogradskogo (Leningradskogo) gubernskogo komiteta), f. 9620 (Sovet po delam religioznykh kul'tov)
TsGAIPD-SPb., f. 24 (Leningradskii oblastnoi komitet KPSS), f. 25 (Leningradskii gorodskoi komitet KPSS), f. K-881 (Leningradskii gorodskoi komitet VLKSM)
TsGALI-SPb., f. 105 (Upravlenie kul'tury ispolkoma Lengorsoveta), f. 229 (VOOPIiK), f. 268 (Bol'shoi dramaticheskii teatr), f. 341 (Leningradskoe otdelenie Soyuza arkhitektorov)
TsGANTD-SPb., f. 36 (Lenproekt), f. 388 (APU Lenoblispolkoma)

Kushkova, Anna, 'Chto eli sovetskie evrei, ili k voprosu o "kulinarnom" izmerenii etnicheskoi identichnosti' (unpublished MS, 2009)

Mukhin, Dmitry, 'Mgnoven'ya' (unpublished MS, *c.* 2007)

Tsipursky, Gleb, 'Youth Cafes in Moscow: Western Culture in the Soviet Capital during the Early Socialist Sixties' (unpublished MS, 2012)

*Interview transcripts*

St Petersburg Academic Classical High School, Folklore Department Archive

Bologoe interviews, 2001: No. 1 (f., about 20)
Interviewers: A. Tarabukina and A. Lityagin. Courtesy Irina Nazarova.
SPbAG AKF Bologoe-01 PF1

Narva and Estonia interviews, 2011: No. 7 (man b. 1948), No. 8 (woman b. 1965), No. 18 (woman b. 1966), No. 23 (woman aged 30), No. 57 (woman b. 1993)
Interviewers: Mariya Akmetova, Ol'ga Burdakova, Elena Dobrovol'skaya, Natalia Galetkina, Larisa Gerasimova, Vera Grunina, Mikhail Lurye, Liliya Matvievskaya, Mariya Minakova, Marina Avila Reese, Elena Rootam-Val'ter, Yuliya Tamm, Anna Tyagunova
SPbAG AKF NE PF7 etc.

Oxford Life History Archive

Interviewers: AB Andy Byford; AK Alexandra Kasatkina; AP Alexandra Piir; CK Catriona Kelly; EK Ekaterina Izmestieva; IN Irina Nazarova; MS Marina Samsonova; NG Natalia Galetkina; SA Svetlana Amosova

Oxf/AHRC Evp-07 PF1–PF3 IN (2 informants)
Oxf/AHRC SPb-07 PF1–PF2 AK (2 informants)
Oxf/AHRC SPb-08 PF1 – SPb-09 PF17 AP (17 informants)

Oxf/AHRC SPb-11 PF1 – PF20 EI (20 informants)
Oxf/AHRC SPb-07 PF1 – SPb-12 PF12 CK (12 informants)
Oxf/AHRC SPb-07 PF1 – SPb-10 PF62 IN (48 informants)
Oxf/AHRC SPb-10 PF1 – SPb-12 PF44 MS (44 informants)
Oxf/AHRC SPb-10 PF1 – SPb-11 PF4 NG (4 informants)
Oxf/AHRC SPb-07 PF1 – SPb-08 PF18 SA (12 informants)

Oxf/AHRC UK-07 PF11 AB (woman b. Perm', 1966)
Oxf/AHRC UK-08 PF22 AB (woman b. Leningrad, 1938)
Oxf/AHRC UK-08 PF26 AB (woman b. Latvia, 1940s)
Oxf/AHRC UK-08 PF32 AB (woman b. Tallinn, mid-1960s)
Oxf/AHRC UK-08 PF42 AB (woman b. Leningrad, 1974)
Oxf/AHRC UK-08 PF44 AB (woman b. Leningrad, 1983)
Oxf/AHRC UK-08 PF52 AB (woman b. Irkutsk, 1958)
Oxf/AHRC UK-08 PF 57 AB (woman b. Leningrad, 1970)
Oxf/AHRC UK-08 PF60 AB (woman b. Uzbekistan, 1943)
Oxf/AHRC UK-08 PF62 AB (woman b. Podmoskov'e, 1949)
Oxf/AHRC UK-08 PF64 AB (woman b. Russian Far East, 1959)
Oxf/AHRC UK-08 PF 66 AB (woman b. Leningrad, 1974)
Oxf/AHRC UK-08 PF69 AB (inf. 1 man b. Latvia, 1955; inf. 2 woman b. Latvia, 1940)
Oxf/AHRC UK-08 PF80 AB (man b. Leningrad, 1972)
Oxf/AHRC UK-08 PF1 – PF2 CK (2 informants)

Oxf/Lev SPb-02 PF1 – SPb-06 PF84 AP (44 informants)


*Published sources*


Akhmetova, Mariya, and Mikhail Lur'e, 'Field Materials from Bologoe', *Forum for Anthropology and Culture* 1 (2004), http://anthropologie.kunstkamera.ru/en/index/8_5/

Alekseev, Nikita, 'Piterskie khroniki', http://magazines.russ.ru/zvezda/2006/12/al5.html

*Almanach de St Pétersbourg. Cour, monde et ville, 1910* (1910)

Almedingen, Edith Martha, *I Remember St Petersburg* (London, 1969)

Alymov, Sergei, '"Perestroika" in the Russian Provinces', *Forum for Anthropology and Culture* 7 (2012)

Antonov, V. V. and A. V. Kobak, *Svyatyni Sankt-Peterburga: Entsiklopediya khristianskikh khramov* (2010)

Appadurai, Arjun (ed.), *The Social Life of Things: Commodities in Cultural Perspective* (Cambridge, 1996)

Applebaum, Anne, *Iron Curtain: The Crushing of Eastern Europe, 1944–56* (London, 2012)

Argenbright, R., 'Avtomobilshchina: Driven to the Brink in Moscow', *Urban Geography* 29.7 (2008), pp. 683–704

Artem'ev, A. Yu., *O Dukhe i Dushe Peterburga* (2003)

Astvatsaturov, Aleksei, *Skuns-Kamera* (2011)

Avdeev, V. I., *Zhilishchnoe khozyaistvo Leningrada v tsifrakh i faktakh* (1969)

Azarova, Katerina, *L'Appartement communitaire: l'histoire cachée du logement soviétique* (Paris, 2007)

Bachelard, Gaston, *La poétique de l'espace* (Paris, 1967)

Baiburin, Albert, 'Ъ (Materialy k kul'turnoi istorii tverdogo znaka)', www.elzabair.ru/cntnt/lmenu/biblioteka/lyubimye_s1/bajburin_a.html

——. and Alexandra Piir, 'Happy Holidays: Remembering Soviet Festivals', in Balina and Dobrenko (eds), *Petrified Utopia*, pp. 161–86

Balina, Marina and Evgeny Dobrenko (eds), *Petrified Utopia: Happiness Soviet Style* (London, 2009)

Barskova, Polina, 'The Fluid Margins: Flâneurs of the Karpovka River', in Matich (ed.), *Petersburg/Petersburg*, pp. 283–304

Baryshnikov, Mikhail and Martha Swope, *Baryshnikov at Work: Mikhail Baryshnikov Discusses His Roles* (London, 1978)

Baryshnikova, M. N., *Delovoi mir Sankt-Peterburga: Istoricheskii spravochnik* (2000)

Basina, M., *Nash Leningrad* (1957)

Bassin, Mark, Christopher Ely and Melissa T. Stockdale (eds), *Space, Place, and Power in Modern Russia: Essays in the New Spatial History* (DeKalb, IL, 2010)

Bassin, Mark and Catriona Kelly (eds), *Soviet and Post-Soviet Identities* (Cambridge, 2012)

Baudrillard, Jean, *The System of Objects* [*Le Système des objets*, 1968], trans. James Benedict (London, 1996)
Beaumont, Matthew and Gregory Dart (eds), *Restless Cities* (London, 2010)
Bechtolsheim, Hubert von, *Leningrad: Die Biographie einer Stadt* (Munich, 1980)
Beiner, Guy, *Remembering the Year of the French: Irish Folk History and Social Memory* (Madison, WI, 2007)
Belinsky, A. I. (ed.), *Pis'ma proshlogo veka: Semeinaia khronika* (2008)
Bérard, Ewa (ed.), *Saint-Pétersbourg, une fenêtre sur la Russie: ville, modernisation, modernité, 1900–1935* (Paris, 2000)
Berdahl, Daphne, '(N) Ostalgie' for the Present: Memory, Longing, and East German Things', *Ethnos* 64.2 (1999), pp. 192–211
Berg, Mikhail, 'Neofitsial'naya leningradskaya literatura i emigratsiya', www.mberg.net/neof/.
Berggol'ts, Ol'ga, *Dnevnye zvezdy* (1971)
———. *Izbrannye proizvedeniya* (1983)
———. *Ol'ga: Zapretnyi dnevnik* (2010)
Bertash, A. V. (ed.), *Zemlya Nevskaya pravoslavnaya: pravoslavnye khramy prigorodnykh raionov Sankt-Peterburga i Leningradskoi oblasti* (2000)
Beumers, Birgit, *Pop Culture Russia! Media, Arts, and Lifestyle* (Santa Barbara, 2005)
Beumers, Birgit and Nancy Condee (eds), *The Cinema of Alexander Sokurov* (London, 2011)
Bidlack, Richard and Nikita Lomagin (eds), *The Leningrad Blockade, 1941–44: A New Documentary History from the Soviet Archives* (New Haven, 2011)
Bitov, Andrei, *Pushkinskii dom* [1978] (M., 2007)
———. *Kniga puteshestvii po Imperii* (1985–1999), www.litmir.net/br/?b=91009&p=1
Bittner, Stephen, *The Many Lives of Khrushchev's Thaw: Experience and Memory in Moscow's Arbat* (Ithaca, NY, 2008)
*The Blue Lagoon Anthology of Modern Russian Poetry*, ed. Konstantin Kuz'minsky and Gregory Kovalev (5 vols.; Blue Lagoon, FL, 1980–86)
Bobyshev, Dmitry, *Ya zdes' (chelovekotekst)* (M., 2003)
Bogdanov, Igor', *Leningradskii leksikon* (Moscow and St Petersburg: Tsentropoligraf, 2008)
Bogdanov, Konstantin, 'The Queue as Narrative: A Soviet Case Study', in Albert Baiburin, Catriona Kelly, and Nikolai Vakhtin (eds), *Russian Anthropology after the Collapse of Communism* (London, 2012, pp. 77–102
———. 'Istoriya odnogo prazdnika: Sovetskoe shampanskoe', *Antropologicheskii forum* 16 (2012), pp. 367–78
Bogemskaya, K. G. et al. (eds), *Samodeyatel'noe khudozhestvennoe tvorchestvo v SSSR: ocherki istorii 1917–1932 gg.* (2000)
Boitsova, Ol'ga, *Lyubitel'skaya fotografiya v gorodskoi kul'ture Rossii kontsa XX veka (vizual'no-antropologicheskii analiz) Avtoreferat dissertatsii na soiskanie uchenoi stepeni kandidata nauk. Sankt-Peterburg: Muzei antropologii i etnografii im. Petra Velikogo (Kunstkamera)* (2010)
Bol'shakova, S. E., *Pod pokrovom Smolenskoi ikony Bozhiei Materi* (2009)
Borisova, Maiya, *Stikhi o Leningrade* (1967)
———. *Interesnee peshkom* (2003) (reprinted 2006: see also http://lib.1september.ru/2006/14/15.htm)
Borodkin, L., *Sila velikikh traditsii* (M., 1963)
Bourdieu, Pierre, *Distinction: A Social Critique of the Judgements of Taste* [La Distinction: critique sociale du jugement, 1979], trans. Richard Nice (London: Routledge, 1984)
Boym, Svetlana, *Common Places: Mythologies of Everyday Life in Russian Culture* (Cambridge, MA, 1994)
———. *The Future of Nostalgia* (NY, 2001)
———. *Ninochka* (NY, 2003)
Bren, Paulina, *The Greengrocer and His TV: The Culture of Communism after the 1968 Prague Spring* (Ithaca, NY, 2010)
Brodsky, Joseph, *Less Than One* (Harmondsworth, 1987)
———. *Sochineniya*, ed. Gennady Komarov and Yakov Gordin (7 vols.; 2nd edn; 1997)
———. *Stikhotvoreniya i poemy*, ed. Lev Losev (2 vols.; 2011) ('Biblioteka poeta' series) (See also http://brodsky.ouc.ru/)
Brudny, V. I., *Obryady vchera i segodnya* (1968)
Brudny, Yitzhak, *Reinventing Russia: Russian Nationalism and the Soviet State, 1953–1991* (Cambridge, MA, 1998)
Buckler, Julie, *Mapping St Petersburg: Imperial Text and Cityshape* (Princeton, NJ, 2005)
Burawoy, Michael and Katherine Verdery, *Uncertain Transitions: Ethnographies of Change in a Post-Socialist World* (Lanham, MA, 1999)

Burlak, V. N., *Tainstvennyi Peterburg* (M., 2003)

Bushnell, John, *Moscow Graffiti* (London, 1990)

Caldwell, Melissa L., 'The Taste of Nationalism: Food Politics in Post-Socialist Moscow', *Ethnos* 67.3 (2002), pp. 295–319

——, 'Domesticating the French Fry: McDonald's and Consumerism in Moscow', in James L. Watson and Melissa L. Caldwell (eds), *The Cultural Politics of Food and Eating: A Reader* (Oxford, 2005), pp. 180–96

——. *Dacha Idylls: Living Organically in Russia's Countryside* (Berkeley, CA, 2011)

Catrell, David T., *Leningrad: A Case Study of Soviet Urban Government* (New York, 1968)

Cerwinske, Laura, *Russian Imperial Style* (London, 1990)

Cherepnina, N. Yu. and M. V. Shkarovsky, *Spravochnik po istorii pravoslavnykh monastyrei i soborov g. Sankt-Peterburga 1917–1945 gg. (po dokumentam TsGA SPb.)* (1996)

——. *Pravoslavnye khramy Sankt-Peterburga, 1917–1945* (1999)

Chuikina, Sof'ya, *Dvoryanskaya pamyat': "byvshie" v sovetskom gorode (Leningrad 1920-e – 1930-e gg.)* (2006)

Clark, Katerina, *Petersburg, Crucible of Revolution* (Cambridge, MA, 1995)

Clarke, Simon (ed.), *Conflict and Change in the Russian Industrial Enterprise* (Cheltenham, 1996)

——. *Making Ends Meet in Contemporary Russia: Secondary Employment, Subsidiary Agriculture, and Social Networks* (Cheltenham, 2002)

Collier, Stephen J., *Post-Soviet Social: Neoliberalism, Social Modernity, Biopolitics* (Princeton, NJ, 2011)

Condee, Nancy, *Soviet Hieroglyphics: Visual Culture in Late Twentieth-Century Russia* (Bloomington, IN, 1995)

——. *The Imperial Trace: Recent Russian Cinema* (NY, 2010)

Confino, Alon, and Peter Fritzsche (eds), *The Work of Memory: New Directions in the Study of German Society and Culture* (Urbana and Chicago, 2002)

Corsini, Ray Pierre, *Caviar for Breakfast* (NY, 1965; London, 1967)

Constanzo, Susan, 'Reclaiming the Stage: Amateur Theater-Studio Audiences in the Late Soviet Era', *Slavic Review*, 57.2 (1998), pp. 398–424

Crapanzano, Vincent, *Tuhami: Portrait of a Moroccan* (Chicago, 1980)

Cross, Anthony (ed.), *St Petersburg and the British: The City through the Eyes of British Visitors and Residents* (London, 2008)

Crowley, David, *Warsaw* (London, 2003)

Czaplicka, John, Nida Gelazis, and Blair A. Ruble (eds), *Cities after the Fall of Communism: Reshaping Cultural Landscapes and European Identity* (Washington, DC, 2009)

Davidson, Alan, *North Atlantic Seafood* (Harmondsworth, 1986)

Davidson, Pamela, 'Recipes from the Soviet Union', in Alan Davidson, *North Atlantic Seafood* (Harmondsworth, 1986), pp. 338–57

——. 'Food and Community in Soviet Russia: From Bulgarian Beans to Polish Plums', in *Moving Worlds: A Journal of Transcultural Writings* 2, pp. 90–8

Davies, Richard and Matilda Moreton, *Wooden Churches: Travelling in the Russian North* (London, 2011)

Demidov, A., 'Improvizatsii Leonida Yakobsona', *Teatr* 12 (1971), pp. 69–79

Derviz, Tat'yana, *Ryadom s bol'shoi istoriei: Ocherki chastnoi zhizni XX veka* (2011)

*10 pyatiletok Leningrada*, comp. A. N. Afanas'ev and N. V. Kumicheva (1980)

Devyatova, Yuliya, and Vladimir Kurennoi, 'Peterburgskie kommunalki', *LPan* 10 (1991), pp. 33–4

Dewhirst, Martin, and Robert Farrell, *The Soviet Censorship* (Metuchen, NJ, 1973)

Dixon, Megan, 'The Baltic Pearl in the Window to Europe: St. Petersburg's Chinese Quarter', Ph.D., University of Oregon, 2008, https://scholarsbank.uoregon.edu/xmlui/bitstream/handle/1794/9172/Dixon_Megan_PhD_Fall08.pdf?sequence=1

——. 'Gazprom versus the Skyline: Spatial Displacement and Social Contention in St. Petersburg', *International Journal of Urban and Regional Research*, 34:1 (2010), pp. 35–54

*Dmitry Likhachev i ego epokha: Vospominaninya. Esse. Fotografii*, ed. E. G. Vodolazkin (2nd edn; 2006)

Dobrovol'skaya, G. N., *Baletmeister Leonid Yakobson* (1968)

Dodin, Lev, *Repetitsii p'esy bez nazvaniya* (2004)

——. *Puteshestvie bez kontsa: dialogi s mirom* (2009)

——. *Puteshestvie bez kontsa: pogruzhenie v miry* (2010)

Dolgopolov, Viktor, *Zdravstvui, drug!* (M., 1957)

*Domovodstvo: izdanie dlya dosuga* (M., 1998)

Donovan, Victoria, '*Nestolichnaya kul'tura*: Regional and National Identity in Post-1961 Russian Culture', D.Phil Thesis, University of Oxford, 2011

Dovlatov, Sergei, *Sobranie sochinenii v 4 tt.* (1999) (see also www.sergeidovlatov.com/books/)
Dragomoshchenko, Arkady, 'Peterburg na polyakh', *Russkii zhurnal*, 13 March 2003, http://old.russ.ru:8081/ist_sovr/tour/2030313_drag-pr.html
Druzhinin, P. A., *Ideologiya i filologiya: Leningrad 1940-e gody: dokumental'noe issledovanie* (2 vols.; M., 2012)
Dudakov, Valery, 'Istoriya negotsii', *Antikvariat* 2 (2006), pp. 110–13
Dzeniskevich, A. R., *Blokada i politika* (2003)
———. (ed.), *O blokade Leningrada v Rossii i za rubezhom* (2005)
Edele, Mark, *Soviet Veterans of the Second World War. A Popular Movement in an Authoritarian Society, 1941–1991* (Oxford, 2008)
Edel'man, Ol'ga, 'Protsess Iosifa Brodskogo', *Novyi Mir* no. 1 (2007), http://magazines.russ.ru/novyi_mi/2007/1/ei11.html
Edmonds, Richard, *Russian Vistas: The Record of a Springtime Journey to Moscow, Leningrad, Kiev, Stalingrad, the Black Sea and the Caucasus* (London, 1958)
Egoshina, Ol'ga, *Akterskie tetradi Innokentiya Smoktunovskogo* (M., 2004)
Enakiev, F. E., *Zadachi preobrazovaniya S-Peterburga* (1912)
Etkind, Alexander, 'Post-Soviet Hauntology: Cultural Memory of the Soviet Terror', *Constellations: An International Journal of Critical and Democratic Theory* 16.1 (2009), pp. 182–200, www.mml.cam.ac.uk/slavonic/staff/ae264/constellations.pdf
———. 'A Parable of Misrecognition: "Anagnorisis" and the Return of the Repressed from the Gulag', *Russian Review* 68.4 (2009), pp. 623–40
———. 'Stories of the Undead in the Land of the Unburied: Magical Historicism in Contemporary Russian Fiction', *Slavic Review* 68.3 (2009), pp. 631–58
Etkind, Alexander and Mark Lipovetsky, 'Vozvrashchenie tritona: Sovetskaya katastrofa i post-sovetskii roman', *Novoe literaturnoe obozrenie* 94 (2009), pp. 174–206
Ezrahi, Christine, *Swans of the Kremlin: Ballet and Power in Soviet Russia* (Pittsburgh, 2012)
Fallowell, Duncan, *One Hot Summer in St Petersburg* (London, 1995)
Fehérváry, Krisztina, 'American Kitchens, Luxury Bathrooms, and the Search for a "Normal" Life in Postsocialist Hungary', *Ethnos* 67.3 (2002), pp. 369–40
Figes, Orlando, *The Whisperers* (London, 2007)
Filippov, Andrei, *Chastushki Leningradskoi oblasti v nazidanie, sobrannye s 1984 g. po raznym vesyam Rossii, peremeshchennye v Leningradskuyu oblast' i pozdnee raskrashennye. Nabor iz 8 otkrytok* (St Petersburg, n. d.)
Filtzer, Donald, *Soviet Workers and De-Stalinization: The Consolidation of the Modern System of Soviet Production Relations, 1953–1964* (Cambridge, 1992)
———. *Soviet Workers and the Collapse of Perestroika: The Soviet Labour Process and Gorbachev's Reforms, 1985–1991* (Cambridge, 1994)
Firsov, Boris, *Televidenie glazami sotsiologa* (M., 1971)
———. *Raznomyslie v SSSR: 1940-e – 1960-e gody* (2008)
———. 'Leningradskie kollektsionery kak kul'turno-istoricheskii fenomen', *Neprikosnovennyi zapas* 2 (64) (2009), http://magazines.russ.ru/nz/2009/2/fi14-pr.html
Fishzon, Anna, 'Confessions of a *psikhopatka*: Opera Fandom and the Melodramatic Sensibility in *Fin-de-siècle* Russia', *Russian Review* 71 (2012), pp. 100–21.
Fitzpatrick, Sheila, *Everyday Stalinism* (New York, 1999)
Ford, Ford Madox, *The Soul of London* (London, 1913)
Forty, Adrian and Susanne Küchler, *The Art of Forgetting (Materializing Culture)* (Oxford, 1999)
Fox, Kate, *Watching the English: The Hidden Rules of English Behaviour* (London, 2004)
French, R. A. and F. E. Ian Hamilton (eds), *The Socialist City: Spatial Structure and Urban Policy* (Chichester, 1979)
Fridman, Ya., 'Razgovory ni o chem na piterskoi kukhne', http://zhurnal.lib.ru/f/fridman_j_i/petersburgerkitchenstories.shtml
Frisch, Michael, *A Shared Authority: Essays on the Craft and Meaning of Oral and Public History* (Albany, NY, 1990)
Frolov, A. I., *Vokzaly Sankt-Peterburga* (2003)
Frow, John, *Time and Commodity Culture: Essays in Cultural Theory and Postmodernity* (Oxford, 1997)
Fürst, Juliane, *Stalin's Last Generation: Post-War Youth and the Emergence of Mature Socialism* (Oxford, 2010)
Gakkel', Ya. Ya., *Za chetvert' veka* (M. and L., 1945)
Gal'perin, Yuri, *Most cherez Letu* (2011)
Gandel'sman, Vladimir, *Novye rifmy* (2003), www.vavilon.ru/texts/prim/gandelsman4.html#8

Gardimer, Svetlana, 'Kartinki iz zhizni evreiskogo Leningrada', www.kontinent.org/article_rus_47756c408e42d.html

Geist, Johann Friedrich, and Klaus Kürvers, *Das Berliner Mietshaus* (3 vols.; Munich, 1980–89)

*General'nyi plan razvitiya Leningrada* (1966)

*Geometriya prirody: vystavka khudozhnika Aleksandra Baturina, 17–31 iyulya 1997 g.* (1997)

George, Arthur, with Elena George, *St Petersburg: A History* (Stroud, 2006)

*Georgy Tovstonogov repetiruet i uchit*, transcribed Semen Losev (2006)

Gerasimova, E. Yu., 'Sovetskaya kommunal'naya kvartira kak sotsial'nyi institute: istoriko-sotsiologicheskii analiz (na materialakh Petrograda-Leningrada, 1917–1991. Avtoreferat dissertatsii na soiskanie uchenoi stepeni sotsiologicheskikh nauk', St Petersburg: Institut sotsiologii RAN, 2000

Gerasimova, Olesya, '"Piterskomu separatistu mesto v toi kamere"', *Kommersant-Vlast'*, 23 July 2012, www.kommersant.ru/vlast/67753?d03b46c0

German, Mikhail, *Slozhnoe proshedshee* (2000)

Gessen, Masha, *Perfect Rigour: A Genius and the Mathematical Breakthrough of the Century* (London, 2011)

Ginzburg, Lidiya, *Zapisnye knizhki. Vospominaniya. Esse* (2002)

——. *Prokhodyashchie kharaktery: proza voennykh let. Zapiski blokadnogo cheloveka*, ed. E. Van Baskirk and A. Zorin (M., 2011)

Glowka, Detlef, *Schulreform und Gesellschaft in der Sowjetunion, 1958–1968* (Stuttgart, 1970)

*Glubinnaya Rossiya: 2000–2002*, ed. V. L. Glazychev (M., 2003)

Glushchenko, Irina, *Obshchepit: Mikoyan i sovetskaya kukhnya* (M., 2010)

Golubchikov, Oleg, 'Cities of the Russian North-West in a New Space Economy: Global Forces, Local Contexts', D.Phil Thesis, University of Oxford, 2007

Gorbovsky, Gleb, *Ostyvshie sledy: zapiski literatora* (1991)

Gornyi, Sergei, *Sankt-Peterburg: Videniya*, ed. A. M. Konechnyi (2000)

Gorodnitsky, Aleksandr, 'Iskrennii donos, ot serdtsa, segodnya uzhe ne vernesh'', www.novayagazeta.ru/data/2008/color04/06.html

*Gorodskaya vlast' Sankt-Peterburga: Biokhronika trekh stoletii* (2007)

Gorsuch, Anne, *All This is Your World: Soviet Tourism at Home and Abroad after Stalin* (Oxford, 2011)

Gorsuch, Anne and Diane Koenker (eds), *Turizm: The Russian and East European Tourist under Capitalism and Socialism* (Ithaca, NY, 2006)

Goscilo, Helena and Vlad Strukov, *Celebrity and Glamour in Contemporary Russia: Shocking Chic* (London, 2011)

Graham, Loren, *Science and the Soviet Social Order* (Cambridge, MA, 1996)

Granin, Daniil, *Leningradskii katalog* (1986)

——. *Sobranie sochinenii v 5 tomakh* (1989–90)

——. *Kerogaz i vse drugie: Leningradskii katalog* (M., 2003)

Granin, Daniil and Ales' Adamovich, *Blokadnaya kniga* (2 vols.; M., 2005)

*Granitsa i lyudi: vospominaniya sovetskikh pereselentsev Priladozhskoi Karelii* (2005)

Grigor'eva, Anna, *Leningrad-Peterburgu: Shtrikhi biografii. Memuary. Legendy*. Avtor-sostavitel' E. B. Belodubrovsky (2008)

Gronow, Jukka, *Caviar with Champagne: Common Luxury and the Ideals of the Good Life in Stalin's Russia* (Oxford, 2003)

Gubin, Dmitry, Lev Lur'e, and Igor' Poroshin, *Real'nyi Peterburg* (1999)

Gudkov, Lev, *Negativnaya identichnost'* (M., 2004)

Guelman, Vladimir [as Gel'man, Vladimir], 'Politics Beyond the Golden Ring: What Might We Learn from Studies of Russia's Regionalism?', in Markku Kivinen and Katri Pynnöniemi (eds), *Beyond the Garden Ring: Discussions of Russian Regionalism* (Helsinki, 2002), pp. 14–40

Gurevich, German, 'Vospominaniya', www.gergur.ru/work/226/

Gurova, Ol'ga, *Sovetskoe nizhnee bel'e: mezhdu ideologiei i povsednevnost'yu* (M., 2008)

Gusentsova, T., Dobrynina, I., *Puteshestvie po Vyborgskoi storone. Peterburgskie etyudy* (2007)

Hafen, Uli, *Das Regime und die Dandys. Russische Gaunerchansons von Lenin bis Putin* (Berlin, 2010)

Hann, Christopher (ed.), *Postsocialism: Ideals, Ideologies and Practices in Eurasia* (2nd edn; London, 2007)

Hann, Christopher and Elizabeth Dunn (eds), *Civil Society: Challenging Western Models* (2nd edn; London, 2005)

Harris, Steven, '"I Know All the Secrets of My Neighbors": The Quest for Privacy in the Era of the Separate Apartment', in *Borders of Socialism: Private Spheres of Soviet Russia*, ed. Lewis H. Siegelbaum (New York, 2006), pp. 171–89

Hathersley, Owen, *A Guide to the New Ruins of Great Britain* (London, 2010)

Hazan, Eric, *L'Invention de Paris* (Paris, 2002)
Healey, Daniel, *Homosexual Desire in Revolutionary Russia: The Regulation of Sexual and Gender Dissent* (Chicago, 2001)
Heinonen, Maarit, Jouko Nikula, Inna Kopoteva and Leo Granberg (eds), *Reflecting Transformation in Post-Socialist Rural Areas* (Cambridge, 2007)
Hellberg-Hirn, Elena, *Imperial Imprints: Post-Soviet St Petersburg* (Helsinki, 2003)
Herzfeld, Michael, *A Place in History: Social and Monumental Time in a Cretan Town* (Princeton, NJ, 1991)
——. *The Body Impolitic: Artisans and Artifice in the Global Hierarchy of Value* (Chicago, 2004)
Hingley, Ronald, *Under Soviet Skins: An Untourist's Report* (London, 1961)
Hobsbawm, Eric, and Terence Ranger (eds), *The Invention of Tradition* (Cambridge, 1983)
Hodgson, Katharine, 'Kitezh and the Commune: Recurrent Themes in the Work of Ol'ga Berggol'ts', *The Slavonic and East European Review*, 74.1 (1996), pp. 1–18
——. *Voicing the Soviet Experience: The Poetry of Ol'ga Berggol'ts* (Oxford, 2003)
Hödjestrand, Tova, 'The Soviet-Russian Production of Homelessness: *propiska*, housing, privatisation', www.anthrobase.com/Txt/H/Hoejdestrand_T_01.htm
Hufen, Uli, *Das Regime und die Dandys: Russische Gaunerchansons von Lenin bis Putin* (Berlin, 2010)
Humphrey, Caroline, 'Traders, "Disorder", and Citizenship Regimes in Provincial Russia', in Burawoy and Verdery (eds), *Uncertain Transition*, pp. 22–42
——. *The Unmaking of Soviet Life: Everyday Economies after Socialism* (Ithaca, NY, 2002)
——. 'Sovereignty and Ways of Life: the *marshrut* System in the City of Ulan-Ude, Russia', in David Nugent and Joan Vincent (eds), *A Companion to the Anthropology of Politics* (London, 2004), pp. 418–36
Il'in, Ivan, *Ispoved' kochevnika* (2007)
*Itogi Vsesoyuznoi perepisi naseleniya 1959 g.* vol. 1: *RSFSR* (M., 1963)
*Itogi Vsesoyuznoi perepisi naseleniya 1979 g.: Statisticheskii sbornik* vol. 1 (M., 1989)
*Itogi Vserossiiskoii perepisi naseleniya 2002 g.* (14 vols.: M., 2004–2005)
Ivanov, Boris, *Sochineniya* (2 vols.; M., 2009)
Izmozik, V. S., *Peshkom po Millionnoi* (2004)
Jacobs, Jane, *The Death and Life of Great American Cities* (1961; reprint, London, 1994)
Jenks, Andrew, 'A Metro on the Mount: The Underground as a Church of Soviet Civilization', *Technology and Culture* 41.4 (2000), pp. 697–724
Jersild, Austin, 'The Soviet State as Imperial Scavenger: "Catch Up and Surpass" in the Transnational Socialist Bloc, 1950–1960', *American Historical Review* 116.1 (2011), pp. 109–32
Johnson, Emily, *How St Petersburg Learned to Study Itself: The Russian Idea of Kraevedenie* (University Park, PA, 2006)
Jones, Polly (ed.), *The Dilemmas of De-Stalinization* (London, 2006)
——. 'From the Secret Speech to the Burial of Stalin: Real and Ideal Responses to De-Stalinization', in Jones (ed.), *The Dilemmas of De-Stalinization*, pp. 41–63
——. 'Memories of Terror or Terrorizing Memories?' *Slavonic and East European Review* 86.2 (2008), pp. 346–71
Kaganov, Grigory, *Sankt-Peterburg: obrazy prostranstva* (1995)
Kan, Aleksandr, 'Leningradskii rok-klub: zametki ochevidtsa', www.bbc.co.uk/russian/society/2011/03/110320_5floor_rock_club.shtml
——. *Poka ne nachalsya dzhaz* (2008)
Kaneff, Deema, and Pamela Leonard, *Post-Socialist Peasant? Rural and Urban Constructions of Identity in Eastern Europe, East Asia and the former Soviet Union* (Basingstoke, 2002)
Karnaukhov, Sergei, 'Pokhorony edy: zametki o prodovol'stvennoi korzine 1990 goda', *Novoe literaturnoe obozrenie* 84 (2007), http://magazines.russ.ru/nlo/2007/84/ka25.html
Kasatkina, Aleksandra, 'Sadovodcheskie nekommercheskie tovarishchestva: opyt postroeniya grazhdanskogo obshchestva na otdel'no vzyatom klochke zemli' (2009), www.cogita.ru/issledovaniya/.
——. 'Kategoriya "sovetskoe" v sovremennykh sadovodcheskikh tovarishchestvakh', *Konstruiruya "sovetskoe"? Politicheskoe soznanie, povsednevnye praktiki, novye identichnosti: Materialy nauchnoi konferentsii studentov i aspirantov, 20–21 aprelya 2012 g., Evropeiskii universitet v Sankt-Peterburge* (2012), pp. 72–7
Katerli, Nina, 'Sennaya ploshchad", *Zvezda* 7 (1991): http://lib.rus.ec/b/261039
Kavanagh, Julie, *Rudolf Nureyev: The Life* (London, 2007)
Kelly, Catriona, *Refining Russia: Advice Literature, Polite Culture, and Gender from Catherine to Yeltsin* (Oxford, 2001)
——. *Comrade Pavlik: The Rise and Fall of a Soviet Boy Hero* (London, 2005)

———. 'Roskosh' ili neobkhodimost': tovary dlya detei v khrushchevskuyu i brezhnevskuyu epokhu', *Teoriya mody* 8 (2008), pp. 140–85

———. *Children's World: Growing Up in Russia, 1890–1991* (New Haven, 2008)

———. 'City Texts: Writing on Walls in St Petersburg', in 'National Identity in Russia: Newsletter', Spring 2010, www.mod-langs.ox.ac.uk/russian/nationalism

———. '"A Dissonant Note on the Neva": Historical Memory and City Identity in Russia's Second Capital During the Post-Stalin Era', *Journal of Eurasian Studies* 1.1 (2010), pp. 72–83

———. '"The Hermitage and My Own Front Door": Local Identities in St Petersburg', *Ab Imperio* 4 (2010), http://abimperio.net/cgi-bin/aishow.pl?idlang=1&state=shown&idnumb=88

———. 'The Leningrad Affair: Remembering the "Communist Alternative" in the Second Capital', *Slavonica* 17 (2011), pp. 103–22

———. 'Making a Home on the Neva: Domestic Space, Memory, and Local Identity in Leningrad and St. Petersburg, 1957–present', *Laboratorium* 3 (2011), http://soclabo.org/eng/journal/11/3/vers/240/

———. 'Leningradskaya kukhnya/la cuisine leningradaise – protivorechie v terminakh?', *Antropologicheskii forum* 15 (2012), pp. 241–78

———. 'Socialist Churches: Heritage Preservation and "Cultic Buildings" in Leningrad, 1924–1940', *Slavic Review* 4 (2012, forthcoming)

———. '"The Traditions of Our History": "Tradition" as Framework for National Identity in Post-Stalinist and Post-Soviet Russia', in Philip Bullock, Claudio Ingerflom, Isabelle Ohayon and Anna Weinstein (eds), *Solidarities and Loyalties in Russian Culture* (London, 2012, forthcoming)

———. '"V podlive otrazhayetsya salyut": obytovlenie lokal'noi pamyati v sovremennoi peterburgskoi poezii (1995–2010)', in Henrieke Stahl and Marion Rutz (eds), *Imidzh. Dialog. Eksperiment* (Trier, forthcoming)

———. '"The Most European City in Russia": St Petersburg as Post-Imperial Capital' (forthcoming)

Kettering, Karen, '"Ever More Cosy and Comfortable": Stalinism and the Soviet Domestic Interior, 1928–1938', *Design History* 10.2 (1997), pp. 119–35

Khapaeva, Dina, *Goticheskoe obshchestvo* (2nd edn; M. 2007)

Khentova, S.M., *Shostakovich v Petrograde-Leningrade* (1979), in the series 'Vydayushchiesya deyateli nauki i kul'tury v Peterburge-Petrograde-Leningrade'

King, David, *The Commissar Vanishes: The Falsification of Photographs and Art in Stalin's Russia* (Edinburgh, 1997)

Kivinen, Markku and Katri Pynnöniemi (eds), *Beyond the Garden Ring: Discussions of Russian Regionalism* (Helsinki, 2002)

Kirschenbaum, Lisa, *The Legacy of the Siege of Leningrad: 1941–1945: Myth, Memories, and Monuments* (Cambridge, 2006)

Knauff, Bruce M. (ed.), *Critically Modern: Alternatives, Alterities, Anthropologies* (Bloomington, IN, 2002)

Kobak, Aleksandr V. and Yury M. Piryutko, *Istoricheskie kladbishcha Sankt-Peterburga* (2009)

Koenker, Diane, 'Whose Right to Rest? Contesting the Family Vacation in the Postwar Soviet Union', *Comparative Studies in Society and History* 51.2 (2009), pp. 401–25

Koivunen, Pia, 'The 1957 Moscow Youth Festival: Propagating a New, Peaceful Image of the Soviet Union', in Melanie Ilic and Jeremy Smith (eds), *Soviet State and Society Under Nikita Khrushchev* (L., 2009), pp. 46–65

Kolker, Yuri, 'Passeizm i gumannost'' (lecture given at a private seminar, 30 May 1981), http://yuri-kolker.narod.ru/articles/Passeism.htm

———. 'Leningradskii Klub-81', http://yuri-kolker.narod.ru/articles/Club-81.htm

———. 'Moi kochegarki', http://yuri-kolker-up-to-date.narod.ru/prose/my_boiler_rooms.htm

———. 'Parkhatogo mogila ispravit', http://yuri-kolker-up-to-date.narod.ru/prose/IM_AS_1.htm

Kolonitsky, Boris, *Simvoly vlasti i bor'ba za vlast': k izucheniyu politicheskoĭ kul'tury rossiiskoi revoliutsii 1917 goda* (2001)

———. *Tragicheskaya erotika: obrazy imperatorskoi sem'i v gody Pervoi Mirovoi voiny* (M., 2010)

Kondratieva, Tamara, *Kormit' i pravit': o vlasti v Rossii* (M., 2006)

*Konkurs na sostavlenie proekta zhilmassiva v Leningrade* (1929)

Könönen, Maija, *Four Ways of Writing the City: St. Petersburg-Leningrad as a Metaphor in the Poetry of Joseph Brodsky* (Helsinki, 2003)

Koposov, Nikolai, *Pamyat' strogogo rezhima* (M., 2011)

Korzun, V. P. and D. M. Kolevatov, 'Professorskaya sem'ya: stil' zhizni, rolevye funktsii v pole nauchnoi povsednevnosti', in *Antropologiya akademicheskoi zhizni*, vol. 2, ed. G. A. Komarova (M., 2010)

Kostsinsky, Kirill, *V teni Bol'shogo doma. Vospominaniya* (Tenafly, NJ, 1987)

Kotsyubinsky, Daniil, 'Peterburg v XXI veke: nezavisimoe gosudarstvo, chlen Evrosoyuza', 'Ekho Moskvy', 20 April 2012, www.echomsk.spb.ru/blogs/kotsubinsky/5704.php

Krivulin, Viktor, *Okhota na mamonta* (1998)

*Kto est' kto v Sankt-Peterburge*, ed. V. K. Vasil'ev, O. S. Kuzin, I. Yu. Svetov, and V. B. Ugryumov (2006)

Kuleshov, E. V., 'Sobiratelskaya rabota v Tikhvine: aksiologiya gorodskogo prostranstva', *Zhivaya starina* 1 (2001), pp. 13–15

———. '"A Tikhvin togda malen'kii byl . . ."', *Geopanorama russkoi kultury: Provintsiya i ee lokalnye teksty* (M. 2004), pp. 161–78

Kupriyanov, Pavel, and Sadovnikova, Larisa, 'Historical Zaryadye as Remembered by Locals: Cultural Meanings of City Spaces', in Baiburin, Kelly, and Vakhtin (eds), *Russian Anthropology after the Collapse of Communism*, pp. 220–53

Kuraev, Mikhail, 'Bardak ili zhizn' kak zhizn'?', *Kontinent* 102 (1999), http://magazines.russ.ru/continent/1999/102/ku15.html

———. 'Belyi polotnyannyi portfel'chik', *Zvezda* 9 (2001), http://magazines.russ.ru/zvezda/2001/9/kuraev.html

Kurbatov, Yu. I., *Petrograd. Leningrad. Sankt-Petevburg. Arkhiteckturno-gradostroitel'nye uroki* (2008)

Kusheva, E. N. and B. A. Romanov, *Perepiska 1940–1957 gg.*, ed. V. M. Paneyakh (2010)

Kushkova, Anna, 'V tsentre stola: zenit i zakat salata "Oliv'e"', *Novoe literaturnoe obozrenie* 76 (2005), http://magazines.russ.ru/nlo/2005/76/ku23.html

———. 'Surviving in the Time of Deficit: Food and the Narrative Construction of a "Soviet Identity"', in Bassin and Kelly (eds), *Soviet and Post-Soviet Identities* (Cambridge, 2012), pp. 276–95

Kushner, Aleksandr, *Pryamaya rech'* (1975)

———. *Dnevnye sni* (1986)

Lapin, Vladimir, *Zvuki i zapakhi Sankt-Peterburga* (2007)

Lavrov, Aleksandr, 'D. Travin. *Ocherki noveishei istorii Rossii* (2010)' (review/response) http://zhurnal.lib.ru/l/lawrow_a_w/znatxwsjuprawduinichegokromeprawdy.shtml

———. 'Deti Pobedy, Literaturnaya gazeta, 25 May 2011', www.lgz.ru/article/N21--6323---2011-05-25-/Deti-ProbedЬI16230

Lebina, N. B., *Povsednevnaya zhizn' sovetskogo goroda: normy i anomalii. 1920–1930-e gody* (1999)

Lebina, N. B. and A. N. Chistikov, *Obyvatel' i reformy: Kartiny povsednevnoi zhizni gorozhan* (2003)

Lebina, N. B. and V. S. Izmozik, *Peterburg sovetskii: "novyi chelovek" v starom prostranstve. Sotsial'no-arkhitekturnoe mikroistoricheskoe issledovanie* (2010)

Ledeneva, Alena, *Russia's Economy of Favours: Blat, Networking and Informal Exchange* (Cambridge, 1998)

———. *How Russia Really Works: The Informal Practices that Shaped Post-Soviet Politics and Business* (Ithaca, NY, 2006)

*Leningrad*, ed. N. V. Baranov (1943)

*Leningrad: Fotoal'bom* (1964)

*Leningrad: Putevoditel'*, ed. V. A. Vityazeva, B. M. Kirikov (1988)

*Leningrad i Leningradskaya oblast' v tsifrakh: statisticheskii sbornik* (1974)

*Leningrad Province in the First Half of 2005: Biannual Monitoring Review* (St Petersburg State University and Helsinki School of Economics), http://cemat.aalto.fi/fi/electronic/economicmonitoring/reports/leningrad/2000–2005/leningradpr_nov05_eng.pdf

*Leningrad Province in the First Half of 2007: Biannual Monitoring Review* (St Petersburg State University and Helsinki School of Economics), http://cemat.aalto.fi/fi/electronic/economicmonitoring/reports/leningrad/2006–2009/leningrad1h2007eng.pdf

*Leningradskii andergraund: zhivopis', fotografiya, rok-muzyka*, ed. Valery Val'ran (2003)

*Leningradskii fotoandergraund*, ed. Valery Val'ran (2007)

*Leningradskii gorodskoi sovet deputatov trudyashchikhsya. Ispolnitel'nyi komitet. Arkhitekturno-planirovochnoe upravlenie. Gosudarstvennaya inspektsiya po okhrane pamyatnikov Leningrada: Nauchnye soobshcheniya* (1959)

*Leningradskii literaturnyi andergraund*, comp. Mikhail Karasik (2003)

*Leningradskii martirolog* (1937–1938) (online version, http://visz.nlr.ru/search/stat.html)

*Leningradskoe delo*, ed. V. I. Demidov and V. A. Kutuzov (1990)

*Leningrad: Vidy goroda*, comp. M. E. Kunin, designed by G. D. Elifanov, photographs by M. A. Velichko, S. P. Ivanov, M. A. Mitskevich (M., 1954)

*Leningradskaya oblast' 1994: kratkii statisticheskii sbornik* (1995)

*Leningradskaya promyshlennost' za 50 let* (1967)

*Leonid Yakobson: tvorcheskii put' baletmeistera, ego balety, miniatyury, ispolniteli* (L. and M., 1965)

Leonidova, Kseniya, *Peterburg astrologicheskii. Astrologicheskii putevoditel' po gorodu* (1999)

*LES: Leningrad: Entsiklopedicheskii spravochnik* (M. and L., 1957)

*Lesnoi: ischeznuvshii mir*, comp. Ivan Fonyakov et al. (2011)
Leving, Yury, *Vokzal-garazh-ambar. Vladimir Nabokov i poetika russkogo urbanizma* (2004)
Levinton, Georgy, and Nikolai Vakhtin, 'Ot redaktorov', in Georgy Levinton and Nikolai Vakhtin, *AB: 60: k 60-letiyu Al'berta Kashfullovicha Baiburina* (2007), pp. 9–19
Likhachev, Dmitry S., 'Chetvertoe izmerenie', *Literaturnaya gazeta* 68 (10 June 1965), p. 2.
——. 'Ansambli Leningrada', *LP* 1 August 1965, p. 1
——. *Vospominaniya. Razdum'ya. Raboty raznykh let* (3 vols.; 2006)
Lonkila, Markku, 'Driving at Democracy in Russia: Protest Activities of St Petersburg Car Drivers' Associations', *Europe-Asia Studies*, 63.2 (2011), pp. 291–309
Losev, Lev, *Meandr: Memuarnaya proza* (M., 2010)
——. *Sobrannoe* (Ekaterinburg, 2000)
Loskutova, Marina (ed.), *Pamyat' o blokade: svidetel'stva ochevidtsev i istoricheskoe soznanie obshchestva* (M., 2006)
Lotman, Lidiya, *Vospominaniya* (2007)
Lotman, Yury, 'Simvolika Peterburga i problemy semiotiki goroda', *Izbrannye stat'i* (Tallinn, 1992–1993), vol. 1, pp. 9–22
——. and Boris Uspensky, *Perepiska* (M., 2008)
Lovell, Stephen, *The Russian Reading Revolution: Print Culture in the Soviet and Post-Soviet Eras* (Basingstoke, 2000)
——. *Summerfolk: A History of the Dacha, 1710–2000* (Ithaca, NY, 2003)
Low, Setha M., and Denise Lawrence-Zuñiga (eds), *The Anthropology of Space and Place: Locating Culture* (Oxford, 2003)
Lukas, Olga, *Porebrik iz bordyurnogo kamnya* and *Novyi porebrik iz bordyurnogo kamnya* (SPb., 2011)
Lur'e, Lev, 'Kak Nevskii prospekt pobedil ploshchad' Proletarskoi Diktatury', *Zvezda* no. 8 (1998), pp. 210–13
——. 'Andropovskii nazhim', *Zvezda* no. 4 (2000), pp. 230–3
——. *Peterburg: putevoditel' (seriya "Afisha")* (M., 2011)
Lur'e, Mikhail, 'Graffery', in *Opyt povsednevnosti. Pamyati S. Yu. Rumyantseva* (M. and SPb., 2005), pp. 251–64
——. 'Subkul'tura grafferov v Rossii', in *Detskii fol'klor i kul'tura detstva* (2006), pp. 196–208
Lur'e, Vadim F., *Mikrotoponimika Leningrada-Pitera*, www.ruthenia.ru/folktee/CYBERSTOL/I_AM/microtop.html
Lygo, Emily, *Leningrad Poetry 1953–1975: The Thaw Generation* (Frankfurt, 2010)
*Lyubitel'skii klub kollektsionera: problemy, resheniya* (M., 1989)
MacFadyen, David, *Songs for Fat People* (Montreal, 2001)
——. *Red Stars* (Montreal, 2001)
——. *Estrada?!* (Montreal, 2002)
McMichael, Polly, 'Prehistories and Afterlives: The Packaging and Re-packaging of Soviet Rock', *Popular Music and Society*, 32.3, pp. 331–50
——. 'After All, You're a Rock Star (At Least, That's What They Say)', *Slavonic and East European Review* 83.4 (2005), pp. 664–84
MacMillan, Margaret, *The Uses and Abuses of History* (London, 2009)
Makarova, Natalia, with Gennady Smakov and Dina Makarova, *A Dance Autobiography* (London, 1980)
Makhrovskaya, A. V., *Rekonstruktsiya zhilykh raionov Leningrada* (M., 1974)
Mally, Lynn, *Revolutionary Acts: Amateur Theatre and the Soviet State, 1917–1938* (Ithaca, NY, 2000)
Mandel'shtam, Roal'd, *Sobranie stikhotvorenii* (2006)
Manning, Paul, 'The Theory of the *Café Peripheral*: Laghidze's Waters and Peripheral Urban Modernity', *Forum for Anthropology and Culture* 7 (2012, forthcoming)
Manuylov, Aleksandr, 'The Practices of "Privacy" in a South Russian Village: A Case Study of Stepnoe, Krasnodar Region', in Baiburin, Kelly, and Vakhtin (eds), *Russian Anthropology after the Collapse of Communism* (London, 2012), pp. 130–54
Maramzin, Vladimir, *Smeshnee, chem prezhde* (Berlin, 1978)
Massey, Doreen, *World City* (Cambridge, 2007)
Massie, Suzanne, *The Living Mirror: Five Young Poets from Leningrad* (NY, 1972)
*Materialy k istorii blokady Leningrada. Trudy GMISPb.: Issledovaniya i materialy* 5 (2000)
Matich, Olga (ed.), *Petersburg/Petersburg: Novel and City, 1900–1921* (Madison, WI, 2010)
Melikhov, Aleksandr, 'Izgnanie iz Edema: ispoved' evreya', *Novyi Mir* 1 (1994), http://magazines.russ.ru/novyi_mi/1994/1/melih.html
Mel'nikov, V. A., and E. S. Mozhenok, *Komarovskii nekropol'* (St Petersburg, 2000)
Mel'nikova, Ekaterina, 'Svoya chuzhaya istoriya: finskaya Kareliya glazami sovetskikh pereselentsev', *Neprikosnovennyi zapas* 2 (2009), http://magazines.russ.ru/nz/2009/2/me4.html

Merridale, Catherine, *Night of Stone: Death and Memory in Russia* (London, 2001)
——. *Ivan's War: Life and Death in the Red Army, 1939–1945* (London, 2005)
Meshcherina, E. Yu., *Ustnaya istoriya i biografiya: zhenskii vzglyad* (Moscow, 2004)
Metter, Izrail', *Izbrannoe* (1999)
Michina, Barry P. and Cheryl Anne Richards, *Person to Person: Fieldwork, Dialogue, and the Hermeneutic Method* (Albany, NY, 1996)
Millar, James R. (ed.), *Politics, Work, and Daily Life in the USSR* (Cambridge, 1987)
Miller, Daniel, *Material Culture and Mass Consumption* (Oxford, 1987)
——. *The Comfort of Things* (Cambridge, 2008)
*Mit'ki: 25-letie*, ed. Larisa Skobina (2010)
Mittseev, Mikhail, 'Moya pervaya vstrecha s Leningradom i Universitetom', www.spbu.ru/files/upload/alumni/phys54/PhisFac1954Vosp.htm
*Mnogonatsional'nyi Peterburg: Etnografiya. Religiya. Narody*, ed. I. I. Shangina, N. V. Revunenkova, N. V. Yukhneva (2002)
*Moya Petrogradskaya storona* [I] [a collection of essays by local schoolchildren] (1996)
*Moya Petrogradskaya storona* [II] [a second collection of essays by local schoolchildren] (1998)
Mravinsky, Evgeny, 'Tridtsat' let s muzykoi Shostakovicha' (3 May 1966), *Dmitry Shostakovich* (M., 1967), www.mravinsky.org/pages/dsch30.htm
*Muzei – anti-muzei. Disskussiya* (Borey Art Center, 1995)
Nabokov, Vladimir, *Speak, Memory* (Harmondsworth, 1969)
Naiman, Anatoly, *Poeziya i nepravda: roman* (M., 1998)
——. *O statuyakh i lyudakh* (M., 2006)
——. [as Nayman, Anatoly], *Remembering Anna Akhmatova*, trans. Wendy Rosslyn (London, 1991)
*Naselenie Leningrada* (M. 1981)
*Nash gorod Leningrad* (1968)
Nefedova, Tatiana, *Sel'skaya Rossiya na pereput'e: geograficheskie ocherki* (M., 2003)
Nefedova, Tatiana and Andrey Treivish, *Regions of Russia and Other European Countries in Transition in [the] Early 90s* (M., 1994)
Nefedova, Tatiana, Pavel Polyan, and Andrey Treivish (eds), *Gorod i derevnya v Evropeiskoi Rossii: Sto let peremen* (M., 2001)
Nefedova, Tatiana and Judith Pallot, 'The Multiplicity of Second Home Development in the Russian Federation: A Case of "Seasonal Suburbanization"?', in Roca, Zoran (ed.), *Second Home Tourism in Europe: Lifestyle Issues and Policy Responses* (London, 2012), pp. 91–120
Nepomnyashchy, A., *Gorod, v kotorom my zhivem* (1958)
'Nevskii prospekt do i posle velikoi kofeinoi revolyutsii: interv'yu s Viktorom Krivulinym', *Pchela* (1996), www.pchela.ru/podshiv/6/coffee.htm
Nielsen, Finn Sivert, *The Eye of the Whirlwind: Russian Identity and Soviet Nation-Building. Quests for Meaning in a Soviet Metropolis* (Oslo, 1987), www.anthrobase.com/Txt/N/Nielsen_F_S_03.htm
Nikitin, Vladimir A., *Optimizm pamyati: Leningrad 70-kh gg.* (2000)
Nivat, Anne, *La Maison haute: Des russes d'aujourd'hui* (Paris, 2002)
Nivat, Georges (ed.), *Les sites de la mémoire russe*, vol. 1 (Paris, 2011)
*Nomen est omen. Sbornik statei k 60-letiyu Nikolaya Borisovicha Vakhtina. Ot neposlushnykh uchenikov* (SPb., 2010)
Nora, Pierre, *Les Lieux de mémoire* (3 vols.; Paris, 1984–92)
Novick, Peter, *The Holocaust in American Life* (NY, 1999)
*Novyi khudozhestvennyi Peterburg. Spravochno-analiticheskii sbornik*, ed. O. Leikind, D. Severyukhin (2004)
Obertreis, Julia, *Tränen des Sozialismus: Wohnen in Leningrad zwischen Alltag und Utopie, 1917–1937* (Cologne, 2004)
O'Brien, David J., Stephen K. Wegren and Valeri V. Patsiorkovski, 'Contemporary Rural Responses to Reform from Above', *Russian Review* 63.2 (2004), pp. 256–76
*Obshchestvennaya zhizn' v Leningrade v gody perestroiki, 1985–1991*, ed. E. K. Zelinskaya, O. N. Ansberg, and A. D. Margolis (2009)
*Ocherki soremennogo sovetskogo iskusstva: sbornik statei po arkhitekture, zhivopisi, grafike i prikladnomu iskusstvu* (M., 1975)
Osorina, Mariya V., *Sekretnyi mir detei (v prostranstve mira vzroslykh)* (1999)
Orttung, Robert, *From Leningrad to St. Petersburg: Democratization in a Russian City* (New York, 1995)
Oushakine, Serguei, '"We're Nostalgic, But We're Not Crazy". Retrofitting the Past in Post-Soviet Russia', *Russian Review* 66.3 (2007), pp. 451–82
——. *The Patriotism of Despair: Nation, War, and Loss in Russia* (Ithaca, NY, 2009)

Pachenkov, Oleg, Zoya Solov'eva, and Mariya Kudryavtseva, 'Ekonomicheskie strategii adaptatsii predstavitelei "nizshikh sloev" bol'shogo goroda v usloviyakh transformatsii', on the site 'Khudozhestvennyi proekt bloshinyi rynok' (see below), www.bloxa.ru/articles/russia/spb/text10/
Palei, Marina, *Kabiriya s Obvodnogo kanala* (1991)
Pallot, Judith and Tatiana Nefedova, 'Trajectories in People's Farming in Moscow oblast during the Post-Socialist Transformation', *Journal of Rural Studies* 19.3 (2003), pp. 345–62
———. 'Geographical Differentiation in Household Plot Production in Russia', *Eurasian Geography and Economics* 44.1 (2003), pp. 40–64
———. *Russia's Unknown Agriculture: Household Production in Post-Socialist Rural Russia* (Oxford, 2007)
Pamuk, Orhan, *Istanbul*, trans. Maureen Freely (London, 2005)
Panteleev, L., and Lidiya Chukovskaya, *Perepiska 1929–1987*, ed. E. Ts. Chukovskaya (M., 2011)
Paperno, Irina, *Chernyshevsky and the Age of Realism: A Study in the Semiotics of Behavior* (Stanford, CA, 1988)
———. 'Dreams of Terror: Dreams from Stalinist Russia as a Historical Source', *Kritika* 7.4 (2006), pp. 793–824
———. *Stories of the Soviet Experience: Memoirs, Diaries, Dreams* (Ithaca, NY, 2009)
Papernyi, Vladimir, *Kul'tura "Dva"* (Ann Arbor, 1984)
Parfenov, Leonid (ed.), *Namedni: Nasha era, 1961–1970* (M., 2010)
———. *Namedni: Nasha era, 1971–1980* (M., 2010)
———. *Namedni: Nasha era, 1981–1990* (M., 2010)
Patico, Jennifer, *Consumption and Social Change in a Post-Soviet Middle Class* (Stanford, CA, 2008)
Pashkova, T. I., *Vtoraya Sankt-Peterburgskaya gimnaziya: Ocherki istorii* (2010)
Patryshev, Vladimir, 'Rodnoi zavod', http://patryshev.com.literatura.
Peeling, Siobhan, 'Displacement, Deviance and Civic Identity: Migrants into Leningrad at the End of the Second World War', *Forum for Anthropology and Culture* 6 (2010), pp. 201–14
*Pervyi v strane*. Comp. K. L. Emel'yanova (1964)
Pesmen, Dale, *Russia and Soul* (Ithaca, NY, 2000)
*Peterburg: istoriya torgovli. Khudozhestvenno-istoricheskii al'bom*, comp. N. N. Smirnov (3 vols.; 2002–2003)
*Peterburg kak kino*, ed. L. Arkus and K. Shavlovsky (2011)
*Peterburg-Leningrad. Al'bom*, comp. G. N. Savin, text written by N. A. Bartenev (1967)
*Peterburgskii balet 1903–2003*, ed. A. Degen, I. Stupnikov (2003)
*Peterburgskii tramvai: istoriya i sovremennost'* (2007)
Petro, Nicolai N., *Crafting Democracy: How Novgorod Has Coped with Rapid Social Change* (Ithaca, NY, 2004)
*Petrograd. Statisticheskie dannye, otnosyashchiesya k gorodu Petrogradu i Petrogradskomu gorodskomu khozyaistvu. (V diagrammakh) Sostavleno Statistichekim Upravleniem Petrogradskoi Gorodskoi Upravoi* (1916)
Petrov-Vodkin, Kuz'ma, *Prostranstvo Evklida* (2000)
Piir, Aleksandra, 'What is a Courtyard For? Generations and the Use of Space in Backyard Leningrad', *Forum for Anthropology and Culture* 4 (2006), pp. 311–45
Platt, Kevin M. F., *Terror and Greatness: Ivan and Peter as Russian Myths* (Ithaca, NY, 2011)
Pokshishevskaya, Galina, 'Tovarnye znaki iz Leningrada: vospominaniya ochevidtsa', www.advertology.ru/print25257.htm
Popov, Valery, *Zapomnite nas takimi* (2003)
*Portrety rezhisserov*, ed. Yu. A. Smirnov-Nesvitsky (M., 1977)
*Post-Soviet Art and Architecture*, ed. Alexey Yurasovsky and Sophie Ovenden (London, 1994)
*Pravovoe gosudarstvo i organy vnutrennikh del* (Sankt-Peterburgskii yuridicheskii institut, 1995)
*Prazdniki nashei ulitsy*, comp. V. L. Bulvanker (1967)
*Proekt razmeshcheniya zhilishchnogo, kul'turno-bytovogo stroitel'stva i inzhinernogo oborudovaniya raionov novoi zastroiki g. Leningrada i ego prigorodov na 1971–1972 gg.* (Mimeographed circular, Proektnyi institut 'Lenproekt', 1969)
Prokofiev, Sergei, *Avtobiografiya* (2nd edn; M., 1982)
*Prostranstvo Timura: K 50-letiyu Timura Novikova* (SPb. and NY, 2008)
Przhepyurko, Leonid, 'Leningradskie prikoly', http://world.lib.ru/p/przhepjurko_l/leningradskie-prikoly.shtml
Puteshestvie po Leningradu [board game], 1979
Pyle, William, 'The Ownership of Industrial Land in Russian Cities: Explaining Patterns of Privatization Across Regions and Firms', NCEEER Working Paper, 2011, www.nceeer.org/papers.html

Qualls, Karl D., *From Ruins to Reconstruction: Urban Identity in Soviet Sevastopol after World War II* (Ithaca, NY, 2009)
Raikin, Arkady, *Bez grima* (M., 2006)
*Raiony leningradskoi oblasti: Statisticheskii sbornik* (1995)
Rajagopalan, Sudha, *Indian Films in Soviet Cinemas: The Culture of Movie-Going after Stalin* (Bloomington, IN, 2009)
Raleigh, Donald, *Soviet Baby Boomers: An Oral History of Russia's Cold War Generation* (Oxford, 2012)
Rau, Santha Rama, *My Russian Journey* (London, 1959)
Rausing, Sigrid, *History, Memory, and Identity in Post-Soviet Estonia: The End of a Collective Farm* (Oxford, 2004)
Reid, Anna, *The Siege of Leningrad* (London, 2011)
Reid, Susan, 'Who Will Beat Whom? Soviet Popular Reception of the American National Exhibition in Moscow, 1959', *Kritika* 9.4 (2008), pp. 855–904
——. 'Communist Comfort: Socialist Modernism and the Making of Cosy Homes in the Khrushchev-Era Soviet Union', *Gender and History* 21.3 (2009), pp. 465–98
——. '"Happy Housewarming!" Moving into Khrushchev-Era Apartments', in Marina Balina and Evgeny Dobrenko (eds), *Petrified Utopia*, pp. 133–60
Rein, Evgeny, *Mne skuchno bez Dovlatova* (1997)
Ries, Nancy, *Russian Talk: Culture and Conversation During Perestroika* (Ithaca, NY, 1997)
Rivkin-Fish, Michele, *Women's Health in Post-Soviet Russia: the Poltiics of Intervention* (Bloomington, IN, 2005)
Robinson, Logan, *An American in Leningrad* (NY, 1982)
Robinson, Mikhail, *Sud'by akademicheskoi elity: otechestvennoe slavyanovedenie v 1920-kh gg.* (M., 2004)
Rogers, Douglas, *The Old Faith and the Russian Land: A Historical Ethnography of Ethics in the Urals* (Ithaca, NY, 2009)
——. 'Postsocialisms Unbound: Connections, Critiques, Comparisons', *SR* 69 (2010), pp. 1–15
Rozhansky, F. V., 'Sleng khippi' (1992), www.philology.ru/linguistics2/rozhansky-92.htm
Ruble, Blair, *Leningrad: Shaping a Soviet City* (NY, 1990)
*Ruf' Zernova: Chetyre zhizni. Sbornik vospominanii*, ed. N. Serman (M., 2011)
*Rukovoditeli Sankt-Peterburga* (2003)
*Russkie stikhi 1950–2000. Antologiya*, ed. I. Akmet'ev, G. Lukomnikov, V. Orlov, A. Uritsky (2 vols.; M., 2010)
Ryklin, Mikhail, 'Luchshii v mire', *Wiener Slavistischer Almanach*, 1995, www.topos.ru/article/3812.
——. 'Metrodiskurs', www.topos.ru/article/4123
Sadof'ev, Igor', *Pesnya o Rodine* (1953)
*St Petersburg Painted by F. de Haenen, Described by G. Dobson* (London, 1910)
Salmi, Anna-Maria, *Social Networks and Everyday Practices in Russia* (Helsinki, 2006)
Saraeva-Bondar', A. M., *Siluety vremeni* (1999)
Sarkizova, Oksana, and Olga Shevchenko, '"They Came, Shot Everyone, and That's the End of It": Local Memory, Amateur Photography, and the Legacy of State Violence in Novocherkassk', *Slavonica* 11.2 (2011), pp. 85–102
Savitsky, Stanislav, *Andergraund: istoriya i mify leningradskoi neofitsial'noi literatury* (M., 2002)
——. *Vzglyad na peterburgskoe iskusstvo 2000-kh godov* (2011)
Schlögel, Karl, *Moskau lesen* (Berlin, 1984)
——. *Petersburg: Laboratorium der Moderne* (Munich, 2002)
——. *Terror und Traum: Moskau 1937* (Munich, 2008)
Schlögel, Karl, Frithjof Benjamin Schenk and Markus Ackeret (eds), *Sankt Petersburg. Schauplätze einer Stadtgeschichte* (Frankfurt on Main, 2007)
Scholl, Tim, *From Petipa to Balanchine: Classical Revival and the Modernization of Ballet* (London, 1993)
Schönle, Andreas, *Architecture of Oblivion: Ruins and Historical Consciousness in Modern Russia* (DeKalb, IL, 2011)
Schönle, Andreas and Julia Hell (eds), *Ruins of Modernity* (Durham, NC, 2010)
Sen'kin-Tolstyi, Ya. M., *Ferdinand, ili Novyi Radishchev* (2nd edn; M., 2008)
Sergeev, V. N., 'Pishchevaya promyshlennost' Rossii v rynochnoi ekonomike (1990–2003 gg.)', *Pishchevaya promyshlennost'* 1 (2004), pp. 44–6
Shchepanskaya, Tat'yana, *Kul'tura dorogi v russkoi miforitual'noi traditsii XIX–XX vv.* (M., 2003)
——. *Sistema: teksty i traditsii subkul'tury* (M., 2004)
Shcherba, A.N. *Voennaia promyshlennost' Leningrada v 20–30-e gody* (1999)

Shefner, Vadim, *Skazki dlya umnykh* (1987)
Shevchenko, Olga, *Crisis and the Everyday in Postsocialist Moscow* (Bloomington, IN, 2009)
Shevtsova, Maria, *Dodin and the Maly Drama Theatre: Process to Performance* (London, 2004)
Shkarovsky, M. V., *Sankt-Peterburgskaia eparkhiia v dvadtsatom veke v svete arkhivnykh materialov* (2000)
———. *Tserkov' zovet k zashchite Rodiny: religioznaya zhizn' Leningrada i Severo-Zapada v gody Velikoi Otechestvennoi voiny* (2005)
Shlapentokh, Vladimir, *Public and Private Life of the Soviet People: Changing Values in Post-Stalin Russia* (New York, 1989)
Shmulyar, Oksana, 'Networking into a Business Career: A New Generation of Russian Managers' (2002), www.anthrobase.com/Txt/S/Shmulyar_O_01.htm
Shpakovskaya, Larisa, 'Starye veshchi. Tsennost': mezhdu gosudarstvom i obshchestvom', *Neprikosnovennyi zapas* 1 (33) (2004), http://magazines.russ.ru/nz/2004/1/shpak14.html
Shtern, Lyudmila, *Leaving Leningrad* (Hanover, MA, 2001)
———. *Brodsky: Osya, Iosif, Joseph* (2005)
Shtyrkov, Sergei and Jeanne Kormina. 'Believers' Letters as Advertising: St Xenia of Petersburg's 'national Reception Centre', *Forum for Anthropology and Culture* 6 (2011), pp. 115–43
Shvarts, Elena, *Sochineniya* (2 vols.; 2002)
Shvarts, Vsevolod S. (ed.), *Leningrad: Khudozhestvennye pamyatniki. Ocherki* (1956)
Siegelbaum, Lewis, *Cars for Comrades: The Life of the Soviet Automobile* (Ithaca, NY, 2008)
Sil'man, Tamara, and Vladimir Admoni, *Vospominaniya: Roman* (1993)
Sindalovsky, Naum A., *Peterburgskii fol'klor* (1994)
———. *Peterburg v fol'klore* (1999)
———. *Peterburg: ot doma k domu, ot legendy k legende, putevoditel'* (2000)
Sirotinina, Svetlana, 'The Moscow Station, St Petersburg: Between "Europe" and the Russia of the Tsars', *National Identity in Russia from 1961: Project Newsletter*, no. 2 (November 2008), pp. 7–11. www.mod-langs.ox.ac.uk/russian/nationalism/newsletter.htm
Skakov, Nariman, 'A Tribute to Otherness: The Art of Galim Madanov', *National Identity in Russia from 1961: Newsletter* 2 (2008), pp. 14–16
Skobkina, Larisa (ed.), *Leningrad 70-e v litsakh i lichnostyakh* (n.d. [1989?])
Slater, Wendy, *The Many Deaths of Tsar Nicholas II: Relics, Remains and the Romanovs* (London, 2007)
Slepakova, Nonna, *Izbrannoe* (3 vols.; 2006)
———. *Stikhotvoreniya i poemy* (2012)
Slezkine, Yuri, *The Jewish Century* (Princeton, NJ, 2004)
Smirnov, Igor', *Genezis (filosofskie ocherki po sotsiokul'turnoi nachinatel'nosti)* (2006)
———. *Deistvuyushchie litsa* (2008)
Smirnova, T. M., *Natsional'nost' – piterskie. Natsional'nye men'shinstva Peterburga i Leningradskoi oblasti v XX veke* (2002)
Smith, G. S., *Songs to Seven Strings* (Bloomington, IN, 1984)
Smith, Jeremy (ed.), *Beyond the Limits: The Concept of Space in Russian History and Culture* (Helsinki, 1999)
Smith, Mark B., *Property of Communists: The Urban Housing Programme from Stalin to Khrushchev* (DeKalb, IL, 2010)
Smolyak, Ol'ga, 'Sovetskie nesuny', *Otechestvennye zapiski* 1 (2012), www.strana-oz.ru/2012/1/sovetskie-nesuny.
Smyth, C. Piazzi, *Three Cities in Russia* (2 vols.; London, 1862)
Snyder, Timothy, *Bloodlands: Europe between Hitler and Stalin* (New York, 2010)
Sobchak, Anatoly, *Iz Leningrada v Peterburg: puteshestvie vo vremeni i prostranstve* (1999)
Soja, Edward W., *Thirdspace: Journeys to Los Angeles and other Real-and-Imagined Places* (Oxford, 1996)
Sokolov, Yu. A., *Trezvost'. Protivokurenie. Metodicheskie rekomendatsii* (1989), video.sbnt.ru/vl/books/U.A.Sokolov-Trezvost.Protivokurenie.doc
Sokolova, Anna, 'Funerals without a Body: The Transformation of the Traditional Burial Rite', *Forum for Anthropology and Culture* 7 (2012), pp. 231–46
Soloukhin, Vladimir, *Slavyanskaya tetrad'* (M., 1972)
Sonne, Paul, 'Cold War Consumption: The Soviet Consumer and the American Product', M.Phil. thesis, University of Oxford (2009)
Sotnikov, N., *Obraztsovyi gorod* (1934)
*Sotsial'naya istoriya Sankt-Peterburga*, ed. V. N. Solov'ev (2005)

'Soviet and Russian Blockbuster Films' (article cluster), ed. Birgit Beumers, *Slavic Review* 62.3 (2003), pp. 441–524
*Spisok abonentov LGTS [Leningradsko gorodskoi telefonnoi sluzhby]* (1988)
'SSSR, rabochii klass vos'midesyatykh godov: Interv'yu s rabochim L'vom Korotkinym', *Grani* vol. 132 (1984), pp. 186–99
Stanyukovich, Maria, 'Stoit li zanimat'sya etnografiei v segodnyashnei Rossii', *Antropologicheskii forum* 3 (2007), pp. 83–90
Starosel'skaya, Natal'ya, *Tovstonogov* (Zhizn' zamechatel'nykh lyudei) (M., 2004)
*Statisticheskii spravochnik po kommunal'nomu khozyaistvu Leningrada i Leningradskoi oblasti* (1930)
Steblin-Kamensky, M.I., *Iz zapisnykh knizhek* (2009)
Steinberg, Mark D., *Petersburg fin de siècle* (New Haven, 2011)
Stern, Elizabeth H., 'Keepers of Classical Balletic Tradition: The Preservation and Evolution of Ballet in Early Soviet Russia', M.Phil Thesis, University of Oxford, 2011
*Stikhi v Peterburge: 21 vek*, ed. Lyudmila Zubova and Vyacheslav Kuritsyn (2005)
Stites, Richard, *Revolutionary Dreams: Utopian Vision and Experimental Life in the Russian Revolution* (New York, 1989)
——. *Russian Popular Culture: Entertainment and Society since 1900* (Cambridge, 1992)
Stogov, Il'ya, *Macho ne plachut* (2001), www.erlib.com/Нлья_Стогов/Мачо_не_плачут/
Stratanovsky, Sergei, *Stikhi* (1993), www.vavilon.ru/texts/stratanovsky1-7.html#10
*Sumerki Saigona*, ed. Yu. Valieva (2009)
Svetlov, S. V., *Peterburgskaya zhizn' v kontse XIX stoletiya*, ed. A. M. Konechnyi (1998)
Taigin, Boris, 'Po goryachim sledam (Otryvki iz dnevnika pisatelya)', ed. Boris Ivanov, *Nevskii arkhiv* 5 (2001), pp. 526–49
Tapp, Alyson, '"The Streetcar Prattle of Life": Reading and Riding St Petersburg's Trams', in Matich (ed.), *Petersburg/Petersburg*, pp. 123–48
Tareev, V. '"Ispravlyat"' li istoriyu pamyatnika?', *LPan* 10 (1984), p. 25
*Teatr Leonida Yakobsona: Stat'i, vospominaniya, fotomaterialy* (2010)
Thornycroft, Joanna [as Dzhoanna Tornikroft], 'Dom na Fontanke', *Antikvariat* 2 (2006), pp. 50–5
Thubron, Colin, *Among the Russians* (London, 1985)
Tikhonov, Nikolai, *Stikhotvoreniya i poemy* (1981)
Tikhonov, Nikolai, *SS v 7 tt.* (M., 1973–6)
Timenchik, Roman, 'K simvolike tramvaya v russkoi poezii', *Trudy po znakovym sistemam* 21 (1987), pp. 135–43
Todorova, Maria N., and Zsusza Gille, *Post-Communist Nostalgia* (NY, 2010)
Tokareva, Marina, '"Stoilo zhit": interv'yu s Andreem Bitovym', *NV* 1 January 1992, p. 3
Tomchin, G. A., *Razvitie Peterburga: Vid s pravogo berega* (2003)
Toporov, Viktor, *Dvoinoe dno: Priznan'ya skandalista* (M., 1999)
Toporov, Vladimir N., 'Peterburg i "Peterburgskii tekst" russkoi literatury' (1971, 1993), *Peterburgskii tekst russkoi literatury: Izbrannye trudy* (2003), pp. 7–118
Tovstonogov, Georgy, *O professii rezhissera* (2nd edn; M., 1966)
——. *Zerkalo stseny. 1. O professii rezhissera* (1984)
Tsendrovskaya, S. N., 'Krestovskii ostrov ot nepa [sic] do snyatiya blokady', *Nevskii arkhiv* 2 (1995), pp. 80–95
Tuan, Yi-Fu, *Space and Place: The Perspective of Experience* (Minneapolis, MN, 1977)
Uflyand, Vladimir, *"Esli Bog poshlet mne chitatelei"* (1999)
*U nas v Leningrade: o primetakh vremeni. Rasskazyvayut zhurnalisty, khudozhniki, fotografy* (1961)
Utekhin, Il'ya, *Ocherki kommunal'nogo byta* (2nd edn: M., 2004)
——. 'Memories of Leningrad's Blockade: Testimonies from Two Generations', *Forum for Anthropology and Culture* no. 4 (2007), pp. 281–310
Vaganova, Agrippina, *Osnovy klassicheskogo tantsa* (L., 1934)
Vail', Petr, *Genii mesta* (M., 1999)
Vail', Petr and Aleksandr, Genis, *1960-e: Mir sovetskogo cheloveka* (Ann Arbor, 1988)
Vakhtin, Boris, *Portret neznakomtsa: sochineniya* (2010)
Vakhtin, Nikolai, 'Malen'kii dvoinoi', in A. Yu. Veselova, M. L. Lur'e (eds), *Kratkii illyustrirovannyi slovar' klishe i stereotipov* [K 60-letiyu P. A. Klubkova] (2009), pp. 74–5
Vakser, Aleksandr Z., *Leningrad poslevoennyi: 1945–1982 gg.* (2005)
Vasil'eva, Evelina Karlovna, *The Young People of Leningrad: School and Work Options and Attitudes* (White Plains, NY, 1975)
*V budushchee voz'mut ne vsekh*, comp. Allen Tager (2010)

Velikonja, Mitja, 'Lost in Transition: Nostalgia for Socialism in Post-Socialist Countries', *East European Politics and Societies* 23.4 (2009), pp. 535–51

Veller, Mikhail, *Khochu byt' dvornikom* (Tallinn, 1983) (see also http://lib.ru/WELLER)

———. *Rasskazy* (2003)

———. *Legendy Nevskogo prospekta* (M., 2010)

Verdery, Katherine, *What Was Socialism, and What Comes Next* (Princeton, NJ, 1996)

———. *The Political Lives of Dead Bodies: Reburial and Post-Socialist Change* (Ithaca, NY, 1999)

Vershlovsky, S., *Peterburgskaya shkola: portret vypusknika* (1999)

Vertinsky, Aleksandr, *Zapiski russkogo P'ero* (NY, 1982)

Vihavainen, Rosa, *Homeowners' Associations in Russia after the 2005 Housing Reform* (Helsinki, 2009), www.iut.nu/members/Russia/HomeownerAssociations_Russia_2009.pdf

Vikhavainen, T. [=Vihavainen, Timo] (ed.), *Normy i tsennosti povsednevnoi zhizni: Stanovlenie sotsialisticheskogo obraza zhizni v Rossii, 1920–30-e gody* (2000)

Vinogradov, Oleg, 'Dva spektaklya', in *Muzyka i khoreografiya sovremennogo baleta: sbornik statei*, 2, ed. L. D. Kremshevskaya (1977)

Visser, Oane, 'Household Plots and Their Symbiosis with Large Farm Enterprises in Russia' (paper for the Land, Poverty and Social Development conference, 2006), www.intra1.iss.nl/content/download/3629/35316/file/visser.pdf

Vlasov, P. V., *Moi Peterburg: Istoriya odnogo doma* (2007)

Volkomorov, Innokenty, *Legendy filfaka* (2009)

Volkonskaya, Sof'ya (as Princess Peter Wolkonsky), *The Way of Bitterness* (London, 1931)

Volkov, Solomon, *Istoriya kul'tury SPb: s osnovaniya do nashikh dnei* (M., 2001) [English-language edition as *St Petersburg: a Cultural History* (NY, 1996)]

Volkov, Vadim, *Violent Entrepreneurs: The Use of Force in the Making of Russian Capitalism* (Ithaca, NY, 2002)

———. *Silovoe predprinimatel'stvo: XXI vek* (2011)

Vonderau, Asta, *Leben im "neuen Europa": Konsum, Lebenstil und Körpertechniken im Postsozialismus* (Bielefeld, 2010)

Voronina, Tat'yana, 'Pamyat' o BAMe: Tematicheskie dominanty v interv'yu s byvshimi stroitelyami', *Neprikosnovennyi zapas* no. 2 (2009), http://magazines.russ.ru/nz/2009/2/vo5-pr.html

*Vospominaniya o L. N. Belovoi. Trudy GMISPb.: Issledovaniya i materialy* 9 (2004)

Voznesensky, L. A., *Istiny radi* (M., 2004)

Voz'yanov, Andrei, 'Tramvainye fanaty i (provintsial'naya) urbanistichnost' ', *Antropologicheskii forum* 15 (2011), pp. 359–87

———. ' "Proizvodstvo passazhira" v sovetskom transporte 1960-e–1970-e gg.', *Konstruiruya "sovetskoe"? Politicheskoe soznanie, povsednevnye praktiki, novye identichnosti: Materialy nauchnoi konferentsii studentov i aspirantov, 20–21 aprelya 2012 g., Evropeiskii universitet v Sankt-Peterburge* (2012), pp. 26–32

Waldstein, Maxim, *The Soviet Empire of Signs: A History of the Tartu School of Semiotics* (Saarbrücken, 2008)

Watts, Julian, 'Heritage and Enterprise Culture in Archangel, Northern Russia', in Ruth Mandel and Caroline Humphrey (eds), *Markets and Moralities: Ethnographies of Postsocialism* (Oxford, 2002), pp. 53–74

Werth, Alexander, *Leningrad* (London, 1944)

White, Anne, *Small Town Russia: Post-Communist Livelihoods and Identities; A Portrait of the Intelligentsia in Achit, Bednodemyanovsk and Zubtsov* (London, 2004)

White, Elizabeth, 'After the War was Over: The Civilian Return to Leningrad', *Europe-Asia Studies* 59.7 (2007), pp. 1145–61

Widdis, Emma, *Visions of a New Land: Soviet Film from the Revolution to the Second World War* (New Haven, 2003)

Worsdall, Frank, *The Glasgow Tenement* (Glasgow, 1989)

Yampolsky, Mikhail, 'In the Shadow of Monuments: Notes on Iconoclasm and Time', in Condee (ed.), *Soviet Hieroglyphics*, pp. 93–112

Yarov, Sergei, *Konformizm v sovetskoi Rossii: Petrograd 1917–1920-kh godov* (2006)

———. *Blokadnaya etika: Predstavleniya o morali v Leningrade, 1941–1942 gg.* (2011)

Yerushalmi, Y. H., *Zakhor: Jewish History and Jewish Memory* (Seattle, 1982)

Yukhneva, E., *Peterburgskie dokhodnye doma: Ocherki iz istorii byta* (2008)

Yurchak, Alexei, *Everything Was Forever, Until it Was No More* (Princeton, NJ, 2006)

———. 'Necro-Utopia: The Politics of Indistinction and the Art of the Non-Soviet', *Current Anthropology*, 49.2 (2008), pp. 199–224

Zaharchenko, Tatiana, 'Environmental Policy in the Soviet Union', *Environmental Law and Policy Journal*, 14.1 (1990), environs.law.ucdavis.edu/issues/14/1/articles/zaharchenko.pdf

Zakharova, Larisa, 'Fabriquer le bon goût: La Maison des modèles de Léningrad à l'époque de Hruščev', *Cahiers du monde russe* 47.1–2 (2006), pp. 195–226

——. 'Dior in Moscow: A Taste for Luxury in Soviet Fashion under Khrushchev', in D. Crowley and S. E. Reid (eds), *Pleasures in Socialism: Leisure and Luxury in the Eastern Bloc* (DeKalb, IL, 2010)

——. *S'habiller à la soviétique: la mode et le dégel en URSS* (Paris, 2011)

Zavisca, Jane, *Housing the New Russia* (Ithaca, NY, 2012)

Zdravomyslova, Elena, 'Leningradskii Saigon: prostranstvo negativnoi svobody', *NLO* 100 (2009), http://magazines.russ.ru/nlo/2009/100/el47.html

*Zhilishchnyi kodeks Rossiiskoi Federatsii* [2004] *Po sostoyaniyu na 1 marta 2010 g.* (M., 2010)

Zholkovsky, Alexander, 'Otdel'nost', granitsa, razrezhennost', tsel'nost': Zametki ob ikonike stikha', *Znamya* 12 (2010), http://magazines.russ.ru/zvezda/2010/12/z18.html

Zhuk, Sergei, *Rock and Roll in the Rocket City: The West, Identity, and Ideology in Soviet Dniepropetrovsk* (Washington, DC, 2010)

Zimin, Dmitri and Michael Bradshaw, 'Economic Performance, Public Policies and Living Standards in Northwestern Russia', in Markku Kivinen and Katri Pynnöniemi (eds), *Beyond the Garden Ring: Discussions of Russian Regionalism* (Helsinki, 2002), pp. 195–204

Zinovieff, Sofka, *Red Princess: A Revolutionary Life* (London, 2007)

Zitzewitz, Josephine von, 'The "Religious Renaissance" of the 1970s and its Repercussions on the Soviet Literary Process', D.Phil Thesis, University of Oxford, 2009

Zukin, Sharon, *Landscapes of Power: From Detroit to Disney World* (Berkeley, CA, 1991)

——. *Naked City: The Death and Life of Authentic Urban Places* (NY, 2010)

## *Filmography*

Asanova, Dinara, *The Woodpecker Doesn't Get Headaches* [Ne bolit golova u dyatla, 1975]

——. *His Wife's Left Him* [Zhena ushla, 1979]

Averbakh, Leonid, *Degree of Risk* [Stepen' riska, 1968]

——. *Monologue* [Monolog, 1972]

——. *The Voice* [Golos, 1982]

Averbakh, Leonid, and Igor' Maslennikov, *The Private Life of Valentin Kuzaev* [Chastnaya zhizn' Kuzyaeva Valentina, 1966]

Balabanov, Aleksei, *Brother* [Brat, 1997]

——. *Of Freaks and Men* [Pro urodov i lyudei, 1998]

——. *Brother 2* [Brat 2, 2000]

Daneliya, Georgy, *I Stride Round Moscow* [Ya shagayu po Moskve, 1964]

——. *Autumn Marathon* [Osennii marafon, 1979]

Heifetz, Joseph, *Married for the First Time* [Vpervye zamuzhem, 1980]

Kosakovsky, Viktor, *Hush!* [Tishe, 2003]

Kozintsev, Grigory, *Hamlet* [Gamlet, 1964]

——. *King Lear* [Korol' Lir, 1970]

Mel'nikov, Vitaly, *Mother's Gone and Got Married* [Mama vyshla zamuzh, 1969]

Panfilov, Gleb, *Request Permission to Speak* [Proshu slova, 1975]

Potyomkin, Sergei, *City with No Sun* [Gorod bez solntsa, 2005]

Ryazanov, El'dar, *The Irony of Fate* [Ironiya sud'by, 1975]

Sheshukov, Igor', *Viktor Krokhin's Second Try* [Vtoraya popytka Viktora Krokhina, 1978/1987]

——. *The Red Arrow* [Krasnaya strela, 1986]

Sokolov, Viktor, *A Day of Sunshine and Rain* [Den' solntsa i dozhdya, 1969]

Teptsov, Oleg, *The Gentleman Artist* [Gospodin oformitel', 1988]

Uchitel', Aleksei, *The Stroll* [Progulka, 2003]

## *Audio*

Andrea Zemskov-Zuge, Tat'yana Voronina, Il'ya Utekhin, *Golosa blokadnogo pokoleniya. Posobie k zanyatiyam po ustnoi istorii* (CD-Rom. European University, St Petersburg, 2005)

*Websites*

babs71.livejournal.com (regular and well-informed posts about Leningrad and Petersburg history, by a local)

'City Walls' (information about architectural history, street by street; in Russian), www.citywalls.ru/street_index.html

'Evgeny Aleksandrovich Mravinsky', www.mravinsky.org/pages/main.htm

'Khudozhestvennyi proekt Bloshinyi rynok: vystavka-yarmarka', www.bloxa.ru/

'Kommunal'naya kvartira: Virtual'nyi muzei sovetskogo byta/Communal Living in Russia: A Virtual Museum of Soviet Everyday Life', by Ilya Utekhin, Alice Nakhimovsky, Slava Paperno, and Nancy Ries, www.kommunalka.spb.ru/

'Mapping Petersburg' (site with information about places associated with the 'Silver Age'), http://petersburg.berkeley.edu/

'Natsional'nyi korpus russkogo yazyka', www.ruscorpora.ru

'Neizvestnyi sotsrealizm: Poiski i otkrytiya' (site on Leningrad 'official' artists), www.leningradartist.com/index_r.html

'Ostrov Sokurova' (the official site of Alexander Sokurov), http://sokurov.spb.ru/

*Peterburgskie starosti* online journal, http://spbstarosti.ru/

'Pro Arte' art and exhibition project, www.proarte.ru/

Dmitry Shostakovich official site, www.shostakovich.ru/

TsGAKFFD (St Petersburg photoarchive, with interactive selection of materials from their vast holdings), www.photoarchive.spb.ru

Village (local listing and city news magazine), www.the-village.ru/tags/Санкт-Петербург

See also the Facebook pages of Petersburg or ex-Leningrad writers such as Arkady Bliumbaum, Mikhail Iossel, Lev Lurie, Stanislav Savitsky, and the 'Saint Petersburg' page (city views, including retro material)

# Index